COMPANION ENCYCLOPEDIA OF PSYCHOLOGY

COMPANION
ENCYCLOPEDIA
OF
PSYCHOLOGY

Volume 1

EDITED BY

Andrew M. Colman

London and New York

First published in 1994
by Routledge
11 New Fetter Lane, London EC4P 4EE
29 West 35th Street, New York, NY 10001

© 1994 Routledge

Typeset in 10/12 pt Times Compugraphic by
Mathematical Composition Setters Ltd, Salisbury, Wiltshire
Printed in England by Clays Ltd, St Ives plc
Printed on acid free paper

British Library Cataloguing in Publication Data
A catalogue record for this book is available from the British Library.

Library of Congress Cataloging-in-Publication Data
A catalog record for this book is available on request.

ISBN 0–415–06446–5 (*set*)
ISBN 0–415–10704–0 (*Volume 1*)
ISBN 0–415–10705–9 (*Volume 2*)

CONTENTS

EDITOR'S PREFACE

What is there to say about a book of more than half a million words, containing 60-something separate contributions by 70-something authors from more than half a dozen different countries? Those who have qualms about all multi-authored books because of their inevitable non-uniformity of style and lack of narrative unity should note that I have just described the best-selling and arguably the most deeply respected book ever published – a book that has already been translated into over 300 languages. I was referring, of course, to the Bible, which the *Companion Encyclopedia of Psychology* resembles in at least one other respect: the arrangement of its contents is to a large extent arbitrary, which means that no one (apart from the editor) is expected to read it from beginning to end; any section or chapter may safely be browsed. In the case of the *Companion Encyclopedia of Psychology*, however, I recommend readers who are new to the subject to read my introductory chapter 1.1 before tackling any of the others.

Psychology is a uniquely diverse discipline, ranging from biological aspects of behaviour on the one hand to social psychology on the other, and from basic research to the applied professions of clinical, counselling, educational (school), industrial (occupational), organizational, and forensic (criminological) psychology. The sheer quantity of information in psychological journals has been increasing exponentially since the 1960s and far exceeds any individual's capacity to absorb it. But over the same period, a number of fundamental problems have been solved, and theoretical consolidation is evident in several branches of the discipline. The time could hardly be more propitious for an introductory survey of psychology and its associated professions, broader in scope and deeper in penetration than any previous survey, written by leading authorities in plain language but without condescension or over-simplification.

The *Companion Encyclopedia of Psychology* seeks to provide just such an authoritative, in-depth reference work covering all major branches of psychological research and professional practice. It is aimed at a thoughtful but not necessarily specialist readership, including seriously interested members of the general reading public as well as students and teachers of psychology and a wide range of other subjects with psychology components, including medicine, nursing, sociology, social work, and education.

The contents of the encyclopedia are arranged thematically (rather than alphabetically) into thirteen sections, corresponding to the topics that appear most often as discrete modules in contemporary psychology courses. The section headings and the topics within them were not chosen arbitrarily but were distilled from a preliminary survey of undergraduate course outlines obtained from a number of departments of psychology in the United States and Britain and the contents pages of the leading introductory texts.

Every section (apart from the first) begins with a brief introduction designed to orient the reader, to outline the contents of the section, to point out useful cross-references to other chapters and sections of the encyclopedia, and occasionally to explain important technical terms and concepts that crop up in the chapters that follow. The introduction to each section is followed by five or six self-contained chapters, and there are suggestions for further reading and up to fifty references at the end of each chapter. Every topic is covered by a full-length chapter written by an acknowledged authority who is an active researcher or practitioner in the relevant field; the list of contributors includes a remarkable number of the world's most eminent psychologists. The book contains numerous illustrations, a full and detailed index, and a glossary of technical terms.

I am grateful to Jonathan Price, formerly of Routledge, for his support and sensible advice on numerous points, to Kathleen Harman, for several helpful suggestions, to Kathy Smith, for practical assistance, to Briony Pulford, for help with the glossary, to Christine Firth, for her remarkably thoughtful copy-editing, and above all to my seventy-five contributors, scattered across three continents, for the spectacular quality of their contributions.

ANDREW M. COLMAN

NOTES ON CONTRIBUTORS

JOHN ANNETT is Professor of Psychology at Warwick University. He took his doctorate at Oxford in 1959, has taught at the Universities of Sheffield, Aberdeen and Hull and was Professor of Psychology at the Open University. His current research interest is in motor imagery and other 'cognitive' aspects of motor skills. He is chairman of the Motor Skills Research Exchange and Psychology Editor of the Journal of Sport Sciences. Among his publications are *Feedback and Human Behaviour* (1969) and *Training in Transferable Skills* (1989).

MICHAEL ARGYLE is Emeritus Reader in Social Psychology at Oxford University, a fellow of Wolfson College, Oxford and Emeritus Professor at Oxford Brookes University. He has been Chairman of the Social Psychology section of the British Psychological Society and Visiting Professor at various universities in the United States, Canada, Australia, and elsewhere. He is the author of *The Psychology of Interpersonal Behaviour* (4th edn, 1983), *Bodily Communication* (2nd edn, 1988), *The Social Psychology of Work* (2nd edn, 1989), *The Social Psychology of Everyday Life* (1992), *Psychology and Social Class* and other books and papers.

ALAN BADDELEY is Director of the Medical Research Council Applied Psychology Unit in Cambridge, and Professor of Cognitive Psychology at Cambridge University. He previously taught at the universities of Sussex and Stirling, and has been president of the Experimental Psychology Society and the European Society for Cognitive Psychology. His books include *The Psychology of Memory* (1976), *Your Memory: A User's Guide* (1982), *Working Memory* (1986), and *Human Memory: Theory and Practice* (1990).

DONALD M. BAER is the Roy A. Roberts Distinguished Professor of Human Development and Family Life, and of Psychology, at the University of Kansas, Lawrence. He took his doctorate at the University of Chicago in 1957, and taught at the University of Washington in Seattle before beginning his current employment with the University of Kansas in 1965. He has also taught briefly at universities in Canada, Australia, Japan, and Brazil. He has published many articles on behaviour analysis and its application, especially to problems of children, and on its use as a theoretical framework for the study of child development. He has served as president of the international Association for Behavior Analysis. His most persistent research and conceptual target has been the problem of securing appropriately generalized results from clinical interventions into behaviour problems.

JOHN BANCROFT qualified in medicine from Cambridge University and St George's Hospital, London, and completed psychiatric training at the Maudsley Hospital, London. He was Clinical Reader in Psychiatry at Oxford University before joining the Medical Research Council Reproductive Biology Unit in Edinburgh in 1976. He has been involved in research into human sexuality and the clinical management of its problems for most of his career. His current research interest is the relationship between reproductive hormones and the well-being and sexuality of women. He is the author of *Human Sexuality and its Problems* (2nd edn, 1989).

SIMON BARON-COHEN studied human sciences at New College, Oxford, followed by a doctorate in experimental psychology at University College London. He has taught at University College London and the Institute of Psychiatry, London, where he is currently Senior Lecturer in Developmental Psychology. He is co-editor (with H. Tager-Flusberg and D. J. Cohen) of *Understanding Other Minds: Perspectives from Autism* (1993), and co-author (with P. Bolton) of *Autism: the facts* (1993).

SUSAN BLACKMORE studied psychology and physiology at St Hilda's College, Oxford, took her doctorate in parapsychology at the University of Surrey and then worked at Bristol and Bath Universities and as a writer and broadcaster. She is Senior Lecturer in Psychology at the University of the West of England at Bristol. Her current research interests are the origins of belief in the paranormal and near-death experiences. She is the author of *Beyond the Body: An Investigation of Out-of-the-Body Experiences* (1982), *The Adventures of a Parapsychologist* (1986), and *Dying to Live: Science and the Near-Death Experience* (1993).

JOHN E. BLUNDELL studied for his doctorate at the Institute of Neurology, University of London. He is the director of a research group at Leeds University specializing in the control of human appetite with particular reference to the relationships among nutrition, physiology, and behaviour. He is the author of a science citation classic on the role of the neurotransmitter serotonin in appetite control entitled "Is there a role for Serotonin (5-hydroxytryptamine) in feeding?" (*International Journal of Obesity*, 1977, *1*, 15–42) and has been awarded the 25th International Prize in Modern Nutrition (1992).

RUPERT BROWN is Reader in Social Psychology at the University of Kent, Canterbury. He is editor of the European Monograph series in social psychology and the author of *Contact and Conflict in Intergroup Encounters* (1986) and *Group Processes: Dynamics Within and Between Groups* (1988).

PETER BULL is a Senior Lecturer in Psychology at the University of York, with special responsibility for teaching social psychology. He is a graduate both of Trinity College, Oxford, and of the University of Exeter, where he also obtained his PhD in psychology. He was elected a Fellow of the British Psychological Society in 1989. He is the author of *Body Movement and Interpersonal Communication* (1983), *Posture and Gesture* (1987) and (with Derek Roger) *Conversation: An Interdisciplinary Perspective* (1989).

GEORGE BUTTERWORTH took his doctorate in psychology at the University of Oxford. He is Professor of Psychology at the University of Sussex. He has published many articles on development in infancy and is currently researching the origins of referential communication in babies. He has been editor of the *British Journal of Developmental Psychology* (1989–93) and chairman of the Scientific Affairs Board of the British Psychological Society (1992–95). He edited *Infancy and Epistemology* (1982).

CONNIE CAHILL studied psychology and philosophy at University College, Dublin. She is now a member of the Cognitive Neuropsychiatry Project at the Medical Research Council Cyclotron Unit and University College London. Her clinical experience and research interests lie chiefly within the domains of mental illness, in particular schizophrenia, and neuropsychology.

JOHN C. CAVANAUGH is Professor and Chairperson of the Department of Individual and Family Studies at the University of Delaware. His research interests include cognitive ageing, self-evaluation of memory, and cognitive impairment. He is co-editor (with Jan Sinnott) of *Bridging Paradigms: Positive Development in Adulthood and Cognitive Aging* (1991) and author of *Adult Development and Aging* (2nd edn, 1993).

JOHN C. COLEMAN obtained his PhD from the University of London. He is also trained as a clinical psychologist. He is currently the Director of the Trust for the Study of Adolescence, an independent charity and research organization based in Brighton, England. He is the editor of the *Journal of Adolescence*. His most recent books are *The Nature of Adolescence* (2nd edn, 1990) and *Youth Policy in the 1990s* (1992).

ANDREW M. COLMAN is Reader in Psychology at the University of Leicester, having previously taught at Cape Town and Rhodes Universities, South Africa. He is the founder and former editor of the journal *Current Psychology*; he is currently Chief Examiner for the British Psychological Society's Qualifying Examination. His books include *Game Theory and Experimental Games: The Study of Strategic Interaction* (1982), *Facts,*

Fallacies and Frauds in Psychology (1987), and *What is Psychology? The Inside Story* (2nd edn, 1988).

PETER J. COOPER is the Lecturer in Psychopathology in the Departments of Psychiatry and Experimental Psychology at the University of Cambridge. He conducted his doctoral research and received clinical training in the Department of Psychiatry of the University of Oxford. His research has principally concerned psychiatric aspects of obstetrics and gynaecology, and eating disorders. He has published in psychiatry and psychology journals on the nature, epidemiology, assessment, and treatment of eating disorders. His books include *Bulimia Nervosa: A Guide to Recovery* (1993) and (co-edited with A. Stein) *Feeding Problems and Eating Disorders in Children and Adolescents* (1992).

MARY CRAWFORD is Professor of Psychology and Graduate Director of Women's Studies at the University of South Carolina. She received her PhD in experimental psychology from the University of Delaware. She is active in the Division on the Psychology of Women of the American Psychological Association and in many organizations concerned with gender equity and feminist scholarship. She is Book Review Editor for *Psychology of Women Quarterly*, a member of the international editorial advisory board of *Feminism and Psychology*, and Research Director for the Women's College Coalition. She is a fellow of the American Psychological Association and the American Psychological Society. Her publications include the book (co-edited with M. Gentry) *Gender and Thought: Psychological Perspectives* (1989).

ROBERT T. CROYLE is Associate Professor of Psychology at the University of Utah, Salt Lake City. He took his doctorate in psychology from Princeton University, New Jersey, and has taught at Williams College and the University of Washington. He has published articles on attitude change, judgement biases, and health-related memory, and is co-editor (with J. A. Skelton) of *Mental Representation in Health and Illness* (1991).

FRANCIS C. DANE is Associate Professor and Chair of Psychology at Mercer University in Macon, Georgia. He currently serves as secretary/treasurer of the Society for the Advancement of Social Psychology; his research concerns jury decision-making. He is the author of *Common and Uncommon Sense of Social Psychology* (1988) and *Research Methods* (1990) and co-author (with K. Deaux and L. S. Wrightsman) of *Social Psychology in the 90s* (6th edn, 1993).

PETER C. DODWELL is Professor of Psychology at Queen's University, Kingston, Ontario. He was educated at Oxford University, receiving his doctorate in 1958. He has spent most of his professional career at Queen's, but has also taught at the University of London and at Harvard; he has held fellowships and other positions at universities in the United States, the United Kingdom, Australia, and New Zealand. He has been president of the Canadian Psychological Association, and edited the *Canadian Journal of Psychology* and *Spatial Vision*. He is a fellow of the Royal Society of Canada. He has published five books, including *Visual Pattern Recognition* (1970) and (as co-editor with T. M. Caelli) *Figural Synthesis* (1984).

ALICE H. EAGLY obtained a doctorate in social psychology from the University of Michigan. She is Professor of Psychological Sciences at Purdue University, Indiana, USA. A past president of the Society for Personality and Social Psychology, she is a member of the editorial boards of several social psychology journals. She is the author of numerous articles and book chapters on attitudes as well as gender and sex differences. She is co-author (with Shelly Chaiken) of *The Psychology of Attitudes* (1993).

K. ANDERS ERICSSON is the Dr Edward Conradi Eminent Scholar Chair in Psychology at the Florida State University, Tallahassee. He is the co-author (with Herbert A. Simon) of *Protocol Analysis: Verbal Reports as Data* (1984), which appeared in a second revised edition in 1993. He is the co-editor (with Jacqui Smith) of *Toward a General Theory of Expertise: Prospects and Limits* (1991).

JONATHAN St B. T. EVANS is Professor of Cognitive Psychology at the University of the South West in Plymouth. Since completing his doctorate at University College London in 1972, he has researched and published extensively in the psychology of human reasoning and judgement with particular emphasis on the study of biases. He is author of three books on human reasoning, including *Bias in Human Reasoning: Causes and Consequences* (1989); and (with others) *Human Reasoning: The Psychology of Deduction*.

BRIAN S. EVERITT is Professor of Behavioural Statistics at the Institute of Psychiatry, London. He is the author of *An Introduction to Latent Variable Models* (1984), *Statistical Methods for Medical Investigations* (1989), and *The Analysis of Contingency Tables* (2nd edn, 1992); he is co-author (with G. Dunn) of *Applied Multivariate Data Analysis* (1991). He is currently working on a third edition of his book on *Cluster Analysis*.

H. J. EYSENCK   Professor Emeritus Hans Eysenck was born in Berlin in 1916. He left Germany in 1934 and took his PhD in psychology at University College London in 1942. He founded the Department of Psychology in the newly created Institute of Psychiatry in 1955, being appointed Professor of Psychology in the University of London in the same year. He received the Distinguished Scientist Award of the American Psychological Society in 1988. His work has been concerned mainly with individual differences of personality and intelligence, behavioural genetics, psychophysiology, behaviour therapy, and clinical psychology generally. He has written nearly 1,000 articles; he founded and edited two journals, *Behaviour Research and Therapy* and *Personality and Individual Differences*. Among his 70 books is *Personality and Individual Differences: A Natural Science Approach* (co-authored with Michael W. Eysenck, 1985).

MICHAEL W. EYSENCK is Professor of Psychology and Head of Department at Royal Holloway and Bedford New College, University of London, at Egham, Surrey. He has been Visiting Professor at the University of South Florida. He was the founding editor of the *European Journal of Cognitive Psychology*. He has published approximately 80 articles and book chapters, mainly in the area of anxiety and cognition. He is the author of 18 books, including *Attention and Arousal: Cognition and Performance* (1982) and *Anxiety: The Cognitive Perspective* (1992); he is co-author (with M. T. Keane) of *Cognitive Psychology: A Student's Handbook* (1990).

RAYMOND E. FANCHER is Professor of Psychology at York University, Ontario, Canada and Executive Officer of CHEIRON (The International Society for History of the Behavioral and Social Sciences). His writing on the history of psychology includes *Psychoanalytic Psychology: The Development of Freud's Thought* (1973), *The Intelligence Men: Makers of the IQ Controversy* (1985), and *Pioneers of Psychology* (2nd edn, 1990). He is currently writing a biography of Francis Galton.

PETER FONAGY took his doctorate in psychology at University College London and has been on the staff of its Department of Psychology since 1976. He is currently Freud Memorial Professor of Psychoanalysis at University College London. He is a clinical psychologist and psychoanalyst and member of the British Psycho-Analytical Society. He is coordinator of research at the Anna Freud Centre (Hampstead Child Therapy Clinic) and is a member of the Executive Council of the International Psychoanalytic Association. He has published articles in both psychoanalytic and psychological journals on numerous clinical and theoretical topics. He is co-author (with A. Higgitt) of *Personality Theory and Clinical Practice* (1984) and co-editor (with J. Sandler and E. S. Pearson) of *Freud's "On Narcissism": An Introduction* (1991).

DAVID FONTANA is Reader in Educational Psychology in the School of Education, University of Wales at Cardiff, and Professor Catedratico in the Department of Child Education, University of Minho, Portugal. A Fellow of the British Psychological Society and a Chartered Psychologist, he is the author of over 100 scientific papers and articles, and serves on the editorial boards of a number of psychological journals. He has written 15 books, including *The Education of the Young Child* (1984), *Behaviourism and Learning Theory in Education* (1984), *Classroom Control* (1985), *Teaching and Personality* (1986), *Psychology for Teachers* (1988), *Managing Stress*

(1989), and *Your Growing Child: From Birth to Adolescence* (1990). His books have been translated over 30 times into all major European languages.

LESLEY FREDERIKSON has a BSc with a psychology major from Massey University, New Zealand, and a DPhil from the University of York, England. She was a Research Fellow for the New Zealand Federation of University Women from 1990 to 1992, studying the communication of information within doctor–patient interaction. She is currently a Research Fellow in the Psychology Department of Massey University studying the effects of post-traumatic stress disorder.

CHRIS FRITH studied psychology at Cambridge and the Institute of Psychiatry in London. From 1975 to 1990 he worked on the neuropsychology of schizophrenia with Tim Crow's group at the Clinical Research Centre, Northwick Park Hospital, London. Currently he is working on functional brain imaging at the Medical Research Council Cyclotron Unit and holds an MRC grant at the Psychology Department of University College London, where he is Visiting Professor. He is author of *The Cognitive Neuropsychology of Schizophrenia* (1992).

ANTHONY GALE is Professor of Psychology at Southampton University, and was president of the British Psychological Society. His research includes physiological studies of information processing and personality, participant observation of family life, and conceptual issues in applied psychology. He has also published critical papers on the teaching of psychology and the failure of psychologists to deploy psychological principles and ethics in the education and treatment of students. He is co-editor (with A. J. Chapman) of *Psychology and Social Problems* (1984) and (with A. Vetere) of *Ecological Studies of Family Life* (1987).

ALAN GARNHAM read Psychology, Philosophy, and Physiology at Oxford University before obtaining a DPhil in Experimental Psychology from Sussex University. He has since worked as a Research Fellow at Sussex University and as a Lecturer at Reading and Sussex Universities. His principal research interests are in psycholinguistics; he is currently engaged in research on the interpretation of anaphoric expressions and on syntactic analysis and ambiguity. In addition to publishing numerous journal articles and book chapters, he is the author of *Psycholinguistics: Central Topics* (1985), *Mental Models as Representations of Discourse and Text* (1987), *Artificial Intelligence: An Introduction* (1988), *The Mind in Action* (1991), and co-author (with Jane Oakhill) of *Becoming a Skilled Reader* (1988).

ROBERT J. GATCHEL is Professor of Psychiatry and Rehabilitation Science at the University of Texas Southwestern Medical Center at Dallas. He received his BA from the State University of New York at Stony Brook, and his PhD in clinical psychology from the University of Wisconsin. He has conducted extensive research on psychophysiological concomitants of stress and emotion, clinical applications of biofeedback and self-regulation techniques, and the assessment and treatment of chronic low back pain disability. He is on the editorial board of numerous journals, and is a fellow of the American Psychological Association and the Academy of Behavioral Medicine Research, as well as various other professional societies. He is the author of over 100 scientific publications and chapters, and has authored or edited 10 books, including (as co-author with A. Baum and D. S. Krantz) *An Introduction to Health Psychology* (1989).

RUSSELL G. GEEN is Curators' Professor of Psychology at the University of Missouri, Columbia. A graduate of the University of Wisconsin (PhD, 1967), he was editor of the *Journal of Research in Personality* from 1977 to 1988 and became editor of the *Journal of Personality and Social Psychology: Personality Processes and Individual Differences* in 1991. He has published five books, including (as co-author with W. Beatty and R. M. Arkin) *Human Motivation* (1984) and is the author of *Human Aggression* (1990).

ANTHONY M. GRAZIANO received his PhD in clinical psychology from Purdue University, Indiana, in 1961. He completed a postdoctoral fellowship in child psychology at the Devereux Foundation before joining the faculty at the University of Bridgeport, Connecticut, where he directed several clinical research programmes with severely disturbed children. He has been on the faculty at the State University of New York at Buffalo since 1969, where he has served as the Director of Clinical Training and is the Co-Director of the Research Center for Children and Youth. He has published extensively on psychological treatment of disturbed children and their families and has written seven books, including (as co-author with Michael Raulin) *Research Methods: A Process of Inquiry* (2nd edn, 1993).

LEONARD W. HAMILTON received his doctorate in biopsychology from the University of Chicago and is now Professor of Psychology at Rutgers University in New Brunswick, New Jersey. He has published articles on the limbic system and behavioural inhibition and is co-author (with C. R. Timmons) of a textbook entitled *Principles of Behavioral Pharmacology: A Biopsychological Approach* (1990).

SARAH E. HAMPSON is Research Scientist at Oregon Research Institute, Eugene, Oregon. Prior to moving to the United States, she was a Lecturer at Birkbeck College, University of London. The second edition of her book, *The Construction of Personality: An Introduction*, was published in 1988.

ISABEL R. HARGREAVES received her PhD at the Department of Psychology, University College of North Wales, Bangor. She has been working as a Clinical Psychologist in Adult Mental Health in Gwynedd since 1984 and is also the Deputy Director of the North Wales Clinical Psychology

Course. Her main clinical interests are cognitions and how they affect emotional states.

MIKE G. HARRIS obtained his PhD in psychology from the University of Bristol in 1980, after undergraduate courses in medical physiology and neurobiology, and several years as a professional musician. Since 1980 he has taught perception at the University of Birmingham, where he is currently Head of the Cognitive Science MSc course and a Director of the Cognitive Science Research Centre. His research interests centre on the psychophysical and computational study of early visual processes, with a particular interest in the analysis and usage of retinal motion, and cricket.

ANDREW J. HILL is Senior Lecturer in Behavioural Sciences at Leeds University Medical School. His doctorate was on hunger motivation and he has published extensively on this issue. Other research interests include the psychology of food cravings, and the emergence of dieting and weight control during childhood and adolescence.

J. ALLAN HOBSON is a Professor of Psychiatry at Harvard Medical School and Director of the Laboratory of Neurophysiology, Massachusetts Mental Health Center. A prominent figure in modern brain science, his major research has been on the neurobiology of the sleeping brain. He has won the prestigious von Humboldt award of the Max Planck Society. He is the author of *The Dreaming Brain* (1988) and *Sleep* (1989).

CLIVE R. HOLLIN took his doctorate in psychology at the University of East London in 1980, after which he worked as a prison psychologist, then as a university lecturer. He currently holds the joint post of Senior Lecturer in Psychology at the University of Birmingham and Research Psychologist in the Youth Treatment Service. He is a fellow of the British Psychological Society and a Chartered Psychologist. He is co-editor of the journal *Psychology, Crime, and Law*. The author or editor of 11 books, including *Psychology and Crime* (1989), he has published numerous research articles, particularly on delinquency. His next book will be an ambitious attempt to blend core concepts from psychology and criminology in the search for a grand theory of criminal behaviour.

WENDY HOLLWAY taught in the Department of Occupational Psychology, Birkbeck College, University of London, for nine years and is now a Senior Lecturer at the University of Bradford. She is an associate fellow of the British Psychological Society and a Chartered Psychologist. She has published articles on the history of work psychology as it relates to current practices, books and articles on psychological theory and method concerning the understanding of subjectivity and gender, and articles concerning gender relations and discrimination in organizations. She is the author of

Work Psychology and Organisational Behaviour: Managing the Individual at Work (1991).

GLYN W. HUMPHREYS obtained a BSc and PhD from the University of Bristol. From 1979 to 1989 he was a Lecturer, then Senior Lecturer and Professor, in the Department of Psychology at Birkbeck College, London. Since 1989 he has been Professor of Cognitive Psychology at the University of Birmingham, where he is currently Head of the School of Psychology. He was the editor of the *Quarterly Journal of Experimental Psychology* from 1989 to 1993, and is a board member of *Cognitive Neuropsychology, Mind and Language*, and the *Journal of Experimental Psychology: Human Perception and Performance*. He initiated a new journal of *Visual Cognition*, beginning in 1994. His research interests are in the interlocking of cognitive science, cognitive neuropsychology and experimental psychology, particularly in the field of visual cognition.

KLAUS JONAS took his doctorate in social psychology at the University of Tübingen, Germany. His current research concerns the prediction of health-related behaviours from social attitudes. He has published articles on health-related topics and on social stereotypes in the *European Journal of Social Psychology* and other journals.

DANIEL KIMBLE is Professor of Psychology and Neuroscience at the University of Oregon. He took his doctorate in psychology at the University of Michigan in 1961 and after a postdoctoral stay at Stanford University, California, joined the faculty at the University of Oregon in 1963. He was named a fellow in the American Association for the Advancement of Science in 1988. He has published numerous articles on the role of the hippocampus in behaviour and on the functional effects of brain grafts in mammals. He is the author of several texts in biological psychology, his most recent book being *Biological Psychology* (2nd edn, 1992).

PAUL KLINE is Professor of Psychometrics in the University of Exeter. He is the author of numerous books and papers in the fields of psychometrics, psychoanalysis, human intelligence, and the philosophy of psychology. Among his most recent works is the *Handbook of Psychological Testing* (1992).

C. P. KYRIACOU   Charalambos Kyriacou is Reader in the Department of Genetics, University of Leicester. He began his career as a psychologist and obtained his doctorate in behaviour genetics at Sheffield University. After periods at Brandeis University, Massachusetts, and in the Psychology Department at Edinburgh University, he moved to Leicester in 1984. His current research interests are in the molecular genetic analysis of behaviour. He is the co-editor (with B. Holland) of *Genetics and Society* (1993).

DONALD LAMING is Lecturer in Experimental Psychology at the University of Cambridge. He is the author of *Information Theory of Choice-Reaction Times* (1968), *Mathematical Psychology* (1973), and *Sensory Analysis* (1986). He is currently engaged on a book which applies the principles of sensory judgement to social issues.

JOHN LAZARUS took his PhD at the University of Wales and is currently at the Department of Psychology, University of Newcastle upon Tyne. His research interests are vigilance, anti-predator behaviour, sampling, sexual strategies, and parental care. In addition to his theoretical and experimental work, he has conducted fieldwork in Britain, Iceland, Australia, and Tanzania.

WILLEM J. M. LEVELT is Director of the Max Planck Institute for Psycholinguistics, Nijmegen, The Netherlands, and Professor of Psycholinguistics at Nijmegen University. He is author of *On Binocular Rivalry* (1968), *Formal Grammars in Linguistics and Psycholinguistics* (three volumes, 1974), and *Speaking: From Intention to Articulation* (1989).

ELIZABETH F. LOFTUS is Professor of Psychology and Adjunct Professor of Law at the University of Washington, Seattle. She took her doctorate in psychology at Stanford University, California. She is the author of 16 books, including *Eyewitness Testimony* (1979) and co-author (with K. Ketchman) of *Witness for the Defense* (1991).

GEOFFREY LOWE is Senior Lecturer in Psychology at the University of Hull. He was previously at the University of Nottingham and Visiting Professor at the University of Tennessee. He is an assistant editor of *The Psychologist*. He has published articles on alcohol and related drugs in *Psychopharmacology*, *British Journal of Addiction*, and *Addiction Research*, and has recently completed a book on *Adolescent Drinking and Family Life*.

NICHOLAS J. MACKINTOSH is Professor of Experimental Psychology at the University of Cambridge and a fellow of King's College, Cambridge. He has previously taught at the University of Oxford, Dalhousie University, Nova Scotia, and the University of Sussex, and, more briefly, at the University of Hawaii, the University of Pennsylvania, and at Bryn Mawr College. He has written several books on animal learning, including *The Psychology of Animal Learning* (1974) and *Conditioning and Associative Learning* (1983), and is currently writing one on human intelligence.

A. W. MACRAE Sandy MacRae is Lecturer in Psychology at the University of Birmingham, where he studies human performance, and sensory psychophysics. He has taught measurement theory, statistics, and research methods to undergraduate and graduate psychologists and to scientists in various industries since 1965. He is a member of UK, US and international (ISO) technical committees concerned with sensory evaluation methods for food and drink.

SARA MEADOWS is Senior Lecturer in Education in the School of Education at the University of Bristol. She is the editor of *Developing Thinking* (1983) and the author of *Understanding Child Development* (1986) and *The Child as Thinker* (1993), which is a 200,000 word version of her contribution to this volume. She is co-author (with Asher Cashdan) of *Helping Children Think and Learn* (1988).

BRIAN C. J. MOORE is Reader in Auditory Perception in the Department of Experimental Psychology, University of Cambridge. He is a fellow of the Acoustical Society of America and a Visiting Consulting Professor in the Department of Bioengineering, University of Ulster. He is the author of *An Introduction to the Psychology of Hearing* (3rd edn, 1989).

WILLIAM L. OLIVER received his doctorate at the University of Colorado and has done postgraduate research at the Learning, Research, and Development Center in Pittsburgh, Pennsylvania. He is currently Assistant Professor of Psychology at Florida State University. He is pursuing research on skill acquisition and computer models of learning and memory.

BRIAN PARKINSON studied psychology as an undergraduate and postgraduate at Manchester University, where he received his PhD in 1983. He is currently Lecturer in Psychology at the University of Leicester. His interests concern the interrelations between the everyday use of emotional concepts and more formal psychological theories of emotion. His most recent research concerns role-prescribed emotion in the workplace and strategies of expressive management among high-contact service employees.

GRAHAM E. POWELL is Director of Clinical Psychology Training at the University of Surrey. He qualified as a clinical psychologist at the Institute of Psychiatry, Maudsley Hospital, London, and is Director of Counselling Services to a British Police Force. He co-edited (with S. J. E. Lindsay) the first British textbook on clinical psychology, *A Handbook of Clinical Adult Psychology* (2nd edn, 1993). He is currently working on an analysis of the psychological factors underlying rate of progress in neurological rehabilitation.

MICHAEL L. RAULIN received his PhD in clinical psychology from the University of Wisconsin, Madison, in 1977. He joined the faculty of the State University of New York at Buffalo in 1978, where he is currently the Director of Clinical Training and the Administrative Director of the Psychological Services Center. He has published articles on schizophrenia and risk factors for schizophrenia, neurological impact of drug abuse, illusory correlations, and professional development. He is co-author (with Anthony Graziano) of *Research Methods: A Process of Inquiry* (2nd edn, 1993).

HARVEY RICHARD SCHIFFMAN is Professor of Psychology at Rutgers, The State University, New Brunswick, New Jersey. He received his PhD from the University of North Carolina at Chapel Hill. He has published articles on space perception, visual illusions, and the perception of time. He is the author of *Sensation and Perception: An Integrated Approach* (3rd edn, 1990).

DAVID J. SCHNEIDER is Professor of Psychology and Department Chair at Rice University, Houston, Texas. He obtained his PhD from Stanford University, California (1966) and has also taught at Amherst College, Brandeis University, Stanford University, Indiana University, and University of Texas at San Antonio. He is editor of the journal *Social Cognition*. He is the author of *Person Perception* (1979) and *Introduction to Social Psychology* (1988).

PETER B. SMITH is Reader in Social Psychology at the University of Sussex. His current interests are in cross-cultural studies in the fields of social and organizational psychology; he is associate editor of the *Journal of Cross-Cultural Psychology*. He is the author of *Groups Within Organisations* (1973) and *Group Processes and Personal Change* (1980), and co-author (with M. F. Peterson) of *Leadership, Organisations and Culture* (1988) and (with M. H. Bond) of *Social Psychology Across Cultures* (1993).

PETER K. SMITH is Professor of Psychology at the University of Sheffield. He has researched extensively on the topic of children's play, and is currently working on ways of dealing with bullying in schools. He is the co-author (with Kevin Connolly) of *The Ecology of Preschool Behaviour* (1980), and (with Helen Cowie) of *Understanding Children's Development* (2nd edn, 1991). He is co-editor (with D. A. Thompson) of *Practical Approaches to Bullying* (1991).

ROBERT J. STERNBERG is IBM Professor of Psychology and Education at Yale University. He won the American Psychological Association's Distinguished Scientific Award for an Early Career Contribution to Psychology in 1981 and also its Boyd R. McCandless Young Scientist Award of the Division of Developmental Psychology in 1982. He is the editor of the journal *Psychological Bulletin*. He is the author of *Beyond IQ: A Triarchic Theory of Human Intelligence* (1985) and *Metaphors of Mind: Conceptions of the Nature of Intelligence* (1990).

RICHARD STEVENS is Senior Lecturer and currently Head of the Department of Psychology at the Open University in Milton Keynes, Buckinghamshire. Previously he taught at Trinity College, Dublin, and the University of California. For several years he was chairperson of the Association for

Humanistic Psychology and is at present developing an integrated theory of human action (trimodal theory). He is the author of *Freud and Psychoanalysis* (1983), *Erik Erikson* (1983), and *Personal Worlds* (1986), and the co-editor (with Hedy Brown) of *Social Behaviour and Experience* (1976).

DAVID D. STRETCH   After a first degree in psychology from the University College of North Wales (at Bangor), David Stretch completed an MSc in mathematical psychology at Stirling, and a PhD at Birmingham, where he studied the mathematical modelling of memory. He then held a variety of positions at the University of Newcastle upon Tyne and also worked for Newcastle Area Health Authority. In 1986 he joined the Psychiatry Department at Leicester University as a Lecturer in Psychology, specializing in statistical modelling and research design. Because of this expertise, he has been associated with publications in a wide area of psychology; he still manages to continue research into psychometrics, axiomatic measurement theory, and other areas of mathematical psychology.

WOLFGANG STROEBE received a doctorate in experimental psychology from the University of Münster, Germany, and in social psychology from the London School of Economics. He has held academic positions in Britain, the United States, and Germany, and is now Professor at the University of Utrecht in The Netherlands. A past president of the European Association of Experimental Social Psychology and a member of the editorial boards of social psychology journals in the United States, Britain, and Germany, he has written numerous books and chapters on attitude change, group productivity, and health psychology. He is co-editor (with W. Meyer) of *Social Psychology and Economics* (1982); he is co-author (with M. S. Stroebe) of *Bereavement and Health: The Psychological and Physical Consequences of Partner Loss* (1987) and (with M. Hewson) of the *European Review of Social Psychology* (1992).

C. ROBIN TIMMONS received her masters degree in biopsychology and her doctorate in developmental psychology from Rutgers University, New Brunswick, New Jersey. She is now Associate Professor of Psychology at Drew University, Madison, New Jersey. She has published articles on the development of behavioural inhibition and memory in infants, and is co-author (with L. W. Hamilton) of a textbook entitled *Principles of Behavioral Pharmacology: A Biopsychological Approach* (1990).

RHODA K. UNGER is Professor of Psychology and Director of the Honors Program at Montclair State College in New Jersey. She received her PhD in experimental psychology from Harvard University, and was the first recipient of the Carolyn Wood Sherif Award from the Division on the Psychology of Women of the American Psychological Association. She is also the recipient of two Distinguished Publication Awards from the Association for Women in Psychology. She is active in various feminist organizations within psychology and has lectured extensively in the United States and abroad. She has published six books; she is the author of *Female and Male* (1979). co-editor (with V. E. O'Leary and B. S. Wallston) of *Women, Gender, and Social Psychology* (1985), and editor of *Representations: Social Constructions of Gender* (1989).

JAMES VIVIAN received his doctorate in social psychology at Boston College, Massachusetts, and is currently a research fellow in social psychology at the University of Kent, Canterbury. His current research is concerned with intergroup contact.

GRAHAM F. WAGSTAFF is Senior Lecturer in Psychology at the University of Liverpool. His main research and teaching interests are in social psychology and he has a particular interest in social psychological and forensic aspects of hypnosis. He is one of the founder members of the British Society of Experimental and Clinical Hypnosis. He has published widely in the area of hypnosis and is author of *Hypnosis, Compliance and Belief* (1981). He is currently writing a book on the psychology and philosophy of justice.

JOHN WEINMAN is Professor of Psychology as Applied to Medicine at the United Medical and Dental Schools of Guy's and St Thomas' Hospital in the University of London. He first trained in clinical psychology at the Royal Free Hospital, London, and then obtained his doctorate at the Institute of Neurology after four years' full-time research with the Medical Research Council. He is the editor-in-chief of *Psychology and Health: An International Journal*. He is the author of *An Outline of Psychology as Applied to Medicine* (1987) and the editor of several other books on aspects of health psychology.

J. MARK G. WILLIAMS is Professor of Clinical Psychology at the University College of North Wales, Bangor, having been Research Scientist at the Medical Research Council's Applied Psychology Unit in Cambridge. He is also an Anglican priest, and interested in the interface of psychology with religion. He is co-author (with F. N. Watts, C. MacLeod, and A. Mathews) of *Cognitive Psychology and Emotional Disorders* (1988) and author of *The Psychological Treatment of Depression: A Guide to the Theory and Practice of Cognitive Behaviour Therapy* (2nd edn, 1992).

COMPANION ENCYCLOPEDIA
OF PSYCHOLOGY
VOLUME 1

1
INTRODUCTION

1.1

WHAT IS PSYCHOLOGY?

Andrew M. Colman
University of Leicester, England

Origin of the word
  "psychology"
Historical background
Related disciplines and practices
  Psychiatry
  Psychoanalysis
  Philosophy
Classification of research and
  fields of applied psychology
Research methods
  Case studies
  Naturalistic observations
  Survey research
Quasi-experiments and
  correlational studies
Controlled experiments
Some key concepts
  Experimental and control
  groups
  Statistical significance
  Correlation
  Cognition
A note to readers
Further reading
References

The authoritative *Oxford English Dictionary* defines psychology as "the science of the nature, functions, and phenomena of the human soul or mind". Nowadays, most psychologists would object to the last part of that definition, because the human soul is no longer regarded as the concern of psychology, and also because human and animal behaviour (which are ignored by the above definition) have come to be regarded as essential components of the discipline. Although any definition of psychology is bound to be controversial, even among psychologists, the following renovated version of the *OED* definition comes as close to encapsulating the essence of psychology as is possible in a few words: psychology is the science of the nature, functions, and phenomena of behaviour and mental experience. Underlying this definition is the fundamental assumption, which is supported by evidence

3

throughout this encyclopedia, that behaviour and mental experience are governed by rational laws that we can discover and understand.

Associated with the scientific discipline of psychology are a number of professions of applied psychology, including clinical, counselling, educational (school), industrial (occupational), organizational, and forensic (criminological) psychology – see chapters 13.1 (Graham E. Powell), 13.2 (David Fontana), 13.3 (Wendy Hollway), and 13.4 (Clive R. Hollin). Whereas academic psychologists work mainly in universities, colleges, and other teaching and research establishments, professional psychologists work in a wider variety of settings, including hospitals and clinics, counselling agencies, commercial and industrial companies, prisons and correctional institutions, government departments, and in private practice.

In both its academic and professional forms, psychology has been increasing in popularity since the Second World War. The number of students choosing to study psychology has been rising steadily for several decades in industrialized and developing countries, and whenever surveys are conducted to try to find out why students choose psychology, the most common reason by far turns out to be interest in its subject matter, rather than career prospects or any other considerations (Radford, 1991). In just one decade between 1980 and the early 1990s the total number of practising psychologists in the world rose from about a quarter of a million to well over half a million (Rosenzweig, 1992). Although these figures are impressive, it is worth pointing out that there are still about twelve times as many medical practitioners in the world as there are psychologists.

ORIGIN OF THE WORD "PSYCHOLOGY"

The word "psychology" was formed from two Greek words. The first, *psyche*, originally meant "breath" but later acquired the additional meaning "soul", because breathing was thought to indicate that the soul had not yet left the body, and later still (during the seventeenth century) broadened further in meaning to include "mind". The equivalent Latin word *anima*, from which the English words "animal" and "animate" are derived, also started life meaning "breath" and later evolved the additional meaning "mind". The second Greek word, *logos*, originally meant "word" and later expanded in meaning to include "discourse" and eventually "science". According to its Greek roots, therefore, psychology is literally the science of the mind.

In later Greek mythology, the soul is personified by Psyche (with a capital P), a young woman loved by Eros, the god of love. Eros marries her on condition that they spend time together only at night and that she never sees his face. Goaded by her jealous sisters to steal a glance, Psyche lights an oil lamp one night while Eros is asleep and falls in love with him at first sight, but she is so startled by his beauty that she accidentally spills a drop of oil on his shoulder and awakens him, whereupon he immediately abandons her. To win

4

him back, Psyche is forced to endure many trials and dangers, but eventually she is transformed into a goddess and joins Eros in heavenly bliss. In this myth, Psyche symbolizes the human soul, suffering hardship and struggle in life but re-awakening after death in a new, better existence, like a caterpillar transformed into a butterfly. This explains why Psyche is generally depicted in works of art with butterfly wings or sometimes simply as a butterfly (see Figure 1).

The Latin word *psychologia* emerged from obscure origins in Germany in the sixteenth century; it was used by Philip Melanchthon, Otto Casmann, and Rudolf Goeckel, but no one is certain who coined it or exactly when it was first used. The English word "psychology" made its first appearance near the end of the seventeenth century in *The Physical Dictionary: Wherein the terms of Anatomy, the names and causes of Diseases, chyrugical Instruments and their Use; are accurately Describ'd* (Blankaart, 1693), which was the second edition of the English translation of Steven Blankaart's *Lexicon Medicum, Graeco-Latinum*, originally published in 1679. Blankaart refers to "*Anthropologia*, the Description of Man, or the Doctrin concerning him [which is divided] into Two Parts; viz. *Anatomy*, which treats of the Body, and *Psychology*, which treats of the Soul" (p. 13, italics and capitals in original). The word "psychology" was used sporadically throughout the eighteenth and early nineteenth centuries – the English philosopher and physician David Hartley (1749), for example, wrote of "Psychology, or the Theory of the human Mind, with that of the intellectual Principles of Brute Animals" (p. 354, capitals in original) – but it was not until the 1830s that it began to be used frequently and came to be widely understood.

Figure 1 The Chartered Psychologists' logo of the British Psychological Society, showing Psyche, the personification of the human soul, with butterfly wings for reasons explained in the text

HISTORICAL BACKGROUND

Although psychology has been recognized as an independent discipline for little more than a century (see chapter 1.2, Raymond E. Fancher), psychological speculations and practices can be found in the records of the most ancient civilizations. The Ebers papyrus, an ancient Egyptian document devoted to medical matters dating from before 1500 BC, for example, describes practices strikingly similar to modern hypnosis (see chapter 11.2, Graham F. Wagstaff), and a later Egyptian scroll records in detail the speech and behaviour of a young boy who was hypnotized while he fixed his gaze on a luminous object (Ellenberger, 1970).

There are even occasional records in ancient documents of scientific experiments designed to settle psychological questions. The earliest is contained in *The Histories* of Herodotus, the world's first history book, which was completed in about 429 BC (Herodotus, 1972). According to Herodotus (part 1, book 2, para. 2), the experiment was performed by the ancient Egyptian Pharaoh Psammetichus I in the seventh century BC to determine whether human beings have an inborn capacity for speech, and if so, which particular language is innate. He ordered two infants to be brought up in a remote place by a shepherd who was forbidden to speak in their presence. After two years the children began to speak, and the word that they repeated most often was *becos*, which turned out to be the Phrygian word for "bread". Psammetichus concluded that the capacity for speech is inborn and that the innate, natural language of human beings is Phrygian.

The questions that Psammetichus's experiment was intended to answer seem quaint and foolish in the present day, and his experiment was certainly poorly designed and methodologically unsound – even in his own time critics pointed out that the children may merely have been imitating the bleating of goats. But what is striking is that it was a psychological experiment none the less; in its conceptual structure and methodology it is strikingly similar to the highly regarded experiments of William H. Thorpe (1958), who reared birds in isolation from members of their own species in order to discover the innate features of their songs.

Before psychology emerged as an independent discipline in Germany in the late nineteenth century, it existed for a long time as a branch of philosophy that was called "mental philosophy" to distinguish it from "natural philosophy" (which is now called physics). During the eighteenth and nineteenth centuries, developments in the biological sciences began to suggest empirical approaches (approaches involving observation and experiment) to some of the problems of mental philosophy, and towards the end of that period psychology finally reached maturity and gained its independence as a separate discipline in its own right. Although psychology is barely a century old as a discipline, psychological speculation, practice, and even research clearly have much older pedigrees. That is what the German psychologist Hermann

Ebbinghaus (1908) meant by his frequently quoted remark that "psychology has a long past but a short history" (p. 1).

The first systematic investigations of psychological problems were carried out in ancient Greece by the pre-Socratic philosophers of the sixth and fifth centuries BC. They did not have any concept of an individual soul or mind – that arose in later Greek philosophy, especially under the influence of Aristotle – but they were the first to understand that the brain plays an important role in mental experience. In particular, they understood that our eyes cannot see and our ears cannot hear without the help of our brains, and by contributing this crucial insight the pre-Socratics paved the way for the scientific study of sensation and perception (see section 3).

The pre-Socratics were also the first to develop a theory to explain the fact that people differ from one another not only physically but also psychologically, that is, not only in appearance but also in temperament, or what psychologists now call personality (see section 7). According to their doctrine of the four temperaments, people were thought to be more or less sanguine (optimistic), melancholic (depressive), choleric (short-tempered), or phlegmatic (apathetic) according to the mixture in their bodies of four humours or fluids, called blood (*sanguis*), black bile (*melaina chole*), yellow bile (*chole*), and phlegm (*phlegma*). The doctrine of the four temperaments held sway for centuries, but the biochemical basis of the theory finally collapsed during the Renaissance when researchers began to discover the rudimentary facts of human physiology. The underlying typology, though not the theory of humours that sought to explain it, survives in some modern theories of personality (see chapters 7.2, Sarah E. Hampson, and 7.3, H. J. Eysenck). The contribution of the pre-Socratics, which can hardly be overestimated, was historically important not so much because of the answers that they gave, but because they thought to ask the questions at all.

Physiology became established as a field of research during the second half of the eighteenth century, after the introduction of the microscope and post-mortem examinations, which had formerly been banned by the Church. During the following decades, enormous advances were made in understanding the brain and nervous system (see chapter 2.3, Daniel Kimble) and evolutionary aspects of behaviour (see chapter 2.2, John Lazarus). The prevailing currents of philosophical and biological research gradually converged towards the emergence of psychology as an independent discipline, and that event finally occurred in Germany in the 1880s. The year in which the independent discipline of psychology is usually said to have been born is 1879, when Wilhelm Wundt opened the first psychological laboratory in Leipzig. The history of psychology is discussed in greater detail in chapter 1.2 (Raymond E. Fancher).

RELATED DISCIPLINES AND PRACTICES

In order to present a clear picture of the nature and scope of psychology, it is useful to distinguish it from a few related practices and professions with which it is often confused. The following brief comments should help to map out the intellectual terrain and eliminate certain common fallacies. (For more detail and further distinctions, see Colman, 1988, chap. 1.)

Psychiatry

As its name suggests, psychiatry (from the Greek *psyche*, meaning mind, and *iatros*, meaning doctor) is a branch of medicine concerned with mental disorders – their classification, aetiology (causes), diagnosis, treatment, and prevention. Anyone intending to qualify as a psychiatrist must first undergo a full medical training and then specialize in psychiatry, which is simply a medical specialism among many others, including cardiology, dermatology, and gynaecology.

Psychology, in contrast, is not a medical specialism, and psychologists are not medically trained. Furthermore, most of psychology is concerned with normal behaviour and mental life rather than with mental disorders. A small part of academic psychology is, however, concerned with mental disorders (section 10), and one of the professions of psychology, clinical psychology (chapter 13.1, Graham E. Powell) involves the treatment of mentally disordered patients. In Britain, the United States, and elsewhere, the work of clinical psychologists has tended over the years to resemble that of psychiatrists more and more closely. Because of their different backgrounds and training, however, psychiatrists tend to favour more medically oriented interpretations of mental disorders and more physical forms of treatment than do most clinical psychologists.

Psychoanalysis

Psychoanalysis is a theory of mental structure and function and a method of psychotherapy based on the writings of Sigmund Freud and his followers (see chapters 7.4, Richard Stevens, and 13.5, Peter Fonagy). As a theory, psychoanalysis focuses primarily on unconscious mental processes and the various defence mechanisms that people use to repress them. As a therapeutic method, psychoanalysis involves the client in three or more 50-minute sessions per week for several years. During the analytic sessions a number of specialized techniques are used to help the client uncover repressed thoughts and feelings, understand why they were repressed, and accept them consciously.

Psychoanalysts are not necessarily trained in psychology or psychiatry; their training involves undergoing psychoanalysis themselves. Conversely, it is also true to say that most psychologists and psychiatrists have no formal qualifications in psychoanalysis; but many of them, especially in parts of continental Europe and the Third World, are influenced to varying degrees by psychoanalytic ideas and approaches. Most – though by no means all – British and American psychologists, on the other hand, hold attitudes towards psychoanalysis ranging from indifference to open hostility.

Philosophy

Many of the problems that non-psychologists assume to fall within the scope of psychology are really philosophical problems. These are questions that must be tackled by rational argument rather than by experiments or observations of behaviour. Although psychology was once a branch of philosophy called "mental philosophy", the psychological offspring has grown up to be quite distinct in its subject matter from its distinguished philosophical parent. Psychology, in contrast to philosophy, is devoted to empirical questions, that is, questions that can, in principle at least, be decided by observations of real-world facts and events.

Some of the traditional problems of philosophy are confusingly tied up with what might at first appear to be psychological issues. The most obvious example is the mind–body problem, which has exercised philosophers throughout the modern period and is still unresolved. This problem relates to the puzzling relationship and apparent interaction between mental experiences and the physical world. How can mental experiences such as desires, which are entirely immaterial, produce physical effects like bodily movements – in other words, how can a thought move a muscle? And how can physical injuries to our bodies produce the non-physical mental experiences we call pains? These are irreducibly philosophical questions, in spite of their superficial resemblance to psychological problems, because they could not be solved, even in principle, by empirical investigations of any kind, or at least that is what most philosophers and psychologists believe.

A second obvious group of questions, which are even more unambiguously philosophical rather than psychological, are moral or ethical problems. A branch of philosophy called *ethics* is devoted to questions of morality and general issues of right and wrong. Is it always wrong to tell lies? Is euthanasia immoral? Questions of this type, once again, are impossible in principle to answer through empirical observations of behaviour, and they therefore fall beyond the scope of psychology. Factual questions about moral attitudes and behaviour, and how they develop in children, are legitimate topics for psychological research, but questions about how people *ought* to behave belong to the field of ethics within the discipline of philosophy. It goes almost without saying that psychologists ought to be, and generally are, concerned about moral issues that arise in psychological research and practice (see chapter 12.6, Anthony Gale).

9

One trivial source of confusion is worth commenting on at this point. In Britain, the United States, and many other countries, universities traditionally confer the degree of Doctor of Philosophy (PhD or DPhil) rather than "Doctor of Psychology" for advanced studies in psychology. The degree of Doctor of Philosophy is the standard doctoral degree, not only in psychology and philosophy, but also in physics, chemistry, biology, history, archaeology, and most other arts, science, and social science subjects. A person with a doctorate in any subject can legitimately use the title of doctor, but for obscure historical reasons medical practitioners in the United Kingdom and many other countries are allowed to call themselves doctors even if they do not hold doctoral degrees in any subject.

CLASSIFICATION OF RESEARCH AND FIELDS OF APPLIED PSYCHOLOGY

The fundamental aim of research in psychology can be stated quite simply: it is to discover and understand the nature, functions, and phenomena of behaviour and mental experience. It is like any other branch of scientific research inasmuch as it aims to enlarge our knowledge and understanding of the world; what distinguishes it from other areas of scientific research is the subject matter with which it deals, namely behaviour and mental experience. Psychologists who are engaged in basic research, like basic researchers in other disciplines, pursue knowledge and understanding as ends in themselves. The value of a basic research contribution is judged (or ought to be judged) according to the amount of light that it casts on an aspect of behaviour or mental experience that was previously unknown or imperfectly understood, rather than according to its assumed practical usefulness.

In contrast to this, the various fields of applied psychology and their associated professions (see section 13) are driven by quite different and much more practical aims. They are concerned with applications of psychology to practical problems of everyday life rather than theoretical problems of understanding and explanation. Applied psychology relies partly on basic research findings, which sometimes turn out to be useful in practice, and partly on the results of applied research specifically designed to answer practical questions.

In clinical psychology (see chapter 13.1, Graham E. Powell), the findings of basic and applied research into the classification, aetiology, diagnosis, treatment, and prevention of mental disorders are put to use in an effort to deal with these problems more effectively. In educational (school) psychology (see chapter 13.2, David Fontana), research into problems of learning, adjustment, and behaviour among schoolchildren is applied in an effort to provide practical help to teachers, parents, and children with learning or behaviour problems. In industrial (occupational) and organizational psychology (see chapter 13.3, Wendy Hollway), research into the well-being and efficiency of people at work and into organizational behaviour is applied to problems arising in those settings. In forensic (criminological) psychology (see chapter 13.4, Clive R. Hollin), research into all aspects of criminal behaviour is applied in an effort to solve practical problems of crime and punishment.

Psychological research can be classified in many different ways, but all classifications are arbitrary and conjectural. The system of classification that has been adopted in this encyclopedia is not necessarily more rational than any other, but it corresponds as closely as possible, according to a preliminary survey that was carried out, to the way the discipline is divided up for teaching purposes in degree courses in the United States and Britain (Boneau, 1990; Watts, 1990). The section headings reflect a hybrid classification, based partly on the types of psychological processes under investigation (sensation and perception, cognition, learning and skills, emotion and motivation, individual differences and personality, social psychology), partly on levels of analysis (biological aspects of behaviour, developmental psychology), and partly on characteristics of the individuals under investigation (abnormal psychology).

Psychology repudiates all attempts to divide its subject matter into watertight compartments, so some seepage between chapters and even between sections has been condoned in this encyclopedia, and unsurprisingly a section devoted to "special topics" turned out to be necessary because certain obviously important topics refused to fit into any of the other sections. Furthermore, research methods and statistics transcend the classification outlined in the previous paragraph, and it would be inappropriate to classify them as "special topics" because they could hardly be more general, but they are integral to the discipline and are taught in all reputable degree courses, so a further section in this encyclopedia is devoted to them. And for the sake of completeness, a final section deals with the professions of psychology.

RESEARCH METHODS

Research in psychology, as in any other science, always begins with a question that needs answering. The question may arise from the natural curiosity of the researcher, from a formal theory that generates a testable prediction, or from something puzzling thrown up by the findings of previous research. Provided that it relates to behaviour or mental experience and is an empirical question that can be tackled by collecting objective evidence, it is a legitimate problem for psychological research. What follows is a brief outline of the main research methods used in psychology (for a more extended discussion along the same lines, see Colman, 1988, chap. 4).

Case studies

A case study is a relatively primitive research method. In psychology, it involves a detailed investigation of a single individual, or occasionally a single social organization. Research of this kind is common in abnormal psychology (see section 10) and comparatively rare in other branches of the discipline. The data reported in case studies may be derived from interviews, diaries, case histories, medical records, questionnaires and other psychometric tests, or direct observations of behaviour. The findings of case studies can be interesting and valuable, but they often suffer from problems of generalizability, because one individual's response to a particular treatment (for example) is not necessarily the same as another's. The accumulation of evidence from a number of case studies, especially if they are reported by independent investigators, can sometimes mitigate this problem. (For more detail on case studies, see chapter 12.5, Francis C. Dane.)

Naturalistic observations

Naturalistic observations, which are discussed in more detail in chapter 12.5, are widely used in ethological research (see chapter 2.2, John Lazarus) and, less commonly, in certain areas of developmental and social psychology (sections 8 and 9). They involve careful observations and recordings of the behaviour of animals or people in their natural habitats. Unlike case studies, which typically include data from interviews and psychometric tests, naturalistic observations are generally non-interactive inasmuch as the investigator tries to avoid influencing the behaviour that is being observed.

Naturalistic observations are often open-ended and exploratory in spirit, but they are sometimes useful for answering specifically focused questions. The range of psychological phenomena for which this method of research is suitable is rather limited, although where it is applicable it often yields important findings about everyday behaviour in natural environments, and it can sometimes serve as a useful corrective to the findings of artificial laboratory studies. The methods of recording observations are, however, often relatively crude and subjective, and this sometimes calls into question the validity of the findings.

Survey research

Survey research (see chapter 12.5, Francis C. Dane) is useful for investigating psychological phenomena in specific sections of a population or in different populations. When it is confined to single populations it usually involves comparisons between groups defined by demographic variables such as age, sex, social class, education, marital status, ethnic identity, and geographical location. It is used, in particular, to answer questions about the incidence, prevalence, and distribution of mental disorders, behaviour patterns, attitudes, opinions, beliefs, and personality characteristics. The most common sources of data in survey research are interviews and questionnaires.

To ensure that the individuals studied are truly representative of the population groups to which they belong, survey researchers use sophisticated methods of sampling. The ideal method of sampling, from a theoretical point of view, is simple random sampling, in which every member of the population has an equal chance of inclusion. In practice, simple random sampling is seldom used because of the difficulty of compiling a sampling frame (a list of all members of the population from which to make the random selection) and the further problem of persuading all of the selected subjects to participate in the survey. As a consequence, the most common sampling technique in psychological survey research, and also in market research and opinion polling, is quota sampling. This involves selecting individuals more or less arbitrarily to fill predetermined quotas, matching the proportions in the population at large according to age, sex, social class, or whatever criteria are thought to be important for the research.

Quasi-experiments and correlational studies

Quasi-experiments resemble controlled experiments (see below) in so far as they are designed to answer questions about cause and effect, but they lack the full control of conjectured causes and extraneous variables that is characteristic of controlled experiments. Correlational research focuses on non-causal questions about the relationship between variables – intelligence and creativity, introversion and self-esteem, gender and verbal ability, and so on. Both of these research methods, which are discussed in more depth in chapter 12.4 (Michael L. Raulin and Anthony M. Graziano), focus on the relationship between two or more factors over which the investigator has imperfect or non-existent control.

Neither of these research methods can conclusively settle questions about cause and effect, but valuable information about the relationship between variables can often be obtained, and it is sometimes reasonable to draw tentative inferences about probable causal effects from quasi-experiments.

Controlled experiments

Controlled experimentation (see chapters 12.1, David D. Stretch, and 12.2, Brian S. Everitt) is the most important research method in psychology, not because experiments are necessarily more objective or precise than other methods, but because they alone allow firm conclusions to be drawn about cause and effect. The defining properties of an experiment are the manipulation of the conjectured cause, called the *independent variable* because it is varied independently by the experimenter, and control of extraneous variables that might also influence the behaviour under investigation, which is called the *dependent variable*. Most experiments take place in laboratory environments, where manipulation and control can be implemented most efficiently, but field experiments conducted in naturalistic settings are sometimes carried out when laboratory experiments are infeasible or undesirable for special reasons.

In a well-controlled experiment, *all* extraneous variables are controlled while the independent variable is manipulated; in factorial designs, more than one independent variable is manipulated simultaneously (chapter 12.2, Brian S. Everitt). In psychology, experimental control is usually achieved through randomization: subjects are randomly assigned to treatment conditions, so that any pre-existing differences between subjects are distributed according to the laws of chance, and subjects in all treatment conditions are then treated identically apart from the deliberate manipulation of the independent variable. This allows statistical methods to be used to evaluate the significance, in relation to chance, of any resulting difference that might be observed in the dependent variable (see chapters 12.1, David D. Stretch, and 12.3, A. W. MacRae).

The purpose of inferential statistics is usually to calculate the probability of obtaining, by chance alone, a difference as large as the one observed, and thereby to provide a rational basis for deciding whether or not the difference is *statistically significant*. The logical connection between experimental control through randomization and statistical inference is explained in detail in Colman (1988, chap. 4).

SOME KEY CONCEPTS

The chapters that follow this introductory section deal with all major areas of psychological research and practice, from biological aspects of behaviour, through sensation and perception, to cognition, learning and skills, emotion and motivation, individual differences and personality, developmental, social, and abnormal psychology, special topics, research methods and statistics, and the professions of psychology. The chapters in each of these sections can be read without any background knowledge beyond a handful of key concepts that crop up again and again and are of sufficient importance to merit brief explanation in this chapter. Several have already been dealt with, but there are a few more that deserve mention.

Experimental and control groups

All experimental research, and most non-experimental research as well, involves comparisons (see chapter 12.1, David D. Stretch). To test the hypothesis that a particular drug produces improvement in patients with a certain mental disorder, for example, it is not sufficient to measure the improvement in patients who have been administered the drug, because any observed improvement might be due to something quite different, for example spontaneous remission (natural improvement due merely to the passage of time). A well-designed experiment would involve not only an experimental group, containing patients who would receive the drug, but also a comparison group of patients, as closely comparable to the experimental group as possible, treated identically to the experimental subjects except that they would not receive the drug.

The comparison group, which is usually made comparable to the experimental group by randomly assigning subjects to the two groups by tossing a coin or using some other randomizing device, is called a control group. Most psychological experiments involve comparisons between experimental and control groups, though other designs are possible (see chapters 12.1, David D. Stretch, and 12.2, Brian S. Everitt). In the example of the previous paragraph, the ideal experiment would be double-blind, with neither the experimenter nor the patients knowing which of the pills contained the drug and which were merely placebos (inactive dummy pills) until after the results had been recorded. This would ensure that any statistically significant difference that was observed between the experimental and control groups could not be due to biased expectations of the experimenters or subjects.

Statistical significance

This concept has been touched on above. A research finding is said to be statistically significant if the probability of obtaining such an extreme finding by chance alone is sufficiently small, by convention usually less than 1 in 20 (the 5 per cent significance level, sometimes written $p < .05$). If a research finding is statistically significant, then the researcher is justified in concluding that the observed effect is "real" and not due merely to chance. If, on the other hand, it is not statistically significant, then chance cannot be ruled out as an explanation and it is impossible to draw any firm conclusion from the result. For a full explanation of this concept, see chapter 12.3 (A. W. MacRae).

Correlation

Two variables are said to be positively correlated if high scores on one of them tend to go with high scores on the other, and low scores on one with low scores on the other, like people's heights and weights. The usual statistical index of correlation, which is symbolized by r, ranges from 1.00 for perfect positive correlation, through zero for no correlation between unrelated variables, to -1.00 for perfect negative correlation. The heights and weights of adults in Britain are positively correlated. According to a survey of a representative sample of 10,000 men and women, which yielded results very similar to findings reported in the United States, the correlations are in fact .47 for men and .35 for women (Knight, 1984), and both of these correlations are of course statistically significant. For more on correlation, see chapter 12.3 (A. W. MacRae).

Cognition

Cognition (from the Latin *cognoscere*, to apprehend) is a rather elastic term used in psychology to refer to attention, thinking, problem-solving, remembering, and other mental processes that can be broadly described as information processing. When psychologists refer to the cognitive aspects of a psychological process, they are often implicitly stressing the mental activity involved in the phenomenon rather than its purely outward, behavioural manifestations. Cognitive psychology (see section 4) is an area of psychological research in its own right, or more precisely a loosely connected set of research areas, but almost every other area of psychological research has cognitive approaches, theories, or aspects, which are frequently referred to in every section of this encyclopedia.

Cognitive science, which should not be confused with cognition or cognitive psychology, is a relatively recent umbrella term for an interdisciplinary endeavour, involving cognitive psychology, the brain sciences, computer science, artificial intelligence, linguistics, and philosophy, to construct theoretical models of information processing (see chapter 4.5, Alan Garnham). Although the activities of cognitive psychologists and cognitive scientists overlap and intersect, their aims and methodologies, and the general flavour of their approaches, are quite distinct.

A NOTE TO READERS

Contributors to this encyclopedia were selected on the basis of their acknowledged expertise in their own fields and their proven ability to communicate their ideas in lively and readable prose. Their expertise is beyond question: they are all leading researchers or practitioners in the areas about which they have written, and never before have so many academic and applied psychologists of such eminence contributed in depth to a single reference work. The contributors were asked to deal with their topics as thoroughly as possible in the space available (about 7,500 words) and to write informatively and entertainingly, at a level accessible to attentive but not necessarily specialist readers. They were requested to assume no prior knowledge on the part of their readers and to explain all technical terminology that they found it necessary to introduce. They were asked to aim for as encyclopedic a presentation of their topics as the constraints of space and level of difficulty permitted, and above all to write with clarity and vigour. Readers will form their own opinions as to how successfully the contributors have achieved these multiple goals.

The totality of the chapters that follow provide a better answer to the question "What is Psychology?" than has been provided by this chapter. There is a limit to how much can usefully be said *about* psychology without getting down to specific examples of what psychologists do. The only way of gaining a proper insight into psychology, or any other discipline for that matter, is by examining its actual content. This encyclopedia provides an overview of the subject matter of psychology written by active researchers and practitioners in every major area of the discipline and its associated practices and professions.

FURTHER READING

Atkinson, R. L., Atkinson, R. C., Smith, E. E., Bem, D. J., & Hilgard, E. R. (1990). *Introduction to psychology* (10th edn). New York: Harcourt Brace Jovanovich.

Colman, A. M. (1988). *What is psychology? The inside story* (2nd edn). London: Hutchinson.

Feldman, R. S. (1992). *Elements of psychology*. New York: McGraw-Hill.

Gross, R. (1992). *Psychology: The science of mind and behaviour* (2nd edn). London: Hodder & Stoughton.

Koch, S., & Leary, D. E. (Eds) (1992). *A century of psychology as science* (2nd edn). Washington, DC: American Psychological Association.

REFERENCES

Blankaart, S. (1693). *The physical dictionary: Wherein the terms of anatomy, the names and causes of diseases, chyrugical instruments and their use; are accurately describ'd* (2nd edn). London: Samuel Crouch (original work in Latin published 1679 by Johannis ten Hoorn, Amsterdam).

Boneau, C. A. (1990). Psychological literacy: A first approximation. *American Psychologist, 45*, 891–900.

Colman, A. M. (1988). *What is psychology? The inside story* (2nd edn). London: Hutchinson.

Ebbinghaus, H. (1908). *Abriss der Psychologie*. Leipzig: Veit.

Ellenberger, H. F. (1970). *The discovery of the unconscious: the history and evolution of dynamic psychiatry*. New York: Basic Books.

Hartley, D. (1749). *Observations on man, his frame, his duty, and his expectations*. London: Tegg.

Herodotus (1972). *The histories* (A. de Sélincourt, trans.). Harmondsworth: Penguin (original work completed *c*.429 BC).

Knight, I. (1984). *The heights and weights of adults in Great Britain*. London: Her Majesty's Stationery Office.

Radford, J. (Ed.) (1991). *The choice of psychology*, Group of Teachers of Psychology Occasional Papers, vol. 12. Leicester: British Psychological Society.

Rosenzweig, M. R. (Ed.) (1992). *International psychological science: Progress, problems, and prospects.* Washington, DC: American Psychological Association.

Thorpe, W. H. (1958). The learning of song patterns by birds, with special reference to the song of the chaffinch *Fringilla coelebs. Ibis, 100,* 535–570.

Watts, F. N. (Ed.) (1990). *The undergraduate curriculum in psychology: Proceedings of a symposium held at the London Conference of the British Psychological Society on 20 December 1988,* Group of Teachers of Psychology Occasional Papers, vol. 9. Leicester: British Psychological Society.

1.2

HISTORICAL BACKGROUND OF PSYCHOLOGY

Raymond E. Fancher
York University, Ontario, Canada

Classical foundations	Wundt and the formal
Descartes and mind–body	establishment of experimental
dualism	psychology
British associationism	Introspection and the problem
Continental nativism	of consciousness
Studies of sensation and	Darwinian influences on
perception	psychology
Fechner and psychophysics	Brain science
	The unconscious
	Further reading
	References

While psychology has existed as an independent academic and scientific discipline for little more than a century, it has extensive foundations in mental philosophy dating from the ancient Greeks. Psychology has never had a single dominating figure to revolutionize and define it, as physics had its Newton or biology its Darwin. Instead, modern psychology is the product of innumerable investigations in a wide variety of fields including physics, biology, physiology, politics, mathematics, and medicine, as well as several branches of philosophy. This brief survey of psychology's complex history cannot be comprehensive, but will focus on a representative selection of its major figures.

19

CLASSICAL FOUNDATIONS

The word "psychology" derives from the ancient Greek *psyche*, originally denoting "breath" but coming by the fourth century BC to signify the animating agency in living organisms, the "soul". The two greatest intellectual figures of that time, Plato (*c*.427–347 BC) and Aristotle (384–322 BC), established contrasting traditions in mental philosophy, each of which contributed importantly to the development of modern psychology.

Plato posited two separate realms of knowledge. The *phenomenal* realm (from the Greek *phenomena*, "appearances") is based on the ordinary senses, is constantly in flux, and produces knowledge that is often illusory. The other and higher realm, revealed through the innate rational and logical faculties of the mind, consists of permanent and ideal "forms" – for example the mathematical axioms, or the regularities discovered by the Pythagoreans to underlie impressions of musical harmony and aesthetic proportion. Plato taught that knowledge of these forms is innate in the human infant, but is not immediately accessible and must be "recollected" through experience and the education of the rational faculties.

Aristotle posited a hierarchy of functions in the souls of various living organisms, with the simplest organisms such as plants having *vegetative souls*, capable only of nourishment and reproduction. Animals, with further capacities for locomotion, sensation, and imagination or memory, also possessed *animal souls* (alternatively called the *sensitive souls*). Human beings were granted further *rational souls*, enabling them to reason logically and to take on the highest human virtues.

Without denying the importance of the rational soul, Aristotle devoted considerable attention to the "lower" psychological functions of sensation and memory. He argued that the five basic senses (sight, hearing, touch, taste, and smell) record accurate impressions of objects in the external world, much as soft sealing wax takes on the impression of a signet ring that is pressed into it. Aristotle further argued that sensory impressions leave behind permanent traces in memory, which are connected or *associated* with each other in such a way that the conscious recollection of one may arouse another because of its *similarity* (the memory of a rose may give rise to the idea of another flower), its *contrast* (the idea of cold may arouse that of hot), or the *contiguity* of their original impressions (the memory of a rose may arouse that of the garden in which it was seen). Because of the relatively greater attention Aristotle paid to knowledge gained through the senses, he is often classified as an *empiricist* compared to Plato the *rationalist*.

In one respect, the ancient Greeks' psychological thought contrasts markedly with the modern viewpoint. For them, the functions of the soul were taken to be ultimate explanatory units; that is, living organisms reproduced, moved, or reasoned *because* they possessed vegetative, animal, or rational souls, and the causal analysis went no further. The Greeks hypothesized an animate universe in which even purely physical phenomena were given "psychological" explanations; for example, a falling body presumably gained speed as it fell (an accurate observation of the acceleration due to gravity) because it experienced increasing "jubilation" or excitation while approaching ever closer to its natural "home", the earth. This animism, of course, is diametrically opposed to the modern practice of explaining psychological functions in terms of antecedent physical causes; for example, different emotions are presumed to result from different physical events in the brain or nervous system.

The transition from animism to mechanism did not begin in earnest until the seventeenth century, when physical theorists such as Galileo Galilei (1564–1642) conceptualized the physical universe as composed of material particles in interactive motion with each other, and obeying mathematical laws. Inevitably, the tendency toward mechanistic and mathematical analysis was gradually extended to biological phenomena, as when the British physician William Harvey (1578–1657) analysed the heart as a pumping mechanism while arguing that the blood must circulate in the body instead of being constantly created and dissipated anew. The French philosopher and mathematician René Descartes (1596–1650) was a leader in extending mechanistic explanations even further, to psychological functions.

DESCARTES AND MIND–BODY DUALISM

After observing some mechanical statues that were set in motion by the flow of water in pipes within them, Descartes argued that *animate motion* might be similarly explained by the flow of cerebrospinal fluid (which he called "animal spirits") through the body's nerves and into the muscles, causing them to swell and hence to move. Descartes further believed (mistakenly) that the nerves contained minute filaments capable of being tugged at their ends by the vibrations of physical stimuli impinging on the sense receptors. He hypothesized that these tugged filaments opened valves in the brain, allowing quantities of animal spirit (stored in the brain's ventricles) to flow through the motor nerves to the muscles. Although incorrect in mechanistic detail, Descartes here suggested the basic idea for the stimulus–response sequence we now call the *reflex*.

In his posthumously published *Treatise on Man*, Descartes extended this "hydraulic" neurological model to provide mechanistic explanations of several psychological phenomena. He attributed the *emotions*, for example, to agitations or currents in the pool of animal spirits in the brain, causing the fluid to flow towards or away from the nerve openings with greater or lesser force. He suggested that *sleep* occurs when the animal spirits drain partially from the brain, causing its tissues to become flaccid and the nerve fibres to become slack and unresponsive; only occasional "eddies" in the remaining spirits can momentarily tighten an isolated fibre and give rise to the transient experience of a dream. While wrong, these formulations were correctable by further observation and experiment, and they set the pattern for future mechanistic analyses. Descartes argued persuasively that mechanistic explanations could be provided for all of the functions traditionally attributed to the vegetative and animal souls.

For the classical functions of the rational soul, however, Descartes was unwilling to suggest mechanistic explanations. He believed that reason, volition, and consciousness are beyond the scope of mechanistic explanation, and constitute a separate domain which may be understood only through rational contemplation. Echoing Plato, Descartes argued that the rational mind comes equipped at birth with its own supply of *innate ideas* – concepts such as "infinity", "perfection", or "unity", as well as the geometrical axioms – which are more certainly true than the impressions left by sensory experience. Descartes further argued that the immaterial mind interacts with the physical body in ways that may be either cooperative or antagonistic. This postulation of an *interactive dualism* between the mechanical body and the immaterial mind set much of the debate for the subsequent development of psychology.

BRITISH ASSOCIATIONISM

Descartes's philosophy aroused differing reactions in Britain and on the continent. In Britain several major figures referred to collectively as the *British associationists* accepted the basic principles of mechanistic analysis but rejected the notion of innate ideas. They argued that all ideas including the most abstract had to have an ultimate basis in experience.

A major initiator of this strongly empiricist position, John Locke (1632–1704), was troubled by the proliferation of competing religious dogmas and sought in *An Essay Concerning Human Understanding* (1690) to assess the capabilities and limitations of the human mind for discerning truth. A protégé of the physicist and Royal Society founder Robert Boyle (1627–1691), Locke particularly respected the emerging experimental methods of the physical scientists, and their habit of sharing information in scientific societies.

Contrary to Plato and Descartes, Locke saw the mind at birth as a *tabula rasa* or blank slate. Following Aristotle, he asserted that concrete experiences – which may be either *sensations* of objects in the physical world or *reflections* of the mind's own operations – impress upon the mind differing permanent traces or *ideas*. The results of single experiences or *simple ideas* may merge to form *complex ideas*, as when the simple ideas of roundness, redness, and sweetness combine in the complex idea of an apple. While accepting that simple ideas may be combined in the imagination to produce complex ideas that have never been actually experienced, Locke insisted that all of the simple components must have been previously experienced.

22

Impressed by the success of the new physics in explaining the world as the result of physical particles in motion and interaction with each other, Locke classified the characteristics of those particles – solidity, extension, shape, and mobility – as the *primary qualities* of the physical world. He asserted that physical objects truly "have" these qualities, and the truest picture of the world is constructed in terms of them. Other features of objects – for example colours, sounds, temperatures, tastes, and odours – reside as much in the perceiving apparatus of the mind as in the objects themselves, and hence Locke referred to them as *secondary qualities*. He saw the ideas produced by secondary qualities as less certain than those of the primary qualities. For example, if one simultaneously immerses the right hand in hot and the left hand in cold water, before placing both in tepid water, the tepid water will seem simultaneously cool to the right and warm to the left. The water's "true" temperature lies not in its secondary qualities of warmth or cold as perceived by the senses, but rather in its primary qualities: the vibrations of its particles. Thus one of the major impediments to true knowledge lies in excessive reliance on secondary qualities.

Locke saw further impediments in the fact that any one person's experience of the world is inevitably incomplete, and to some degree random. Thus for each individual the *association of ideas* is to some degree idiosyncratic. Some of each person's associations have a genuine, "natural" conjunction with each other, while others are interconnected only because of "artificial" causes such as chance or social custom. For example, the simple ideas of colour, scent, and shape that become associated in the complex idea of a rose occur together naturally, while those of bogeymen and darkness do not. But children who have been repeatedly told that bogeymen inhabit the darkness may (mistakenly) come to associate darkness and danger together just as firmly as they (correctly) associate the qualities of a rose.

Because each individual's experience is limited as well as partly random, Locke saw great benefit in societies that provide for the sharing of experience. His models here were scientific groups like the Royal Society, but he also believed that political organizations could work most effectively on similar principles: absolute authority should be vested in no single individual, but in the collective judgements of individuals each committed to pursuing the truth themselves, while respecting the knowledge of others similarly committed.

Several British mental philosophers built upon Locke's foundation. The Irish bishop George Berkeley (1685–1753) applied Locke's empiricist and associationist principles to the analysis of visual depth perception, and argued that three-dimensional vision is not innate but acquired through experience: one learns to associate the impressions of objects at varying distances with concurrent sensations of muscular movements in the eyes and body as one moves towards or away from the objects. Berkeley differed from Locke, however, by disputing the distinction between primary and secondary qualities. He claimed that *all* sensory ideas – including those of solidity, extension, and so on – are essentially mental creations.

The Scotsman David Hume (1711–1776) echoed Aristotle in positing *laws of association* that determine the conditions under which ideas become linked together. Ideas experienced either simultaneously or in close succession to each other become connected because of the law of *association by contiguity*; ideas that resemble each other become linked through the law of *association by similarity*. Hume denied the existence of any meaningful relationships among ideas apart from their connectedness through contiguity and similarity. In one of his most provocative analyses, he explained the notion of *causality* as the mere expectation that patterns of association experienced in the past will continue in the future: although one may see one billiard ball strike another and have the impression that the impact *causes* the second to move, one never has direct evidence of the causality. All one really knows, argued Hume, is that certain sequences of impact and subsequent motion have occurred in the past, and one implicitly assumes that similar sequences will continue to occur in the future.

In the nineteenth century the associationist tradition was continued by James Mill (1773–1836) and his son John Stuart Mill (1806–1873), who insisted that most of the important individual differences among people with regard to character and intellect arise not because of innate differences, but because of differences in their experiences and associations.

CONTINENTAL NATIVISM

While universally recognized as partially valid, British associationism was perceived by many, particularly in the Germanic countries, as too limited. They developed an opposing tradition, accentuating the active qualities of the mind itself in creating experience, and the nativist and rationalist aspects of Descartes's philosophy.

Locke's contemporary Gottfried Wilhelm Leibniz (1646–1716) wrote his *New Essays on Human Understanding* as an explicit response to Locke's *Essay*. Disputing the *tabula rasa* metaphor for the human mind at birth, Leibniz proposed instead a veined block of marble whose internal lines of cleavage predispose it to be sculpted more easily into some shapes than others. The sculptor's chisel blows – equivalent to the mind's concrete experiences – are necessary to expose and refine the latent shapes within, but they do not completely create them. Leibniz argued that the human mind carries innately within it certain "necessary truths" such as the mathematical and logical axioms, which predispose it to experience the world in the way it does. Casting himself as a latter-day Plato against the Aristotelian Locke, Leibniz argued that forms are innate in the human mind as particular inclinations, dispositions, and potentialities.

Leibniz did not deny that the mind sometimes responds to the world in the

24

mechanical, associationistic fashion described by Locke, a process Leibniz referred to as simple *perception*. But he argued that when the mind focuses its full conscious attention on ideas — a process he designated as *apperception* — the results go farther. As experiences are apperceived in terms of the necessary truths, genuine mental creativity may occur.

These ideas were further developed by the German philosopher Immanuel Kant (1724–1804), who was stimulated by Hume's sceptical analysis of the notion of causality. Forced to agree with Hume that causality cannot be proven to exist in the external world, but nevertheless seeing the subjective conviction of causality as an inescapable aspect of human experience, Kant argued that it must be an innate contribution of the mind. He postulated two domains of reality: an external, *noumenal world*, consisting of "things-in-themselves" that exist independently of human experience; and an inner and subjective *phenomenal world* that is created by the mind after interacting with the noumenal world. While Kant presumed them to exist, things-in-themselves can never be known directly, for they are automatically transformed by the mind into "phenomena" or "appearances".

Kant further stipulated that the mind, in creating its phenomena, inevitably organizes the world in terms of the *intuitions* of space and time, and the *categories* defining quality, quantity, relationship, and mode. Among the innate categories of relationship is the concept of causality. Thus human beings experience the world as organized in time and space and as operating according to causal laws, not because the noumenal world is necessarily that way, but because the mind can do nothing but structure its experience in that way.

From a Kantian perspective, conscious sensations of the world cannot be taken as literal impressions or reproductions of objects, but must be recognized as the creations of an active mind. In emphasizing the importance of central mental processes as subjects to study and analyse, Kant helped set the stage for a new discipline of psychology. Ironically, however, Kant also asserted that because such mental processes could not be experimentally manipulated or made subject to mathematical description, psychology could never assume the status of a true "science" like physics. This assumption was shortly challenged by increasingly sophisticated empirical investigations of the sensory and perceptual processes.

STUDIES OF SENSATION AND PERCEPTION

In the early nineteenth century, scientific attention focused on a number of situations in which conscious experience was demonstrably different in some way from the "objective" properties of the stimulus giving rise to the experience. Among the most dramatic of these were *optical illusions*, such as Figure 1 where the two horizontal lines are measurably equal in length, yet produce a compelling subjective impression of difference. The observer's "false"

Figure 1   The Müller-Lyer illusion

conviction of difference is something that has been added to the experience by the sensory-perceptual processes. In the post-Kantian philosophical climate, this addition assumed importance as a further example of the independent contribution of mind to conscious experience.

A related development was the discovery of the *law of specific nerve energies*: the fact that each sensory nerve conveys only one kind of sensation. Thus the optic nerve produces visual sensations of light regardless of whether it is originally activated by actual light falling on the retina, by tactile pressure on the eyeball, or by any other sort of stimulation. Although proposed by the Scottish scientist Charles Bell (1774–1842) in 1811, the law was not fully appreciated until the 1830s in Germany following its promotion by the physiologist Johannes Müller (1801–1858). This was no historical accident, for Kant's philosophy had created a receptive climate in Germany for appreciating the law's implication that a particular sensation may not be taken as an infallible representation of external "reality". When one experiences a particular visual sensation, it means only that the visual nerve has been stimulated by some means or other, without specifying what that means was.

Further, nineteenth-century physicists demonstrated the value of analysing the universe as composed of various waves and energies which, like Kantian things-in-themselves, are not immediately apprehendable by the senses. Light or sound waves, for example, are not consciously experienced as waves but as sights or sounds. But while the wave-like qualities of such stimuli were not *directly* perceivable by the senses, they were becoming increasingly so *indirectly* through new measurement techniques that could provide numerical values for frequencies and wavelengths. Thus the physical world of the scientists was like Kant's noumenal world, in being only indirectly knowable by the senses, after being transformed into conscious "phenomena" of sight or sound. But unlike Kant's noumenal world, the scientists' physical universe was still precisely describable in mathematical and other scientific terminology.

Hermann Helmholtz (1821–1894) integrated many of these trends while laying major foundations for a truly experimental psychology. In analyses of the senses of vision and hearing, Helmholtz emphasized the numerous distortions and transformations undergone by stimulation from the time it originally impinges on the nervous system, until it produces meaningful conscious perceptions. He saw these transformations as occurring successively at a *physical* level (e.g., where the eye operates as an optical device to produce an image of an external stimulus on the retina); a *physiological* level (where the image on the retina stimulates the optic nerve and brain to produce differentiated sensations of light); and a *psychological* level (where sensations of light become interpreted as meaningful perceptions of specific objects).

Helmholtz's physical analyses of the eye emphasized the *imperfections* of that organ as an optical device: for example, its chromatic aberration, astigmatism, narrow field of focus, and blind spot. Because of these, the pattern of light waves on the retina is not a perfect reproduction of the stimulus in external "reality". Transformations at the physiological level are even more dramatic, as the light waves on the retina give rise to various specific sensations of light and colour. To account for many of the puzzling aspects of *colour mixing* that occur at this level, Helmholtz invoked the *trichromatic theory*. This extended the law of specific nerve energies by positing three specific types of visual receptors in the retina, respectively responding most strongly to light waves in the red, green, or blue-violet ranges of the spectrum. This theory explained, for example, why an identical sensation of whiteness can be produced by many different combinations of coloured lights, including the various pairs of *complementary colours* (e.g., red mixed with blue-green, or yellow with blue-violet), or by the complete spectral mix of normal sunlight. Helmholtz argued that "whiteness" results whenever all three types of receptors are stimulated at once, a result produced by each of the light mixtures described above. In discussing this theory, Helmholtz explicitly emphasized the "Kantian" fact that here once again experience fails to perfectly reflect external reality, since widely varying combinations of "objective" stimulation by light waves all produce identical sensations of whiteness.

At Helmholtz's final, psychological level of transformation, sensations of colour become recognized as meaningful perceptions of specific objects, a process that is learned rather than innate. Helmholtz hypothesized that perceptions follow a process of *unconscious inference*, which operates much like logical reasoning except at an unconscious level, and enables one to interpret and adapt to the world automatically. Thus one learns automatically to make use of the fact that a progressively diminishing image on the retina is associated with an object increasingly difficult to reach, and which therefore is moving progressively farther away. While investigating perceptual learning, Helmholtz conduced classic studies of *perceptual adaptation* showing how individuals wearing distorting spectacles could shortly learn to adapt to the distortions, and to respond to the changed input automatically and normally.

In sum, Helmholtz impressively demonstrated that many of the creative and transformative processes of the "Kantian" mind could be precisely described and empirically investigated in the laboratory. Helmholtz's compatriot Gustav Theodor Fechner (1801–1887) soon went even further in contesting Kant's limitations on psychology by showing how a psychological quality – namely the subjective impression of *intensity of stimulation* – could be quantified and subjected to mathematical analysis.

FECHNER AND PSYCHOPHYSICS

The basic observation underlying Fechner's programme of *psychophysics* was that small increments in stimulation are subjectively more noticeable when the background levels of that same stimulation are relatively low. Thus a lighted match completely transforms a dark room but scarcely alters a brightly lit one, or the proverbial dropped pin rings out against complete silence but is overwhelmed by a background din. Aspects of this phenomenon had already been investigated in the 1840s by Fechner's Leipzig colleague Ernst Heinrich Weber (1795–1878). Weber discovered that judges could make accurate discriminations of heavier from lighter weights only when the difference was at least one-thirtieth the weight of the heavier one. That is, a weight of 29 drams could be reliably judged as lighter than one of 30 drams, but one of 59 drams could not be differentiated from one of 60; in that case the difference had to be at least 2 drams in order to exceed the critical fraction. A similar condition prevailed in judging the relative lengths of straight lines, except that here the necessary minimum fraction of difference was 1/100 instead of 1/30.

Weber and Fechner hypothesized that other sense modalities would have their own particular critical fraction defining their *just noticeable difference* (commonly abbreviated *jnd*), and here was the basic clue that Fechner needed to posit a general mathematical law. He argued that one may determine the lowest intensity of a physical stimulus that can be detected at all, and define that as the zero point or *absolute threshold* of a ratio scale of subjective intensities. Each subsequent increase in physical stimulation equal to the critical fraction or jnd may then be taken as an increase of one unit on the scale. And when the unit increases in subjective intensity are plotted against the unit increases in the "objective" physical intensity necessary to produce them, a mathematically regular curve occurs showing that each successive jnd requires a proportionately larger increase in physical stimulation. Fechner recognized that this relationship could be expressed in terms of the general formula

$$S = k \log P$$

where S equals the subjective intensity in jnd units, P equals the physical intensity of the stimulus in objective units, and k equals a constant which will vary from sense to sense depending on their particular critical fractions.

By quantifying and mathematizing subjective stimulus intensities, Fechner showed that there was at least one way in which the methods of the established physical sciences could be applied to a psychological variable. For this reason Fechner's *Elements of Psychophysics* – the 1860 book in which he introduced his psychophysical formula – is rightfully considered one of the founding documents of experimental psychology.

WUNDT AND THE FORMAL ESTABLISHMENT OF EXPERIMENTAL PSYCHOLOGY

While Helmholtz and Fechner laid the foundations for an experimental psychology, Wilhelm Wundt (1832–1920) built on them by introducing the first textbook and laboratory explicitly devoted to the new enterprise. While serving as Helmholtz's assistant at Heidelberg in 1861, Wundt conducted a home experiment testing his own ability to judge the position of a clock's pendulum at the exact instant of a bell's chime. He discovered that invariably his subjective judgement placed the pendulum at a point it actually did not reach until one-tenth of a second after the chime had sounded; that is, there was a brief delay between the sound of the chime and his conscious observation of the pendulum's location. Wundt accounted for the tenth of a second as the time necessary for an act of *attention* to occur. Here was yet another example of the successful experimental measurement of a psychological variable.

Familiar with Fechner's psychophysics as well as Helmholtz's studies of sensation and perception, Wundt recognized that there now existed a variety of established experimental approaches to psychological problems; in 1862 he tentatively proposed the establishment of a new discipline of experimental psychology (which he called "physiological psychology"). In 1874 he published *Principles of Physiological Psychology*, a two-volume compendium of the growing body of research on the relations between bodily states and consciousness, which was quickly recognized as an appropriate textbook for the new field. After becoming Professor of Philosophy at Leipzig, Wundt in 1879 established a formal research institute in experimental psychology – the first place to which students could come and earn PhD degrees by conducting research in the new field. In 1881 he established *Philosophische Studien*, a journal for publishing the new institute's research. Now experimental psychology had a formal institutional base, and students from around the world began coming to Leipzig to take advantage of it. Many returned home to establish their own laboratories, and the new discipline was well underway.

But while Wundt thus "established" experimental psychology, he also expressed reservations about its range of applicability. Most of the experimental studies actually conducted in his laboratory were straightforward extensions of Fechner's psychophysics, or variations of reaction-time experiments. In a few studies subjects used *introspection* to analyse their conscious states during the experimental procedures, in terms of varying combinations of specifiable *sensations* and *feelings*. But while accepting such introspective analysis as useful descriptively, Wundt also cautioned that it was essentially unverifiable by objective means, and subject to distortions by memory. Accordingly he restricted introspection to simple and immediately recallable experimental situations, or to the generation of hypotheses that could be further tested by non-introspective methods.

Wundt further believed that the highest and most complex mental processes, such as thinking and memory, could never be adequately studied by introspection or any other, less problematic experimental means. He thought that such processes could be approached only naturalistically, through historical and comparative linguistic analyses. He devoted the final years of his life to a programme he called *Völkerpsychologie*, which approached the higher mental processes through the study of the collective products of human culture: myth, religion, custom, and especially language. Thus in the end Wundt echoed Descartes, by proposing two methods of psychological analysis: an experimental and physicalistic mode for the lower psychological functions, and another, non-experimental mode for the highest functions and consciousness itself.

INTROSPECTION AND THE PROBLEM OF CONSCIOUSNESS

Wundt's reservations notwithstanding, two of his students carried the techniques of introspection well beyond the bounds he had set for them. Edward B. Titchener (1867–1927), who became Professor of Psychology at Cornell University following his apprenticeship with Wundt, promoted a *structural psychology* whose major goal was the systematic introspective analysis of consciousness into its presumed "elements" of sensation and feeling. Oswald Külpe (1862–1915) together with colleagues at the University of Würzburg attempted introspective analyses of several of the higher processes, and conscious states of readiness and attention.

While these efforts helped to get experimental psychology established in the universities, they came under attack (as Wundt predicted) for a variety of different reasons. Titchener's "atomism" and "elementism" was challenged by the influential American psychologist William James (1842–1910), who argued that consciousness has an ever-changing, stream-like quality whose essence can never be captured atomistically; privately, he sarcastically referred to Titchenerian psychologists as "barbarians". The *Gestalt psychologists*, led by Max Wertheimer (1880–1943), Kurt Koffka (1886–1941), and Wolfgang Köhler (1887–1967), reversed Titchener's basic strategy. Instead of starting with simple elements and trying to show how they combine to create wholes, the Gestaltists began with wholes such as musical melodies or organized visual patterns, and showed how the individual parts (e.g., musical notes) function within those wholes.

As is well known, a more radical assault on introspection in general came from the *behaviourists*, led by the American John B. Watson (1878–1958). Reportedly a poor introspector as a graduate student, whose results did not accord with others, Watson reacted strongly against the subjectivity and unverifiability of introspective reports. Starting with his 1913 article "Psychology as the Behaviorist Views It", Watson argued not only against introspection as a technique, but also against consciousness itself as a legitimate object of scientific investigation. Psychologists, he asserted, should restrict their analyses to publicly observable events. In effect, Watson and the behaviourists tried to change the definition of psychology from the traditional "science of consciousness" (or "mind") to the "science of behaviour". Watson's message found a particularly receptive audience in the United States of America, where from the 1930s to the 1950s behaviourism dominated academic psychology departments.

As a substitute for introspection as psychology's primary analytic tool, Watson proposed the *conditional reflex* (sometimes called the *conditioned reflex*) as introduced by the Russian physiologist Ivan Pavlov (1849–1936) in his studies of acquired salivary reflexes in dogs. Watson extended the conditional reflex model in his theory of *conditional emotional reactions* in humans, according to which the vast majority of all emotional reactions are the result of early and often accidental pairings of neutral stimuli with early arousals of fear, rage, or love. Later, studies of so called "Pavlovian", "classical", or "respondent conditioning" came to be supplemented by the "operant conditioning" pioneered by the most famous latter-day behaviourist, B. F. Skinner (1904–1990).

While Wundt had declared that the highest mental processes would have to be studied by the non-experimental methods of *Völkerpsychologie*, and the Watsonian behaviourists essentially ruled them beyond the bounds of psychology altogether, a more positive approach to the issue was taken by Hermann Ebbinghaus (1850–1909). After being inspired by a chance reading of Fechner's *Elements of Psychophysics*, Ebbinghaus sought to bring a similarly mathematical approach to the study of memory – one of Wundt's supposedly non-experimental subjects. In order to provide stimuli for memorization that would be "neutral" – that is, equally unfamiliar or unmeaningful to a subject before the experiment – Ebbinghaus constructed some 2,300 *nonsense syllables*: consonant-vowel-consonant combinations that were not real words, such as "taz", "bok", or "lef".

Serving as his own subject, Ebbinghaus measured the time required to memorize various lists of syllables. Then he allowed varying periods of time to elapse before *re*-memorizing each list, again measuring the required times. Relearning was generally quicker than the original memorization, and when the amounts of the "savings" in learning time were plotted against the lengths of the interval between the two tests, a *forgetting curve* was revealed. Memory tended to decline most rapidly immediately after the original learning: for example, for one series of lists, savings were 58 per cent after twenty minutes, 44 per cent after one hour, 36 per cent after eight hours, and 34 per cent after one day. Ebbinghaus did not fail to note that this curve resembled the logarithmic shape of Fechner's psychophysical law. *On Memory* (his 1885 monograph describing the work) is regarded as a classic for being the first work to show how a "higher" mental process could be studied experimentally without relying on introspection.

Wundt could (and did) argue that Ebbinghaus's nonsense syllables were merely parodies of normal mental stimuli, and that normal meaningful memory had still evaded laboratory study. But this objection was widely overlooked by the new generations of psychologists, and experimental psychology seemed to have outgrown Wundt's restrictions just as his own approach had outgrown Kant's. During the 1980s, however, echoes of Wundt's cry against the sterility of experimental, laboratory approaches to many psychological issues were beginning to be heard (e.g., Gergen, 1985). Few contemporary psychologists are still willing to accept the behaviourists' proscription of consciousness from their subject matter. Thus psychology's classical problem since Descartes − the question of whether consciousness and higher mental processes can be studied by the same general techniques as the "hard" sciences, or whether they require their own, non-experimental approaches − is still unresolved and seems likely to remain so for the foreseeable future.

DARWINIAN INFLUENCES ON PSYCHOLOGY

The experimental psychology discussed so far aimed to study what may be characterized as the human mind in general. Even as that psychology was developing, however, the revolutionary implications of Charles Darwin's (1809−1882) theory of *evolution by natural selection* were reverberating throughout the new field, and suggesting alternative foci of interest.

Darwin introduced his basic evolutionary theory in *On the Origin of Species* (1859), but did not himself discuss explicitly psychological issues until 1871, in *The Descent of Man, and Selection in Relation to Sex*. There he asserted explicitly for the first time that humans have descended from animal ancestors, and supported his argument by citing many ways in which "lower" animals possess at least the rudiments of human mental functions. He concluded that the differences between human and animal mentality, great as they might be, are of degree rather than kind. In *The Expression of Emotion in Man and Animals* (1872) he made the complementary case, namely that in their emotional expression human beings betray many inherited remnants of their "animality", that is, their evolutionary history.

In stressing the evolutionary interrelatedness of humans with animal species, Darwin implied that human psychological functions could no longer be looked upon as essentially distinct. In his wake the study of animal behaviour gained new significance, and the subdiscipline of *comparative psychology* arose in consequence. Darwin's younger friend George Romanes (1848–1894) argued in *Animal Intelligence* (1882) and *Mental Evolution in Animals* (1883) that the comparative study of psychological functions in animals could shed light on their human counterparts in the same way that comparative anatomy had furthered the understanding of human bodily structures. The new respect accorded to animal studies also helped prepare the field for the behaviourists, whose investigations of learning and conditioning usually employed animal subjects.

Developments of a different kind followed from Darwin's assertion that evolution proceeds by the natural selection of adaptive *variations* within breeding populations. In this context, small but inheritable *differences* among members of a species assume great importance, for they provide the basis of future evolution. Here was the logical basis for a *differential psychology*, concerned with the discovery and measurement of potentially inheritable individual differences in psychological qualities.

Darwin's cousin Francis Galton (1822–1911) pioneered this new field, largely in the service of the *eugenics movement* which he founded and named. Galton proposed to accelerate the progress of human evolution by identifying those individuals highest in "natural ability", and encouraging them to intermarry and procreate at a higher rate than the rest of the population. (Darwin, who recognized this project as more akin to the "artificial selection" practised by animal breeders than to the "natural selection" that produces genuine and enduring species changes, remained politely sceptical about the viability of many of his cousin's eugenic plans.)

In the interest of his eugenic programme, Galton introduced several ideas that were momentous for the emerging psychology. Seeking a quantitative measure of resemblance between relatives of varying degrees, he invented the techniques of *statistical correlation* and *regression analysis*. He conducted the first, crude studies comparing similarities between biological as opposed to adoptive relatives, and between monozygotic (identical) as opposed to dizygotic (non-identical) twins. Galton's interpretation of these studies – that they demonstrated the greater power of heredity over environment in producing the most important individual differences among human beings – was controversial from the first. The debate about the relative importance of *nature and nurture* (a phrase first popularized by Galton) has raged unabated ever since. But however their results are interpreted, Galton's statistical and experimental procedures continue to form the basis for the modern discipline of *behaviour genetics*.

Also to further his eugenic vision, Galton introduced the first *intelligence tests*, measures intended to identify young men and women with the highest degrees of inheritable natural ability, who would be encouraged to intermarry and have many children. In devising his tests Galton drew heavily on the technology of the new experimental psychology, and assumed that measures of reaction time and sensory acuity would reflect underlying and presumably inheritable differences in the efficiency of the brain and nervous system. These physiologically oriented measures, which Galton introduced in his *Anthropometric Laboratory* of the mid-1880s, turned out not to correlate significantly with measures of intellectual accomplishment.

The first practically useful tests of intelligence were introduced in 1905, by the French psychologist Alfred Binet (1857–1911) and his younger colleague Théodore Simon (1873–1961). Working to establish measures of mental retardation in children, Binet and Simon employed direct tests of higher-order mental functioning including vocabulary, logical reasoning, and memory to define developmental norms. These norms could be used to assign an *intellectual level* or *mental age* for each tested child, to be compared with his or her actual age. In this way, relative retardation or advancement from the "normal" rate of development could be estimated. Although mental age has ceased to be the criterion used in modern intelligence tests, the same types of items continue to be used.

Much debate has ensued over the nature and determinants of the "intelligence" measured by Binet-type intelligence tests. One influential interpretation was proposed by Charles Spearman (1863–1945), a Wundt student whose reading of Galton led him to focus on the importance of individual differences, and who became Britain's first professor of psychology at University College London. Noting the positive correlations among a wide variety of different types of intelligence measures, Spearman argued for the existence of an inherited factor of *general intelligence* (*"g"*) underlying all intellectual acts. The American L. L. Thurstone (1887–1955) countered that intelligence is actually a congeries of more specific abilities, essentially independent of one another, in his theory of *primary mental abilities.* Questions of how "intelligence" is structured, and whether it is primarily innate or acquired, continue to dominate the attention of many psychologists.

BRAIN SCIENCE

No historical account of psychology would be complete without mentioning the contributions of medical practitioners to an understanding of the brain as the "organ of the mind". Because of its unimpressive appearance and insensitivity to tactile pressure, the brain was regarded by many influential figures from Aristotle onwards as lacking important psychological functions. Only in the late eighteenth century did the German physician Franz Josef Gall (1758–1828) systematically compare the brains of different species, and definitively establish the general fact that higher mental functions were associated with relatively larger and more complex brains. More controversial was Gall's *phrenology*, his theory that specific psychological faculties were localized in specific subregions or "organs" of the human brain. As phrenology came to be a popular fad, diagrams and models abounded dividing the head into specific regions for faculties such as "amativeness" (the cerebellar region), "acquisitiveness" (just above the ears), or "verbal memory" (just behind the eyes). Professional phrenologists, occupying a social role similar to that now held by diagnostic psychologists, gave readings of their clients' character and abilities, based on the bumps and depressions in their skulls presumably reflecting underlying brain shapes.

Phrenology came under scientific attack following ablation experiments on animal brains in the 1820s by Pierre Flourens (1794–1867). Flourens observed that the deficits remaining after recovery were *not* those that would be predicted by phrenology: cerebellar ablations produced a loss of coordinated movement rather than a decrease in "amativeness", for example, and removal of cortical tissue resulted in an apparently generalized loss of sensory ability and "will". Only the phrenologists' organ of "verbal memory" attracted a modicum of scientific support over the years, thanks to a small number of poorly documented cases in which injury to that area had apparently produced language deficits. Then in 1860, Paul Broca (1824–1880) publicly dissected the brain of a patient who had lost the power of discursive speech, and found a large lesion in the left frontal lobe, just behind the eye. Subsequent studies quickly confirmed the localization of speech functions in this region.

The "new phrenology" gained momentum in 1870, when Gustav Fritsch (1837–1927) and Eduard Hitzig (1839–1907) produced specific movements as they electrically stimulated specific parts of what has come to be called the *motor strip* on the exposed cortex of a dog. Subsequent experiments by the Scottish neurologist David Ferrier (1843–1928), using both ablations and electrical stimulation, revealed the existence of a *sensory strip* immediately adjacent to the motor strip, as well as a *visual area* in the occipital lobe, and an *auditory area* in the temporal lobe. This research tradition was continued by Wilder Penfield (1891–1976), who stimulated the exposed cortex of conscious epileptic surgical patients, and found that specific regions of the *interpretive cortex* in the temporal lobe were involved in producing feelings such as anxiety, guilt, familiarity or strangeness. The brain is now recognized as largely if not completely localized in function, although the specific functions (except for language or "verbal memory" in Broca's area) bear scant resemblance to the faculties originally posited by Gall and the phrenologists.

THE UNCONSCIOUS

Another major contribution from medical practitioners was an appreciation of unconscious psychological factors. Early followers of the German physician Franz Anton Mesmer (1734–1815) showed that many persons could be placed in trance-like states, which we now call *hypnosis*, in which they showed heightened suggestibility. Upon command, such subjects experienced dramatic physical effects such as paralyses and anaesthesias, but lost memory for them upon awakening from their trances. Moreover, they sometimes demonstrated *post-hypnotic suggestion*, as they continued to act upon certain suggestions after the trance, but without memory that the suggestions had been made. Here was clear evidence for the effect of motives acting outside of conscious awareness.

In the late 1800s the French neurologist Jean Martin Charcot (1825–1893) noted parallels between hypnotic effects and the symptoms of *hysteria*, a malady marked by selective amnesias and physical complaints including paralyses and anaesthesias. Although these symptoms resembled the effects of neurological lesions, they occurred in the absence of demonstrable organic damage. Charcot attributed both hysterical symptoms and hypnotic effects to a generalized weakness of the nervous system.

Although Charcot's theory was quickly discredited, his student Sigmund Freud (1856–1939) followed up with his theory of *psychoanalysis*, one of the most powerful cultural influences of the first half of the twentieth century. Through investigations of not only hysteria and hypnosis, but also such "everyday" phenomena as dreams and apparently unmotivated accidents or "slips", Freud discerned the pervasive influence of impulses and wishes of which a person is totally unaware, and which moreover may conflict directly with conscious desires. Many of the details of Freud's formulation, including his emphasis on the sexual nature of many such "repressed" impulses, have remained controversial. Nevertheless his general point – that psychology cannot be restricted to the analysis of merely conscious experience, but must also account for the existence and influence of unconscious factors – is widely accepted.

From varied roots such as these, psychology has evolved into the complex discipline whose breadth and diversity is amply illustrated in the chapters ahead.

FURTHER READING

Fancher, R. E. (1990). *Pioneers of psychology* (2nd edn). New York: Norton.
Hearnshaw, L. S. (1964). *A short history of British psychology*. London: Methuen.
Hothersall, D. (1990). *History of psychology* (2nd edn). New York: McGraw-Hill.
Murray, D. J. (1988). *A history of western psychology*. Englewood Cliffs, NJ: Prentice-Hall.
Robinson, D. N. (1981). *An intellectual history of psychology*. New York: Macmillan.

REFERENCES

Aristotle (1947). *De anima (On the soul)*. In R. McKeon (Ed.) *Introduction to Aristotle* (pp. 145–235). New York: Modern Library.
Darwin, C. (1859). *On the origin of species, by means of natural selection, or the preservation of favoured races in the struggle for life*. London: Murray.

Darwin, C. (1871). *The descent of man, and selection in relation to sex.* London: Murray.

Darwin, C. (1872). *The expression of emotion in man and animals.* London: Murray.

Descartes, R. (1972). *Treatise of man.* Cambridge, MA: Harvard University Press (originally published 1664 as *Traité de l'homme*).

Ebbinghaus, H. (1964). *Memory.* New York: Dover (originally published 1885 as *Über das Gedächtnis*).

Fechner, G. T. (1966). *Elements of psychophysics.* New York: Holt, Rinehart & Winston (originally published 1860 as *Elemente der Psychophysik*).

Gergen, K. J. (1985). Social psychology and the phoenix of unreality. In S. Koch & D. Leary (Eds) *A century of psychology as science* (pp. 528–557). New York: McGraw-Hill.

Jowett, B. (1937). *The dialogues of Plato translated into English.* New York: Random House.

Kahl, R. (Ed.) (1971). *Selected writings of Hermann von Helmholtz.* Middletown, CT: Wesleyan University Press.

Leibniz, G. W. (1949). *New essays on human understanding.* Lasalle, IL: Open Court (originally published 1765 as *Nouveaux essais sur l'entendement humain*).

Locke, J. (1961). *An essay concerning human understanding.* New York: Dutton (originally published 1690).

Romanes, G. (1882). *Animal intelligence.* London: Kegan Paul, Trench.

Romanes, G (1969). *Mental evolution in animals.* New York: AMS Press (originally published 1883).

Smith, N. K. (Ed.) (1958). *Descartes: Philosophical writings.* New York: Modern Library.

Watson, J. B. (1913). Psychology as the behaviorist views it. *Psychological Review,* *20*, 158–177.

Wundt, W. (1904). *Principles of physiological psychology.* London: Swan Sonnenschein (originally published 1874 as *Grundzüge der physiologischen Psychologie*).

2
BIOLOGICAL ASPECTS OF BEHAVIOUR

INTRODUCTION

This section is concerned with aspects of psychology that are related to biology. Research in this area overlaps with many of the biological sciences, including ecology (the study of the relationship between organisms and their environments), ethology (the study of behaviour in natural habitats), evolutionary biology, genetics, neurophysiology (the study of the functions of the nervous system), molecular biology, pharmacology (the study of drugs), sociobiology (the study of the biological bases of social behaviour), and zoology.

Human life always begins with the fertilization of a woman's ovum (egg) by a man's sperm, and the fertilized egg contains all the genetic information necessary for the development of a new human being. The elementary principles of genetics were first investigated by an Austrian monk and amateur botanist, Gregor Mendel (1822–1884), who published his findings in 1866, but it was not until 1953 that the molecular basis of the genetic code was worked out by Francis Crick (1916–) and James Watson (1928–) in England.

Every cell in the human body, apart from the sex cells in the testes and ovaries, carries 23 pairs of chromosomes, and the chromosomes contain tightly coiled molecules of deoxyribonucleic acid (DNA). The DNA encodes the genetic information in the form of some 100,000 units, called genes, about 70 per cent of which are expressed in the nervous system and hence can potentially affect behaviour. Modern techniques of genetic engineering enable researchers to uncoil DNA molecules, cut them into pieces, recombine them with strands of DNA from other sources, and insert them into host organisms where they reproduce themselves and control the production of proteins just like ordinary DNA. Behaviour genetics has its own armoury of techniques, operating at the behavioural as well as the biochemical level, to study the influence of heredity on behaviour.

In chapter 2.1 C. P. Kyriacou outlines the main research methods and findings of both human and animal behaviour genetics, including work using advanced techniques of molecular biology. His outline covers what is known about hereditary aspects of human intelligence and mental disorders, together with various aspects of animal behaviour, including learning, biological rhythms, and sexual behaviour. Anyone who reads chapter 2.1 will realize that this is an area of research where rapid and exciting developments are taking place. Molecular neurobiology, which is still in its precocious infancy, may well become the major life science in the twenty-first century, as Kyriacou predicts.

In chapter 2.2 John Lazarus focuses on evolutionary aspects of human and animal behaviour. According to the theory of evolution by natural selection, the most influential theory in the history of biology, which was popularized by Charles Darwin in 1859 and adapted in the light of subsequent discoveries in the field of genetics, the frequency of a gene in a population increases if it improves the Darwinian fitness – the chances of survival and reproduction – of the individuals that possess it. The theory is almost tautological, in the sense that it seems self-evident that genes that improve fitness *must* increase in relative frequency, because the organisms that inherit them will produce more offspring and therefore more copies of their genes; but certain well-known forms of behaviour, which are certainly hereditary, seem to contradict the theory of natural selection. A familiar example (one could say a garden variety) is the alarm call of a bird that sees a predator such as a cat; this behaviour attracts the attention of the predator and *reduces* the individual bird's chances of survival and reproduction. Lazarus provides an explanation for this and several other evolutionary paradoxes in the context of a comprehensive introduction to behavioural ecology – a branch of psychology devoted to understanding adaptive behaviour in the light of its evolutionary development.

Daniel Kimble's survey in chapter 2.3 of the human nervous system and brain begins with an account of the structure and functions of the basic cellular units, the nerve cells called neurons in the nervous system and brain, and the processes by which they send and receive electrical signals (these neural signalling processes are also explained in detail in chapter 2.5). Chapter 2.3 continues with a detailed account, from the most elementary starting-point up to an advanced level, of functional neuroanatomy – the functions of the major anatomical units of the nervous system and brain. For more information on the physiology of vision, hearing, and the skin, body, and chemical senses, see chapters 3.1 (Peter C. Dodwell), 3.3 (Brian C. J. Moore), and 3.4 (Harvey R. Schiffman) respectively; and for more information on bodily processes associated with emotion and sex, see chapters 6.1 (Brian Parkinson) and 6.4 (John Bancroft).

In chapter 2.4 J. Allan Hobson focuses on sleep and dreaming. These processes have received considerable attention from psychologists since 1952, when a graduate student at the University of Chicago, Eugene Aserinsky, first reported rapid eye movements (REMs) behind the closed eyelids of people who were sleeping; William Dement and Nathaniel Kleitman subsequently confirmed that REM sleep is normally associated with vivid dreaming. Hobson summarizes what is known about the behavioural and physiological properties of sleep, the psychological features of dreams, the physiological processes of dreaming, and the main hypotheses that have been put forward regarding the functions of both sleep and dreaming. For a discussion of Freud's theory of dreams, see also chapter 7.4 (Richard Stevens).

Finally, chapter 2.5 is devoted to psychopharmacology, the study of the psychological effects of drugs. Leonard W. Hamilton and C. Robin Timmons begin by classifying psychoactive drugs and discussing their biochemical action in the brain. They then discuss in detail drugs that affect moods and states of consciousness (central nervous system stimulants, central nervous system depressants, and hallucinogens) and drugs that are used to treat behavioural disorders (antipsychotics, anti-anxiety drugs, and antidepressants). The chapter includes some comments on drug abuse and addiction; on that subject see also chapter 10.5 (Geoffrey Lowe).

A.M.C.

2.1

HEREDITY AND BEHAVIOUR GENETICS

C. P. Kyriacou
University of Leicester, England

The genetic analysis of behaviour has a long history, beginning with the twin studies conducted by Galton (1869) in the nineteenth century. In the 1920s, with the environmentalism of J. B. Watson dominating the intellectual atmosphere within psychology, a few islands of nativism were to be found, the most important being in the laboratories of E. Tolman and R. C. Tryon. In a two-generation artificial selection experiment, Tolman produced evidence that rat "intelligence", as measured by the number of errors made by rats trying to find their way around a maze, had a significant genetic component. Tryon extended and improved the procedure and produced his famous "maze-bright" and "maze-dull" lines within a few generations of selection (Tryon, 1940).

In the 1950s investigators began in earnest their attempts to get to grips with "behavioural genes". Margaret Bastock and Aubrey Manning studied the genetics of behaviour in the fruit fly *Drosophila*. They concentrated on the stereotyped "fixed-action-patterns" that make up the courtship interactions of the male and female. By investigating these instinctive behavioural "elements", they reasoned that the genetic substrate for behaviour would be more evident, compared to more complex motor programmes where learning might be involved. P. L. Broadhurst, at the Maudsley Hospital in London, also began selecting for "emotional" versus "non-emotional" rats in an open-field arena. Clearly there was a "psychological" perspective to this work, as the Maudsley reactive and non-reactive strains (as the two selected lines were called) could, at least at face value, provide an animal model for "neurotic" behaviour. Tolman, Tryon, and these British workers in the 1950s were truly pioneers, but converts to the cause of behaviour genetics were rather thin on the ground.

In this review, I shall attempt to assess the more significant developments in the area. A number of excellent textbooks exist to introduce the reader, including Plomin, Defries, and McClearn (1990) and Hay (1985). The latter part of the discussion that follows will draw heavily on molecular biology, which is becoming increasingly important in behaviour genetics.

NATURE AND NURTURE

Any behaviour requires movement, and motor structures such as muscles, glands, etc., are built by genes. Thus all behaviour has a strong genetic component. The interesting question is whether behavioural *differences* between individuals are due predominantly to genetic or to environmental factors, and what is the scale of their respective contributions. Let us consider the case of "identical" or monozygotic (MZ) twins. They have all their genes in common, but environmental influences mean that we can usually tell them apart quite easily, simply by looking at them. So even when there are no genetic differences, the environment can produce differences between two individual "clones". This example illustrates how the environment can mould differences in even genetically identical individuals. The obvious conclusion is that whatever behavioural or morphological character you examine, environment and genes always interact to produce the final product − the phenotype. What the behaviour geneticist wants to know is the relative contribution of each, the evolutionary history of the behavioural trait, and the underlying molecular, biochemical, and physiological mechanisms that mediate the expression of the behaviour.

QUANTITATIVE GENETICS

There are a number of basic methods used by behavioural geneticists which

43

range from the simple to the almost intractable. Mendel's law of segregation illustrates how any character (or phenotype) that is determined by a single locus (a position on a chromosome at which a gene is situated) will segregate in a 3 : 1 ratio in the F_2 (second filial) generation, assuming complete dominance of one of the alleles (an allele is simply one form of a gene). Mendel worked out his law of segregation using pea plant characteristics. Some behavioural characters show similar patterns of inheritance, for example the *waltzer* mutant mice which are neurologically abnormal, and behaviourally uncoordinated, and thus appear to "waltz". However, most naturally occurring behavioural differences that are observed between different people or different animals will not be due to single genetic differences, and the study of these behavioural characters requires the discipline of quantitative genetics.

One way of determining the approximate number of genes that might be determining a difference in a behavioural phenotype is to use a selection experiment. Starting from a genetically variable strain which is heterozygous at many loci, the organisms under study (usually flies, mice, or rats) are selected simultaneously for both high and low levels of a particular trait (aggression, sex drive, intelligence), and then bred together for several or many generations, selecting at each cycle. Imagine that after a few generations a peak and a depth of performance is reached in the two bidirectionally selected lines and no amount of subsequent selection can elevate or reduce the performance. This would argue that perhaps only one or two genes were segregating in the founder populations, and that they very soon became homozygous during the selection procedure. If the response to selection is slow, and small improvements and decrements are continually being made at every generation of selection, then it is clear that many genes are involved in the behavioural character under study. These genes will be continually "reshuffled" with the meiotic recombination that occurs during sexual reproduction and realigned within the "high" and "low" strains.

Imagine two highly inbred strains of animals, say mice. They have been maintained by brother–sister mating for many years and so each can be considered to be homozygous at every gene locus. The two lines show differences in the level of a particular behaviour, let us say aggression. By measuring the behavioural scores of progeny of the F_1, F_2, and the two back-crosses (where the F_1 is crossed back to each parent), it is possible by using simple mathematics to extract some very useful information about what is called the "genetic architecture" of a behavioural trait. This information includes the additive genetic component, A, the dominance component D, and the environmental component, E. To illustrate what "additive" and "dominance" mean, imagine two strains of mice; one has an aggression score of 10 arbitrary units and the other of zero. If the F_1 hybrid between the two strains had a mean score of 5 units then there is complete additivity. If the hybrids produce a score of 6 units then the deviation from the mean value is $6 - 5 = 1$ giving a dominance value of $+1$ unit. If we examine the phenotypic variances from the different crosses, we can obtain a measure of the genetic component of variation V_G (which is the additive genetic component V_A plus the dominance component V_D) and of the environmental variation V_E. Thus, the phenotypic variation that we see in a trait, V_P, equals

$$V_P = V_A + V_D + V_E$$

and the heritability (h^2) of a character is the ratio of the genetic variation to the total phenotypic variation:

$$h^2 = V_G/V_P.$$

This is sometimes called the broad heritability (h_B^2). The narrow heritability (h_N^2) is the ratio of the additive genetic variation divided by the total phenotypic variation:

$$h_N^2 = V_A/V_P.$$

h_N^2 is an important statistic for animal and plant breeders, because if a character has a high narrow heritability there are presumably lots of genes available that produce predictable additive effects. Thus two large animals should produce large progeny of intermediate size between them. The dominance component V_D is an irritant to the breeder, because it is pushing scores towards one or other parent unpredictably, because of segregation. Thus for selection experiments to work, a reasonable amount of predictable additive genetic variation must be present.

There are more sophisticated crossing schemes available for obtaining measures of V_A, V_D, V_E, such as the diallel cross and the triple test cross. The triple test cross, for example, can estimate the epistatic genetic component, which is the non-additive interaction of alleles at more than one locus. Let us take locus A' which can have allele A or a and locus B' which can have allele B or b. If certain combinations of these alleles produce completely unpredictable phenotypic scores, then epistatis or gene interactions are occurring.

The quantitative methods are an art in themselves and have reached high levels of complexity. The one thing that should always be borne in mind, however, from the simplest F_1, F_2 and back-cross method to the most esoteric multivariate path technique, is that all these analyses have implicit assumptions that are often unrealistic.

METHODOLOGY FOR HUMANS

Allied to these quantitative models are the three major methods used for human behavioural genetic analyses, which are twin, family, and adoption studies. As an example let us take the intelligence quotient, IQ. If you measured the IQ of pairs of monozygotic (MZ) twins and compared them with pairs of fraternal or dizygotic (DZ) twins, then if IQ has a heritable component, the MZ correlation should be greater than the DZ correlation. This is because MZ twins share all their genes, whereas DZ twins share on average only half their genetic endowment. However, it must be remembered that MZ twins have a more uniform uterine environment than DZ twins, and may also be treated more similarly than DZ twins within their family, because they look more similar and because they are always of the same sex. Thus it is conceivable that the more similar environment enjoyed by MZ twins from conception onwards may be the cause of more similar phenotypic scores in MZ compared to DZ twins. However, such evidence as exists concerning the possibility of more equal postnatal environments for MZ over DZ twins is equivocal (reviewed in Plomin et al., 1990).

Related to the twin method is the family study, where the similarities in the behavioural phenotype between two individuals of known genetic relatedness are compared. The parent/offspring correlation in IQ or any other character is underscored by a coefficient of genetic relatedness of .50 which reflects the number of genes shared by father or mother and each child. Siblings also share an average of half their genomes whereas grandparents with grandchildren have a coefficient of relatedness of .25. Half siblings, who share one parent only, like the grandparent/grandchild case, enjoy a coefficient of .25. Thus if we correlate IQ scores between fathers and sons, for example, and there is a strong heritable component to IQ, then the correlation should be higher than that between first cousins, who share .125 of their genomes. The first step in trying to assess whether genetic differences give phenotypic differences in human behaviour is to examine family relationships. If the correlation does not improve with the increasing degree of relatedness, then it is unlikely that the genetic component is significant.

The third method in human behaviour genetics is the adoption method. Here we are interested in unrelated individuals who live together, usually an adopted child and its non-biological parents. Any phenotypic correlation will be due to their shared home environment. A second relevant group is represented by genetically related individuals who for one reason or another are separated early in life and are raised in different families. However, in both these cases there are some complications. Perhaps an adoption agency selectively places a child into a "suitable" family, or perhaps identical twins are raised apart, but in two related families, for example one twin in an aunt's home and the other in the mother's. Perhaps such shared familial situations tend to make these twins more similar than they might otherwise have been.

Let us now turn to some of the important behavioural phenotypes that have been analysed in humans. What we would like to do eventually is to isolate the genes for high IQ, for example, or for extraversion and introversion as another example, and find out what types of proteins these genes encode. Regrettably this is not possible at present with humans.

HUMAN BEHAVIOUR GENETICS

The behavioural phenotypes that are commonly studied are cognitive abilities such as IQ, and the psychopathologies such as schizophrenia and unipolar and bipolar depression. However, a range of other personality variables have also been studied, together with such talents as musical ability, creativity, and so on.

Intelligence IQ

A large number of twin studies have been performed, including the famous (or infamous) studies of Cyril Burt. Burt's results have been challenged and are generally believed to be fraudulent. I refer any interested reader to a critical review of the whole affair by Joynson (1989). However, the fact that one of a large number of twin studies may not be reliable does not weaken the conclusions that are obtained from examining the results of all the other twin studies. Clearly IQ variation has a considerable genetic component. Figure 1 summarizes the IQ correlations taken from studies of various family relationships and reviewed by Bouchard and McGue (1981). MZ twins have a correlation in IQ that clusters around .85 whereas DZ twins have correlations ranging from .50 to .70, which is slightly higher than that for full siblings. The difference between the correlation for DZ twins (.60) and siblings (.47) suggest that DZ twins, because of their age similarity, have a more similar environment than ordinary siblings. (In Figure 1 "midparent IQ" is the average of the parents' IQ; "midoffspring IQ" is the average of the offspring's IQ.) From Figure 1 we can see that one or two of the correlations are not quite what would be predicted based on a simple additive genetic model with no environmental influence. Siblings reared apart should have a higher correlation in IQ than .24, perhaps as high as .50. Although only two of these studies are reported, the apparent significant environmental contribution implied is amply supported by the last four sets of correlations in Figure 1, which are taken from adoption studies. Significant correlations between .19 and .29 again reflect the environmental contribution to IQ scores.

The difference between MZ and DZ correlations is about .26 (.86 − .60) and reflects half the genetic variation in IQ (because DZ twins share half their genes whereas MZ twins share all their genes). By doubling this figure we obtain an approximate broad heritability of .52. Thus the conclusion from all these studies is that about half the phenotypic variation in IQ is due to genetic differences, and half to environment. Can we isolate or even count the number of genes involved? Not directly. However, in a mammal about 70 per cent of all genes are expressed in the nervous system (John & Miklos, 1988). This tells us that natural selection invests a huge amount in brains. We might consider that the most conservative estimate of the number of human

47

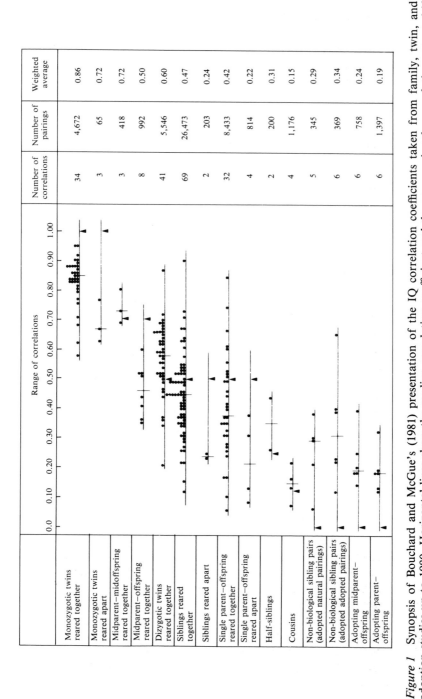

Figure 1 Synopsis of Bouchard and McGue's (1981) presentation of the IQ correlation coefficients taken from family, twin, and adoption studies up to 1980. Horizontal lines show the median correlation coefficient and the arrows give the correlation expected if IQ variation were completely due to additive genetic variation with no environmental component.

Source: Reproduced from Plomin, Defries, and McClearn, 1990, and based on Bouchard and McGue, 1981. Reproduced with permission from both sources

genes is 100,000. Consequently up to 70,000 of these genes might be expressed in the nervous system, and we could imagine that many of these genes have a function. Furthermore, we know from molecular population genetic analysis that all of these genes would be represented by more than one allele at the DNA level. Some of this variation in DNA sequence will be "silent" and not produce any amino acid changes in brain cell proteins. Some of these DNA variants will be neutral and change the amino acid sequence but with no effect on the proteins being produced. However, some variants will alter the amino acid sequence and perhaps also alter the activity of the nerve cell proteins. Therefore if 10 per cent of these genes have different alleles segregating in the population and 10 per cent of these alleles in turn give changes in the nervous system, then perhaps 700 genes will be potentially contributing to differences in neural performance and inevitably to IQ. Not all of these hypothetical 700 genes will be segregating within the native British or American population, but by even these conservative estimates it is obvious that many genes will be contributing to the variation we see in IQ: some of these genes will push IQ scores up and some will push them down.

While at present we cannot hope to identify or isolate IQ genes that are segregating in normal populations, can we nevertheless understand how the environment which determines fully half of IQ variation acts on the phenotype? A clue comes from Figure 1 where unrelated children raised together produce an overall correlation of .32. This does suggest that about one-third of the total IQ variation is due to the shared family environment. Several reports suggest that the influence of the shared environment drops sharply between the teenage and early adult years (Plomin, 1988). This implies that shared home environment is a significant influence on the heritability of IQ early in life, but recedes as children grow up and move to different environments. It is comforting therefore that these correlations reflect such intuitively "sensible" features in the development of young adults.

Developmental studies

In some investigations cognitive ability has been studied longitudinally with the children's abilities measured as they mature. The Louisville twin study is probably the best known (Wilson, 1983). For twenty years, 500 pairs of twins were tested at three-month intervals between the ages of 3 and 24 months using the Bayley Scales of mental and motor development. Various IQ tests were given at roughly one-year intervals from the ages of 3 to 9 years and then again at 15 years. Until the age of 6 months, the MZ twin correlation does not exceed that of DZ twins. By 3 years of age the difference is still small, .77 for MZ twins, .67 for DZ twins. The heritability of IQ increases until about the age of 6 years and then declines (Wilson, 1983; see also Figure 2). As genes are not transcribed constantly, but are switched on and off at different stages of development this may reflect an underlying temporal

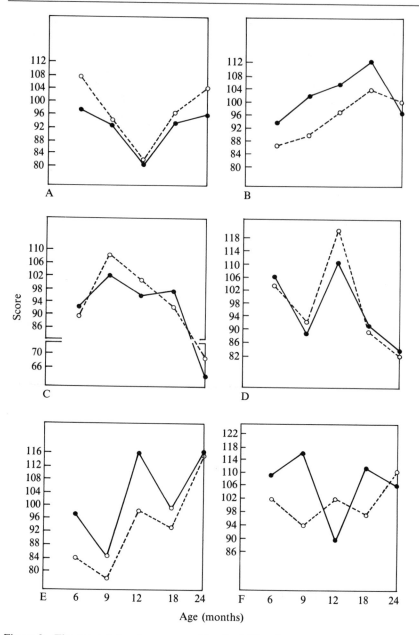

Figure 2 The mental development profiles for MZ twins between the ages of 6 and 24 months from the Louisville twin study (Wilson, 1983). The pairs A to E show high similarity whereas pair F does not

Source: Reproduced from Plomin et al., 1990, and based on Wilson, 1983. Reproduced with permission from both sources

regulation of neurally acting genes. Another well-known longitudinal study, the Colorado adoption project, was set up in 1975 (Plomin & Defries, 1985). The children are tested at yearly intervals with a battery of cognitive and physical tests, making this the most complete adoption project so far undertaken. Plomin, Defries and Fulker (1988) were able to confirm with their adoptees Wilson's (1983) twin study findings on the increase in heritability of IQ until middle childhood. A large number of multivariate analyses have been applied to this and other longitudinal projects. One can barely pick up an issue of the journal *Behavior Genetics* without finding yet another complex analytical technique being used. It is not appropriate to address these statistical models in this review, especially as I am not competent to make judgements on them. However, some of the basic features of these models and their results are described in Plomin et al.'s (1990) text.

Race and IQ

One cannot leave the subject of the genetic basis of IQ without some reference to the racial question, raised most prominently by Jensen. The average IQ difference between blacks and whites in the United States is about one standard deviation (or 15 IQ points). If the variance in IQ is at least partly genetic, could the difference between the two populations be genetic? Jensen (1972) argued that blacks may be genetically inferior in IQ to whites, and so the various government educational programmes that were set up with the intention of boosting scholastic achievement in disadvantaged children were doomed to failure. Jensen argued that because the heritability of IQ is high, there was little room left for the environment to improve performance. However, one could just as easily argue that short-sightedness is highly heritable, but can be corrected by using the appropriate environmental intervention, that is, by wearing glasses. Thus a highly heritable character need not be immune from improvement by the environment. The evidence presented for and against a predominantly genetic explanation of the racial differences in IQ is evenly balanced (see Loehlin, Lindzey, & Spuhler, 1975).

Behavioural genetic analyses have also been performed on more specific mental performance measures including verbal comprehension, fluency, reasoning, spatial abilities, school achievement, and reading (see Nichols, 1978). Generally the heritabilities for such behavioural indices are rather smaller than those for IQ.

Psychopathology

Schizophrenia

The second major behaviour genetic adventure with human subjects concerns the work with schizophrenia. Instead of correlating the scores of two relatives as one does for IQ, the investigator looks for concordances between relatives. If one twin has the disease, does the other? However, there are some intrinsic problems with the study of all psychopathologies. First, the diagnosis of schizophrenia can vary from country to country (Gottesman & Shields, 1982). Second, a subject may not have schizophrenia when tested, but might develop it later in life. Quantitative analysis is also difficult because one is not dealing with an absolute score as in IQ. Thus measures of heritability of schizophrenia are very approximate.

Gottesman and Shields (1982) reviewed the various family, twin, and adoption studies up to that period. While schizophrenia in the general population affects 1 per cent of people, the children of schizophrenics have a 10 per cent liability for the disease. From a variety of twin studies (Gottesman & Shields, 1982; Kendler & Robinette, 1983) the concordance rates for MZ twins varied from 31 to 58 per cent and from 6.5 to 27 per cent for DZ twins. Taking the lower figure of 31 per cent for MZ twins, this suggests a strong environmental component, as identical genotypes are, more often than not, discordant for schizophrenia. Doubling the difference between the MZ and DZ concordances gives a rough estimate of heritability which, depending on which studies you take, can approach .50.

Adoption studies

Heston (1966) examined the adopted-away children of 47 severely affected women. The children were raised in families free of any obvious psychopathology, but of the 47, 5 were clearly schizophrenic and another 4 showed schizophrenic symptoms. Thus 9 out of 47 of the children of the affected mothers could be considered to show some form of the disease. The control group of 50 adoptees of normal mothers gave no incidence of schizophrenic symptoms. These results, which confirm the genetic hypothesis, have been reproduced in a number of other studies.

Wender, Rosenthal, Kety, Schulsinger, and Welner (1974) reported a study in Denmark where adoptees whose biological parents were not schizophrenic were fostered in homes in which at least one of the parents was schizophrenic. The results showed that the schizophrenic environment itself was not enough to increase the prevalence of schizophrenia in the children. Wender, Rosenthal, and Kety (1968) compared three groups: biological parents raising their own schizophrenic children; adoptive parents rearing their schizophrenic adoptees; and adoptive parents rearing unaffected adoptees.

Higher frequencies of schizophrenia were found in the biological parents of schizophrenics compared to the adoptive parents of schizophrenics. However, these adoptive parents of schizophrenic children were given higher schizophrenia ratings than adoptive parents with unaffected children, suggesting that raising a schizophrenic child can produce schizophrenic symptoms in otherwise healthy parents.

Molecular genetics of psychopathologies

Since the late 1980s, the power of molecular genetics has been brought to bear on schizophrenia. Sherrington et al. (1988) raised the possibility that a dominant gene on chromosome 5 appeared to be involved in the appearance of schizophrenia in a number of Icelandic and English families. However, a number of subsequent studies failed to confirm this linkage of a major gene for schizophrenia to chromosome 5 (reviewed in Byerley, 1989). However, schizophrenia may show genetic heterogeneity in that several different major loci can mutate and each mutation can by itself produce schizophrenia. If different genes have been mutated in different families, the end point in all the families is similar, that is, a high incidence of schizophrenia. Pedigree analysis of different families would then produce exactly the type of apparently contradictory findings mentioned above.

Similar inconsistencies appear in the molecular genetic literature for manic depression. Egeland et al. (1987) reported that within the reproductively isolated Amish community of Pennsylvania, a gene linked to the tip of the short arm of chromosome 11 appeared to be implicated in the high incidence of bipolar depression. However, further analysis of these data failed to confirm the linkage to chromosome 11 and studies of other pedigrees also excluded chromosome 11. Still further investigations have suggested that manic depression may be linked to the X chromosome (reviewed by Robertson, 1989; Gershon, Martineo, Goldin, & Gejman, 1990; Hodgkinson, Mullan, & Gurling 1990). The conclusion forced upon us is that manic depression represents a genetically heterogeneous set of syndromes with a similar phenotypic end-point. However, what is beyond doubt is that manic depressive psychosis has a strong genetic component as demonstrated from the results of twin, family, and adoption studies (see Plomin et al., 1990, for a review).

Family, twin, and adoption studies have also been applied to alcoholism, delinquency, and various forms of antisocial behaviour. In these psychopathologies, as in childhood hyperactivity, extraversion and neuroticism, musical ability, and sexual orientation, significant genetic components are implicated. In fact it is difficult to escape the conclusion that genetic variation plays a very important role in just about every form of behaviour that has been studied.

ANIMAL BEHAVIOUR GENETICS

Historically, there have been two major schools of thought in animal behaviour genetics. One school is interested in the genetic analysis of behaviour and its evolutionary implications. The other approach has sought to use genetic analysis to study the neural mechanisms that underlie behaviour. Thus the evolutionary school tends to concentrate on polygenic characters, while the neurobiological school focuses more on single genes. It has become quite clear over the years that single genes have quite a lot to offer in the understanding of behaviour from an evolutionary perspective.

Interspecific studies

One way of analysing behaviour that may have a genetic basis is to examine fixed-action patterns, instinctive behavioural elements which may be relatively unmodified by experience and therefore easy to study genetically. If two species show a difference in behaviour, and can be crossed together to obtain F_1 and F_2 and back-cross progeny, then simple Mendelian ratios will reflect the existence of a single gene difference in behaviour. Examples of this are few and far between. Interspecific genetics is difficult precisely because of the reproductive barriers that have evolved to keep the species' gene pools apart. However, molecular techniques now allow us to move a gene from species A to species B and observe the consequences. I shall discuss below the potential of this exciting new methodology for analysing species-specific behaviour.

Intra-species comparisons

A more fruitful approach is to examine different inbred strains within a species. The genetic architecture (as discussed above) has been obtained for many different behavioural characteristics in many different organisms, for example aggression, locomotor activity, emotional behaviour, sexual behaviour, learning ability, and so on – the list is almost endless. Rarely is it that a single gene determines the difference in behaviour between two strains of mice, for example, and quantitative methods can be used to examine the contributions of the additive genetic component A, the dominance component D, etc. I mentioned earlier that if there is plenty of additive genetic variation then it is easy to select for high or low levels of a character. Imagine now that natural selection has done the job for us on a characteristic, such as rapid learning ability in flies, so that smart flies are "fitter" and selected over dumb ones. What shall we see in the genetic architecture for learning in these flies? We should see an absence of additive genetic variation as natural selection has "used up" the variation in the additively acting "smart" genes.

I shall give one classic example of this approach. Fulker (1966) studied the mating propensity of male fruit flies from several inbred lines which differed in the average number of females mated per unit time. Male mating behaviour is a major fitness character and would be expected to be under strong selection for high levels of sexual performance. Using the diallel cross method, Fulker indeed showed that the additive component was low compared to the dominance component. This is one of the first applications of the diallel cross to behaviour, and fortunately it came up with a reasonable answer, thereby verifying the method. Many different types of similar experiments have been performed and space does not permit a detailed discussion of these experiments. Instead I refer the interested reader to the relevant sections of Hay's (1985) text.

Artificial selection studies can also produce estimates of heritability. Most behaviours respond to selection, and again, large numbers of studies have been reported, especially on invertebrates because the generation time is so much faster than mammals. A character that shows a rapid response to selection in both the high and low direction, as in Tryon's (1940) experiment, suggests that the character is probably determined by one or a few segregating genes. A more measured response, such as that obtained by Manning (1961) in his selection study for fast and slow fruit fly mating, implies that many genes are contributing to the phenotype. An asymmetric response to selection, as also obtained by Manning, where he obtained a response for slow mating but not for fast mating, is also informative. It suggests that natural selection has already selected the additively acting genes that determine fast mating, and it is therefore difficult to improve on this "ceiling" with further selection.

Selection experiments together with inter-strain analyses produce a useful picture of genetic architecture and invoke the past evolutionary history of a behavioural trait. Identifying specific genes in a polygenic system is difficult and has usually been limited to calculating the contributions to the phenotypic variation of the different chromosomes. This can be performed quite readily in the fruit fly where it is possible to track intact chromosomes through several generations without having the inconvenience of recombination. For example, a fly's third chromosome from strain B can be placed into a background where chromosomes 1, 2 and 4 are from strain A and the hybrid fly can be examined to see whether the B chromosome produces B-like behaviour. This has been used in many studies and is the first step in identifying specific genes within a polygenic system. To identify and map polygenes that determine behavioural differences between strains requires many markers on each chromosome to which linkage of the behavioural genes can be assigned. Polymorphic molecular markers have been developed, which are pieces of DNA that differ between strain A and B, and linkage of the behavioural phenotype to the markers can be performed using standard segregation analysis.

55

Single genes and behaviour

A simpler way forward is to analyse behaviour by using single gene mutations. For example, the *ebony* gene in *Drosophila melanogaster* affects body colour, visual behaviour, sexual behaviour, and locomotor activity (Kyriacou, Burnet, & Connolly 1978; Kyriacou, 1985). The biochemical lesion induced in *ebony* mutants obviously affects the pathway that is recruited in the normal expression of all these different phenotypes. Thus *ebony* is a pleiotropic gene. Molecular analysis of the *ebony* gene reveals that it encodes an enzyme required both for the normal tanning of the cuticle (hence the dark body colour in the mutant), and also in nervous tissue (hence the behavioural defects). Furthermore, *ebony* is of interest to evolutionary biologists because *ebony* mutants are found in nature even though the mutants themselves mate poorly given their visual defect (males cannot follow the female during the courtship display). Yet heterozygous *ebony* males are at a significant mating advantage to both the wild-type and *ebony* mutants, and therefore the *ebony* gene continues to segregate in natural and artificial laboratory populations (Kyriacou, 1985). This hybrid vigour in the sexual behaviour of the heterozygotes maintains the *ebony* polymorphism (Kyriacou, 1985), and has evolutionary implications as it maintains genetic variation at the *ebony* locus. Examples of morphological mutations like *ebony*, which are of relevance to psychologists and evolutionary biologists, are rather rare.

Single gene mutations in mice include about 300 that affect neurological functioning, for example *waltzer*, *twirler*, *reeler*, etc. These mice were highly prized in Victorian times for their bizarre behaviours, and the mutants have given some insights into cerebellar, inner ear, and neural crest development. However, the interest in these "behavioural" genes is at present developmental rather than psychological (Hay, 1985).

A breakthrough in single gene research came when Seymour Benzer (1973) advocated the use of mutagenesis and mass screening techniques in order to induce new mutations in the behavioural systems of choice. *Drosophila* was ideally suited to such a venture and Benzer, using ingenious devices and amusing names for his new mutants, induced neurological mutants (*ether-a-go-go*, *drop dead*), sexual behaviour mutations (*coitus interruptus*), flight and visual mutants, etc. He also extended a technique called "fate-mapping" to locate the primary anatomical site of action of a mutant gene. After the first generation of mutations had been produced, some of Benzer's students began to study complex behavioural phenotypes, such as learning, biological rhythmicity, and courtship behaviour.

Learning

The demonstration that flies could be classically conditioned en masse to associate electric shock with odour laid the foundation for the subsequent isolation of mutant flies which learned poorly or failed to learn at all (Quinn & Greenspan, 1984). Several such mutants, *dunce* (*dnc*), *rutabaga* (*rut*), *amnesiac* (*amn*), *turnip* (*tur*), etc., also showed defects in other tests that were designed to measure aspects of learning mediated by different sensory modalities (see Kyriacou & Hall, 1993, for review). This suggested that the mutations were acting centrally within the nervous system because more than one sensory modality was affected. Biochemical and molecular characterization of *dnc* and *rut* (see Davis & Dauwalder, 1991) revealed that these genes encoded enzymes from the cyclic adenose monophosphate (cAMP) second messenger signalling system. This is particularly interesting as the cAMP pathway appears to be implicated in the cellular mechanisms that underlie learning in the mollusc *Aplysia*, much studied by Kandel and his colleagues. The *dnc* gene appears to be expressed particularly prominently in the region of the fly brain known as the mushroom bodies (Davis & Dauwalder, 1991). Surgical lesion of these regions in higher insects such as the hymenoptera leads to memory defects (Erber, Masuhr, & Menzel, 1980).

In addition, the number of mushroom body fibres rises in the first week of the adult fly's life (see Balling, Technau, & Heisenberg, 1987). Flies raised in a sensory deprived environment show reduction in the number of these fibres compared to flies raised in an enriched environment. However, *dnc* and *rut* mutants do not show this experience-dependent increase in fibre number when raised in enriched and deprived environments. Consequently, these learning mutants have helped to identify the biochemical cellular, and anatomical substrates of learning, and have been shown to be involved in the critical periods when sensory experiences can mould the fly's brain. Flies are evidently not born knowing all they need to know.

Biological rhythms

In 1971 Konopka and Benzer induced three mutations that altered the periodicity of the fly's circadian clock. The three mutations shortened, lengthened, or obliterated the fly's 24-hour rhythmic behaviour as measured by pupal to adult eclosion and locomotor activity cycles (Konopka & Benzer, 1971; see also Figure 3). All three mutations mapped to the same spot on the X chromosome, in other words, they were all alleles of a single locus which was called the *period* (*per*) gene. Thus the per^s variant has a short 19-hour cycle, per^{L1} mutant has a long 29-hour rhythm, and the per^{01} fly is arrhythmic (see Figure 3). The three mutations also disrupt a one-minute (ultradian) cycle found in the male's courtship song: per^s males have a short 40-second cycle, per^{L1} males have a long 80-second cycle and per^{01} males are arrhythmic (Kyriacou & Hall, 1993). Finally the *per* mutants also affect the fly's 10-day egg-to-adult developmental cycle in a predictable manner with per^s mutants developing faster than the wild-type and per^{L1} mutants

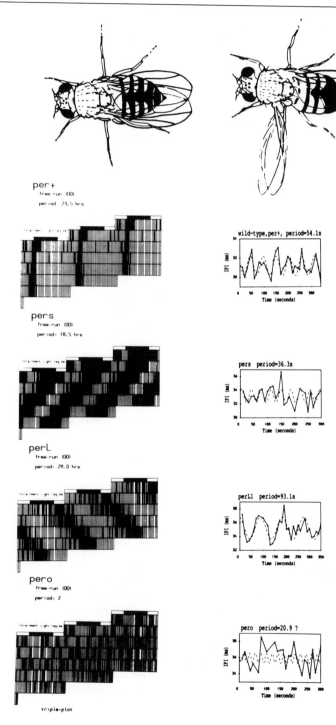

58

developing more slowly, while per^{01} mutants give a somewhat erratic profile (Kyriacou & Hall, 1993). Thus the *per* gene appears to control biological timing in a rather general way. The *per* gene was cloned and sequenced (see Kyriacou & Hall, 1993, for review) and encodes a 1,200-amino-acid protein of unknown function. It has some similarities to two other proteins that are believed to act as transcription factors. Transcription factors are proteins that act to switch on or off other genes. The *per* messenger RNA (mRNA) cycles in abundance with a circadian period, as does the *per* protein (mRNA is the molecule that enables protein to be synthesized from a gene). There is good evidence that the *per* protein feeds back on itself and negatively regulates its own mRNA transcription. Consequently the current model of *per's* action is as follows. As the *per* protein is made it reaches a critical concentration, and then blocks more of its own mRNA transcription. As the mRNA is blocked, so less protein is translated, giving the mRNA and protein cycles that are observed. Imagine now that *per* encodes a transcription factor which turns on or off all the other downstream genes required to get the animal behaving rhythmically. As the *per* protein waxes and wanes, batteries of these genes will be turned on or off in unison, giving circadian cycling of many different behaviours. The per^s protein achieves its critical concentration 5 hours earlier than the wild-type *per* protein because it may be more stable, and the per^{L1} protein 5 hours later than the normal protein because it may be less stable. In per^{01} mutants the *per* protein is truncated to 450 amino acids and therefore must have very low activity.

The *per* gene is expressed in many organs of the fly and in fact many of these structures have been shown in the past to have circadian cycles in their physiology (see Hall & Kyriacou, 1990). The *per* gene is expressed in the

---

Figure 3 The phenotypic effects of the *per* mutants in *Drosophila melanogaster*. The locomotor activity profile (actogram) is given on the left and the song cycle on the right. The activity data are triple plotted with day 1 on the top row, days 1 and 2 on the next row, days 1, 2, and 3 on the next, with days 2, 3, and 4, then 3, 4, and 5, then 4, 5, and 6, etc. on the subsequent rows. Each vertical line represents the amount of activity in a 30-minute time bin. The darker the shade the more intense the activity. The flies were allowed to "free-run" in constant darkness after first being maintained in a 12-hour light, 12-hour dark environmental light cycle. The times of lights on and off before the free-run are represented by the horizontal black and white lines above the actogram. Note how the wild-type (per^+) fly becomes active at about the same time each day, whereas the per^s mutant begins activity at approximately 5 hours earlier each day, and the per^{L1} mutant about 5 hours later. The per^{01} mutant is arrhythmic (insomniac!). To the right are presented the song rhythms of the males carrying the different *per* alleles. The males wing vibration produces pulses (see also legend to Figure 4) with an interpulse interval (IPI) which oscillates with a *period* of approximately 55 seconds in per^+, 36 seconds in per^s, 93 seconds in per^{L1}, and a weak non-significant 21-second cycle is obtained in per^{01}. The plots represent the mean IPIs for each 10 seconds of time for about 5 minutes of courtship

brain and visual system of the fly, and certain cells called "lateral" neurons appear to be particularly important in mediating circadian locomotor activity. Thus the marriage of behaviour and molecular biology has, in this case, produced a real insight into the cellular mechanisms that are involved in determining one of life's ubiquitous features.

Sexual behaviour

The courtship song cycle of male fruit flies (Figure 3) is also affected by the *per* mutations mentioned above (Kyriacou & Hall, 1989). The song cycle is functionally important and a 60-second cycle appears to enhance the *D. melanogaster*'s female's receptivity, while a 35-second cycle will enhance a *D. simulans* female's receptivity to *D. simulans* males (Kyriacou & Hall, 1986). Males from *D. simulans* (which is a closely related sympatric species to *D. melanogaster*) sing with a 35-second cycle. Thus the song cycle may act as part of a species recognition mechanism with the different species of *Drosophila* females preferring the song cycles of their conspecific males. Interspecific crosses reveal that the species difference in song cycles between *D. melanogaster* and *D. simulans* (60 seconds versus 35 seconds) map to the *X* chromosome. This suggests that perhaps it is the sex-linked (*X* chromosome) *per* gene, that may differ in the two species and be causing the behavioural difference between them. This was confirmed by taking the cloned *D. simulans per* gene and transforming it into a *D. melanogaster per^{01}* arrhythmic mutant (Wheeler et al., 1991). Not only were locomotor activity cycles restored in the transgenic *per^{01} D. melanogaster* fly, but also the song cycle produced by the transgenic males revealed the 40-second *D. simulans* rhythm. Thus the species-specific behaviour of one species (*D. simulans*) was transferred to another (*D. melanogaster*) by shunting one gene between the two species. This remarkable result shows that an apparently complex species-specific sexual behaviour, which may by its nature be implicated in speciation, can be determined by a single gene. A song cycle is superimposed upon the basic structure of the courtship song. Males vibrate their wings and produce a series of pulses with interpulse intervals (IPI) that are on average 30–40 ms (milliseconds) in *D. melanogaster* and 40–60 ms in *D. simulans* (Kyriacou & Hall, 1986; see also Figure 4). These IPI lengths cycle with the *per* determined period in the two species. However, two mutations also affect the characteristics of the song structure itself. The *cacophony* (*cac*) and *dissonance* (*diss*) mutations, both which are sex-linked (Kulkarni & Hall, 1987; Kulkarni, Steinlauf, & Hall, 1988) lead to abnormal pulses being produced (Figure 4). The *cac* pulses are polycyclic and have a large amplitude, while *diss* pulses may be monocyclic at the beginning of a song burst but degenerate, becoming polycyclic towards the end, often with an increasing amplitude (see Figure 4). The *cac* and *diss* mutations map to two independent loci, both of which have other mutant alleles that affect vision. Thus *cac* is

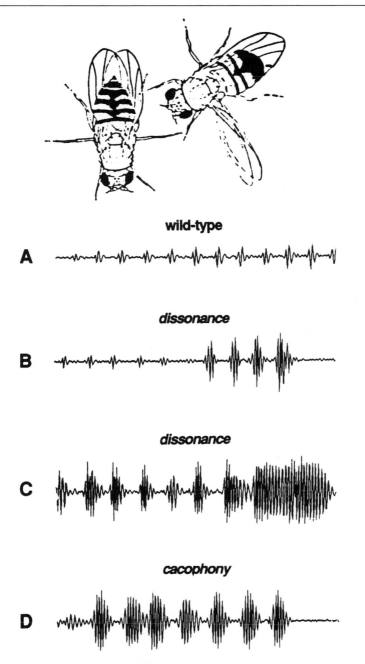

Figure 4 The song pulses of wild-type, *dissonance* (diss) and *cacophony* (cac)
mutant males
Source: Reproduced from Kyriacou, 1990, and based on Kulkarni et al., 1988. Reproduced with
permission from both sources

a mutant allele of a gene called *L(1)L13* which has another mutant allele called *night-blind-A (nbA)* (Kulkarni & Hall, 1987). The *diss* mutation is a mutant allele of the *no-on-transient A (nonA)* locus, but *nonA* mutants have defective vision but normal songs (Rendahl, Jones, Kulkarni, Bagully, & Hall, 1992), whereas the *diss* mutant does have a visual defect (Kulkarni & Hall, 1987). The *diss* mutation is now formally designated as *nonA*^{diss} to show that it is a mutant allele of the *nonA* locus. The *nonA* gene has been cloned and sequenced (Jones & Rubin, 1990) and it appears to encode a protein that may be able to bind to RNA. Such proteins can play a regulatory role and often show rapid evolution between species (Kyriacou, 1992). However, this does not give us any biochemical insight into the possible nature of the *diss* protein. It is remarkable, however, that two different song mutants, *cac* and *diss*, are both alleles of visual loci, demonstrating a neurogenetic connection between the visual and song mechanisms during development.

Drosophila, for many, is the organism of choice because its genetics and molecular biology is well developed compared to the mouse, for example, and its behaviour is complex enough to interest a psychologist and a zoologist. The nematode worm *Caenorhabdytis elegans* also has a lot to offer the neurogeneticist in that its molecular biology and genetics are as well understood as that of the fly. The nematode's behaviour, however, is much simpler than *Drosophila* but for studying the development of the nervous system the nematode is in a league of its own (Way, 1990). This is because the development of each of the worm's neurons has been documented in detail. Behaviour such as touch reception has been analysed using mutations; more recently rhythmic behaviour has also come under scrutiny. Perhaps by the turn of the millennium someone will be able to teach the nematodes to learn, opening up the neuromolecular dissection of learning in a very simple nervous system.

Aplysia egg-laying behaviour

The molecular analysis of the egg-laying behaviour of *Aplysia* has provided some major insights into the control of complex behaviours. Egg laying is a highly stereotyped behaviour pattern and is expressed sequentially (see Figure 5). The behaviour consists of a change in the locomotor activity and eating patterns of the snail and an increase in its heart and breathing rate. The oviduct extrudes a string of eggs which the mouth grasps, and with a series of side-to-side movements the egg string is pulled out by the mouth. Mucus is secreted on to the eggs, and with a final head movement the eggs are deposited on a solid substrate (see Figure 5). The complete sequence of this highly stereotyped behaviour pattern can be generated by injecting an extract, which is produced from two clusters of neurons positioned above the abdominal ganglion, the "bag" cells. The factor that produces this complex

Figure 5 Egg-laying behaviour in *Aplysia*. The egg string is extruded by contractions of the oviduct (1), is placed in the mouth (2), and mucus is secreted on the string with side-to-side head movements, while the string is being drawn out (3). The egg string is finally deposited on a substrate (4)

Source: Reproduced with permission from Scheller and Axel, 1984

behavioural repertoire is a 36-amino-acid peptide called egg-laying hormone (ELH). Scheller and Axel (1984) were able to clone the gene for ELH (see Figure 6). When they examined the DNA sequence they found that it potentially encoded several different peptides, one of which was ELH, but also three others α, β, and acidic peptides. In fact the gene, once translated into the precursor polypeptide, could potentially release ten or eleven different peptides. Scheller realized that if different patterns of peptides could be released from this precursor protein, then a huge combination of different behaviours could be switched on in the snail. Imagine that each of the peptides can alter the firing patterns of the different neurons important for the expression of the egg-laying-behaviour repertoire. The potential for a

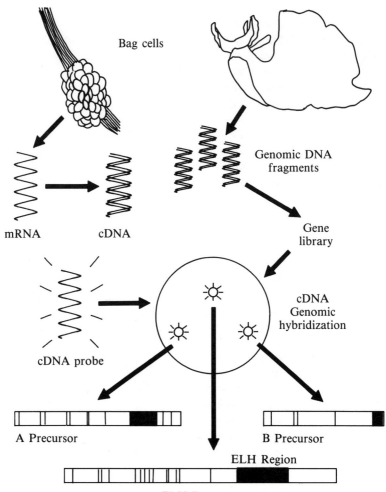

Bag cells

Genomic DNA fragments

mRNA   cDNA

Gene library

cDNA probe

cDNA Genomic hybridization

A Precursor   B Precursor

ELH Region

ELH Precursor

§*QFigure 6* Isolation of the *Aplysia ELH* gene family. The bag cells produce messenger RNA (mRNA) which is used to make the complementary double-stranded DNA (cDNA). This cDNA molecule acts as a probe when labelled with a radioisotope. The genomic DNA from *Aplysia* is cut with restriction enzymes into small pieces and the fragments are recombined with a vector (a plasmid or virus) to form a gene library. The genomic DNA fragments can then be probed with the cDNA, which will hybridize to any complementary DNA and light it up. Three positives are obtained which encoded the *ELH*, A, and B precursor peptides (see text). The *ELH* peptide is represented in the *ELH* precursor as the darker shading. Similar regions are also present in the A and B precursors (see text)

Source: Reproduced with permission from Kyriacou, 1990

precursor protein to generate complex behaviour is enormous with over 1,000 combinations of different peptides possible. This work with *Aplysia* was the first application of molecular biology to complex behaviour. A strong evolutionary component is also present in this investigation, as Scheller and Axel (1984) originally found three similar genes, the *ELH* precursor gene, and the *A* and *B* precursor genes (see Figure 6). The *A* and *B* peptides were produced in the atrial gland and appeared to control the release of *ELH*. The fact that the gene sequences of the *ELH*, *A*, and *B* genes were similar, suggested that they evolved by a process of duplication of the original ancestral *ELH* gene. The *A* and *B* genes began to diverge from the *ELH* gene, and from each other, eventually taking on different, but related regulatory function. Other *Aplysia* species do not have *A* and *B* genes, suggesting that the *ELH* locus indeed represents the ancestral DNA.

CONCLUSIONS

Genetic analysis of behaviour can be performed at many different levels, from the evolutionary to the biochemical. With humans, the methods used are limited to making statements about whether a particular behavioural phenotype has a genetic component or not. With animals, the whole range of genetic, biochemical, physiological, and molecular techniques can be applied to answer penetrating questions about the evolution and the neural control of a behavioural pattern. In the twenty-first century it appears that molecular neurobiology will become the major life science. No one scientist can possibly be an expert in all the different subjects that are required for an integrated understanding of behaviour. Therefore psychologists, zoologists, biochemists, molecular biologists, and geneticists will have to begin to formulate ways of communicating with each other, free of the jargon peculiar to their own particular speciality. They have a lot to offer one another, and I hope that my modest contribution in these pages contributes to the dialogue.

FURTHER READING

Fuller, J. L., & Thompson, W. R. (1978). *Foundations of behavior genetics*. St Louis, MO: Mosby.

Greenspan, R. J. (Ed.) (1990). Genetics in the study of the nervous system. *Seminars in the Neuroscience, 12*(3), 143–241.

Hall, J. C. (1982). Genetics of the nervous system in *Drosophila. Quarterly Review of Biophysics, 15*, 223–479.

Plomin, R. (1990). The role of inheritance in behavior. *Science, 248*, 183–188.

Vogler, G. P. (Ed.) (1992). Human developmental behaviour genetics. *Behavior Genetics, 22*(2), 189–244.

REFERENCES

Balling, A., Technau, G. M., & Heisenberg, M. (1987). Are the structural changes in adult *Drosophila* mushroom bodies memory traces? Studies in biochemical learning mutants. *Journal of Neurogenetics, 4,* 64–73.

Benzer, S. (1973). Genetic dissection of behavior. *Scientific American, 229*(6), 24–37.

Bouchard, T. J. Jr, & McGue, M. (1981). Familial studies of intelligence: A review. *Science, 212,* 1055–1059.

Byerley, W. F. (1989). Genetic linkage revisited. *Nature, 340,* 340–341.

Davis, R. L., & Dauwalder, B. (1991). The *Drosophila dunce* locus: Learning and memory genes in the fly. *Trends in Genetics, 7,* 224–229.

Egeland, J. A., Gerhardt, D. S., Pauls, D. L., Sussex, J. N., Kidd, K. K., Allen, C. K., Hosteller, A. M., & Housman, D. E. (1987). Bipolar affective disorders linked to DNA markers on chromosome 11. *Nature, 325,* 783–787.

Erber, J., Masuhr, R., & Menzel, R. (1980). Localization of short-term memory in bee (*Apis mellifera*). *Physiological Entomology, 5,* 343–358.

Fulker, D. W. (1966). Mating speed in male *Drosphila melanogaster*: A psychogenetic analysis. *Science, 153,* 203–205.

Galton, F. (1869). *Hereditary genius: An inquiry into its laws and consequences.* London: Macmillan.

Gershon, E. S., Martineo, M., Goldin, L. R., & Gejman, P. V. (1990). Genetic mapping of common diseases. The challenges of manic-depressive illness and schizophrenia. *Trends in Genetics, 6,* 282–287.

Gottesman, I. I., & Shields, J. (1982). *Schizophrenia: The epigenetic puzzle.* Cambridge: Cambridge University Press.

Hall, J. C., & Kyriacou, C. P. (1990). Genetics of biological rhythms in *Drosophila. Advances in Insect Physiology, 22,* 221–298.

Hay, D. A. (1985). *Essentials of behaviour genetics.* Oxford: Basil Blackwell.

Heston, L. L. (1966). Psychiatric disorders in foster home reared children of schizophrenic mothers. *British Journal Psychiatry, 112,* 819–825.

Hodgkinson, S., Mullan, M. J., & Gurling, H. M. D. (1990). The role of genetic factors in the etiology of the affective disorders. *Behavior Genetics, 20,* 235–250.

Jensen, A. R. (1972). *Genetics and education.* New York: Harper & Row.

John, B., & Miklos, G. (1988). *The eukaryote genome in development and evolution.* Sydney: Allen & Unwin.

Jones, R. K., & Rubin, G. M. (1990). Molecular analysis of *no-on-transient A*, a gene required for normal vision in *Drosophila. Neuron, 4,* 711–723.

Joynson, R. B. (1989). *The Burt affair.* London: Routledge.

Kendler, K. S., & Robinette, C. D. (1983). Schizophrenia in the National Academy of Sciences – National Research Council twin registry: A 16 year update. *American Journal of Psychiatry, 140,* 1521–1563.

Konopka, R. J., & Benzer, S. (1971). Clock mutants of *Drosophila melanogaster. Proceedings of the National Academy of Sciences USA, 68,* 2112–2116.

Kulkarni, S. J., & Hall, J. C. (1987). Behavioral and cytogenetic analysis of the *cacophony* courtship song mutant and interacting genetic variants in *Drosophila melanogaster. Genetics, 115,* 461–475.

Kulkarni, S. J., Steinlauf, A. F., & Hall, J. C. (1988). The *dissonance* mutant of courtship song in *Drosophila melanogaster*: Isolation, behaviour and cytogenetics. *Genetics, 118,* 267–285.

Kyriacou, C. P. (1985). Long-term *ebony* polymorphisms: A comparison of the contributions of behavioral and non-behavioral fitness characters. *Behavior Genetics, 15,* 165–180.

Kyriacou, C. P. (1990). Genetic and molecular analysis of eukaryote behaviour. *Seminars in the Neurosciences, 22*, 217–229.

Kyriacou, C. P. (1992). Sex variations. *Trends in Genetics, 8*, 261–263.

Kyriacou, C. P., & Hall, J. C. (1986). Inter-specific genetic control of courtship song production and reception in *Drosophila*. *Science, 232*, 494–497.

—— (1989). Spectral analysis of *Drosophila* courtship song rhythms. *Animal Behaviour, 37*, 850–859.

—— (1993). Genetic and molecular analysis of *Drosophila* behaviour. *Advances in Genetics*, in press.

Kyriacou, C. P., Burnet, B., & Connolly, K. (1978). The behavioural basis of overdominance in competitive mating success at the *ebony* locus of *Drosophila melanogaster*. *Animal Behaviour, 26*, 1195–1206.

Loehlin, J. C., Lindzey, G., & Spuhler, J. N. (1975). *Race differences in intelligence*. San Francisco, CA: Freeman.

Manning, A. (1961). The effects of artificial selection of mating speed in *Drosophila melanogaster*. *Animal Behaviour, 9*, 82–91.

Nichols, R. C. (1978). Twin studies of ability, personality and interests. *Homo, 29*, 158–173.

Plomin, R. (1988). The nature and nurture of cognitive abilities. In R. J. Sternberg (Ed.) *Advances in the psychology of human intelligence* (pp. 1–33). Hillsdale, NJ: Lawrence Erlbaum.

Plomin, R., & Defries, J. C. (1985). *Origins of individual differences in infancy: The Colorado Adoption Project*. New York: Academic Press.

Plomin, R., Defries, J. C., & Fulker, D. W. (1988). *Nature and nurture during infancy and early childhood*. New York: Cambridge University Press.

Plomin, R., Defries, J. C., & McClearn, G. E. (1990). *Behavioral genetics: A primer* (2nd edn). New York: Freeman.

Quinn, W. G., & Greenspan, R. J. (1984). Learning and courtship in *Drosphila*: Two stories with mutants. *Annual Review of the Neurosciences, 21*, 67–93.

Rendahl, K. G., Jones, K. R., Kulkarni, S. J., Bagully, S. H., & Hall, J. C. (1992). The *dissonance* mutation at the *no-on-transient-A* locus of *Drosophila melanogaster*: Genetic conctrol of courtship song and visual behaviors by a protein with putative RNA-binding motifs. *Journal of Neuroscience, 12*, 390–407.

Robertson M. (1989). False start on manic-depression. *Nature, 342*, 222.

Scheller, R. J., & Axel, R. (1984). How genes control an innate behavior. *Scientific American, 290*(3), 44–52.

Sherrington, R., Brynjolfsson, J., Petursson, J., Potter, M., Duddlestone, K., Baraclough, B. B., Wasmuth, J. J., Dobbs, M., & Gurling, H. M. D. (1988). Localization of a susceptibility locus for schizophrenia on chromosome 5. *Nature, 336*, 164–167.

Tryon, R. C. (1940). Genetic differences in maze learning ability in rats. *National Society for the Study of Education 39th Yearbook, 39*, 111–119.

Way, J. C. (1990). Determination of cell type in the nervous system. *Seminars in the Neurosciences, 2*, 173–184.

Wender, P. H., Rosenthal, D., & Kety, S. S. (1968). A psychiatric assessment of the adoptive parents of schizophrenics. In D. Rosenthal & S. Kety (Eds) *The transmission of schizophrenia* (pp. 235–250). Oxford: Pergamon.

Wender, P. H., Rosenthal, D., Kety, S. S., Schulsinger, F., & Welner, J. (1974). Cross-fostering: A research strategy for clarifying the role of genetic and experimental factors in the etiology of schizophrenia. *Archives of General Psychiatry, 30*, 121–128.

Wheeler, D. A., Kyriacou, C. P., Greenacre, M. L., Yu, Q., Rutila, J. E., Rosbash, M., & Hall, J. C. (1991). Molecular transfer of a species-specific courtship behaviour from *Drosophila simulans* to *Drosophila melanogaster*. *Science, 251*, 1082–1085.

Wilson, R. S. (1983). The Louisville Twin Study: Developmental synchronies in behavior. *Child Development, 54*, 298–316.

2.2

BEHAVIOURAL ECOLOGY AND EVOLUTION

John Lazarus

University of Newcastle upon Tyne, England

Theory in behavioural ecology
  Natural selection, fitness, and
    reproductive success
  Adaptation, optimization,
    and theoretical modelling
  Selection pressures
  Evolutionary stability and
    social behaviour
  The role of genetics
The scope of behavioural
  ecology
  Selfishness: why don't
    animals fight more fiercely?

Cooperation: why should
  animals benefit others?
Altruism: why should animals
  sacrifice themselves for
  others?
Sex and parental care
  Competition for mates
  Mate choice
  Parental investment and
    mating strategies
Methods and prospects
Acknowledgement
Further reading
References

The aim of psychology is to understand the nature of behaviour and mental processes, and much of psychological endeavour is concerned with understanding causation; the conditions – social, environmental, physiological, or genetic – that are responsible for some behaviour, attitude, thought, or emotion. What environmental events cause an individual to behave aggressively, for example; what stimulates a male to court a female?

But for psychologists and biologists there is another kind of question, a "why?" kind of question. *Why* should certain events in the environment make an individual aggressive? Why, in general, do animals behave the way they do and not otherwise? Is there some common organizing principle that will provide an answer to all the disparate "Whys"?

There is such a principle: the process of evolution by *natural selection*. Species have evolved as a result of small accumulated changes in prior forms and, as a result of Darwin's (1859) insights, we know that the major force for such change has been the process of natural selection. The enormous importance of Darwin's theory is that it gives us a guiding principle for understanding the nature of life: the principle of *adaptation*. An adaptation is some feature of the animal's structure, physiology, or behaviour that solves some problem in its life. Darwin's theory of natural selection may not seem capable of predicting anything very profound or precise about behaviour but since the mid-1960s it has been enormously powerful in generating new theories to explain both the broad principles by which animals live their lives and the exquisite detail of their moment-to-moment decision-making. *Behavioural ecology* is the branch of psychology whose aim is to understand behaviour in terms of a history of evolutionary forces favouring adaptation.

THEORY IN BEHAVIOURAL ECOLOGY

Natural selection, fitness, and reproductive success

Darwin's (1859) theory of natural selection forms the starting-point for all further theorizing, and the logical structure of the theory is shown in Figure 1. Dawkins (1986) illuminates the theory brilliantly.

Natural selection predicts that phenotypic characters that increase *fitness*, compared to some alternative, will increase in frequency in the population. The fitness of an individual is a measure of its success at replicating itself in the next generation and can be measured as its *lifetime reproductive success* – the number of offspring it produces in its lifetime. A major aim of behavioural ecology is to test predictions about the way in which behaviour influences lifetime reproductive success.

As an example of the way in which natural selection moulds behaviour, imagine a gazelle that visits a waterhole to drink but in doing so runs some risk of predation by lions. How often will the gazelle go to drink if its behavioural decisions are the result of generations of natural selection acting on the decisions of its ancestors? We would expect the gazelle to make a trade-off between predation risk and the risk to its survival from dehydration (survival, to natural selection, being a means to the end of increasing reproductive success). An obvious prediction, therefore, is that drinking frequency will decline as the gazelle's perceived predation risk increases (e.g., as it detects lions more often by the waterhole) and increase as its water requirement becomes more pressing (for example, at higher temperatures). The gazelle's *optimal* decision – the precise drinking frequency that maximizes its survival chances as a result of both risks combined – can be predicted only

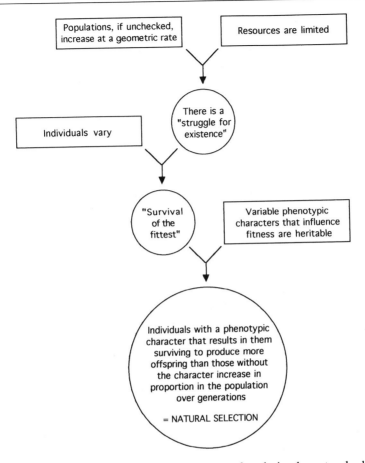

Figure 1 The structure of Darwin's (1859) theory of evolution by natural selection. Observations known to Darwin are shown in rectangles and Darwin's inferences in circles. A "phenotypic character" is simply some aspect of the individual's structure, physiology, or behaviour
Source: After Lazarus, 1987

if we know how the risk of death from predation and from dehydration are each influenced by drinking frequency. We would then have a *common currency* for the two conflicting consequences of drinking and would be able to calculate the rate of drinking that minimized the overall risk of death. An example where this is possible will be given later.

It is therefore possible to develop predictions about behaviour directly and simply from the theory of natural selection. This example also introduces the ubiquitous problem of *trade-offs*. In animal as in human life there are no free lunches and every investment in behaviour that brings some increase in fitness is accompanied by two kinds of disadvantage, or *fitness cost*. First, as in the

71

gazelle's waterhole problem, the behaviour itself has costs as well as benefits; and second, there are always other, competing, demands on the individual's time that are being postponed. The drinking gazelle, for example, is taking valuable time out from feeding.

It is important to be clear about what is meant by an animal's "decisions" or "strategies". These terms describe choices made at the behavioural level and imply nothing about the cognitive processes involved, conscious or otherwise.

Adaptation, optimization, and theoretical modelling

Ideally, predictions in behavioural ecology would be made in terms of the influence of behaviour on lifetime reproductive success, and yet this is often difficult. For qualitative predictions of the kind "Waterhole visits will diminish as lion density increases", there is little problem. It can safely be assumed that more lions mean greater predation risk and that fewer waterhole visits will reduce that risk.

The problem comes with the more ambitious aim of testing whether animals have evolved optimal solutions to their problems, solutions that maximize fitness (Krebs & Kacelnik, 1991). If the effect of some behaviour on fitness cannot be measured, then we must look for some other consequence of behaviour that can be measured and that is assumed to be maximized when fitness is maximized.

For example, Parker (1978) developed a model to predict how long a male dung fly would copulate with a female on the assumption that he is selected to maximize the number of eggs fertilized per unit time. Parker found quite a good agreement between predicted and observed copulation time, which supports the hypothesis that natural selection has optimized copulation time in this species (Box 1). Note that the quantity assumed to be maximized here is not lifetime reproductive success but fertilization rate during some short period, and that the two quantities may not be optimized by the same behavioural option. This is because the short-term measure ignores costs borne later (e.g., predation risk while copulating), which influence the lifetime optimal value.

What should we conclude if the data did not fit the prediction? We could infer either that male copulation time is not optimized or that one or more of the model's assumptions are incorrect.

72

Box 1   The marginal value theorem and
          copulation time in the dung fly

Parker's (1978) model employs a theorem, the marginal value theorem (Charnov, 1976), which is used widely in behavioural ecology to predict how animals exploit resources, and gives a flavour of the optimality approach. It starts with the fact that resources (in this case females) are distributed patchily and that the male must travel from female to female in order to mate. While copulating he fertilizes eggs at a diminishing rate, as Parker discovered by interrupting copulating pairs at different times. When he moves to a new female he therefore swaps a low fertilization rate for a travel period with a zero rate followed by a period with a new female at an initially high rate.

When should he leave one female and seek out another in order to maximize fertilization rate? The solution is shown graphically in Figure 2. The rate of fertilization, taking into account both travel time and copulation time, can be drawn as a straight line on a graph of the number of eggs fertilized against time, starting with the onset of travel from the last female. The maximum fertilization rate is realized when this line just touches the diminishing returns curve of the number of eggs fertilized, and the optimal copulation time is the time at which this rate is achieved. The male is incapable of achieving a rate greater than this (a steeper line), and if the line was below this the male would have a lower fertilization rate than he was capable of achieving.

Parker's data and the predicted optimal copulation time are shown in Figure 2. The observed copulation time of 35.5 minutes is close to the predicted time of 41.4 minutes. Possible reasons for the discrepancy are discussed in the text.

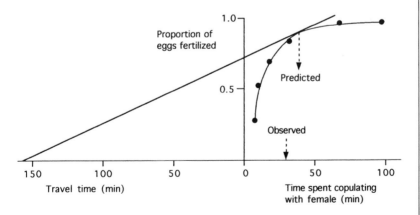

Figure 2   Predicting optimal copulation time in the male dung fly using the marginal value theorem. The average travel time between females (156.5 minutes) is shown to the left of the vertical axis, followed by the time spent copulating to the right of the vertical axis. When the male stops copulating the next cycle of travel and copulation begins
Source: Redrawn from Parker, 1978

73

How damaging would it be for the general belief in the adaptiveness of behaviour if we concluded that male copulation time was not optimal? First, optimality in copulation might have been compromised by a competing demand, such as hiding from predators. This would mean that the wrong criterion for optimality had been chosen, since it was the joint allocation of time devoted to copulation and hiding that had been selected, just as we expected the gazelle's waterhole problem to be solved in terms of two conflicting demands. A study demonstrating adaptive trade-offs between gathering resources and avoiding predation is described in Box 2.

Second, there might be some *constraint* that prevents an optimal solution

---

Box 2   Measuring a feeding-predation trade-off
in a common currency: patch choice in an ant species

Animals of many species will choose a food patch giving a lower rate of food intake if by doing so they avoid a predation risk, thereby demonstrating their ability to trade-off conflicting demands in an adaptive manner. The study coming closest to measuring such conflicting demands in a common fitness currency is that by Nonacs and Dill (1990) on the ant *Lasius pallitarsis*.

In this elegant study ants were given the choice of foraging from two sites with liquid diets differing in concentration, and therefore in the volume of nutrient that could be carried back to the colony by each ant worker on each foraging trip. The path from the colony to the more concentrated solution sometimes contained a larger predatory ant and a worker had a 1 in 57 chance of being killed if it chose this path.

The common currency employed for the consequences of food gathering and predation risk was the growth in mass of the colony. Foraging increased growth by the production of new eggs and the growth of larvae, while predation reduced growth by loss of worker adults. While eggs, larvae, and adults may not be exactly equivalent in terms of colony fitness, fast colony growth is certainly important for survival and reproduction.

Ants tended to forage from the patch that gave the greater net colony growth, taking into account both egg and larval gains and adult losses. More impressively, risky and safe patches were valued equally when a colony growth of 0.98 mg was balanced by the loss of one worker, weighing on average 1.37 mg. Given a range of worker weights of 0.90–2.20 mg and the fact that worker size is not too important for the job of gathering liquid food, workers have done impressively well at the job of maximizing colony growth.

---

being reached (Krebs & Kacelnik, 1991). In the present example it might be a constraint on the ability of the male to control the behaviour of the female. Finally, the behaviour might be sub-optimal for two reasons even though there are no constraints or competing demands. First, environmental factors influencing the optimum might have changed too recently or be fluctuating too fast to have been tracked by selection. Second, the behaviour may be correlated with another trait, more important for fitness, whose optimal value does not coexist with that of the behaviour in question (Price & Langen, 1992).

As Darwin (1872) himself made clear, natural selection does not predict optimization, but only that the option most enhancing fitness, of those available in the population, will come to predominate:

> Natural selection tends only to make each organic being as perfect as, or slightly more perfect than, the other inhabitants of the same country with which it comes into competition. . . . Natural selection will not produce absolute perfection, nor do we always meet, as far as we can judge, with this high standard under nature. (p. 163)

The merit of optimization models, however, is that they provide precise and testable predictions and a sensible starting-point for the investigation of adaptation; there is no sense in developing a model that predicts, say, 90 per cent of an optimal value. Where they fail, a study of the possibilities outlined above leads to a fuller understanding. Quite often, however, such models are vindicated by the data, often enough for us to realize now that animals have a quite astonishing ability to achieve optimal solutions to complex problems.

Selection pressures

A selection pressure is a feature of the animal's environment that influences fitness by acting on features of its phenotype. For the gazelle at the waterhole, for example, predation is a selection pressure on its drinking behaviour. A selection pressure can itself be an adaptation. For example, the mating strategy of male red deer is to defend a number of females from other males in a harem, but this is possible only because females congregate on the best swards to graze. Food dispersion and predation are selection pressures on female congregation which, in turn, is a selection pressure on the male's mating strategy (Emlen & Oring, 1977). Feeding efficiency and predator avoidance are ubiquitous selection pressures on behaviour.

Evolutionary stability and social behaviour

The optimal value for, say, the time to be spent grazing by a goose will be influenced by many factors, but is unlikely to be affected by the grazing times of other geese. Social behaviour, however, is different in an important way.

75

The fitness consequences of a social act depend on the response it receives, and its fate under natural selection therefore depends on the relative frequency with which it encounters different responses. Selection is then said to be *frequency-dependent*.

Imagine, for example, two strategies for competing over resources. The first is to fight for it viciously, the second to threaten the opponent but to withdraw if things get nasty. If most of the population threaten, a rare fighter will do well since it beats every threatener it meets, and most of its opponents are threateners. Natural selection therefore favours fighters and they increase in frequency. As they do so, however, they meet each other more often as opponents and now lose some encounters, often sustaining injury. The success of fighting therefore depends on its frequency in the population. What will be the outcome? Will fighters take over the entire population or will they wipe each other out, leaving only the more peaceful threateners? Could both strategies coexist in the population at stable frequencies, or might the evolutionary outcome be an endless cycle of fluctuating frequencies? The answer to this particular problem is given later, but more generally we wish to know if there is a *stable* outcome to the evolutionary history of some social action and, if so, what it will be.

A stable set of strategies may not achieve their greatest fitness (i.e., be optimal) at stability and yet it is stable frequencies that we expect to find in nature since, by definition, these are the ones that endure. Natural selection therefore tends to produce stable behavioural strategies and not necessarily optimal ones. Maynard Smith (1976a) developed these ideas first in the context of competitive behaviour and coined the term *evolutionarily stable strategy* (ESS) for the strategy observed in the stable state. The concept of evolutionary stability is now seen to be fundamental to an understanding of the evolution of social behaviour, and is arguably the most important contribution to the study of behavioural evolution since Darwin's theory of natural selection (Maynard Smith, 1982).

The role of genetics

The evolution of behaviour by natural selection requires that behaviour is heritable but not that it is fully determined by genes. In fact much behavioural variability is a result of animals responding adaptively to variations in the environment. What is inherited by the fitter individuals is then a set of learning rules that produces more adaptive responses to environmental input. For example, ants make adaptive patch choices as a result of nutrient and predation risk experiences on the patches (Box 2).

THE SCOPE OF BEHAVIOURAL ECOLOGY

A major division in the subject matter of behavioural ecology is that between social and non-social behaviour, study of the former being termed *sociobiology*.

Acquisition of resources, such as food, is an animal's most pressing non-social problem (although it becomes a social problem if individuals compete or cooperate in gathering resources). One approach to studying optimality in resource acquisition has been exemplified by the male dung fly's copulation time problem (Box 1), which is treated as a non-social problem since the female is assumed to take a passive role. This area is reviewed by Krebs & Kacelnik (1991).

Social behaviour influencing survival can be classified in terms of the *benefits* and *costs* to the fitness of the actor and recipient of the social act (Hamilton, 1964), where benefit means an increase in fitness and cost a decrease. Figure 3 illustrates the four possible outcomes defined in this way. The terms used there are familiar in the context of human motivation, but in behavioural ecology they are defined solely in terms of the consequences of action for fitness and imply nothing about motives or emotions. Spite, in which neither party benefits, is at best a rare occurrence in the animal world (Lazarus, 1987).

In discussing social behaviour I shall concentrate on some major problems that remained unsolved until the development since the 1960s of new theories that have revolutionized our understanding of behavioural evolution.

Selfishness: why don't animals fight more fiercely?

Since natural selection favours competitive success, the evolution of selfishness is not difficult to understand. The problem is not to understand why animals are competitive but why they are not more so; why aggressive disputes are not more injurious and why they often involve merely display. The large carnivores, for example, refrain from attacking each other in the way they treat their prey. The answer briefly is that hawkish tactics of all-out

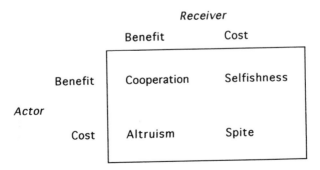

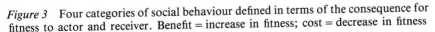

Figure 3 Four categories of social behaviour defined in terms of the consequence for fitness to actor and receiver. Benefit = increase in fitness; cost = decrease in fitness

attack carry a risk of injury and are therefore often unstable, as Maynard Smith (1976a) demonstrated. The essence of the argument, and of the method employed, can be appreciated by considering the very simplest of his models.

Imagine two strategies for competition over a resource, "Hawk" and "Dove" (Maynard Smith, 1976a) — like the fighter and threatener described above — which involve three tactics: display, escalate (with a risk of injury), and retreat. A Hawk always escalates a fight until either it is injured, and loses, or its opponent retreats. A Dove displays but if its opponent escalates it retreats before getting injured. When two Hawks meet each is equally likely to win the resource, which increases fitness by an amount V, whereas injury reduces it by W. Similarly, when two Doves compete each is equally likely to win after a period of display which costs them both T units of fitness due to the time and energy involved.

To analyse the evolutionary outcome Maynard Smith (1976a) employed the methods of game theory, which already had a long history of application to human social interaction. The average change in fitness (or "payoff") to Hawk and Dove of fighting each type of opponent is cast in a *payoff matrix* as shown in Figure 4. For example, when a Hawk meets another Hawk it wins (payoff $= V$) and loses (payoff $= -W$) with equal probability, giving a mean payoff of $(V - W)/2$. When a Dove meets another Dove it is equally likely to win ($V - T$) or lose ($-T$), resulting in a mean payoff of $(V/2) - T$. We now seek an evolutionarily stable strategy, or ESS; that is, a strategy which, if adopted by most members of the population, has a greater payoff than any other strategy in the game.

We examine the case where $W > V$, since we are interested in the fate of hawkish behaviour, which is greater when $W > V$ than when the reverse is true. With this scenario a Hawk mutant arising in a population of Doves would have a payoff of V (Figure 4) while Doves gain only $((V/2) - T)$ in fights against each other. Since $V > ((V/2) - T)$ selection favours Hawks, which will therefore increase in frequency over generations. In the same way

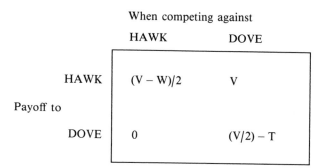

When competing against

	HAWK	DOVE
HAWK	$(V - W)/2$	V
DOVE	0	$(V/2) - T$

Payoff to

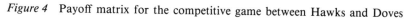

Figure 4 Payoff matrix for the competitive game between Hawks and Doves

a Dove mutant in a population of Hawks fares better than the dominant strategy, since $0 > (V - W)/2$. This means that the stable outcome is a mixture of Hawks and Doves — a *mixed ESS* — at frequencies which give the two strategies equal payoff. This simple model shows that all-out attack is not necessarily favoured by natural selection because of the injuries sustained when most individuals are hawkish.

Since this pioneering use of game theory, more realistic models have been developed incorporating real-life differences between individuals. For example, individuals differ in their ability to win an encounter as a function of their size and strength and may use reliable indicators of strength to assess their chances of winning an escalated contest, the weaker animal withdrawing before it risks injury. Common toads assess each other's size by listening to the depth of their opponents' croaks, since large males reliably produce deeper croaks (Davies & Halliday, 1978).

Cooperation: why should animals benefit others?

Why should an individual behave so as to increase the fitness of another, even if it benefits in the process itself? It is not difficult to think of cases where cooperation is obviously adaptive. Wolves hunting together in a coordinated pack, for example, can bring down a large animal like a moose, a task almost impossible for a single animal. However, a more subtle problem remains. Why don't animals that receive the fruits of cooperation without reciprocating replace those that give as well as receive?

The answer to this problem was provided by Axelrod and Hamilton (1981) and their solution shows once more the importance of ESS thinking. If individuals meet only once, then selection will favour a selfish strategy which "defects" on the system of cooperation. However, if individuals meet repeatedly, and can modify their behaviour as a function of past experience, then more subtle strategies can develop in which defectors can be penalized. Axelrod and Hamilton found that a simple strategy, TIT FOR TAT, was an ESS in competition against many others, provided that the probability of individuals meeting again was sufficiently high. TIT FOR TAT cooperates on the first encounter and then does on every subsequent encounter whatever its opponent did on the previous encounter. It is therefore a strategy of cooperation based on reciprocity. Several examples of reciprocity have now been studied in detail, including the sharing of blood by vampire bats.

Altruism: why should animals sacrifice themselves for others?

The suicidal sting of the honeybee; the sharing of food by lions; the alarm call that warns others but attracts the attention of a predator: how can natural selection explain such behaviour when its mechanism is based on selfish competition, the very antithesis of altruism (Figure 3)?

Until the 1960s it was commonly believed that natural selection could act at the level of the group or species. In this climate Wynne-Edwards (1962) argued that altruism would be selected if it aided population survival by preventing overexploitation of resources. He made the analogy of the advantage of setting fishing limits to maintain fish stocks for the long-term benefit of all fishing fleets.

The problem with this argument is that a selfish individual in a group of altruists would have a greater reproductive success, so that selfishness would be favoured by selection and spread through the population (Maynard Smith, 1976b). The evolutionary origins of altruism must therefore be sought at the level of the individual or in some cases, as we shall see, at the level of the gene (Dawkins, 1989).

One origin for altruism is as a component of cooperation. When the mutual benefit of cooperation is realized by the reciprocation of altruistic acts (Trivers, 1971) then each altruistic act is explicable in the wider context of Axelrod and Hamilton's (1981) theory of cooperation described above.

To appreciate the second major way in which altruism might evolve we must abandon the Darwinian notion of the individual as the unit of selection. Whilst selection pressures act directly on the individual's phenotype, the heritable unit responsible for changes in phenotype frequencies over time is the gene (Dawkins, 1989).

A special property of social behaviour is that it affects the fitness not only of the performer but also of the recipient of the social act. Now, if the recipient bears the same genes that influenced the act in the performer, the evolutionary fate of the behaviour in question will be determined by its consequences for the fitness of both parties, since both bear the relevant genetic material. The behaviour pattern will be favoured by natural selection as long as it results in the genes controlling it having a greater chance of replication into the next generation. It follows that the unit upon which natural selection acts is, most generally, the gene rather than the individual.

The benefit arising from altruistic behaviour relies on the beneficiary of the altruism bearing the altruistic gene. The commonest way in which individuals come to share the same genes is by inheriting them by recent common descent. A parental gene, for example, has a probability of .5 (i.e., a 50–50 chance) of appearing in one of its offspring, and full siblings have the same chance of sharing a gene by common descent from a parent. This probability is termed the *coefficient of relatedness*, r.

Now, suppose an altruistic act produces a cost C to the actor and a benefit B to the recipient, to which it is related by r. The genes promoting altruism will be benefited if the relative contains them, which it does with probability r. So, on average, the benefit of such acts to the relevant genes is equal to Br. For natural selection to favour the altruistic act its benefit must outweigh its cost, so that the condition favouring altruism between relatives can be expressed as $Br > C$. For altruism between full sibs ($r = .5$) to be favoured, for example, the benefit must be greater than twice the cost.

This gene-centred view, and the condition derived from it above for the evolution of altruism (Hamilton, 1964), has necessitated a new measure to replace the Darwinian concept of individual fitness. Hamilton introduced the concept of *inclusive fitness*, which takes into account the effects of social acts directed towards and received from relatives, and Maynard Smith coined the term *kin selection* to describe the action of natural selection on interactions between relatives. Since altruism between relatives is common in nature these ideas have thrown light on a great variety of social actions, from parental care to alarm calls and from cooperative breeding in birds and mammals (Emlen, 1991) to the ultimate altruism of the worker castes of ants, bees and wasps which forgo reproduction to raise their sisters (Box 2).

Sex and parental care

In moving from the analysis of social strategies of survival to those of reproduction and parental care we encounter a far more complex set of problems. In the first place, sexual and parental strategies generally involve more than a single interaction. Individuals may form relationships with sexual partners for one or more breeding episodes in order to raise offspring, so that long-term strategies of exploitation and cooperation become possible. Long-term strategies also characterize the parent–offspring relationship (Clutton-Brock, 1991; Trivers, 1974).

Second, we need to understand the evolution of two sets of interdependent strategies, male and female. This means a search for three ESSs, each of which depends on the outcome of the other two: one for males, one for females, and one for the combination of male and female strategies. This is a formidable task with much still to be achieved. At present we understand the major evolutionary forces determining sexual and parental strategies, and some of the variation in these strategies across the animal kingdom in terms of the costs and benefits to the individuals involved. In addition, quantitative studies have revealed the detailed workings of selection on particular aspects of sexual and parental behaviour in a number of species (e.g., Davies, 1992).

Understanding the different reproductive strategies of males and females starts with a simple principle. An individual can enhance its reproductive success by increasing the number of offspring that it brings into the world and by improving the survival chances of each offspring. This starting-point leads us to predict the existence of competition for mates and mate choice: a preference for mates that produce more or fitter offspring (Lazarus, 1987). Mate choice, in turn, favours advertisement of the attributes of favoured sexual partners. The evolutionary forces favouring mate competition and mate choice are termed, respectively, *intra-sexual* and *inter-sexual selection*.

Competition for mates and mate choice are ubiquitous in nature but are sexually biased, males commonly competing for females and females exercising a choice between males. Why are the sex roles generally arranged in this way?

Competition for mates

These questions are matters of current debate but the first major contribution was made by Trivers (1972), a century after Darwin's (1871) pioneering work on sexual selection. Trivers showed the central importance of parental care for the evolution of sexual strategies and his argument stems from the fundamental difference between the sexes. Males are defined as the sex producing a large number of small gametes – sperms – while females produce a small number of large gametes – eggs. The gamete is the first act of *parental investment* (PI) that a parent makes in its offspring, PI being defined as any act by a parent that increases the fitness of its offspring at the cost of the parent's ability to produce other offspring (Trivers, 1972).

The sex difference in gamete size means that a male's initial PI in his offspring is less than the female's. Since an offspring is less costly for a male to produce it follows that the male's optimal number of offspring, and therefore his optimal number of matings, is greater than the female's (Trivers, 1972). With the usual 1 : 1 sex ratio, and the rapid rate at which sperm can be renewed compared to eggs, competition between males for access to females is therefore inevitable. Consequently, intra-sexual selection favours greater size and strength in males, and the evolution of weapons such as the antlers of male deer. In the primates, for example, sexual dimorphism in body size increases with the number of females per male in a breeding group (Figure 5; Clutton-Brock, Harvey, & Rudder, 1977). Where this sex ratio is higher males can increase their reproductive success to a greater extent by competing successfully for females with other males, so this relationship can be understood as the result of intra-sexual selection. It is also an example of the *comparative method*, by which cross-species comparisons provide evidence relating to adaptive hypotheses (Harvey & Pagel, 1991).

Males have also evolved methods of *sperm competition*, designed to prevent the sperm of competitors from reaching a female's eggs. Insects flush out the sperm of other males from the female with their penis before inseminating her, or cement up her genital opening after copulation. Male birds copulate with their mates more frequently if they are likely to have mated recently with another male (Birkhead & Møller, 1991). Another strategy is to guard the female from other males. The male dung fly, for example, guards the female between copulation and egg laying to prevent his sperm being removed by a later male, and this guarding period is part of the "travel time" involved in his optimal copulation time problem (Box 1).

Clutton-Brock and Vincent (1991) argue that competition is determined by the relative rates of reproduction of the two sexes. The sex that completes its

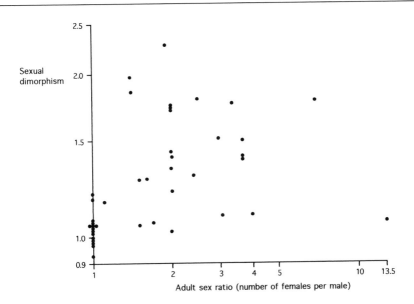

Figure 5 The degree of sexual dimorphism (male weight/female weight) increases with the average number of females per male in a breeding group across 42 primate species. Each point is a different species
Source: Redrawn from Clutton-Brock, Harvey, and Rudder, 1977

parental duties and is free to breed again more quickly will, on average, have more members in the breeding population, whose *operational sex ratio* (Emlen & Oring, 1977) will thus be biased towards that sex. The majority sex will therefore compete for the sex in the minority, which becomes a *limiting resource* for the majority sex.

Where females bear the major parental burden, as in mammals, we therefore expect males to be the sexually competing sex, as is the case. While in mammals the arguments based on relative PI and relative reproductive rates therefore make the same prediction, mating patterns in fish are more satisfactorily explained in terms of reproductive rates. In many fish species the male cares for the developing eggs and yet males still compete for females. This is partly because males are able to guard batches of eggs at the same time as courting females, so that parental duties do not limit their time in the breeding population (Gross & Sargent, 1985).

Mate choice

The exertion of some choice on the part of the female seems a law almost as general as the eagerness of the male. (Darwin, 1871)

83

Delilah was a floosy...
She wasn't choosy.
(Ira Gershwin)

Female choice of male partners also follows from the above arguments based on sex differences in PI and reproductive rates. If males attempt to mate with more than one female, or if the operational sex ratio is male biased, then females will be courted by a number of males and have the opportunity to choose between them. Darwin (1871) did not explain the evolution of female preferences, but later theorists have shown how preference for a male trait, and the trait itself, can coevolve to produce exaggerated male characters like the peacock's tail. This has been a controversial issue, involving the idea that a preferred male trait must "handicap" the male in order to indicate his true fitness to a female (reviewed by Maynard Smith, 1991). Females may select males for the resources they can give the young or for traits of high fitness their offspring will inherit.

Parental investment and mating strategies

The sex difference in gamete size can explain sex differences in competition and mate choice where there is no further parental investment in the young. However, as Trivers (1972) argued, it is the sex difference in *total* PI that influences mating strategies. A parent will be selected to continue investing in its offspring as long as the net benefit (i.e., benefit minus cost) of this option exceeds that of deserting the young and seeking new breeding opportunities elsewhere (Clutton-Brock, 1991). This is a complex problem since the consequences of desertion for offspring survival may depend crucially on whether the other parent also deserts, so that desertion decisions will be selected to take into account the desertion decisions of the partner. Once again, ESS analysis and game theory are the analytical tools for tackling this problem (Lazarus, 1990; Maynard Smith, 1977).

However, the broad taxonomic variation in parental care and mating patterns can be understood as coevolved adaptations following the rules outlined above. Compare, for example, the commonest patterns shown by birds and mammals. The majority of bird species are monogamous, with males competing for the superior breeding territories preferred by females (Vehrencamp & Bradbury, 1984). The male commonly helps his mate to care for the eggs and young although he has the opportunity to desert her after copulation. Male care is probably favoured because of the importance of parental feeding for offspring survival, a view supported by the greater incidence of male care in species with altricial young, which require feeding in the nest, compared to those with precocial young (such as ducklings) which are able to feed for themselves soon after hatching. Furthermore, experimental removal of the male in a number of altricial species reduces offspring fitness (Clutton-Brock, 1991).

In mammals, female lactation frees the male from the requirement of feeding the young and consequently male care and monogamy are rare in this group, polygyny and promiscuity being the common mating systems.

This kind of cost-benefit analysis does not provide the whole answer, however, since male strategies of PI may be constrained as a result of female choice. If females reject a male who is already mated, because of the disadvantage of sharing his parental duties with another female, then monogamy may be imposed on males. However, a female may accept an already mated male if he can offer her sufficient resources to compensate for the disadvantage of sharing (Vehrencamp and Bradbury, 1984).

METHODS AND PROSPECTS

As we have seen, behavioural ecologists generate predictions by verbal arguments and mathematical models based on the theory of natural selection. Predictions are tested by observations and experiments that relate behaviour to environmental influences and its consequences for some component of the individual's fitness. Alternatively, predictions can be tested by comparing the adaptations of different species operating under different selection pressures and constraints (e.g., Figure 5). Such comparisons represent natural experiments offered by the evolutionary process (Harvey & Pagel, 1991).

Exciting new insights are offered by DNA fingerprinting, a technique that allows the relatedness between individuals to be determined with confidence. It is showing, for example, that males of supposedly monogamous species like the house sparrow are sneaking off to sire offspring on neighbouring territories.

These methods are demonstrating how far adaptive decision making penetrates into all aspects of an animal's life.

ACKNOWLEDGEMENT

I am grateful to Stuart Laws for preparing the figures.

FURTHER READING

Dawkins, R. (1989). *The selfish gene* (2nd edn). Oxford: Oxford University Press.
Krebs, J. R., & Davies, N. B. (1987). *An introduction to behavioural ecology* (2nd edn). Oxford: Basil Blackwell.

REFERENCES

Axelrod, R., & Hamilton, W. D. (1981). The evolution of cooperation. *Science, 211*, 1390–1396.
Birkhead, T. R., & Møller, A. P. (1991). *Sperm competition in birds*. London: Academic Press.
Charnov, E. L. (1976). Optimal foraging: The marginal value theorem. *Theoretical Population Biology, 9*, 129–136.
Clutton-Brock, T. H. (1991). *The evolution of parental care*. Princeton, NJ: Princeton University Press.
Clutton-Brock, T. H., & Vincent, A. C. J. (1991). Sexual selection and the potential reproductive rates of males and females. *Nature, London, 351*, 58–60.
Clutton-Brock, T. H., Harvey, P. H., & Rudder, B. (1977). Sexual dimorphism, socionomic sex ratio and body weight in primates. *Nature, London, 269*, 797–800.
Darwin, C. (1859). *The origin of species by means of natural selection, or the preservation of favoured races in the struggle for life* (1st edn). London: John Murray.
Darwin, C. (1871). *The descent of man, and selection in relation to sex*. London: John Murray.
Darwin, C. (1872). *The origin of species by means of natural selection, or the preservation of favoured races in the struggle for life* (6th edn). London: John Murray.
Davies, N. B. (1992). *Dunnock behaviour and social evolution*. Oxford: Oxford University Press.
Davies, N. B., & Halliday, T. R. (1978). Deep croaks and fighting assessment in toads *Bufo bufo*. *Nature, London, 274*, 683–685.
Dawkins, R. (1986). *The blind watchmaker*. Harlow: Longman.
Hawkins, R. (1989). *The selfish gene* (2nd edn). Oxford: Oxford University Press.
Emlen, S. T. (1991). Evolution of cooperative breeding in birds and mammals. In J. R. Krebs & N. B. Davies (Eds) *Behavioural ecology: An evolutionary approach* (3rd edn, pp. 301–337). Oxford: Basil Blackwell.
Emlen, S. T., & Oring, L. W. (1977). Ecology, sexual selection and the evolution of mating systems. *Science, 197*, 215–223.
Gross, M. R., & Sargent, R. C. (1985). The evolution of male and female parental care in fishes. *American Zoologist, 25*, 807–822.
Hamilton, W. D. (1964). The genetical evolution of social behaviour, I and II. *Journal of Theoretical Biology, 7*, 1–16, 17–52.
Harvey, P. H., & Pagel, M. D. (1991). *The comparative method in evolutionary biology*. Oxford: Oxford University Press.
Krebs, J. R., & Kacelnik, A. (1991). Decision-making. In J. R. Krebs & N. B. Davies (Eds) *Behavioural ecology: An evolutionary approach* (3rd edn, pp. 105–136). Oxford: Basil Blackwell.
Lazarus, J. (1987). The concepts of sociobiology. In H. Beloff & A. M. Colman (Eds) *Psychology survey 6* (pp. 192–217). Leicester: British Psychological Society.
Lazarus, J. (1990). The logic of mate desertion. *Animal Behaviour, 39*, 672–684.
Maynard Smith, J. (1976a). Evolution and the theory of games. *American Scientist, 64*, 41–45.
Maynard Smith, J. (1976b). Group selection. *Quarterly Review of Biology, 51*, 277–283.
Maynard Smith, J. (1977). Parental investment: A prospective analysis. *Animal Behaviour, 25*, 1–9.
Maynard Smith, J. (1982). *Evolution and the theory of games*. Cambridge: Cambridge University Press.

Maynard Smith, J. (1991). Theories of sexual selection. *Trends in Ecology and Evolution*, *6*, 146–151.

Nonacs, P., & Dill, L. M. (1990). Mortality risk vs. food quality trade-offs in a common currency: Ant patch preferences. *Ecology*, *71*, 1886–1892.

Parker, G. A. (1978). Searching for mates. In J. R. Krebs & N. B. Davies (Eds) *Behavioural ecology: An evolutionary approach* (1st edn, pp. 214–244). Oxford: Basil Blackwell.

Price, T., & Langen, T. (1992). Evolution of correlated characters. *Trends in Ecology and Evolution*, *7*, 307–310.

Trivers, R. (1971). The evolution of reciprocal altruism. *Quarterly Review of Biology*, *46*, 35–57.

Trivers, R. (1972). Parental investment and sexual selection. In B. Campbell (Ed.) *Sexual selection and the descent of man 1871–1971* (pp. 136–179). Chicago, IL: Aldine.

Trivers, R. (1974). Parent–offspring conflict. *American Zoologist*, *14*, 249–264.

Vehrencamp, S. L., & Bradbury, J. W. (1984). Mating systems and ecology. In J. R. Krebs & N. B. Davies (Eds) *Behavioural ecology: An evolutionary approach* (2nd edn, pp. 251–278). Oxford: Basil Blackwell.

Wynne-Edwards, V. C. (1962). *Animal dispersion in relation to social behaviour*. Edinburgh: Oliver & Boyd.

2.3

THE NERVOUS SYSTEM AND THE BRAIN

Daniel Kimble

University of Oregon, USA

The human nervous system consists of the brain, spinal cord, and peripheral nervous system, and is composed of many billions of cells. There are two distinctive cell types in the nervous system, *neurons* and *neuroglial* cells. Neurons, of which there are estimated to be at least 10^{11} in the human brain, are specialized to process, transmit, and store information. These functions depend on two basic attributes of neurons, their capacity to generate and conduct electrical signals and their ability to manufacture, secrete, and respond to a variety of chemical substances. It is estimated that there are several times as many neuroglial (glial) cells as neurons in the nervous system. Although glial cells do not produce nerve impulses, they are essential to the proper operation of the nervous system. Different types of glial cells are known to serve to (1) provide structural support and possibly guidance for migrating neurons during embryonic development; (2) produce the insulating myelin sheath around the axons of many neurons; and (3) remove debris and secrete neurotrophic factors following injury to the nervous system. It is axiomatic among modern researchers that all of our observable behaviour, as well as all of our thoughts, emotions, and dreams – in short, all mental life – is generated by activity of neurons and glial cells in the nervous system.

STRUCTURE AND FUNCTION OF NEURONS

Neurons come in a variety of shapes and sizes, but (with rare exceptions) they all share certain morphological features. The neuronal cell body contains the nucleus, which in turn contains the genetic material of the cell. Outside the nucleus in the cytoplasm of the cell can be found cellular components necessary for the synthesis of proteins. It is instructive to realize that once differentiated, neurons in mammals do not again undergo mitosis (cell division). Thus, many neurons in long-lived species survive for many decades. Glial cells, on the other hand, retain the capacity to undergo mitosis, as do most other cell types in the body. In vertebrates, processes (branches) from the neuronal cell termed *dendrites* serve as important sites for synaptic contacts from other neurons, as does the cell body itself. Some synapses are also found on axon terminals. On some neurons in the cerebral cortex and hippocampus, dendrites are studded with *dendritic spines*. These spines are common sites for synapses. The shape and number of spines are abnormal in some neurological conditions, and have been demonstrated to increase in number in enriched environments in laboratory rats (Greenough, 1975). The *axon* is the output segment of the neuron. Axons also emerge from the cell body, often branch several times, forming *axon collaterals*, and form specialized *axon terminals* which make contact with postsynaptic cells, either other neurons, muscle cells, or gland cells.

In order to understand the ability of the neuron to conduct electrical signals, it is necessary to consider the structure of the cell membrane. The neuronal cell membrane is similar to other animal cell membranes in many ways, but with significant specializations. Neuronal membranes are composed of a *lipid* bilayer to which are attached sugars, proteins, and glycoproteins. It is the particular mix of proteins that define different functional regions of the cell membrane.

Electrical signalling by neurons

An electrical potential of 60–70 millivolts occurs across the neuronal membrane, caused by a slightly unequal distribution of *ions* (charged particles produced by the dissociation of substances in the watery medium of the brain). In all cases known, the interior of the neuron is negative with respect to the outer surface of the membrane. The basic form of communication in the nervous system is by means of electrical signals generated and conducted by neurons. These signals in turn cause the release of chemical neurotransmitter substances as the electrical signal invades the axon terminals. Two basic classes of electrical signals can be recorded in the nervous system: *nerve impulses*, occurring primarily in the axon of the sending neuron, and *postsynaptic potentials*, produced primarily in the dendrites and cell body of the receiving neuron. Postsynaptic potentials can be either excitatory or inhibitory, while nerve impulses are excitatory only.

Four ion species are involved in producing these electric signals: sodium, potassium, chloride, and calcium. Sodium, potassium, and calcium are all positively charged ions (*cations*), while chloride carries a negative charge and is termed an *anion*. Modern understanding of the role of ion movements underlying electric signalling in neurons stems from the pioneering research of Andrew Hodgkin and Alan Huxley at Cambridge University in the 1950s and 1960s (Hodgkin, 1964; Hodgkin & Huxley, 1952). Although precise details vary among different neurons, it appears universally true that the movement of sodium ions from the outer surface of the cell membrane to the interior of the neuron is responsible for initiating a nerve impulse. The movement of potassium ions from the interior of the cell to the outer surface of the membrane underlies the restoration of the original resting potential, setting the stage for subsequent nerve impulses. Ion movement takes place through specialized *ion channels*, usually, but not always, specific for a particular ion species. Ion channels regulate the flow of ions across the neuronal membrane by changing their shape slightly in response to voltage changes across the membrane, the presence of specific chemical neurotransmitters, or both. In the axon the movement of ions through ion channels is regulated by the moment-to-moment voltage across the membrane. At synapses located in the dendrites and cell body, the presence of neurotransmitters regulates ion movement.

Sodium and potassium also participate in postsynaptic potentials. Whether the resulting potential is inhibitory or excitatory depends on the direction of movement of these cations. Outward movement of cations (e.g., potassium) is inhibitory, moving the potential across the membrane further away from the point where a nerve impulse can be produced (termed a *hyperpolarizing event*). Inward movement of cations (e.g., sodium), is excitatory for the opposite reason, and is termed a *depolarizing event*. Chloride is primarily involved in inhibitory postsynaptic potentials by moving inward, hyperpolarizing the membrane.

Calcium is involved in a multitude of cellular functions. For example, the release of chemical neurotransmitter by a nerve impulse is calcium dependent. Calcium ions are also involved in many cellular responses to neurotransmitters. In many of these processes, a *second messenger system* is activated by the binding of a neurotransmitter to specialized receptors located on the external surface of the neuronal membrane. Several different second messenger systems are known to be present in the nervous system. The richness of the responses to various neurotransmitters available to the neuron makes the neuron an extremely flexible information signalling device.

Once initiated, nerve impulses travel down the axon toward the axon terminals where neurotransmitter release occurs. The conduction speed of a nerve impulse depends on the diameter of the axon and the degree to which it is myelinated (covered in a fatty sheath). Larger axons and heavy myelination both increase conduction speed. In warm-blooded animals, axonal conduction rates vary from less than 1 m/sec to over 100 m/sec.

Synapses

The invasion of the axon terminals by the nerve impulse initiates a series of events at the *synapse*. A synapse is a junction between neurons, consisting of the *presynaptic* axon terminal, a small gap or *synaptic cleft* that separates the cells involved, and a *postsynaptic* receptive region. Both electrical and chemical synapses are known to exist in vertebrates. At electrical synapses, the presynaptic neuron passes on the nerve impulse to the postsynaptic neuron through specialized ion channels in the two cells that line up directly across from one another, allowing for passage of ionic current with little loss of signal strength. Chemical synapses are more common in the brains of vertebrates than electrical synapses, and have attracted most of the research efforts since 1920. Chemical neurotransmitters are stored in *synaptic vesicles* in the axon terminals, and are released as the nerve impulse invades the axon terminals. Calcium ions are directly responsible for neurotransmitter release. The depolarization caused by the nerve impulse opens ion channels located in the axon terminals. Calcium ions then enter the terminal and cause the release of the neurotransmitter (Llinas, 1982). Neurotransmitter molecules then diffuse across the synaptic cleft and interact with specific *synaptic receptor molecules* located in the membrane of the postsynaptic neuron. This results either in the direct change in shape of ion channels (as in the case of the neurotransmitter acetylcholine) or, more commonly, in the activation of one or more second messenger systems within the postsynaptic cell. One of the main results of second messenger activation is also a change in ion channel shape. Thus, either directly or indirectly, neurotransmitters influence ion movement across the postsynaptic membrane by altering the shape of the proteins that form the ion channels. The resultant *postsynaptic potentials* can be either excitatory or inhibitory, depending on the identity of the ion channels involved. Although both nerve impulses and postsynaptic potentials are caused by ionic currents across the membrane, they are quite different in several respects. Table 1 lists some of these differences.

Whether or not the combined effect of the postsynaptic potentials on a

Table 1 Comparison of nerve impulses and postsynaptic potentials

	Nerve impluses	*Postsynaptic potentials*
Amplitude	Approximately 110 mV	< 1 mV to 15–20 mV
Direction	Always depolarizing	Either hyperpolarizing or depolarizing
Duration	1–10 msec	Up to several minutes
Propagation	Without decrement	With decrement
Ion channels	Voltage regulated sodium and potassium	Chemically regulated sodium potassium, chloride

given neuron results in a change in the rate of production of nerve impulses in that neuron depends on the moment to moment algebraic summing of depolarizing and hyperpolarizing events in that neuron. Such activity is constantly occurring in the nervous system. If sufficient depolarization is produced, an increase in the firing rate will occur in the postsynaptic neuron. If hyperpolarization dominates, the postsynaptic cell will be silenced or will reduce its firing rate. An individual neuron may make as many as 100,000 or more synaptic contacts with other neurons.

The current list of neurotransmitters is certain to be incomplete, as new candidates are added to the list from time to time. Strong evidence exists for at least ten neurotransmitters. These include *acetylcholine* and biogenic amines such as *noradrenaline (norepinephrine)*, *adrenalin (epinephrine)*, *dopamine*, *serotonin*, and *histamine*. Another group includes some amino acids and their derivatives such as *gamma-amino butyric acid (GABA)*, *glutamate*, *glycine*, and *aspartate*. There appear to be two or more different varieties of receptors for each neurotransmitter. The variety of available neurotransmitters and receptors provides the nervous system with remarkable flexibility of action.

FUNCTIONAL NEUROANATOMY

Historical perspective

Knowledge of the structure of the nervous system has accumulated over centuries. An early authority was Galen (AD 129–199), a physician, who placed great importance on the cavities in the brain (what we know now as the *ventricles*), rather than the brain itself. Galen suggested that these cavities contained the fluids or "spirits" that governed our actions. The legacy of these erroneous ideas lingered into the nineteenth century. The first known drawings of the human brain made directly from cadavers are found in *De Humani Corporis Fabrica*, which was written by the Flemish anatomist Andreas Vesalius (1514–1564), and published in 1543. Although gradual progress was made between the sixteenth and nineteenth centuries, it was not until the end of the nineteenth century that substantial knowledge about the structure of neurons and glial cells was available. Two individuals can be singled out in this regard, Italian anatomist Camillo Golgi (1843–1926), and Spanish anatomist Santiago Ramón y Cajal (1852–1934). These two shared the Nobel Prize for medicine in 1906. Ironically, Ramón y Cajal, using a staining procedure developed by Golgi, demonstrated beyond doubt that the nervous system is composed of individual cells and is not a reticulum or network of connected elements as Golgi had proposed. The development of the electron microscope in the middle of the twentieth century, along with other technical advances, ushered in the modern period of neuroanatomy, which remains an extremely active and changing field.

Divisions of the nervous system

The nervous system can be divided into two connected parts, the central nervous system (CNS), consisting of the brain and spinal cord, and the peripheral nervous system (PNS), composed of the cranial and spinal nerves and the autonomic nervous system (ANS) (Figure 1). Over 99 per cent of all neurons and glial cells are in the CNS. Nevertheless, the PNS contains elements vital to normal functioning. For example, all of the nerves that convey sensory impressions from the skin and many sense organs belong to the peripheral nervous system (the sensory neurons in the retina of the eye, however, belong to the central nervous system). The axons of the motor nerves that innervate the muscles of the body are also part of the PNS. Also, the autonomic nervous system that innervates various internal organs and whose activity is prominent in emotional responses is an element of the PNS. The ANS in turn is composed of two distinct divisions, the sympathetic

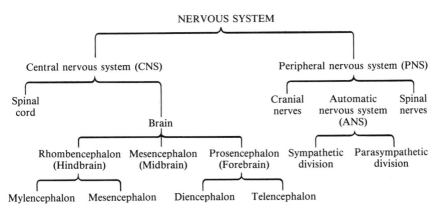

Figure 1 Main divisions of the human nervous system

93

division, whose activity accompanies emergency, energy expending situations ("fight or flight"), and the parasympathetic division.

Functions of the autonomic nervous system

In general, parasympathetic activity tends to produce results that oppose those of the sympathetic division; thus the parasympathetic division is more active during energy conserving times, as when we rest or digest food. Thus, sympathetic activity increases the rate and force with which the heart beats, while parasympathetic activity does the opposite. No simple generalization can cover all of the activities of the ANS, however, and both divisions are known to work together in some cases. For example, both erection and ejaculation are crucial for successful reproduction by male vertebrates. The changes in blood flow required for erection are regulated by nerves belonging to the parasympathetic division, while ejaculation is controlled by nerves from the sympathetic division. These two divisions must thus operate in a coordinated sequence.

Cranial and spinal nerves

The remainder of the PNS in humans is made up of 12 pairs of cranial nerves and 31 pairs of spinal nerves. The cranial nerves, designated by Roman numerals, are listed in Table 2, along with their main functions. The spinal nerves innervate skeletal muscles (those attached to bones, as opposed to smooth muscles such as in the gut), mediating both sensation and motor control via separate neuronal pathways. Spinal nerves are named for the region of the vertebral column from which they emerge; thus there are eight pairs of cervical nerves, twelve pairs of thoracic nerves, five pairs of lumbar

Table 2 Cranial nerves

	Nerve	*Main functions*
I	Olfactory	Perception of odours
II	Optic	Vision
III	Oculomotor	Regulation of eye movements
IV	Trochlear	Regulation of eye movements
V	Trigeminal	Face sensations; chewing
VI	Abducens	Regulation of eye movements
VII	Facial	Taste sensations; face movements
VIII	Auditory	Hearing; equilibrium
IX	Glossopharyngeal	Taste sensations; swallowing
X	Vagus	Internal organ sensation and control
XI	Accessory	Vocal cord; neck movements
XII	Hypoglossal	Tongue movements

nerves, five pairs of sacral nerves, and one pair of coccygeal nerves. As determined in the nineteenth century by Charles Bell (1774–1842) in England, and François Magendie (1783–1855) in France, each spinal nerve has two divisions, or roots. The dorsal (rear) root contains sensory neurons from the skin, joint, and muscles, while the ventral (front) root contains the axons of motor neurons which activate the muscles. This early discovery, known as *the law of roots*, encouraged workers at the time to seek other specializations in the nervous system. Sensory pathways that carry nerve impulses from the periphery to the CNS are also known as *afferent*, while *efferent* neurons, such as the motor neurons in the ventral root, carry nerve impulses from the CNS to the periphery. The terms afferent and efferent are also used with respect to neurons entering and leaving various areas of the brain and spinal cord.

Divisions of the brain

The human brain has evolved into the most complex living organ in the known universe, and our knowledge of its structure and function is, naturally, incomplete. Nevertheless, some consistent findings have emerged from basic research that comes from the examination of patients from the neurological clinic, from laboratory work with animals, and other sources.

The basic divisions of the human brain start to form during the first five weeks of fetal life, when the neural tube changes its shape to form five bulbous enlargements which are recognized as the basic divisions of the brain. Early in development, the most posterior division is the *rhombencephalon* or *hindbrain* (*cephalon* means "head"). The rhombencephalon further divides to form the *myelencephalon* and the *metencephalon*. The middle of the five divisions is the *mesencephalon* or *midbrain*. The most anterior enlargement is the *prosencephalon*, or *forebrain*. About the fifth week of gestation this divides to form the final two divisions, the *diencephalon* and the *telencephalon*. These five divisions plus the spinal cord provide a meaningful organization for the vertebrate nervous system (see Figure 1).

The entire CNS, brain and spinal cord, is surrounded by a covering of three membranes or *meninges*. The outermost of these is the *dura mater*, a tough, fibrous sheet of cells. The innermost layer, directly in contact with the underlying tissue is the thin, delicate, transparent *pia mater*. In between the pia mater and the dura mater is the *arachnoid layer*. Between the dura mater and the pia mater is the subarachnoid space, filled with cerebrospinal fluid (CSF), secreted by specialized cells in the ventricles. The meninges and CSF protect the brain, cushioning it to some extent from blows to the skull.

Hindbrain structures

Several notable regions of the brain are located in the hindbrain. These are

95

the *medulla oblongata*, and the *pons* (see Figure 2). The medulla oblongata forms a core within the hindbrain, while the pons ("bridge") is the name given to the ventral and anterior portion of the hindbrain. Both the medulla oblongata and the pons contain ascending and descending nerve tracts as well as nuclei (clusters of neuronal cell bodies with associated glia) serving both motor and sensory functions. Several cranial nerves enter and leave the hindbrain. The pons is involved in processes of sleep and dreaming. It contains cholinergic neurons which are thought to help usher in rapid eye movement (REM) sleep, a periodic phase of sleep proven in humans to correlate highly with reports of dreaming. Injections of acetylcholine into the pons reliably produce REM sleep in experimental animals (Hobson, 1988).

Another major brain component develops from the dorsal surface of the hindbrain, the *cerebellum* ("little brain"). The cerebellum is critically involved in many functions including the modification and guidance of co-ordinated movements, and the maintenance of postural balance and muscle tone. There are two features of the cerebellum worth noting. First, it operates

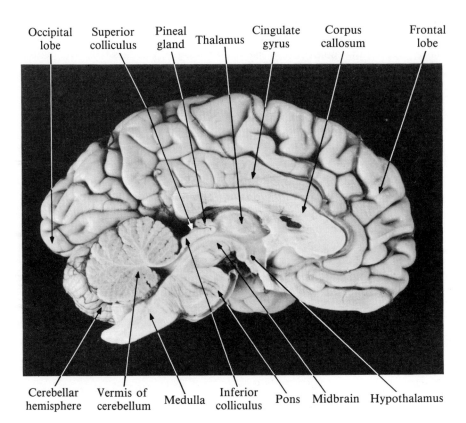

Figure 2 Left side of human brain as viewed from the medial surface

without intruding on our consciousness. For example, patients with cerebellar damage may stumble and fall, but they do not feel dizzy. Similarly, input from various sensory systems (vision, equilibrium, etc.) enters the cerebellum but does not produce any conscious awareness such as is generated by input into the sensory regions of the cerebral cortex. Second, the cerebellum is believed to act indirectly to carry out its functions. Output from the cerebellum, carried by *Purkinje* neurons, does not go to motor neurons directly, but to other intermediate components of the motor system, such as those in the brain stem and cerebral cortex.

Beginning in the hindbrain and extending well into the midbrain is the *reticular formation*, a network ("reticulum") of neurons thought to be critical for regulating levels of consciousness and attention through their influence on forebrain structures such as the cerebral cortex and hippocampus. Damage to the reticular formation, as can occur with tumours or severe blows to the head, can produce coma and even death. Neurons in this system are involved in the production of different stages of consciousness such as sleep and waking.

Midbrain structures

The hindbrain merges into the midbrain at the anterior end of the pons. The dorsal surface of the midbrain is marked by two structures, the *inferior* and *superior colliculi* ("little hills", singular *colliculus*). There is an inferior colliculus and a superior colliculus on each side of the midline. The superior colliculi are composed of two regions, a superficial and a deeper part. The superficial region receives input from neurons of the optic nerve, visual regions of the cerebral cortex and a region of the frontal lobes termed the *frontal eye fields*. The superficial layers are concerned with orienting responses to visual stimuli, but probably play no significant role in image formation. The deeper layers of the superior colliculi do not receive input directly from the optic nerve, but do receive input from several different brain regions. The deeper layers seem to be concerned with orienting to stimuli in various modalities (Wurtz & Albano, 1980). The inferior colliculi are part of the auditory pathway and relay information originating in the ear to the medial geniculate nucleus in the thalamus.

The internal core of the midbrain contains portions of the reticular formation, including the *locus ceruleus* ("blue place"). This important nucleus contains about 20,000 neurons in humans, and axons go from the locus ceruleus throughout the forebrain, innervating virtually all regions of the cerebral cortex and hippocampus. The widespread influence of these nuclei (there is one on each side of the brain) has attracted considerable theoretical interest in the role of the locus ceruleus in control of waking and sleeping, forebrain arousal and attentional mechanisms. The main neurotransmitter found in neurons originating in the locus ceruleus is noradrenalin.

Other important structures in the midbrain include a series of midbrain nuclei, the *raphe* ("seam") nuclei and the *substantia nigra* ("black substance"). Raphe neurons secrete *serotonin* as their major neurotransmitter, while those of the *substantia nigra* use *dopamine*. The raphe nuclei are, like the locus ceruleus, concerned with regulation of states of waking and sleeping, while the substantia nigra is part of the motor control system. The raphe nuclei are located along the midline. Degeneration of neurons in the substantia nigra is found in *Parkinson's disease*, a condition characterized by involuntary tremors of the limbs and torso, profound slowness in initiating and performing movements, and a shuffling walk. As is true of the hindbrain, the midbrain also contains many ascending and descending nerve tracts, as well as various nuclei involved in a variety of functions. For example, the *central grey* is the name given to a series of nuclei located at the centre of the midbrain. These neurons are known to be involved in the reception and modulation of pain sensations.

Forebrain structures

During development the forebrain forms two structures, the *diencephalon* and the *telencephalon*. The diencephalon is the more caudal of these two. These are the most recently evolved parts of the brain, and contain those regions thought to be most directly involved in higher mental functions such as perception, thinking, language, etc. It should be kept in mind, however, that without the normal functioning of the phylogenetically older parts of the brain, such as the reticular formation, these so-called "higher" structures cannot operate normally. Although some localization of function may be possible within the brain, the interaction of systems located throughout the brain and spinal cord are necessary for the production of all but the simplest of reflex behaviours. Nevertheless, the size of the cerebral cortex in humans, other primates, and some other mammals such as the cetaceans attests to the fundamental importance of this and other forebrain structures in the emergence of sophisticated mental operations seen in these species.

The junction of midbrain and the diencephalon in humans is marked on the dorsal surface of the brain by the *pineal gland*. This tiny, unpaired organ has attracted attention since the time of René Descartes (1596–1650), who suggested that the pineal gland was the location within the brain where mind and body interacted. Its function remains obscure in humans, although it is known that this gland participates in the control of annual reproductive cycles in hamsters and in the regulation of daily activity-rest rhythms in some species of birds. There is speculation that the pineal gland in humans may influence the timing of puberty and also play a role in *seasonal affective disorder* (SAD), a form of depression linked to the short day length.

The *thalamus* ("room") and the *hypothalamus* ("below the room") comprise two major regions of the diencephalon. These are major components of the brain and house nuclei involved in many different functions. The thalamus, for example, contains neurons that participate in the processing of information from each of the different senses (except that of olfaction). Thus, the *lateral geniculate nucleus* receives input from the optic nerve and sends and receives messages to and from regions of the cerebral cortex involved in vision. The *medial geniculate* nucleus performs similar functions within the auditory system. Other nuclei are concerned with other senses. Some nuclei in the thalamus participate in *non-specific* (not related to any specific sensory system) input that reaches the cerebral cortex from the reticular formation. The hypothalamus, located just below the thalamus, contains a rich variety of nuclei and nerve tracts involved in many diverse activities such as eating, drinking, temperature regulation, reproductive functions, and timing of various rhythmic activities in the body. Also, the hypothalamus contains *neurosecretory neurons* that release *hypothalamic hormones* into a specialized, local blood system that carries these hormones directly to the *anterior pituitary gland* attached to the base of the hypothalamus. Hypothalamic hormones regulate the synthesis and release of hormones from the anterior pituitary. The hormones released from the anterior pituitary in turn travel in the general blood supply to influence other organs in the body such as the gonads and adrenal glands. This arrangement means that mental and emotional events can directly influence the hormonal system via hypothalamic hormones. Also, hormones secreted by the gonads, adrenal glands, and other *endocrine* organs can penetrate to the brain and influence neural circuits and thus affect behaviour, mood, and thoughts, as well as further release of hypothalamic hormones.

Another important group of structures in the forebrain are the *basal ganglia*; this group includes the *caudate* ("comet") *nucleus*, the *globus pallidus* ("pale globe"), and the *putamen* ("peachstone"). The basal ganglia are known to be involved in the initiation and execution of movements, although it is probable that these structures are also active in many other functions as well. Axons from substantia nigra neurons to the basal ganglia degenerate in Parkinson's disease, while in *Huntington's chorea* neurons in the basal ganglia itself degenerate.

Another loosely associated group of brain structures are identified as the *limbic* ("border") *system*, named by the French physician Paul Broca (1824–1880), who observed that these structures tend to form a border or ring around the medial face of the cerebral hemisphere (Nauta & Feirtag, 1986). Structures generally included in the limbic system include the *hippocampus* ("seahorse"), *amygdala* ("almond"), *septal nuclei*, and *cingulate* ("belt") gyrus (see Figure 3). The limbic system has been a focus for research for many years, and a number of theories have been proposed regarding limbic system function. The hippocampus is known to be an important component in a medial temporal lobe memory system that participates in the processing of memories of events in an individual's life. Damage to the hippocampus in humans, such as occurs as an aftermath of some viral brain infections produces a profound *anterograde amnesia* (loss of memory for events occurring after the damage), and considerable *retrograde amnesia* (loss of memory for prior events) as well.

Functions of the amygdala, septal nuclei, and cingulate gyrus are poorly understood, but it is likely that all, particularly the amygdala, play some role in the attachment of emotional significance to various stimuli. Removal of the temporal lobes, including the amygdala (a cluster of several different

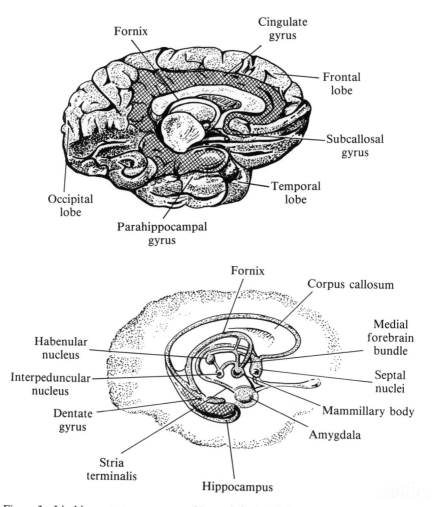

Figure 3 Limbic system structures. *Upper left*: Medial view of left hemisphere, showing cingulate gyrus, parahippocampal gyrus, and fornix. *Lower right*: View of limbic system structures not visible from the medial surface: hippocampus, dentate gyrus, amygdala, septal nuclei, and mammillary body

nuclei buried in the tip of the temporal lobe) is known to produce dramatic changes in the emotionality of monkeys. The constellation of symptoms produced by bilateral temporal lobe removal is known as the Klüver-Bucy syndrome after the workers who first noted these changes in the 1930s (Klüver & Bucy, 1939). Although rare, this syndrome has also been noted in humans following bilateral temporal lobe damage.

Cerebral cortex

The most impressive evolutionary advance in mammalian brains is seen in the dramatic increase in the size and complexity of the cerebral cortex. Nowhere is this more evident than in the primate order, particularly in humans. A progression index developed to assign numbers to the degree of evolution of different brain regions (Stephan, 1972) accords the human cerebral cortex a score of 156. The cerebral cortex of the chimpanzee, our nearest existing relative, receives a 60. The human hippocampus, by contrast, scores 17, and the cerebellum 4. As can be seen in Figure 4, the cerebral cortex entirely covers the rest of the brain of the two cerebral hemispheres. The cortex of primates and several other mammals is so greatly enlarged that it folds in on itself, forming the characteristic ridges or *gyri*, and fissures or *sulci*. Containing

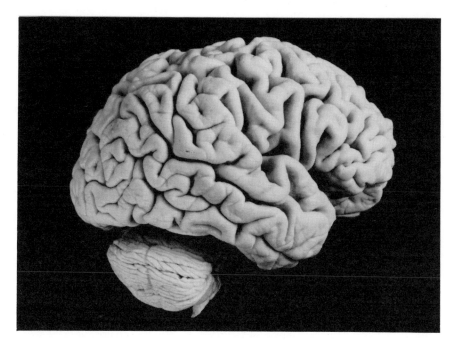

Figure 4 Human brain as seen from posterior aspect, showing gyri and sulci

101

over 10^{10} neurons, and perhaps five to ten times that many glia cells, the cerebral cortex is a multi-layered sheet of cells some 2.5–4 mm in thickness. By convention, six layers of cells and their processes can be distinguished, although most schemes also identify several sub-layers (see Figure 5). Because of its appearance in fresh brain tissue, the cortex itself is called *grey matter*, while the underlying layer of axons covered with myelin is termed *white matter*.

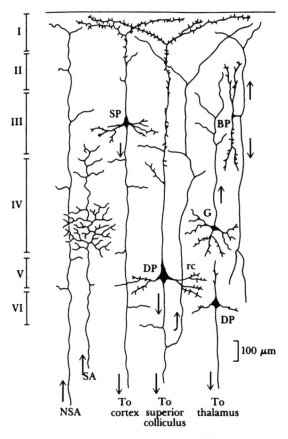

Figure 5 Neuronal cell types in cerebral cortex. Drawing based on Golgi stained cells. Abbreviations: NSA = non-specific afferent; SA = specific afferent; SP = superficial pyramidal cell; DP = deep pyramidal cell; BP = bipolar cell; G = granule cell; rc = recurrent collateral axon branches. Roman numerals at left refer to layers of the cortex

Cell types in the cortex

Although neurons in the cerebral cortex display many different shapes, a useful classification divides cortical neurons into one of two categories – pyramidal and non-pyramidal or stellate cells (Peters & Jones, 1984). Figure 6 shows these cell types as revealed by Golgi staining. The pyramidal neurons are widely viewed as the primary output or "executive" neurons in the cortex. Although originally named because of the shape of the cell body, some pyramidal cells actually have spherical or ovoid cell body shapes. Pyramidal cells are generally oriented perpendicular to the surface of the brain, and characterized by a single large apical dendrite which extends vertically from the top or apex of the cell body and several basal dendrites which extend from the base of the cell body in a horizontal fashion. These dendrites, particularly the apical dendrites, are usually studded with hundreds of dendritic spines. Dendritic spines are suspected of being one of the main places where brain changes underlying learning happen (e.g., Baudry & Lynch, 1987; Kandel, 1991a, 1991b). The axon of pyramidal cells typically emerges from the base of the cell body and usually (but not always) joins the underlying white

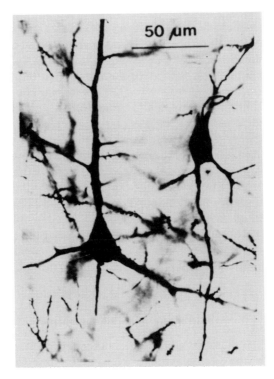

Figure 6 Photograph of Golgi stained pyramidal neuron (lower left), and stellate cell (upper right)

103

matter and projects to other regions of the brain. These projections can be to the opposite hemisphere of the brain, via the large interconnecting band, the *corpus callosum,* or other interhemispheric nerve tracts such as the anterior and posterior commissures. Other pyramidal cells project to subcortical areas, or to other regions of the same hemisphere. Some pyramidal neurons project several centimetres to synapse with motor neurons in the spinal cord.

A wide variety of neurons fall into the non-pyramidal or stellate cell category. Non-pyramidal cells lack the prominent apical dendrite. A variety of cell body shapes, dendritic branches and axonal ramification have been noted for these cells. While pyramidal neurons can send axons long distances in the brain and are therefore viewed as output neurons from the cortex, most non-pyramidal neurons have axons that branch and synapse in a much more localized fashion, and generally do not leave the region where their parent cell body is found. Thus, it is assumed that non-pyramidal neurons primarily perform local circuit duties within the cortex.

Functional columns in the cortex

Considerable evidence suggests that much of the cerebral cortex is organized into *functional columns* of neurons which, within a given column, all share some closely related function. For example, it is known that in the visual cortex of cats and monkeys vertical columns exist that respond primarily to impulses from one eye or the other (*ocular dominance columns*), while still other columns contain neurons that respond primarily to lines or edges with narrowly defined orientations (*orientation columns*) (Hubel & Wiesel, 1979). In the somatosensory cortex, columns with similar response properties have also been identified. These vertically oriented columns have been suggested to form the basic neural modules that underlie functional organization throughout widespread regions of the cortex (Mountcastle, 1979). The size of these columns varies from 30 to 500 micrometres (millionths of a metre) in diameter, and contain from a few hundred to a few thousand neurons. These columns were originally determined by recording the responses of individual neurons while presenting various stimuli to the animal. In recent years, various anatomical techniques have confirmed the existence of these columns.

Architectonic maps of the cortex

In the early part of the twentieth century, various neuroanatomists proposed different maps of the cerebral cortex based on their observations of regional differences in cell structure as seen with the light microscope. Most of these *architectonic maps* are of historical interest only, but the one produced by Korbinian Brodmann in 1909 continues to be used by modern workers, and

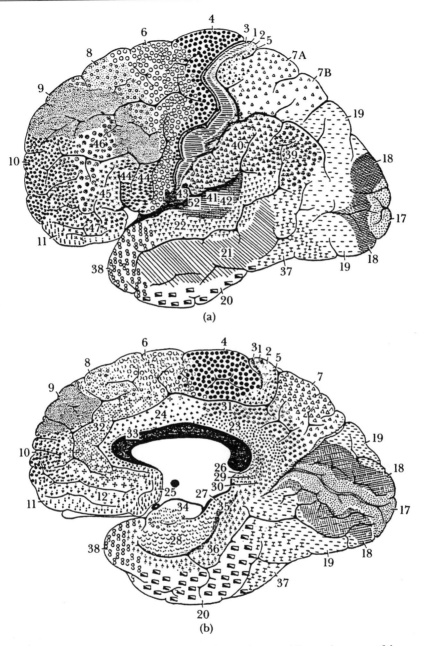

Figure 7 Brodmann numbering system for various architectonic areas of human cortex

Brodmann numbers still serve as useful referents to various regions of the human brain (see Figure 7).

Functional regions of the cortex

Our knowledge of functional distinctions among various regions of the cortex has accumulated gradually over the past 150 years. In fact, many brain researchers, perhaps put off by the eccentric claims of localization of function proposed by phrenologists such as Gall and Spurzheim in the nineteenth century, rejected the idea of localization of function until well into the twentieth century. More recently, however, the evidence for functional modules, albeit often involving dispersed circuits in the cortex, is now compelling. The first major evidence for localization of function in the human brain was Broca's discovery in 1861 that severe *aphasia* (loss of language function) was associated with damage to the posterior region of the *left* frontal lobe. This discovery not only provided an impetus for further thinking about localization of function but also, for the first time, suggested that the right and left cerebral hemispheres of human beings were not identical in function. As Broca put it, *"Nous parlons avec l'hémisphère gauche!"* ("We speak with the left hemisphere!") (Kandel, 1977, p. 10). Over a century was to pass before it was recognized that the right and left cerebral hemispheres were not structural mirror images either (Geschwind & Levitsky, 1968). In particular, a structure in the temporal lobe of humans known as the *planum temporale* (temporal plane) is larger in the left hemisphere in about 71 per cent of human brains, larger in the right in about 15 per cent of cases, and about the same size in 14 per cent (Witelson, 1983). Other anatomical asymmetries have also been observed, although their functional significance remains uncertain (Kolb & Whishaw, 1990).

Information concerning possible functional differences between the left and right cerebral hemispheres in humans has come from study of neurological patients with unilateral brain damage, neurosurgical patients, and studies of normal subjects using brain imaging techniques such as *positron emission tomography* (PET scanning). In addition, one notable series of experiments has been performed on epileptic patients who have had the major intercerebral commissures surgically cut to stop the spread of seizure activity from one hemisphere to the other. Such surgery allows an experimenter to present visual and tactile stimuli to each hemisphere independently, taking advantages of the anatomical organization of the sensory pathways involved. These experiments, conducted by Roger Sperry and his colleagues (e.g., Gazzaniga & Le Doux, 1978; Sperry, 1968; 1982) have shown that under laboratory conditions, each hemisphere can display "two independent streams of conscious awareness, one in each hemisphere" (Sperry, 1968). Such patients have also reinforced the view that the left hemisphere is, in most individuals, specialized to mediate language *production*, while the right hemisphere tends to be superior in various pattern perception skills such as recognition of faces and visual patterns that cannot be easily given a verbal label. Controversy exists concerning the capacity of the minor (usually right) hemisphere to *comprehend* language, although there is agreement that it is considerably more limited than is that of the dominant hemisphere.

Modern brain imaging techniques such as positron emission tomography have opened new research possibilities for exploring localization of function in the conscious human brain. For example, PET scans of subjects responding to verbal stimuli have shown those specific areas of the brain that are more active as subjects perform different language related tasks. These studies are forcing the revision of theories of brain organization dating back to the nineteenth century (Petersen, Fox, Posner, Mintun, & Raichle, 1988). Prospects for understanding the functions of the human brain have never been brighter.

FURTHER READING

Adelman, G. (Ed.) (1987). *Encyclopedia of neuroscience* (2 vols). Boston, MA: Birkhäuser.

Kandel, E. R., Schwartz, J. H., & Jessell, T. M. (Eds) (1991). *Principles of neural science* (3rd edn). New York: Elsevier.

Kimble, D. P. (1992). *Biological psychology* (2nd edn). Orlando, FL: Harcourt Brace Jovanovich.

Kolb, B., & Whishaw, I. Q. (1990). *Fundamentals of human neuropsychology* (3rd edn). New York: Freeman.

Nauta, W. J. H., & Feirtag, M. (1986) *Fundamental neuroanatomy*. New York: Freeman.

REFERENCES

Baudry, M., & Lynch, G. (1987). Properties and substrates of mammalian memory systems. In H. Y. Meltzer (Ed.) *Psychopharmacology: The third generation of progress* (pp. 449–462). New York: Raven.

Gazzaniga, M. S., & Le Doux, J. E. (1978). *The integrated mind*. New York: Plenum.

Geschwind, N., & Levitsky, W. (1968). Human brain: Left–right asymmetries in temporal speech region. *Science, 161*, 186–187.

Greenough, W. T. (1975). Experiential modification of the developing brain. *American Scientist, 63*, 37–46.

Hobson, J. A. (1988). *The dreaming brain*. New York: Basic Books.

Hodgkin, A. L. (1964). *The conduction of the nerve impulse*. Liverpool: Liverpool University Press.

Hodgkin, A. L., & Huxley, A. F. (1952). A quantitative description of membrane current and its application to conduction and excitation in nerves. *Journal of Physiology, 117*, 500–544.

Hubel, D. H., & Wiesel, T. N. (1979). Brain mechanisms of vision. *Scientific American, 241*, 150–162.

Kandel, E. R. (Ed.) (1977). *Handbook of physiology: A critical, comprehensive presentation of physiological knowledge and concepts* (2nd edn, sectn 1, vol. 1). Bethesda, MD: American Physiological Society.

Kandel, E. R. (1991a). Brain and behavior. In E. R. Kandel, J. H. Schwartz, & T. M. Jessell (Eds) *Principles of neural science* (3rd edn, pp. 5–17). New York: Elsevier.

Kandel, E. R. (1991b). Cellular mechanisms of learning and the biological basis of individuality. In E. R. Kandel, J. H. Schwartz, & T. M. Jessell (Eds) *Principles of neural science* (3rd edn, pp. 1009–1030). New York: Elsevier.

Klüver, H., & Bucy, P. C. (1939). Preliminary analysis of functions of the temporal lobe in monkeys. *Archives of Neurology and Psychiatry, 42*, 979–1000.

Kolb, B., & Whishaw, I. Q. (1990). *Fundamentals of human neuropsychology* (3rd edn). New York: Freeman.

Llinas, R. R. (1982). Calcium in synaptic transmission. *Scientific American, 247*, 38–47.

Mountcastle, V. B. (1979). An organizing principle for cerebral function: The unit module and the distributed system. In F. O. Schmitt & F. G. Worden (Eds) *The neuroscience fourth study program* (pp. 21–41). Cambridge, MA: Massachusetts Institute of Technology Press.

Nauta, W. J. H., & Feirtag, M. (1986). *Fundamental neuroanatomy*. New York: Freeman.

Peters, A., & Jones, E. G. (1984). Classification of cortical neurons. In A. Peters & E. G. Jones (Eds) *The cerebral cortex: vol. 1. Cellular components of the cerebral cortex* (pp. 107–121). New York: Plenum.

Petersen, S. E., Fox, P. T., Posner, M. I., Mintun, M., & Raichle, M. E. (1988). Positron emission tomographic studies of the cortical anatomy of single-word processing. *Nature, 331*, 585–589.

Sperry, R. W. (1968). Hemispheric deconnection and unity in conscious awareness. *American Psychologist, 23*, 723–733.

Sperry, R. W. (1982). Some effects of disconnecting the cerebral hemispheres. *Science, 217*, 1223–1226.

Stephan, H. (1972). Evolution of primate brains: A comparative anatomical investigation. In T. Tuttle (Ed.) *The functional and evolutionary biology of primates* (pp. 155–174). Chicago, IL: Aldine-Atherton.

Witelson, S. F. (1983). Bumps on the brain: Right–left anatomic asymmetry as a key to functional lateralization. In S. J. Segalowitz (Ed.) *Language functions and brain organization* (pp. 117–144). New York: Academic Press.

Wurtz, R. H., & Albano, J. E. (1980). Visual-motor function of the primate superior colliculus. *Annual Review of Neuroscience, 3*, 189–226.

2.4

SLEEP AND DREAMING

J. Allan Hobson

Harvard Medical School, Massachusetts, USA

With its increasing emphasis upon functional questions, sleep research has entered a new and exciting third phase. Since sleep had never been objectively studied in any detail prior to the beginning of its first phase in about 1950, it was to be expected that much of the early work in the field would be descriptive. (For reviews of the early work, see Jouvet, 1972; Moruzzi, 1972.) Sleep proved a more complex behaviour than such distinguished physiologists as Pavlov (1960) and Sherrington (1955) had imagined, and, even in the 1990s, new discoveries continue to be made, especially in the clinical realm. In the second phase of sleep research, beginning about 1960, specific mechanistic theories began to be enunciated and tested. New cellular and molecular research techniques produced a spate of findings that have gained conceptual and empirical coherence (Hobson, Lydic, & Baghdoyan, 1986; Hobson, 1988; Steriade and Hobson, 1976). While incomplete, the mechanistic approach is still going strong, promising to inform – and be informed by – the third phase research on sleep function that has recently been initiated (see reviews, Hobson, 1988, 1989).

Sleep is regarded as an evolutionarily recent, emergent, and "higher" function of the brain. In its fully developed form in humans – a cycle of dreamless Non-Rapid Eye Movement (NREM) sleep followed by Rapid Eye Movement sleep accompanied by dreaming – sleep is clearly a complex function; yet, even in unicellular organisms or single cells, sleeplike behaviour is present, organized differentially over time in sequential phases of rest and activity responsiveness and unresponsiveness (Aschoff, 1965a; Moore-Ede, Czeisler, & Richardson, 1983). The circadian rhythm (of about one day in length) is the best-known example of the temporal organization of physiological functions, but rhythms with shorter (infradian) and longer (ultradian) periods are now widely recognized. Thus, it would seem that the rhythm of rest and activity (the primordia of sleeping and waking) is one of the most universal and basic features of life.

While rest states are seen in all organisms, sleep as we define and measure it in warm-blooded mammals has many significant features not seen in lower animals. Thus, although the reptiles and birds have both high-voltage and low-frequency electroencephalogram (EEG) patterns and diminished responsiveness (as in mammalian NREM sleep), they evince no REM phase despite having all the brain-stem structures used by mammals to activate their brains periodically in sleep. The only exceptions are birds, who show brief REM episodes in the first few days after hatching. They lose this sleep state as they mature, thus paralleling the dramatic decline in sleep – and especially REM – that occurs in the early development of all young mammals (Roffwarg, Muzio, & Dement 1966). Amphibians have none of the sleep features of mammals and, unless their temperature falls, they remain constantly alert even when immobile and relaxed for long periods of time.

I begin this chapter by defining the states of waking, NREM, and REM sleep and their behavioural, electrographic, and psychological activity changes that allow for the investigation of the functional implications of sleep and dreaming. I shall then describe the most recent findings regarding the functional roles of the different states of the brain-mind, not only because they are exciting in their novelty, but also because they strongly support some of our common-sense notions about the importance of sleep. Whatever ultimately stands as the truth of the matter, it is already clear that sleep is a global organismic phenomenon, and its study can integrate in an illuminating way many domains of behavioural and psychological science with neurobiology.

SLEEP

Behavioural and psychological definition of sleep

Sleep is a behavioural state of homeothermic (warm-blooded) vertebrate mammals defined by characteristic changes in posture; raised sensory thresholds; and distinctive electrographic signs. Sleep is usually associated with a marked diminution of motor activity and with the assumption of recumbent postures. Typically the eyes close and the somatic musculature becomes relaxed. As sleep deepens, threshold to external stimulation increases and animals become progressively more unresponsive to external stimuli (see Figure 1).

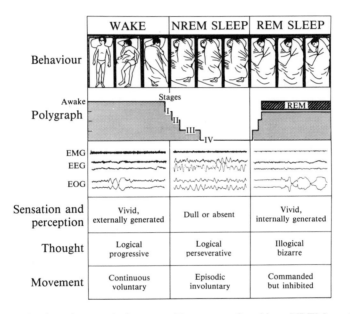

Figure 1 Behavioural states in humans. The states of waking, NREM, and REM sleep have behavioural, polygraphic, and psychological manifestations which are depicted here. In the behavioural channel, posture shifts – detectable by timelapse photography or video – can be seen to occur during waking and in concert with phase changes of the sleep cycle. Two different mechanisms account for sleep immobility: disfacilitation (during states I–IV of NREM sleep) and inhibition (during REM sleep). In dreams, we imagine that we move but we do not. The sequence of these stages is schematically represented in the polygraph channel and sample tracings are also shown. Three variables are used to distinguish these states: the electromyograph (EMG), which is the highest in waking, intermediate in NREM sleep, and lowest in REM sleep; the electroencephalogram (EEG) and electrooculogram (EOG), which are both activated in waking and REM sleep, and inactivated in NREM sleep. Each sample record is about 20 sec long. Other subjective and objective state variables are described in the three lower channels

The sensori-motor aspects of sleep may be seen in other conditions such us narcosis and hypothermia but are distinguished from these non-sleep states by their relative reversibility: the increased response threshold to stimuli can always be overcome, and sleeping animals can quickly regain both upright postures and alertness following sufficiently strong stimuli. The distinction of sleep from states of torpor (in those cold-blooded animals that cannot regulate their core body temperature) has a similar evolutionary history to the neural structures mediating the electrographic signs of sleep. Critical brain parts include the cerebral cortex and thalamus whose complex evolution underlies the distinctive EEG features of sleep in the higher vertebrate mammals. Sleep constitutes the state of entry to and exit from hibernation in those mammalian species who regulate temperature at lower levels during winter.

In humans, it is now clear that mental activity undergoes a progressive and systematic reorganization throughout sleep. On first falling asleep individuals may progressively lose awareness of the outside world and experience micro-hallucinations and illusions of movement of the body in space; after sleep onset, mental activity persists but is described as thought-like and persevera-tive if it can be recalled at all upon awakening. These four correlated features − (1) the assumption of recumbent, or inert postures; (2) the increase in response threshold to stimulation; (3) the evolution of distinctive electroen-cephalographic features; and (4) the decrease in efficiency of mental activity − together constitute the fundamental features of the initial stages of sleep in humans. All animals whose sleep may be properly distinguished from states of torpor share the first three features.

Physiological aspects of sleep

The conditions described above do not persist throughout the sleep of most animals; rather, there is a complex reorganization of behavioural, physio-logical, and psychological events within each sleep bout. To detect this process, it is convenient to record the brain activity by means of an electroen-cephalogram (EEG) from the surface of the head (or directly from the cor-tical structures of the brain), to record the movement of the eyes by means of the electrooculogram (EOG), and to record muscle tone by means of the electromyogram (EMG). These three electrographic parameters allow one to distinguish sleep from waking and to distinguish two distinctive and cyclically recurrent phases within sleep, NREM (non-rapid eye movement) and REM (rapid eye movement) sleep. NREM, or synchronized sleep, is characterized by a change in the EEG from a low-amplitude, high-frequency pattern to a high-amplitude, low-frequency pattern. The degree to which the EEG is progressively synchronized (that is, of high voltage and low frequency) can be subdivided into four stages in humans (see Table 1). At the same time that

Table 1 EEG frequency and voltage characteristics of NREM sleep stages I–IV

Sleep stage	Frequency	Voltage
I	4–7 cycles per second (cps) (theta range)	arrhythmic < 50 mV
II	12–15 cps (spindle complexes)	peaks at 100 mV
III	1–4 cps (with spindle complexes)	> 100 mV
IV	1–3 cps (delta range)	150–250 mV

the EEG frequency is decreasing and the voltage increasing, muscle tone progressively declines and may be lost in most of the somatic musculature.

After varying amounts of time (depending upon the size of the animal and its brain), this progressive set of changes in the EEG reverses itself and the EEG finally resumes the low voltage, fast character previously seen in waking. Instead of waking, however, behavioural sleep persists; muscle tone (at first passively decreased) is now actively inhibited; and there arise in the electrooculogram stereotyped bursts of saccadic eye movement called rapid eye movements (the REMs, which give this sleep state the name REM sleep). This phase of sleep has also been called activated sleep (to signal the EEG low voltage, high frequency shared by REM and waking) and paradoxical sleep (to signal the maintenance of increased threshold to arousal in the face of the activated brain).

In all mammals (including aquatic, arboreal, and flying species) sleep is organized in this cyclic fashion: sleep is initiated by NREM and punctuated by REM at regular intervals. Most animals compose a sleep bout out of three or more such cycles, and in mature humans the average nocturnal sleep period consists of four to five such cycles, each of 90–100 min duration. After a prolonged period of wake activity (as in humans), the first cycles are characterized by NREM phase enhancement (a preponderance of high-voltage, slow wave activity) while the last cycles show more REM phase enhancement (low-voltage, fast wave activity). The period is of fixed length across any and all sleep periods.

Recent progress in the cellular neurophysiology of sleep

Since the early 1960s the neurobiological mechanisms of sleep have been investigated in experimental animals using lesion, stimulation, and single-cell recording techniques. The results are of great psychological significance because they demonstrate a clear correspondence between the states of the

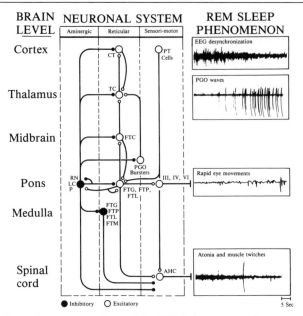

Figure 2   Schematic representation of the REM sleep generation process. The electrographic signs of REM sleep in the cat are shown in the four boxes on the right. A distributed network involves cells at many brain levels (left). The network is represented as comprising three neuronal systems (centre) that mediate REM sleep electrographic phenomena (right). Postulated inhibitory connections are shown as *solid circles*; postulated excitatory connections as *open circles*. In this diagram no distinction is made between neurotransmission and neuromodulatory functions of the depicted neurons. It should be noted that the actual synaptic signs of many of the aminergic and reticular pathways remain to be demonstrated, and in many cases, the neuronal architecture is known to be far more complex than indicated here (e.g., the thalamas and cortex). Two additive effects of the marked reduction in firing rate by aminergic neurons at REM sleep onset are postulated: disinhibition (through removal of negative restraint) and facilitation (through positive feedback). The net result is strong tonic and phasic activation of reticular and sensori-motor neurons in REM sleep. REM sleep phenomena are postulated to be mediated as follows: EEG desynchronization results from a net tonic increase in reticular, thalamocortical, and cortical neuronal firing rates. PGO waves (see text) are the result of tonic disinhibition and phasic excitation of burst cells in the lateral pontomesencephalic tegmentum. Rapid eye movements are the consequence of physic firing by reticular and vestibular cells; the latter (not shown) directly excite oculomotor neurons. Muscular atonia is the consequence of tonic postsynaptic inhibition of spinal anterior horn cells by the pontomedullary reticular formation. Muscle twitches occur when excitation by reticular and pyramidal tract motoneurons phasically overcomes the tonic inhibition of the anterior horn cells. Anatomical abbreviations: RN, raphé nuclei; LC, locus coeruleus; P, peribrachial region; FTC, central tegmental field; FTG, gigantocellular tegmental field; FTL, lateral tegmental field; FTM, magnocellular tegmental field; FTP, parvocellular tegmental field; TC, thalamocortical; CT, cortical; PT cell, pyramidal cell; III, oculomotor; IV, trochlear; V, trigmenial motor nuclei; AHC, anterior horn cell

Source: Modified from Hobson, Lydic, and Baghdoyan, 1986

114

brain and the states of the mind. While debate continues on the precise architecture and dynamics of the NREM–REM sleep cycle control system, there is widespread agreement on the following points: the critical neurons are localized in the brain stem, principally the pontine tegmentum (as Jouvet originally suggested in 1962), but the critical neurons are more widely distributed and more heterogeneous than originally thought. They are gathered in numerous nuclei and have a diverse chemical constitution and connectivity (see Figure 2). This explains one of the great puzzles of sleep research: why REM sleep, whose control is clearly localized in the pons, can be neither completely abolished by local electrolytic lesions nor consistently evoked by local electrical stimulation. Aminergic neurones enhance waking and suppress REM sleep. Thus drugs which augment noradrenergic and/or serotonergic activity tend to increase arousal but impede REM sleep, suggesting a cholinergic-aminergic, push-pull oscillatory system of sleeping and waking (Karczmar, Longo, & De Carolis, 1970). Recent experiments indicate that REM sleep can be increased for over a week following a single microscopic injection of cholinergic drug into the brain stem. Cholinergic neurons enhance some REM sleep events, and all or part of the REM sleep phase can be cholinergically stimulated.

DREAMING

Dreaming is a distinctive mental state that occurs periodically in normal human sleep. Typical dream reports include such psychological features as hallucinations, delusions, cognitive abnormalities, emotional intensification, and amnesia. These five remarkable features of dreaming have invited its comparison to abnormal states of mind occurring during waking in certain clinical conditions, especially schizophrenia and the organic mental syndromes, in particular delirium (see Table 2). The exploration of dreaming therefore constitutes not only an aspect of mind–body (psychophysiological)

Table 2 Some formal cognitive aspects of dreaming

Mental faculty	*Dream characteristics*
Orientation	Discontinuity and incongruity of times, places and persons
Memory	Amnesia for over 95% of dreams
Thinking	Insight and logic impaired
	Inferences uncertain and inaccurate
Sensory perceptions	Intense visual illusion
	Continuous illusion of motion
Visceral perceptions	Weak or absent sense of smell, taste and pain
Emotions	Labile with intensification of anxiety, anger and elation
	Weak or absent sadness, shame and guilt

interaction but also a model approach to the study of mental illness. An obvious problem is that the unconformable nature of all subjective experience is compounded by difficult access to the mind in sleep. The recent development of sleep laboratory techniques has given the study of dreaming a more instrumental and systematic character, and the emerging picture encourages psychophysiological integration.

Psychological features of dreaming

Dreams are characterized by vivid and fully formed hallucinatory imagery with the visual sensory domain predominant: auditory, tactile, and movement sensations are also prominent in most dream reports. Compared with the intense involvement of these sensori-motor domains, taste and smell are underrepresented and reports of pain are exceedingly rare despite the involvement of dreamers in frightening and even physically mutilating scenarios.

Dreaming is properly considered delusional because subjects have virtually no insight regarding the true nature of the state in which they have these unusual sensory experiences. The tendency is thus great to consider dream events as if they were completely real even though they are promptly recognized as fabrications when recalled in subsequent waking states. This is all the more surprising since the uncritical belief in the reality of dream events must overcome high degrees of improbability and even physical impossibility.

The lack of insight that makes dreams delusional is part of a broader set of cognitive disturbances. Dreams are characterized by marked uncertainties (with explicit vagueness); discontinuities (with unexplained changes of subject, actions, and setting); impossibilities (with defiance of physical law) and improbabilities; and incongruities (with social inappropriateness and cognitive illogicality). Dream characters and dream objects may be banal or altogether fantastic and impossible collages of existing reality; they may behave normally or indulge in the most absurd, improbable, or impossible actions in settings either familiar or bearing only the faintest resemblances to those of real life. To explain these unique and remarkable dream features illogical thought processes such as non sequiturs, post-hoc explanations, and mythical, metaphorical, and symbolic interpretations are the norm.

Memory undergoes a paradoxical intensification and suppression: recall is intensified within the dream as remote characters, scenes, events, and concerns are knitted into the fanciful and evanescent fabric of the dream. Dreams can thus be said to be hypermnesic (extraordinary memory recall) within the state itself; this increased access to memory within the state of dreaming contrasts markedly with the virtual impossibility of recovering the dream product after the state has terminated. On awakening even from a dream in progress, subjects have difficulty holding the vivid experiences in short-term memory long enough to give a report or transcribe the dream

116

scenario in detail. It can be conservatively stated that at least 95 per cent of all dream mentation is totally forgotten.

Emotion fluctuates widely in association with the abnormal and vivid mental content of dreaming: anxiety, fear, and surprise are common affects which undergo marked intensification during dreams. Obsessional concerns are common with dreamers focusing their worry about nudity, missed trains, unpacked suitcases, and a host of other incomplete arrangements. Depressive affects are markedly underrepresented, with shame and guilt playing a relatively small part.

The definition and characterization of dreaming given here serves to differentiate it from other kinds of mental activities that may occur in sleep. Fleeting images accompanied by the sensation of falling (but unsustained by a narrative plot and sequential action) characterize mental activity at sleep onset. Once sleep is established, mentation assumes a thought-like character which is usually perseverative and unprogressive as the sleeper reviews daytime activities and concerns in a persistent, repetitive manner. Such sleep "thinking" is unaccompanied by either vivid visual imagery or bizarre cognitive feature. Sustained dream scenarios occur only after these two forms of mental activity have subsided. Dreaming then alternates with thought-like mentation at 90–100-minute intervals throughout the night. Recall of dreams and other forms of mental activity in sleep depends upon prompt awakening from the state in which the mental activity occurs; retention of such recall further depends upon the instrumental act of verbally reporting or transcribing the dream narration.

Dreaming and REM sleep

In 1953 Aserinsky and Kleitman noted that the sleep of children was interrupted periodically by activation of the EEG and by bursts of saccadic eye movement, the so-called rapid eye movements, or REMs, of sleep (see Figures 1 and 2). Dement (1955) confirmed the hypothesis that these periods of brain activation during sleep were correlated with dreaming as defined above. When normal subjects were aroused from REM sleep, they gave detailed reports of dream activity. The capacity to recall dreams appeared to be related to the nature of the awakening process; subjects who learned to obtain a fully aroused state without moving increased their recall capacity. Within the REM period, dream intensity tended to parallel the intensity of other physiological events, especially the eye movements; arousal during REM sleep with the eye movement activity yielded reports fulfilling the definition of dreaming given here in 90–95 per cent of the cases. When scored for vividness, emotionality, and imagined physical activity, measures were correlated positively with the quantitative intensity of the eye movement in the REM sleep just prior to awakening. Awakening during REM sleep without eye movement yielded reports of lesser intensity in about 70 per cent of the awakenings. These figures dropped to 5–10 per cent when awakenings were made during non-REM sleep.

Awakenings from non-REM sleep yielded reports of mental activity in about 50 per cent of the trials, but a large proportion of these reports were of perseverative, thought-like mental activity. Reports qualitatively indistinguishable from dreaming were obtained from stage I sleep at sleep onset, a phase of sleep without sustained eye movements; but these reports were quantitatively less impressive in duration and intensity than those obtained from emergent REM sleep periods later in the night.

Estimations of dream duration correlate positively with the time spent in REM sleep prior to arousal. When subjects were aroused after only 5 minutes of REM sleep, they gave shorter reports; after 15 minutes had elapsed, reports were considerably longer and more detailed. Thus it would appear, despite intensification and contraction of duration estimates within individual dream scenarios, that overall correlation between time estimation of dream duration and real time elapsed in REM sleep is quite good.

To test the resistance of memory to dreams, awakenings were performed in the non-REM sleep phase at intervals following the termination of REM. The incidence of reported dreams dropped to non-REM levels within 5 minutes of the end of a REM cycle, indicating the extremely fragile state of memory and highlighting the strong state dependency of recall upon arousal from REM sleep.

Psychophysiological theories of dreaming

The simplest and most direct approach to the correlation of dream mentation with the physiological state of the sleeping brain is to assume a formal isomorphism between the subjective and objective levels of description. By isomorphism is meant a similarity of form in the psychological and physiological domains. For example, subjective experience of visually formed imagery in dreams implicates the activation of the same perceptual elements in the visual system that operate in the waking state. Other details of psychophysiological correlation are assumed to obey the same general law; for example, the vivid hallucinated sensation of moving within dreams is assumed to be related to patterned activation of motor systems and those central brain structures that control the perception of position and changes in position of the body in space during the waking state. When we look at the physiological level for patterned activation of the visual motor and vestibular systems, we find that powerful, highly coordinated excitatory processes are recordable in oculomotor nerves, the middle ear, and visual sensory centres.

To be fully adequate, a psychophysiological hypothesis has to account for the following processes (see Figure 3a,b).

1 *Activation* The brain has to be turned on and kept internally activated

118

to support dream mentation throughout the REM sleep episode. A possible mechanism is the disinhibition of sensori-motor circuits (see Figure 2 and Figure 3b).

2 *Input blockade*   Input from the outside world to an internally activated brain has to be prevented in order for sleep and the illusions of dreaming to be maintained. This is accomplished in at least two ways. One is the inhibition of the group Ia nerves, which impedes access to the central nervous system from signals of peripheral origin; this presynaptic inhibition has also been recorded throughout the brain stem and thalamus. The second mechanism for excluding sensory input is obstruction which occupies the higher levels of sensory circuits with internally generated messages.

3 *Output blockade*   The internally activated and actively deafferented brain must also quell motor outputs to prevent the disruption of sleep by stimulation created by movement and to halt the enactment of dreamed motor commands. This is accomplished by postsynaptic inhibition of motoneurons in the spinal cord and brain stem. By these three processes, the brain is thus made ready to process information arising from within, to exclude data coming from without, and not to act upon the internally generated information.

4 *Internal signal generation*   It remains to provide the activated but disconnected brain with internal signals which it then processes as if they came from the outside world. This appears to occur in part by a mechanism intrinsic to brain activation: the reciprocal interaction of aminergic and cholinergic neurons in the brain stem. In most mammals including humans, the so-called PGO waves – P, pons, G, (lateral) geniculate; and O, occipital cortex – present themselves as candidates for an internally generated information signal arising at the level of the pontine brain stem (see Figure 2, second box on right, PGO waves). In association with oculomotor activity, strong pulses of excitation are conducted to visual and association cortices and the thalamus. It is now known that these PGO waves are generated by cellular activity which faithfully replicates generated eye movements at the level of the brain stem. Thus not only is internal information generated but also the information has the accompanying eye movements to create spatial specificity. According to the activation-synthesis hypothesis of dreaming, the now autoactivated and autostimulated brain processes these signals and interprets them in terms of information stored in memory.

The precise neural basis of the cognitive disturbances occurring in dreaming is not understood. It is tempting to see these failures as perhaps related to the cessation of activity in the aminergic neurons (which enhance waking and suppress REM sleep). This arrest of aminergic neuronal activity would affect the entire brain by depriving it of the tonic modulatory influence of norepinephrine (noradrenaline) and serotonin. It is speculated that this tonic modulatory influence may be essential to attentional processes, including the capacity to organize information in a logical and coherent manner and to achieve full self-awareness. In the absence of external cues and internal modulatory influences, the activated forebrain would interpret its internally generated signals as if they were real. By a similar mechanism it may be speculated that the synthesized dream product is unremembered. That is, the activated forebrain circuits which mediated the dream experience are simply not instructed to keep a record of the transaction. Aminergic interneurons are also postulated to regulate mnemonic instruction as they send signals to create memory to the vast postsynaptic domain in waking (when they are active) but not in dreaming (where they are inactive). Current models of learning and memory at the cellular level evoke the intervention of an aminergic interneuron. Thus, the attribution of dream amnesia to the loss of aminergic modulation is consistent with these hypotheses.

This activation-synthesis model of dreaming and the reciprocal interaction theory of sleep cycle control to which it is linked are both incomplete and controversial. They both represent working hypotheses about the

REM SLEEP AND DREAMING

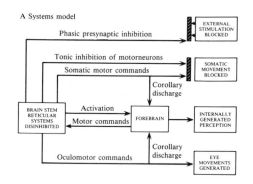

Figure 3a Systems model As a result of disinhibition caused by cessation of aminergic neuronal firing, brain stem reticular systems become autoactive. Their outputs have effects including depolarization of afferent terminals causing phasic presynaptic inhibition and blockade of external stimuli, especially during the burst of REM; postsynaptic hyperpolarization causing tonic inhibition of moto-neurons which effectively counteract concomitant motor commands so that somatic movement is blocked. Only the oculomotor commands are read out as eye movements because the moto-neurons are not inhibited. The forebrain, activated by the reticular formation and also aminergically disinhibited, receives efferent copy or corollary discharge information about somatic motor and oculomotor commands from which it may synthesize such internally generated perceptions as visual imagery and the sensation of movement, both which typify dream mentation. The forebrain may, in turn, generate its own motor commands which help to perpetuate the process via positive feedback to the reticular formation

fundamental physiology of sleep and the way in which that physiology may help us to understand unique features of the dream process. The attribution of automaticity to the control system and the feature of randomness in the information generator model should not be taken to exclude the meaningful nature of the synthetic process carried out by the dreaming brain. By definition, the brain/mind of each dreamer is obliged to make as much sense as is possible of its internally generated signals under the adverse working conditions of REM sleep. Thus, the dream product for each individual may contain unique stylistic psychological features and concerns and may thus be worthy of scrutiny by the individual to review life strategies. But the new theory challenges the psychoanalytic idea that the many meaningless aspects of dream mentation are the result of an active effort to disguise the meaning of unconscious wishes (which are in turn postulated to be the driving force of dreaming). Instead, it ascribes these defective cognitive properties of dreaming to unusual operating features of the internally activated, autostimulated brain during REM sleep.

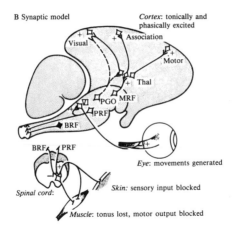

Figure 3b Synaptic model Some of the directly and indirectly disinhibited neuronal systems are schematized together with their supposed contributions to REM sleep phenomena. At the level of the brain stem, five neuronal types are illustrated: midbrain reticular neurons (MRF) projecting to thalamus convey tonic and phasic activating signals rostrally; burst cells in the peribrachial region (PGO) convey phasic activation and specific eye movement information to the geniculate body and cortex (dashed line indicates uncertainty of direct projection); pontine reticular formation (PRF) neurons transmit phasic activation signals to oculomotor neurons (VI) and spinal cord which generate eye movements, twitches of extremities, and presynaptic inhibition; bulbar reticular formation (BRF) neurons send tonic hyperpolarizing signals to motor neurons in spinal cord. As a consequence of these descending influences, sensory input and motor output are blocked at the level of the spinal cord. At the level of the forebrain, visual association and motor cortex neurons all receive tonic and phasic activation signals from non-specific and specific thalamic relay cells

FUNCTIONS OF SLEEP AND DREAMING

The main achievements since the mid-1960s have been in describing previously unsuspected sleep phenomena and in detailing the neural mechanisms by which sleep is controlled. While incomplete and still controversial, schemata of the type outlined earlier in the chapter will almost certainly be more confidently established in the near future. Completely without definitive supporting evidence, however, are the multiple functional theories that the diversity of new findings relevant to sleep phenomena and sleep mechanisms have produced.

These theories can be conveniently considered in four categories: the behavioural, the developmental, the metabolic, and the informational. (The informational level is discussed later in the chapter).

At the *behavioural level*, it is clear that sleep serves to suppress activity at times of the day when the likelihood of accomplishing a given specific goal is relatively low; finding food (self-preservation) and mates (furthering of the species) are clearly less likely to go well in sighted animals when light levels are low. Such activity also has a high energy cost in homeothermic animals when temperature is low. Thus the efficiency of sleep is clear (at the behavioural level). Correspondingly, the enforced nature of sleep and its relation to nesting activity clearly serves to unite animals in a family or pair-bonded situation that may foster sexual behaviour and promote nurturance and development of the young. Incredibly, scientists who study animal behaviour (ethologists) have not conducted systematic investigations of such ecological notions of sleep. The recognition of sleep as a behaviour by ethologists, especially neuroethologists, has not yet occurred. The current development of remote and portable monitoring systems makes this a promising area of investigation.

At the *developmental level*, it is certainly significant that sleep is the major state of existence in the life of the immature animal. For example, the newborn human sleeps 16 hours a day and half of this period is devoted to REM. This indicates not only a preponderance of sleep in the immature animal but also a disproportionate allowance of time to the REM phase. The newborn human devotes a full 8 hours to REM sleep each day. In further contradistinction to the adult profile, REM sleep may occur immediately at sleep onset. As indicated earlier, the length of the cycle is a function of brain size within and across species so that, in the newborn human infant, cycle length is 45 minutes as against 90 minutes in the adult state.

The high proportion of sleep in REM at birth is complemented by even higher levels during the last trimester of mammalian life in utero. During later stages of development the total amount of sleep will decrease to one-half and the amount of each sleep devoted to REM will decrease to one-quarter of the neonatal level. At the same time the period length of the NREM–REM cycle doubles (from 45 to 90 minutes). In immature animals both NREM and

REM sleep show important quantitative differences from the adult state: slow waves are less well developed at birth and become more distinctively differentiated as brain and behavioural competence increase. The muscle inhibition of REM sleep is considerably less well established at birth than at maturity and the phasic muscle twitches, which are only faintly visible in most adult mammals, are dramatically and clearly evident in the immature members of the species. Thus both the allocation of time and the qualitative appearance of sleep change dramatically during development.

A function of REM sleep for the developing organisms could be guaranteed activation of neural circuits underlying elemental behaviours. It is attractive to think of the evolutionary advantages of guaranteeing the organized activation of the complex systems of the brain before the organism has developed the full capability of testing them in the real world. An associated idea is that of behavioural rehearsal. In the developing and in the adult animal REM sleep could guarantee maintenance of circuits critical for survival whether or not they were called upon for use during the wake state.

At the *metabolic level*, the fact that the early cycles are predominantly composed of slow wave sleep has given rise to the notion that this sleep stage may serve to rest the body and be responsive to the duration of the preceding wake period. The low-voltage fast (or REM) phase of sleep (which is recovered later) may have more to do with anabolic processes and be related to the function of the brain itself.

The recurrent cycles of NREM and REM sleep are accompanied by major changes in all physiological systems of the body. During NREM sleep there are decreases in blood pressure, heart rate, and respiratory rate and pulsatile release of growth and sex hormones from the pituitary. The concomitance of these events gives further credence to the notion that NREM sleep may be functionally associated with constructive processes benefiting the somatic tissues.

REM sleep is associated with activation of other physiological functions: heart rate, blood pressure, and respiratory rate and irregularity all increase. Penile erection in males and clitoral engorgement in females accompany the brain and autonomic activation of this phase, and although the somatic musculature is actively inhibited, small twitches of the facial, digital, and even major proximal skeletal muscles may be observed. It is unlikely that these features simply denote a functional state of rest.

It has been demonstrated that slow wave sleep is associated with appreciable savings of energy in many neural structures. The decrease in action potential generation by many central neurons is associated with decreases in cerebral blood flow and cerebral metabolism. It seems unlikely, however, that such modest energy savings can be the sole or major function of sleep since they are all lost or reversed during the REM phase. In REM, however, the arrest of firing by aminergic neurons could allow replenishment of neurotransmitter levels or of synthetic enzymes needed to assure the synaptic efficiency of attentional systems in the wake state.

SPECIFIC FUNCTIONAL HYPOTHESES

Effects of sleep deprivation

Because mental lapses and fatigue are the well-known sequelae of even moderate sleep deprivation, common sense has long held that sleep is as essential to effective information processing as it is to energy homeostasis. But, because convincing experimental models of these phenomena have not been available, the underlying pathophysiology (functional changes) of the deficit states and the mediating variables of sleep's supposed benefits have not been elucidated. The discovery of sleep's periodic NREM and REM phases retarded progress in this area, by inducing scientists to make fruitless attempts to differentiate between a hypothetical energy-restoration function for NREM sleep and a cognitive or information-processing function for REM sleep.

Long-term sleep deprivation in rats has recently been shown to produce impaired thermoregulation, metabolic dyscontrol, and death. Studies by Rechtschaffen and co-workers (1989a, 1989b) demonstrated this by selectively depriving rats of either REM sleep or both NREM and REM sleep (Gilliland, Bergmann, & Rechtschaffen, 1989; Kushida, Bergmann, & Rechtschaffen, 1989). After one week of total sleep deprivation, rats show a progressive weight loss, which occurs even in the face of increased food intake. The progressive weight loss, which becomes more pronounced after two weeks, appears to be a syndrome of metabolic dyscontrol, which causes more and more calories to be consumed in a vain attempt to restore lost energy homeostasis. When deprivation is stopped, recovery is prompt and complete (Everson et al., 1989). En route to each rat's demise at about four weeks of deprivation, body weight plummets, while food consumption soars, and the body temperature becomes progressively more unstable.

These observations provide an excellent model for the investigation of what appears to be a progressive failure of energy-regulating mechanisms within the brain. One attractive hypothesis is that sleep deprivation causes a progressive loss of aminergic synaptic firing power, resulting from over-driving the sympathetic system on the one hand, and denying the respite from neurotransmitter release that normally occurs in sleep. According to this interpretation, aminergic discharge and/or transmitter release would increase as an initial response to sleep deprivation. However, as the sleep-deprived brain becomes more and more depleted of its sympathetic neurotransmitters, first cognitive, then thermal, and finally homeostatic caloric systems would fail. These and other hypotheses involving sleep-dependent neuroendocrine

124

responses (such as growth hormone release) can be tested in the new sleep paradigm.

Temperature regulation

Sleep onset normally occurs on the descending limb of the curve describing the circadian body temperature rhythm, and a further drop in body temperature occurs with the first episode of NREM sleep. Furthermore, two distinct thermal adaptations, shallow torpor (a temperature drop occurring daily in small mammals) and hibernation (a more profound and prolonged seasonal drop in body temperature) occur during NREM sleep (Heller, Glotzbach, Grahn, & Radehe, 1988). These facts combine to favour the view that sleep is part of a continuum of diverse energy conservation strategies used by mammals to cope with varying levels and sources of heat and light. Whatever benefits sleep may accrue for tomorrow, one clear function is to conserve calories for today.

In addition to a drop in body temperature, reduced responsiveness to changes in ambient temperature is also observed in NREM sleep; shivering in response to cold and sweating in response to heat are both diminished. Heller and co-workers at Stanford (1988) and Parmeggiani and colleagues in Bologna (1988) have shown that the responsiveness of temperature sensor neurons in the preoptic hypothalamus dips to a lower level in NREM sleep than in waking, and bottoms out in REM sleep. In sleep, the animal apparently changes its behaviour as a substitute for its neuronal thermostat – an unlikely high-cost manoeuvre for a small short-term calorie saving.

Daily observations in human body temperature of $1.5°C$ were observed in the first phase of sleep research and led to the discovery of the circadian rhythm (Aschoff, 1965b). The circadian rhythm of temperature has been shown to be tightly coupled to the circadian rhythm of sleep and waking, and the degree to which these can be dissociated continues to be debated. The dual oscillator theory suggests there is one oscillator for body temperature and another for sleep. While the two oscillators can be dissociated both surgically and chemically (Jouvet et al., 1988), the cellular and molecular basis of the circadian oscillator and the mechanism of its coupling to the other oscillators remains to be fathomed.

Immune system

It is well known that humans with an infectious disease become sleepy, but the mechanism of this effect and its functional significance are not understood. Is this a consequence of increasing demands upon the sympathetic nervous system and upon energy metabolism, with more calories diverted to defensive processes? The work in this newly developing area of sleep and immune function interaction are studying particularly the capacity of interleukin-1 to promote sleep.

These experiments grew out of major work initiated by John Pappenheimer and colleagues (1975), which identified the NREM sleep-promoting factor (S) in the spinal fluid of sleep-deprived goats and rabbits as a muramyl dipeptide (MDP). Muramyl peptides are not found in brain cells but are the building blocks of bacterial cell walls. They are responsible for raising body temperature (pyrogenic) and stimulating the immune system, in addition to having sleep-inducing effects (somnogenic), which appear to be at least partially independent of their pyrogenicity (Krueger, Walter, & Levin, 1985b). One particularly intriguing finding is the capacity of MDP to compete with serotonin at its binding sites on both the central nervous system and immune system cells, suggesting a common mechanism linking MDP's sleep-promoting and immunostimulatory effects (Silverman & Karnovsky, 1989).

Interleukin-1 is an immunostimulatory and somnogenic peptide which is endogenous, being produced by brain glial cells and macrophages. Both interleukin-1 and MDP enhance tumorcidal and bacteriocidal activity. Interleukin-1 alters sleep in a manner similar to muramyl peptides; time spent in NREM sleep, amplitude of the EEG slow waves, and duration of individual episodes of sleep are all increased by this compound (Krueger, Walter, Dinarello, & Chedid, 1985a). However, because time spent in REM sleep is markedly decreased by both compounds, their contribution to the physiology of normal sleep remains uncertain.

Cognition

Work on the cognitive neuroscience of sleep is tantalizing, but most of its promise remains unfulfilled. Early results indicated that learning (i.e., conditioned avoidance) in rats is followed by increases in REM sleep and is impaired by deprivation of REM sleep (Bloch, 1973; Fishbein, Kastaniotis, & Chattman, 1974; Smith, Kitahama, Valatx, & Jouvet, 1974). Efforts to further detail these findings revealed that the increase in REM sleep following conditioned avoidance is quite prolonged (Smith, Young, & Young, 1980; Smith & Lapp, 1986), and that REM sleep must occur at particular times after training in order for learning to occur.

In studies with humans, two interesting new findings using the deprivation technique substantiate the idea that sleep improves cognitive competence. Mikulincer, Babkoff, Caspy, & Sing (1989) showed that measures of attention, concentration, affect, and motivation declined with increasing sleep loss and that all these measures were powerfully sensitive to time of day. The problem with such studies is that their strongly correlative findings (brains do not work well when sleepy) do not establish the causal hypothesis (brains work well because of sleep).

Contrary to common sense and most sleep research findings, the provocative theory of Crick and Mitchison (1983) states that we have REM sleep (and dreams) to forget. The theory addresses a long-standing problem in neuropsychology: how brains distinguish between trivial and important associations and memories. (Hartley, 1801; Luria, 1968). There are two different ways through interactions in the brain that such sorting could occur. Procedural memories (dealing with a series of actions) might be reinforced through the interaction of a fixed repertoire of motor commands (issued automatically by the brain stem during REM sleep) and synaptic hotspot residues of the day's sensori-motor experience. Declarative memories might be reinforced through interaction with fixed action programmes of emotional and vegetative behaviours programmed in the limbic systems. Our dreams clearly reflect some such integrative process: they are constantly animated and we move through diverse settings, combining both recent and remote experience in an emotional climate often fraught with strong feelings of anxiety and fear.

The problem with these attractive ideas is that they are most difficult to test experimentally in living animals. Thus one of the most attractive aspects of the Crick-Mitchison theory is its heuristic resort to neural net behaviour in computerized brain simulations. Another option for the cognitive neuroscience of sleep is a more imaginative use of "experiments of nature", for

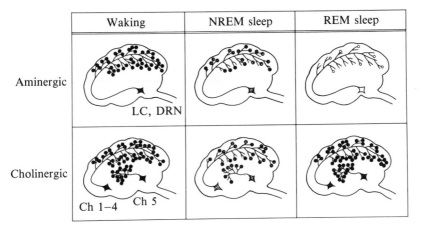

Figure 4a State-dependent changes in aminergic and cholinergic neuronal function. Schematic representation of progressive decrease of aminergic neurotransmitter release in cerebral cortex as animal passes from waking through NREM to REM sleep. Cortical concentrations of norepinphrine (noradrenaline) and serotonin are highest in waking, lowest in REM sleep, and intermediate in NREM sleep. Top panel illustrates sagittal sections of the brain with aminergic neurons of nucleus locus coeruleus (noradrenergic) and dorsal raphe nucleus (serotonergic). Bottom panel illustrates cholinergic neurons in basal forebrain and peribrachial pontine tegmentum. Cholinergic neurons release levels of acetycholine as high in REM as they are in waking; release in NREM sleep is lower

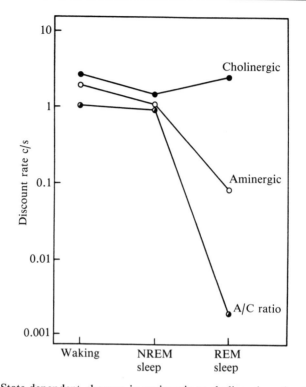

Figure 4b State-dependent changes in aminergic-to-cholinergic ratio. Quantitative estimate of aminergic (A) and cholinergic (C) neurotransmitter concentrations may be derived from single-unit recording studies and by direct and indirect measurements of neurotransmitter release. Because values are similar and parallel in waking and NREM sleep but diverge in REM sleep, the ratio of the two values amplifies the difference between REM and the other two states. Values of A are computed by averaging mean rate of putatively noradrenergic and serotonergic neurons recorded by microelectrodes in brain stem of cats. Inferred decrease in release has been confirmed voltametrically, for serotonin, in waking and in REM sleep. Values of C are computed by averaging mean rate of unidentified cortical neurons. These estimates are compatible with direct measurements of acetylcholine release from cerebral cortex

example, the clinical study of patients with brain lesions. While brain-stem-lesion patients lose REM sleep entirely, cortical lesion patients lose only dreaming. Are there differences in what such different kinds of patients can learn (or at least not forget)?

When the metabolic and developmental implications of our rapidly increasing knowledge of sleep mechanism are considered at the *informational level*, other intriguing theories can be enunciated. For example, if the brain is only slightly decreased in level of activity during slow-wave sleep and increases activity again (during REM sleep), but with a change of information processing mode during REM sleep, it is possible to imagine that later stages of the learning process may be enhanced during sleep. To be more specific, the cerebral cortex may benefit differentially from the NREM and REM phases of sleep. The activity of aminergic brain stem neurons (and direct measurements of neurotransmitter release in the forebrain) indicated that the activated states of waking and REM sleep are at diametrically opposite poles: the ratio of aminergic activity (high in waking and lowest in REM sleep) to cholinergic activity (high in both waking and in REM sleep) therefore places NREM sleep in a functionally intermediary position (see Figure 4a,b).

Since aminergic and cholinergic neurotransmitters not only influence neural events at the membrane level but also influence the metabolic activity of the cytoplasm and nucleus (via second messengers), it is the postsynaptic change in mode of operation of the entire brain that may contain the secret of the functional specificity of NREM and REM sleep. Sleep could be thus a programme for the comparison of genetically determined organizational priorities of the brain with the external experience of the animal. The upshot of this idea is that information already stored in memory is compared with recent inputs such that the memory stores can be corrected and updated. Related notions include consolidation of memory and the elimination of unwanted or spurious information.

Now that the metabolic differentiation of REM sleep and waking has been detailed at the level of single cells and specific neurotransmitters, it is possible to envisage a new line of functional investigations in which the consequences of metabolic switching can be specifically tested with respect to protein metabolism in the brain.

CONCLUSION

Modern sleep research has evolved from an early, descriptive phase in the human sleep lab through an increasingly detailed and precise analysis of the cellular and molecular mechanisms that regulate the NREM–REM cycle in experimental animals. The fruit of this two-pronged attack is a completely new approach to our understanding of exceptional mental states, like dreaming with its many formal similarities to mental illness, in terms of specific brain processes. Now attention is being focused upon functional questions in studies of animals subjected to experimental deprivation and in experiments of nature which result in human sleep disorders. Evidence from all these sources converges to suggest that sleep is a complex, neurological strategy for simultaneously promoting energy regulation and automatic information processing by the brain.

ACKNOWLEDGEMENTS

This chapter is based on articles by the author, which first appeared in the following publications.

Hobson, J. A. (1987). Dreaming. In G. Adelman (Ed.) *Encyclopedia of neuroscience* (vol. 1, pp. 338–340). Boston, MA: Birkhauser.

Hobson, J. A. (1987). Sleep. In G. Adelman (Ed.) *Encyclopedia of neuroscience* (vol. 2, pp. 1097–1101). Boston, MA: Birkhauser.

Hobson, J. A. (1988). Homeostasis and heteroplasticity: Functional significance of behavioral state sequences. In R. Lydic & J. F. Biebuyck (Eds) *The clinical physiology of sleep* (pp. 199–200). Bethesda, MD: American Physiological Society.

Hobson, J. A. (1990). Sleep and dreaming. *Journal of Neuroscience, 10*, 371–382.

FURTHER READING

Bootzin, R., Kihistrom, J., & Schachter, D. (Eds) (1990). *Sleep and cognition.* Washington, DC: American Psychological Association.

Cohen, D. B. (1979). *Sleep and dreaming: Origins, nature and functions.* Oxford: Pergamon.

Hobson, J. A. (1988). *The dreaming brain.* New York: Basic Books.

Hobson, J. A. (1989). *Sleep.* New York: Scientific American Library.

REFERENCES

Aschoff, J. (1965a). *Circadian clocks.* Amsterdam: North-Holland.

Aschoff, J. (1965b). Circadian rhythms in man. *Science, 148*, 1427–1432.

Aserinsky, E., & Kleitman, N. (1953). Regularly occurring periods of eye motility and concomitant phenomena during sleep. *Science, 118*, 273–274.

Bloch, V. (1973). Cerebral activation and memory fixation. *Archives de Italiennes Biologie, 111*, 577–590.

Crick, F., & Mitchison, G. (1983). The function of dream sleep. *Nature, 304*, 111–114.

Dement, W. (1955). Dream recall and eye movements during sleep in schizophrenics and normals. *Journal of Nervous and Mental Disease, 122*, 263–269.

Everson, C. A., Gilliland, M. A., Kushida, C. A., Pilcher, J. J., Fang, V. S., Refetoff, S., Bergmann, B. M., & Rechtschaffen, A. (1989). Sleep deprivation in the rat: IX. Recovery. *Sleep, 12*, 60–67.

Fishbein, W., Kastaniotis, C., & Chattman, D. (1974). Paradoxical sleep: Prolonged augmentation following learning. *Brain Research, 79*, 61–77.

Gilliland, M. A., Bergmann, B. M., & Rechtschaffen, A. (1989). Sleep deprivation in the rat: VII. High EEG amplitude sleep deprivation. *Sleep, 12*, 53–59.

Hartley, D. (1801). *Observations on man, his frame, his duty and his expectations.* London: Johnson.

Heller, C. G., Glotzbach, S., Grahn, D. & Radehe, C. (1988). Sleep dependent changes in the thermo-regulatory system. In R. Lydic & J. F. Biebuyck (Eds) *Clinical physiology of sleep* (pp. 145–158). Bethesda, MD: American Physiological Society.

Hobson, J. A. (1988). *The dreaming brain.* New York: Basic Books.

Hobson, J. A. (1989). *Sleep.* New York: Scientific American Library.

Hobson, J. A., Lydic, R., & Baghdoyan, H. A. (1986). Evolving concepts of sleep generation: From brain centers to neuronal populations (with commentaries). *Behavioral and Brain Sciences*, *9*, 371–448.

Jouvet, M. (1962). Récherche sur les structures nerveuses et les mécanismes responsables des differentes phases du sommeil physiologique. *Archives de Italiennes Biologie*, *100*, 125–206.

Jouvet, M. (1972). The role of monoamines and acetylcholine-containing neurons in the regulation of the sleep-waking cycle. *Ergebn. Physiology Biol. Chem. Exp. Pharmakol.*, *64*, 166–307.

Jouvet, M., Buda, L., Denges, M., Kitahama, K., Sallanon, M., & Sastre, J. (1988). Hypothalamic regulation of paradoxical sleep. In T. Onian (Ed.) *Neurobiology of sleep–wakefulness cycle* (pp. 1–17). Metsniereba, Tbilisi: Georgian Academy of Sciences.

Karczmar, A. G., Longo, V. G., & De Carolis, A. S. (1970). A pharmacological model of paradoxical sleep: The role of cholinergic and monoamine systems. *Physiological Behavior*, *5*, 175–182.

Krueger, J. M., Walter, J., Dinarello, C. A., & Chedid, L. (1985a). Induction of slow-wave sleep by interleukin-1. In M. J. Kluger, J. J. Oppenheim, & M. C. Powanda (Eds) *The physiologic, metabolic and immunologic actions of interleukin-1* (pp. 161–170). New York: Liss.

Krueger, J. M., Walter, J., & Levin, C. (1985b). Factor S and related somnogens: An immune theory for slow-wave sleep. In D. J. McGinty, R. Drucker-Colin, A. Morrison, & P. L. Parmeggiani (Eds) *Brain mechanisms of sleep* (pp. 253–275). New York: Raven.

Kushida, C. A., Bergmann, B. M., & Rechtschaffen, R. (1989). Sleep deprivation in the rat: IV. Paradoxical sleep deprivation. *Sleep*, *12*, 22–30.

Luria, A. R. (1968). *The mind of a mnemonist*. Cambridge, MA: Harvard University Press.

Mikulincer, M., Babkoff, H., Caspy, T., & Sing, H. (1989). The effects of 72 hours of sleep loss on psychological variables. *British Journal of Psychology*, *80*, 145–162.

Moore-Ede, M. C., Czeisler, C. A., & Richardson, G. S. (1983). Circadian timekeeping in health and disease. *New England Journal of Medicine*, *309*, 469–476.

Moruzzi, G. (1972). The sleep–waking cycle. *Ergeb. Physiol. Biol. Chem. Exp. Pharmakol.*, *64*, 1–165.

Pappenheimer, J. R., Koski, G., Fenci, V., Karnovsky, M. L., & Krueger, J. (1975). Extraction of sleep-promoting factor S from cerebrospinal fluid and from brain of sleep-deprived animals. *Journal of Neurophysiology*, *38*, 1299–1311.

Parmeggiani, P. L. (1988). Thermoregulation during sleep from the viewpoint of homeostasis. In R. Lydic & J. F. Biebuyck (Eds) *Clinical physiology of sleep* (pp. 159–170). Bethesda, MD: American Physiological Society.

Pavlov, I. P. (1960). *Conditioned reflexes: An investigation of the physiological activity of the cerebral cortex* (G. V. Anrep, trans.). New York: Dover.

Rechtschaffen, A., Bergmann, B. M., Everson, C. A., Kushida, C. A., & Gilliland, M. A. (1989a). Sleep deprivation in the rat: I. Conceptual issues. *Sleep*, *12*, 1–4.

Rechtschaffen, A., Bergmann, B. M., Everson, C. A., Kushida, C. A., & Gilliland, M. A. (1989b). Sleep deprivation in the rat: X. Integration and discussion of the findings. *Sleep*, *12*, 68–87.

Roffwarg, H. P., Muzio, J. M., & Dement, W. C. (1966). Ontogenetic development of the human sleep–dream cycle. *Science*, *152*, 604–619.

Sherrington, C. (1955). *Man on his nature*. New York: Doubleday.

131

Silverman, D. H. S., & Karnovsky, M. L. (1989). Serotonin and peptide neuro-modulators: Recent disorders and new ideas. In A. Meister (Ed.) *Advances in enzymology*. New York: Wiley.

Smith, C., & Lapp, L. (1986). Prolonged increases in both PS and number of REMs following a shuttle avoidance task. *Physiological Behavior*, *36*(6), 1053–1057.

Smith, C., Kitahama, K., Valatx, J. L., & Jouvet, M. (1974). Increased paradoxical sleep in mice during acquisition of a shock avoidance task. *Brain Research*, *77*, 221–230.

Smith, C., Young, J., & Young, W. (1980). Prolonged increases in paradoxical sleep during and after avoidance-task acquisition. *Sleep*, *3*(1), 67–81.

Steraide, M., & Hobson, J. A. (1976). Neuronal activity during the sleep–waking cycle. *Progress in Neurobiology*, *6*, 155–376.

2.5

PSYCHOPHARMACOLOGY

*Leonard W. Hamilton and
C. Robin Timmons*
Rutgers University, New Jersey, USA

**Classification of psychoactive
 drugs**
**Some principles of
 pharmacology**
**Mechanisms of drug action in
 the brain**
**Mechanisms of drug actions on
 behaviour**
Drugs that alter moods and
 states of consciousness
Central nervous system
 stimulants
Central nervous system
 depressants
Hallucinogens
Some observations on
 abuse and addiction
Drugs used to treat disorders
 of behaviour
Antipsychotics
Anti-anxiety drugs
Antidepressants
Future directions
Further reading
References

The human experience is frequently characterized by our feelings towards certain aspects of our environment. We are frightened by things we do not understand, calmed by familiarity, anxious in the face of uncertainty, exhilarated by our accomplishments, and depressed by our losses. Gradually, over the course of our individual development, we come to expect certain situations to produce certain types of feelings.

There are many chemical substances that have the power to alter this relationship between environment and feeling. Anxiety can be transformed into tranquillity, exhilaration into sobriety, and torpor into vigour. When these substances are administered in a formal manner, they are called *drugs*, and the study of the effects of these drugs on mood and other behaviours defines the field of *psychopharmacology*.

Historically, the more common chemical substances that change behaviour were plant products that were widely available and self-administered. Tea and opium were available in the Orient; tobacco and coffee in the Americas; and alcohol throughout the world. The substances were valued by each culture for the effects that they had on behaviour, but each culture also developed written or unwritten guidelines to regulate the use of the substances.

In addition to the commonly available plants, each geographic region has more obscure plants that may contain psychologically active substances. Information about the identifying features and effectiveness of these plants was passed on to family elders and to religious leaders. These individuals became valued for their knowledge of the effects of chemical substances, and became the informal practitioners of *folk medicine*. This gave way to the development of still more knowledge of these effects, and to the gradual development of formal medical practitioners.

We now have literally hundreds of different drugs that are known to change behaviour. Some of these have been borrowed directly from folk medicine and simply represent the modern processing and reformulation of a drug application that may be centuries old. Others have been discovered by accident when a chemical reaction has gone awry or when a drug has been administered to treat one malady and it ends up being effective for some totally different problem. Although important contributions have been made from both of these sources, the vast majority of our modern drugs have been developed through systematic research on the relationships among drugs, behaviour, and the underlying chemistry of the brain.

CLASSIFICATION OF PSYCHOACTIVE DRUGS

Psychoactive drugs have two basic uses: to alter mood and states of consciousness, and to treat psychopathology. Table 1 lists some examples of each type of drug.

Drugs that are used to alter moods and general states of consciousness can be divided into three broad categories based on the type of change they produce in the nervous system. Stimulant drugs produce an exaggeration of the conditions that are normally associated with alert wakefulness; in high dosages, these drugs produce overt seizure activity. Depressant drugs produce an exaggeration of the conditions that are normally associated with relaxation and sleep; in high dosages these drugs can produce unconsciousness. Hallucinogens produce a distortion of normal perception and thought processes; in high dosages these drugs can produce episodes of behaviour that can be characterized as psychotic. Although there are exceptions, a general rule is that these drugs produce their effects rather immediately by direct action on the neurons of the brain.

134

Table 1 Psychoactive drugs

Drug class	Example drugs	Primary mechanism of action
Drugs used to alter moods and states of consciousness		
STIMULANTS (produce psychomotor arousal; treat attention deficit disorder)		
Sympathomimetics	Dextroamphetamine Methylphenidate Cocaine	Monoamine (DA & NE) agonist, increase release, block re-uptake
Cholinomimetics	Nicotine	Ach agonist (high dose blocks)
Xanthines	Caffeine	Block adenosine receptors, GABA antagonist
Convulsants	Strychnine	Glycine antagonist
DEPRESSANTS (produce sedation; treat pain, anxiety, sleep disorders)		
Opioids	Morphine, Codeine Heroin, Methadone	Endogenous opiate agonist
Barbiturates	Secobarbital	GABA agonist
Barbiturate-like	Meprobamate	Similar to Barbiturates
Organic solvents	Alcohol, Ether	Disrupt neuronal membrane; may facilitate GABA
HALLUCINOGENIC (produce distorted perception)		
NE-like	Mescaline	Alter 5HT activity
5HT-like	Lysergic acid diethylamide (LSD)	Alter 5HT activity
Other	Marijuana, Anti-cholinergics, Phencyclidine (PCP)	Varied mechanisms, but many have endogenous receptors
Drugs used to treat psychological disorders		
ANTIPSYCHOTICS (treat schizophrenia; also delirium and dementia)		
Phenothiazines	Chlorpromazine	Block DA receptors
Butyrophenones	Haloperidol	Block DA receptors
Other	Clozapine	Block DA receptors
ANTIDEPRESSANTS (treat depression and bipolar disorder)		
Tricyclics		Block NE and 5HT re-uptake
(secondary)	Nortriptyline	(primarily block NE)
(tertiary)	Imipramine Clomipramine	(primarily block 5HT)
Heterocyclics	Fluoxetine	Block NE and 5HT re-uptake
MAO inhibitors	Phenelzine Tranylcypromine	Inhibit monoamine oxidase
Lithium	Lithium	Stabilizes synapses
ANTI-ANXIETY (treat acute and chronic anxiety; also sleep disturbances)		
Benzodiazepines	Alprazolam Diazepam	Facilitate GABA
Other	Buspirone	Decrease 5HT activity

Notes: Ach = acetylcholine
DA = dopamine
5HT = 5-hydroxytryptamine
GABA = gamma amino butyric acid
MAO = monoamine oxidase
NE = norepinephrine (noradrenaline)

Drugs that are used to treat psychopathology can also be divided into three broad categories based on the types of symptoms that they can ameliorate. The anti-anxiety drugs are used to treat the day-to-day fears and anxieties of individuals who lead basically normal lives. The antidepressant drugs are used to treat feelings of negative affect that may range from mild melancholy to abject depression accompanied by suicidal tendencies. Finally, the antipyschotic drugs are used to treat severe forms of mental illness, most notably schizophrenia, in which patients lose contact with reality and engage in behaviours that fall considerably outside the realm of normality. Again, there are exceptions, but a general rule is that these drugs tend to act indirectly: although they have immediate effects on the neurons of the brain, the therapeutic effects often require several weeks to appear, suggesting that the behavioural changes must await some long-term, chronic adjustment of the neurons to the drug's actions (i.e., *neuromodulation*).

There are many drugs that are not listed in the general classification schema of Table 1. Such a table can never remain complete for very long because new drugs are continually being developed, new applications may be found for some drugs, old drugs are sometimes phased out of the marketplace, and new theory may change the boundaries of classification. Detailed and current information that would expand this table is compiled regularly and published in a variety of sources (e.g., *Goodman and Gilman's The Pharmacological Bases of Therapeutics* and the *Physicians' Desk Reference*). Paperback summaries of this information for prescription and non-prescription drugs are available from bookshops and libraries. We shall return to Table 1 later for a discussion of the mechanisms of actions for these drugs.

SOME PRINCIPLES OF PHARMACOLOGY

In order for a drug to have an effect on behaviour, it must come into contact with the appropriate neurons in the brain. This can be accomplished in numerous ways, and the decision about the route of administration is based on a combination of factors including convenience, effects of the drug on local tissue, solubility of the drug, ionic characteristics of the drug, size of the drug molecule, and vulnerability of the drug to metabolism. The most common mode of administration is *oral*, with the drug being absorbed into the bloodstream through the walls of the stomach and intestines. *Subcutaneous*, *transdermal*, and *intramuscular* routes tend to produce slower and more sustained rates of delivery. *Inhalation* of drug vapours or injection of drugs directly into the bloodstream (*intra-arterial* or *intravenous*) tend to produce very rapid onset of the drug effects. Minute quantities of drugs can be injected directly into the brain (*intracranial*) or into the spinal cord (*intrathecal*) to produce rapid effects that are restricted to the local area of injection.

136

The duration of drug action is determined primarily by the rate of metabolic inactivation of the drug. Most commonly, the drugs are metabolized into some inactive form by enzymes that are produced by the liver, the digestive tract, or by the nervous system tissue per se. These drug metabolites are removed from the body as waste products in the bowel, in the urine, through the skin, or by exhalation through the lungs. Drugs can sometimes be present in the body but have little or no effect because the drug molecules have been sequestered into a metabolically inactive *pool*. Examples of such pools include the bladder, fat deposits, or chemical bonding of drug molecules to larger protein molecules.

The relationship between the dosage of a drug and the response to that drug poses one of the thorniest problems in psychopharmacology. Common experience can provide a general description of the dose–response effect: for example, a sip of coffee will be subthreshold and will not help a student stay awake to study; a cupful will certainly help, and two might be better; five or six cups might lead to tremor and anxiety. These different responses to caffeine reflect the different concentrations of the drug in the blood. Technically, the lowest dose required to produce the desired effect (in 50 per cent of the subjects) is termed the *minimum effective dose* (MED-50), and a dosage that is lethal to 50 per cent of the subjects (the LD-50) is an index of the toxicity of the drug. The safety factor of a drug, the *therapeutic index*, is the ratio of LD-50/MED-50, which should be a large number (10 or more) to indicate that a *lethal dose* would be many times higher than the recommended dose.

Within the effective dose range, the responses may still be complicated. Typically, doubling the dosage does not double the effect, and many drugs show a bipolar *dose–response curve* as shown in Figure 1. In the case of caffeine, for example, moderate doses can enhance typing skills but heavier doses begin to increase the number of errors. Furthermore, on tasks that are not well practised, even low doses may impair performance; the dose–response relationship is determined as much by the details of the response as the details of the drug's biochemistry.

The effects of a particular drug dosage also depend on the condition of the subject when the drug is administered. The *law of initial values* is an old concept that was first formulated to describe the effects of drugs on the cardiovascular system. Some drugs, for example, may be very effective in lowering blood pressure, but only if the blood pressure is abnormally high to begin with. This concept applies equally well in psychopharmacology, and is frequently referred to as the *rate–dependency* effect. Individuals who are already highly aroused may respond adversely to even small doses of a stimulant drug because it effectively increases the arousal to a level that interferes with performance. Similarly, many drugs that have antidepressant or antianxiety effects may produce relatively little change in the mood of individuals who are not suffering from depression or anxiety.

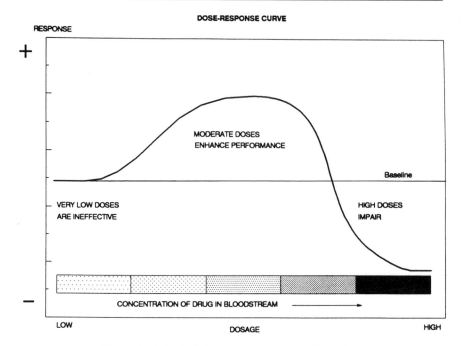

Figure 1 A typical dose–response curve for a drug

A particularly interesting drug effect is one that can occur when the dosage is zero. The *placebo* effect (placebo is Latin for "I will please") occurs when an inactive substance such as saline or a sugar capsule is represented as a drug, and leads to the relief of symptoms. This does not necessarily mean that either the initial symptoms or the relief of symptoms was imaginary. In the case of pain relief, for example, it is now clear that placebo effects are the result of the body's release of endogenous opiates in response to the belief that a drug was given. This type of behavioural effect is almost certainly a regular occurrence that increases or decreases the impact of real drug effects.

Given the intricate nature of the dose–response relationship, it should come as no surprise that subject variables play an important role. From childhood through senescence, there occur systematic changes in metabolism, body weight, and neurochemistry which can alter the effects of drugs. Hormonal differences between males and females, systematic differences in certain enzymes, and even cultural and climatic differences can further alter the effects of drugs. Finally, the individual's history of drug use may also produce long-term changes in metabolism of certain drugs that can either reduce their effectiveness (*tolerance*) or, less commonly, increase their effectiveness (*sensitization*). These contributing factors rarely appear on the labels of either prescription or non-prescription drugs, but should always be considered for patients who do not represent a typical category.

Drugs are not magic bullets: even under the most carefully controlled conditions, a particular drug can influence either multiple neurotransmitter systems or multiple systems that use the same neurotransmitter. The pattern of this combination of effects can change with drug dosage. As a result, drugs frequently have undesirable *side-effects*, but these complications may diminish with time or be controlled by adjusting the drug dosage. In many cases, the side-effects of the drug may mimic the symptoms of some other disorder, for example, a drug that successfully treats depression might cause anxiety. The existence of side-effects simply means that the effects of the drug on the brain are influencing pathways that are not specifically a part of the problem that was diagnosed.

The utility of any particular drug or elixir can be determined empirically. The successful treatment of previous patients can provide information about the most appropriate route of administration and dosage to use and the types of side-effects to watch for. For example, if it is observed that alcohol can reduce anxiety, the clinician might suggest that the anxious patient have a glass of wine with dinner. These types of observations and decisions have been useful in the development of folk medicines, but modern pharmacology relies more heavily on theory and mechanism. The development of a new and better drug treatment requires an understanding of both the disease process (i.e., the brain structures that are dysfunctional) and the way in which the drug alters this process (i.e., the neurochemical actions of the drug.) We turn now to a discussion of these mechanisms.

MECHANISMS OF DRUG ACTION IN THE BRAIN

One of the most elegant experiments in the history of pharmacology was performed in the mid-nineteenth century by a French physiologist, Claude Bernard (1813–1878). Explorers had brought back *curare*, a compound that native South Americans used as a poison on their blowgun darts to paralyse large mammals. Bernard was able to demonstrate that curare did not influence either the nerve fibres or the muscle fibres, but rather acted at the junction between these two structures (Bernard & Pelouze, 1850).

Several decades later, the English physiologist, Sir Charles S. Sherrington (1857–1952) studied the special properties of the junction between one neuron and the next, and coined the term *synapse* to label this gap (Sherrington, 1897). He observed that the transmission of messages through the synapse differed in several ways from electric transmission through the nerve fibre: (1) messages passed in only one direction, (2) messages were changed as they travelled through the synapse, (3) messages were delayed at the synapse by 0.5 millisecond, and (4) some messages inhibited other messages. Knowledge of electricity was still in its infancy, but it was known that electric signals could not mimic these features of the synapse.

At the beginning of the twentieth century, several researchers began to suspect that the transmission of messages across the synapse might involve chemicals. Many chemicals were known to influence the activity of the nervous system, and some of these (e.g., *acetylcholine* and *noradrenaline*) were present in the body. Although these chemicals could influence neuronal activity in laboratory preparations, there was no proof that they served as messengers under normal circumstances. The method of proof finally came to one of the researchers in a dream, and the German-American biochemist Otto Loewi (1873–1961) went into his laboratory on Easter Sunday in 1921 to perform the critical experiment.

Loewi's experiment was elegant and simple (Loewi, 1921). He dissected one frog's heart with a portion of the vagus nerve attached, a second heart without the vagus nerve, and placed them into separate containers of saline. Both hearts continued beating and, as expected from previous observations, electric stimulation of the vagus nerve caused the beating of the first heart to slow down. The clever part of the experiment was the pumping of the saline from the first beaker into the second. When this was done, the second heart also slowed down when the vagus nerve of the first heart was stimulated. There was no electric connection between the two hearts, and the only possible way that the message could be transmitted from one to the other was through the release of a chemical messenger into the surrounding fluid. Loewi dubbed the substance *Vagusstoff* (which turned out to be acetylcholine) and was later awarded the Nobel Prize for this first demonstration of the *chemical transmission* of neural messages.

Chemical messages could account for the special properties of the synapse observed by Sherrington (1897). The release of a chemical messenger by one neuron on to the next would restrict the flow of information to one direction. Specific types of chemical messengers might be expected to inhibit rather than excite the next neuron. The chemical message would not be expected to maintain the specific temporal features of the volley of impulses that caused its release. Finally, the time required for the release and delivery of the chemical message could easily account for the 0.5-millisecond delay that Sherrington had observed. Despite all of these explanations, it still required a bold imagination in the 1920s to believe that tiny neurons could release several hundred chemical messages per second to conduct the complex functions of the nervous system.

Because of its accessibility and known functions, the peripheral autonomic nervous system became the natural choice as a test system for studying chemical transmission. Following Loewi's experiment, it soon became apparent that acetylcholine served as a chemical messenger in several locations. It was released not only on to the heart muscle by the vagus nerve, but also on to the smooth muscles of all the organs and glands served by the

140

parasympathetic system. Furthermore, acetylcholine was the messenger at the synapses in both the sympathetic and parasympathetic ganglia. It was also the messenger at the nerve—muscle junction for the striated muscles of voluntary movement (where the receptors can be blocked by curare, as in Bernard's experiment). But it became clear that acetylcholine was not the only neurotransmitter. Some other substance was being released on to the smooth muscles by the fibres of the sympathetic system, and that substance was determined to be noradrenaline, a substance very closely related to adrenaline, the hormone of the adrenal gland.

Now, the logic and the power of chemical transmission began to unfold. When different systems were anatomically separate as in the case of the separate locations of the sympathetic and parasympathetic ganglia, the same neurotransmitter could be used without confusion. But when two opposing systems projected to the same organ, for example the heart, then the release of different chemical messengers (e.g., acetylcholine to slow the heartbeat; noradrenaline to speed the heartbeat) could determine the different functions. But the autonomic nervous system was not going to yield all of the answers this simply.

A particular transmitter substance did not always produce the same effect. In the case of acetylcholine, there were two *receptor* types, *muscarinic* and *nicotinic*, which responded to different aspects of the molecule. Similarly, in the case of noradrenaline, there were also two receptor types, termed *alpha* and *beta*. The early researchers were eager to categorize these different receptor types into functional categories. The initial suspicions that acetylcholine was always inhibitory and noradrenaline was always excitatory had already been disconfirmed. The discovery of different receptor types for each compound held the possibility that these could be classified as excitatory or inhibitory. But it was not to be — the specific receptor type is strictly for encoding the arrival of a message, and that message can be used as either a signal for excitation or inhibition.

While the details of chemical transmission were unfolding, other brain researchers had sought to relate anatomic structures of the brain to specific behavioural functions. Considerable progress was made in this effort, and research continues to sharpen the structure—function relationships. However, the discovery of chemical transmission required that yet another layer of organization be added — neurons within a particular anatomic structure could have different neurotransmitters.

One of the clearest examples of this was a set of experiments done by S. P. Grossman in 1960. Previous research had demonstrated that lesions of the lateral hypothalamus produced a dramatic reduction in both eating and drinking, whereas electric stimulation elicited both eating and drinking. Grossman was able to separate these functions by applying different chemicals directly into the lateral hypothalamus through a chronically implanted cannula. Drugs that mimic acetylcholine elicited drinking only, whereas drugs that mimic noradrenaline elicited eating only. Drugs that block acetyl-choline receptors reduced drinking in thirsty rats, whereas drugs that block noradrenaline receptors reduced eating in hungry rats. These results provided a finer grained analysis than the experiments that were based strictly on anatomy. Within the anatomic boundaries of the lateral hypothalamus are chemically coded functions for eating (noradrenergic) and drinking (cholinergic).

Given the knowledge that chemical coding at synapses is superimposed on anatomic subdivisions, we can now begin to understand how drugs can produce their specific effects on behaviour. The third column of Table 1 describes the action of the drug at the level of the individual neuron or synapse as illustrated in Figure 2. As more of the blanks in this table are filled, we gain a better understanding of the relationship between behaviour and its underlying pharmacologic bases. Drugs can be classified, for example, as *mimickers* of neurotransmitters, *blockers* of receptors, *facilitators* of neuro-transmitter release, *presynaptic blockers* of activity, *inhibitors* of specific enzymes, and so forth. The list of neurotransmitters grew slowly at first

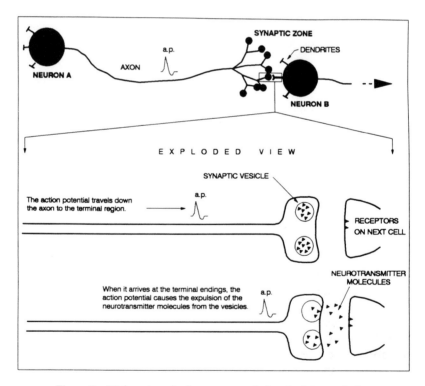

Figure 2 Major steps in the process of chemical transmission

Table 2 Some of the many neurotransmitters

Acetylcholine	Peptides (several dozen)
Serotonin	Enkephalins (opiate-like)
Adrenaline	Leu-enkephalin
Dopamine	Met-enkephalin
Noradrenaline	
Amino acids	GABA
Aspartate	Histamine
Glycine	Carbon monoxide
Glutamate	Nitric oxide
Others	Others

Note: GABA = gamma amino butyric acid

(acetylcholine, noradrenaline, dopamine), but since the early 1980s the list has exploded to more than 100 different chemicals (see Table 2).

Drugs that influence behaviour must do so by influencing the brain, and there are several features of the brain that have contributed to a widespread misunderstanding of its basic character. Neurons, unlike most other cells, do not undergo cell division, so the brain contains virtually all of its cells at the time of birth. These cells are already committed to the general *structure–function relationships* that are seen in the adult brain, thus encouraging the view of the brain as a stable, organized set of neural circuits with individual experiences simply selecting different combinations of existing pathways; not unlike the structure of a computer (the hardware) that can be used for a host of different functions (the software).

This view of the brain as a static set of complex circuits is wrong. Although the general features and structure–function relationships are fixed, the details of neuronal actions are dynamic and constantly changing. When certain activity in the brain acts repeatedly to produce some behaviour, the circuits that are active can undergo physical changes (e.g., increased production of neurotransmitter molecules, expansion of the branching terminals of the axons, increased complexity of the receiving dendritic tree, increased number of receptors, etc.) which result in the enhanced efficiency of the system. The behaviour that is produced can produce changes in the environment, and changes in the environment (whether mediated by behaviour or not) can, in turn, produce changes in the brain.

A good way to conceptualize this (see Figure 3) is to view the brain, behaviour, and the environment as an interacting triangle, with each dimension influencing the other two (cf. Hamilton & Timmons, 1990). These interpenetrating effects require a more complex view of the results of various experimental manipulations. Although a particular drug may produce a very specific change in behaviour, we must not fall into the trap of viewing this as a singular effect. The neuronal systems that were directly influenced by the

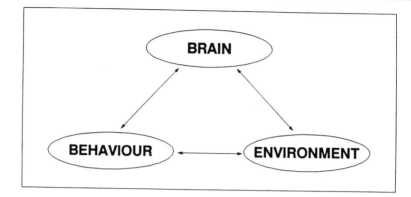

Figure 3 The brain, behaviour, and environment interact continually, and each changes the other two

drug will also undergo a longer-term change as a result of the drug's presence (and absence). The resulting behaviour will change the environment and that change will change other aspects of behaviour, and so forth. An appreciation of this dynamic interaction helps to provide a more complete understanding of the effects of drugs on behaviour.

The discipline of psychopharmacology in its modern form arose from the convergence of two separate areas of study: first, the growing information about neurotransmission and the drugs that influenced it, and second, B. F. Skinner's development of *operant conditioning* techniques for the study of behaviour. Skinner's methodology (e.g., Reynolds, 1975) provided powerful methods for analysing behavioural change, and numerous animal models began to emerge for the screening of potentially useful drugs. The antipsychotic drugs rather specifically interfered with conditioned emotional responses, anti-anxiety drugs blocked the normal response to punishment, stimulant and depressant drugs changed general levels of activity, and so forth. The efficiency of these procedures greatly facilitated the accumulation of knowledge about the effects of drugs on behaviour, and became an indispensable link in the pathway of drugs from the chemist's bench to the pharmacist's shelf.

MECHANISMS OF DRUG ACTIONS ON BEHAVIOUR

Drugs that alter moods and states of consciousness

Central nervous system stimulants

Drugs can be classified as stimulants based on their ability to produce behavioural arousal, characteristic patterns of electroencephalographic

144

(EEG) arousal, increases in motor activity, or some combination of these. These changes can be accomplished by several different mechanisms of action.

The so-called convulsant drugs such as *strychnine*, *picrotoxin*, and *pentylenetetrazol* are representative of the different modes of action. Strychnine blocks the receptors for *glycine*, an inhibitory neurotransmitter. Picrotoxin reduces chloride permeability through its actions on the *GABA receptor complex*. (Gamma amino butyric acid, or GABA, is the most widespread neurotransmitter in the brain.) Pentylenetetrazol decreases the recovery time between action potentials by increasing potassium permeability of the axon. Drugs such as *caffeine*, *theophylline*, and *theobromine* (present in coffee, tea, and chocolate) stimulate the activity of neurons by increasing the calcium permeability of membranes. Note that all of these drugs produce rather general effects that can influence neurons irrespective of the particular neurotransmitter system, and the state induced by these drugs is sometimes referred to as *non-specific arousal*. In low to moderate dosages they can enhance learning and performance in a wide variety of situations, but with higher dosages, behaviour is impaired and dangerous seizures can be induced.

The *amphetamines* and *cocaine* may be the best-known stimulant drugs, and both categories have rather specific effects on neurons that release dopamine or noradrenaline. Although the effects are not entirely specific, amphetamine stimulates these neurons by promoting the release of these neurotransmitters, while cocaine tends to block their reuptake. The restriction of the drug effects to a certain class of neurons is mirrored by a more specific change in behaviour. Some non-specific arousal can be observed, but these two types of drugs have a profound effect in situations that involve specific behavioural responses that result in reward.

Central nervous system depressants

Drugs that are classified as central nervous system (CNS) depressants appear to act on two major neurotransmitter systems. One of the neurotransmitters of sleep is *serotonin*, and certain drugs that enhance the activity of serotonin can induce drowsiness and sleep. The other important neurotransmitter is *GABA*, and the more common sedative and hypnotic drugs (e.g., the *benzodiazepines*, *barbiturates*, and *alcohol*) tend to produce their effects by acting on the GABA receptor complex. Acting on a special receptor site, they facilitate the action of GABA and inhibit neuronal activity by increasing the permeability of the neuronal membranes to chloride ions.

The *narcotic* drugs deserve special mention as CNS depressants. Extracts of the opium poppy have been used for thousands of years for both medicinal (pain relief) and recreational (general sense of well-being) effects. *Opium* (a mixture of *morphine* and *codeine*) is naturally occurring, whereas *heroin* is a synthetic drug. The powerful effects of these drugs could not be explained by their actions on any of the known neurotransmitters. Finally, in the 1970s, it was determined that some neurons had specific receptors for these compounds, and that the body produced a variety of different substances (some chemical neurotransmitters and some hormones) that acted like the narcotic drugs. These endogenous morphine-like substances, termed *endorphins*, are released in response to various types of pain or stress.

Hallucinogens

Although drugs that stimulate or depress the general activity of the brain lead to changes in the interaction with the environment, these changes tend to be more quantitative than qualitative. Hallucinogens, on the other hand, produce fundamental changes in the sensorium. Visual and auditory distortions and imagery may be experienced. Tactile sensations may occur without stimulus. In some cases there may occur a conflation of experiences, called synesthesia, in which visual experiences may be "heard" or tactile experiences "seen" in ways that almost never occur in the absence of the drug. The drugs that produce these changes are derived from a variety of different plant sources as well as synthetic sources and tend to produce changes in many different neurotransmitter systems. The mechanism of action that causes the hallucinations remains clouded, but there is a growing consensus that these drugs act on serotonin receptors.

Some observations on abuse and addiction

If a drug is administered repeatedly, there is frequently a reduction in the effectiveness of the drug, called tolerance. This can occur through several different mechanisms: (1) liver enzymes may be induced to speed up drug degradation; (2) presynaptic neurons may increase or decrease the production of neurotransmitters; (3) postsynaptic neurons may increase or decrease the number of receptors; and (4) opposing systems may increase or decrease their activity. Typically, more than one of these countermeasures is launched, and the brain's activity gradually becomes more normalized despite the presence of the drug.

Tolerance sets the stage for another phenomenon. If the drug administration is suddenly stopped, the mechanisms of tolerance are unmasked and *withdrawal symptoms* occur. As a result of the mechanisms of tolerance, the brain functions more normally in the presence of a drug than in its absence.

The types of tolerance described above are referred to as *pharmacological tolerance*. These mechanisms cannot always account for the observed decline in response to the drug. For example, amphetamine reduces the amount of milk that rats will drink during a daily session, but by the tenth day, drinking has returned to normal levels. However, if the drug is administered alone for ten days, and milk is offered on the eleventh day, the drug still suppresses

146

drinking. The return to normal drinking requires learning to perform the behaviour in the presence of the drug. This type of effect is known as *behavioural tolerance* (Carlton & Wolgin, 1971).

The facts that many drugs have direct rewarding effects and that tolerance can develop to these rewarding effects can lead to motivation for *self-administration* of drugs. Drugs that have the capacity to produce such motivation typically share three characteristics: they act on the central nervous system, they act rapidly, and the cessation of use produces withdrawal symptoms. These characteristics can produce an *acquired motivational state* (i.e., a desire or motivation for the effects of the drug) which can lead to addiction or abuse of the drug. The narcotic drugs are among the most potent in this regard.

Just as some individuals may be more sensitive to the effects of a drug because of differences in metabolism, specific neurotransmitter activity, or other subject variables, so might some individuals be more susceptible to acquiring the motivational states that we call addiction or substance abuse. There is growing evidence that this susceptibility may have a genetic basis. In the case of alcohol abuse, for example, there is a clear tendency for sons of alcoholics to be more likely to become alcoholics, and preliminary evidence points to a genetic defect that may alter the response to reward (e.g., Blum, 1991). This and related evidence may soon provide a physiologic basis for the somewhat ill-chosen term, *addictive personality*.

Drugs used to treat disorders of behaviour

Antipsychotics

The discovery of the drugs that are used to treat psychoses (primarily *schizophrenia*) followed a strange and fascinating pathway. A French surgeon, Henri Laborit, was convinced in the 1940s that many of the deaths associated with surgery could be attributed to the patients' own fears about the dangers of surgery (see Palfai & Jankiewicz, 1991, p. 10). Attempts to reduce this distress with sedatives or by blocking the autonomic nervous system were only marginally effective. Laborit concluded that what was needed was a drug that could dissolve the fear response itself – in his words, a Pavlovian deconditioner. His search led to one of the newly developed anti-histamine compounds (promethazine), and a variant of this compound, *chlorpromazine*, proved to be dramatically effective. Patients who received this drug pre-surgically were calm, minimally sedated, and the incidence of deaths from surgical shock was greatly reduced.

Soon, of course, the use of chlorpromazine spread to the psychiatric clinic and was found to produce an equally dramatic reversal of the symptoms of schizophrenia. Chlorpromazine and related *phenothiazine* drugs were responsible for the release of hundreds of thousands of patients from institutions where they otherwise would have spent the remainder of their lives in heavy sedation, in strait-jackets, or other restraints. The patients were not cured, but for many, they were able for the first time in years to engage in relatively normal day-to-day interactions.

Laborit's characterization of chlorpromazine as a Pavlovian deconditioner was upheld. In proper doses, the phenothiazines can specifically reduce signalled avoidance responding in animals while not influencing the direct response to an aversive stimulus. More recently, an even more specific animal (and human) model of this disorder has been developed by Jeffrey Gray and his colleagues at the University of London (see Baruch, Hemsley, & Gray, 1988). They view much of the anxiety associated with schizophrenia as being the result of a discordance between current perceptions and perceived regularities of past events. For example, normal individuals who have heard 30 presentations of a bell do not readily acquire a conditional response (sometimes called a conditioned response) if this bell is now paired with electric shock – a phenomenon known as *latent inhibition*. Patients suffering from schizophrenia are impaired in latent inhibition, and this deficit is normalized by chlorpromazine.

These antipsychotic drugs produce a variety of effects on neurons, but almost certainly produce their beneficial effects by blocking the *D2 receptor* for dopamine. When all of the drugs in common clinical use are rank-ordered according to their potency, the rank-ordering is identical to that achieved when they are rank-ordered according to their ability to block the D2 receptor. A similar order is obtained when they are ranked according to their specific ability to inhibit avoidance responding, and given time, there will almost certainly be a similar concordance when rank-ordered in terms of their effects on latent inhibition.

These close relationships between clinically useful drugs, animal models, affinity to specific receptors, and theoretical models of neurotransmitters and behaviour have brought us to a point where it is not unrealistic to suppose that schizophrenia can be understood in the foreseeable future, perhaps even prevented or cured.

Anti-anxiety drugs

The success of chlorpromazine in dissolving the acute fears that surround surgery as well as the pervasive fears that torment the psychotic mind led to the search for milder drugs that could allay more commonplace anxieties. The barbiturate drugs (and alcohol) had been used with some success, but dosages that reduced anxiety also produced troublesome side-effects of sedation. This situation led to the marketing of *meprobamate*, which was claimed to ease anxiety without sedation. This drug became very popular, even though it was in fact just a mild barbiturate that had as many sedative effects as the other drugs in this class.

148

Although meprobamate did not live up to its initial promise, the claims of specificity did promote the search for other drugs that could have these effects. By the early 1960s two such drugs (*chlordiazepoxide* and *diazepam*) had been discovered. Marketed under the trade names of Librium and Valium, these drugs quickly became the most widely prescribed drugs of their time.

Chlordiazepoxide and related *benzodiazepine* compounds were initially termed minor tranquillizers (as contrasted with the antipsychotics that were known as major tranquillizers), but this terminology fell into disfavour and they are now known simply as anti-anxiety compounds. Nearly all of the compounds in this class act by facilitating the activity of the neurotransmitter GABA. The so-called GABA receptor complex is a complicated structure that has a GABA site, a sedative/convulsant site, and a benzodiazepine site. There is now growing evidence that the brain manufactures its own anti-anxiety compounds that are released during periods of stress.

Antidepressants

Antidepressants are drugs that help to reverse mood states which are characterized by sadness, lack of self-esteem, and general depression. A variety of animal models of this disorder has linked depression to the *monoamines*, especially noradrenaline and serotonin.

The first drugs to be used in the treatment of depression were discovered by accident. Tuberculosis patients who were being treated with a new drug called iproniazid seemed to be enjoying a remarkable recovery, but it was soon learned that while their tuberculosis remained unaffected, their understandable mood of depression was being elevated by the drug. It was later learned that *iproniazid* and related drugs inhibit the activity of an enzyme known as *monoamine oxidase* (MAO), and tend to gradually elevate the level of activity of neurons that utilize dopamine or noradrenaline as neurotransmitters.

The search for better and safer drugs to treat depression led to the discovery of a class of compounds called the *tricyclic antidepressants*, so named because their basic chemical structure includes three carbon rings. Most of these compounds appear to act by blocking the re-uptake of dopamine and noradrenaline, but some of them also block the re-uptake of serotonin, some block serotonin alone, and some have no known effect on any of these systems.

Some patients who suffer from depression also have recurrent episodes of manic behaviour. This disorder, known as *bipolar disorder*, is treated most successfully by the administration of *lithium* salts. Lithium tends to stabilize the neurons, preventing the development of mania that is usually followed by a period of deep depression. The neuronal mechanism remains somewhat mysterious, although recent evidence suggests that lithium blocks the

149

synthesis of a *second messenger*, a neuronal compound that promotes long-term changes in the general capacity for synaptic activity (Lickey & Gordon, 1991, chap. 14).

FUTURE DIRECTIONS

The future of psychopharmacology contains many challenges. Certainly one of the major challenges is to understand the biological bases of substance abuse in sufficient detail to allow the prevention and treatment of these devastating disorders. The foundations for this are already in place: the neurotransmitters and anatomic circuitry of the reward system are known in some detail; the psychology of reward and motivational systems has unravelled many of the behavioural contributions to substance abuse; and genetic studies have begun to demonstrate the possibility of predicting and understanding individual differences in the vulnerability of these systems (Kaplan & Sadock, 1985; Lickey & Gordon, 1991).

A second set of challenges involves the development of more specific drugs ("magic bullets") which can restore the victims of depression, schizophrenia, anxiety, and other disorders to normality. Again, the development of these drugs will require a detailed understanding of the neurotransmitters, specific receptor types, and sophisticated understanding of the behavioural contributions to the disorders.

A third, related set of challenges will be to provide drugs that treat and otherwise modify behaviours that are of day-to-day concern for many people: drugs that can facilitate memory, counteract the effects of ageing on cognitive abilities, normalize food intake, and so forth. Some might claim that the availability of more drugs will serve only to exacerbate the problems that we already face with drug abuse. However, drug use and abuse are as old as humankind, and we can only benefit from a better understanding of the effects of drugs on the brain's control of behaviour.

FURTHER READING

Andreasen, N. C. (1984). *The broken brain: The biological revolution in psychiatry*. New York: Harper & Row.

Hamilton, L. W., & Timmons, C. R. (1990). *Principles of behavioral pharmacology: A biopsychological perspective*. Englewood Cliffs, NJ: Prentice-Hall.

Kalat, J. W. (1992). *Biological psychology* (4th edn). Belmont, CA: Wadsworth.

Lickey, M. E., & Gordon, B. (1991). *Medicine and mental illness*. New York: Freeman.

Snyder, S. H. (1986). *Drugs and the brain*. New York: Scientific American.

REFERENCES

Baruch, I., Hemsley, D. R., & Gray, J. (1988). Differential performance of acute and chronic schizophrenics in the latent inhibition task. *Journal of Nervous and Mental Diseases*, *176*, 598–606.

Bernard, C., & Pelouze, T. J. (1850). Recherches sur le curare. *Comptes Rendus Hebdomadaires des Séances de l'Academie des Sciences*, Paris, *31*, 533–537.

Blum, K. (1991). *Alcohol and the addictive brain*. New York: Free Press.

Carlton, P. L., & Wolgin, D. L. (1971). Contingent tolerance to the anorexigenic effects of amphetamine. *Physiology and Behavior*, *7*, 221–223.

Gilman, A. G., Goodman, L. S., & Gilman, A. (Eds) (1980). *Goodman and Gilman's the pharmacological basis of therapeutics* (6th edn). New York: Macmillan.

Grossman, S. P. (1960). Eating or drinking elicited by direct adrenergic or cholinergic stimulation of hypothalamus. *Science*, *132*, 301–302.

Hamilton, L. W., & Timmons, C. R. (1990). *Principles of behavioral pharmacology: A biopsychological perspective*. Englewood Cliffs, NJ: Prentice-Hall.

Kaplan, H. I., & Sadock, B. J. (Eds) (1985). *Comprehensive textbook of psychiatry*. Baltimore, MD: Williams & Wilkins.

Lickey, M. E., & Gordon, B. (1991). *Medicine and mental illness*. New York: Freeman.

Loewi, O. (1921). Über humorale Übertragbarkeit der Herznervenwirkung. *Pflügers Archiv für die gesamte Physiologie des Menschen und der Tiere*, *189*, 239–242.

Palfai, T., & Jankiewicz, H. (1991). *Drugs and human behavior*. Dubuque, IA: Wm C. Brown.

Physicians' desk reference (1992). Oradell, NJ: Medical Economics.

Reynolds, G. S. (1975). *A primer of operant conditioning*. Glenview, IL: Scott, Foresman.

Sherrington, C. S. (1897). The central nervous system. In M. Foster (Ed.) *A text book of physiology* (7th edn, vol. 3). London: Macmillan.

3
SENSATION AND PERCEPTION

INTRODUCTION

Sensation, in the terminology of contemporary psychology, is the acquisition of "raw" information by the body's external and internal sense organs. Sensation is traditionally distinguished from perception, which is the processing and interpretation of sensations. It is worth pointing out, however, that many psychologists and philosophers deny the possibility of a "raw" sensation without any processing or interpretation, so the distinction, though well established by custom and practice, is in fact scientifically and philosophically controversial or even dubious.

This is perhaps the most difficult section of the encyclopedia, but it contains some of the most substantial contributions in the whole of psychology. The two facts are not unrelated: it is largely because sensation and perception have been more thoroughly researched than other psychological phenomena that our understanding of them is relatively advanced and therefore far from simple. They were the first areas of psychology to receive sustained experimental investigation: in Leipzig, Germany, the pioneering research of the physiologist Ernst Heinrich Weber (published in 1846) and of the philosopher-mystic Gustav Theodor Fechner (published in 1860) established mathematical laws of sensation that formed the basis of what is nowadays called psychophysics (chapter 3.5).

In chapter 3.1 Peter C. Dodwell outlines the fundamental processes of vision, the sense modality that has attracted by far the most attention from researchers. His discussion begins with the unresolved controversy over nativism (the doctrine that our perceptual capacities are inborn) versus empiricism (the doctrine that nothing is innate in the mind); for a historical perspective on that debate see chapter 1.2 (Raymond E. Fancher). He then describes the physiology of the visual system, and all the major phenomena of vision, including space and object perception, perceptual illusions, and stereoscopic depth perception.

In chapter 3.2 Mike G. Harris and Glyn W. Humphreys provide an introduction to modern computational theories of vision, focusing chiefly on object perception. This approach seeks to show in detail how the pattern of light falling on the retinas of the eyes is (or could be) transformed into a symbolic representation of the objects in the field of vision; this has turned out to be a vastly more complicated and challenging enterprise than anyone had anticipated. For a further discussion of computational theories of vision in the context of formal models of psychological processes in general, see chapter 4.5 (Alan Garnham).

In chapter 3.3 Brian C. J. Moore provides a comprehensive survey of hearing, from the structure and function of the auditory system to the perception of loudness, pitch, and timbre, the temporal resolution of the ear, and the localization of sounds in space. In chapter 3.4 Harvey R. Schiffman introduces the skin senses (touch and pressure, temperature, and pain), the body senses (the internal sensations of posture, location, movement, and balance that are called kinaesthesis and the vestibular sense), and the chemical senses (taste and smell). Finally, in chapter 3.5 Donald Laming explains the fundamental methods and findings of psychophysics, which deals with the relationship between the strength of (psychological) sensations and the intensity of the (physical) stimuli that give rise to them, hence the term *psychophysics*. The relationship is obviously not straightforward, because if you walk into a dark room and switch on one, and then another, 60-watt light bulb, the room does not seem twice as brightly lit when the physical intensity of the light is doubled. The relationship turns out to be governed by intriguing mathematical laws that are explained in chapter 3.5.

A.M.C.

3.1

FUNDAMENTAL PROCESSES IN VISION

Peter C. Dodwell

Queen's University, Ontario, Canada

Reading a book, hearing a familiar song, recognizing a friend's face – all are characteristic acts of perception which occur so effortlessly that we take them for granted. Yet the study of perception is a major field in modern psychology, and one that is full of new and interesting challenges. In order to understand the processes of seeing we have to understand the nature of the physical events that give rise to perception, the physiological processes that record them, and the psychological abilities of the perceiver that make sense of them.

Perception is the primary process by means of which we obtain knowledge of the world: it has been estimated that more than 80 per cent of it is accounted for by vision. Certainly the visual system is by far the most thoroughly studied of the senses (conventionally five are recognized: sight, hearing, taste, touch, and smell) and the best understood. Perception is a skill, or set of skills, not simply the passive recording of external stimulation

155

(Gibson, 1966). A perceiving organism is more like a map-reader than a camera. What we so easily accept in perceiving and understanding the world involves complex processes at many levels. Psychological research on seeing extends all the way from the study of the electrical activity of single cells in the eye or brain, to colour vision, the perception of objects and events, learning to read, and understanding the complexity of an air traffic controller's video console.

The early investigation of perception, as with so much of psychology, started with philosophical speculation about how the senses work, and what role they might play in the acquisition of knowledge. Much of this early work involved intellectual justification for claiming that our senses supply reliable and valid knowledge about the world and ourselves. It was only in the middle of the nineteenth century that the scientific and experimental study of these matters came into being, and some of the first psychological laboratories were established in Germany for the study of the senses, including vision, in the second half of the nineteenth century (Boring, 1950).

NATIVISM AND EMPIRICISM

Two themes dominated the early psychological research on vision, themes that were derived from established philosophical traditions. On the one hand there was the view, derived from the British *empiricist* philosophers of the seventeenth and eighteenth centuries, principally John Locke (1632–1704), George Berkeley (1685–1753), and David Hume (1711–1776), that all our knowledge is based ultimately on the senses, the elementary sensations being as it were the building blocks of knowledge, all else being secondary, influenced by habit, assumption, memory, and the like. These would help to build up our representation of the world – this view is also called "constructivist" – but the primary elements of knowledge are even so given in the simple "raw" sensations.

In contrast was the nativist position, deriving from the rationalism of the French philosopher René Descartes (1596–1650), which claimed that the senses are fallible, all true knowledge thus needing to be grounded in clear thinking, reasoning, and the innate capacity to order and refine the messages of the senses. These opposed views are still reflected in the theoretical and practical activities of modern psychologists, but in the 1890s they dominated the field to a remarkable degree. On the one hand Hermann von Helmholtz (1821–1894), the great physicist and psychologist, held that all sensory stimulation is inherently ambiguous, and true perception required the active participation of the perceiver in order to succeed (he called this process "unconscious inference"), and on the other hand stood the physiologist Ewald Hering (1834–1918), champion of the notion that understanding of psychological processes was mainly dependent on the investigation of the neural activity supporting it, thus having an innate basis.

156

In the present day, it would be difficult to find a supporter of either of these positions in their simple form, but they still exist as the poles, as it were, of the spectrum of theoretical positions perceptual psychologists adopt. It is now much more a matter of investigating the manner in which innate processes interact with, or are influenced by, experience of different kinds, and in this regard we shall see that much progress has been made.

THE PHYSIOLOGY OF THE VISUAL SYSTEM

There is a well-defined area of the brain and its associated "inputs" which is known as the primary visual system (Dreher & Robinson, 1991). It is illustrated in Figure 1. The eyes are, of course, the organs by means of which we gain visual access to the world; we say that light is the "adequate stimulus" to vision. Visual sensations can be produced in other ways, for example by

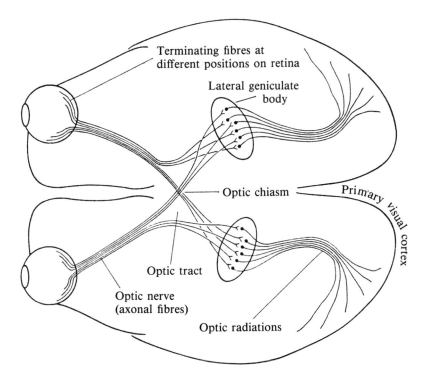

Figure 1 The basic layout of the human "primary visual system", greatly simplified. Light enters the eyes, is captured and transduced into physiological signals at the retina, which is a multi-layered neural complex at the back of the eye. These signals are transmitted to the visual area of the brain, also called the occipital cortex

157

chemical, thermal, or mechanical means, but these do not supply reliable and interpretable information about the world in the same way as light. A great deal is known about the physiological substrate to vision and this knowledge is fundamental to our understanding of how we see, what constitutes "normal" perception, and how the mature perceptual system develops.

The central nervous system is made up of many sorts of specialized cells, or neurons, which record, transmit, and modify signals that are essentially electrical pulses. Neurons are connected together, and the manner and place of these connections determine different physiological systems. In the case of vision, specialized neurons in the retina of the eye receive light, and cause neural signals to be generated that are transmitted through the various pathways (illustrated in Figure 1) to the posterior portion of the brain. Notice that there are various relay stations on the way to the brain cortex, at which information is sorted and refined. Of particular importance are the retina, that light-sensitive area at the back of the eye on to which light is focused by the optical lens at the front of the eye (see Figure 2) and the lateral geniculate bodies of the midbrain, where signals from the two eyes are first "mixed". The whole anatomical and physiological basis for vision is one of extraordinary complexity and delicacy, and it is mainly since the early 1960s that a detailed knowledge of how it works has been attained.

The major breakthrough came with the ability to record from single neurons in different parts of the system, starting with its peripheral part, namely the retina of the eye, and culminating in the impressive work of David Hubel and Torsten Wiesel of Harvard University who, in 1962, first reported on recordings from single neurons in the brain cortex of the cat. For this they justly earned a Nobel Prize (Hubel & Wiesel, 1962).

The interconnections of neurons in the brain are so dense and complex that

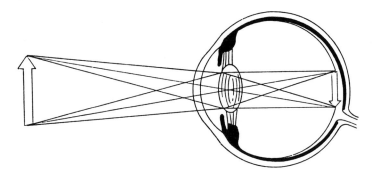

Figure 2 A diagram of the eyeball. Light enters through the pupil and is focused into sharp images on the retina by the lens. This part of the visual apparatus is much like a camera; or perhaps we should more truthfully say that the camera is like an eye

one might well despair of ever being able to understand what the function of individual neurons might be. Yet the remarkable discovery of Hubel and Wiesel was that usually this function is not too difficult to describe and analyse. Before them it had been widely accepted that the connections at birth between neurons must be essentially random, and that it would be the function of experience to "tune up" the system so that it could deal adequately with the information supplied to it through the eyes. Indeed this was the basis of a celebrated and widely accepted theory of perceptual learning due to the Canadian psychologist D. O. Hebb (1949). These developments are discussed in Dodwell (1970).

Hubel and Wiesel were able to show that most neurons in the primary visual area of the brain are specialized so that they respond to quite specific features of the environment. Like the ganglion cells of the retina, each cortical cell has a *retinal receptive field*, that is, a circumscribed and usually small area of the retina to which it responds. Moreover most of them are activated by short lines at a particular orientation within the receptive field. For example, there are some cells that respond to a horizontal line at the centre of the visual field, others prefer vertical or diagonal lines in other parts of the field, and so on. The important point is that they all have a definite preference, which can be quite readily defined. What the role of these *feature detectors* may be in the larger scheme of visual perception, and how they are to be understood as the building blocks for the development of a mature perceiving organism, are questions we shall defer for the moment. One of the most telling of Hubel and Wiesel's discoveries was the fact that the high degree of specificity in *stimulus coding*, as it is called, is innate in the kitten. They found that young kittens, prior to any visual experience, have in place a coding system with many of the features of adult vision. To be sure it is not so precise, and it can be modified to some degree by experience, but basically the system is in place at birth. There is good reason to suppose that what is true of the kitten is true of other mammals, including humans. Thus the empiricism of the psychologist Hebb was to a great extent overtaken by the discoveries of Hubel and Wiesel (and subsequently very many other investigators) concerning the actual physiological mechanisms in place at birth.

Does this mean that nativism has won the day? No, because we shall see later that the built-in coding system is itself subject to modification in the light of experience. This will demonstrate how in modern research the simplistic division between nativism and empiricism has been replaced by a far more sophisticated and informative account of how innate factors interact with experienced events to shape the mature visual system – and the adult perceiver (Cronly-Dillon, 1991).

Since Hubel and Wiesel's discoveries, much more has been discovered about how the visual brain works. The different sensory qualities of contour, movement, colour, and depth have all been found to be processed in anatomically distinct "channels" which even have separate "maps" in different

159

parts of the brain cortex (Maunsell & Newsome, 1987). Certain "higher order" neurons that are sensitive to more complicated aspects of the visual field than simple oriented line segments have been identified, even some that respond to hands, moving human bodies, and faces (Perrett et al., 1985)! We shall have to pass over this exciting work in the interest of describing other important and less specialized aspects of the visual system.

This brief survey of the physiological basis of vision has shown that the broad outline of the areas of the brain involved in seeing are well known, and that the detailed operation of many of the individual parts is understood, at least as far as the operations of the neurons in them is concerned. This is only a basis, however, and there is much more to learn about the nature of seeing, and how its properties have been investigated and understood.

THE VISUAL WORLD: SPACE AND OBJECT PERCEPTION

The most obvious property of our visual world is that it is extended in space and time. The spatial character is to be understood in terms of the formation of a sharp image of the visual scene on the retina of the eye (Figure 2). This spatial image is reproduced, at least approximately, in the visual cortex of the brain (Figure 1). We call the image in the eye the "retinal image"; some but by no means all the properties of seeing can be understood in terms of it. The retinal image depends on the optical properties of both the environment and the eye. As Figure 3 shows, the size of the image depends on the distance between eye and object, but we know very well that perceived size does not vary to anything like the degree to be expected in these terms. Your friends do not suddenly shrink in size as they move away from you! This discrepancy between what the retinal image might lead one to expect, and the actual "phenomenological" appearance (that is, how things really appear to the observer) is called *perceptual constancy*, and occurs not only for size, but also for shape, colour, and brightness, among others. In each case what is meant by constancy is the fact that what one sees (the phenomenon) is far *less* variable than what an analysis of the optical and other physical features of the stimulating environment would lead one to expect. To take another

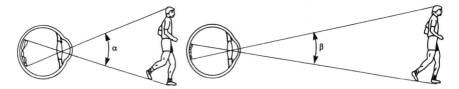

Figure 3 The retinal image, and visual angle. The size of the retinal image is measured in terms of *visual angle*, which is clearly dependent on both physical size, and distance

example, consider the appearance of a book with a blue cover. You look at it in bright daylight, or in the artificial illumination of a neon lamp, you stretch out the arm that holds it, or turn it away from you. In each case the stimulation reaching your retina implies (if it does not demand) that what you see should vary markedly. Yet what you do see is a book with quite stable visual characteristics. Constancy has done its job without your cooperation or awareness. It is factors of this sort that led Helmholtz to talk of "unconscious inference", and empiricists generally to question whether a simple account of the physiological processing systems involved could ever reach a satisfactory account of the nature of perception (Rock, 1984).

A more general aspect of the empiricist stance, stemming from the views of Bishop Berkeley, one of the empiricist philosophers who did so much to establish one pole of the theoretical debate discussed above, is this: the retinal image is essentially *ambiguous*; many different stimulus configurations could in principle give rise to one and the same retinal image (a wine bottle viewed from 50 cm versus a half-bottle viewed from 40 cm, for example). Therefore some *non-visual* information must be added to the visual to achieve veridical perception. The roles of different cues, both visual and non-visual, in achieving both a true representation of the world, and in manipulating our perceptions in amusing and sometimes confusing ways, were explored by a group of American psychologists who called themselves *transactionalists*. For them perception was a transaction between observer and environment – yet another twist on the empiricist theme (Kilpatrick, 1961). Results of their research can be seen in the distorted rooms and similar illusory displays to be found in many a science centre. The best known of these is a distorted room in which, from a certain vantage point, the retinal image is identical to that which would be produced by a normal "four square" room. When the room is viewed from this point, it does indeed appear normal, and we may have difficulty in being persuaded otherwise. In such a room strong illusions of size and distance can be induced. All this shows with remarkable force how easy it is to manipulate visual cues to yield non-veridical percepts. It demonstrates how much we are creatures of habit, in this case the cognitive habits induced by the properties of our stable visual surroundings.

Our perceptual world is indeed usually very stable, yields few surprises, and is not subject to misinterpretation. No doubt this is why non-psychologists normally pay little attention to how they perceive, and may be surprised that there is so much about perception that requires investigation and explanation. It is stable because most of our percepts are *overdetermined*; visual cues are mutually consistent and are reinforced by tactile, auditory, and other information about what is in the world. Only a philosopher would question whether the object in front of us is really a solid table, or the person we're talking to a robot. The world is just too consistent for us to worry about such things. But it is still true that we take a great deal on trust. It is not difficult to break the trust, and doing so can be revealing.

161

PERCEPTUAL ILLUSIONS

Everyone is familiar with visual illusions of different types. A small sample of the best known is shown in Figures 4–6. Far from being mere party amusements, these illusions can help us to understand quite a bit about perception. First, why do we call them illusions? Because, as with the distorted room, there is a discrepancy between what common sense, habit, or geometrical intuition tells us should be seen, and what we actually see. Consider the Müller-Lyer illusion of Figure 4a. The two horizontal lines are of equal length, yet are seen as different. It has been proposed that the illusion is induced by false intimations of perspective (as in the Ponzo illusion, Figure 4e), yet this cannot be the whole story, as other versions of the Müller-Lyer, as in Figure 4b–d, do not share the perspective interpretation. Perhaps illusions are caused by the way information is coded by physiological mechanisms in some cases, or by the way the layout is interpreted, or by simple misinterpretation of distance cues. Study of the illusions is important, but the fact is they seem to raise almost as many questions as they answer. No one theory of the illusions has gained universal acceptance; perhaps their main challenge is in reminding us of the many different factors that can enter into perceptual processing, and alerting us to the need to be flexible in thinking about how we come to know the world through seeing.

Some aspects of perception can be understood if we know about the coding

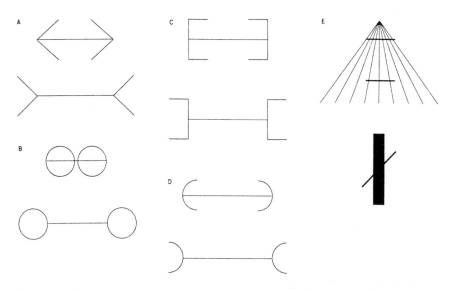

Figure 4 Some of the best-known simple visual illusions (of which there are hundreds). 4a, the Müller-Lyer illusion, is perhaps the best known, and most studied, of them all. 4b–d show some variations on the same theme. Figure 4e is the Ponzo illusion (top) and the Poggendorf (bottom)

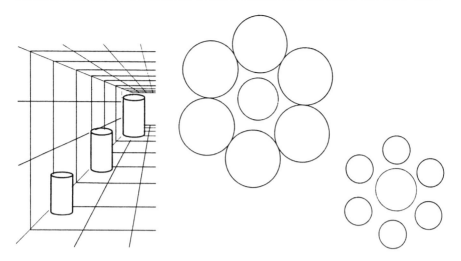

Figure 5 Two illusions of size, induced by context; the one case by perspective (giving a false impression of distance, so "size constancy" is operative), in the other distortion is due to strong relative size cues

of features, as in colour vision or the elementary contour elements as studied by Hubel and Wiesel. Others require an understanding of how different cues, to depth and distance for instance, interact to affect what is seen (Figure 5). Still others, like the distorted room, require us to consider how our habits of thought and expectations – unconscious inferences – determine what we see. The study of illusion is like a workshop for the meshing together of all the different sorts of influence that bear on perception.

GESTALT PSYCHOLOGY

The study of illusions certainly seems to favour an eclectic and empiricist approach to perception. Yet there have been influential movements in psychology that have denied that position. Gestalt psychology was one of them; it asserted the primacy of organizational phenomena, yet denied the role of experience in building up perception. The German word *Gestalt* means "configuration", and identifies the main tenet of that school of psychology, namely that the nature of perception is *holistic*; it is not to be understood by breaking it into elementary parts. The elements of Figure 6a and b for example fall "naturally" into a certain organization. We seem to have no control over this, and it occurs without effort on our part. The Gestalt psychologists maintained that this is no accident; for them the visual field was determined by a set of organizational principles that are simply a part of the way the brain works (Köhler, 1929). This school of psychology arose at a

163

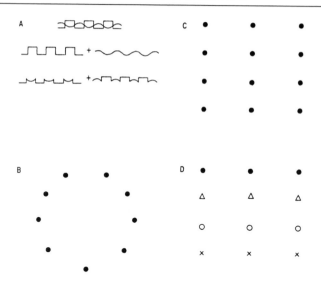

Figure 6 Four classical Gestalt demonstrations of "natural" perceptual organization. In 6a, the top form is organized into a "square wave" and a "sinusoid" rather
than into the equally possible decomposition shown at the bottom of the figure. No
one would fail to see the circular organization of 6b. In 6c organization into columns
is mediated by proximity, but in 6d the proximity is overridden by similarity of the
elements in each row. There are a dozen or so Gestalt "principles" of organization,
that seem to describe most instances of such natural organization

time when little was known about the operations of the visual brain. Indeed
Gestalt psychologists held theories about brain activity that are now known
to be false. For this reason the school fell into disrepute, yet it provided a
brilliant set of demonstrations of organizational phenomena in perception
that are still valid, and pose a challenge to modern theories of perception.

Figure 7 illustrates some displays with a strong Gestalt flavour (commonly
true of many cartoons, incidentally), but if one thinks about it, the organization here is not merely automatic, it relies on our interpretation of the elements in the displays. In fact a major weakness of the Gestalt theory was its
failure to take account of the many factors that impinge on perception.
Indeed it denied them, and was quite nativistic in approach. It is worth a
place in the history of perception, however, not only for the power of the
demonstrations it spawned, but also as a warning of the dangers of being too
narrow in the range of influences one is willing to allow in trying to understand perception. There was a resurgence of interest in the Gestalt approach
some years ago (see Kubovy & Pomerantz, 1981).

Figure 7 There are strong Gestalt principles at work in these cartoons, but notice that they also depend on a strong element of interpretation (meaningfulness) for their effect

GIBSON'S PERCEPTUAL THEORY

The theoretical position of J. J. Gibson was strongly influenced by Gestalt psychology, although in some ways it was very different (Gibson, 1950, 1966). He, like the Gestalt theorists, was disenchanted by the traditional empiricist approach in which elements of sensory experience are somehow glued together to yield the coherent, one-piece perceptual world of normal experience. What is this glue? Nobody knows. Gibson argued that it is unnecessary to know, because the glue does not exist. He came to this conclusion as a young US Air Force psychologist during the Second World War, attempting to use his knowledge of the psychology of perception to aid in the training of pilots. Traditional theory was of no help, but he was struck by the fact that the information they *used* in flying their machines was nevertheless readily identified and described. Given this background, it is not surprising that Gibson concentrated his attention on movement, and concluded that information contained in moving displays (in traditional terms, the motion of the retinal image) was of decisive importance, for instance in the landing of an aircraft. From this he reached the idea that information in "whole field" displays gives valid and salient information about the true state of the world.

Here is an example of a typical Gibsonian demonstration: take a wire coat-hanger and bend it into an arbitrary, but fairly complicated, shape. "Shadowcast" this on a screen with a single light source, and have an observer view the screen only. What will be seen is a flat squiggly shape. Now start to rotate the hanger (about a vertical axis), and the three-dimensional nature of the shape "leaps out". This has all the punch and convincingness of a Gestalt demonstration. No analysis of the local element movements gives the effect. It is a true "whole-field" phenomenon. Gibson argued that such whole field displays very often contained *gradients* of information, in the case of motion the different parts of the field would move at different rates, thereby signalling the true layout of the world. Figure 8 gives an indication of another such motion gradient. Other gradients, for example of perspective and texture, were likewise held to be the basis for veridical perception, as in Figure 9.

In his early work, Gibson called this "global psychophysics", the idea being that the visual stimulation arising from the world had a coherence that was not dependent on the observer's own knowledge or activity (one sees the close relationship to Gestalt theory) but was inherent in what he called the *optic array*, that is, the physical structure of the light impinging on the observer's eye (rather than being a function of brain organization, as in the Gestalt account). All this is very true, and there is no doubt that Gibson's ideas had a fundamental effect on our understanding of the nature of perception, and especially on the importance of analysing the stimulus properties to which organisms are sensitive, and to which they respond. This aspect of his work has had a profound influence in a surprising place, namely in the

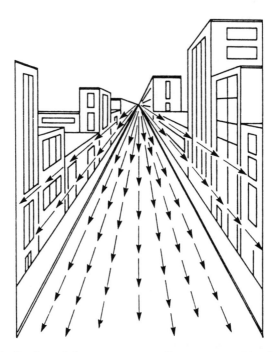

Figure 8 An indication of the movement gradients generated by "straight ahead" motion of the observer. The relative velocity of different elements in the field is indicated by the lengths of the arrows. Such relative motion provides gradients of stimulation that contain valid information about the world, as Gibson demonstrated

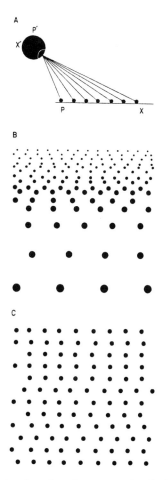

Figure 9 Texture gradients also give strong cues to depth and slant. 9a indicates how, optically, the texture of 9b would be generated. 9c has no texture gradient, and supplies no depth information

field of computational and machine vision, and artificial intelligence (see Banks & Krajicek, 1991).

Gibson was successful in demonstrating the important role gradients can play in perception. As with any successful theory, however, there is a danger of claiming too much. While a great deal can be understood in these terms, it is going too far to claim, as Gibson did, that the whole of perception can be captured in this net. There are phenomena of constancy, and the illusions, which do not fit easily into the Gibsonian view. Likewise it would be difficult to account for more symbolic perceptual activities like reading, or artistic representation, along these lines.

Gibson always claimed that his ideas were powerful enough to encompass everything, but his programme was never wholly successful. On the other hand his influence has been great, and beneficial. By insisting on the careful definition of the properties of the light impinging on the eye he established a new standard of perceptual analysis. Like the Gestalt psychologists he insisted on the organized quality of our perceptions, but unlike them he was not at all interested in the physiological substrate of perception. He felt that undue concern with that substrate would tend to make us ask the wrong questions about perception.

Gibson was very modern in his insistence that perception is to be understood as the basis for action, for defining the ecological niche of the organism, and for understanding both organism and environment as a single interacting system. He argued that too much concern with the physiology would simply displace concern from the places where it was most needed. In view of the amazing advances in knowledge of the physiological substrate in recent years, and the extent to which it has influenced practical and theoretical understanding of vision, this stance may seem bizarre, yet we owe an immense debt of gratitude to Gibson for freeing us from the "piecemeal, instantaneous frozen section" view of sensory stimulation that was the traditional view before his time. It is now understood that the dynamic, whole-field sensory continuum contains far richer sources of information than we thought (Cutting, 1987; Wallach, 1987). Modern research has capitalized on this change in the way stimulation is treated.

PERCEPTUAL PLASTICITY AND LEARNING

Both Gestalt psychology and Gibson's theory deny the role of "constructive" learning in perception, yet there is a long tradition, and ample evidence, attesting to its importance. Following the lead provided by Hebb (1949), a vast amount of research has been done to assess the matter. This has been of several kinds, including work on perceptual development in infancy and with young animals raised in specialized environments, and studying the ways in which adults respond to distortions of their normal perceptual "diet". The findings complement other methods of studying perception in mature organisms.

Initial work, starting in the early 1960s, attempted to assess the effects of restriction on the rearing of young animals. Thus kittens, for example, were raised in the dark for some weeks or months, and an assessment was then made of their visual capacities. The results were inconclusive, because it was never possible to prove that the visual apparatus was functioning properly after such treatment. But surely the point of such research was to show that the system was not normal? The problem was that researchers were looking for changes that could be attributed to lack of experience, which were expected to occur in the brain, but the damage caused by restricted vision probably was also occurring in the periphery (at the retina, for example). In that case even if central (brain) malfunction had been induced, there was no way of separating its effects from the peripheral effects, so the results were bound to be of little theoretical interest. A more promising approach was to rear animals in specialized environments rather than just in the dark, and to look for changes in behaviour subsequently. A number of ingenious studies along these lines were undertaken, especially in the laboratory of Richard Held at Brandeis University, and subsequently at the Massachusetts Institute of Technology (Held, 1965). The tests of visual function were behavioural and functional and had some intriguing results, but a still more promising line of attack became available with the development of the single-neuron recording methods described above.

Hubel and Wiesel had shown, even in their first classic paper, that many of the neurons in the cat's visual cortex are binocular, that is to say, a given neuron would have receptive fields in both eyes, so could be made to respond to similar features presented to either the left or the right eye not only separately, but also in combination. This implies an amazing degree of coordination in the anatomical arrangements, even in the newborn kitten. They found, by a technique of restricted rearing, that the balance between the two eyes could be disrupted. A kitten reared with artificial squint, so that the coordination between the eyes was lost, no longer showed regular binocular responding. This work was taken further by others who were able to show that kittens (and other mammals) could be reared so as to produce essentially two "monocular" visual brains, that is, to have no neurons capable of responding to both eyes, and indeed having a restricted capacity to respond only to a limited set of visual features, such as horizontal contours in one eye, vertical in the other. Of great interest is the fact that the plasticity of the brain is greatest in the very young organism (about the first three months of life in the kitten) and later on disappears almost entirely. This and similar work is reviewed in Blakemore (1978). This work led to the study of binocular abnormalities in human infants, and to programmes attempting to relieve such conditions.

Research on plasticity shows how new techniques have made it possible to answer old questions in new ways, and to cast light on matters of theoretical as well as practical significance. It also shows how psychological questions can become the province of other scientists' research, which in turn leads to further psychological advance.

A somewhat different approach to plasticity is found in studies of adult responses to novel stimulation. In the 1890s George Stratton asked what the perceptual effect of inverting the retinal image would be. This can be achieved by optical means, so that the image on the retina really is "upside down". Remember that the normal retinal image is upside down, according to our conventional reckoning of orientation with respect to gravity (Figure 2). Stratton's manipulation reversed this, so we can say that the retinal

169

image, although in one sense now "upright", was nevertheless opposite to what we normally experience. The immediate effect of the reversal is to make the visual world appear inverted, perhaps not surprisingly, as we know that there is at least an approximate map of the retinal surface in its cortical representation. What is quite amazing is the extent to which the human observer can adapt to this major distortion of visual appearances. Stratton wore the reversing spectacles for periods of several days, and his descriptions of the course of changes in how he perceived the world are fascinating (Stratton 1897). At first the disruption was great; he would bump into furniture, see his hands and feet in the "wrong" places, and move in the wrong directions. It would be difficult to point to objects, pick them up, and so on. Yet over the course of days many of these anomalies disappeared. The world never seemed quite normal, to be sure, but his success in adapting to it was incontrovertible. On removing the devices (having been careful to allow no "normal" vision during their use) a reverse distortion appeared in the normal world, to which re-adaptation had to occur.

Over the years many other psychologists have repeated experiments similar to Stratton's (Dolezal, 1982; Kohler, 1964) sometimes with much less radical distortions than his. It has been found that adaptation to "mild" distortions, ones for instance in which the retinal image is simply displaced and/or stretched, rather than being inverted, can occur quite rapidly and be essentially complete. Debate has raged about whether these adaptations are true visual effects, some theorists believing that the adaptations occur in the felt position of the head and limbs, for example, rather than in the visual representation itself. Interestingly enough, we can here see another facet of the nativist–empiricist division in perceptual psychology. Nativists tend to insist, given the well-established anatomical connections between retina and cortex, that nothing as feeble as a behavioural manipulation would be capable of affecting the transfer of information from one to the other (the "telephone switchboard" theory of visual function). For them, it is much easier to conceive of the plasticity as occurring in other modalities such as "felt limb position" or touch. Empiricists, on the other hand, have no such difficulty. Indeed plasticity, even at the physiological level, has now been demonstrated so convincingly that there is no a priori reason to deny its function in the visual representation. Further details on this debate can be found in Dodwell (1992). It may be mentioned that plasticity, or adaptability, is demonstrated in everyday life in the experience of people who wear corrective glasses. These change the sharpness with which images are projected on the retina, but also distort, to a greater or less degree, other characteristics, such as size and apparent distance. Yet virtually everyone, after an initial period of adjustment, is able to wear them and to adapt perfectly to the visual world.

THE NATURE OF PERCEPTUAL LEARNING

Unlike the Gestalt psychologists, Gibson did not deny that perceptual learning has a role to play in the production of a mature organism. Rather, he maintained that the nature of this learning is quite different from what the traditional empiricist account tells us. That account says that perceptual elements – cues – are atomistic, local, and in themselves essentially meaningless. Memory, habit, inference, and insight supply what is missing to construct the meaningful world. According to Gibson, the environment (the optic array in the first instance) supplies us with a much richer and more usable source of information; in fact in his view all the information needed to know and live in the world we normally inhabit. Perceptual learning, according to him, consists not in the gluing together of sensory "atoms", but in coming to differentiate and discriminate among the features of the environment, represented in the optic array. Indeed in his last major work, on "ecological optics", he maintained that virtually all cognitive activity could be analysed into components of discrimination within that array (Gibson, 1979).

Where's the truth? To most psychologists and philosophers of mind it seems inherently unlikely that one can understand cognition, of which perception is but the "front end", without resort to concepts that reach beyond the ground of "ecological validity" (Fodor & Pylyshyn, 1988). At the same time this is not to deny the importance of higher, more global concepts of stimulus attributes than the traditional theory allowed. It does not seem unreasonable to suggest that there are two different sorts of perceptual learning, one constructive, or synthetic, and another that, while not "destructive", is analytic in the Gibsonian sense. Synthetic perceptual learning might well be needed to account for the infant's ability to coordinate sights and sounds in forming concepts of *object permanency*, long held to be a constructive activity, whereas analytic processes might be involved in learning to discriminate between the faces of two distinct adults in the infant's environment. In the adult world a form of synthetic activity must be involved in learning the categories of *stamen* and *pistil*, for example, botanical categories defined much more by their functional attributes than by perceived characteristics. A more analytic form of discrimination learning, on the other hand, would be involved in learning to tell the difference between two shades of red, say *carmine* and *crimson*, or the difference between two vintages of wine (a favourite example of Gibson's). There is no good reason to restrict the number of different types of perceptual learning that are theoretically possible. If the study of perception has taught us anything, it is that a narrow focus on one point of view, valuable as it may be in furthering theory, runs the risk of distorting the truth.

171

BINOCULAR VISION AND DEPTH PERCEPTION

A remarkable fact about the normal visual system is that we have two eyes, each of which performs well on its own, but which function together to produce single visual images to which, as is easily shown, both eyes contribute. A look at the binocular system provides a suitable end-piece to this brief account of basic processes in vision, supplying as it does variations on most of the themes we have touched on.

At the centre of each retina is a small patch densely furnished with receptor cells which is called the *fovea*. It is the patch that is stimulated by that point in the visual field on which we fixate, and is mainly concerned with the detection of fine detail (and colour, but that is another story). The two eyes are independently mobile in their sockets, but by a near-automatic mechanism will converge in their lines of sight so that the same point is fixated by both (except in those unusual experimental situations in which psychologists cause different features to be presented to the two eyes). When properly fixated at some specific distance, we say that *corresponding points* in the two eyes are stimulated by features in the world that are at the same distance away as the fixation point. Objects nearer or farther therefore stimulate *non*-corresponding points, and it is a remarkable fact that in that case, the non-correspondence, provided it is not too great, gives rise to a totally new visual quality known as *stereoscopic* depth. Everyone will have seen this quality in the commercial stereoscopes so beloved of the Victorian era and still to be found as "Viewmasters" and the like. These involve the separate presentation to the two eyes of slightly different pictures (the two halves of a *stereogram*) which simulate the disparities present in real left and right-eye views of a scene.

What is the physiological basis for stereodepth perception? It was mentioned earlier that Hubel and Wiesel found most cells in the visual cortex to be binocularly driven. In their work it was assumed that the receptive fields in the two eyes were stimulating corresponding points in the two retinas. Yet it did not take long for Barlow and others to show, in the cat and subsequently in other mammals, that those binocular neurons can be divided into different classes, according to whether and by how much their "preferred" receptive fields are in non-corresponding parts of the two retinas (Barlow, Blakemore, & Pettigrew, 1967). The non-correspondence of the left and right eye retinal receptive fields are related to the distance at which "preferred" features are located. So we have here the physiological basis for coding stereodepth in the activity of single neurons.

That, in a sense, is only the beginning of the matter. Extensive research with humans has revealed a large and interesting field of inquiry with many puzzling and unexpected features. For example, how is it that we have two retinal images, but one visual world? What role does learning play in the production of stereoscopic depth effects? We know that there are many different cues to depth, such as perspective, texture gradient, relative size, and interposition (one object nearer than another can obscure a part of it), and it seems these are subject to learning at least to some extent – *pace* Gibson. Yet it has been found that "pure stereoscopic depth" can be produced where there is no possibility of learning or interpretation playing a role. Stereograms have been designed in such a way that each half, that is to say the field presented to each separate eye, contains no regular pattern information and appears random, yet when the two halves are fused together a "binocular image" stands out from the fused background. These stereograms were first studied by the Hungarian-American psychologist Bela Julesz, and have led to the conclusion, supported by the physiological work described above, that there is an elementary stereo-detection code built into the mammalian visual system, just like the colour and contour coding systems described earlier (Julesz, 1971).

There are still many puzzling things about fused single vision. Is there genuine fusion of the images in the two eyes, or does one eye's image *suppress* the other? There is evidence for both processes! Hold your right thumb up about 30 cm from your nose, and fixate it carefully, so you see it as a single thumb (i.e., fused). Now hold up your left thumb behind the right one, at about 60 cm, carefully maintaining fixation on the near one. What do you see? Two sort of "ghost" thumbs, one to the right and one to the left of the near (fused) thumb (Figure 10). By alternately closing the left and right eyes you will be able to convince yourself that the ghost on the left is due to stimulation of the left eye, and that on the right comes from the right eye. If you are really careful, you can now fixate on the far thumb, and again you will see the two ghosts, but this time the right ghost is in the left eye, and conversely. These are called uncrossed and crossed disparity images respectively.

What are the ghosts? they are partially suppressed images of the full left and right eye images. Normally these are completely suppressed and we notice only the single, fused binocular images. If you think about it, your visual field must be full of such suppressed images, of which you are usually completely unaware. So suppression is a fact, fusion is a fact, the likely physiological basis for it is known, and the marvellous integration of the two processes allows us to see unconfabulated images, with the additional advantage of a new and reliable cue to depth.

As was mentioned, there are many other cues to depth and distance, most of which can override stereodepth. For example if you reverse the two parts of a stereogram in a stereoscope, so the right eye sees the left eye's view and vice versa, you will still see good depth if the scene depicted is of a rich natural scene like a landscape or building. Here *interpretation* clearly takes precedence over the built-in processing system for stereodepth which, on its own, should produce reversed depth impressions.

So, binocular vision and depth perception show in miniature, as it were, many of the characteristics of visual perception as a whole; we know

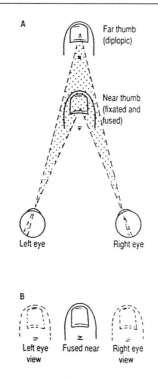

Figure 10   The fused view of the near thumb, and the two "ghost" images to the left and right (see text for further explanation)

something of the physiological substrate, its phenomenology tells us important things about what is going on (suppression and fusion, for example), and it even supplies evidence of how important experience and interpretation can be in reaching a coherent and seamless view of the perceptual world.

CONCLUSION

The wide scope of research in perception, the ways it can aid us in understanding the intricacies of the perceptual apparatus, how it is used to inform us about the world, and how it is "tuned up" in the course of development have been our main themes. I have also tried to give some idea of the flavour of modern theorizing in the psychology of perception, for it is after all this which guides us in our attempts to understand both the apparatus and its function. If the emphasis has seemed at times to be heavily on the physiological side, this is because advances in understanding of the physiological substrate of vision have been so impressive since the 1950s. Yet I would be the last to argue that all we need to know about perception is exhausted by this knowledge, and I hope that has come through in my account too.

Nativism and empiricism still are the primary poles in the theoretical dialogue about the nature of perception. They seem to be in some way quite intractable, and are most unlikely to go away. This is not because they do not involve factual differences which can be settled by experimentation. Such differences exist of course, but the debate between the two poles is largely theoretical if not metaphysical, and reflects a difference in the predilection of individual scientists for accounting for perceptual phenomena on one basis or another. From that point of view we are not much further ahead than were Helmholtz and Hering in the 1880s, even though our store of detailed knowledge about the visual system and about perception is now vastly greater than theirs.

What are the primary problems that await solution in the psychology of perception? One without doubt is the question of the "seamless web" of perceptual experience (Dodwell, 1992). We have plenty of ideas and information about the processing of visual information, especially as this is evinced in the activity of single cells in the visual system, but not too many yet about its integration into the meaningful objects and events of our normal cognitive world. Some powerful ideas come from the recent field of computational vision; readers will have to decide for themselves how successful this enterprise is in that regard. Another primary question has to do with the fitting of our internal representation of the world to the external reality (Andrews, 1964). I have not said much about this, as it is an area of research still in its infancy, but one which no doubt will grow in time to match its importance as an epistemological problem (Dodwell & Humphrey, 1990).

What is that problem? We know much about the transduction of physical energy into neural signals, quite a bit about how these are transmitted to the brain, yet almost nothing about how the signals come to represent reality, as surely they must. Is this an empirical problem capable of scientific resolution? In some respects it certainly is, but nothing I have written about, for instance, will account for the fact that straight lines look straight. Indeed much of what we know about sensory coding seems to suggest that "straightness" is quite foreign to the operation of the physiological system. Many cells "prefer" short line segments, but how these are integrated into the global contours of the visual field is not accounted for by that fact. Mathematical modelling, involving integration of these line elements in "vector fields" may supply the answer (Hoffman, 1966; Hoffman & Dodwell, 1985). Yet there it is; straight lines look straight, and this is especially puzzling because if we put on a distorting lens (even an ordinary spectacle lens) that causes the line to look bent, we adapt pretty soon, so that it again looks straight! This is basically the same puzzle that beset the Gestalt psychologist Koffka in the 1930s. He asked "Why does a tree look like a tree?" (Koffka, 1935). One might say that this is too broad and general a question to be answered scientifically, like the question "What is life?" But, like that question, ours is too urgent to be neglected. Gibson had his answer (it is all in the optical array; no other sources of information are relevant). The empiricists, following Berkeley and Helmholtz, had their answer too (it is all in the mind, depending on the individual's experiences of the world), and other psychologists have made similarly sweeping pronouncements. I hope that I have been able to show that all such answers are too simple. Perception is a many-faceted beast, and answers to its many problems need to be sought in different places, and at different levels of function; sensory, organizational, cognitive. This is the reason why the study of perception is so rich and rewarding. We can be sure that it will continue to pose puzzles to the researcher for the foreseeable future. To perceive seems effortless. To understand perception is nevertheless a great challenge.

FURTHER READING

Dodwell, P. C. (1990). *Perception.* In R. Lockhart, J. Grusec, & J. Waller (Eds) *Foundations of perception* (chap. 5). Toronto: Copp Clark Pitman.
Gregory, R. L. (1966). *Eye and brain.* New York: McGraw-Hill.
Hubel, D. H. (1987). *Eye, brain and vision.* New York: Freeman.
Rock, I. (1984). *Perception.* New York: Scientific American.
Schiffman, H. R. (1982). *Sensation and perception: An integrated approach* (2nd edn). New York: Wiley.

REFERENCES

Andrews, D. P. (1964). Error-correcting perceptual mechanisms. *Quarterly Journal of Experimental Psychology, 16,* 104–115.
Banks, W. P., & Krajicek, D. (1991). Perception. *Annual Review of Psychology, 42,* 305–331.
Barlow, H. B., Blakemore, C., & Pettigrew, J. O. (1967). The neural mechanism of binocular depth discrimination. *Journal of Physiology, 193,* 327–342.
Blakemore, C. (1978). Maturation and modification in the developing visual system. In R. Held, H. Liebowitz, & H. Teuber (Eds) *Handbook of sensory physiology: Perception* (vol. 8., pp. 377–436). New York: Springer.
Boring, E. (1950). *A history of experimental psychology.* New York: Appleton-Century-Crofts.
Cronly-Dillon, J. R. (Ed.) (1991). *Vision and visual dysfunction* (general ed. J. R. Cronly-Dillon): *vol. 11. Development and plasticity in the visual system.* London: Macmillan.
Cutting, J. E. (1987). Perception and information. *Annual Review of Psychology, 38,* 61–90.
Dodwell, P. C. (1970). *Visual pattern recognition.* New York: Holt, Rinehart & Winston.
Dodwell, P. C. (1992). Perspectives and transformations. *Canadian Journal of Psychology, 46,* 510–538.
Dodwell, P. C., & Humphrey, G. K. (1990). A functional theory of the McCollough effect. *Psychological Review, 97,* 78–89.
Dolezal, H. (1982). *Living in a world transformed.* New York: Academic Press.

Dreher, B., & Robinson, S. R. (Eds) (1991). *Vision and visual dysfunction* (general ed. J. R. Cronly-Dillon): *vol. 3. Neuroanatomy of the visual pathways and their development.* London: Macmillan.

Fodor, J. A., & Pylyshyn, Z. W. (1988). Connectionism and cognitive architecture. *Cognition, 89*, 3–71.

Gibson, E. J. (1988). Exploratory behaviour in the development of perceiving, acting and acquiring of knowledge. *Annual Review of Psychology, 39*, 1–41.

Gibson, J. J. (1950). *The perception of the visual world.* Boston, MA: Houghton Mifflin.

Gibson, J. J. (1966). *The senses considered as perceptual systems.* Boston, MA: Houghton Mifflin.

Gibson, J. J. (1979). *The ecological approach to visual perception.* Boston, MA: Houghton Mifflin.

Hebb, D. O. (1949). *The organization of behavior.* New York: Wiley.

Held, R. (1965) Plasticity in sensorimotor systems. *Scientific American, 213*(5), 84–94.

Hoffman, W. C. (1966). The Lie algebra of visual perception. *Journal of Mathematical Psychology, 3*, 65–98.

Hoffman, W. C., & Dodwell, P. C. (1985). Geometric psychology generates the visual gestalt. *Canadian Journal of Psychology, 39*, 491–528.

Hubel, D. H., & Wiesel, T. N. (1962). Receptive fields, binocular interaction and functional architecture in the cat's visual cortex. *Journal of Physiology, 160*, 106–115.

Julesz, B. (1971). *Foundations of cyclopean perception.* Chicago, IL: Chicago University Press.

Kilpatrick, F. P. (1961). *Explorations in transactional psychology.* New York: New York University Press.

Koffka, K. (1935). *The principles of Gestalt psychology.* New York: Harcourt Brace & World.

Kohler, I. (1964). The formation and transformation of the perceptual world. *Psychological Issues, 3*, 1–173 (original German, 1951).

Köhler, W. (1929). *Gestalt psychology.* New York: Liveright.

Kubovy, M., & Pomerantz, J. R. (Eds) (1981). *Perceptual organization.* Hillsdale, NJ: Lawrence Erlbaum.

Maunsell, J. H. R., & Newsome, W. T. (1987). Visual processing in monkey extrastriate cortex. *Annual Review of Neuroscience, 10*, 363–401.

Perrett, D. I., Smith, P. A. J., Potter, D. D., Mistlin, A. J., Head, A. S., Milner, A. D., & Jeeves, M. A. (1985). Visual cells in the temporal cortex sensitive to face view and gaze direction. *Proceedings of the Royal Society of London*, B, *223*, 293–317.

Rock, I. (1984). *Perception.* New York: Scientific American.

Stratton, G. M. (1897). Vision without inversion of the retinal image. *Psychological Review, 4*, 341–360; 463–481.

Wallach, H. (1987). Perceiving a stable environment when one moves. *Annual Review of Psychology, 38*, 1–27.

3.2

COMPUTATIONAL THEORIES OF VISION

Mike G. Harris and Glyn W. Humphreys
University of Birmingham, England

Marr's computational framework for object recognition
The raw primal sketch
Edge detection
The detection of luminance discontinuities
Making edge assertions
Comments, criticisms, and extensions
The full primal sketch
Comments, criticisms, and extensions

The $2\frac{1}{2}$ D sketch
Comments, criticisms, and extensions
Object representation
Accessing models from the $2\frac{1}{2}$ D sketch
Comments, criticisms, and extensions
Biederman: recognition by components (RBC) theory
Conclusions
Further reading
References

Imagine a pond surrounded by children throwing stones into the water. As each stone lands, it creates an expanding pattern of ripples on the surface. Sometimes several stones land at the same time, so that the surface is thrown into a complex, ever-changing pattern. Now consider the problems of working out how big each stone was and where it landed in the pond, given the seemingly artificial constraints that you cannot see or hear and that your only contact with the world is through your two index fingers, which you are allowed to dip into water to feel the ripples drifting by.

This simple scene offers a fairly direct analogy with hearing and, more generally, with senses such as vision, where information about the world is conveyed indirectly to the perceiver. The point is that to solve the problems set by the analogy, and more importantly to understand a good solution, you would need to know about the relationships between stones and ripples and about how they are represented in the patterns arriving at your fingertips. You would also need to be very specific about the kinds of information you are trying to extract. Information in the above context means those aspects of the ripples that are useful to a specific task: if you were interested in the size of the stones it might be the size of the ripples, but if you were interested in where they landed it might be the difference in the time of arrival of a particular ripple at the two fingers. These two ingredients – an understanding of the relationships between the stimulus and the object that produced it, and a proper specification of the problem that you are trying to solve – form the essential basis of a computational theory, which is simply a principled description of those aspects of the stimulus that are potentially useful to completing a specified task. The thrust of a computational theory is thus not just to explain *how* things work, but *why* they work the way they do.

A computational theory is an abstract description of the relationships between world, stimulus and task. It is the first, and most important, step in understanding some aspect of perception but it is not, by itself, enough. Having identified the aspects of the stimulus that are important to a particular task we must also think about how these aspects might be extracted, represented, and processed, and about how each stage might actually be carried out. These additional steps are generally important because a given computational theory may suggest several different ways to proceed. To psychologists, the additional steps are absolutely essential because psychologists are interested not only in how a problem *might* be solved, but also in how it *is* solved within the brain. A computational theory can identify only the theoretical constraints on what is possible and, to take into account the biological constraints on what is practicable, we must use it to derive a specific representation and a neurally plausible implementation.

Since a computational theory is just an abstract description, it has nothing inherently to do with computers and, in that sense, the name is unfortunate. However, even more confusingly, computational theories almost invariably lead to working computer models and the models and the theories together make up the computational approach to vision. Working computer models obviously provide a rigorous test of a particular implementation but they also have another important role, which follows indirectly from the fact that we cannot hope to develop a single computational theory of vision, because vision is not a single task. Vision is like a service industry which contributes to a broad range of behaviours including, among others, navigation, balance, object recognition, and the guidance of social interaction. Each of these different types of behaviours consists of many tasks, each requiring its own computational theory, so that the computational approach is inevitably very modular. If we are to gain a full understanding of vision rather than just its

179

parts, we must also have an overall framework that specifies the interactions between the modules. The development of large-scale computer models, which combine several modules in the simulation of substantial aspects of perception, is thus an essential adjunct of the computational approach.

MARR'S COMPUTATIONAL FRAMEWORK FOR OBJECT RECOGNITION

Since a general overview of computational theories would inevitably be very superficial, this chapter concentrates upon the single theme of object recognition, outlining some of the recent developments in this one important area. Rather than following an historical sequence, the material is structured around the framework developed by the late David Marr (Marr, 1982), who first popularized the computational approach, and whose framework (outlined in Figure 1) remains the widest ranging computational account of visual object recognition.

Marr's framework starts from the idea that such useful attributes of a three-dimensional (3D) scene as surface markings, object boundaries, and

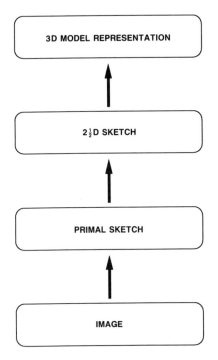

Figure 1   The levels of representation mediating object recognition, proposed by Marr (1982)

shadows can all be recovered from the basic retinal input by locating and describing the places where the intensity of the image changes relatively abruptly from place to place. He argued that these properties could be captured in something he termed a primal sketch. Two stages of deriving the primal sketch were distinguished. The raw primal sketch involves coding and locating individual intensity changes within a map based on the retina. The full primal sketch involves a more elaborate description in which the individual edge fragments are grouped into more meaningful clusters relating to surfaces. At the next stage, information about the distance and layout of each surface were added using a variety of techniques, or "depth cues". The resulting representation is termed the $2\frac{1}{2}$D sketch because it describes only the *visible* parts of the scene and is thus not fully three-dimensional. The $2\frac{1}{2}$D sketch will not serve for object recognition, however, because this requires that the input representation of the object be mapped against a representation stored in memory. Since the $2\frac{1}{2}$D sketch changes with the observer's viewpoint, it could be matched with memory only if representations were stored for all encountered views. To lessen the memory requirements of this process, Marr suggested that a further representation be constructed, which he termed a 3D model description. In this representation the parts of objects are coded relative to some salient part of the object itself, so that the resultant description remains the same across different views.

This framework is obviously "bottom-up" in nature, being concerned primarily with how information is extracted and built up into useful descriptions from the basic retinal input. Thus, the early stages of the framework make only very general assumptions about the structure of the external world, and do not call upon knowledge about specific objects. This contrasts sharply with the alternative "top-down" approach, where knowledge about specific objects or scenes can be used to facilitate, or even bypass, some of the earlier descriptive stages. While a bottom-up framework is not an inevitable consequence of the computational approach, it has certainly dominated recent research, at least partly because it is easier to derive computational theories for the early stages of perception where the relationships between the stimulus and the world are much easier to specify.

THE RAW PRIMAL SKETCH

Edge detection

The Marr and Hildreth (1980) account of edge detection is one of the earliest computational theories and is worth considering in some detail as an excellent example of the computational approach. When asked to sketch an object, most people begin with a simple line drawing rather than by shading in solid regions of colour. This is reasonable because the line drawing emphasizes two useful kinds of edge—object boundaries, which economically convey the object's overall shape, and the edges delineating the position and shape of detailed features and surface markings. Faced with the problem of recognizing, rather than depicting, an object, we can apply the logic in reverse and begin with a description based on edges. In general, these will appear in an image as places where the luminance changes fairly abruptly from place to place. Such changes are called luminance discontinuities. Of course, a description of these discontinuities is by no means complete because not all edges will produce discontinuities – some will, for example, be occluded – and not all discontinuities will correspond to real features of the object – some will, for example, correspond to shadows. The second of these problems, at least, can be solved by breaking the task into two stages: first locating and describing the luminance discontinuities in the image, then deciding which of them correspond to object features. The better the description produced in the first stage, the easier the second stage will be. For example, shadows tend to produce relative broad luminance discontinuities, so they can be distinguished from edges if the steepness of the change is known.

The detection of luminance discontinuities

The best way to find luminance discontinuities is simply to subtract the amount of light at one point in the image from that at adjacent points because, by definition, this subtraction will give a non-zero result in the presence of a luminance discontinuity. This process is known technically as spatial differentiation. However, there are three complications to be overcome:

1 Because luminance discontinuities occur at different spatial scales (sharp or gradual) and because no single scale of comparison can detect them all, several comparisons need to be made simultaneously at a range of different scales.
2 Because discontinuities can occur at any orientation, comparisons need to be made simultaneously at all orientations.
3 Images are inherently "noisy" so that, even under perfect viewing conditions, luminance varies randomly from place to place. Spatial differentiation is very sensitive to this noise and will tend to signal many spurious luminance discontinuities. To avoid this, the image must be "smoothed" by calculating the *average* luminance over a small area before making the comparison. The exact size of the area is crucial because averaging over a large area will blur out the discontinuities, while averaging over a small area won't reduce the noise. The best compromise is to calculate a *weighted* average – so that the luminance near the point of interest contributes a lot to the average, and more remote points contribute relatively

little. The ideal weighting function is the Gaussian (or Normal) distribution, familiar in statistics, since it averages over a wide area but assigns most of the weight to a small region near the centre.

As shown in Figure 2, the receptive field of a typical retinal ganglion cell (the type of cell that signals the result of retinal processing to higher visual centres) seems to embody all these requirements. The two sub-regions average the light over adjacent areas of the image, the antagonistic arrangement of the sub-regions takes the difference between these averages, and the circular shape ensures that the comparisons are made at all orientations. At each point on the retina, there are retinal ganglion cells with different sized receptive fields, so that the comparisons are done simultaneously at a range of spatial scales.

According to Marr and Hildreth's computational theory, retinal processes have evolved to emphasize luminance discontinuities – a task that requires Gaussian smoothing followed by spatial differentiation. An individual retinal ganglion cell performs these operations at one point in the image and an array of similar cells, one at each point, analyses the whole image. At a more technical level, the analysis predicts the precise form of the receptive field profile shown in Figure 2b, and psychophysical studies of human observers (e.g., Wilson & Bergen, 1979) confirm that the mechanisms underlying edge detection have sensitivity profiles which are very close approximations to this prediction.

The position of luminance discontinuities is normally given by the position of "zero-crossings" in the description resulting from smoothing and differentiation (Figure 2c), so that the problem of detecting edges becomes the problem of detecting zero-crossings. Zero-crossings can be detected in a biologically plausible way by wiring together groups of retinal ganglion cells in the manner shown in Figure 3. Cells with on- and off-centre receptive fields forming two adjacent, parallel rows are connected by a logical "AND" so that an output occurs only when both rows are simultaneously responding positively, a situation that generally occurs only in the presence of an appropriately oriented zero-crossing. The resulting device – a model of the "simple" cells which form the first stage of processing in the visual cortex – would thus function as an "oriented zero-crossing detector". Individual simple cells do indeed have the required oriented receptive fields and, for each retinal position, there are many simple cells with receptive fields covering the full range of orientations (Hubel & Wiesel, 1962, 1968) and spatial scales (Tootell, Silverman, & De Valois, 1981).

Making edge assertions

The result of these processes is a set of zero-crossing maps of the image, each depicting a different spatial scale. The final stage of the analysis is to convert

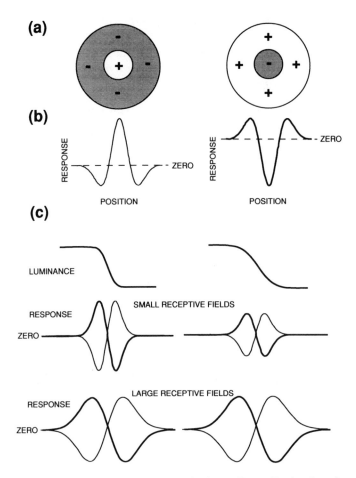

Figure 2 (a) The receptive field of typical retinal ganglion cells. A microelectrode is placed in or close to a cell and its response is monitored while a small spot of light is moved about the retina. The receptive field is the area of the retina in which the light causes a change in the cell's response. Under diffuse lighting conditions, retinal ganglion cells have a spontaneous background firing rate. A small spot of light may cause an increase (excitatory, indicated by a +) or a decrease (inhibitory, indicated by a −) in response, depending on its position within the receptive field. The example on the left is an "on-centre" cell, in which the central sub-region is excitatory. That on the right is an "off-centre" cell. An equal number of both types is found in the retina. (b) The receptive field sensitivity profiles of the cells in (a), indicating the precise sensitivity of the cell to light at each position in the receptive field. The profile shown is that predicted by Marr's analysis and is known mathematically as $\nabla^2 G$ (del-squared G). It is produced by differentiating a Gaussian function twice and (in the case of the on-centre cell) inverting the result. (The second differentiation is needed so that spatial comparisons are performed at all orientations.) (c) The pattern of response in an array of retinal ganglion cells to luminance discontinuities at different spatial scales. Two different sizes of receptive field are shown, corresponding to $\nabla^2 G$ derived from Gaussian functions of two different widths (standard deviations). The bolder line represents the response of on-centre cells, the finer line that of off-centre cells

184

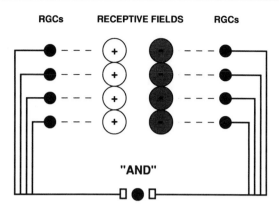

Figure 3 Marr's model of a cortical simple cell as an "oriented zero-crossing detector". Two sets of retinal ganglion cells (RGCs), one consisting of on-centre cells and the other of off-centre cells, with suitably positioned receptive fields are wired together by a logical "AND". The resulting simple cell responds only when *both* sets of RGCs are active. For clarity, only the centre sub-regions of the receptive fields are shown

this complex description of the image into a single, symbolic description which captures the layout of object features in the world. Unlike noise, real object features will tend to produce zero-crossings at more than one spatial scale, and so "edge assertions" are made only where the zero-crossing maps coincide. Each edge assertion can then be described in terms of its position, contrast, orientation, scale, and so forth, by analysing the pattern of response across the different maps. For example, it is clear from Figure 2c, that the pattern of response at different spatial scales conveys information about the slope of the edge.

It is important to recognize that the final result of all this processing – the raw primal sketch – is a list of *symbols* which make assertions about the external world and which can be conveniently manipulated by further processes. It thus has a very different status from the simple, zero-crossing maps which only describe the image. In Marr's original framework, the raw primal sketch is the basis for all subsequent analysis, and higher level processes have no access to the zero-crossing maps on which it is based.

Comments, criticisms, and extensions

On the face of it, the computational theory that underpins the above account of edge detection is a simple statement about the descriptive usefulness of luminance discontinuities. At a deeper level, however, the entire analysis is

185

driven by the proper understanding of the relationships between edges and images that the computational theory requires. Thus, the theory leads directly to the constraints that emphasize smoothing and differentiation and to the processes that distinguish edges from random noise. Indeed, precisely the same computational theory underpins the edge detection routines that are currently popular in computer vision (e.g., Canny, 1986) though here, because biological constraints are unimportant, the final representation and implementation is rather different. From a psychological viewpoint, the theory describes the *why*, as well as *how*, of visual processing and should be compared with earlier accounts of simple cells as "feature detectors" (e.g., Hubel & Wiesel, 1962) which, lacking any computational theory, assigned far too much responsibility to the responses of individual cells.

The account so far deals only with static images and thus takes no account of the information provided by the smooth transformations, or flow patterns, which accompany movement of the observer through the world (see, for example, Gibson, 1979). This information could, in principle, be recovered later by analysing the changes in a sequence of raw primal sketches (Ullman, 1979) but there are also several computational accounts of how motion can be extracted directly from the image (Adelson & Movshon, 1982; Heeger, 1987; Marr & Ullman, 1981). Marr and Ullman's account, for example, emphasizes the role of temporal differentiation (comparisons over time, rather than across position) and leads directly to an implementation requiring only a small refinement of the scheme outlined above. Although the original computational theory deals only with motion direction, it can easily be extended to encompass speed (Harris, 1986), leading to a *dynamic* raw primal sketch in which each edge assertion includes a description of its image velocity.

More serious criticisms of Marr and Hildreth's model begin with the details of the implementation. Neurophysiological studies (Robson, 1980) show that the receptive fields of retinal ganglion cells do not have precisely the form illustrated in Figure 2b, but that this property is more compatible with cortical mechanisms, which have elongated receptive fields and are thus already selective for stimulus orientation (Hawken & Parker, 1987). More importantly, although cortical simple cells do combine the outputs of several retinal ganglion cells, there is little evidence of the logical AND operation which is so important to Marr's way of making edge assertion (Hochstein & Spitzer, 1984). In general, while retaining the basic notions of smoothing and differentiation, recent accounts have provided alternative accounts of subsequent processing (e.g., Watson & Ahumada 1989; Watt & Morgan, 1985). To take a specific example, Watt and Morgan point out that the positions of zero-crossings can be misleading in noisy images and argue instead for more reliable descriptions based on the position and size of the peaks and troughs in the response patterns shown in Figure 2c. Originally, these descriptive primitives were used only to derive edge assertions like those of Marr but

Watt (1991) developed a rather more general computational theory based on the simple principle that rare events are the most informative. This leads to a process of statistical image description in which the mean and standard deviation (i.e., variability) of some image property are calculated, and only those features that have significantly unusual properties contribute to the final description. According to this more general view, the peaks and troughs in Figure 2c are simply rare responses which are consequently selected for further processing.

THE FULL PRIMAL SKETCH

All computational theories of early visual processing begin with an initial description which, like the raw primal sketch, emphasizes localized variations in image luminance. The same principle seems to apply within the visual system in that all retinal and most cortical cells have localized receptive fields so that each processes only a small region of the image. The resulting computational or neural representation is therefore very fragmentary, rather like a partly solved jigsaw in which the individual pieces preserve the informative features of the image but fail to capture the meaningful structure of the scene in terms of surfaces and objects.

The computational theory behind the recovery of this large-scale structure, as proposed by Marr, is based on two very simple but very powerful constraints. First, matter is coherent so that symbols that are close together in the image will usually belong to the same object. Second, symbols that share a common descriptive attribute will usually have a common physical cause. So, for example, symbols sharing similar orientations might first be grouped together to form larger-scale symbols with new descriptive attributes such as shape and texture, and the process might then be repeated upon these new symbols. Such simple and powerful grouping not only reveals additional image properties, such as texture gradients which are potentially useful in inferring depth (see below), but it also allows the recognition of additional object boundaries as places where the new image property changes abruptly from place to place.

Comments, criticisms, and extensions

The full primal sketch provides a functional explanation for the perceptual grouping strategies illustrated in Figure 4, which were extensively studied by the Gestalt psychologists (e.g., Wertheimer, 1912). On the basis of demonstrations such as those illustrated in Figure 4, the Gestalt psychologists drew up a set of principles of grouping, stating that (for instance) items tend to group if they are close to one another (the law of proximity), are similar (the law of similarity), make a good form, continue a single edge (good continuation), have a common pattern of motion (common fate). These

187

demonstrations provided a comprehensive description of the rules by which human observers cluster individual stimulus elements into coherent structures but, because they were confined to artificial stimuli and laboratory phenomena, say nothing about why grouping is a *necessary* perceptual stage. Of course, within any account such as Marr's, grouping is a necessary process because edge descriptions will be fragmentary. Grouping also helps the visual system to deal with incomplete data and with complex scenes, where the images of different objects may occlude each other. For example, grouping two edges by good continuation enables the visual system to register the presence of a single large object when a smaller object is placed in front of it.

Early attempts to develop computer vision systems, prior to Marr's work,

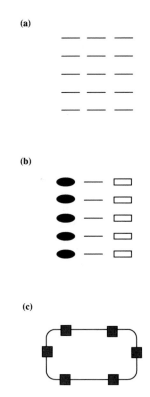

Figure 4 Examples of Gestalt properties of proximity (a), similarity (b), and good continuation (c). In (a) horizontal lines tend to be seen rather than vertical lines, because the elements in the horizontal lines are closer together. In (b) vertical lines tend to be seen, even though the vertical elements are further apart from the horizontal elements, because the vertically aligned elements are identical while the horizontally aligned elements differ. Thus the vertical elements group more strongly by similarity. In (c) the background oblong is seen beneath the smaller squares because the broken contour of the oblong can be grouped by good continuation

also paid considerable attention to grouping phenomena, and attempted to implement grouping procedures in terms of simple interactions between edges and junctions in shapes. These attempts, epitomized in the work on the so-called "blocks world", involved the development of programs to segment displays comprising a fixed set of object types (cylinders, wedges, pyramids, and so forth), on the basis of simple rules governing the relations between the lines in the images (e.g., Clowes, 1971; Guzman, 1968). This work was limited, in that it used highly simplified representations of the world, and so failed to confront the many problems encountered with real images. It also tended to adopt solutions specific to its own limited domain, rather than developing more general-purpose algorithms that serve across different domains.

Marr's account, with its emphasis of the computational constraints involved both in coding edges and subsequently in grouping edges together, provides a richer description of the input, and this is necessary if robust and generalizable procedures are to be developed (across different contrasts, scale, and so forth). More recently, Watt's (1991) account, computing statistical summaries at each stage of description and identifying unusual elements for the next stage, also offers a promising, and more general, refinement of the theory.

Marr's account of how the full primal sketch is derived emphasizes that grouping takes place within a two-dimensional representation, coded in retinal co-ordinates. Recent empirical research suggests that this is not the case, however, and that visual grouping processes may employ quite "deep" assumptions about the three-dimensional structure of the world. For instance, differences in the three-dimensional structure of block figures give rise to the instantaneous perception of an "odd-man-out", even when there are no two-dimensional orientation differences present (Enns & Rensink, 1990; see also Figure 5). This suggests rapid coding of the spatial relations

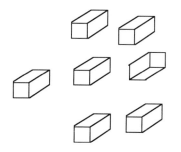

Figure 5 Example of rapid "pop out" of a block differing in its 3D orientation from the background, even though there are no 2D orientation differences present. This indicates that grouping and segmentation of the blocks is operating using 3D rather than 2D representations

between edges in three- rather than two-dimensions across the visual field. Also, by assuming that the world is three-dimensional, and that the corners of solid objects often form right angles, the three-dimensional structure of objects can be coded rapidly, with little other spatial information required (Perkins, 1968).

In contrast to our understanding of the neural mechanisms mediating the coding of the raw primal sketch, our understanding of the neural mechanisms involved in the full primal sketch is limited. Workers have shown that cells within area V2 of the cortex, an area taking input directly from the primary visual cortex, respond to the presence of an "illusory" contour between two co-linear edges (e.g., they respond to the illusory bar present in the Kanisza figure shown in Figure 6; Peterhans & von der Heydt, 1989). This suggests that cells in V2 play a role in grouping between co-linear edges coded at different retinal locations. Little is known about the ways in which neural mechanisms implement three-dimensional constraints on grouping.

One of the reasons for the relative sparsity of knowledge about the neurophysiological mechanisms mediating grouping is that, to date, neurophysiological studies have largely examined the response properties of single neurons whereas grouping probably involves interactions between neurons (e.g., two neurons in the primary visual cortex pooling their outputs into a common cell that responds to continuation between the lines activating the primary cortex neurons). Studies examining the properties of groups of neurons suggest that the time-locking of cell responses may be important in linking cells together in response to Gestalt properties in the environment (e.g., Gray & Singer, 1989). Such time-locking of responses may in turn impose constraints on visual grouping (e.g., it may limit the number of groups that can be maintained without interference). The exploration of the computational constraints thus imposed is only just beginning (e.g., Hummel & Biederman, 1992). One promising avenue for research here concerns attempts to implement processes dependent on the interaction between

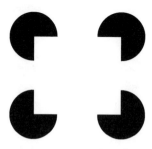

Figure 6   A Kanisza square. An illusory contour is seen joining the pacmen together. Neurophysiological evidence indicates that such contours are computed as early as area V2 in the cortex

190

neurons within "connectionist" models. These models generate intelligent behaviour from interactions between large numbers of computationally simple processing units, which (for example) summate activity from their "input" cells and pass on either excitatory or inhibitory input to their "output" cells. Since it is the pattern of interaction within a network of such cells that underlies behaviour, such models may provide valid ways to capture grouping processes in vision. Attempts to simulate completion phenomena in V2 cells, for instance, have been made by Grossberg and his colleagues (e.g., Grossberg & Mingolla, 1985).

THE $2\frac{1}{2}$D SKETCH

One of the most difficult problems faced by any sophisticated visual system is the need to reconstruct a depthy description of the world from flat retinal images. The main contribution of psychologists to this area has been the identification of the many different types of information – termed depth cues – which are useful to this task, while, recently, the computational approach has provided more precise theories of how (and, of course, why) each of these cues is used. For example, computational theories now exist for the recovery of 3D shape, at least under certain conditions, from linear perspective (Clowes, 1971; Draper, 1981; Huffman, 1971; Kanade, 1981; Waltz, 1975), shading (Horn, 1977), texture (Blake & Marinos, 1990) and motion (Clocksin, 1980; Koenderink, 1986; Longuet-Higgins & Prazdny, 1980; Rieger & Lawton, 1985; Waxman & Wohn, 1988). Again, rather than considering each of these rather superficially, we shall concentrate upon just one important example, that of stereopsis (literally "solid vision").

Stereopsis relies upon the fact that we have two separate views of the world, one for each eye, taken from slightly different viewpoints. As you can readily confirm by opening and closing each eye alternately, these two views are slightly different – and these differences, called disparities, contain information about the distance of objects in the world. The analysis of stereopsis is, in principle, very simple: one simply compares the two images, detects and measures the disparities, and analyses the disparities to recover depth. A problem, however, arises at the first, comparison, stage. Provided the images have already been recognized, it is easy to compare the positions of some identifiable feature in the two images but, at least in a bottom-up framework, stereopsis is supposed to be an *aid* to recognition, rather than a consequence. In fact, many years ago Julesz (1971) demonstrated that stereopsis can occur prior to recognition using an elegant stimulus called the random dot stereogram. Each eye is presented separately with essentially the same pattern of randomly positioned dots, the only difference between them being that, in one image, a region of dots (say a square) is displaced slightly to one side. This introduces a disparity which human observers can detect, so that they experience a compelling impression of the displaced region standing out in

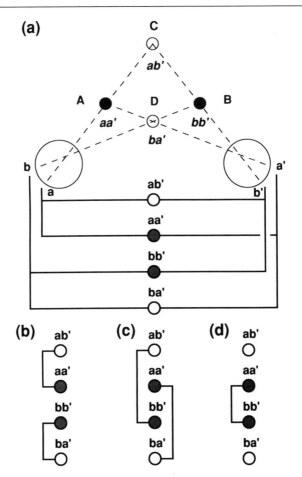

Figure 7 The correspondence problem. (a) Two objects (A and B) produce two images (a and b) in the left eye and two images (a' and b') in the right eye. When these images are correctly matched (*aa'* and *bb'*), the objects are seen in their correct positions. However, it is also possible to match the images incorrectly (*ab'* and *ba'*), in which case the objects are seen in incorrect positions (C and D). Binocular cells (ab', aa', bb', and ba') each combines one of the images from each of the eyes and thus make all possible matches (i.e., each cell responds because it has an appropriate stimulus in both of its receptive fields). (b)–(d) show the connections between the binocular cells needed to implement Marr and Poggio's (1976) solution to the correspondence problem. (b) *Only one object is visible along each line of sight* from the left eye, so *inhibitory* connections are made between aa' and ab', and between ba' and bb'. (c) The same rule for the right eye results in *inhibitory* connections between bb' and ab', and between ba' and aa'. (d) *Depth varies slowly*, so *excitatory* connections are made between aa' and bb', since they are in the same depth plane

192

depth from the background. Since the individual images are completely unstructured and contain no recognizable features, stereopsis can occur without prior recognition of the images.

Random dot stereograms emphasize the basic problem of stereopsis: since each image may contain several thousand dots, how does the visual system work out which dot in one image corresponds with which dot in the other? This is known as the correspondence problem. Getting the correspondence wrong (making a "false match"), as illustrated for a very simple case in Figure 7, is equivalent to seeing an object at the wrong position. Although the correspondence problem appears formidable, Marr and Poggio's (1976) computational theory argues that it can be solved by recognizing just two fundamental constraints. First, only one object can usually be seen at any one time along each line of sight, so that many potential correspondences are mutually incompatible. Second, objects generally have relatively smooth surfaces, so that distance will usually vary rather gradually from place to place. (Note that this is just the inverse of the familiar argument that object boundaries are rare and thus informative.)

These simple constraints translate almost directly into a recipe for solving the correspondence problem: first make all possible matches between the two images and then weaken those that are mutually incompatible while strengthening those that are likely to occur together. This recipe translates equally directly into the plausible neural implementation illustrated at the bottom of Figure 7. Binocular units — which receive input from both eyes — make all possible matches by responding whenever an appropriate feature occurs at the appropriate positions in both images. These units are interconnected by inhibitory and excitatory links which implement the second part of the recipe, so that units representing the same line of sight inhibit each other, while those representing the same distance, or "depth plane", excite each other. When the resulting neural network is presented with a random dot stereogram many units initially respond but, as the inhibitory and excitatory interconnections exert their influence, it rapidly settles down to a stable state in which only those units representing the correct 3D interpretation continue to respond.

Comments, criticisms, and extensions

The model outlined above is, in fact, a rather early attempt chosen for its clarity and because it provides a good example of a connectionist approach to a particular visual processing problem. More recent accounts (e.g., Marr & Poggio, 1979; Pollard, Mayhew, & Frisby, 1985) have considered whether correspondence matches should be based on the primal sketch or whether they should have access to the earlier zero-crossing maps so that matches can first be made at coarse spatial scales and then progressively refined. They have also introduced the concept of "disparity gradient", which is a convenient way to represent the way that distance in the world changes across position in the image and thus provides a convenient measure for the constraint on smoothness of depth variation. None the less, such developments can be viewed essentially as refinements of the same basic computational theory.

Work on the $2\frac{1}{2}$D sketch has by and large emphasized single processes (or modules) that provide depthy representations of stimuli – stereopsis being a prime example. It remains poorly understood how the different forms of input to such a representation might be combined, what the representation so formed might specify, and what purposes it might serve. Marr (1982) suggested that such a representation might be useful for action, since it would specify the relative depth of the surface of the object to the viewer. In this way, the $2\frac{1}{2}$D sketch would serve a different computational purpose from the 3D model description, which, being viewpoint invariant, cannot be used to guide actions directly, but which is useful for recognition. However, different input modules provide information suiting subtly different purposes. For example, stereopsis can provide accurate information about the relative distances of surfaces from an observer, but it is less suited to providing information about the tilt and slant of each point on the surface. In contrast, surface tilt and slant can be reliably provided by movement information. Hence it is possible that different tasks are dependent on different input modules, and that combination of the inputs to form a single representation is not useful.

OBJECT REPRESENTATION

No matter how efficient and rich the description produced in the stages described so far, the most fundamental and difficult step in visual recognition is the matching of this description to some pre-stored representation of an object. This is the very essence of recognition, allowing us to mobilize our existing knowledge and thus to make sense of the world. The processes involved in matching the viewer-centred representation provided by the $2\frac{1}{2}$D sketch to stored representations are so complex that computational theories can provide only very general constraints. However, two basic requirements on any general method of representing objects are, first, that it be flexible enough to capture a wide range (if not all) recognizable objects, and second, that it be easily accessible from the types of representation available from the image. Of course, these requirements work both ways – a good way to represent objects will almost certainly suggest an appropriate way to describe the image, while a good way to describe the image will constrain the plausible ways of representing objects.

The representation provided by the $2\frac{1}{2}$D sketch is viewer-centred, describing the scene from one particular viewpoint, whereas pre-stored representations must obviously be much more general, describing the basic 3D structure of an object in such a way that its appearance from *any* viewpoint can easily be obtained. One effective way to achieve this is to describe the object, or a significant component of it, in relation to some axis – perhaps an axis of symmetry, or along which the object is most elongated or, failing these, an external reference such as vertical. Marr and Nishihara (1978) developed this basic idea into a representational scheme based upon generalized cones. A generalized cone has three components – an axis of description, a description of the cross-section at right-angles to this axis, and a description of how this basic cross-section varies along the axis. Thus, for example, the shape of a milk bottle would be completely described by an axis running lengthways through its centre, a circular cross-section, and a simple mathematical function specifying how the radius of the circle varies along the axis from top to bottom. Allowing that complex objects can be broken down into simpler 3D components, one can imagine similar descriptions of basic tree-shapes, or human beings – indeed almost anything can be represented by this scheme, although it is obviously more appropriate for some objects than for others.

Accessing models from the $2\frac{1}{2}$D sketch

A primary aim in coding the parts of an object relative to an axis is to derive a representation that is robust to the effects of changing viewpoint. For example, let us suppose that a coffee pot is coded as having a semi-circular handle connecting along the main elongated axis of the pot, with a lip on the other side of the main axis. This description of the parts relative to the main axis remains the same as the pot is rotated during the action of pouring, even though the description of the pot on the retina changes with the angle of rotation. All that is needed is that the main axis can be coded as such across the different orientations.

Of course, many common objects contain multiple axes: while the main axis of a coffee pot may be the axis of elongation determined by its height, there are other major axes for each of the parts – e.g., axes of symmetry for the handle and for the lip. The coffee pot can serve as the "object" for the visual system, if the other axes are coded as parts relative to the main axis of the pot. However, it is also possible for the lip to serve as the "object", in which case the parts might be the curved outer lines of the lip which are coded relative to the main axis of symmetry down the centre. These different descriptions might be used on different occasions. The lip might be taken as the "object" if the task is to discriminate the type of lip on the particular pot; however, if the task is to discriminate the type of coffee pot, then the lip would be coded as a part relative to whole pot.

The above discussion suggests that it might be useful to encode objects hierarchically, with each "part" nested relative to the main axis of the next-most global whole. For instance, this would allow an observer to focus upon a part, or to re-orient attention from a part to a whole, according to the task

195

at hand. Marr and Nishihara's (1978) representation scheme allows this to take place.

Marr and Nishihara also recognized that such representations should probably not be static. For many objects, the locations of parts change as the whole object moves. Too rigid a coding of the location of a part to the whole could lead to the object becoming unrecognizable when it moves. In fact, human vision copes extremely well with motion of parts of objects, and can even use relative motion of parts as an important cue in recognizing complex perceptual wholes. Thus, in a classic demonstration, Johansson (1973) had stooges walk with light-points attached to the main joints of their bodies. Observers could see only the light-points as the stooges moved but they nevertheless gained the instantaneous impression of human beings walking. This instantaneous impression could be gained only if the coding of parts to the whole were sensitive to the ways in which the parts are articulated during movement of the object. Marr and Nishihara suggested that the locations of the parts of objects were coded with some degree of freedom of movement.

Comments, criticisms, and extensions

Marr and Nishihara's scheme for high-level object representations itself depends on adequate procedures for finding appropriate axes and for segmenting whole objects into suitable parts. Marr and Nishihara suggested that such segmentation may involve finding points of high concavity (sharp bends) along the bounding contour of an object, and segmenting the object at those points. The parts may then be coded as the regions divided by each region of concavity. Subsequent workers (e.g., Hoffman & Richards, 1984) have developed the formal computational theory demonstrating mathematically why regions of concavity provide reliable segmentation cues, and have demonstrated empirically that such regions are used for parsing wholes into parts in human vision.

Other empirical research shows that objects can be identified most rapidly at particular levels of specificity. For instance, cats may be identified first as animals, then as cats and then as a particular breed of cat (e.g., Rosch, Mervis, Gray, Johnson, & Boyes-Bream, 1976). This meshes with the notion of a hierarchical representation, with more specific representations being generated lower in the representational hierarchy. Hierarchical representations may also be computationally useful in that they allow fast access to more general levels of representational knowledge, and thus general categorization to be made rapidly.

Biederman: recognition by components (RBC) theory

Later researchers have queried details of Marr's account of object representation and recognition. One noteworthy extension was suggested by Biederman

(1987). Biederman's account differs in two fundamental ways from that proposed by Marr. First, instead of generalized cones, Biederman suggests that objects are represented in terms of a limited set of specific "geons" (which can be thought of as specific instances of generalized cones). Second, geons are derived by combining "non-accidental properties" typically found in images, for example a straight line in an image will generally indicate a straight 3D edge, a symmetrical region in the image will generally indicate a symmetrical 3D surface. These 2D image properties are reliable in the sense that they almost always indicate a related 3D property of the world.

Geons are specified by describing both the cross-section and the axis of a part of an object in terms of simple dichotomies (e.g., straight *vs* curved, symmetrical *vs* asymmetrical): there is no need to describe the degree of curvature or the actual shape of any symmetry. This provides a vocabulary of 36 geons, and objects can be described as a set of geons and their relationships. Recognition thus becomes a matter of (1) segmenting the image into regions (as done by Marr & Nishihara, 1978), (2) describing the regions in terms of their properties (straight, symmetrical, and so forth) to obtain a suitable description, and then (3) matching this description to a pre-stored geon-based description of known objects. The important point here, however, is that the initial descriptions can be obtained directly from a 2D representation (say the full primal sketch) because the whole scheme is based upon non-accidental image properties: there is no need to derive a $2\frac{1}{2}$D sketch.

Biederman's scheme is computationally useful in a number of ways. First, since it uses non-accidental properties of edges to drive the recognition process, it is robust to random noise in images. Second, since the coding of geons depends on qualitative rather than metric differences in image primitives, recognition does not depend on accurate metric representation (though whether visually guided actions to objects depend on metric information is perhaps another matter). Third, qualitative differences between the geon types are relatively constant across a wide range of image variations. It follows that the same descriptions of an object can be derived across a wide range of viewpoints, doing away with the need to generate complex 3D model representations to ease memory constraints on recognition.

In a number of ways, then, Biederman's account amounts to a different computational theory from that proposed by Marr, based on the realization that some 2D properties of images provide reliable information about the 3D structure of the world. Relevant empirical research indicates that object recognition may operate directly from 2D image properties (Biederman & Ju, 1988), though the extent to which it does so may differ according to the nature of the object (e.g., surface information may become useful when objects have to be differentiated within classes of visually similar neighbours; Price & Humphreys, 1989). Both edge-based processes, of the type suggested

197

by Biederman, and surface-based processes, such as those proposed by Marr, may play a role in human object recognition.

CONCLUSIONS

From the examples considered, it should be clear that the product of a computational theory is, in practice, a set of specific constraints. An analysis of the stimulus, for example, may reveal constraints on its structure which may be exploited by building general assumptions into the analytic processes. Such is the case in edge detection and stereopsis, where the relationship between the images and the world leads almost directly to suggestions about specific neural processes, and the computational theory provides the link between neurophysiological, psychophysical, and computer modelling data. In other cases, the constraints emerge mainly from an analysis of the task, rather than the stimulus. Here, as in the case of object representation, the constraints typically function at a higher level and, although they are usually too general to suggest specific neural implementations, they none the less usefully restrict the range of possible solutions.

The computational approach that we have discussed in most detail, that of David Marr, was unremittingly bottom-up in emphasis. It sought to maximize the processing of image data, making only general assumptions about the nature of the perceptual world, rather than using assumptions about specific objects. In part, this may have been a reaction against the earlier "blocks world" research, which tended towards solutions too particular to the stimulus domain to be generally applicable. However, attempts to implement the processing algorithms proposed by Marr have not yet led to clear practical successes, and researchers are beginning again to consider whether top-down, domain-specific knowledge might be utilized (though, in contrast to the "blocks world" research, this would now be based on a thorough analysis of real-world image properties). This trend has been encouraged by two of the recent developments we have mentioned. One is the development of connectionist models of visual processing. In many instances, connectionist models incorporate feedback from higher-level representations to early representations, which can serve to constrain the "hypotheses" suggested by early visual processing. Within the models, the role of top-down feedback becomes more important as bottom-up information becomes more degenerate (e.g., McClelland, 1987), consistent with much evidence for top-down effects in vision. The second development stems from the work of researchers such as Biederman, who has argued that stored knowledge about objects may be contacted directly from 2D information in the image, without the elaboration of $2\frac{1}{2}$D or 3D descriptions. Direct edge-based activation provides a route for the early mobilization of object knowledge, and such early mobilization is clearly important if top-down processing is to play a role in normal object recognition. Indeed, the coupling of fast edge-based processes to Marr and Nishihara's scheme of hierarchical object representation may provide one way to generate rapid object categorization and top-down feedback using categorical knowledge.

In sum, we may expect to see a continuing and substantial modification of the specific framework proposed by Marr. Nevertheless, his general approach, and in particular the argument for computational theories, is likely to remain as one of the most important contributions of research in artificial intelligence to psychological theory. Such theories are able to guide empirical and theoretical research, even if the detailed models specified at any one time later turn out to be wrong.

FURTHER READING

Bowden, M. A. (1987). *Artificial intelligence & natural man* (2nd edn). London: Massachusetts Institute of Technology Press.

Fischler, M. A., & Firschein, O. (Eds) (1987). *Readings in computer vision: Issues, problems, principles, and paradigms.* Los Altos, CA: Morgan Kaufmann.

Green, P., & Bruce, V. (1991). *Visual perception* (2nd edn). London: Lawrence Erlbaum.

Marr, D. (1982). *Vision: A computational investigation into human representation and processing of visual information.* San Francisco, CA: Freeman.

Watt, R. J. (1991). *Understanding vision.* London: Academic Press.

REFERENCES

Adelson, E. H., & Movshon, J. A. (1982). Phenomenal coherence of moving visual patterns. *Nature, 300,* 523–525.

Biederman, I. (1987). Recognition-by-components: A theory of human image understanding. *Psychological Review, 94,* 115–147.

Biederman, I., & Ju, G. (1988). Surface versus edge-based determinants of visual recognition. *Cognitive Psychology, 20,* 38–64.

Blake, A., & Marinos, C. (1990) Shape from texture: Estimation, isotropy and moments. *Artificial Intelligence, 45,* 323–380.

Canny, J. F. (1986). A computational approach to edge detection. *IEEE Transactions on Pattern Analysis and Machine Intelligence, 8,* 679–698.

Clocksin, W. H. (1980). Perception of surface slant and edge labels from optical flow: A computational approach. *Perception, 9,* 253–269.

Clowes, M. B. (1971). On seeing things. *Artificial Intelligence, 21,* 79–116.

Draper, S. W. (1981). The use of gradient and dual space in line-drawing interpretation. *Artificial Intelligence, 17,* 461–508.

Enns, J., & Rensink, R. A. (1990). Influence of scene-based properties on visual search. *Science, 247,* 721–723.

Gibson, J. J. (1979). *The ecological approach to visual perception.* Boston, MA: Houghton Mifflin.

Gray, C. M., & Singer, W. (1989). Stimulus specific neuronal oscillations in orientation columns of cat visual cortex. *Proceedings of the National Academy of Science, 86,* 1698–1702.

Grossberg, S., & Mingolla, E. (1985). Natural dynamics of perceptual grouping: texture boundaries and emergent segmentations. *Perception and Psychophysics*, *38*, 141–161.

Guzman, A. (1968). Decomposition of a visual scene into three-dimensional bodies. *Proceedings of the American Federation of Information Processing Studies Fall Joint Conference*, *33*, 291–304.

Harris, M. G. (1986). The perception of moving stimuli: A model of spatiotemporal coding in human vision. *Vision Research*, *26*, 1281–1287.

Hawken, M. J., & Parker, A. J. (1987). Spatial properties of neurons in the monkey striate cortex. *Proceedings of the Royal Society of London* B, *231*, 251–288.

Heeger, D. J. (1987). Model for the extraction of image flow. *Journal of the Optical Society of America*, *4A*, 1455–1471.

Hochstein, S., & Spitzer, H. (1984). Zero-crossing detectors in monkey cortex? *Biological Cybernetics*, *51*, 195–199.

Hoffman, D. D., & Richards, W. A. (1984). Parts of recognition. *Cognition*, *18*, 65–96.

Horn, B. K. P. (1977) Understanding image intensities. *Artificial Intelligence*, *8*, 201–231.

Hubel, D. H., & Wiesel, T. N. (1962). Receptive fields, binocular interaction and functional architecture in the cat's visual cortex. *Journal of Physiology*, *160*, 106–154.

Hubel, D. H., & Wiesel, T. N. (1968). Receptive fields and functional architecture in the cat's visual cortex. *Journal of Physiology*, *195*, 215–243.

Huffman, D. A. (1971). Impossible objects as nonsense sentences. *Machine Intelligence*, *6*, 295–324.

Hummel, J. E., & Biederman, I. (1992). Dynamic binding in a neural network for shape recognition. *Psychological Review*, *99*, 480–517.

Johansson, G. (1973). Visual perception of biological motion and a model for its analysis. *Perception and Psychophysics*, *14*, 201–211.

Julesz, B. (1971). *Foundations of cyclopean perception*. Chicago, IL: University of Chicago Press.

Kanade, T. (1981). Recovery of the 3-D shape of an object from a single view. *Artificial Intelligence*, *17*, 409–460.

Koenderink, J. J. (1986). Optic flow. *Vision Research*, *26*, 161–180.

Longuet-Higgins, H. C., & Prazdny, K. (1980). The interpretation of a moving retinal image. *Proceedings of the Royal Society of London*, B, *208*, 385–397.

McClelland, J. L. (1987). The case for interactionism in language processing. In M. Coltheart (Ed.) *Attention and performance XII* (pp. 3–36). London: Lawrence Erlbaum.

Marr, D. (1982). *Vision: A computational investigation into human representation and processing of visual information*. San Francisco, CA: Freeman.

Marr, D., & Hildreth, E. (1980). Theory of edge detection. *Proceedings of the Royal Society of London*, B, *207*, 187–217.

Marr, D., & Nishihara, K. H. (1978). Representation and recognition of the spatial organisation of three-dimensional shapes. *Proceedings of the Royal Society of London*, B, *200*, 269–294.

Marr, D., & Poggio, T. (1976). Cooperative computation of stereo disparity. *Science*, *194*, 283–287.

Marr, D., & Poggio, T. (1979). A theory of human stereo vision. *Proceedings of the Royal Society of London*, B, *204*, 301–328.

Marr, D., & Ullman, S. (1981). Directional selectivity and its use in early visual processing. *Proceedings of the Royal Society of London*, B, *211*, 151–180.

Perkins, D. N. (1968). Cubic corners. *MIT Research Laboratory of Electronics Quarterly Progress Report*, *89*, 207–214.

Peterhans, E., & von der Heydt, R. (1989). Mechanisms of contour perception in monkey visual cortex 2: Contours bridging gaps. *Journal of Neuroscience*, *9*, 1749–1763.

Pollard, S. B., Mayhew, J. E. W., & Frisby, J. P. (1985). PMF: A stereo correspondence algorithm using a disparity gradient limit. *Perception*, *14*, 449–470.

Price, C. J., & Humphreys, G. W. (1989). The effects of surface detail on object categorization and naming. *Quarterly Journal of Experimental Psychology*, *41A*, 797–828.

Rieger, J. H., & Lawton, D. T. (1985). Processing differential image motion. *Journal of the Optical Society of America*, *2A*, 354–360.

Robson J. G. (1980). Neural images: The physiological basis of spatial vision. In C. S. Harris (Ed.) *Visual coding and adaptability* (pp. 177–214). Hillsdale, NJ: Lawrence Erlbaum.

Rosch, E., Mervis, C. B., Gray, W. D., Johnson, D. M., & Boyes-Bream, P. (1976). Basic objects in natural categories. *Cognitive Psychology*, *8*, 382–439.

Tootell, R. B., Silverman, M. S., & De Valois, R. L. (1981). Spatial frequency columns in striate visual cortex. *Science*, *214*, 813–815.

Ullman, S. (1979). *The interpretation of visual motion*. Cambridge, MA: Massachusetts Institute of Technology Press.

Waltz, D. (1975). Understanding line drawings as scenes with shadows. In P. H. Winston (Ed.) *The psychology of computer vision* (pp. 19–91). New York: McGraw-Hill.

Watson, A. B., & Ahumada, A. J. (1989). A hexagonal orthogonal-oriented pyramid as a model of image representation in the visual cortex. *IEEE Transactions on Biomedical Engineering*, *36*, 97–106.

Watt, R. J. (1991). *Understanding vision*. London: Academic Press.

Watt, R. J., & Morgan, M. J. (1985). A theory of the primitive spatial code in human vision. *Vision Research*, *25*, 1661–1674.

Waxman, A. M., & Wohn, K. (1988). Image flow theory: A framework for 3-D inference from time-varying imagery. In C. Brown (Ed.) *Advances in computer vision* (vol. 1, pp. 165–224). Hillsdale, NJ: Lawrence Erlbaum.

Wertheimer, M. (1912). Experimentalle Studien über der Sehen von Bewegung. *Zeitschrift für Psychologie*, *61*, 161–265. Translated in T. Shipley (Ed.) (1961) *Classics in psychology*. New York: Philosophical Library.

Wilson, H. R., & Bergen, J. R. (1979). A four mechanism model for threshold spatial vision. *Vision research*, *19*, 19–32.

3.3

HEARING

Brian C. J. Moore
University of Cambridge, England

This chapter is mainly concerned with the perception of sound by normally hearing and hearing-impaired people. However, to reach an understanding of the mechanisms involved in auditory perception, it is helpful to have a basic understanding of the physical nature of sounds and of the physiology of the peripheral auditory system. Hence the chapter starts with a brief review of those topics.

THE PHYSICAL CHARACTERISTICS OF SOUNDS

Fourier analysis

Sound usually originates from the motion or vibration of an object. This motion is impressed upon the surrounding medium (usually air) as a pattern of changes in pressure. The pressure changes are transmitted through the medium and may be heard as sound. One of the simplest types of sound is the sinusoid. For a sinusoid, the pressure variation as a function of time, $P(t)$, is described by the equation

$$P(t) = A \sin(2\pi f t)$$

where t is time, A is the peak amplitude (maximum deviation from the mean atmospheric pressure), and f is the frequency of the sound in Hz (number of cycles per second). A sinusoid has a "pure" tone quality, like the sound produced by a tuning fork, and is also called a "pure tone" or "simple tone".

Although any sound can be described in terms of sound pressure as a function of time (often called the waveform of the sound), it is often more convenient, and more meaningful, to describe sound in a different way, based on a theorem by Fourier, who proved that any complex waveform (with certain restrictions) can be analysed, or broken down, into a series of sinusoids with specific frequencies and amplitudes. Such an analysis is called Fourier analysis, and each sinusoid is called a (Fourier) component of the complex sound. A plot of the magnitudes of the components as a function of frequency is referred to as the spectrum of the sound.

The simplest type of complex sound to which Fourier analysis can be applied is one which is periodic, repeating regularly as a function of time. Such a sound is composed of a number of sinusoids, each of which has a frequency that is an integral multiple of the frequency of a common (not necessarily present) fundamental component. The fundamental component has a frequency equal to the repetition rate of the complex waveform as a whole. The frequency components of the complex sound are known as harmonics and are numbered, the fundamental being given harmonic number 1. The nth harmonic has a frequency which is n times that of the fundamental.

One of the reasons for representing sounds in terms of their sinusoidal components is that people can, to a limited extent, perform a similar analysis. For example, two simultaneous sinusoids, whose frequencies are not too close, will usually be heard as two separate tones each with its own pitch rather than as a single complex sound.

The measurement of sound level

The instruments used to measure the magnitudes of sounds, such as microphones, normally respond to changes in air pressure. However, the auditory system can deal with a huge range of sound pressures. This makes it inconvenient to deal with sound pressures directly. Instead a logarithmic measure expressing the ratio of two pressures is used – the decibel. One pressure, P_0, is chosen as a reference and the other pressure, P_1, is expressed relative to this. The number of decibels (dB) corresponding to a given ratio of acoustic pressure is

number of dB $= 20 \log_{10}(P_1/P_0)$.

When the magnitude of a sound is specified in dB, it is customary to use the word "level" to refer to its magnitude. The reference pressure most commonly used is 2×10^{-5} Newtons per square metre (N/m^2). A sound level specified using this reference level is referred to as a sound pressure level (SPL). The reference sound level, 0 dB SPL, is a low sound level which was chosen to be close to the average human threshold for detecting a 1,000-Hz sinusoid. Normal conversation typically has a level of 65–70 dB SPL, while a rock band may produce potentially damaging levels as high as 120 dB SPL.

BASIC STRUCTURE AND FUNCTION OF THE AUDITORY SYSTEM

The outer and middle ear

Figure 1 shows the structure of the peripheral part of the human auditory system. The outer ear is composed of the pinna (the part we actually see) and the auditory canal or meatus. Sound travels down the meatus and causes the eardrum, or tympanic membrane, to vibrate. These vibrations are transmitted through the middle ear by three small bones, the ossicles, to a membrane-covered opening (the oval window) in the bony wall of the spiral-shaped structure of the inner ear – the cochlea. Damage to the middle ear, or obstruction of the ear canal, leads to a partial hearing loss known as conductive deafness. Its effects are similar to a simple attenuation of the sound, and it can often be treated medically.

The inner ear and the basilar membrane

The cochlea is divided along its length by the basilar membrane, which moves in response to sound. The response of the basilar membrane to sinusoidal stimulation takes the form of a travelling wave which moves along the membrane, with an amplitude that increases at first and then decreases rather abruptly. The basic form of the wave is illustrated in Figure 2, which shows

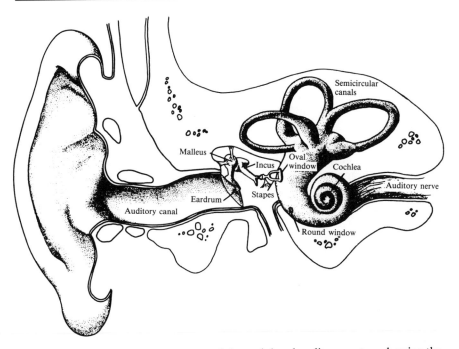

Figure 1 Illustration of the structure of the peripheral auditory system showing the
outer, middle and inner ear
Source: Lindsay and Norman, 1972, by permission of the authors

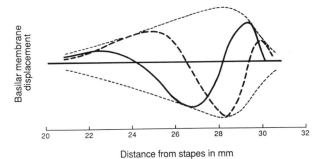

Figure 2 The instantaneous displacement of the basilar membrane at two successive
instants in time, derived from a cochlear model. The pattern moves from left to right,
building up gradually with distance, and decaying rapidly beyond the point of
maximal displacement. The dotted line represents the envelope traced out by the
amplitude peaks in the waveform
Source: Redrawn from von Békésy, 1947

205

the instantaneous displacement of the basilar membrane (derived from a cochlear model, described by von Békésy, 1947) for two successive instants in time, in response to a 200-Hz sinusoid. This figure also shows the line joining the amplitude peaks, which is called the envelope. The envelope shows a peak at a particular position on the basilar membrane.

The position of the peak in the pattern of vibration differs according to the frequency of stimulation. High-frequency sounds (around 15,000 Hz) produce a peak near the oval window, while low-frequency sounds (around 50 Hz) produce a peak towards the other end (the apex). Intermediate frequencies produce peaks at intermediate places. Thus, each point on the basilar membrane is "tuned" to a particular frequency. When a sound is composed of several sinusoids with different frequencies, each sinusoid produces a peak at its own characteristic place on the basilar membrane. In effect, the cochlea behaves like a Fourier analyser, although with a less than perfect frequency-analysing power.

Measurements of basilar membrane vibration have shown that the basilar membrane is much more sharply tuned than originally found by von Békésy (1960). The sharpness of tuning of the basilar membrane depends critically on physiological condition; the better the condition, the sharper is the tuning (Khanna & Leonard, 1982; Robles, Ruggero, & Rich, 1986). In a normal, healthy ear, each point on the basilar membrane is sharply tuned, responding with high sensitivity to a limited range of frequencies, and requiring higher and higher sound intensities to produce a response as the frequency is made higher or lower. The sharp tuning and high sensitivity probably reflect an active process; that is, they do not result simply from the mechanical properties of the basilar membrane and surrounding fluid, but depend on biological structures actively influencing the mechanics (for reviews, see Pickles, 1986, 1988; Yates, 1986). Damage to the cochlea can weaken or destroy the active process, leading to a type of hearing loss known as cochlear hearing loss. This results not only in a loss of sensitivity to weak sounds (an elevation of the absolute threshold), but also in changes in the way that supra-threshold sounds are perceived. Cochlear hearing loss usually cannot be helped by medical treatment.

Between the basilar membrane and the tectorial membrane are hair cells, which form part of a structure called the organ of Corti (see Figure 3). The hair cells are divided into two groups by an arch known as the tunnel of Corti. Those on the side of the arch closest to the outside of the cochlea are known as outer hair cells, and are arranged in three rows in the cat and up to five rows in humans. The hair cells on the other side of the arch form a single row, and are known as inner hair cells. There are about 25,000 outer hair cells, while there are about 3,500 inner hair cells. The tectorial membrane, which has a gelatinous structure, lies above the hairs. When the basilar membrane moves up and down, a shearing motion is created between the basilar membrane and the tectorial membrane. As a result the hairs at the

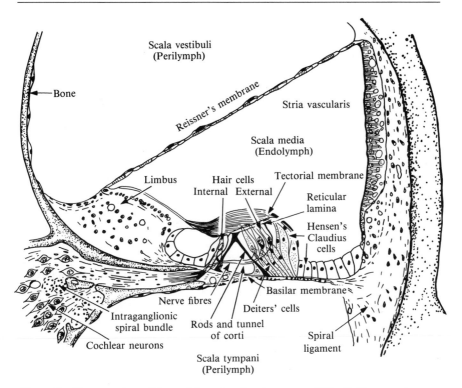

Figure 3 Cross-section of the cochlea, showing the organ of Corti. The receptors are the hair cells lying on either side of the tunnel of Corti
Source: Redrawn from Davis, 1962

tops of the hair cells are displaced. It is thought that this leads to excitation of the inner hair cells, which leads in turn to the generation of action potentials in the neurons of the auditory nerve. Thus the inner hair cells act to transduce mechanical movements into neural activity.

The main role of the outer hair cells may be actively to influence the mechanics of the cochlea, so as to produce high sensitivity and sharp tuning. There is even evidence that the outer hair cells have a motor function, changing their length and shape in response to electrical stimulation (for a review see Pickles, 1988). Cochlear hearing loss is often associated with damage to the outer hair cells.

NEURAL RESPONSES IN THE AUDITORY NERVE

Information in the auditory nerve is carried in three main ways:

1 In terms of the rate of firing (action potentials per second) within

individual neurons. Generally, increases in sound level result in increases in firing rate.

2 In terms of the distribution of activity across neurons. This reflects the fact that each neuron is tuned to a particular frequency range.

3 In terms of the detailed time pattern of firing of individual neurons. The second and third of these will be described in more detail.

Tuning curves in the auditory nerve

Each neuron in the auditory nerve derives its activity from one or more hair cells lying at a particular place on the basilar membrane. Thus, the neurons are "tuned". This is often illustrated by a tuning curve, which shows the response threshold of a single neuron as a function of frequency. This curve is also known as the frequency-threshold curve (FTC). Some typical tuning curves are presented in Figure 4. The frequency at which the threshold of a neuron is lowest is called the characteristic frequency (CF). It appears that the sharpness of tuning of the basilar membrane is essentially the same as the sharpness of tuning of single neurons in the auditory nerve (Khanna & Leonard, 1982; Robles et al., 1986; Sellick, Patuzzi, & Johnstone, 1982).

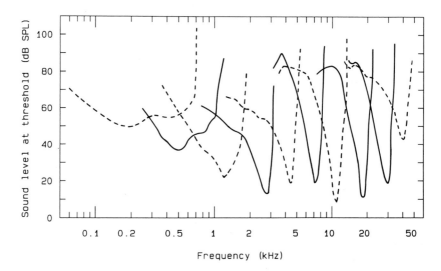

Figure 4 A sample of tuning curves (also called frequency-threshold curves) obtained from single neurons in the auditory nerve of anaesthetized cats. Each curve shows results for one neuron. The sound level required for threshold is plotted as a function of the stimulus frequency (logarithmic scale)
Source: Redrawn from Palmer, 1987

Phase locking

Nerve firings tend to be phase locked or synchronized to the time pattern of the stimulating waveform. A given neuron does not necessarily fire on every cycle of the stimulus but, when firings do occur, they occur at roughly the same phase of the waveform each time (e.g., close to a peak). Thus the time intervals between firings are (approximately) integral multiples of the period of the stimulating waveform. For example, a 500-Hz sinusoid has a period of 2 milliseconds (2 ms), and the intervals between nerve firings in response to it are grouped around 2 ms, 4 ms, 6 ms, and 8 ms. Phase locking becomes less precise at high frequencies, and in most mammals cannot be measured for frequencies above about 5 kHz.

THE ACTION OF THE EAR AS A FREQUENCY ANALYSER

A major characteristic of the auditory system is that it acts as a limited-resolution frequency analyser; complex sounds are broken down into their sinusoidal frequency components. The initial basis of this frequency analysis almost certainly depends upon the tuning which is observed on the basilar membrane. Largely as a consequence of this analysis, we are able to hear one sound in the presence of another sound with a different frequency. This ability is known as frequency selectivity or frequency resolution.

Measurement of the ear's frequency selectivity

Important sounds are sometimes rendered inaudible by other sounds, a process known as "masking". Masking may be considered as a failure of frequency selectivity, and it can be used as a tool to measure the frequency selectivity of the ear. One conception of masking, which has had both theoretical and practical success, assumes that the auditory system contains a bank of overlapping band-pass filters, with adjacent, ordered, centre frequencies (Fletcher, 1940; Patterson & Moore, 1986). The filters are called the "auditory filters". In the simple case of a sinusoidal signal presented in a background noise, it is assumed that the observer detects the signal using the filter whose output has the highest signal-to-masker ratio. The signal is detected if that ratio exceeds a certain value. In most practical situations, the filter involved has a centre frequency close to that of the signal.

A good deal of work has been directed towards determining the characteristics of the auditory filters; the most important characteristic for a given filter is the relative response to different frequencies, sometimes referred to as the "shape" of the filter. One method uses a psychophysical analogue of the method used by neurophysiologists to determine a neural tuning curve. The resulting curves are often called psychophysical tuning curves (PTCs). The signal used is a sinusoid which is usually presented at a very low level, say 10 dB above the absolute threshold. It is assumed that this will excite only a small number of nerve fibres with characteristic frequencies (CFs) close to that of the signal. Thus, to a first approximation, only one auditory filter will be involved in detecting the signal. The masker is either a sinusoid or a noise containing a narrow range of frequencies.

To determine a PTC the signal is fixed in frequency and level, and the level of the masker required to mask the signal is determined, for various centre frequencies of the masker. If it is assumed that the signal will be masked when the masker produces a fixed amount of activity in the neurons that would otherwise respond to the signal, then the curve mapped out in this way is analogous to the neural tuning curve. Some examples are given in Figure 5. Returning to the concept of the auditory filter, we can think of the PTC as representing the masker level required to produce a fixed output from the filter centred at the signal frequency. Thus the filter "shape" can be obtained simply by turning the tuning curve upside-down.

An alternative method of determining the auditory filter shape has been described by Patterson (1976). The method is illustrated in Figure 6. The signal is fixed in frequency, and the masker is a noise with a bandstop or notch centred at the signal frequency. The deviation of each edge of the notch from the signal frequency is denoted by Δf. The threshold of the signal is

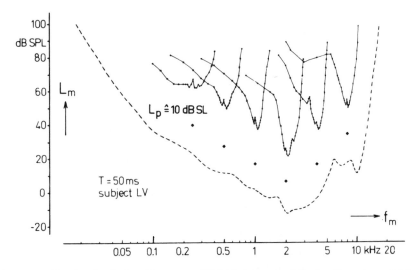

Figure 5 Psychophysical tuning curves (PTCs) determined in simultaneous masking using sinusoidal signals 10 dB above absolute threshold (called 10 dB SL). For each curve the solid diamond below it indicates the frequency and level of the signal. The masker was a sinusoid which had a fixed starting phase relationship to the 50-ms signal. The masker level required for threshold is plotted as a function of masker frequency. The dashed line shows the absolute threshold for the signal

Source: From Vogten, 1974, by permission of the author

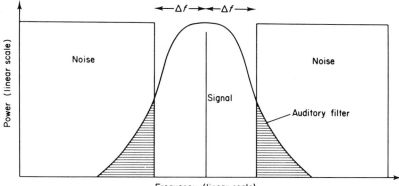

Figure 6 Schematic illustration of the method used by Patterson (1976) to determine auditory filter shape. The threshold of the sinusoidal signal is measured as a function of the width of a spectral notch in the noise masker. The amount of noise passing through the auditory filter centred at the signal frequency is proportional to the shaded areas
Source: Moore, 1989

determined as a function of notch width. Usually the notch is symmetrically placed around the signal frequency and the analysis assumes that the auditory filter is symmetric on a linear frequency scale. This assumption seems reasonable at moderate sound levels (Patterson & Moore, 1986).

As the width of the notch is increased, less and less noise passes through the auditory filter; thus, the threshold of the signal drops, that is, improves. The amount of noise passing through the auditory filter is proportional to the area under the filter in the frequency range covered by the noise. This is shown as the shaded areas in Figure 6. Given the assumption that threshold corresponds to a constant signal-to-masker ratio at the output of the auditory filter, the change in threshold with notch width indicates how the area under the filter varies with Δf. From this, it is possible to derive the shape of the filter itself. The method can also be extended to the case where the filter is not assumed to be symmetric, provided certain assumptions are made about the general form of the filter (Patterson & Moore, 1986).

A typical auditory filter shape obtained using Patterson's method is shown in Figure 7, for a centre frequency of 1 kHz. Notice that the filter is symmetrical on the linear frequency scale used; this is only the case at moderate sound levels. The sharpness of a filter is often described by its equivalent rectangular bandwidth (ERB). This is defined as the frequency range covered by a rectangular filter with the same peak value and which passes the same total power of white noise (a sound containing equal energy at all frequencies). The ERB of the auditory filter increases with increasing centre frequency. However, when expressed as a proportion of centre frequency the band-

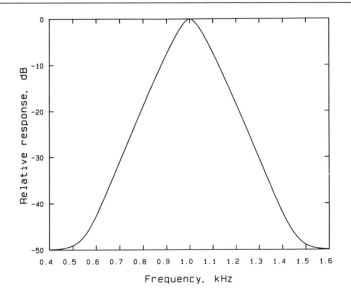

Figure 7 A typical auditory filter shape derived using Patterson's notched-noise method

width tends to be narrowest at middle to high frequencies. Over the range 100 to 8,000 Hz, and at moderate sound levels, the ERB (in Hz), is well approximated by

ERB = 24.7(4.37F + 1)

where F is frequency in kHz (Glasberg & Moore, 1990).

Frequency selectivity in the hearing impaired

There is now considerable evidence that in people with hearing impairments of cochlear origin there is a loss of frequency selectivity. This type of hearing loss is quite common, especially in elderly people. In general, higher absolute thresholds tend to be associated with broader auditory filters. Figure 8 shows a comparison of auditory filter shapes obtained separately from each ear of six subjects, each with a cochlear hearing loss in one ear only (data from Glasberg & Moore, 1986). The upper panels show filter shapes for the normal ears and the lower panels show filter shapes for the impaired ears, which had threshold elevations at the test frequency (1 kHz) ranging from about 40 to 60 dB. Losses were relatively flat as a function of frequency. A notched-noise masker was used, as described earlier, and the same noise level was used for testing all ears. It is clear that the auditory filters are considerably broader in the impaired ears. The most obvious feature is that the lower skirts of the filters are consistently and considerably less sharp than normal in the impaired ears.

A consequence of reduced frequency selectivity is a greater susceptibility to masking by interfering sounds. This may partly account for the fact that people with cochlear hearing loss often complain of difficulty in understanding speech in noise.

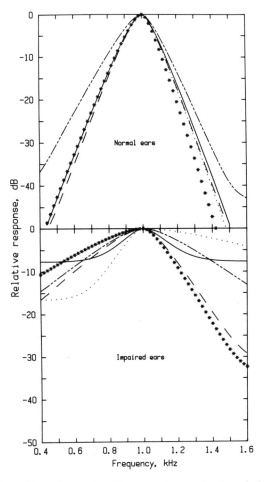

Figure 8 Auditory filter shapes for the normal ears (top) and the impaired ears (bottom) of six subjects with unilateral cochlear impairments. The impaired ear of subject DJ had too little frequency selectivity for a filter shape to be determined
Source: Glasberg and Moore, 1986

213

THE PERCEPTION OF LOUDNESS

Equal-loudness contours

In describing the perception of sound it is useful to have some kind of scale which allows one to compare the loudness of different sounds. A first step towards this is to construct equal-loudness contours for sinusoids of different frequencies. Say, for example, we take a standard tone of 1 kHz, at a level of 40 dB SPL, and ask the listener to adjust the level of a second tone (say, 2 kHz) so that it sounds equally loud. If we repeat this for many different frequencies of the second tone, then the sound level required, plotted as a function of frequency, maps out an equal-loudness contour. The level of the 1-kHz standard sound defines the loudness level, in phons. If we repeat this procedure, for different levels of the 1-kHz standard tone, then we will map out a family of equal loudness contours. Such a family is shown in Figure 9. Note that the contours resemble the absolute threshold curve (lowest curve in the figure) at low levels, but tend to become flatter at high levels.

The role of frequency selectivity in determining loudness

It has been known for many years that if the total intensity of a complex sound is fixed, its loudness depends on the frequency range over which the

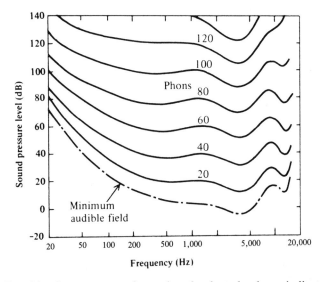

Figure 9 Equal-loudness contours for various loudness levels, as indicated on each curve. The dashed-dotted curve shows the absolute threshold (minimum audible field)
Source: Moore, 1989. Original data from Robinson and Dadson, 1956

sound extends. The basic mechanism underlying this seems to be the same auditory filter as is revealed in masking experiments. Consider as an example a noise whose total intensity is held constant while the bandwidth is varied. The loudness of the noise can be estimated indirectly by asking the listener to adjust the intensity of a second sound, with a fixed bandwidth, so that it sounds equally loud. The two sounds are presented successively. When the bandwidth of the noise is less than a certain value, the loudness is roughly independent of bandwidth. However, as the bandwidth is increased beyond a certain point, the loudness starts to increase. This is illustrated in Figure 10, for several different overall levels of the noise. The bandwidth at which loudness starts to increase is known as the critical bandwidth for loudness summation. Its value is approximately the same as the ERB of the auditory filter. A model which explains this effect is described by Moore and Glasberg (1986).

Loudness perception and recruitment in impaired ears

Cochlear hearing loss is usually associated with an abnormality of loudness perception known as loudness recruitment. Although the absolute threshold

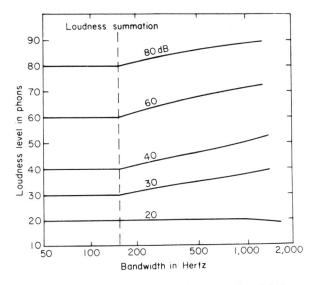

Figure 10 The loudness level of a band of noise centred at 1 kHz, measured as a function of the width of the band. For each of the curves the overall level was held constant, and is indicated in the figure. The dashed line shows that the bandwidth at which loudness begins to increase is the same at all levels tested (except that no increase occurs at the lowest level)

Source: Redrawn from Feldtkeller and Zwicker, 1956

may be elevated, the rate of growth of loudness with intensity is more rapid than normal, so that at high intensities a sound appears as loud in an impaired ear as it would in a normal ear. The effect is most easily demonstrated when only one ear of a person is affected, since then loudness matches can be made between the two ears, but it can be detected in other ways. The presence of recruitment can limit the usefulness of conventional hearing aids, since if the gain of the aid is set so as to make sounds of low intensity clearly audible, sounds of high intensity will be uncomfortably loud. Hearing aids incorporating automatic gain control (AGC), especially multi-band AGC, can be useful in alleviating this effect (Laurence, Moore, & Glasberg, 1983; Moore, 1987).

Loudness recruitment can probably be explained in terms of responses on the basilar membrane. In normal ears the active mechanism amplifies the response to weak sounds, but has progressively less effect at high sound levels. In impaired ears, this mechanism is damaged or inoperative. Thus weak sounds may not be detected, but the response to strong sounds is almost normal (Moore, 1989; Yates, 1990).

THE PERCEPTION OF PITCH

The pitch of sinusoids

Pitch is defined as that attribute of auditory sensation in terms of which sounds may be ordered on a musical scale, that is, that attribute in which variations constitute melody. For sinusoids (pure tones) the pitch is largely determined by the frequency; the higher the frequency the higher the pitch. One of the classic debates in hearing theory is concerned with the mechanisms underlying the perception of pitch. One theory, called the place theory, suggests that pitch is related to the position of maximum vibration on the basilar membrane, which is coded in terms of the relative activity of neurons with different CFs. Shifts in frequency will be detected as changes in the amount of activity at the place where the activity changes most. The alternative theory, the temporal theory, suggests that pitch is determined by the time-pattern of neural spikes (phase locking).

One major fact that these theories have to account for is our remarkably fine acuity in detecting frequency changes. This ability is called frequency discrimination, and is not to be confused with frequency selectivity. For two tones of 500 ms duration presented successively, a difference of about 3 Hz (or less in trained subjects) can be detected at a centre frequency of 1 kHz. It has been suggested that tuning curves (or auditory filters) are not sufficiently sharp to account for this fine acuity in terms of the place theory (Moore & Glasberg, 1986). A further difficulty for the place theory is that frequency discrimination worsens abruptly above 4–5 kHz (Moore, 1973). Neither neural measures of frequency selectivity (such as tuning curves) nor

216

psychophysical measures of frequency selectivity (such as PTCs or auditory filter shapes) show any abrupt change there.

These facts can be explained by assuming that temporal mechanisms are dominant at frequencies below 4–5 kHz. Changes in frequency discrimination with centre frequency (and with tone duration) can be predicted from the information available in inter-spike intervals (Goldstein & Srulovicz, 1977). The worsening performance at 4–5 kHz corresponds well with the frequency at which the temporal information ceases to be available. Studies of our perception of musical intervals also indicate a change in mechanism around 4–5 kHz. Below this, a sequence of pure tones with appropriate frequencies conveys a clear sense of melody. Above this, the sense of musical interval and of melody is lost, although the changes in frequency may still be heard.

The evidence, then, supports the idea that, for pure tones, pitch perception and discrimination are determined primarily by temporal information for frequencies below 4–5 kHz, and by place information for frequencies above this. The important frequencies for the perception of music and speech lie in the frequency range where temporal information is available.

The pitch perception of complex tones

In general, any complex sound that is periodic has a pitch, provided that the waveform repetition rate lies in the range 20–16,000 Hz. If a listener is asked to adjust the frequency of a sinusoid so that its pitch matches that of a complex tone, the frequency is usually set close to the fundamental frequency of the complex. In other words, the pitch of the complex tone is the same as the pitch of its fundamental sinusoidal component. Remarkably, however, the fundamental component does not have to be present for this pitch to be heard; removing the fundamental component from a complex sound does not generally change its pitch, although the tone quality may be slightly altered. This is called the "phenomenon of the missing fundamental". It seems that the low pitch of a complex tone is somehow derived from its higher harmonics.

Most modern theories of pitch perception assume a two-stage process. In the first stage, the stimulus is passed through an array of filters (the auditory filters). These resolve (separate) the lower harmonics, but usually do not resolve the higher harmonics. In the second stage, the pitch is derived by a central processor from the pattern of the output of the auditory filters. The central processor may make use of the distribution of activity across auditory filters, the time patterns at the outputs of the filters, or both of these (Goldstein, 1973; Moore, 1989; Moore & Glasberg, 1986; Terhardt, 1974). In essence, the pitch corresponding to the missing fundamental appears to be derived by a kind of pattern recognition process from information conveyed by harmonics above the fundamental.

217

THE PERCEPTION OF TIMBRE

Timbre may be defined as the characteristic quality of sound that distin-guishes one voice or musical instrument from another (when their pitches and loudnesses are the same). Timbre depends on several different physical properties of sound, including

1 Whether the sound is periodic, having a tonal quality for repetition rates from about 20 to 16,000 Hz, or irregular and having a noise-like quality.
2 Whether the sound is continuous or interrupted. For sounds that have short durations the exact way in which the sound is turned on and off can play an important role. For example, in the case of sounds produced by stringed instruments, a rapid onset (a fast rise time) is usually perceived as a struck or plucked string, whereas a gradual onset is heard as a bowed string.
3 The distribution of energy over frequency, and changes in the distribution with time. This is the correlate of timbre that has been studied most widely. Sounds containing predominantly high frequencies have a "sharp" timbre, whereas those containing mainly low frequencies sound "dull" or "mellow". This is another example of the action of the ear as a frequency analyser. The components in a complex sound will be partially separated by the auditory filters, and the distribution of activity at the output of the filters, as a function of filter centre frequency, determines timbre.

THE TEMPORAL RESOLUTION OF THE EAR

The auditory system is particularly well adapted to detecting changes in sounds as a function of time. The limits of this ability reflect the temporal resolution of the ear. One measure of this requires the subject to detect a brief gap in a relatively long duration sound. Many gap-detection experi-ments have used white noise as a stimulus; this noise contains equal energy at all frequencies. The results generally agree quite well, the threshold value being 2 to 3 ms (Penner, 1977; Plomp, 1964). More recently, gap thresholds have been measured for bandpass noises, to determine whether gap threshold varies with centre frequency. Unfortunately, when a noise band is abruptly switched off and on, to produce the gap, energy is spread to frequencies out-side the nominal bandwidth of the noise. In order to prevent the detection of this "spectral splatter", which could give rise to artificially low thresholds, the noise bands have been presented in a continuous noise designed to mask the splatter (Fitzgibbons & Wightman, 1982; Shailer & Moore, 1983). Some results from Shailer and Moore (1983) are plotted in Figure 11.

The value of the gap threshold increases monotonically with decreasing centre frequency. At high frequencies the gap threshold is similar to that found for white noise, suggesting that subjects make use primarily of high

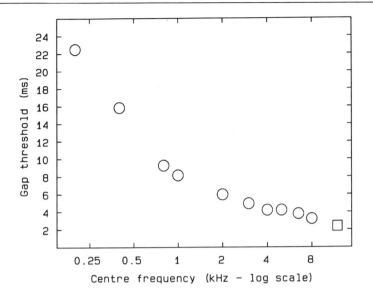

Figure 11   Thresholds for the detection of a temporal gap in a bandpass noise
stimulus, as a function of the centre frequency of the noise
Source: Data from Shailer and Moore, 1983

frequencies when detecting gaps in white noise. The increase in gap threshold
at low frequencies may be connected with temporal fluctuations in the noise
bands. The auditory filters have narrower bandwidths at low frequencies,
and so each filter passes only a small range of frequencies; at low frequencies
the output is a narrow band of noise. A narrow band of noise resembles a
sinusoid that is fluctuating in amplitude from moment to moment. The
narrower the bandwidth, the slower are the fluctuations. Slow fluctuations in
the noise, especially "dips" in the envelope, may be confused with the gap
that is to be detected. Thus, the increase in gap threshold at low frequencies
may be explained by the decrease in auditory filter bandwidth, and the
resulting slow fluctuations at the output of the auditory filter.

Another way of measuring temporal resolution is to determine the
threshold for detecting amplitude modulation (changes in amplitude over
time) as a function of modulation rate; the resulting function is known as the
temporal modulation transfer function (TMTF). When the modulated
stimulus is white noise, modulation thresholds are small (i.e., sensitivity is
high) for modulation rates up to about 50 Hz, and thresholds increase
progressively beyond that (Viemeister, 1979). Modulation is not detectable at
all for rates above about 500–1,000 Hz.

THE LOCALIZATION OF SOUNDS

Binaural cues

It has long been recognized that slight differences in the sounds reaching the two ears can be used as cues in sound localization. The two major cues are differences in the time of arrival at the two ears and differences in intensity at the two ears. For example, a sound coming from the left will arrive first at the left ear and be more intense in the left ear. For steady sinusoidal stimulation, differences in time of arrival can be detected and used to judge location only at frequencies below about 1,500 Hz. At low frequencies, very small changes in relative time of arrival at the two ears can be detected, of about 10–20 μs, which is equivalent to a movement of the sound source of 1–2° laterally.

Intensity differences between the two ears are primarily useful at high frequencies. This is because low frequencies bend or diffract around the head, so that there is little difference in intensity at the two ears whatever the location of the sound source. At high frequencies the head casts more of an acoustic "shadow", and above 2–3 kHz the intensity differences are sufficient to provide useful cues. For complex sounds, containing a range of frequencies, the difference in spectral patterning at the two ears may also be important.

The idea that sound localization is based on interaural time differences at low frequencies and interaural intensity differences at high frequencies has been called the "duplex theory" of sound localization, and it dates back to Lord Rayleigh (1907). However, it has been realized that it is not quite correct (Hafter, 1984). Complex sounds containing only high frequencies (above 1,500 Hz) can be localized on the basis of interaural time delays, provided that they have an appropriate temporal structure. For example, a single click can be localized in this way no matter what its frequency content. Periodic sounds containing only high-frequency harmonics can also be localized on the basis of interaural time differences, provided that the envelope repetition rate is below about 600 Hz (Neutzel & Hafter, 1981). Since many of the complex sounds we encounter in everyday life have envelope repetition rates below 600 Hz, interaural time differences will be used for localization in most listening situations.

The role of the pinna

Binaural cues are not sufficient to account for all of our localization abilities. For example, a simple difference in time or intensity will not define whether a sound is coming from in front or behind, or above or below, but people can clearly make such judgements. It has been shown that the pinnae play an important role in sound localization (Batteau, 1967). They do so because the spectra of sounds entering the ear are modified by the pinnae in a way which depends upon the direction of the sound source. This direction-dependent filtering provides cues for sound source location. The cues occur mainly at high frequencies, above about 6 kHz. The pinnae are important not only for localization, but also for judging whether a sound comes from within the head or from the outside world. A sound is judged as coming from outside only if the spectral transformations characteristic of the pinnae are imposed on the sound. Thus sounds heard through headphones are normally judged as being inside the head; the pinnae do not have their normal effect on the sound when headphones are worn. However, sounds delivered by headphones can be made to appear to come from outside the head if the signals delivered to the headphones are prerecorded on a dummy head or synthetically processed (filtered) so as to mimic the normal action of the pinnae. Such processing can also create the impression of a sound coming from any desired direction in space.

The precedence effect

In everyday conditions, the sound from a given source reaches the ears by many different paths. Some of it arrives via a direct path, but a great deal may only reach the ears after reflections from one or more surfaces. However, people are not normally aware of these reflections or echoes, and they do not appear to impair the ability to localize sound sources. The reason for this seems to lie in a phenomenon known as the precedence effect (Wallach, Newman, & Rosenzweig, 1949). When several similar sounds reach our ears in close succession (i.e., the direct sound and its echoes) the sounds are perceptually fused into a single sound, and the location of the total sound is primarily determined by the location of the first (direct) sound. Thus the echoes have little influence on the perception of direction, although they may influence the timbre and loudness of the sound.

Sound localization in the hearing impaired

Most hearing losses result in some degradation in sound localization (Durlach, Thompson, & Colburn, 1981). However, there may be considerable individual differences even in people with similar amounts of hearing loss. In general, tumours in the auditory nerve, or damage higher up in the auditory pathways, lead to greater localization problems than cochlear losses. Most hearing-impaired people show a reduced ability to use interaural time and intensity differences. In addition, people with high-frequency hearing losses are generally unable to make use of the directional information provided by the pinnae. Hearing aid users also suffer in this respect, since, even if the microphone is appropriately placed within the pinna, the response of most aids is limited to frequencies below 6 kHz.

FURTHER READING

Bregman, A. S. (1990). *Auditory scene analysis: The perceptual organisation of sound.* Cambridge, MA: Bradford.

Moore, B. C. J. (1986). *Frequency selectivity in hearing.* London: Academic Press.

Moore, B. C. J. (1989). *An introduction to the psychology of hearing* (3rd edn). London: Academic Press.

Pickles, J. O. (1988). *An introduction to the physiology of hearing* (2nd edn). London: Academic Press.

REFERENCES

Batteau, D. W. (1967). The role of the Pinna in human localization. *Proceedings of the Royal Society*, B, *168*, 158–180.

Davis, H. (1962). Advances in the neurophysiology and neuroanatomy of the cochlea. *Journal of the Acoustical Society of America*, *34*, 1377–1385.

Durlach, N. I., Thompson, C. L., & Colburn, H. S. (1981). Binaural interaction in impaired listeners. *Audiology*, *20*, 181–211.

Feldtkeller, R., & Zwicker, E. (1956). *Das Ohr als Nachrichtenempfänger.* Stuttgart: S. Hirzel.

Fitzgibbons, P. J., & Wightman, F. L. (1982). Gap detection in normal and hearing-impaired listeners. *Journal of the Acoustical Society of America*, *72*, 761–765.

Fletcher, H. (1940). Auditory patterns. *Reviews of Modern Physics*, *12*, 47–65.

Glasberg, B. R., & Moore, B. C. J. (1986). Auditory filter shapes in subjects with unilateral and bilateral cochlear impairments. *Journal of the Acoustical Society of America*, *79*, 1020–1033.

Glasberg, B. R., & Moore, B. C. J. (1990). Derivation of auditory filter shapes from notched-noise data. *Hearing Research*, *47*, 103–138.

Goldstein, J. L. (1973). An optimum processor theory for the central formation of the pitch of complex tones. *Journal of the Acoustical Society of America*, *54*, 1496–1516.

Goldstein, J. L., & Srulovicz, P. (1977). Auditory-nerve spike intervals as an adequate basis for aural frequency measurement. In E. F. Evans & J. P. Wilson (Ed.) *Psychophysics and physiology of hearing* (pp. 337–346). London: Academic Press.

Hafter, E. R. (1984). Spatial hearing and the duplex theory: How viable? In G. M. Edelman, W. E. Gall, & W. M. Cowan (Eds) *Dynamic aspects of neocortical function* (pp. 425–448). New York: Wiley.

Khanna, S. M., & Leonard, D. G. B. (1982). Basilar membrane tuning in the cat cochlea. *Science*, *215*, 305–306.

Laurence, R. F., Moore, B. C. J., & Glasberg, B. R. (1983). A comparison of behind-the-ear high-fidelity linear aids and two-channel compression hearing aids in the laboratory and in everyday life. *British Journal of Audiology*, *17*, 31–48.

Lindsay, P. H., & Norman, D. A. (1972). *Human information processing.* New York and London: Academic Press.

Moore, B. C. J. (1973). Frequency difference limens for short-duration tones. *Journal of the Acoustical Society of America*, *54*, 610–619.

Moore, B. C. J. (1987). Design and evaluation of a two-channel compression hearing aid. *Journal of Rehabilitation Research and Development*, *24*, 181–192.

Moore, B. C. J. (1989). *An introduction to the psychology of hearing* (3rd edn). London: Academic Press.

Moore, B. C. J., & Glasberg, B. R. (1986). The role of frequency selectivity in the perception of loudness, pitch and time. In B. C. J. Moore (Ed.) *Frequency selectivity in hearing* (pp. 251–308). London: Academic Press.

Neutzel, J. M., & Hafter, E. R. (1981). Lateralization of complex waveforms: Spectral effects. *Journal of the Acoustical Society of America, 69,* 1112–1118.

Palmer, A. R. (1987). Physiology of the cochlear nerve and cochlear nucleus. In M. P. Haggard & E. F. Evans (Eds) *Hearing* (pp. 838–855). Edinburgh: Churchill Livingstone.

Patterson, R. D. (1976). Auditory filter shapes derived with noise stimuli. *Journal of the Acoustical Society of America, 59,* 640–654.

Patterson, R. D., & Moore, B. C. J. (1986). Auditory filters and excitation patterns as representations of frequency resolution. In B. C. J. Moore (Ed.) *Frequency selectivity in hearing* (pp. 123–177). London: Academic Press.

Penner, M. J. (1977). Detection of temporal gaps in noise as a measure of the decay of auditory sensation. *Journal of the Acoustical Society of America, 61,* 552–557.

Pickles, J. O. (1986). The neurophysiological basis of frequency selectivity. In B. C. J. Moore (Ed.) *Frequency selectivity in hearing* (pp. 51–121). London: Academic Press.

Pickles, J. O. (1988). *An introduction to the physiology of hearing* (2nd edn). London: Academic Press.

Plomp, R. (1964). The rate of decay of auditory sensation. *Journal of the Acoustical Society of America, 36,* 277–282.

Rayleigh, Lord (1907). On our perception of sound direction. *Philosophical Magazine, 13,* 214–232.

Robinson, D. W., & Dadson, R. S. (1956). A re-determination of the equal-loudness relations for pure tones. *British Journal of Applied Physics, 7,* 166–181.

Robles, L., Ruggero, M. A., & Rich, N. C. (1986). Basilar membrane mechanics at the base of the chinchilla cochlea: I. Input–output functions, tuning curves, and response phases. *Journal of the Acoustical Society of America, 80,* 1364–1374.

Sellick, P. M., Patuzzi, R., & Johnstone, B. M. (1982). Measurement of basilar membrane motion in the guinea pig using the Mössbauer technique. *Journal of the Acoustical Society of America, 72,* 131–141.

Shailer, M. J., & Moore, B. C. J. (1983). Gap detection as a function of frequency, bandwidth and level. *Journal of the Acoustical Society of America, 74,* 467–473.

Terhardt, E. (1974). Pitch, consonance, and harmony. *Journal of the Acoustical Soeiety of America, 55,* 1061–1069.

Viemeister, N. F. (1979). Temporal modulation transfer functions based on modulation thresholds. *Journal of the Acoustical Society of America, 66,* 1364–1380.

Vogten, L. L. M. (1974). Pure-tone masking: A new result from a new method. In E. Zwicker & E. Terhardt (Eds) *Facts and models in hearing* (pp. 142–155). Berlin: Springer-Verlag.

von Békésy, G. (1947). The variations of phase along the basilar membrane with sinusoidal vibrations. *Journal of the Acoustical Society of America, 19,* 452–460.

von Békésy, G. (1960). *Experiments in hearing* (E. G. Wever, trans.). New York: McGraw-Hill.

Wallace, H., Newman, E. B., & Rosenzweig, M. R. (1949). The precedence effect in sound localization. *Journal of Experimental Psychology, 27,* 339–368.

Yates, G. K. (1986). Frequency selectivity in the auditory periphery. In B. C. J. Moore (Ed.) *Frequency selectivity in hearing* (pp. 1–50). London: Academic Press.

Yates, G. K. (1990). Basilar membrane nonlinearity and its influence on auditory nerve rate-intensity functions. *Hearing Researeh, 50,* 145–162.

3.4

THE SKIN, BODY, AND CHEMICAL SENSES

Harvey Richard Schiffman
Rutgers University, New Jersey, USA

This chapter covers four basic sensory systems: the skin sense, the general body sense, and the related senses of taste and smell. In examining the skin sense we shall deal with how stimulation by touch, temperature, and pain informs about the nature of surfaces and objects that come in contact with our skin. We shall also examine the ability to perceive the spatial position of our limbs and the "sense of balance" − the overall location of the body and head in space. Finally we shall deal with our capacities to taste chemicals when they dissolve in our mouth and stimulate the tongue and to smell gaseous chemicals when they reach our nasal passages.

THE SKIN

The skin of the human, serving both as a sensory organ and a protective surface, is by far the largest organ of the body. It forms a covering for the entire body: a person 6 feet tall, of average weight and body build, possesses about 2 square metres or 3,000 square inches of skin area. The skin is also the most versatile sensory organ of the body, serving as a flexible and renewable shield against many forms of foreign agents, infections, and mechanical injuries. It retains vital body fluids, it wards off harmful solar radiations, it helps to regulate and stabilize internal body temperature by retarding heat loss or cooling the body, and of course, by providing different sensations, the skin informs the organism of what is directly adjacent to the body, especially the presence of potentially harmful stimuli.

The sensory effect of stimulation of the skin is termed *cutaneous sensitivity* and three primary cutaneous qualities have been identified: pressure or touch (also called contact, tactual, or tactile stimulation), temperature (cold or warm), and pain. It has been proposed that the different sensory qualities are mediated by different specialized receptors embedded within the layers of the skin. Some of the proposed receptor types are sketched in Figure 1. The majority of the skin surface is covered with hairs and the presumed major sensory receptors for hairy skin regions are called *basket cells* because they resemble a woven basket wrapped around the bottom of the hair shaft embedded within the inner skin layer. The primary sensory receptors for the much more sparse hairless or *glabrous skin* of the body − certain facial regions including the lips and mouth, palms of the hands, and soles of the feet − are a class of specialized structures called *encapsulated end organs*, which come in a wide variety of forms. The major form embedded in glabrous skin are *Pacinian corpuscles* which have an onion-like appearance (other presumed cutaneous receptors are Meissner's corpuscles and tactile disks for touch, and Ruffini endings for warmth and Krause end bulbs for cold). Additionally, both hairy and hairless skin regions contain receptors called *free nerve endings* that lack specialized receptor cells and are unattached to any specific skin region. Free nerve endings are found almost

225

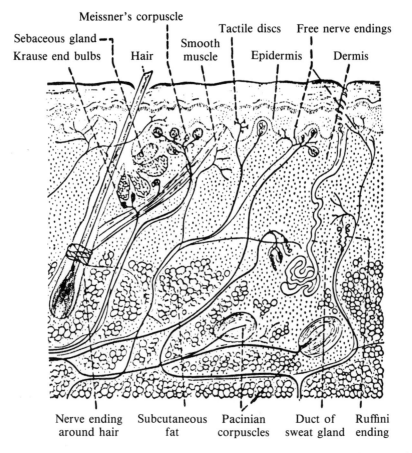

Meissner's corpuscle

Sebaceous gland

Krause end bulbs | Hair | Smooth muscle

Tactile discs | Free nerve endings

Epidermis | Dermis

Nerve ending around hair | Subcutaneous fat | Pacinian corpuscles | Duct of sweat gland | Ruffini ending

Figure 1 Composite diagram of the skin in cross-section, showing chief layers, epidermis, dermis, and subcutaneous tissue, and a hair follicle and its supporting structures. Also shown are several kinds of nerve endings and receptors that are embedded within the skin
Source: Gardner, 1947, revised from H. R. Schiffman, 1990

everywhere within the skin surface and by far are the most common skin receptor.

All three types of receptors, the basket cells, the Pacininan corpuscles, and the free nerve endings, yield some sort of pressure or touch sensation when stimulated. It thus appears that a given cutaneous pressure sensation may be produced by a number of different specialized receptors in the skin rather than a single one. Moreover it is not clear whether stimulation of a particular type of skin receptor exclusively initiates a specific cutaneous touch sensation. For example, the cornea of the eye contains only free nerve endings but it is very sensitive to pressure, temperature, and pain. It must be concluded that, in general, highly specialized receptors do not appear to be necessary to receive a particular type of stimulus or elicit a specific class of sensation.

It should also be noted that all regions of the skin are not uniformly sensitive to all forms of cutaneous stimulation. Some areas may be sensitive to warm and relatively insensitive to cold stimuli or the reverse; whereas most regions of the skin may be sensitive to pain, different regions may be more sensitive to painful stimulation than others.

Touch and pressure

Touch localization

The skin is extremely sensitive to light pressure. Indeed under ideal conditions, displacements of the skin less than 0.001 mm (0.00004 in.) can result in a sensation of pressure or touch. However, as with thermal and painful stimulation, the sensitivity to touch or pressure stimulation also varies considerably from one region of the body to another. Drawing from common experience we easily recognize that it takes more contact or pressure to feel something on the thigh or the sole of the foot than on the finger tips or on the face. In a classic experiment on a related ability – *point localization* – Weinstein (1968) stimulated observers with fine nylon filaments, to obtain measures of the ability to localize pressure sensations applied to various regions of the skin. As Figure 2 indicates, point localization largely varies with the region of the body stimulated. Since a major function of the skin is to inform the organism of what is directly adjacent to it, it is not surprising that generally, stimulation of the more mobile, exploratory skin regions of the body, endowed with finer muscular control – e.g., the hands and mouth – results in more accurate point localization. For example, stimulation of the fingertip or the lip is extremely well localized, producing an error in the observer's perception of where the stimulus was applied of only about 2 millimetres. In contrast, stimulation of the upper arm, thigh or back produces an error of localization of more than a centimetre.

Two-point threshold

Another means of demonstrating the sensitivity of the skin to touch stimulation is to assess the *two-point threshold*, which refers to the smallest separation of two discrete but adjacent points of stimulation on the skin that just produces two distinct impressions of touch. That is, if they were placed any closer together they would produce a single touch sensation. As with the ability to localize a single stimulus, more mobile regions are more sensitive and have lower two-point thresholds.

227

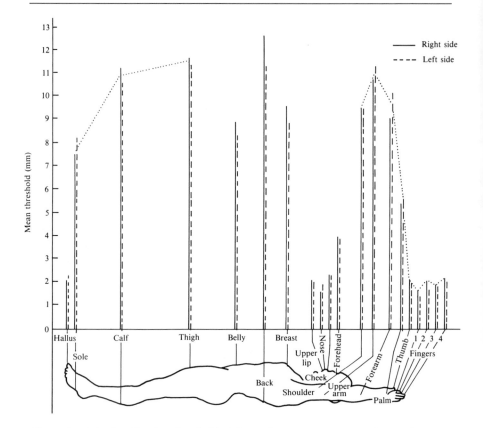
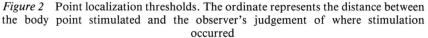

Figure 2 Point localization thresholds. The ordinate represents the distance between the body point stimulated and the observer's judgement of where stimulation occurred

Source: Weinstein, 1968, p. 204. Reproduced by courtesy of Charles C. Thomas, publisher, Springfield, Illinois

Adaptation to touch

It should be noted that continued steady pressure or touch stimulation may result in a decrease or even a complete elimination of a sensation. Clearly even after a short while, we do not usually feel the pressure of our watch-band on the wrist or the clothes against our body. That is, touch sensations undergo *adaptation*. The course of adaptation varies with a number of factors, particularly the size, intensity, and the region of the skin under continuous contact. But touch sensations can be quickly restored by some movement or an abrupt change in the stimulation against the skin.

228

The skin and brain

The efficiency and the variability of the skin in such tasks as point localization and the two-point threshold is highly correlated with the particular skin region's density of nerve fibres and its connection to the brain. Some skin regions such as those of the fingers, lips, and tongue are more densely supplied with nerve fibres; hence, they are more sensitive than other skin areas such as the shoulders; moreover they are correspondingly represented by larger areas in the sensory brain – a cortical region called the *somatosensory cortex* – responsible for receiving and processing touch or pressure stimulation.

The Braille system

The skin, when actively employed, is capable of extracting complex kinds of information from small changes in pressure or touch. One example is the Braille reading system devised by Louis Braille in the nineteenth century. The Braille alphabet is composed of dots embossed on a surface that can be "read" by the skin of the fingertips. As shown in Figure 3, various combinations of dots are used to represent letters and words. By moving the fingertip

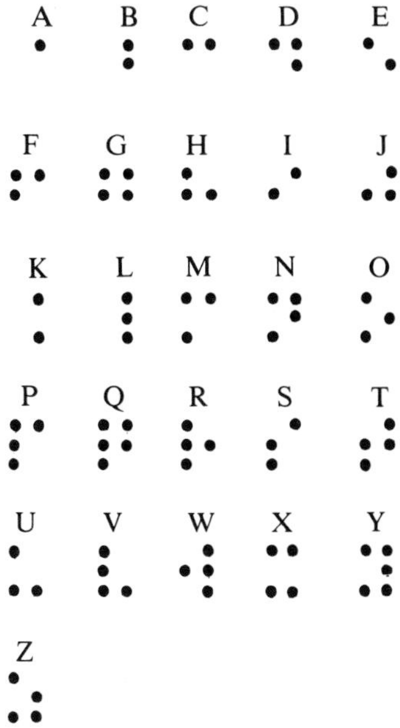

Figure 3   The Braille alphabet. Various combinations of from one to six embossed dots are used to represent letters and short words. Each dot is raised 1 mm above the surface and the dot separations are 2.3 mm

over the raised surface of Braille writing, the experienced adult Braille reader can reach 100 words or more per minute (e.g., Kennedy, 1984).

The Tadoma method

The Braille system enables a blind individual to "read" with the skin. Touch may also be used by some individuals who are both blind and deaf to communicate speech by using the *Tadoma* method of speech reception (Loomis & Lederman, 1986; Reed, Dohrty, Braida, & Durlach, 1982). In the Tadoma method the "listener" places his or her hand in contact with specific parts of the speaker's lips, jaw and neck so that the hand receives some of the complex patterns of vibration stimulation in the airflow and lip and jaw movements produced by the speaker's vocalizations (see Figure 4). If the rate of speech is slow, use of the Tadoma system permits a well-experienced "listener" to reach a modest but useful level of speech comprehension.

Tactile visual substitution system

While we have outlined only two kinds of information extracted from touch stimulation it should be clear that on the basis of touch alone it is possible

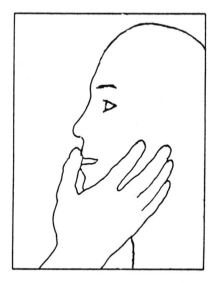

Figure 4 Hand placement using the Tadoma method of speech perception. As the speaker talks the "listener" can directly pick up information that is closely tied to articulation, such as oral air flow and lip and jaw movement

Source: Revised from Loomis and Lederman, 1986, based on Reed, Doherty, Braida, and Durlach, 1982

to perceive complex and spatially detailed forms of environmental stimulation. Indeed it is possible to convert a visual image into a direct tactual display on the skin by using a technology called the *Tactile visual substitution system*. Specifically, a video camera records a scene containing an array of objects; then the image of the scene is electronically transformed and reproduced into a succession of vibratory impressions on the skin surface (usually the back). With experience, especially when they can control the scanning pattern of the video camera, observers are able to interpret the pattern of stimulations as representing specific objects, and they can even perceive the location of objects relative to each other within a spatial framework. The authors of this technology appropriately term this functional use of tactual stimulation, "seeing with the skin" (White, Saunders, Scadden, Bach-y-Rita, & Collins, 1970).

Tactual stereognosis

Finally, in this context of the meaningful extraction of environmental information from touch, we must take note of the phenomenon of tactual *stereognosis*, the familiar and extremely accurate ability to perceive three-dimensional shapes by palpation or manipulation by the hands. Indeed, almost effortlessly we can identify objects solely on the basis of how they "feel". In one investigation, Klatsky, Lederman, and Metzger (1985) studied the ability of blindfolded subjects to identify common objects solely by feeling them. The subjects handled 100 common objects, each easily identifiable by name, for example, a paper clip, toothbrush, fork, and screwdriver. The results were impressive with respect to the subjects' accuracy and overall competence in palpation: out of a total of 2,000 judgements, approximately 96 per cent were correct and 94 per cent of the correct judgements occurred within 5 seconds of handling the object.

Temperature

The sensations resulting from the temperature of a surface that is in contact with the skin is also registered by a form of cutaneous stimulation. The surface of the skin is irregularly distributed with spots that are thermally sensitive, some spots more sensitive to warm, other spots more sensitive to cold stimulation.

Adaptation to temperature

As with constant pressure or touch stimulation, thermal sensations from the skin undergo adaptation. Exposure to a moderately warm or cold environment, as in the case of entering a bath or swimming pool, may initially result in a very warm or cold experience, but despite a constant thermal environment, eventually the thermal sensations diminish and the water feels only slightly warm or cool, respectively. Moreover, with prolonged immersion in the warm or cold thermal environment adaptation may be total in which case no thermal sensation may occur until there is a change in its temperature.

Generally the skin surface is adapted to a narrow range of temperatures which fails to yield a warm or cold sensation – a neutral zone of complete thermal adaptation – called *physiological zero*. Normally, physiological zero corresponds to the temperature of the skin which is about $91°F$ ($33°C$). That is, temperatures applied to the skin that are close to $91°F$ feel neither warm

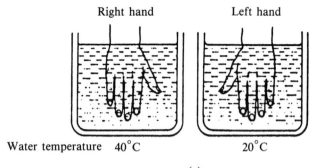

Right hand　　　　Left hand

Water temperature　40°C　　　　20°C

(a)

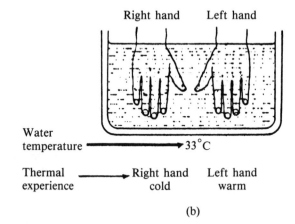

Right hand　Left hand

Water
temperature ━━━━━━━━▶ 33°C

Thermal ━━━━▶ Right hand　Left hand
experience　　　 cold　　　　warm

(b)

Figure 5 Effects of thermal adaptation. (a) Each hand is placed in a separate basin of water and is thermally adapted to a different temperature. (b) When both hands are then placed in the 33°C water, the right hand, previously adapted to warm water, feels cold, and the left hand, previously adapted to cold water, feels warm. These sensory effects of thermal adaptation point out that the skin is not a good indicator of physical temperature

Source: Based on H. R. Schiffman, 1990

232

nor cold (the neutral zone usually extends 2–4°C to either side of physiological zero). But it should be noted that physiological zero can occur with a number of temperatures. A demonstration attributed to John Locke in 1690 makes this point and also points out that the skin is not a good indicator of physical temperature. As outlined in Figure 5, one hand is immersed in a 40°C basin of water, and the other in a 20°C basin and both are allowed to thermally adapt until neither hand feels any thermal sensation. If then both hands are then shifted in to a 33°C basin of water, the water in the 33°C basin will now feel distinctly cold to the hand that was originally in the warm water and warm to the hand that was originally in the cold water. As shown in Figure 5, owing to prior thermal adaptation, the same physical temperature can feel cold to one hand and warm to the other. Thus thermal sensations occur as a result of the relation of the temperature of the skin surface to the temperature of its surroundings rather than from the reception of absolute physical temperature itself.

Pain

It is clear that towards the extremes of thermal stimulation – freezing and boiling – thermal sensations merge with those of pain. This is a biologically adaptive association because intense thermal stimulation can produce tissue damage. Since painful stimuli, in general, are immediately attended to, this helps protect the organism against harmful and even lethal thermal extremes.

Although we recognize that tissue injury is neither a necessary nor a sufficient condition for the experience of pain, generally speaking, most forms of painful stimuli are potentially damaging. Thus a significant benefit from the reception of pain is warning of potential biological harm. Indeed chronic failure to perceive pain is extremely maladaptive: the pernicious physical effects occurring to individuals who lack the sense of pain provide convincing evidence of its overall value to the organism's well-being. Reports of self-inflicted injury due to pathological pain insensitivity, especially in childhood, have included serious, often life-threatening, injury to the skin, flesh, and bones, extensive burns from hot surfaces and liquids, and even chewing off the tip of the tongue (e.g., Melzack, 1973).

The nociceptor

It is generally held that pain results from the excitation of a specialized receptor called a *nociceptor* (from the Latin *nocere*, "to injure"). A nociceptor is a receptor that is activated by stimulation that may produce injury to the body and whose sensations are unpleasant. For a number of reasons, but most importantly because they are found wherever pain spots are located, free nerve ending receptors (introduced earlier) are generally assumed to be nociceptors.

233

Variability in pain perception

It is worth noting that pain is not a single sensation produced by a single or specific stimulus; rather pain may encompass a range of different, unpleasant experiences produced by a wide variety of potentially harmful, noxious events. Moreover, a rather remarkable aspect of pain perception is its extremely variable relationship to the stimulus that elicits it. Indeed the relation between pain and bodily injury extends from injury with no pain to extreme pain with little or no injury. A pain stimulus that is experienced as extreme in one situation may not be so in another. Among the psychological factors that affect this variability in perceiving pain is one's emotional state and level of stress. Thus severe injuries sustained in competitive sports and combat may be accompanied by little or no pain. Clearly there are numerous cognitive, social and cultural factors that markedly affect pain perception. Indeed it is often the case that the same injury produces different effects in different individuals.

Melzack (1973) describes several culturally based initiation rites and rituals (of India and of the North American Plains Indians) that involve suspending and swinging "celebrants" by skewers and hooks that are inserted into their chests and backs as part of religious ceremony. Rather than showing the effects of pain, the celebrants appear more in a state of exaltation and ecstasy. That variability in pain perception may be linked to culture is further supported by some clinical observations following major surgery. One orthopaedic surgeon (cited in H. R. Schiffman, 1990, p. 147), reported that he had performed spinal grafts or fusions (in which bone fragments are chipped from regions of the pelvic bone and placed over vertebrae) on Canadian Indians on one day, and on the next day they walked about as if without any pain. Such stoic behaviour was never observed with members of other cultural groups who underwent the same surgical procedure.

The spinal gate control theory

There are specific pathways to the brain that signal pain. As we noted, free nerve endings are the likely receptors – the nociceptors – for pain in the skin. They are linked to specific fibres connecting to the spinal cord, which in turn contains neurons that also react selectively to noxious stimuli. However, as we noted above, sometimes an environmental event that is usually experienced as painful is barely sensed at all. That is, pain sensation is a highly variable experience. Melzack and Wall (1965, 1982; see also Morris, 1991) have proposed a comprehensive theory that they called the *spinal gate control theory* to explain the general mechanism of pain perception; it also takes into account why pain perception is so variable. Their basic idea is that there is a neural "gate" in the spinal cord that can be opened or closed to

234

allow or inhibit painful stimulation to be sent, by way of specific transmission (T) cells, from the spinal cord to the brain along the specific pain pathways. According to the spinal gate control theory, three interlocking factors control the opening and closing of the spinal gate and the transmission of T cell activity. First, when pain receptors of the skin are sufficiently stimulated, they activate the T cells in the spinal cord which signals the presence of painful stimulation. That is, activity of nociceptors "opens" the spinal gate and increases the sensation of pain. Second, when nociceptor activity (i.e., pain or nociceptor stimulation) is also accompanied by excitations from skin receptors that carry messages concerning non-painful cutaneous stimulation – such as from light touch and stroking of the skin – activity of the pain receptors are inhibited and T cell activity of the spinal cord accordingly decreases. That is, excitation of certain touch-sensitive receptors of the skin "closes" the spinal gate and decreases the sensation of pain. In this case, the neural activity of non-painful stimuli competes with and displaces the neural message from nociceptor activity, thereby reducing the pain sensation. This helps explain why sometimes gently stroking or rubbing the skin around the site of an injury helps reduce the pain, or why scratching is able to briefly relieve an itch (which is a kind of low-grade pain stimulus): such activity stimulates pressure-sensitive receptors and partly closes the spinal gate.

The third factor that exerts control on the spinal gate is a central-cognitive mechanism from the brain itself. Neurons in the brain have pathways back to the spinal cord and by this route can send a message down the spinal cord and close the spinal gate, thus inhibiting the activity of the T cells. It follows that since messages originating from the brain can affect the spinal gate, psychological factors such as stress and emotion, attention and attitude, and other cognitive factors can also exert control over T cell activity and thereby affect pain sensation.

The spinal gate control theory is consistent with a number of phenomena involving pain suppression by cutaneous stimulation. For example, there is evidence that selectively transmitting non-painful touch stimulation such as occurs with therapeutically massaging an injured region or the application of low-intensity electrical pulses – experienced as "tingling" – can reduce chronic cutaneous pain. The spinal gate control theory may also explain the effectiveness as a pain suppressor of *acupuncture*, an ancient Chinese technique in which needles are inserted into various parts of the body. It has been proposed that the needles, when heated, twirled or electrified, send non-painful cutaneous excitations that close the presumed spinal gate.

Endorphins

There is considerable evidence that the body produces natural pain suppressors called *endorphins*. Endorphins are neurotransmitter chemicals manufactured by the body that interact with a particular kind of neuron called an opiate receptor. Opiate receptors act to reduce pain sensation, and in fact, many pain-reducing drugs, especially the opiate drugs (derivatives of opium such as morphine), are specifically administered to stimulate the opiate receptors. Of course, opiate receptors in the body did not evolve to react specifically to opiates or other substances foreign to the body. Rather, it is most likely that the function of opiate receptors is to mediate the body's own capacity to reduce pain. Endorphins (the word is a contraction of "endogenous morphine") are thus chemicals produced by the body itself and serve a biologically significant role in pain management and control.

The clearest evidence for activation of an endogenous pain reducing mechanism comes from animal studies in which unrelenting stress or pain stimulation is applied (e.g., Bolles & Fanselow, 1982; Grau, 1984; Terman, Shavit, Lewis, Cannon, & Liebeskind, 1984). The existence of a human endorphin mechanism is generally accepted, but direct evidence is scarce (Bandura, O'Leary, Taylor, Gauthier, & Gossard, 1987). Of interest to the preceding discussion on the spinal gate control mechanism, is that the spinal cord is highly enriched in opiate receptors. Perhaps endorphins act by inhibiting the release of excitatory substances for neurons carrying information about pain. That is, endorphins may "close" the spinal gate and thereby suppress pain.

THE BODY SENSES

Thus far we have concentrated on the awareness of the environment that surrounds us when contact is made with our skin. However, there is also an immense amount of vital information generated within our bodies. This class of information informs us of such things as the position and movement of our mobile body parts, and it tells us whether we are tilted or erect and whether we are in transit or stationary. There are two sensory mechanisms for receiving and monitoring this kind of information called *kinaesthesis* and the *vestibular sense*.

Kinaesthesis

Kinaesthesis refers to the sensory system that receives and processes information about the posture, location, and movement in space of the limbs and other mobile parts of the jointed skeleton. The sensory mechanism for kinaesthesis makes use of receptors that reside within the joints, muscles, and tendons. The proposed receptors for the joints are *Pacinian corpuscles* (similar to those we encountered within the skin); these lie in the mobile joints of the skeletal system and they are stimulated by mechanical contact between the parts of the joints' surfaces. That is, stimulation of the Pacinian corpuscles occurs with changes in the angles at which the bones of a joint are held relative to each other. In addition, muscles and their attached tendons are well supplied with sensory nerves that react to changes in tension when

236

the muscle fibre is stretched or contracted. Thus with movement of the limbs in space the brain receives information concerning joint movement and the state of muscle tension.

Clearly, the kinaesthetic system provides a source of critical bodily information. Effortlessly, we are aware of, and continuously monitor the position, posture, and the direction of the movement of our limbs in space. Thus we easily scratch an itch that we cannot see, and we walk safely down a flight of steps without gazing directly at our feet.

The vestibular sense

The kinaesthetic information provided by the joints, muscles, and tendons enables the brain to know where the various body parts are relative to one another. Thus being aware of the angles of the toes, ankles, knees, hips, shoulders, and so on, enables an individual to distinguish a crouch from an upright position or from standing on one's tiptoes. Similarly, sensing the angles of the wrist, hand, and finger joints, allows the brain to recognize whether the hand is holding a small or a large object. However, such information does not tell the brain the position of the body, or how it moves with regard to the environment or to gravity. In order to obtain this sort of information the brain requires an additional class of position information.

Saccule and utricle

Awareness of body position, equilibrium, and movement in space arises from the two *vestibular* structures that lie within the inner ear. The first vestibular structure is comprised of two small sacs, the *saccule* and the *utricle*, which are attached to the auditory structures of the inner ear (see Figure 6). These two vestibular sacs are lined with hair-like, *cilia* receptors that are covered with extremely small calcium crystals. When you are relatively stationary and stand upright the force of gravity forces downward movement of the calcium crystals and bends the cilia lining the bottom surface of the sacs; when you abruptly move your head, such as when jumping downward, the mass of calcium particles lags somewhat because of inertial forces, thus bending the cilia lining the top surface of the sacs. In fact, any sort of linear movement bends and excites specific cilia producing a consequent discharge of attached nerve fibres and sends an appropriate message to the brain. Thus in a very real sense the saccule and utricle serve as gravity detectors and inform an individual which way is "up" and which way is "down". They also signal *changes* in movement (i.e., linear acceleration or deceleration) of the body, such as changes in up and down, forward and backward, or side to side movement: that is, they react to starts and stops and changes in motion, as opposed to sustained movement at a constant velocity.

237

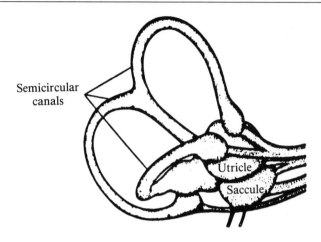

Semicircular
canals

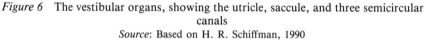

Utricle

Saccule

Figure 6   The vestibular organs, showing the utricle, saccule, and three semicircular
canals
Source: Based on H. R. Schiffman, 1990

Semicircular canals

The second vestibular structure is actually a set of three fluid-filled canals −
called the *semicircular canals* − set at approximately right angles to each
other (see Figure 6). The primary function of the canals is to register information of angular acceleration or rotation of the head. Each canal relates to
a major plane of the body and when stimulated during rotation of the head,
the fluid in the canals moves in relation to the direction and extent of the
rotary changes. Displacement of the fluid within the canals excites specific
receptors that lie within the canals and corresponding signals of the direction
of the rotation are sent to the brain. Thus collectively, the semicircular canals
form a three-coordinate system to which the direction of head rotation can
be referred.

The vestibular system performs vital functions, providing information
concerning gravity and linear and rotary movement, and accordingly assists
in the maintenance of an upright posture. Another function performed by the
vestibular sense is to help stabilize vision by coordinating eye and head position. As we move about through the spatial environment, our head bobs and
weaves continuously. To adjust for changes in the visual imagery due to the
continual head movement, the eyes have to move accordingly. The compensation for the visual changes is accomplished by a complex reflex system that
automatically and smoothly compensates for each head movement by an
equal and opposite movement of the eyes. Thus, for example, if you lock
your gaze at something in the environment while turning your head to the
left, your eyes will move to the right and the visual image of what you have
fixated on remains stabilized. These automatic compensatory eye movements

are initiated by neural signals from the vestibular system to the brain which are relayed to the muscles of the eyes that control their movement. The perceptual result, of course, is that as we move about, the visual scene appears stabilized and fixed on the retina.

Motion sickness

The vestibular system is well-suited to receive stimulation that is typically self-produced by individuals who move about in a three-dimensional environment, subject to the earth's gravity. However, when we take advantage of some of the opportunities provided by passive vehicular transport, such as with ships, cars, trains, and aircraft, we may introduce abnormal motion stimulation that the vestibular sense cannot effectively deal with, and the result is *motion sickness*. Motion sickness is a widespread phenomenon that can be totally disabling, usually accompanied by pallor, dizziness and vertigo, and nausea. A major explanation of motion sickness is that it is the result of a conflict between the main sources of sensory information about the spatial orientation of the head and body (e.g., Young, 1984). That is, the moment-to-moment position information signalled by the visual sense is discrepant or mismatched with that signalled by the vestibular sense. For example, when you are in the cabin of a ship that is in choppy waters, your vestibular sense signals the erratic series of movements that are imposed on your body, while your visual sense signals a relatively stable visual environment. Perhaps more familiar is the strong reaction to reading a book while in a moving vehicle, especially when moving over a bumpy road. In such conditions it is the *conflict* between the visual signals and the passively imposed vestibular signals that produces the motion sickness. To some extent the symptoms of motion sickness may be relieved or reduced if the information provided by the visual sense is made somewhat consistent with the vestibular stimulation. In our sea example, this could be attempted by looking at the rough water and anticipating the movements of the ship (and one's body); but even here the series of abnormal, passively imposed motion signals is often too much of a challenge to the vestibular system for anything but a moderate reduction in the distress experienced.

THE CHEMICAL SENSES: TASTE AND SMELL

Both taste (technically, *gustation*) and smell (*olfaction*) depend on receptors that are normally stimulated by chemical substances, and these receptors are called *chemoreceptors*. Aside from the fact that they both require chemical stimuli, taste and smell are functionally linked. Their close relationship can be easily demonstrated. If the reception for smell is reduced or eliminated by blockage of the air passages of the nose, such as by tightly pinching the nostrils, or as sometimes happens to a person who has caught a common cold (in which an overproduction of mucous results in a congestion of the olfactory sensory cells), two quite different food substances may taste surprisingly similar. For example, under such conditions of reduced smell, raw potato does not taste very different from apple. What this points out, of course, is that many of the "taste" qualities that are ordinarily assigned to foods are in fact due to their odours (Moncrieff, 1951). Moreover it is clear that together, taste and smell interact as a functional unit serving in many dietary activities, such as food seeking and sampling, and ingesting or rejecting substances. However, it is equally clear that taste and smell also possess quite independent functions: thus for many forms of animal life, smell enables the reception of non-nutritive information such as detecting the presence of prey or predator and it is critical for sexual activity, whereas taste aids in the regulation of nutrients, enabling an organism's tongue and mouth to test or "sample" substances prior to ingestion. Accordingly, while we recognize that taste and smell are closely allied senses, for the most part, we shall here treat each sense separately.

Taste

The chemical stimulus

A potential stimulus for taste must be a dissolved or soluble substance that must go into solution on coming in contact with saliva, a requirement that limits taste to water-soluble molecules. For the human there are four basic or primary tastes: sweet, sour, salty, and bitter. Presently there are no precise or exact rules to specify the taste of a substance based on its chemical composition. However, it is generally the case that the salty taste comes from organic salts, especially table salt or sodium chloride (NaCl), the sour taste from acid compounds, the sweet taste from nutrients associated with organic substances such as carbohydrates and amino acids, and the bitter taste from alkaloids (which are usually poisonous). The observation that nutritive substances tend to be sweet, and poisonous substances tend to be bitter, strongly suggests that the ability to sense sweet and bitter is necessary for survival. Likewise a salt taste has a vital adaptive function, playing a unique role in the regulation of body fluid. With insufficient salt we cannot retain water, blood volume plummets, and the heart fails. Indeed as we sometimes recognize in our own dietary activities, a critical loss of sodium stimulates a strong craving for salty foods. It should be noted further that the salt taste also warns against the ingestion of intolerably high concentrations of salt, which can have as serious consequences to the normal functioning of the body as does insufficient salt. Thus we may accept as a very general rule, at least for most naturally occurring substances, that things that have an unpleasant taste are likely to be harmful or even poisonous and usually indigestible, whereas substances that are appealing are likely to be necessary for the metabolism and homeostasis of the body.

Receptors for taste

The basic receptors for taste in the human, called *taste buds*, are specialized structures located in microscopically small pits and grooves throughout the oral cavity but particularly on the surface of the tongue (see Figure 7). A taste bud is composed of taste cells that have finger-like projections called *microvilli* which extend into taste pores and are in direct contact with saliva and chemical solutions applied to the surface of the tongue. The human possesses about 10,000 taste buds, which are generally found in clusters lying within small, but visible elevations on the tongue, called *papillae*.

The tongue and taste sensitivity

Not all papillae are equally responsive to the basic tastes. That is, different regions of the tongue are more sensitive to specific taste stimuli than are others. Figure 8 shows the regional differences in taste sensitivity. The front of the tongue is most sensitive to the sweet taste, the back sides for sour, the front and sides of the tongue are most sensitive to the salt taste, and the front (and especially the soft palate) is most sensitive to bitter. However, it should be noted that although they are not equally sensitive, all areas of the tongue respond to almost all of the basic tastes. Indeed, studies in which sweet, bitter, sour, and salty stimuli were applied to individual taste buds indicate

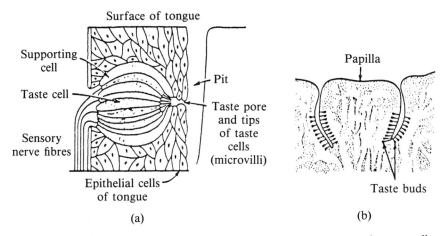

Figure 7 (a) Drawing of a taste bud. Sensory nerve fibres connect to the taste cells; the tips of the taste cells project microvilli into the taste pore. (b) Clusters of taste buds form papillae
Source: Based on H. R. Schiffman, 1990

241

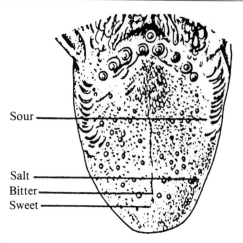

Sour

Salt
Bitter
Sweet

Figure 8 Approximate location on the tongue of regions of greatest taste sensitivities for the four primary taste qualities. For the bitter taste, the soft palate (not shown) is the most sensitive region
Source: Based on data from Collings, 1974

that, with sufficient concentration, a single taste bud will react to more than one taste stimulus (Arvidson & Friberg, 1980; Collings, 1974).

Temperature and taste

Taste sensitivity for a substance is affected not only by its chemical composition but also by a wide variety of stimulus variables, such as its concentration, the area of its application, the age, species, and prior dietary conditions of the taster, and the temperature of the substance. As an example, consider how temperature affects taste sensitivity. Regardless of the basic taste quality of a substance, taste sensitivity is greatest for substances when they are between 22°C and 32°C (about 72°F to 90°F; McBurney, Collings, & Glanz, 1973). This corresponds with the generalization that maximal sensitivity to most compounds occurs in the range between room and body temperature. In general, of course, the cook's caveat applies: food seasoning – salt or sugar – should be adjusted at the temperature at which the food will be served.

Taste adaptation

If the tongue is continually stimulated with an identical solution, sensitivity to that taste declines quickly and may eventually be completely lacking. This decrement in taste sensitivity is due to *adaptation*, an effect of unchanging stimulation that is observed in virtually every sensory modality. For example, after a period of constant stimulation with a bitter solution such as with

242

strong caffeinated black coffee, the bitter taste of the coffee becomes weaker and weaker and may eventually appear tasteless. However, if the coffee is rinsed out and the mouth left unstimulated for a short while, taste sensitivity to coffee is restored in full, thereby reversing the adaptation process.

Adaptation to one taste stimulus can also affect the taste of a different taste stimulus. An unusual example of this is the effect that adaptation to certain substances has on the taste of water. If, for example, your tongue is well adapted to the bitter taste of strong black coffee, a taste of distilled water will taste slightly sweet. Similarly, adaptation to a sweet solution will impart a bitter taste to water. This phenomenon of taste induction has been termed *adaptation-produced potentiation*; it has been shown that each of the four primary tastes can be imparted to water by prior adaptation to certain chemical solutions (McBurney & Shick, 1971).

Conditioned taste aversion

When individuals are exposed – even once – to a substance accompanied by certain unpleasant conditions such as nausea, a powerful and relatively long-lasting aversion to that substance may be created (Garcia, Hankins, & Rusiniak, 1974). The phenomenon is called *conditioned taste aversion* and it is of considerable theoretical and practical interest to psychologists because it shows how a very strong association can be formed after only a single pairing of a stimulus (taste) and a response (sickness). Individuals with a conditioned taste aversion to a food avoid the offending food not so much because they assume that sickness will follow its ingestion but because the food seems to acquire an unpleasant taste.

A serious consequence to conditioned taste aversion, observed with cancer patients undergoing radiation and chemotherapy treatment (which also induces nausea and sickness), is that the patients often acquire taste aversions for foods consumed close to the time of the therapy (Bernstein & Webster, 1980). Accordingly it is advisable that attention be paid to the kind of food consumed close to treatment since long-lasting aversions may develop with any ingested substance, even highly favoured ones.

Smell

The chemical stimulus

In order for a substance to be smelled it must be *volatile*, that is, it must readily vaporize and pass into a gaseous state. In general, the typical chemical stimuli for the olfactory sense are organic substances, usually mixtures of chemical compounds such as the odours emitted by vegetative life, decaying matter, and the scent-producing glands of animals. However, unlike the taste sense there is no agreed upon set of primary odour qualities and the number of distinct odours is immense. Moreover the relationship between the physical and chemical properties of a stimulus and the odour that it arouses is far from clear. In short, there is little agreement about the underlying mechanism that makes specific chemicals excite olfactory receptors and arouse a particular odour. However, it is generally held that a specific set of receptors is *not* exclusively excited by specific chemicals – such as say, a specific set of receptors reacting only to chemicals that we label as "fragrant" and another set of receptors reacting only to chemicals that we label as "spicy", and so on. Instead, it is proposed that the specific neural code for odour quality is based on a *pattern* or response profile of excitations across a number of different receptors; that is, the same olfactory receptors respond to different chemical stimuli but in different ways. In turn, the particular code of neural activity for a particular odour is sent to the olfactory centres of the brain.

Receptors for smell

The sense of smell begins with the inhalation of airborne molecules into the nasal cavity, which then stimulate receptors cells located in the upper reaches of the passages. Figure 9 presents an outline of the main olfactory structures. Although it is not clear how the molecules actually excite the receptor cells,

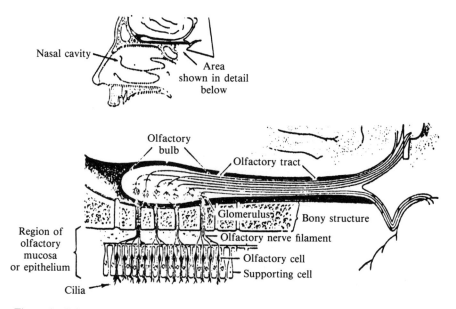

Figure 9 Schematic of anatomy of olfactory system and detail of its cellular structure
Source: Based on H. R. Schiffman, 1990

stimulation probably occurs when the gaseous molecules interact with small cilia on the receptor cells.

Sensitivity of smell

The olfactory system is remarkably sensitive to minute amounts of certain odorants. Indeed, as Mozell (1971) points out, the olfactory system can detect the presence of a smaller number of molecules than can most laboratory methods used for the same purpose. A striking example of this is provided by our sensitivity to *mercaptan*, a foul-smelling compound often added to odorless natural gas as a warning signal of its presence: a concentration of one part of mercaptan per 50 trillion parts of air is detectable (Geldard, 1972, p. 448). Clearly, with respect to the concentration of molecules, smell is the more sensitive of the chemical senses – 10,000 times as sensitive as taste, according to Moncrieff (1951). Even so, the human is much less sensitive to certain odours than are other animals. For example, the average dog possesses a much keener sense of smell than does the average human. The reason is that dogs (and many other mammals) possess many times the olfactory receptors than does the human.

It should be noted in this context that there are differences in sensitivity that are gender and age related. Specifically, females are more sensitive to certain odours than are males. The threshold for Exaltolide, a musk-like synthetic odorant used as a fixative in perfume, is 1,000 times lower for sexually mature women than for males (Doty, Snyder, Huggins, & Lowry, 1981; Vierling & Rock, 1967). In a series of studies, mature males were either *anosmic* (i.e., lacking a sense of smell) to Exaltolide, or barely perceived it (Good, Geary, & Engen, 1976; Vierling & Rock, 1967). It is worth noting here also that there is evidence indicating that females outperform males in the identification as well as the detection of many odours (Doty et al., 1984). In spite of this, the "noses" who work (for only about two hours a day) in French perfume factories are generally men.

While sensitivity to taste shows only a moderate decrease with age, particularly for the sweet and salt taste, overall sensitivity to smell markedly decreases with age (S. S. Schiffman, Moss, & Erickson, 1976). In one study the average ability to identify odours was greatest for individuals between 20 and 40 years and declined markedly thereafter (Doty et al., 1984; Murphy, 1987). It was further observed that 25 per cent of the people tested between the ages of 65 and 68, and nearly 50 per cent of the people tested over the age of 80 years were anosmic, that is, insensitive to odours. Of some interest here is the finding that, at all ages tested, non-smokers outperform smokers on tasks requiring the detection and identification of odours.

Adaptation

As with the other senses, the sense of smell is subject to adaptation; that is, continued exposure to an odorant results in a decline in sensitivity to it. Depending on the particular odour and its concentration, with a sufficient exposure duration, the smell of the odour is almost eliminated (Cain, 1988). Olfactory adaptation is a commonplace experience. Owing to adaptation we are usually not aware of our own objectionable body odours (although we may be painfully aware of the odours of other individuals). Similarly the cooking odours one initially senses when entering the kitchen seem to be gone after a period of continued exposure.

Identification of odours

The human appears to be able to identify certain important characteristics of odours. For example, in studies of odour recognition, women were able to identify their own babies solely on the basis of smell just a few hours after birth (Porter, Balogh, Cernoch, & Franchi, 1986; Porter, Cernoch, & McLaughlin, 1983); newborn babies could discriminate the odour of their own mother's breast and milk from those of a strange mother (Russell, 1976). Russell reported that observers could accurately identify the gender of wearers of undershirts worn for 24 hours by individuals who neither bathed nor used any deodorant or perfume; that is, identification was based on the wearers' perspiration. Similarly, Wallace (1977) found that observers could discriminate males from females with over 80 per cent accuracy by smelling only the perspiration from the person's hand. In addition to the odour of perspiration, Doty, Green, Ram, & Yankell (1982) found that observers were moderately successful in judging a person's gender solely on the basis of his or her breath. Consistent with an earlier point made, females outperformed males on all these tasks.

Memory of odours

Odours have a remarkable capacity to call up long-ago events and memories. However, sometimes they seem to evoke only vague feelings and memories that we feel certain we experienced before, but at the same time we are unsure what they were and when they occurred. This occasional tendency to recognise that an odour is familiar combined with the inability to identify its source is called the *tip-of-the-nose* phenomenon (Lawless & Engen, 1977). Indeed, a striking aspect of our memory of odours is that although the initial identification and recognition of odours is only moderate – not nearly as high as our memory for many visual materials such as pictures – the memories of odours, especially those associated with real-life experiences are quite long lasting. In one experiment on this phenomenon, Engen and Ross (1973)

246

reported that when subjects were given a diverse set of 20 odours of familiar household products, they recognised only about 70 per cent when tested immediately after exposure. However, when tested one year later the average recognition score had dropped only about 5 per cent, indicating that odour memory shows little loss over time (see also Engen, 1987; Shepard, 1967).

Pheromones

For many animals smell provides an important mode of communication. By releasing *pheromones*, complex odorous chemicals that produce specific reactions in other members of the same species, they are able to send such messages as species and colony recognition, sexual arousal and availability, mark scent trails and territorial boundaries. There are two main types of pheromones. *Primers* produce physiological changes such as altering hormonal activity thereby affecting an animal's reproductive cycle and its sexual receptivity. *Releasers* automatically trigger an immediate behavioural response in an animal. They can serve as powerful sexual stimulants that attract sexual partners for the receptive member. Among the more familiar effects of a releaser pheromone in mammals is the female dog in heat attracting mates. Another familiar example of pheromonal activity is the domesticated male cat spraying around the borders of a room marking his territory.

Evidence of pheromonally elicited behaviour in the human is speculative at best. Studies indicate that women who are close friends or who live together tend to have menstrual cycles that are closely synchronized (Graham & McGrew, 1980; McClintock, 1971, 1984; Quadagno, Shubeita, Deck, & Francoeur 1981). There is also supporting evidence that olfactory cues promote the menstrual synchrony (McClintock, 1984; Russell, Switz, & Thompson, 1980) and that the volatile chemicals influencing the timing of menstrual activity are found in human perspiration (Cutler et al., 1986; Preti et al., 1986). However, the functional implications of the odour's influence on human physiology remains unknown.

FURTHER READING

Engen, T. (1987). Remembering odors and their names. *American Scientist, 75,* 497–503.

Finger, T. E., & Silver, W. L. (Eds) (1987). *Neurobiology of taste and smell.* New York: Wiley.

Howard, I. P. (1982). *Human visual orientation.* New York: Wiley.

Klatsky, R. L., Lederman, S. J., & Metzger, V. A. (1985). Identifying objects by touch: An "expert system". *Perception and Psychophysics, 37,* 200–302.

Schiffman, H. R. (1990). *Sensation and perception: An integrated approach.* New York: Wiley.

REFERENCES

Arvidson, K., & Friberg, U. (1980). Human taste: Response and taste bud number in fungiform papillae. *Science, 209*, 806–807.

Bandura, A., O'Leary, A., Taylor, C. B., Gauthier, J., & Gossard, D. (1987). Perceived self-efficacy and pain control: Opioid and nonopioid mechanisms. *Journal of Personality and Social Psychology, 53*, 563–571.

Bernstein, I. L., & Webster, M. M. (1980). Learned taste aversions in humans. *Physiology and Behavior, 25*, 363–366.

Bolles, R. C., & Fanselow, M. S. (1982). Endorphins and behavior. *Annual Review of Psychology, 33*, 87–101.

Cain, W. S. (1988). Olfaction. In R. C. Atkinson, R. J. Herrnstein, G. Lindzey, & R. D. Luce (Eds) *Stevens' handbook of experimental psychology* (2nd edn, vol. 1, pp. 409–459). New York: Wiley.

Collings, V. B. (1974). Human taste response as a function of locus of stimulation on the tongue and soft palate. *Perception and Psychophysics, 16*, 169–174.

Cutler, W. B., Preti, G., Krieger, A., Huggins, G. R., Garcia, C. R., & Lawley, H. J. (1986). Human axillary secretions influence women's menstrual cycles: The role of donor extract from men. *Hormones and Behavior, 20*, 463–473.

Doty, R. L., Snyder, P. J., Huggins, G. R., & Lowry, L. D. (1981). Endocrine, cardiovascular and psychological correlates of olfactory sensitivity changes during the human menstrual cycle. *Journal of Comparative and Physiological Psychology, 95*, 45–60.

Doty, R. L., Green, P. A., Ram, C., & Yankell, S. L. (1982). Communication of gender from human breath odors: Relationship to perceived intensity and pleasantness. *Hormones and Behavior, 16*, 13–22.

Doty, R. L., Shaman, P., Applebaum, S. L., Gilberson, R., Sikorski, L., & Rosenberg, L. (1984). Smell identification ability: Changes with age. *Science, 226*, 1441–1444.

Engen, T. (1987). Remembering odors and their names. *American Scientist, 75*, 497–503.

Engen, T., & Ross, B. M. (1973). Long-term memory of odors with and without verbal descriptions. *Journal of Experimental Psychology, 100*, 221–227.

Garcia, J., Hankins W. G., & Rusiniak, K. W. (1974). Behavioral regulation of the milieu interne in man and rat. *Science, 185*, 824–831.

Gardner, E. (1947). *Fundamentals of neurology*. Philadelphia, PA: Saunders.

Geldard, F. A. (1972). *The human senses* (2nd edn). New York: Wiley.

Good, P. R., Geary, N., & Engen, T. (1976). The effect of estrogen on odor detection. *Chemical Senses and Flavor, 2*, 45–50.

Graham, C. A., & McGraw, W. C. (1980). Menstrual synchrony in female undergraduates living on a coeducational campus. *Psychoneuroendocrinology, 5*, 245–252.

Grau, J. W. (1984). Influence of naloxone on shock-induced freezing and analgesia. *Behavioral Neuroscience, 98*, 278–292.

Howard, I. P. (1982). *Human visual orientation*. New York: Wiley.

Kennedy, J. M. (1984). The tangible world of the blind. *Encyclopaedia Britannica Medical and Health Annual*. Chicago, IL: Encyclopaedia Britannica.

Kenshalo, D. R. (Ed.) (1968). *The skin senses*. Springfield, IL: Charles C. Thomas.

Klatsky, R. L., Lederman, S. J., & Metzger, V. A. (1985). Identifying objects by touch: An "expert system". *Perception and Psychophysics, 37*, 200–302.

Lawless H. T., & Engen, T. (1977). Associations to odors: Interference, mnemonics, and verbal labels. *Journal of Experimental Psychology: Human Learning and Memory, 3*, 52–59.

Loomis, J. M., & Lederman, S. J. (1986). Tactual perception. In K. R. Boff, L. Kaufman, & J. P. Thomas (Eds) *Handbook of perception and human performance, vol. II* (chap. 31, pp. 1–41). New York: Wiley.

McBurney, D. H., & Shick, T. R. (1971). Taste and water taste of twenty-six compounds for man. *Perception and Psychophysics, 10*, 249–252.

McBurney, D. H., Collings, V. B., & Glanz, L. M. (1973). Temperature dependence of human taste responses. *Physiology and Behavior, 11*, 89–94.

McClintock, M. K. (1971). Menstrual synchrony and suppression. *Nature 229*, 244–245.

McClintock, M. K. (1984). Estrous synchrony: Modulation of ovarian cycle length by female pheromones. *Physiology and Behavior, 32*, 701–705.

Melzack, R. (1973). *The puzzle of pain.* New York: Basic Books.

Melzack, R., & Wall, P. D. (1965). Pain mechanisms: A new theory. *Science, 150*, 971–979.

Melzack, R., & Wall, P. D. (1982). *The challenge of pain.* New York: Basic Books.

Moncrieff, R. W. (1951). *The chemical senses.* London: Leonard Hill.

Morris, D. B. (1991). *The culture of pain.* Berkeley, CA: University of California Press.

Mozell, M. M. (1971). Olfaction. In J. W. Kling & L. A. Riggs (Eds) *Experimental psychology* (3rd edn) (pp. 193–222). New York: Holt, Rinehart & Winston.

Murphy, C. (1987). Olfactory psychophysics. In T. E. Finger & W. L. Silver (Eds) *Neurobiology of taste and smell* (pp. 251–273). New York: Wiley.

Porter, R. H., Cernoch, J. M., & McLaughlin, F. J. (1983). Maternal recognition of neonates through olfactory cues. *Physiology and Behavior, 30*, 151–154.

Porter, R. H., Balogh, R. D., Cernoch, J. M., & Franchi, C. (1986). Recognition of kin through characteristic body odors. *Chemical Senses, 11*, 389–395.

Preti, G., Cutler, W. B., Garcia, C. R., Huggins, G. R., & Lawley, H. J. (1986). Human axillary secretions influence women's menstrual cycles: The role of donor extract of females. *Hormones and Behavior, 20*, 474–482.

Quadagno, D. M., Shubeita, H. E., Deck, J., & Francoeur, D. (1981). Influence of male social contacts, exercise and all female living conditions on the menstrual cycle. *Psychoneuroendocrinology, 6*, 239–244.

Reed, C. M., Doherty, M. J., Braida, L. D., & Durlach, N. I. (1982). Analytic study of the Tadoma method: Further experiments with inexperienced observers. *Journal of Speech and Hearing Research, 25*, 216–223.

Russell, M. J. (1976). Human olfactory communication. *Nature, 260*, 520–522.

Russell, M. J., Switz, G. M., & Thompson, K. (1980). Olfactory influence on the human menstrual cycle. *Pharmacology, Biochemistry and Behavior, 13*, 737–738.

Schiffman, H. R. (1990). *Sensation and perception: An integrated approach* (3rd edn). New York: Wiley.

Schiffman, S. S. (1974). Physiochemical correlates of olfactory quality. *Science, 185*, 112–117.

Schiffman, S. S., Moss, J., & Erickson, R. P. (1976). Thresholds of food odors in the elderly. *Experimental Aging Research, 2*, 389–398.

Shepard, R. N. (1967). Recognition memory for words, sentences, and pictures. *Journal of Verbal Learning and Verbal Behavior, 6*, 156–163.

Terman, C. G., Shavit, Y., Lewis, J. W., Cannon, J. T., & Liebeskind, J. C. (1984). Intrinsic mechanisms of pain inhibition: Activation by stress. *Science, 226*, 1270–1277.

Vierling, J. S., & Rock, J. (1967). Variations of olfactory sensitivity to Exaltolide during the menstrual cycle. *Journal of Applied Physiology, 22*, 311–315.

Wallace, P. (1977). Individual discrimination of humans by odor. *Physiology and Behavior, 19*, 577–579.

Weinstein, S. (1968). Intensive and extensive aspects of tactile sensitivity as a function of body part, sex, and laterality. In D. R. Kenshalo (Ed.) *The skin senses* (chap. 10). Springfield, IL: Charles C. Thomas.

White, B. W., Saunders, F. A., Scadden, L., Bach-y-Rita, P., & Collins C. C. (1970). Seeing with the skin. *Perception and Psychophysics, 7*, 23–27.

Young, L. R. (1984). Perception of the body in space: Mechanisms. In I. Darian-Smith (Ed.) *Handbook of physiology: The nervous system, III* (pp. 1023–1066). Bethesda, MD: American Physiological Society.

3.5

PSYCHOPHYSICS

Donald Laming
University of Cambridge, England

Psychophysics is really about the measurement of the strength of internal sensations and I emphasize that *sensation* is a technical term. It must not be confused with the physical magnitude of the stimulus. Three examples will make the distinction clear.

First, you wake up early on a dark winter's morning and put the bedroom light on to see the time. Initially you are dazzled; but after a few seconds your eyes adapt to the light which then seems much less bright. The (physical) luminance of the light is one thing, its apparent (subjective) brightness quite another.

Second, suppose, now, you are listening to TV late at night. Although the volume control has not been touched, the sound nevertheless appears gradually to get louder. If you listen past midnight, your next-door neighbour may well protest about a level of sound that passed unnoticed earlier in the evening. The loudness of the sound as you (and your neighbour) hear it is not the same as the auditory power produced by the TV set's loudspeaker.

Third, there is a trick question: which is heavier, a pound of feathers or a pound of lead? Without thinking, you say "lead" – and are then told that they both weigh the same! But if "heaviness" means the feel of weight as one or the other is picked up, the pound of lead is indeed heavier. Dense materials feel heavier, weight for weight, than materials of lesser density; this is known as the size-weight illusion. In my classroom demonstration a pillow weighing 720 gm is repeatedly judged to be equal to a lead weight somewhere between 30 and 225 gm. The feel of heaviness is distinct from the physical weight of the object.

In what follows I distinguish carefully between the physical measurement of a stimulus – luminance, sound pressure level, weight – and its subjective counterpart – brightness, loudness, heaviness. To emphasize this distinction I use two separate sets of words. Luminance, sound pressure level, and weight can be measured with photometers, sound level meters, and scale pans to whatever accuracy may be desired. But how can one measure internal quantities like brightness, loudness and heaviness? Such measurement is the subject of this chapter.

MEASUREMENTS OF THE DISCRIMINABILITY BETWEEN STIMULI

Suppose you lift a weight of 100 gm and then one of 200 gm; the second weight is obviously heavier. But suppose the second weight is 101 gm? Would the difference be obvious then? As the 100 gm weight is compared with progressively heavier second weights, there comes a point at which the difference is "just noticeable". In 1860 Fechner proposed using that "just noticeable difference" as a unit (like a foot or a pound) to measure internal sensation.

Fechner's idea works like this. Take the 100 gm weight and a selection of heavier weights to discover which of them is just noticeably greater. In an experiment the weights are usually made up by setting a requisite amount of lead shot in wax at the bottom of a tin can. Each weight is housed in an identical can so that there is no visual indication which weight is which. Suppose 105 gm is judged to be just noticeably greater than 100 gm. Now find the weight which is just noticeably greater than 105 gm, and then the weight just noticeably greater than that, and so on. A ladder of weights is constructed in which the step from one weight to the next is always "just noticeable". Fechner proposed using that ladder as a scale of internal sensation.

There are some practical problems of which the most pressing is how to measure "just noticeable differences". It happens that the minimum resolvable difference in weight (and in many other attributes as well) bears a simple relation to the standard weight with which comparison is being made. But the problem of ascertaining the constant ratio which enters into that relation remains. Fechner devoted nine years to experimental research exploring three different methods of measuring that constant ratio; eventually, in 1860, he published his *Elemente der Psychophysik*, a book which did more than any other single publication to make psychology an experimental science. In that book Fechner sketched out a "physics of the mind" which he called *psychophysics*. But the preliminary to any such exploration of mental function must be reliable measurement of internal sensations.

The method of constant stimuli

Suppose a subject lifts two weights, 100 gm and $100 + \Delta$ gm, where Δ is a small increase. After lifting the two weights the subject says which she thinks is greater. Figure 1 presents data from Brown (1910), for the comparison of

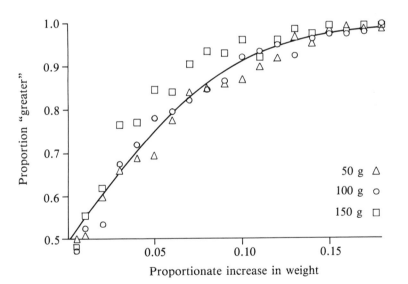

Figure 1 Discrimination of lifted weights by the method of constant stimuli. Each data point shows the proportion of correct judgements in 200 trials. The continuous curve is the upper half of a normal integral
Source: Data from Brown, 1910, Table II, pp. 16–17, Rows M, N, and O; figure from Laming, 1986, p. 22. Copyright Academic Press, 1986. Reproduced by permission

253

standard weights of 50, 100, and 150 gm with a range of percentage increases. The proportion of "greater" judgements increases smoothly throughout this range. This means that there is no precise increase in weight which can obviously be said to be "just noticeably different". Instead, a *just noticeable difference*, more frequently called a *difference threshold* or simply *threshold*, has to be defined as a statistical concept, most often that difference which is judged correctly 75 per cent of the time (though other percentages are sometimes used). The curve in Figure 1 is the upper half of a normal integral, the cumulative function of a normal distribution. When the subject is comparing two separate stimuli, this curve has repeatedly been found to provide a good representation of the way in which the proportion of correct judgements increases with the stimulus difference. This relation was first proposed by Fechner (1860).

The method of limits

In the method of limits there is a standard stimulus (100 gm) which is fixed and a comparison which is increased or decreased by small predetermined steps. The scheme is illustrated in Figure 2. Starting at a value clearly less

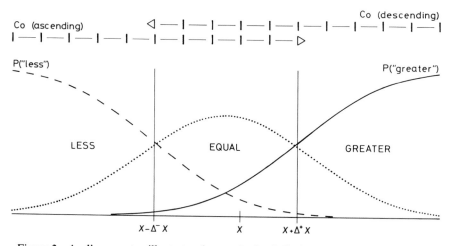

Figure 2 A diagram to illustrate the method of limits. A graduated series of increasing comparison stimuli are successively compared with a fixed standard (X) to determine the point at which "less" gives way to "equal" and the greater point at which "equal" gives way to "greater". Ascending series of comparisons are balanced by an equal number of descending series. The *upper difference threshold* Δ^+X is determined by that value which is judged greater than the standard 50 per cent of the time; likewise the *lower difference threshold* Δ^-X by the value judged "less than" 50 per cent of the time

Source: Laming, 1986, p. 19. Copyright Academic Press, 1986. Reproduced by permission

254

than the standard, the comparison stimulus is increased until the subject says "equal" and then increased further until she says "greater". The objective is to determine what value of the comparison stimulus would be judged less than the standard 50 per cent of the time (the difference $\Delta^- X$ with respect to the standard X in Figure 2 is known as the *lower difference threshold*) and what greater value of the comparison would be judged "greater than", again 50 per cent of the time (giving the *upper difference threshold* $\Delta^+ X$ in Figure 2). Ascending sequences of comparison values are balanced by descending sequences because subjects tend to perseverate their judgements. Ascending series usually give higher estimates of the 50 per cent values than do descending series.

Figure 3 shows a sample of measurements by this method from Kiesow (1925/1926). The stimuli were horizontal lines, about $\frac{1}{3}$ mm thick, drawn in black ink on white paper. The length of the comparison line was varied by covering part of it with another sheet of paper. The open triangles are upper thresholds determined from ascending series of comparison stimuli, and the

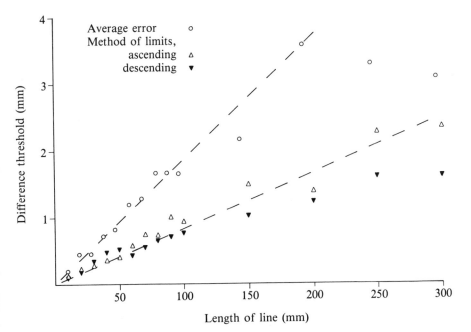

Figure 3 Thresholds for the discrimination of lengths of line by the method of limits and the method of average error. The thresholds by the method of average error (circles) are plotted against the mean adjustment as abscissa, rather than the standard stimulus

Source: The data, all from the same subject, are from Kiesow, 1925/1926; the figure is from Laming, 1986, p. 20. Copyright Academic Press, 1986. Reproduced by permission

filled triangles are from descending series. Most of the estimates from ascending series are greater than the corresponding estimates from descending series.

The method of average error

The circles in Figure 3 are thresholds obtained from the same subject for the same lines drawn on paper, but using the third of Fechner's methods, the method of average error. In this procedure the subject's task is simply to adjust the length of one line (by moving the sheet of paper which partially overlays it) so that it matches the length of another line (the standard). There is some restriction of the subject's opportunity to compare the two lines; they are placed end to end, not side by side. The adjustment of the comparison line to match the standard is, of course, different each time, and several matches are made to each standard length. The threshold is usually taken to be the probable error of adjustment, that is, the absolute error which would be exceeded in 50 per cent of such matches.

The same standard lengths were used as with the method of limits (and are represented in Figure 3 by the abscissa values of the *triangles*); the data from the method of average error (circles) are plotted against *mean adjustment* as abscissa. This manner of presentation shows that the mean adjustment in the method of average error was always less than the standard to be matched; the abscissa values of the circles lie always to the left of the corresponding triangles. It is common for the mean adjustment to deviate from the standard stimulus; the difference is known as the *constant error* to distinguish it from the *variable error* which is different for each separate matching. Constant errors also appear in the other two methods, but are most obvious with average error.

Comparison of the three methods

An immediate problem for Fechner's scheme for measuring internal sensations is that these three methods typically do not give the same value for a just noticeable difference. The method of average error usually gives smaller thresholds than does the method of constant stimuli (e.g., Kellogg, 1929; Wier, Jesteadt, & Green, 1976) provided the threshold is calculated from the variable errors alone. (The data in Figure 3 are absolute errors with respect to the standard stimulus and are inflated by confounding with the constant error.) A possible explanation was suggested by Stephanowitsch (1913) who recorded all the separate comparisons made by subjects while adjusting the length of one line to match another. There were many more comparisons of small differences than of large; this biases the ultimate estimate of the threshold.

Comparisons with the method of limits are uncertain. This method realizes

256

more directly than the other two the nineteenth-century conception of a "threshold" as a limit below which nothing can be perceived – like the threshold in a doorway. That idea is now known to be misconceived (see Laming, 1986, chap. 3; Swets, Tanner, & Birdsall, 1961) and the method has accordingly fallen into disuse. Contemporary practice is based on the picture presented in Figure 1 in which the probability of a correct judgement increases smoothly as the stimulus difference increases. Modern methods aim to estimate some chosen point on this function (often, but not always, the 75 per cent point) with as few trials as possible. This is accomplished by adjusting the comparison stimulus from one trial to the next, up or down, according to the subject's responses. A variety of schemes, sometimes known as *staircase procedures*, have been devised by Cornsweet (1962), Levitt (1971), and others. The ultimate in the efficient use of experimental trials is QUEST (Watson & Pelli, 1983; see also Laming & Marsh, 1988). QUEST achieves its efficiency by utilizing certain prior knowledge about the function in Figure 1.

Weber's Law

Notwithstanding the difficulties in measuring thresholds, one important generalization can be made. In Figure 1 the same percentage increase with respect to standards of 50, 100, 150 gm gives nearly the same proportion of correct responses. This means that the difference threshold increases in proportion to the standard. The same relation is evident in the data from the method of limits in Figure 3.

Let ΔW be the 75 per cent threshold measured at a standard weight W. (ΔW means a small, but not vanishingly small, increment in weight.) Then

$$\Delta W / W = \text{constant.} \tag{1}$$

This is known as *Weber's Law* after E. H. Weber who first enunciated it in 1834. It holds approximately for many stimulus attributes down to about the absolute threshold which is the smallest magnitude of stimulus that can be perceived (see Laming, 1986, pp. 76–77, Table 5.1).

Fechner's Law

Fechner proposed measuring internal sensations in units of "just noticeable differences". Suppose that sensation S increases as the logarithm of the physical stimulus magnitude. If weights are being lifted,

$$S = \log W. \tag{2}$$

If ΔS is the just noticeable increase in heaviness produced by the increase in ΔW in weight,

$$S + \Delta S = \log (W + \Delta W). \tag{3}$$

Subtracting Equation 2 from Equation 3 gives, for the just noticeable increase in sensation,

$$\Delta S = \log (W + \Delta W) - \log W$$
$$= \log (1 + \Delta W / W), \tag{4}$$

because the difference of two logarithms is equal to the logarithm of their ratio.

If, in Equation 4, ΔS is constant, so also is $\Delta W / W$, which is Weber's Law (Equation 1). This means that, if Weber's Law applies to the stimulus attribute in question and just noticeable differences in sensation are taken to be equal, then sensation increases as the logarithm of the physical stimulus magnitude. Equation 2 is known as *Fechner's Law*. I have argued here from Fechner's Law to Weber's Law. Fechner (1860) had to argue in the opposite direction, which is more difficult (see Krantz, 1971; Luce & Edwards, 1958).

"DIRECT" MEASUREMENTS OF SENSATION

Fechner's Law was long accepted as the relation between internal sensation and physical stimulus magnitude, chiefly because there was no serious alternative. But about the year 1930 a practical problem arose in acoustic engineering. The sounds that we ordinarily hear vary over a very wide range, so wide that sound level is conventionally measured in decibels on a logarithmic scale. The quietest sound that can just be heard is rated 0 dB and each tenfold increase in power above that level adds 10 dB to the rating. Table 1 lists some common environmental sounds against their approximate decibel values.

Because the decibel rating increases as the logarithm of the physical power of the sound, it ought to be proportional to the sensation produced. But most people would say that 100 dB (an underground train coming into a station) sounds much more than twice as loud as 50 dB (the background noise of conversation in a library). When acoustic engineers have to explain to their clients how loud things are going to sound, the false impression given by the decibel scale matters.

There were some experiments conducted by acoustic engineers in the early 1930s. A typical trial presented two tones and asked: how many times louder was the second tone than the first? Alternatively the subject might adjust the second tone to be twice or half as loud as the first. The results of those experiments were assembled by S. S. Stevens (1936) into the *sone* scale of loudness. Taking a 1,000 Hz (cycles per second) tone as the standard sound, a tone at

258

Table 1   Decibel levels of some common environmental sounds

Sound	Sound level in dB
Softest audible sound	0
Normal breathing	10
Open country at night	20
Soft whisper	30
Very quiet living room	40
Quiet conversation (e.g., library)	50
Average speaking voice at 5 ft	60
Television, typical sound level	70
Motor car at 65 mph, from 25 ft	80
Motor cycle 25 ft away	90
Underground train entering station	100
Chain saw (unprotected operator)	110
Loud rock group	120
Machine-gun fire at close range	130
Jet engine at take-off, from 100 ft	140

40 dB was defined to have a loudness of 1 sone, at 50 dB 2 sones, at 60 dB 4 sones, at 70 dB 8 sones, and so on, the number of sones doubling with each increase of 10 dB. The loudnesses of other sounds were then measured by matching to a 1,000 Hz tone.

The difference with respect to the decibel scale is worth emphasis. If the intensity (physical power) of a sound is increased tenfold, its dB rating increases always by 10, but its sone rating is doubled. The fixed dB increase for a constant multiplicative increase in intensity makes the dB scale logarithmic, like Fechner's scale of sensation. But the doubling of the sone rating means that it increases as a (mathematical) power of intensity. Put into an equation

$$\text{Loudness in sones} = (10^{-2} A/A_0)^{0.6} \tag{5}$$

where A is the amplitude of the physical sound wave and A_0 is the faintest amplitude that can be heard (0 dB). The sone scale (Equation 5) constituted the first serious alternative to Fechner's Law (Equation 2).

Magnitude estimation

Twenty years later S. S. Stevens (1956, 1957) returned to the problem of measuring sensation and developed his method of *magnitude estimation*. Figure 4 displays the results from an experiment which Stevens (1975) presented as typical.

In this experiment the stimuli, eight 1,000 Hz tones ranging from 40 to 110 dB, were presented one at a time in random order. They were presented

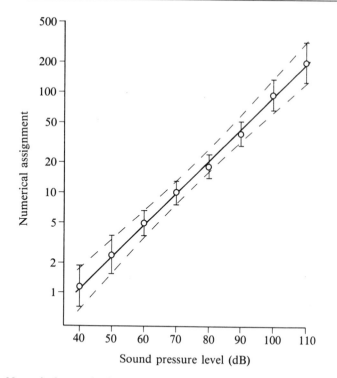

Figure 4 Numerical magnitude estimates of the loudness of a 1000 Hz tone by 32 observers judging each stimulus twice only. The vertical bar through each data point shows the inter-quartile range of the 64 judgements. The broken curves are predictions for the inter-quartile ranges
Source: Adapted and redrawn from S. S. Stevens, 1975, p. 28

twice each to 32 subjects, in a different random order to each subject. The first tone heard was given any number considered appropriate; thereafter, the instruction was "Try to make the ratios between the numbers you assign to the different tones correspond to the ratios between the loudnesses of the tones" (S. S. Stevens, 1956, p. 20). There was no suggestion that there was such a thing as a "correct" response; "We are interested in how loud tones *seem* to be to you, not in some kind of 'accuracy'." (S. S. Stevens, 1956, p. 17). The intention was to record the subject's internal experiences as simply and directly as possible.

Some subjects tended to use larger numbers than others; the numbers in Figure 4 have been scaled so that the geometric mean of each subject's scaled judgements is the same. After scaling, the mean judgements accord closely with the sone scale (Equation 5 above; Figure 4 has been plotted with logarithmic ordinate and abscissa: this way of presenting the data turns the power relation of Equation 5 into a straight line of gradient equal to the exponent). The vertical bars in Figure 4 mark the inter-quartile intervals of the magnitude estimates and the broken curve describes predictions for those intervals. The intervals and their predictions will be discussed later.

Stevens' Power Law

Magnitude estimation was developed by S. S. Stevens (1956) as an experimental procedure after much trial and error. While some psychologists have reported difficulty in replicating the experiment, in the hands of Stevens and his colleagues it has given nicely repeatable results. It has been applied to a very large number of different stimulus attributes; S. S. Stevens (1975, p. 15) lists 33. The results from each attribute conform approximately to an equation of the form

$$\text{Mean magnitude estimate} = aX^b \tag{6}$$

where X is the physical measurement of the stimulus, a a scale factor, and b an exponent characteristic of the attribute. That exponent (b) has been found to vary from 0.33 (brightness) to 3.5 (electric shock). The exponent for length, of which most people have much experience, is approximately 1.0. Equation 6 is known as *Stevens' Power Law*.

Magnitude production

If subjects can systematically assign numbers to stimuli, can they also adjust stimuli to match given numbers? Figure 5 presents an example from S. S. Stevens and Greenbaum (1966).

The stimulus in this experiment was an interval of time marked by a burst of white noise. In the first phase of the experiment ten subjects made two separate judgements each of the durations of twelve different bursts of white noise. Their geometric mean estimates are shown by the open circles in Figure 5 and the standard deviations of these estimates by the lengths of the broken lines. In the second phase of the experiment the same subjects pressed a key to produce a noise burst of appropriate duration in response to each of eight different numbers. Those numbers were chosen in the light of the mean responses in the first phase. The geometric mean productions are shown by the filled circles in Figure 5 and their respective standard deviations (it is now the abscissa value which is set by the subjects) by the continuous straight lines. Both sets of means are approximately linear on this log-log plot in accord with Stevens' Power Law. But the gradients of the two lines (and therefore the values of the exponent in the power law) differ. The mean productions (filled circles) are steeper (higher exponent) than the estimates (open circles).

This difference in gradient, depending on whether magnitudes are being estimated or produced, is usually small, but is, at the same time, highly

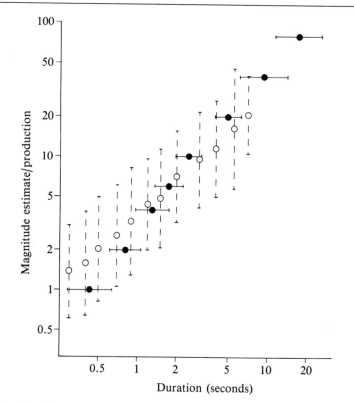

Figure 5 Matching of numbers to the durations of bursts of noise. The open circles are geometric mean magnitude estimates and the filled circles magnitude productions. The vertical and horizontal lines through the data points extend to ±1 standard deviation of the distribution of logarithm matches

Source: Data from S. S. Stevens and Greenbaum, 1966, Table 2, p. 444

systematic. The difference always lies in the direction illustrated in Figure 5, with productions giving a steeper gradient than estimates, and may be succinctly summarized by the dictum "The observer tends to shorten the range of which ever variable he controls" (S. S. Stevens, 1971, p. 426). Stevens and Greenbaum (1966) called this the "regression effect".

Cross-modality matching

If subjects can assign numbers to stimuli and adjust stimuli to match numbers, presumably they can also adjust one stimulus to match another, the stimuli being of quite different kinds. J. C. Stevens, J. D. Mack, and S. S. Stevens (1960) had subjects match values of a number of different attributes to force of handgrip. The subjects squeezed a hand dynamometer to whatever extent seemed to match the intensity of electric current, or white noise, or vibration, or whatever, presented for matching. Figure 6 shows their results.

Other experiments have determined exponent values for numerical estimation of all the attributes represented in Figure 5. Suppose, for example, that the assignment of numbers to a 1,000 Hz tone accords with the equation

$$N = X^b \tag{7}$$

and the assignment to force of handgrip to

$$M = Y^c. \tag{8}$$

If Stevens' Power Law derives from some real transformation of the neural message inside the sensory system, as Stevens (1970) believed, the matching of force of handgrip directly to the loudness of a 1,000 Hz tone should be predictable from Equations 7 and 8. Briefly, when a value of Y is matched to a value of X, the number (N) assigned by Equation 7 should equate to the other number (M) assigned by Equation 8; that is, the force of handgrip

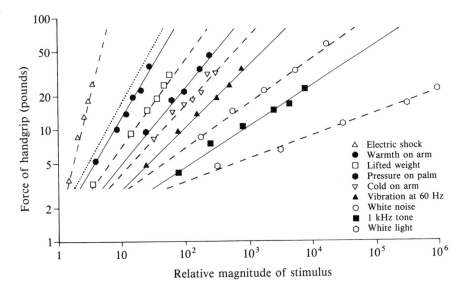

Figure 6 Force of handgrip matched to values of ten other stimulus attributes. Each set of data has been arbitrarily transposed along the abscissa for clarity of presentation. The dotted line represents a gradient of 1
Source: Redrawn from S. S. Stevens, 1966, p. 5

263

Table 2 Calculation of predicted exponents in Figure 6

Stimulus attribute	Numerical estimates (b)	Predicted exponent	Matching by force of handgrip (b/c)
Electric shock	3.5	2.06	2.13
Force of handgrip	1.7(c)	—	—
Warmth on arm	1.6	0.94	0.96
Lifted weight	1.45	0.85	0.79
Pressure on palm	1.1	0.65	0.67
Cold on arm	1.0	0.59	0.60
Vibration at 60 Hz	0.95	0.56	0.56
White noise	0.67	0.39	0.41
1,000 Hz tone	0.67	0.39	0.35
White light	0.33	0.19	0.21

(Y) matched to the sound level (X) should satisfy

$$Y^c = X^b$$

or

$$Y = X^{b/c}. \tag{9}$$

Table 2 sets out calculations which show that this relation holds for the data in Figure 6. The estimates of the magnitude estimation exponents in the second column are taken from the list assembled by S. S. Stevens (1975, p. 15). Dividing each by the exponent for numerical estimation of force of handgrip (row 2, c) gives the predicted value in the third column. This is to be compared with the exponent in the fourth column estimated from the direct matching of force of handgrip with the stimulus attribute in Figure 6. The concordance is very good.

RELATING STEVENS' POWER LAW TO FECHNER'S LAW

A controversy has continued, on and off, ever since S. S. Stevens (1957) enunciated his law. Fechner (1860) had asserted that internal sensations grew as the logarithm of the physical stimulus magnitude (Equation 2), and Stevens proposed instead that they increased as a power function. Which is correct?

First, in principle, it is possible for both to be correct. A more general form of Fechner's Law (Equation 2) would be

$$S = \log a + b \log X \tag{10}$$

writing X for the physical magnitude of some arbitrary stimulus attribute.

Taking antilogarithms on both sides of Equation 10 gives

$$10^S = aX^b, \tag{11}$$

which is Stevens' Power Law (Equation 6) with "10^S" for "Mean magnitude estimate"; taking logarithms on both sides of Equation 6, of course, gives Fechner's Law (Equation 10). So it is possible that the controversy concerns no more than the way in which the mathematics should be formulated – whether the label "sensation" should be attached to magnitude estimates or to their logarithms.

Second, on the other hand, it could be that the logarithmic law and the power function are both wrong. Fechner and Stevens have attached the label "sensation" to different experimental measurements solely by fiat. Some extraneous justification is needed for taking either just noticeable differences or magnitude estimates as the measurement of internal sensation.

Such justification can come only from the role that each plays in some ultimate theory of sensory discrimination or of sensory judgement. It is the task of the natural scientist to describe the state of nature as accurately and succinctly as possible. If in such a theory of sensory discrimination there emerged a fundamental role for some function of the stimulus attribute distinct from the physical measurement (the logarithm, for example), that function might reasonably be taken to measure internal sensation. Likewise, if it were shown that magnitude estimates fulfilled such a role, the label "sensation" might reasonably be attached there. But this matter should not be decided without a careful examination of the results obtained from the different experiments.

In the rest of this chapter I show, first, that Fechner's Law and Stevens' Power Law cannot both be correct. The possible reconciliation sketched above is incompatible with existing experimental results. In fact, sensory discrimination and magnitude estimation study quite distinct psychological processes. Second, the findings about sensory discrimination, especially Weber's Law, which led to Fechner's logarithmic law, can be described more succinctly and comprehensively directly in terms of the physical measurement of the stimulus. Third, Stevens' results from magnitude estimation also admit a more comprehensive description in which the power law results from the way in which the experiment is set up and has no theoretical significance at all.

Reconciling Fechner's and Stevens' laws

If the controversy is solely about the way in which the mathematics should be formulated, then, whichever way that question is ultimately resolved, values on one attribute (X) should map on to values on some other attribute

(Y) according to Equation 9 (Stevens' Power Law), which I rewrite here in the form

$$Y^c = X^b. \tag{12}$$

At the same time, Fechner's Law requires a just noticeable increase in X to equate to an equally noticeable increase in Y. So

$$(Y + \Delta Y)^c = (X + \Delta X)^b. \tag{13}$$

Dividing Equation 13 by Equation 12 leads to

$$(1 + \Delta Y/Y)^c = (1 + \Delta X/X)^b \tag{14}$$

which relates the exponents from magnitude estimation (b, c) to the Weber fractions ($\Delta X/X$, $\Delta Y/Y$) from discrimination experiments. More to the point, the quantities on the left hand side of Equation 14 relate *solely* to attribute Y and those on the right *solely* to attribute X, whatever those attributes might be. It follows that

$$(1 + \Delta X/X)^b = \text{constant} \tag{15}$$

a constant that is independent of the stimulus attribute.

Equation 15 relates the Weber fraction to the magnitude estimation exponent. It was first derived by Teghtsoonian (1971) who tabulated data from nine different attributes. Teghtsoonian's calculated values for the constant range from 0.026 to 0.034, a closer concordance than one might expect in view of the difficulties of pairing different experiments by different experimenters using different apparatus in different laboratories. Careful examination of Teghtsoonian's sources shows that this concordance is, indeed, too good to be true (see Laming, 1989, p. 280).

Figure 7 presents my own collection of some 30 pairs of experimental values. The continuous line, not quite straight, is Equation 15 with the constant set equal to 0.052. The triangles are the particular attributes tabulated by Teghtsoonian (1971), but not necessarily estimated from the same data. Some of those attributes are here represented more than once. The filled symbols are pairings of Weber fractions and exponents from the *same experimenter*, usually from different experiments employing the same apparatus and published together. One might expect these pairings to be more precisely related than the open symbols which are based on two independent sources. But the scatter of the filled symbols is as great as that of the open ones. All that can be said of the predicted relation is that there are no attributes with both a small Weber fraction and a low exponent. Otherwise, there is no relation between the two.

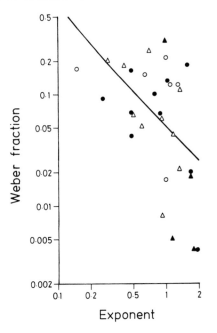

Figure 7 Weber fractions and power law exponents from some 30 pairs of experiments. The filled symbols are those pairs where both quantities have been estimated from the work of the same experimenter; open symbols are pairings of results from different experimenters. The triangles represent those attributes surveyed by Teghtsoonian (1971). The continuous line is Equation 15 with the constant set equal to 0.052

Source: Laming, 1989, p. 280. Copyright 1989 by Cambridge University Press. Reproduced by permission

Variability of magnitude estimates

If sensory discrimination and magnitude estimation were telling us about the *same* underlying psychological process, the precision of the two kinds of judgement should be about the same. The data in Figures 4 and 5 enable two comparisons.

First, the inter-quartile range of log. magnitude estimates in Figure 4 is at a minimum at 80 dB where it is ±0.115 log. units. Individual estimates have been rescaled to eliminate differences of scale in the size of the numbers uttered by different subjects, so this inter-quartile interval relates entirely to intra-subject variation. For comparison with other experiments, it is convenient to convert this interval into an equivalent on the stimulus scale. Since log. loudness varies 0.6 in proportion to differences in log. amplitude (Equation 5), the equivalent interval on the stimulus scale is 0.19 log. units (= 0.115/0.6), which equates to a proportional 0.55 increase in amplitude. A

267

discrimination experiment with comparable stimuli has been reported by Jesteadt, Wier, and Green (1977). They found the Weber fraction for a 1,000 Hz tone at 80 dB to be 0.06 in amplitude units, less by a whole order of magnitude.

Second, the data in Figure 5 (open circles and broken lines) are magnitude estimates and standard deviations for intervals of time marked by bursts of white noise. The standard deviations range from 0.34 to 0.45 log. units (except for the longest duration, which has standard deviation 0.29). The power law exponent estimated from the means is 0.87, so that a standard deviation in log. magnitude estimate of 0.34 is equivalent to 0.39 log. units (= 0.34/0.87) with respect to log. time, that is, an increase of 1.46 or a decrease of 0.59. Discrimination of similar intervals of time has been studied by Treisman (1963) who found the corresponding standard deviation (that is, the threshold according to a criterion of 84 per cent correct) to vary between 0.066 and 0.174 in different experiments. Again, the variability of the magnitude estimates is greater by an order of magnitude.

The two experiments in each comparison employed substantially the same stimuli, so the initial sensory processing must be common. Since magnitude estimates are so much more variable than simple discriminations of "louder" or "softer", the magnitude estimation task must engage some further psychological process which contributes additional variance. The process studied by simple threshold experiments is *sensory discrimination*, and I call the additional process engaged by magnitude estimation *sensory judgement* (Laming, 1991). The standard deviation of magnitude estimates is typically ten times that of threshold discriminations in linear measure. But since variances add in square measure, the real contribution of variance from sensory judgement must be 100 times that from sensory discrimination. The two kinds of experiments, looking respectively at resolving power and at "direct" estimates of magnitude, cannot be studying the same process.

SENSORY DISCRIMINATION

The possibility of justifying one or the other measurement of sensation now depends on there being some fundamental role in sensory discrimination for Fechner's Law or in sensory judgement for Stevens' Power Law. Sensory discrimination lies beyond the scope of this chapter. But recent developments permit the question of the validity of Fechner's Law to be resolved.

A discrimination between two separate stimuli, any two values of an attribute conforming to Weber's Law, may be modelled very accurately by combining Fechner's Law with the normal distribution. Torgerson (1958, chap. 10) has set out the general idea; Thurstone's (1927) "Law of Comparative Judgement" and Tanner and Swets' (1954) signal-detection theory are particular instances of it. This looks at first sight to be the required justification for Fechner's Law; but, unfortunately, the model is not unique. Another

268

model, equally accurate, can be constructed by combining the natural physical measurement of the stimulus, in similar manner, with a χ^2 distribution (Laming, 1986, pp. 71–78). This undermines whatever validity there might have been for Fechner's Law.

The choice between the two models is not, in fact, arbitrary. The first (normal) model works well for discriminations between two separate stimuli. It happens so because, under a logarithmic transform, the χ^2 model transforms into a very close approximation of the normal model (Laming, 1986, pp. 242–254) and, mathematically speaking, this is the reason why Fechner's Law takes the form that it does. But many sensory experiments add a brief increment to an existing stimulus background. The normal model cannot accommodate this different configuration of the stimulus levels to be distinguished, whereas the second (χ^2) model generalizes naturally to a more comprehensive model which takes in the detection of increments as well (Laming, 1986). For this reason the χ^2 model is to be preferred. There is no need, so far as sensory discrimination is concerned, to invoke any fundamental variable distinct from the physical measurement of the stimulus. Fechner's Law does not provide any basis for measuring internal sensations.

NUMERICAL ESTIMATION OF SENSORY MAGNITUDES

Fechner's Law fails to provide a basis for measuring sensation because the experimental phenomena on which it is based admit an alternative, and more comprehensive, account in terms of the physical measurement of the stimulus magnitude. Can the same be accomplished for magnitude estimation and the related procedures on which Stevens' Power Law is based? Note that the consistency check provided by cross-modality matching experiments is not itself sufficient to establish the validity of Stevens' Law. It is merely a constraint which any, and every, explanation has to satisfy.

Explanation of Stevens' Power Law

It is usual practice in magnitude estimation experiments to choose a geometric ladder of stimulus values so that each value is a fixed multiple of the one below it. Since the stimulus attributes commonly employed are those which conform to Weber's Law, this practice ensures that the discriminability of each stimulus from its neighbours is uniform throughout the scale. On a scale of log. stimulus magnitude the values are equally spaced.

It is also common for subjects to use *round* numbers in judging sensory magnitudes: 1, 2, 5, 10, 20, 50, 100, and so on (cf. Baird, Lewis, & Romer, 1975). This means that the numerical responses are also spread, more or less uniformly, on an approximately logarithmic scale. This practice is enhanced by instructing the subjects to judge ratios, as Stevens typically did (S. S. Stevens, 1971, p. 428). All that is now needed to complete a model for magnitude estimation is some scheme for a partially random assignment of numbers to stimulus values. The mapping of numbers on to stimuli is then estimated by regressing *log. number* on to *log. stimulus magnitude*, that is, by using an equation like

$$\log N = \log a + b \log X. \tag{16}$$

When antilogs are taken on both sides of Equation 13, it turns into Equation 6.

When the exponent b is estimated in this manner, its value will be approximately equal to the difference between the largest and smallest of the log. mean numerical estimates (i.e, the range of $\log N$) divided by the difference between the largest and smallest log. stimulus magnitudes (i.e., the range of $\log X$). That suggests looking at the relations between the estimates of the exponents for different stimulus attributes and the ranges of $\log N$ and $\log X$ in the corresponding experiments.

The relation between the exponent and log. stimulus range is plotted in Figure 8. The data points cluster closely around the hyperbola

$$b = 1.48/(\text{Log. Stimulus Range}). \tag{17}$$

This relation was discovered by Poulton (1967), but put into this striking form by Teghtsoonian (1971). If all the points lay exactly on the hyperbola,

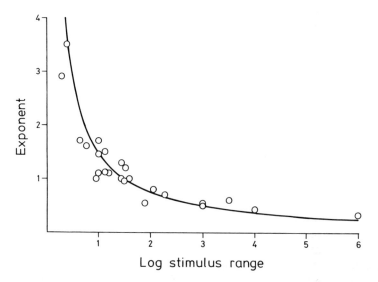

Figure 8 Power law exponents for 24 stimulus attributes plotted against the logarithm of the geometric range of stimulus values employed in the experiments from which the exponents were estimated. The continuous curve is the hyperbola of Equation 17
Source: After Teghtsoonian, 1971, p. 73

Stevens' laboratory was always the same, and that the exponent varied from one stimulus attribute to another solely because the range of stimulus values was different. That is not quite the picture in Figure 8, but very nearly.

The smallest stimulus range in Figure 8 is 2 (for the saturation of yellow) and the largest 1,000,000 (for brightness). So the stimulus ranges vary over 5.7 log. units. The smallest response range is 7.4 (again for saturation of yellow) and the largest is 138.33 (for binaural sound intensity). So the response ranges vary only over 1.27 log. units. It is not quite true to say that the response range is independent of the stimulus range, but the relationship is no more than slight.

Figure 8 suggests that Stevens' experimental results are most succinctly viewed as the mapping of a nearly constant logarithmic range of numbers on to a chosen logarithmic range of stimulus values. The stimulus range is usually chosen to be the largest practicable because this affords the most accurate estimate of the exponent. That largest practicable stimulus range depends on the attribute being studied, and the relation between exponent and stimulus attribute is generated thereby.

Relativity of judgement

If magnitude estimation is a mapping, subject to considerable variability, of a logarithmic range of numbers on to a logarithmic range of stimuli, it needs to be explained how this is accomplished.

Laming (1984) proposed this Principle of Relativity:

All judgements are relative to the immediate context.

In a magnitude estimation experiment the immediate context is the stimulus presented on the preceding trial and the number assigned to it. Judgement of the present stimulus relative to that context is no more than ordinal. This is implicit in the Principle of Relativity for this reason:

Suppose one stimulus is judged to be twice the magnitude of its predecessor. If that predecessor has itself been judged to be three times *its* predecessor, then the present stimulus is six times the stimulus presented two trials ago. Working backwards in this manner, all stimuli can be related to the standard presented at the beginning of the experiment. It is implicit in the Principle of Relativity that such backwards reference is impossible and judgements no better than ordinal.

Suppose, instead, each stimulus to be judged "greater than" or "about equal to" or "less than" its predecessor. If a stimulus is judged "greater than" the one before it, it is given a greater number; if "equal", the same number; if "less than", a smaller number. The question now is how will the numbers fall over a long run of judgements of randomly chosen stimulus values?

Small stimuli will usually be judged smaller than their respective pre-decessors and be assigned smaller numbers. For the complementary reason large stimuli will be assigned larger numbers. If the stimulus values are chosen in geometric progression, spaced equally on a logarithmic scale, and if the subjects are induced to use round numbers, to judge ratios — both these features were frequent in experiments by S. S. Stevens and his colleagues — it is appropriate to think in terms of logarithmic stimulus and response scales. The explanation of Stevens' Power Law above is thereby concordant with the Principle of Relativity, and in what follows I am concerned only with the variability of magnitude estimates. Laming (1984) expressed the conse-quences of the assumption of purely ordinal judgement in a quantitative model. In the interests of simplicity, I present here only a verbal characteriza-tion of that model and two of its predictions.

The estimation of the loudness in Figure 4 used a set of eight 1,000 Hz tones spaced at 10 dB intervals. The softest tone (40 dB) was preceded equally, on different trials, by each of the other seven and that variation in the point of reference increased the variability of the responses to the 40 dB tone. The variance of any one estimate includes a component which increases as the *square* of the (logarithmic) distance of the stimulus being judged from its predecessor. Since the 40 dB tone is more remote from 110 dB than, say, 70 or 80 dB is from either end of the scale, so the overall variability of the judgements is greater for the extreme stimuli (40 and 110 dB) than it is for the central ones. The broken curves in Figure 4 are numerical predictions der-ived by Laming (1984) for this particular experiment.

Autocorrelation of successive judgements

Figure 9 presents certain statistics from a magnitude estimation experiment by Baird, Green, and Luce (1980). The stimuli in this experiment were again 1,000 Hz tones ranging from 40 to 90 dB in steps of 2.5 dB. There were three subjects who made about 2,500 judgements each, randomly distributed over these 21 different stimuli. The statistics in Figure 9 are *autocorrelations* between successive log. numerical estimates in relation to the difference in dB between the corresponding stimulus values.

To explain the notion of correlation: suppose two examiners are each marking the same set of scripts. Examiner X assigns marks x_1, x_2, x_3, and so on, and Examiner Y marks y_1, y_2, y_3, ... to Scripts 1, 2, 3, ... Ideally, one would like these two examiners, each assigning marks independently of the other, to agree closely, because then one would have confidence in their marking. The correlation coefficient measures the closeness of their agreement.

Denote the average of Examiner X's marks by $\bar{x}$. Then $(x_1 - \bar{x})$ is the devi-ation of the mark assigned to Script 1 from that mean, and the average of terms like $(x_1 - \bar{x})^2$ is the variance of Examiner X's marks. If there are n

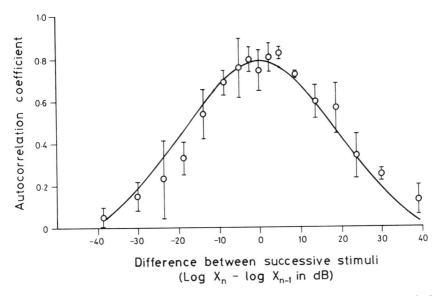

Figure 9 Coefficients of correlation between the logarithms of successive numerical estimates of loudness in relation to the dB difference between the tones. The circles show the mean coefficient from three subjects and the vertical bars extend to ±1 standard deviation. The quadratic curve is the prediction derived by Laming (1984, pp. 168–70)

Source: Adapted and redrawn from Baird, Green, and Luce, 1980, p. 286

scripts in the set to be marked, the variance is most accurately estimated by

$$\Sigma_i \ (x_i - \bar{x})^2/(n - 1) \tag{18}$$

where $i = 1, 2, 3, \ldots$ indexes the different scripts. Similar expressions can be calculated from Examiner Y's marks; one can also calculate the sum of cross-products like $(x_1 - \bar{x}) (y_1 - \bar{y})$. Suppose the two examiners averages are the same. If they also assign the same mark to Script 1, the cross-product will equal $(x_1 - \bar{x})^2$; if they assign the same mark to every script (i.e., they agree perfectly), the average cross-product (dividing by $n - 1$) will equal the variance of each examiner's marks. It is therefore conventional to measure the correlation as the average of the cross-products divided by the geometric average of the variances (which are usually not the same). This leads to the expression

$$\text{Correlation coefficient} = \frac{\Sigma_i (x_i - \bar{x})(y_i - \bar{y})}{\sqrt{[\{\Sigma_i (x_i - \bar{x})^2\} \{\Sigma_i (x_i - \bar{x})^2\}]}} \tag{19}$$

which necessarily lies between +1 (perfect agreement) and −1 (complete disagreement).

In a magnitude estimation experiment there is only a *single* series of numerical judgements, N_i, where i indexes the ordinal number of the trial. Substitute $\log N_i$ for x_i in Formula 19 and $\log N_{i+1}$ for y_i. Each log. numerical judgement is then compared with its successor in the series: this is called *autocorrelation*. It is sensitive to any interdependence between successive judgements and might be indicative of the underlying process by which they are produced. In Figure 9 the pairs of successive judgements are sorted according to the decibel difference between the corresponding stimuli. When there is a large change in the level of the tone, there is little correlation between successive judgements; but when the level varies by no more than ± 5 dB from one stimulus to the next, the logarithms of the successive numbers are correlated about $+0.8$. That is to say, locally high values of log N_i generate high values of $\log N_{i+1}$ on the following trial, and this comes about because the number uttered on trial i is used as a point of reference for the judgement on trial $i + 1$. In fact, $0.64\ (=0.8^2)$ of the variance of log N_{i+1} is inherited from $\log N_i$. On this basis Laming (1984) was able to calculate the quadratic curve in Figure 9 as a model for the correlation coefficients obtained in the experiment. This autocorrelation of successive log. magnitude estimates is the most compelling evidence of all for the Principle of Relativity, that each judgement uses its predecessor as a point of reference.

CONCLUSIONS

To complete this chapter I summarize the conclusions that may be drawn about the various experiments purporting to measure internal sensations and spell out what those conclusions mean for the notion of sensation.

First, there is an essential distinction to be drawn between the physical luminance, power, or weight of the stimulus and the brightness, loudness, and heaviness which one experiences.

Second, Fechner (1860) sought to measure internal sensation in terms of ability to distinguish one stimulus from another. Although the logarithmic transform implicit in Fechner's Law affords a simple and accurate account of a wide range of experimental results concerning the discrimination of one stimulus from another, an equally simple and accurate account may be had from a model based directly on the physical stimulus magnitude (Laming, 1986). Moreover, that equally simple and accurate account generalizes, in a way that the logarithmic model does not, to accommodate a significantly wider range of experimental findings, taking in the detection of increments to an existing stimulus background. There is, therefore, no justification in the study of sensory discrimination for taking Fechner's Law as descriptive of internal sensation.

Third, as an alternative, S. S. Stevens (1957) proposed a power law relation between physical stimulus magnitude and internal sensation. That relation concisely summarized the averaged results of many experiments using magnitude estimation and related procedures by S. S. Stevens and his colleagues. Comparison of the variance of magnitude estimates with the corresponding precision of discrimination in experiments using substantially the same stimuli shows that magnitude estimation studies a different and much more variable process (which I have called *sensory judgement*) than sensory discrimination.

Fourth, as before, a more comprehensive account of S. S. Stevens' results, including, especially, the variability of magnitude estimates, is afforded by the idea that judgements of sensation are no more than ordinal. According to this account, Stevens' Power Law is a by-product of the way that the experiments have been designed and conducted and the value of the power law exponent, different for different stimulus attributes, is determined chiefly by the geometric range of stimulus values used.

The nature of sensation

Finally, existing experiments do not support any measurement of internal sensation analogous to the measurement of length and weight. The most that subjects can validly say is that this light is brighter than that one, this sound louder than that, this weight heavier than that. Fechner's original conception of a "physics of the mind" is not realizable. On the other hand, the experiments by S. S. Stevens and many others addressing this question have provided a wealth of data on how numerical judgements are formulated. Once those data are disentangled from traditional misunderstandings about internal sensation, the way is open for the study of the wide range of mental phenomena subsumed in sensory judgement, a study which is only just beginning.

FURTHER READING

For a detailed account of the psychophysical methods developed by Fechner and others, see
Woodworth, R. S., & Schlosberg, H. (1955). *Experimental psychology*. London: Methuen (chaps 8 and 9); or, even more comprehensive, Guilford, J. P. (1954). *Psychometric methods* (2nd edn). New York: McGraw-Hill.
For a definitive record of S. S. Stevens's contribution to psychophysics, see Stevens, S. S. (1975). *Psychophysics*. New York: Wiley.
For an account of recent developments in sensory discrimination, see Laming, D. (1986). *Sensory analysis*. London: Academic Press.

REFERENCES

Baird, J. C., Green, D. M., & Luce, R. D. (1980). Variability and sequential effects in cross-modality matching of area and loudness. *Journal of Experimental Psychology: Human Perception and Performance*, 6, 277–289.

Baird, J. C., Lewis, C., & Romer, D. (1970). Relative frequencies of numerical responses in ratio estimation. *Perception and Psychophysics*, *8*, 358–362.

Brown, W. (1910). The judgment of difference. *University of California Publications in Psychology*, *1*, 1–71.

Cornsweet, T. N. (1962). The staircase-method in psychophysics. *American Journal of Psychology*, *75*, 485–491.

Cornsweet, T. N. (1970). *Visual perception*. New York: Academic Press.

Fechner, G. T. (1860). *Elemente der Psychophysik* (2 vols). Leipzig: Breitkopf & Härtel. (Vol. 1 trans. by H. E. Adler (1966) *Elements of psychophysics*. New York: Holt, Rinehart & Winston.)

Jesteadt, W., Wier, C. C., & Green, D. M. (1977). Intensity discrimination as a function of frequency and sensation level. *Journal of the Acoustical Society of America*, *61*, 169–177.

Kellogg, W. N. (1929). An experimental comparison of psychophysical methods. *Archives of Psychology*, *17*, whole no. 106.

Kiesow, F. (1925/1926). Über die Vergleichung linearer Strecken und ihre Bezeihung zum Weberschen Gesetze. *Archiv für die gesamte Psychologie*, *52*, 61–90; *53*, 433–446; *56*, 421–451.

Krantz, D. H. (1971). Integration of just-noticeable differences. *Journal of Mathematical Psychology*, *8*, 591–599.

Laming, D. (1984). The relativity of 'absolute' judgements. *British Journal of Mathematical and Statistical Psychology*, *37*, 152–183.

Laming, D. (1986). *Sensory analysis*. London: Academic Press.

Laming, D. (1989). Experimental evidence for Fechner's and Stevens's laws. *Behavioral and Brain Sciences*, *12*, 277–281.

Laming, D. (1991). Reconciling Fechner and Stevens? *Behavioral and Brain Sciences*, *14*, 188–191.

Laming, D., & Marsh, D. (1988). Some performance tests of QUEST on measurements of vibrotactile thresholds. *Perception and Psychophysics*, *44*, 99–107.

Levitt, H. (1971). Transformed up-down methods in psychoacoustics. *Journal of the Acoustical Society of America*, *49*, 467–477.

Luce, R. D., & Edwards, W. (1958). The derivation of subjective scales from just noticeable differences. *Psychological Review*, *65*, 222–237.

Poulton, E. C. (1967). Population norms of top sensory magnitudes and S. S. Stevens' exponents. *Perception and Psychophysics*, *2*, 312–316.

Stephanowitsch, J. (1913). Untersuchung der Herstellung der subjektiven Gleichheit bei der Methode der mittleren Fehler unter Anwendung der Registriermethode. *Psychologische Studien*, *8*, 77–116.

Stevens, J. C., Mack, J. D., and Stevens, S. S. (1960). Growth of sensation on seven continua as measured by force of handgrip. *Journal of Experimental Psychology*, *59*, 60–67.

Stevens, S. S. (1936). A scale for the measurement of a psychological magnitude: Loudness. *Psychological Review*, *43*, 405–416.

Stevens, S. S. (1956). The direct estimation of sensory magnitudes – loudness. *American Journal of Psychology*, *69*, 1–25.

Stevens, S. S. (1957). On the psychophysical law. *Psychological Review*, *64*, 153–181.

Stevens, S. S. (1966). Matching functions between loudness and ten other continua. *Perception and Psychophysics*, *1*, 5–8.

Stevens, S. S. (1970). Neural events and the psychophysical law. *Science*, *170*, 1043–1050.

Stevens, S. S. (1971). Issues in psychophysical measurement. *Psychological Review*, *78*, 426–450.

Stevens, S. S. (1975). *Psychophysics*. New York: Wiley.

Stevens, S. S., & Greenbaum, H. B. (1966). Regression effect in psychophysical judgment. *Perception and Psychophysics, 1*, 439–446.

Swets, J. A., Tanner, W. P., & Birdsall, T. G. (1961). Decision processes in perception. *Psychological Review, 68*, 301–340.

Tanner, W. P., & Swets, J. A. (1954). A decision-making theory of visual detection. *Psychological Review, 61*, 401–409.

Teghtsoonian, R. (1971). On the exponents in Stevens' Law and the constant in Ekman's Law. *Psychological Review, 78*, 71–80.

Thurstone, L. L. (1927). A law of comparative judgment. *Psychological Review, 34*, 273–286.

Torgerson, W. S. (1958). *Theory and methods of scaling*. New York: Wiley.

Treisman, M. (1963). Temporal discrimination and the indifference interval: Implications for a model of the "internal clock". *Psychological Monographs, 77*(576).

Watson, A. B., & Pelli, D. G. (1983). QUEST: A Bayesian adaptive psychometric method. *Perception and Psychophysics, 33*, 113–120.

Weber, E. H. (1834). *De pulsu, resorptione, auditu et tactu. Annotationes anatomicae et physiologicae*. Leipzig: Koehler. (Trans. H. E. Ross & D. J. Murray (1978) *The sense of touch*. London: Academic Press.)

Wier, C. C., Jesteadt, W., & Green, D. M. (1976). A comparison of method-of-adjustment and forced-choice procedures in frequency discrimination. *Perception and Psychophysics, 19*, 75–79.

4
COGNITION

INTRODUCTION

The word "cognition" comes from the Latin *cognoscere*, which means "to apprehend". Cognitive psychology has evolved over the years to include memory, attention, thinking, reasoning, problem solving, and all of the mental processes that can be thought of as essentially forms of information processing – some psychologists include perception within its scope (see chapter 1.1, Andrew M. Colman, for some comments on the definition of cognition and distinctions between cognitive psychology and cognitive science). The five chapters in this section cover the main branches of cognitive psychology, and inevitably there is some overlap between their contents.

In chapter 4.1, which deals with memory, Alan Baddeley distinguishes between sensory memory, working memory, and long-term memory, which have quite distinct properties and functions, and he discusses at some length the real-world implications of the major research findings on working memory and long-term memory in particular. Among the real-world problems that he touches on is the unreliability of eyewitness testimony; further discussion of this is presented in chapter 11.4 (Robert T. Croyle and Elizabeth F. Loftus) and in chapter 13.4 (Clive R. Hollin). Also relevant to memory is chapter 5.3, in which K. Anders Ericsson and William L. Oliver discuss the acquisition of superior memory performance. Two areas on which Alan Baddeley concentrates in chapter 4.1 are prospective memory (remembering to do things) and autobiographical memory (remembering things that have happened in the past). He concludes with some brief comments on the psychoanalytic (Freudian) theory of forgetting as repression, in relation to which interested readers should see also the rather different views put forward in chapters 7.4 (Richard Stevens) and 13.5 (Peter Fonagy).

In chapter 4.2 Michael W. Eysenck provides a general overview of the psychology of attention, including focused auditory and visual attention (attending to an auditory or visual message that is accompanied by distracting signals). This chapter also deals with research into divided attention, absent-mindedness, and vigilance (sustained attention during prolonged, monotonous tasks, such as watching a radar screen for occasional unexpected blips, or proofreading a book looking for typographical errors). Eysenck's discussion of absent-mindedness, in particular, intersects with Baddeley's remarks on the fallibility of memory in chapter 4.1; readers interested in this topic should consult both accounts and also chapter 5.3 (K. Anders Ericsson and William L. Oliver), which deals with cognitive skills.

Willem J. M. Levelt's survey of psycholinguistics in chapter 4.3 covers all of the main areas of research into the psychology of language apart from language acquisition, which is dealt with briefly in chapter 8.2 (Sara Meadows) and chapter 8.1 (George Butterworth). Chapter 4.3 deals with both the encoding of speech (that is, speaking), and its decoding (the understanding of speech), and it contains additional material on reading and sign language. There is a link with chapter 4.5, which contains a discussion of language in relation to artificial intelligence (see below).

Chapter 4.4, in which Jonathan St B. T. Evans discusses thinking and reasoning, lies at the very heart of cognitive psychology. With the help of some fascinating logical puzzles that have been used in experimental investigations, Evans summarizes what is known about problem solving, reasoning, and subjective judgements of probability. There are close links between the contents of this chapter and parts of chapter 5.3 on cognitive skills (K. Anders Ericsson and William L. Oliver).

Finally, in chapter 4.5, which is devoted to artificial intelligence, Alan Garnham discusses certain aspects of thinking, reasoning, and problem solving, though from a slightly different perspective. Research in the field of artificial intelligence attempts to understand these phenomena by designing computers or computer programs that can mimic them. Artificial intelligence involves designing machines to do things that are normally done by minds, including not only thinking and reasoning, but also the manipulation of natural languages, and especially seeing (see chapter 3.2, where Mike G. Harris and Glyn W. Humphreys focus on computational theories of vision).

A.M.C.

4.1

MEMORY

Alan Baddeley

MRC Applied Psychology Unit, Cambridge, England

No one would deny that memory is a faculty of some importance, but just how important? Perhaps the best way of gaining some insight into this is to consider the case of patients who have had the misfortune to become amnesic following brain damage. Any loss of neural tissue will tend to be reflected in slower learning and recall, but certain deficits can have an effect that is quite catastrophic. This was dramatically illustrated in a TV programme made by Jonathan Miller (1986) about Clive Wearing, a very intelligent and cultured musician who became densely amnesic following encephalitis, a brain infection caused by the herpes simplex virus. Clive's illness meant that he was left with a desperately impaired capacity to remember new and ongoing information. Since he could not remember anything from more than a minute or two before, he was perpetually convinced that he had just recovered consciousness. A typical remark would be "Consciousness has come to light since I was standing there . . . I was blind, deaf and dumb . . . everything has suddenly come back". He was found on occasion with a notebook in front of him containing the statement "Have just recovered consciousness 3.15 pm", with 3.15 crossed out and changed to 3.20, 3.25, and so forth. If his wife left the room for five minutes, on her return he would greet her as if he had not seen her for months, asking how long it was that he had been unconscious. In short, he lived in a perpetual present, which he described as "like being dead – all the bloody time!"

He had rather better access to memories that occurred before his illness, but even here his memory was far from good. He had written a book on the early composer Lassus, and could answer a few very general questions on him, but could provide virtually no detail. When shown pictures of Cambridge where he had spent four years, he failed to recognize any of the scenes other than King's College Chapel. His general knowledge was likewise impoverished; he could not recall who had written *Romeo and Juliet*, although he could still talk in a lively and intelligent way on more general issues, such as for example the development of the role of the conductor in early music.

Amidst this desert of impaired memory, one capacity was marvellously preserved, namely his musical skills. His wife returned home one evening to find that he had been visited by his choir, and to see him conducting them with all his old skill through a complex choral piece. He could play the harpsichord and sing and to all intents and purposes appeared to have retained his marvellous musical facility. Despite this, however, his grossly impaired access to his own long-term past, and his incapacity to develop and build up an ongoing picture of experience make life for him "a living hell". A few minutes with Clive is enough to convince one of the enormous importance of memory. We all tend to complain that our memories are terrible; what follows aims to persuade you that far from being terrible the human memory system is superb, although fallible.

MEMORY SYSTEMS

We have so far discussed human memory as if it were a single entity like the lungs or heart. It is much better considered as an alliance of several different systems, all of which have in common the capacity to take in information, store it, and subsequently make it available. We shall begin by suggesting that memory can be divided into three broad categories: *sensory memory, working memory*, and *long-term memory*. A diagram illustrating the relationship between the three is shown in Figure 1. Information is assumed to initially be taken up by a series of sensory memory systems, shown on the left of Figure 1. These are perhaps best considered as part of the processes of perception, and include a brief visual memory system sometimes known as *iconic memory*, and its auditory equivalent *echoic memory*. Little more will be said about them here other than that they play an integral part in our perception of the world. For example, if we had no iconic memory system we would perceive a film at the cinema as a series of still images interspersed with blank intervals, rather than as a continuously moving scene. Similarly, without echoic memory we would not hear a word, or indeed even a single tone as an entity. However, such systems probably do not play an important

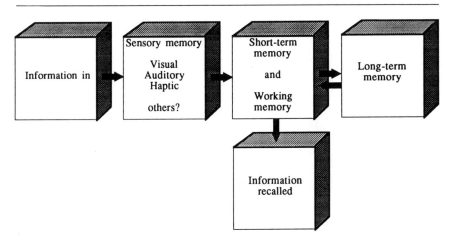

Figure 1 The flow of information through the memory system
Source: Adapted from Atkinson and Shiffrin, 1971

role in those aspects of memory that will concern the rest of this account, and for that reason we shall now move on to talk about working memory.

Working memory

Suppose you were asked to multiply 27 by 9. In order to perform this task by the usual method you need to remember the 27, multiply the 7 by the 9, remember the 3, carry the 6, and so on, eventually coming up with the solution. In reaching that solution you will have to remember small amounts of information for short periods of time, subsequently discarding that information as it ceases to be useful. The system that performs this task of temporarily manipulating information is typically termed *working memory*. It is itself far from unitary, and Figure 2 shows one conceptualization of the structure of working memory.

Working memory is assumed to comprise an attentional coordinating system known as the *Central Executive* aided by a number of subsidiary slave systems of which two are illustrated, namely the *Visuo-spatial Sketchpad*, which is used for setting up and manipulating visual images, and the *Articulatory Loop*, a system that holds and utilizes inner speech.

Some feel for the operation of one's working memory can be gained from attempting the task of working out how many windows there are in your present home. Try it.

Most people attempt to do this task by forming a visual image of their house and then counting the windows either by imagining looking from outside or walking through the house. The Visuo-spatial Sketchpad is the system used for setting up and manipulating the image, the Articulatory Loop is

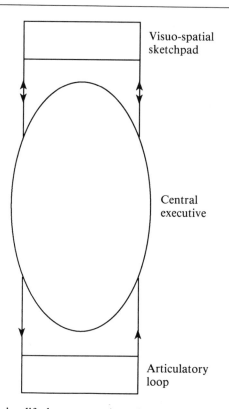

Visuo-spatial
sketchpad

Central
executive

Articulatory
loop

Figure 2 A simplified representation of the working memory model

involved in the process of subvocal counting, while the whole strategy is organized and run by the Central Executive.

The system has been explored over the years using a number of approaches, including that of using a specific task to interfere with a particular part of the system. For example, a visuo-spatial task such as steering a car will interfere with the operation of the sketchpad, and vice versa. A particularly clear example of this occurred when I attempted to drive a car along an American freeway at the same time as listening to an American football game on the radio. As I formed a more and more precise image of the game and its state, I found that the car weaved from side to side because of the interference between the two uses of my sketchpad. I hurriedly switched to a music programme.

A rather intriguing example of the use of the sketchpad came from a study of Japanese abacus experts. In Japan the use of the abacus for mental calculation is common, and practitioners become extremely skilled. With sufficient practice, the expert learns to dispense with the abacus altogether, relying apparently on a visual image. Using methods derived from the study of working memory, two Japanese psychologists, Hatano and Osawa (1983), showed that use of the sketchpad lay at the root of this skill, with the result that it could be disrupted by concurrent visuo-spatial, but not verbal activity.

In contrast, concurrent verbal activity can substantially interfere with the operation of the Articulatory Loop which appears to comprise a system involving two components, a temporary auditory store, and a speech-based rehearsal process. It is possible to get some information about each of these in turn by trying the following short tests. In each case, read the sequence of words, then look away and attempt to repeat them back; then check whether you were able to do this accurately and in the appropriate order. I shall include sequences of both five items and six items in each case:

PEN DAY RIG COW HOT
RIG DAY PEN SUP HOT COW

Now try the next two:

MAP CAN MAX MAD CAP
MAX CAP MAD MAP MAT CAN

Most people find the *MAD MAX* set of words considerably harder than the others. The reason for this is that the memory store involved in temporarily holding strings of unrelated words is based on the phonological or sound characteristics of those words. Words that are similar in sound tend to be confused within this store, leading to poorer performance. Now try the next set:

HARM WIT BOND TWICE YIELD
SOME YIELD BOND TWICE HARM WIT

Now attempt the next set:

ORGANIZATION INDIVIDUAL UNIVERSITY CONSIDERABLE ASSOCIATION

UNIVERSITY INDIVIDUAL ASSOCIATION OPPORTUNITY ORGANIZATION CONSIDERABLE

In this case, people usually find the short words considerably easier than the long ones. The reason here is that we maintain words in our temporary memory store by rehearsing them, subvocally saying them to ourselves. The system of rehearsal operates in real time, and consequently long words are rehearsed more slowly than short, allowing more fading of the memory trace between successive rehearsals.

If you were to stop yourself rehearsing by subvocally repeating some irrelevant words such as "the" while reading and recalling the words, then you would find that your memory performance dropped substantially, but that you avoided both the similarity and the word-length effects. The reason for this is that you need subvocal rehearsal to feed the printed words into your auditory-verbal store. If the subvocal rehearsal system is kept fully occupied repeating the word "the", then the written material does not enter the store, and neither word-length nor similarity effects are found. Instead you rely on some alternative memory in terms of the visual or semantic characteristics of the words, systems that are rather less efficient than the phonological store for briefly retaining this type of material.

By using experiments of this kind we have been able to find out a good deal about the Articulatory Loop system. But what function does the system serve? This problem was made particularly acute by the discovery of patients who have a specific deficit of short-term phonological storage (Shallice & Warrington, 1970; Vallar & Baddeley, 1982). Such patients appear to cope with life remarkably well, raising the dreadful thought that this system may be very useful for keeping experimental psychologists happy but of not much general significance. It might, as my colleague Jim Reason rather unkindly suggested, turn out to be "nothing but a pimple on the face of cognition".

In our research we have been particularly concerned with this question and in particular have been interested in the cognitive abilities of the rare patients who are found to have a very specific deficit in this system. Close investigation shows that such patients do have problems in comprehending certain types of sentences, particularly those in which comprehension requires the listener to hold the surface characteristics of initial words across several intervening words. One example of such material is provided by self-embedded sentences such as "The soldier whom the man had met on the train earlier in the week was wearing a large hat". Such patients have difficulty in working out who was wearing the hat in these circumstances.

A much more dramatic impairment was, however, revealed in a study of such a patient in which she was required to learn phonologically novel items, such as would be the case if you were learning the vocabulary of a foreign language. Our patient proved quite incapable of learning even a single new vocabulary item when these were presented auditorily, although when she was allowed to read the foreign words, she did show some learning, but her learning was by no means as good as that of control subjects matched for age and background. On the other hand, when required to learn to associate pairs of familiar and meaningful words, her learning capacity proved to be quite normal (Baddeley, Papagno, & Vallar, 1988).

It appears then that the short-term phonological memory system is necessary for the long-term learning of novel verbal material. As such, it should play an important role in a child's learning the vocabulary of his or her native language. A colleague, Susan Gathercole, and I explored this question using a sample of children who started school in Cambridge at the age of 4–5 years. We tested the short-term phonological memory of our children by requiring them to echo back spoken unfamiliar nonwords varying in length and complexity. We also tested their vocabulary, speaking a word and requiring them to point to a picture of the item denoted, and in addition measured their non-verbal intelligence and any reading skills they might have acquired. A year later we re-tested them using the same tasks.

When we analysed our results we found a close relationship between performance on the phonological memory task involving non-word repetition and vocabulary score. The relationship was still there when we allowed for other factors such as non-verbal intelligence and slight differences in age. One year later the relationship still held. Furthermore, the increase in vocabulary over the intervening year was predicted by their initial non-word repetition skills (Gathercole & Baddeley, 1988). Our results suggest, therefore, that the short-term phonological store plays a crucial role in the long-term acquisition of language. So if the Articulatory Loop is a pimple on the face of cognition, then it is a rather important pimple!

Long-term memory

We have so far concentrated almost exclusively on one aspect of working memory, the Articulatory Loop subsystem. Space availability forbids the provision of similar detail about the rest of working memory; the interested reader is referred to Baddeley (1986). Meanwhile, we must move on to discuss long-term memory. Once again, it seems unlikely that this reflects a single unitary system, although there is still considerable disagreement as to how long-term memory should be fractionated. We shall begin by discussing two theoretical distinctions that have proved influential in recent years, namely that between *semantic* and *episodic* memory, and that between *procedural* and *declarative* learning. We shall then go on to talk about two aspects of memory that are defined in terms of their real-world manifestations rather than their theoretical underpinning, namely *prospective* memory and *auto-biographical* memory. This will be followed by an analysis of the points at which human memory is particularly vulnerable to bias and distortion.

In the early 1970s the Canadian psychologist Endel Tulving emphasized a distinction between two aspects of memory that, as he points out, had long been implicit in the culture, but had not been explicitly acknowledged by experimental psychologists. He drew a distinction between episodic memory, by which he meant the conscious recollection of personally experienced events, and semantic memory or knowledge of the world (Tulving, 1972). An example of an episodic memory would be my recall of the experience of having breakfast this morning, or of meeting someone a year ago on holiday. Semantic memory, on the other hand, involves such factual knowledge as how many inches there are in a foot, what the capital of France is, or the fact that people often have cornflakes for breakfast.

There is no doubt that, as Tulving points out, there are very many differences between, for example, my memory of watching a rugby game on television yesterday afternoon and my knowing that a rugby team constitutes

15 players. What is, however, much less clear is whether these two examples reflect the operation of quite separate systems within the brain, as Tulving initially suggested, or whether they reflect the same system operating under very different conditions. This latter view might, for example, suggest that semantic memory represents the accumulation of information from many, many episodes or layers of experience, implying that rather than being a separate system, semantic memory is made up from multiple episodic memories.

A distinction that appears to have much stronger experimental support is that between procedural and declarative learning. Procedural learning comprises the acquisition of skills, such as learning to type, whereby demonstration of learning is reflected in the more efficient performance of the skill. In this respect it is different from declarative learning, such as remembering going to a typing class, which is essentially the acquisition of new knowledge or experience. Procedural learning is knowing *how*; declarative learning is knowing *that*.

The most powerful evidence for such a distinction comes from studies of amnesic patients who have a major long-term memory deficit following brain damage. This can be produced by a number of causes including chronic alcoholism, brain damage due to head injury, stroke, or through a viral infection, as was the case with Clive Wearing described earlier. Amnesic patients typically have great difficulty in recalling what they had for breakfast, where they are, or in remembering their way around the house or ward. Typically they would have normal language and normal working memory, and might have a relatively good memory for events occurring well before the onset of their illness or accident. They would, however, show very poor performance on most standard tests of the memory laboratory such as learning lists of words, recalling complex patterns, or recognizing previously presented faces or pictures.

However, despite the general and often profound memory deficit shown, such patients typically show quite normal learning on a remarkably wide range of other tasks. These range from classical conditioning, in which the patient learns to associate a sound with a puff of air and to close his or her eyes in anticipation, through motor skills such as learning to type or for a pianist learning a new tune, to perceptual skills. These might, for example, involve learning to read mirror-writing, or to find anomalies in complex pictures, where performance speeds up with practice, just as it does in people with normal memory. Similarly, a range of puzzles and problem tasks can be acquired at a normal rate, including jigsaw puzzles, and even the solving of complex problems such as the Tower of Hanoi task (Parkin, 1987).

Although such amnesic patients show very poor learning of words, there are certain conditions under which their verbal learning also proves to be normal. One of the most striking of these is one in which the subject is given a series of words to learn, and is then cued to remember them by being presented with a fragment of the original. For example one of the words might be PERFUME. If tested by recognition, with the patient required to say which of a number of words had been presented before, then amnesic patients perform very poorly. However, given the letters P**F*M* and asked to come up with the first word that fits the letter pattern, then the amnesic patient will perform extremely well, showing virtually as much advantage from previously having seen the target word as a normal subject asked to perform in this way.

What all these examples have in common is that they allow the patient to demonstrate learning, without the need for conscious awareness of the learning process. Typically, indeed, amnesic patients will deny having encountered the task before, at the same time as they are showing clear evidence of learning. This therefore seems to argue for two separate aspects of memory, one involving the capacity to reflect on prior experience, a capacity that is grossly impaired in amnesic patients. The second involves the apparently automatic display of learning in tasks where recollection of the learning event is unnecessary; such procedural learning appears to be intact in densely amnesic patients.

Long-term memory therefore appears to involve two separate types of learning: declarative and procedural. Declarative learning appears to be associated with conscious recollection of the past, and its adequate functioning appears to be disrupted by damage to a number of cortical and subcortical structures including the temporal lobes, the hippocampi, and the mamillary bodies. In contrast, damage to these areas does not appear to prevent the more automatic process of procedural learning. Whether procedural learning will ultimately prove to be a single unitary system, or whether procedural tasks merely have in common the fact that they do not require conscious recollection, is still a very open question.

The psychology of memory succeeded in separating itself from the more speculative philosophical approach to memory by dint of simplification. In particular, the father of research on human memory, the nineteenth-century German psychologist Hermann Ebbinghaus, was the first person to demonstrate the possibility of quantitative exploration of the characteristics of human memory. He did so by reducing the complexities of real-world memory to the simple learning by rote of meaningless verbal material, teaching himself to recite long sequences of invented non-words such as TOV, ZIL, and KIJ, and carefully measuring those factors that influenced rate of learning and forgetting (Ebbinghaus, 1913).

REAL-WORLD IMPLICATIONS

The Ebbinghaus tradition played an important role in the development of the psychology of memory, but it has the weakness that it tends to concentrate too heavily on simplified and apparently soluble problems, and to neglect the richness of memory in the world at large. There have been increasing efforts to link the memory laboratory and the world, typically by taking laboratory phenomena and looking for their real-world implications, as for example in the case of our studies on the role of the Articulatory Loop system of working memory. Equally important, however, is a willingness to take aspects of memory that are important in everyday life, and ask what are the implications of these for current theories of memory. I shall briefly describe two such areas, one concerned with *prospective memory*, or remembering to do things, while the other, *autobiographical memory*, refers to our capacity to remember the events of our own lives.

Prospective memory

If people tell you that they have a terrible memory, it typically implies that they are prone to making memory lapses such as forgetting appointments or failing to remember where they have left things around the house. How is this type of memory related to the system studied by psychologists in the laboratory? Arnold Wilkins and I became interested in the problem of studying this in the mid-1970s (Wilkins & Baddeley, 1978). We wanted to simulate the task of remembering to take pills four times a day, and in order to do so Arnold invented a simple but ingenious device. This comprised a light-tight box containing a digital watch and a film. When a button on the box was pressed, the dial of the watch was illuminated and the time registered on the film, which was then moved on. The subjects were instructed to press the button at four specified times each day for a period of a week. We carefully selected two groups of subjects, one that we knew to be very good at remembering lists of words, and one that was rather poor at this task. We were interested in whether the two groups would differ in remembering to "take their pills".

We found that significant differences between the two groups did indeed occur, but that the subjects who were particularly good at remembering words were the least punctual and accurate in pressing the button, a phenomenon we subsequently labelled "the absent-minded professor effect". It seems likely that remembering to do things at the right time depends on things other than having a good general memory. There is, for example, evidence that elderly people become significantly poorer at learning new material, but report fewer memory lapses. While some of this apparent improvement with age may simply be due to the fact that elderly people are more likely to forget their memory lapses before they are asked to report them, other evidence suggests that this is not the only cause. In one study, for example, where subjects were instructed to telephone the experimenter at a specified time in the future, elderly people were consistently more reliable and accurate than the young (Moscovitch, 1982). The reason for this is probably that they have learned to organize their lives in a much more structured way than the young, hence compensating for a memory system that is perhaps not quite what it used to be.

Does remembering to do things therefore depend on an entirely different system from the rest of memory? We now know that this is not the case. In order to obtain a good and reliable estimate of everyday memory problems, Barbara Wilson, who at that time was working at Rivermead Rehabilitation Centre in Oxford, came up with a novel kind of memory test. This involved requiring the patient to perform a number of tasks, each of which attempted to test objectively a situation in which patients report a tendency to memory lapses. For example, they would be required to learn the name of a person in a photograph, to learn a new route, to memorize and subsequently recognize photographs of new people, and to indicate orientation in time and place. In addition, a number of tests of prospective memory were included; for example the patient was asked for some small personal item such as a comb, and this was secreted in a drawer, with the instruction that the patient should remember to ask for it at the end of the test (Wilson, Cockburn, & Baddeley, 1985).

The Rivermead Behavioural Memory Test was subsequently validated using a large number of patients attending the Rehabilitation Centre. It proved to be a good measure of everyday memory, correlating quite highly ($r = .75$) with the observation of memory lapses in the patients made by therapists over many hours of treatment. It also proved to be the case that prospective memory was impaired in those patients who performed poorly on other tests of memory, including such traditional tasks as learning lists of words and recalling complex figures (Wilson, Baddeley, & Cockburn, 1988). Indeed, a subsequent study which applied the test to normal elderly people showed that those items that tested prospective memory were particularly susceptible to the effects of age (Cockburn & Smith, 1988).

In conclusion then, it appears that remembering to do things does depend on the same system as is reflected in standard laboratory memory tasks. In addition, however, it probably depends rather crucially on both the way in which one organizes one's life, and on how important it is to remember that particular feature. Forgetting an appointment, birthday, or anniversary can be hurtful in a way that forgetting an address or telephone number is not; the reason is that forgetting to do things certainly in part reflects the fallibility of our memory, but it also reflects the importance that we place on the event in question.

Autobiographical memory

People often claim of elderly relatives that they have a marvellous memory. When questioned further, this usually means not that they make no errors of prospective memory, but rather that they appear to show an amazing capacity to recollect the events from their earlier life, sometimes prompting the speculation that age somehow enhances early memories. On the whole the evidence does not support this view; elderly people tend to be poorer at recalling both recent and distant events. They are, however, likely to spend rather more time reminiscing about the past, and hence to revive and go over certain old memories in a way that makes them perhaps more accessible than they were during the middle years when attention was focused more firmly on the present and the future.

The capacity to recollect events from one's earlier life is termed *auto-biographical memory*. The systematic study of this aspect of memory began in the 1880s with the work of Sir Francis Galton (1883), but was then neglected until a relatively recent revival of interest. The reason for its neglect is probably the complexity of the topic, with the difficulty of turning rich but potentially unreliable information into readily quantifiable and verifiable results.

In my own case, the development of interest in autobiographical memory stemmed from a discovery that amnesic patients, who were otherwise very similar, might differ quite markedly in their capacity to recollect their own earlier life. In order to explore this further, we adopted the technique origin-ally pioneered by Galton, whereby the patient is given a word such as *river*, and asked to try to recollect some specific personally experienced event that is associated with a river. The resulting memory is then classified as to its richness, specificity, and reliability.

Using these criteria, we found that patients tended to fall into one of three categories. Some patients appeared to have relatively normal memories of the period before their illness, whereas others appeared to view their past as if through a dense cloud. Yet a third group proved to be particularly intriguing since they gave what appeared to be rich and detailed recollections which sub-sequently proved to be quite fictitious. Such confabulating patients were typ-ically those with severe damage to the frontal lobes, coupled with an amnesic deficit. The frontal lobes appear to be responsible among other things for the control of behaviour, for the operation of the central executive component of working memory, for example, and a deficit in this system appears to lead to confabulation. Such confabulation is worth discussing in rather more detail since it has interesting implications for the veracity of autobiographical memory in normal subjects, raising as it does the question of how we separate truth, or approximate truth, from fantasy in recalling our own past.

The confabulated memory sometimes has an amusing and almost sur-realistic character, as in the following recollection produced by a patient, NW, who in response to the cue word *make* described making a gramophone turntable at school. On being re-tested on a later occasion he did not report this, and I attempted to prompt him by mentioning that he had described something made at school, whereupon he produced the following:

ADB: Can you think of anything you made at school that is striking?
NW: An Australian wombat.
ADB: An Australian wombat?
NW: Ashtray, something different.
ADB: That does sound different. How do you make an Australian wombat ashtray?
NW: Get a piece of wood, let your imagination go . . .
ADB: Did you make anything else that you can think of, a bit more conventional?
NW: No I don't think so; I made a daffodil, again in wood. That was all to do with the school play.
ADB: How was it to do with the school play?
NW: There was a bowl of fruit and flowers which had to be given to the queen, Queen Diadem. All the various people had to make a flower. We were told to make something out of wood; I happened to be asked to make the daffodil, one of the easier pieces.

As this particular recollection might suggest, one occasionally wonders whether the patient is not simply teasing the experimenter. I think not, for a number of reasons. First of all, such confabulations are by no means limited to discussions with psychologists. In the case of one of our patients RJ, for example, his wife reported that when he was home one weekend he turned to her in bed and asked

"Why do you keep telling people we are married?"
"But we are married, we've got three children", his wife responded.
"That doesn't necessarily mean we're married".

Whereupon his wife got out of bed and produced the wedding photographs, to which her husband commented, "Well that chap does look like me, but it's not!"

The same patient also would hold with considerable stubbornness to his often misguided memory, insisting for example that he should be in occupational therapy next and not physiotherapy, or that his luggage had been stored in a loft, and climbing on a toilet seat in order to access the non-existent loft. As the last incident implies, he was certainly willing to act on his confabulations, and on one occasion was found wheeling a fellow patient down the road. When stopped he reported that he was taking him to show his friend the sewage works that he was working on. He had indeed been involved in building a sewage works as a civil engineer, but that was many years ago and many miles away.

So why does confabulation occur? We suspect that it requires a combination of two things, first of all an impaired or clouded autobiographical memory, and second, a deficit in that aspect of the central executive of working memory that is necessary for controlling and evaluating behaviour. We believe that given the difficult task of retrieving a specific memory associated with a highly constrained cue word, patients with a deficit in the central executive are unable to access a genuine memory. What they produce instead is some form of association which they accept and elaborate. Without the adequate control of the process of retrieval, what is produced is something rather closer to a free association or a dream.

Normal subjects do not on the whole confabulate, partly because they have better access to their memory trace, and so have less need to invent memories, and partly because they have a much better checking mechanism for the plausibility of whatever their memory might produce. I suspect, however, that this is a matter of degree rather than an absolute difference. On the whole we do not go in for florid confabulation, but in subtler ways our memories can be highly unreliable, and I would like to conclude by reviewing some of the ways in which our memories are fallible.

FALLIBILITY

Memories are systems for storing information, and as such are required to do three things: to take in the necessary information, to store it, and to retrieve it at the appropriate time. Human memory is potentially fallible at each of these points.

Consider first the way in which information is registered in memory. This of course depends on attention. If we do not attend to something, then we are very unlikely to remember it, despite the claims to the contrary of those who try to sell courses of sleep learning and other allegedly painless roads to knowledge. What we attend to is determined by our interests and prejudices, as was demonstrated many years ago by the Princeton social psychologists Hastorf and Cantril (1954). They described a football game between Dartmouth and Princeton that aroused passionate commitment on both sides. Princeton had a particularly talented quarterback who was injured early in the game, a game that subsequently became increasingly violent. Hastorf and Cantril report the account of the game given in the Princeton and Dartmouth college newspapers.

> This observer has never seen quite such a disgusting exhibit of so-called "sport". Both teams were guilty but the blame must be laid primarily on Dartmouth's doorstep. Princeton, obviously the better team, had no reason to rough up Dartmouth. Looking at the situation rationally, we don't see why the [Dartmouth] Indians should make a deliberate attempt to cripple Dick Kazmaier or any other Princeton player. The Dartmouth psychology, however, is not rational itself.

> However, the Dartmouth-Princeton game set the stage for the other type of dirty football. A type which may be termed as an unjustifiable accusation. Dick Kazmaier was injured early in the game . . . after this incident [the coach] instilled the old see-what-they-did-go-get-them attitude into his players. His talk got results. Gene Howard and Jim Millar [from Dartmouth] were both injured. Both had dropped back to pass, had passed, and were standing unprotected in the back field. Result: one bad leg and one leg broken. The game was rough and did get a bit out

of hand in the third quarter. Yet most of the roughing penalties were called against Princeton.

It is not hard to guess which newspaper is which.

But is this a memory effect? Hastorf and Cantril investigated this by showing a film of the game to both Dartmouth and Princeton students, asking them to note when they observed a piece of foul play. In the case of Dartmouth infringements there was a clear difference between the two with Princeton students reporting a mean of 9.8 while the Dartmouth students reported 4.3.

The tendency to see and remember things from an egocentric viewpoint is of course not limited to situations involving conflict. A particularly intriguing example of rather more subtle effects of bias was shown in Neisser's (1981) analysis of the testimony given by John Dean in the Watergate investigation. You may recall that the press were so struck by Dean's apparent capacity to remember specific conversations in great detail that they dubbed him the man with the tape recorder memory. When the actual tape recordings of the conversations subsequently became available it proved possible to check the accuracy of this claim.

In terms of the gist of the conversations, Dean's recollection was in fact reasonably accurate, but the detail showed considerable distortion. The nature of the distortion was interesting in that it typically resulted in Dean's own role being perceived as more important and more central, an egocentric bias that I suspect most of us would show in a similar situation.

To return to our students watching the football game, bias in their viewpoint was clearly one factor, but another could well have been the degree of emotion generated by the "big game". What role does emotion play in memory? This is a point of some importance in the case of a witness recalling a violent crime.

I was telephoned one Sunday evening by someone who introduced himself as a detective from the San Diego Police Force. He was involved in the investigation of a multiple murderer who had the unsavoury habit of slashing his victims' throats. Having killed six people, the seventh survived and identified someone as the attacker. What, I was asked, would be the influence of extreme emotion on the victim's memory?

The answer is that on the whole introducing emotion tends to reduce the accuracy with which an eyewitness can remember a crime; it does not apparently imprint the incident indelibly on the memory, as one might guess. However, when asked if the level of emotion generated in the experimental studies was equivalent to the level that the San Diego slasher's victim was likely to have experienced, I had to admit that it was certainly not. Even the most dedicated experimental psychologists do not, I am happy to say, threaten to cut their subjects' throats, even in the interests of science.

It is clear then that bias and emotion can both cause distortion in what gets into memory. Suppose, however, that information does get into memory, what factors will influence the durability of memory storage? While information on speed of forgetting is still surprisingly sparse, the evidence on the whole suggests that differential rates of forgetting for different kinds of material is not very common. Needless to say, increased forgetting can be produced by brain damage, or by the more temporary effects of a blow on the head. The ability to remember an incident can, however, also be substantially impaired by presenting further interfering or misleading information.

This again has obvious practical implications in the case of eyewitness testimony, and there has been a great deal of interest in the distortions of memory that can be produced when leading questions are inserted into the subsequent interrogation of the witness. Choice of words can for example bias the subject's subsequent recall. In one study, Loftus and Palmer (1974) showed subjects a film of a car crash, and subsequently questioned them about various details. One question concerned the speed at which one car was moving when it hit the other. Some subjects were asked "About how fast were the cars going when they hit each other?", while for others the word "hit" was replaced with "contacted", "bumped", "collided", or "smashed". Estimated speeds ranged from 31.8 miles per hour for "contacted" to 40.8 for "smashed". When questioned a week later as to whether any glass had been broken, subjects who had encountered the word "smashed" were significantly more likely to report, falsely, that glass had been broken.

In other studies, Loftus and her collaborators were able to change subjects' views on a whole range of features of observed incidents, including the colour of cars, whether a stop sign or a yield (give way) sign was present, while in another study many subjects were induced to report the occurrence of a nonexistent barn. In all these cases, the distorted information was introduced parenthetically during an earlier question, and only subsequently probed directly. Subjects do not appear to be aware of the source of their mistake, and allowing them a second guess, or paying them a substantial amount for making the correct response had no effect on the bias.

At this point, Loftus and Palmer began to conclude that a permanent modification had been made in the underlying memory trace, with the old information destroyed by the new. However, as they fully realized, failure to find the old trace did not necessarily mean that it had been destroyed, rather than simply made unavailable.

Indeed a subsequent study by Bekerian and Bowers (1983) showed that the old trace had survived, and given an appropriate method of retrieval, it could be accessed. The studies by Loftus typically involved questioning the subject about the incident in a relatively unstructured way. Bekerian and Bowers showed that if the questions followed the order of the events in strict sequence, then subjects were able to access the original information, and to escape from the bias introduced by subsequent questions. In short, the

Loftus effect is not due to destruction of the memory trace but is due to interfering with its retrieval.

RETRIEVAL

Before discussing further potential distortions in human memory that occur at the retrieval stage, it is perhaps worth describing the process of retrieval in somewhat more detail. One way of doing so is to draw an analogy between human memory and an inanimate storage system such as a library. A library could operate merely as a passive storehouse in which books were piled up as they arrived. Such a system would, however, not be very easy to use unless one virtually always needed one of the last few books to have entered the system. If one needed to access books on the basis of subject, then it is of course essential to have a subject catalogue, and if a book has not been correctly catalogued when it came in, then retrieving it is going to be a very difficult and haphazard process. The secret of a good memory, as of a good library, is that of organization; good learning typically goes with the systematic encoding of incoming material, integrating and relating it to what is already known.

Suppose, however, that one has encoded the material appropriately, what is the process whereby one calls up the right memory at the right time? While we are still some way from fully understanding the retrieval process, one feature is captured by what Tulving has termed *encoding specificity*. On the whole, we access a piece of information by feeding in a fragment of what we wish to recall; the more accurate and complete the fragment, the better the chance of retrieval.

One aspect of this that has been known for centuries is the phenomenon of *context dependency*, the tendency for what is learned in one situation to be best recalled in that situation. The philosopher John Locke recounts the tale of a young man who learned to dance. His lessons always occurred in an attic that had a large trunk. Locke reports that while the young man could dance extremely well in the attic, if the trunk was removed he was no longer able to remember the steps.

How good is the scientific evidence for such context dependency? While there are not too many experiments on memory for dancing, there certainly is evidence that memory may be influenced by context. For example, Duncan Godden and I studied memory in deep-sea divers. We had our divers learn lists of words either on the beach, or 10 feet under the sea, and subsequently recall them in the wet or the dry environment. What we found was that regardless of where they learned the words, they remembered about 40 per cent fewer when they were trying to recall them in the opposite environment (Godden & Baddeley, 1975).

Such a result could have rather dramatic implications; would all our students show dramatically good memory if their examinations were held in the lecture theatre, and will they forget everything once they have left the university? While the latter suggestion may indeed be true, it is probably not a result of context dependency: effects as large as those we obtained occur only with a very dramatic change in environment. Less marked changes can produce detectable effects, but on the whole studies that look at examination performance in the original lecture room versus the novel examination hall do not suggest any major difference in performance.

The comparatively small effect of environmental context under normal conditions probably reflects the fact that when we are learning, the surroundings are probably not a particularly salient feature of the situation. The internal environment, however, can have subtle but powerful effects. Mood, for instance, can have a contextual effect on memory, with subjects in a sad mood typically being much more likely to recollect earlier unhappy events from their life than subjects in a happy mood, and vice versa (Bower, 1981). This can have a powerful effect on depression since it will of course tend to make the sad person even sadder, which in turn will cause him or her to remember even more depressing events, locking the unfortunate person into a vicious spiral of increasingly depressive rumination. This is in fact thought to be an important factor in the maintenance of depression, and some developments in the cognitive treatment of depression are principally concerned to reverse this process.

Other changes in internal states can of course be induced by drugs, producing so-called *state dependency* effects. Such effects can, for example, be produced by alcohol: what is learned drunk is best recalled drunk. Sometimes alcoholics will hide money and drink while in a drunken state, and then forget where it has been located, only to remember once they are drunk again. Such drug-based state dependency played an important role in what is claimed to be the first detective story written, *The Moonstone* by Wilkie Collins (published 1868).

Retrieval then is probably one of the most vulnerable points in human memory, with biased situations leading to failure to recall, or possibly partial recall which in turn is subject to distortion when we try to interpret our incomplete memory. A very nice example of such distortion is given by the Swiss psychologist Jean Piaget, who reports having had a very clear and detailed memory of an incident when he was a baby, whereby an attempt was made to kidnap him and was thwarted by his nursemaid. He reports having a vivid memory of the incident, full of detail. The nursemaid was rewarded for her valour by being given a watch. Many years later she returned the watch to the family saying that she had recently had a religious conversion and wished to confess an earlier sin. It appears that the incident had simply not occurred, but had been invented by her in the hopes of currying favour with her employers. Piaget's vivid "memory", it appears, was constructed from the many accounts he had heard of the incident as he grew up (Loftus, 1979, pp. 62–63).

PSYCHOANALYTIC THEORY

Before concluding, I should say something about one approach to forgetting that has had considerable influence on twentieth-century western culture, namely the psychoanalytic view of forgetting as the result of repression. Freud suggests that much forgetting occurs because the events concerned are associated with unpleasant events that evoke anxiety, and call up an automatic process that bars them from conscious awareness. In his *Psychopathology of Everyday Life*, Freud (1938) reports many incidents which he attributes to repression. I am afraid, however, that attempts to demonstrate repression under more controlled conditions have not proved particularly encouraging (see Baddeley, 1990, chap. 15). There certainly is a general tendency for people recalling their earlier life to remember the pleasant events rather than the unpleasant, at least when they are in a reasonably happy state of mind. Whether this represents active repression, however, is open to question; it is quite possible that this simply reflects a tendency to choose to reflect on and tell others about our successes rather than our failures, leading to pleasant events being rehearsed more. Certainly, attempts to demonstrate the influence of repression under more rigidly controlled conditions tend to suggest that it is not a major feature in the vast amount of forgetting that most people exhibit, although in the rare cases of hysterical amnesia, something much more closely approaching the Freudian explanation probably does apply.

To conclude then, there is no doubt that human memory is eminently fallible. However, its sources of fallibility are often reflections of its strengths. Bias in feeding information into the memory system certainly does occur. However, bias is simply the consequence of selection; if we did not select what was interesting and important, then our memory systems would become overloaded with trivial and irrelevant information.

There is no doubt that forgetting occurs on a massive scale, something that characterizes memory systems in humans but not in computers or libraries. However, such forgetting is on the whole benign. Typically we remember what is salient and important to us, and forget the trivial and irrelevant detail. It is only when such detail subsequently becomes crucial, as in the testimony of an eyewitness, that the fallibility of our memory becomes particularly obvious. In other situations, if we need to remember something in enormous detail, then we write it down.

Finally, retrieval presents a clear bottleneck in our capacity to access what we have previously learned. Even here, however, the context dependency effect means that we are more likely to remember the information that is relevant to the situation we are in, in preference to information that is relevant to some other distant setting, surely a sensible adaptation of a limited retrieval system. In conclusion, I should like to suggest that although eminently fallible, human memory is an elegant system; nobody should be without one.

ACKNOWLEDGEMENT

This chapter is based on my contribution to Thomas Butler's (1989) *Memory: History, Culture and the Mind* published by Basil Blackwell of Oxford. I am grateful to the publisher for permission to reproduce it.

FURTHER READING

Baddeley A. D. (1993). *Your memory: A user's guide*, 2nd edn. Harmondsworth: Penguin.
Baddeley, A. D. (1990). *Human memory: Theory and practice*. Hove: Lawrence Erlbaum.
Cohen, G. (1989). *Memory in the real world*. Hove: Lawrence Erlbaum.
Parkin, A. J. (1987). *Memory and amnesia: An introduction*. Oxford: Basil Blackwell.

REFERENCES

Atkinson, R. C., & Shiffrin, R. M. (1971). The control of short-term memory. *Scientific American*, *225*, 82–90.
Baddeley, A. D. (1982). *Your memory: A user's guide*. Harmondsworth: Penguin.
Baddeley, A. D. (1986). *Working memory*. Oxford: Oxford University Press.
Baddeley, A. D. (1990). *Human memory: Theory and practice*. Hove: Lawrence Erlbaum.
Baddeley, A. D., Papagno, C., & Vallar, G. (1988). When long-term learning depends on short-term storage. *Journal of Memory and Language*, *27*, 586–595.
Bekerian, D. A., & Bowers, J. M. (1983). Eyewitness testimony: Were we misled? *Journal of Experimental Psychology: Human Learning and Memory*, *9*, 139–145.
Bower, G. H. (1981). Mood and memory. *American Psychologist*, *36*, 129–148.
Cockburn, J., & Smith, P. T. (1988). Effects of age and intelligence on everyday memory tasks. In M. M. Gruneberg, P. Morris, & R. N. Sykes (Eds) *Practical aspects of memory: Current research and issues. Clinical and educational implications* (vol. 2, pp. 132–136). Chichester: Wiley.
Ebbinghaus, H. (1913). *Memory* (H. Ruyer & C. E. Bussenius, trans.) New York: Teachers College, Columbia University (original work published 1985).
Freud, S. (1938). Psychopathology of everyday life. In A. A. Brill (Ed.) *The writings of Sigmund Freud*. New York: Modern Library.
Galton, F. (1883). *Inquiries in human faculty and its development*. London: Dent.
Gathercole, S. E., & Baddeley, A. D. (1988). Development of vocabulary in children and short-term phonological memory. *Journal of Memory and Language*, *28*, 200–213.
Godden, D., & Baddeley, A. D. (1975). Context-dependent memory in two natural environments: On land and under water. *British Journal of Psychology*, *66*, 325–331.
Hastorf, A. A., & Cantril, H. (1954). They saw a game: A case study. *Journal of Abnormal and Social Psychology*, *97*, 399–401.

Hatano, G., & Osawa, K. (1983). Digit memory of grant experts in abacus-derived mental calculation. *Cognition, 15*, 95–110.

Loftus, E. F. (1979). *Eyewitness testimony.* Cambridge, MA: Harvard University Press.

Loftus, E. F., & Palmer, J. C. (1974). Reconstruction of automobile destruction: An example of the interaction between language and memory. *Journal of Verbal Learning and Verbal Behavior, 13*, 585–589.

Miller, J. (1986). Interview with Clive Wearing. *Prisoner of Consciousness.* Broadcast in the UK by Channel 4 in the Equinox Series, September.

Moscovitch, M. (1982). A neuropsychological approach to memory and perception. In F. I. M. Craik & S. Trehub (Eds) *Aging and cognitive processes* (pp. 55–78). New York: Plenum.

Neisser, U. (1981). John Dean's memory: A case study. *Cognition, 9*, 1–22.

Parkin, A. J. (1987). *Memory and amnesia: An introduction.* Oxford: Basil Blackwell.

Shallice, T., & Warrington, E. K. (1970). Independent functioning of verbal memory stores: A neuropsychological study. *Quarterly Journal of Experimental Psychology, 22*, 261–273.

Tulving, E. (1972). Episodic and semantic memory. In E. Tulving & W. Donaldson (Eds) *Organization of memory* (pp. 381–403). New York: Academic Press.

Vallar, G., & Baddeley, A. D. (1982). Short-term forgetting and the articulatory loop. *Quarterly Journal of Experimental Psychology, 34A*, 53–60.

Wilkins, A. J., & Baddeley, A. D. (1978). Remembering to recall in everyday life: An approach to absentmindedness. In M. M. Gruneberg, P. E. Morris, & R. N. Sykes (Eds) *Practical aspects of memory* (pp. 27–34). London: Academic Press.

Wilson, B., Baddeley, A. D., & Cockburn, J. (1988). Trials, tribulations and triumphs in the development of a test of everyday memory. In M. M. Gruneberg, P. Morris, & R. N. Sykes (Eds) *Practical aspects of memory: Current research and issues. Memory in everyday life* (vol. 1, pp. 249–254). Chichester: Wiley.

Wilson, B., Cockburn, J., & Baddeley, A. D. (1985). *The Rivermead behavioural memory test.* Bury St Edmunds: Thames Valley Test Company.

4.2

ATTENTION

Michael W. Eysenck

Royal Holloway, University of London, Surrey, England

The term "attention" has been used in a number of different ways. It is sometimes used to mean concentration, as in the expression "Pay attention!" A related use of the term is as a process that varies as a function of an individual's level of arousal: someone who is aroused is attentive to his or her environment, whereas someone who is low in arousal or drowsy is not. However, the most common usage of attention is in connection with selectivity of processing. This usage was emphasized by the nineteenth-century psychologist William James (1890):

> Everyone knows what attention is. It is the taking possession of the mind, in clear and vivid form, of one out of what seem several simultaneously possible objects or trains of thought. Focalisation, concentration, of consciousness are of its essence. It implies withdrawal from some things in order to deal effectively with others. (pp. 403–404)

In order to investigate how efficiently we are able to attend selectively, researchers have conducted much research on focused attention. In such research, subjects are presented with two or more sets of stimuli at the same time. They are instructed to process one set of stimuli while ignoring the other set or sets. The amount of processing of the to-be-ignored stimuli which occurs provides an indication of how successfully attention can be focused on the stimuli that the experimenter has identified as important.

Another issue which is important in attention research concerns the number of things that can be attended to at the same time. Once again, William James (1890) had an important contribution to make:

> The number of things we may attend to is altogether indefinite, depending on the power of the individual intellect, on the form of the apprehension, and on what things are. ... But however numerous the things, they can only be known in a single pulse of consciousness for which they form one complex "object". (p. 405)

In order to investigate the extent to which more than one thing can be attended to at once, it has been customary to carry out studies on divided attention. In essence, subjects are generally presented two stimulus inputs or tasks at the same time. They are instructed to do their best to perform both of the tasks, and their success or otherwise in doing this provides an indication of the capacity of the attentional system.

While the distinction between focused and divided attention is of fundamental importance, there are other distinctions worth noting. First, attention can be directed towards either the external environment or to the internal environment, which consists of our own thoughts. In practice, most of the research on attention has concerned the external environment rather than the internal environment, presumably because researchers can control those aspects of the external environment which receive attention much more readily than they can the internal environment. Second, it is important to distinguish between attentional processes in the various sense modalities. For example, it may be easier to focus attention on a single stimulus input in some modalities than others, and so we really need to consider the various modalities separately. However, only the visual and auditory modalities have been investigated with any thoroughness, and so our coverage will concentrate on those modalities.

FOCUSED AUDITORY ATTENTION

One of the key issues with respect to focused auditory attention is whether it is possible to attend to one auditory message while successfully ignoring other auditory messages that are presented at the same time. This issue was first examined systematically by Cherry (1953), who devised the dichotic listening task. Subjects performing this task listen through headphones which deliver one message to the left ear and a different message to the right ear. They are instructed to repeat back (or shadow) the message presented to one ear while ignoring the message presented to the other ear. Cherry found that the subjects found it reasonably straightforward to follow the instructions even when the two messages were spoken in the same voice, suggesting that auditory selective attention can be very efficient.

Cherry's (1953) most powerful evidence that people can select one of two auditory messages and ignore the other one came when he questioned the subjects afterwards about their knowledge of the unattended message. Rather surprisingly, most subjects had no awareness of the meaning of the to-be-ignored message, and could not repeat a single word or phrase from it. Some subjects were given a to-be-ignored message in reversed speech. Most of them claimed that the message had been in normal speech, but a few subjects argued that there had been "something queer about it". In spite of their ignorance of the content of the non-shadowed message, most subject were aware of some of its basic physical characteristics, such as the sex of the speaker and the intensity of sound.

Broadbent (1958) was impressed by Cherry's (1953) findings, which influenced the theory of attention that he proposed. According to Broadbent, the information-processing system has limited capacity, and so a filter is required in order to prevent that system from becoming overloaded. More specifically, information about the different stimuli in the environment is initially stored briefly in a sensory buffer. Information about one of the stimuli is then selected for further processing by being allowed to pass through the filter. Information about the other stimuli resides in the sensory buffer for a short period of time, and then decays unless selected by the filter.

Broadbent's (1958) theory provides a neat explanation of Cherry's (1953) main findings. The filter selects one of the two messages on the basis of its physical characteristics (e.g., the ear to which it is presented). The non-shadowed message does not pass through the filter, and thus is not processed in terms of its meaning. However, Cherry's data were limited, in that they were based on subjects who had little familiarity with the shadowing task, and who therefore found it very demanding. The importance of familiarity or practice was demonstrated by Underwood (1974). He asked his subjects to detect digits which were presented in either the shadowed or the non-shadowed message. Unpractised subjects detected only approximately 8 per cent of the digits in the non-shadowed message, whereas a highly practised subject managed to detect 67 per cent of the digits in that message. It is difficult to account for the performance of this subject in terms of a filter which prevents processing of non-shadowed stimuli.

Further problems for filter theory stemmed from the work of Allport, Antonis, and Reynolds (1972). They argued that part of the reason why Cherry's subjects had very little knowledge of the to-be-ignored message was because the shadowed and the non-shadowed messages were both presented in the same sense modality (i.e., auditory), and this caused a certain amount of interference. Allport et al.'s subjects shadowed an auditory message; at the same time some of them attempted to learn either auditorily presented words or pictures. Subsequent memory for the auditorily presented words was extremely poor, whereas there was 90 per cent correct performance on a recognition-memory test for the pictures. Thus, contrary to Broadbent's

(1958) filter theory, two inputs presented at the same time can both be processed thoroughly provided that they are in different sense modalities.

Treisman (1964) responded to some of the problems that were becoming apparent in Broadbent's (1958) theory by proposing an attenuation theory. According to attenuation theory, the processing of unattended auditory inputs is typically attenuated or reduced in comparison with the amount of processing of attended inputs. The major contrast with Broadbent's theory is that the unattended message will generally be processed to some degree. More specifically, Treisman argued that the processing of a message starts with an analysis of its physical characteristics (e.g., loudness, sex of speaker) before proceeding to analyses of grammatical structure and meaning. As a consequence, it is most likely that the physical characteristics of an unattended message will be processed and least likely that its meaning will be processed. This is precisely in line with the findings that Cherry (1953) and others obtained.

A rather different theory of attention was proposed by Deutsch and Deutsch (1963). They argued that attended and unattended inputs are both fully analysed, with one input being selected immediately before a response is made. In other words, the filter or bottleneck to which Broadbent referred is placed considerably later in the processing system than Broadbent himself placed it. It has proved surprisingly difficult to evaluate this theory, but the evidence suggests that it is no more than partially correct (see Eysenck, 1984).

Some theoretical views

Johnston and Heinz (1978) argued that most of the earlier theories of focused auditory attention suffered from the limitation of being too inflexible. Instead of claiming that there is a filter or bottleneck at some particular point in the sequence of processing, it is preferable to think in terms of attentional selectivity occurring at various points depending on the particular task that the subject is carrying out. In general terms, selection of one auditory input occurs as early as possible in processing.

Evidence of flexibility in processing was obtained by Johnston and Wilson (1980). They presented pairs of words at the same time, one member of each pair to each ear. The subjects were instructed to detect members of a specified category (e.g., articles of furniture); these were the targets, and they were all ambiguous words with two quite separate meanings. Each target word was accompanied by a non-target word, which was related either to the appropriate (i.e., category-relevant) meaning of the target, or to its inappropriate (i.e., non-category-relevant) meaning, or was unrelated in meaning to the target. In the focused attention condition, subjects knew which ear the targets would be presented to, whereas they did not know this in the divided attention condition.

The findings are shown in Figure 1. In the focused attention condition, the

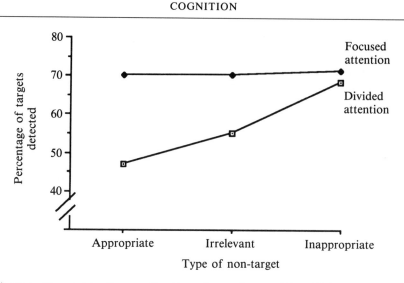

Figure 1 Target detection as a function of attention condition (divided vs. focused) and of type of non-target
Source: Data from Johnston and Wilson, 1980

relationship between the non-target and target words had no effect on subjects' ability to detect targets. This suggests that the non-target words were not processed for meaning. In contrast, when subjects did not know where targets would be presented (i.e., in the divided attention condition), then target detection was facilitated by appropriate non-targets and reduced by inappropriate non-targets. This suggests that the non-targets in this condition were processed for meaning. In other words, there is full processing of all auditory inputs if this is necessary (as in the divided attention condition), but this does not happen if it is not necessary (as in the focused attention condition).

FOCUSED VISUAL ATTENTION

The eye is constructed in such a way that there is a small area of high acuity in the centre of the retina known as the fovea. The fovea consists solely of cone cells. These cells are very sensitive, and as a result visual perception is very clear and precise within the foveal area. However, visual perception is markedly less clear in the periphery of vision. Here there are only rods, which permit motion to be detected but not fine details or colour. Psychologists have argued on the basis of this anatomical evidence that visual perception resembles a spotlight in that everything in the centre of the spotlight (or in the foveal area) can be seen with great clarity, but objects lying outside the beam can be seen imperfectly or not at all. The beams of spotlights are often adjustable so that the width of the beam can be altered within limits, and it has been suggested (e.g., by LaBerge, 1983) that the same is true of focused visual attention.

The most obvious prediction from the spotlight analogy is that visual stimuli falling within the central area of vision should be processed much more thoroughly than those further away from the central area. Some support for this view was obtained by Johnston and Dark (1985). They gave their subjects the task of identifying a rather unclear test word. They discovered that subjects could identify the test word more easily when a prime word (the same word as the test word or one closely related to it in meaning) was presented to the central visual area immediately before the presentation of the test word. However, identification of the test word was not facilitated when the prime word was presented outside of the central visual area. The implication is that very little information was extracted from the prime word when it was presented outside of the visual attentional spotlight.

The notion that the visual spotlight can be either narrow or broad depending on circumstances was explored by LaBerge (1983). His subjects were shown five-letter words, and had to perform a task which required them to focus on either the entire word or just the middle letter of the word. The evidence indicated that the subjects were able to adjust the breadth of the visual spotlight to make it appropriate for the task in hand.

Feature integration theory

Treisman (1988) proposed an interesting feature integration theory of focused visual attention which built on some of her earlier theoretical views. She started by arguing that there is an important distinction between objects (e.g., a tomato, a tree) and the features of objects (e.g., colour, line, orientations). According to her theory, the features of the objects in the visual environment are processed rapidly and in parallel (i.e., all at the same time), and visual attention is not required for this to happen. In contrast, object perception normally involves integrating the features of a given object (e.g., the roundness and redness of a tomato). This necessitates focused attention and involves a serial (i.e., one at a time) process. In other words, focused attention provides the "glue" which allows us to perceive objects rather than meaningless sets of features.

Some of the evidence leading to this theory was reported by Treisman and Gelade (1980). There was a visual display containing between 1 and 30 items, and the subjects had to decide as rapidly as possible whether a specified target was present. In one condition, the target was the letter S, and so was defined by a single feature. Since only rapid parallel feature processing is required to detect the target in this condition, the number of items in the display should not affect detection time. In a second condition, the target was a green letter T. Since this target is defined by a combination of two features (and can thus be rewarded as an object), it should require the serial processing associated

307

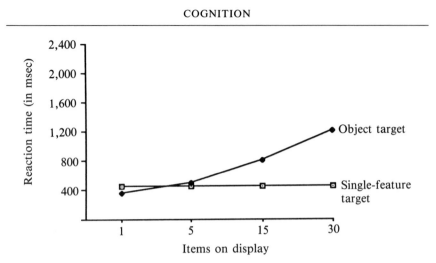

Figure 2 Speed of target detection as a function of target type (single-feature vs. object) and of number of items in the display
Source: Data from Treisman and Gelade, 1980

with focused visual attention. As a consequence, it should take much longer to detect the target when there are several items in the display than when there are only a few.

The findings are shown in Figure 2. It can be seen that performance on the feature-detection task was essentially unaffected by the number of items in the display, whereas performance on the object-detection task was greatly influenced by display size. According to Treisman and Gelade (1980) and Treisman (1988), this difference occurred because focused visual attention was needed on the latter task but not on the former.

Treisman's (1988) feature integration theory has clarified the role of focused visual attention in visual perception. However, as Humphreys and Bruce (1989) pointed out, the theory is in some ways rather oversimplified. More specifically, there are various studies in which subjects were able to identify object targets rapidly without making use of focused attention. What appears to be the case is that feature integration by means of focused attention is needed only when it is relatively difficult to discriminate between the target and non-target stimuli; if the discrimination is easy, then the initial parallel processing of features is adequate.

Inhibitory processes

Our coverage of the processes involved in focused visual attention has been somewhat limited so far, in that we have not considered the possible involvement of inhibitory processes. The position was expressed very well by

Wilhelm Wundt (1874), who founded the first laboratory of experimental psychology in 1879:

> The basic phenomenon of all intellectual achievement is the so-called concentration of attention. It is understandable that in the appraisal of this phenomenon we attach importance first and therefore too exclusively to its positive side, to the grasping and clarification of certain presentations. But for the physiological appraisal it is clear that it is the negative side the inhibition of the inflow of all other disturbing excitations ... which is more important. (p. 481)

In spite of Wundt's (1874) statement, it was only comparatively recently that researchers began to investigate inhibitory processes in attention. This research is reviewed by Tipper (1990), who pointed out that there are at least two visual phenomena that demonstrate the existence of inhibitory processes. The first phenomenon concerns the return of attention. If someone's attention is directed to one area of the visual environment and then to another area, it is difficult for that person to detect a target stimulus which is then presented in the first area. It is as if attention is actively inhibited from returning to an area to which it has been directed.

The second phenomenon seems to involve inhibition of the internal representations of objects. For example, a subject is initially presented with two objects at the same time (e.g., a red book and a blue ball), and instructed to name the blue one. If, on a subsequent trial, the subject has to name the previously ignored object (e.g., the red book), he or she performs this task relatively slowly. Presumably the internal representation of a previously ignored object is inhibited, and it is this which slows performance.

Why do these inhibitory processes exist? The first phenomenon makes sense if we assume that it can be important (e.g., in a dangerous environment) to examine the environment in an efficient way without constantly re-inspecting parts of the environment which have just been examined. The second phenomenon makes sense on the basis that inhibitory processes may facilitate the task of ignoring those objects in the environment which are not relevant to our present purposes.

DIVIDED ATTENTION

How good are we at doing two things at once? We know from experience that it is sometimes relatively easy to do and sometimes almost impossible. For example, nearly everyone can combine walking and chewing gum, but it is very difficult to make sense of a book and a television programme at the same time. Psychologists have attempted to identify the factors that determine how successfully attention can be divided between two tasks, and their attempts are considered in this part of the chapter.

There are several everyday examples which demonstrate that the ability to do two things at once depends heavily on practice. Experienced motorists can generally hold a normal conversation while driving, whereas learner drivers find car driving so demanding that they have little or no spare capacity left over to engage in conversation. In similar fashion, expert typists can hold a conversation or listen to the radio while they type, whereas beginning typists cannot.

Experimental evidence that practice can greatly improve the ability to perform two tasks together was obtained by Spelke, Hirst, and Neisser (1976). They carried out a study on two students (Diane and John) who initially found it extremely difficult to read short stories for comprehension while at the same time writing down words from dictation. More specifically, their reading speed was greatly slowed and their handwriting on the dictation task was very poor. After they had been given 30 hours of practice, however, Diane and John had the same reading speed and level of comprehension whether or not they had to take dictation at the same time. In addition, their handwriting on the dictation task had improved.

Spelke et al. (1976) were impressed by the performance of the two students. However, they did notice that the students did not appear to be taking in the meaning of the words that were presented for dictation. For example, when 20 successive words presented for dictation all belonged to the same category, the students did not realize that fact. John and Diane were given additional practice at this aspect of dictation, so that eventually they could write down the names of the categories to which the dictated words belonged while at the same time reading at high speed and with good comprehension.

The finding that reading for comprehension can be successfully combined with dictation suggests that two reasonably complex tasks can be performed together provided that sufficient practice is provided. More support for this contention comes from Shaffer (1975). He discovered that a highly trained typist could type rapidly and accurately while at the same time repeating back or shadowing an auditory message. However, while Shaffer's findings and those of Spelke et al. (1976) and Allport et al. (1972) appear to indicate that there are no problems with performing two well-practised tasks at once, this is not quite true. As Broadbent (1982) pointed out in a review, there are indications that the two tasks interfered with each other to some extent (e.g., increasing the number of errors on the dictation task).

The level of performance under divided attention conditions does not depend only on the extent to which the tasks have been practised. It depends also on the degree of similarity of the two tasks. Tasks can be similar in a number of ways, including having the same modality of input (e.g., visual or auditory), use of common internal processes (e.g., short-term memory), or similar response requirements. Evidence indicating that divided attention suffers when the two tasks are similar in any of these respects was reviewed by Wickens (1984). Here we consider a single example. Kolers (1972) devised a headgear with a half-silvered mirror. When he was wearing this headgear, he could choose whether to see the visual environment in front of him or behind him. However, he could not see both visual environments at the same time, because the one that he was not attending to directly seemed to disappear.

Another factor that determines how well two tasks can be performed together is the difficulty or complexity of the individual tasks. It is almost self-evident that it would be more difficult to combine complex than simple tasks, and only one study will be mentioned to illustrate the point. Earlier in the chapter we considered the dichotic listening task, in which auditory message to one ear has to be repeated back or shadowed at the same time as a second auditory message is presented to the other ear. Sullivan (1976) considered subjects' ability to detect certain words on the non-shadowed message. Many more words were detected when the shadowed message was easy to comprehend than when it was difficult to comprehend.

Theoretical accounts

The simplest way of attempting to account for the findings from studies of divided attention is to assume that there is some very general central capacity or pool of resources such as attention or effort. Each task makes some demands on those resources. If the combined demands of the two tasks exceeds the available pool of resources, then the tasks will interfere with each other and performance will suffer. On the other hand, if the demands of the two for attention or effort fall below the available level of resources, then the two tasks can be performed successfully at the same time.

Such central capacity theories (e.g., Norman & Bobrow, 1975) obviously provide a potential explanation of the effects of task difficulty on performance in studies of divided attention. They can also accommodate the effects of practice, if one assumes that the demands of any given task are much reduced after prolonged practice. However, central capacity theories do not in general provide a good account of the effects of task similarity, as can be seen in the following example. Segal and Fusella (1970) asked their subjects to think of a visual or an auditory image. While they were thinking of this image, they were given the task of attempting to detect either a visual or an auditory signal The findings are shown in Figure 3. It can be seen that the subjects performed much worse on the auditory signal task when they were thinking about an auditory image than when they were thinking about a visual image. Within the central capacity theory, this suggests that the auditory image task was more demanding of attention or other resources than was the visual image task. However, the results from the visual signal task suggest that the visual image task was more demanding than the auditory image task.

An alternative theoretical approach has been proposed by several theorists (e.g., Eysenck, 1984). In essence, it is proposed that we possess several specific processing mechanisms in addition to a more general processing mechanism such as attention. These specific processing mechanisms all have

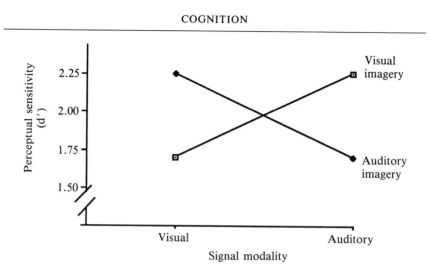

Figure 3   Sensitivity of signal detection as a function of signal modality and of imagery modality
Source: Data from Segal and Fusella, 1970

limited capacity, and may take many different forms. For example, there may be a processing mechanism which is specialized for the processing of auditory information and a different processing mechanism which is specialized for visual information. The reason why performance on the visual signal task is worse when it is combined with visual imagery than with auditory imagery may be because the visual signal task and the visual imagery task together exceed the capacity of the visual processing mechanism. In similar fashion, the auditory signal task and the auditory image task compete for the limited resources of a different specific processing mechanism.

In sum, it is possible to argue that the effects of task difficulty and of practice on dual-task performance are mainly due to the central processor or attentional limitations. In contrast, the effects of task similarity on performance are due to more specific processing mechanisms.

As we have seen, an individual's ability to perform two tasks at the same time can be greatly improved by practice. An important issue here is to identify precisely how practice produces this beneficial effect. According to several theorists (e.g., Logan, 1988; Shiffrin & Schneider, 1977) practice often permits some of the processes involved in task performance to become automatic. There have been disagreements about the definition of an automatic process, but it is generally agreed that automatic processes do not require attention, that they occur rapidly, that they always occur when an appropriate stimulus is presented, and that they do not require conscious awareness. Improved dual-task performance as a result of practice is thought to occur in large measure because of the development of automatic processes which make no demands on attentional resources. Thus, for example, a skilled typist can type and shadow an auditory message at the same time (Shaffer, 1975) because nearly all of the processes involved in typing are automatic, so that there is no need to attend to the movements of the fingers as each letter is typed.

We still do not have a detailed account of how automatic processes develop. However, Logan (1988) has made a start in that direction. He argued that repeated experience with a given stimulus leads to the storage of valuable information about that stimulus and how best to respond to it. In other words, as a result of practice, the appropriate response to a stimulus is stored firmly in memory and can be retrieved very easily. In Logan's own words, "Automaticity is memory retrieval: performance is automatic when it is based on a single-step direct-access retrieval of past solutions from memory" (p. 493).

Logan's (1988) theoretical analysis makes it possible to understand why automatic processes do not require attention, are rapid, and do not involve conscious awareness. They do not require attention because they involve an almost effortless retrieval of well-learned information from memory. They are rapid because the appropriate response is readily accessible in memory. They do not involve conscious awareness because no thought processes intervene between presentation of a stimulus and the retrieval and production of the appropriate response.

ABSENT-MINDEDNESS

According to *Collins English Dictionary*, absent-minded means "preoccupied; forgetful; inattentive", in other words, people are absent-minded when they fail to attend to the task in hand. This common-sense view (which as we shall see has much to recommend it) indicates the value of considering the everyday phenomenon of absent-mindedness in a chapter on attention. Absent-mindedness is often associated with action slips, which involve the performance of unintended actions. There are important reasons for obtaining a good understanding of absent-mindedness in general and action slips in particular: many fatal accidents (e.g., aircraft crashes, workplace deaths) occur as a direct consequence of people's inattention to what they are supposed to be doing.

The most obvious problem that faces the researcher in this area is the difficulty of obtaining adequate numbers of absent-minded actions under laboratory conditions. What is often done is to ask people to keep diary records of any action slips that they detect in their everyday lives. For example, Reason (1979) collected over 400 action slips from 35 individuals, and Reason and Mycielska (1982) managed to obtain a total of 625 action slips from 98 subjects. The most common form of action slip recorded involved storage failure, in which crucial information is forgotten. Here is an example of a storage failure from one of the subjects: "I started to pour a second kettle of boiling water into a teapot full of freshly made tea. I had no recollection of having just made it" (Reason, 1979, p. 74).

Approximately 40 per cent of all of the action slips recorded by Reason (1979) were storage failures. The next most common category of slips was that of test failure, which accounted for 20 per cent of the action slips. Test failure occurs when the progress of a sequence of planned actions is not attended to adequately at some crucial stage in the sequence. Reason quoted the following example of a test failure "I meant to get my car out, but as I passed through my back porch on my way to the garage I stopped to put on my wellington boots and gardening jacket as if to work in the garden" (p. 73). The other major categories identified by Reason (1979) and by Reason and Mycielska (1982) were subroutine failures, discrimination failures, and programme assembly failures. Subroutine failures occur when there are omissions or re-orderings of the various component stages involved in carrying out a given action sequence. Discrimination failures occur when the individual fails to discriminate accurately between two stimuli (e.g., brushing one's teeth with shaving cream rather than with toothpaste). Finally, programme assembly failures involve inappropriate combinations of actions.

It is important to consider some of the limitations of these diary studies. First, only those action slips that were detected by those keeping the diaries were included. There may have been numerous action slips that were either undetected or not remembered subsequently, and so did not appear in the diaries. That means that no great weight can be attached to the percentage figures for the various categories. Second, the number of times that action slips of a particular kind occur is meaningful only in relation to the number of times on which that kind of action slip might have occurred. For example, there may have been relatively few discrimination failures either because people are very good at discriminating between similar stimuli or because people only rarely find themselves in the position of having to discriminate between confusable stimuli.

There is an apparent paradox about action slips, which mostly occur during the action sequences that have been performed numerous times previously and are thus highly practised. Practice generally leads to considerable improvements in performance and to a marked reduction in the number of errors, and yet with action slips precisely the opposite seems to be the case. Reason (1979) provided a potential explanation for this apparent paradox. According to him, people performing unpractised skills tend to use a closed-loop or feedback mode of control in which a central processor or attentional system guides and controls behaviour from start to finish of an action sequence. However, when people become skilled, they tend to make more use of an open-loop mode of control in which motor performance is under the control of pre-arranged instruction sequences or motor programmes. Use of this open-loop mode of control frees the individual's attentional resources to be used for other purposes. The implications so far as action slips are concerned are as follows:

> The performance of a highly practised and largely automatized job liberates the central processor from moment-to-moment control; but since, like Nature, focal attention abhors a vacuum it tends to be 'captured' by some pressing but parallel mental activity so that, on occasion, it fails to switch back to the task in hand at a 'critical decision point' and thus permits the guidance of action to fall by default under the control of 'strong' motor programmes (p. 85).

The essence of Reason's (1979) theoretical position is that action slips generally occur when we place too much reliance on automatic processes in the open-loop mode of control rather than on attentional processes using the closed-loop or feedback mode of control. It is mainly with practised action sequences that we are in a position to be able to rely on automatic processes, and so most action slips are found when such action sequences are being performed Most action slips could be avoided if attentional processes or the central processor were to be used continuously during the performance of every action sequence. However, paying full attention to over-learned actions (e.g., walking down a street) would be wasteful of precious processing resources. What most of us do most of the time is to shift rapidly between automatic and attentional processes as and when necessary. That this is a sensible strategy to adopt is suggested by the fact that the diarists studied by Reason (1979) and by Reason and Mycielska (1982) reported an average of only one action slip per day and probably did not make many more slips than that. In other words, the very occasional action slip is a price which is generally well worth paying in order to free the attentional system from the task of constant monitoring of our habitual actions.

VIGILANCE

Most of the research on attention that has been discussed in this chapter has been concerned with reasonably complex tasks which were performed for relatively short periods of time. However, there are various real-life tasks that differ considerably from those we have been discussing. Inspecting goods moving along a conveyor belt in order to detect faulty ones is an example of a task that is monotonous and long-lasting, and on which action is only occasionally required. Tasks possessing such characteristics pose particular problems for the attentional system, because they require continuous attention in a rather boring situation. Performance on monotonous tasks (often called vigilance tasks) has been studied extensively under laboratory conditions in order to determine how successfully subjects can handle the attentional demands such tasks impose.

The first major programme of research on vigilance was reported by Mackworth (1950). He asked his subjects to observe a clock pointer, and to indicate whenever they detected a double jump in the movements of this pointer. One of his major findings was that there was vigilance decrement, meaning that the likelihood of detecting each double jump of the pointer tended to decrease during the course of the experimental session. At an intuitive level, it seems plausible to assume that the vigilance decrement occurred because the subjects became fatigued and unmotivated as the task proceeds. Mackworth obtained some support for this viewpoint. Subjects who were given the stimulant drug amphetamine generally showed little or no evidence of vigilance decrement, presumably because the drug prevented them from feeling tired. In similar fashion, Mackworth also discovered that providing knowledge of results in terms of signals missed and correctly detected largely prevented vigilance decrement. Knowledge of results probably had this beneficial effect because it helped to maintain motivation.

More direct evidence of the importance of motivation to vigilance performance was obtained by Nachreiner (1977). Some of those participating in a vigilance experiment were told that they would be offered a well-paid part-time job if they performed well on the vigilance task, whereas others were not given this inducement. The motivational effects of the job offer were such that it eliminated vigilance decrement.

Why exactly does the vigilance decrement occur in most circumstances? As Broadbent (1971) pointed out, there are two quite different possibilities which need to be considered. First, the subjects may find it increasingly more difficult to attend fully to the task with the consequence that they become less sensitive to the to-be-detected stimuli or signals (e.g., double jumps of the clock pointer. Second, as time goes by the subjects may become more cautious about reporting signals, i.e., they are more reluctant to accept that a signal has been presented. In order to distinguish between these two possibilities it is necessary to take account of what are known as false alarms. These are the occasions on which a signal is reported in spite of the fact that no signal was actually presented. In general terms, subjects who are rather cautious about reporting signals will make fewer false alarms than those who are less cautious. As Broadbent pointed out, the number of false alarms typically declines during the course of a vigilance task. Analyses that take account of the numbers of correct detections and false alarms indicate that the vigilance decrement is due primarily to increased cautiousness in reporting signals rather than to any reduction in the subject's level of sensitivity to signals.

There has been a steady reduction in vigilance research; probably the single most important reason is that it has proved difficult to identify with any precision the changes in attentional functioning which occur during the course of a vigilance experiment. This has made vigilance research of less theoretical significance than had initially been anticipated. Another reason is that technological advances and other changes within society have reduced the number of workers whose jobs involve sitting passively looking out for stimuli that occur only rarely. Many vigilance tasks formerly performed by humans are nowadays performed by computers. As a consequence, vigilance research has lost some of its practical relevance.

FURTHER READING

Eysenck, M. W., & Keane, M. T. (1990). *Cognitive psychology: A student's handbook*. London: Lawrence Erlbaum.
Gopher, D. (1990). Attention. In M. W. Eysenck (Ed.) *The Blackwell dictionary of cognitive psychology* (pp. 23–28). Oxford: Basil Blackwell.
Hampson, P. J. (1989). Aspects of attention and cognitive science. *Irish Journal of Psychology*, *10*, 261–275.
Johnston, W. A., & Dark, V. J. (1986). Selective attention. *Annual Review of Psychology*, *37*, 43–75.

REFERENCES

Allport, D. A., Antonis, B., & Reynolds, P. (1972). On the division of attention: A disproof of the single channel hypothesis. *Quarterly Journal of Experimental Psychology*, *24*, 225–235.
Broadbent, D. E. (1958). *Perception and communication*. Oxford: Pergamon.
Broadbent, D. E. (1971). *Decision and stress*. London: Academic Press.
Broadbent, D. E. (1982). Task combination and selective intake of information. *Acta Psychologica*, *50*, 253–290.
Cherry, E. C. (1953). Some experiments on the recognition of speech with one and two ears. *Journal of the Acoustical Society of America*, *25*, 975–979.
Deutsch, J. A., & Deutsch, D. (1963). Attention: Some theoretical considerations. *Psychological Review*, *70*, 80–90.
Eysenck, M. W. (1984). *A handbook of cognitive psychology*. London: Lawrence Erlbaum.
Humphreys, G. W., & Bruce, V. (1989). *Visual cognition: Computational, experimental and neuropsychological perspectives*. London: Lawrence Erlbaum.
James, W. (1890). *Principles of psychology*. New York: Holt.
Johnston, W A., & Dark, V. J. (1985). Dissociable domains of selective processing. In M. I. Posner & O. S. M. Marin (Eds) *Mechanisms of attention: Attention and performance* (vol. 10, pp. 487–508) Hillsdale, NJ: Lawrence Erlbaum.
Johnston, W. A., & Heinz, S. P. (1978). Flexibility and capacity demands of attention. *Journal of Experimental Psychology: General*, *107*, 420–435.
Johnston, W. A., & Wilson, J. (1980). Perceptual processing of non-targets in an attention task. *Memory & Cognition*, *8*, 372–377.
Kolers, P. A. (1972). *Aspects of motion perception*. New York: Pergamon.
LaBerge, D. (1983). Spatial extent of attention to letters and words. *Journal of Experimental Psychology: Human Perception and Performance*, *9*, 371–379.
Logan, O. D. (1988). Toward an instance theory of automatisation. *Psychological Review*, *95*, 492–527.
Mackworth, N. H. (1950). Researches in the measurement of human performance. *Medical Research Council special report series 268*.
Nachreiner, F. (1977). Experiments on the validity of vigilance experiments. In R. R. Mackie (Ed.) *Vigilance: Theory, operational performance and physiological correlates* (pp. 569–592). New York: Plenum.
Norman, D. A., & Bobrow, D. G. (1975). On data-limited and resource-limited processes. *Cognitive Psychology*, *7*, 44–64.

Reason, J. T. (1979). Actions not as planned. In G. Underwood & R. Stevens (Eds) *Aspects of consciousness* (pp. 69–96). London: Academic Press.

Reason, J. T., & Mycielska, K. (1982). *Absent-minded? The psychology of mental lapses and everyday errors.* Englewood Cliffs, NJ: Prentice-Hall.

Segal, S. J., & Fusella, V. (1970). Influence of imaged pictures and sounds on detection of visual and auditory signals. *Journal of Experimental Psychology, 83,* 458–464.

Shaffer, L. H. (1975). Multiple attention in continuous verbal tasks. In P. M. A. Rabbitt & S. Dornic (Eds) *Attention and performance* (vol. 5, pp. 243–258). London: Academic Press.

Shiffrin, R. M., & Schneider, W. (1977). Controlled and automatic human information processing: II. Perceptual learning, automatic attending, and a general theory. *Psychological Review, 84,* 127–190.

Spelke, E. S., Hirst, W. C., & Neisser, U. (1976). Skills of divided attention. *Cognition, 4,* 215–230.

Sullivan, L. (1976). Selective attention and secondary message analysis: A reconsideration of Broadbent's filter model of selective attention. *Quarterly Journal of Experimental Psychology, 28,* 167–178.

Tipper, S. P. (1990). Inhibitory processes in attention. In M. W. Eysenck (Ed.) *The Blackwell dictionary of cognitive psychology* (pp. 28–30). Oxford: Basil Blackwell.

Treisman, A. M. (1964). Verbal cues, language, and meaning in selective attention. *American Journal of Psychology, 77,* 206–219.

Treisman, A. M. (1988). Features and objects: The 14th Bartlett Memorial Lecture. *Quarterly Journal of Experimental Psychology, 40A,* 201–237.

Treisman, A. M., & Gelade, G. (1980). A feature-integration theory of attention. *Cognitive Psychology, 12,* 97–136.

Underwood, G. (1974). Moray vs. the rest: The effects of extended shadowing practice. *Quarterly Journal of Experimental Psychology, 26,* 368–372.

Wickens, C. D. (1984). Processing resources in attention. In R. Parasuraman & D. R. Davies (Eds) *Varieties of attention* (pp. 487–516). London: Academic Press.

Wundt, W. (1874). *Grundzüge der physiologischen Psychologie (Principles of physiological psychology).* Berlin: Springer.

4.3

PSYCHOLINGUISTICS

Willem J. M. Levelt

*Max-Planck-Institut für Psycholinguistik, Nijmegen,
The Netherlands*

Conversation	**Speech understanding**
The mental lexicon	Acoustic-phonetic analysis
Speaking	Phonological decoding
Conceptual preparation	Grammatical decoding
Grammatical encoding	Discourse processing
Phonological encoding	**Reading**
Articulation	**Sign language**
Self-monitoring	**Further reading**
	References

Psycholinguistics is the study of the mental processes and skills underlying the production and comprehension of language, and of the acquisition of these skills. This chapter will deal with the former aspect only; for the acquisition of language see the suggested "Further reading" at the end of this chapter.

Although the term "psycholinguistics" was brought into vogue during the 1950s, the psychological study of language use is as old as psychology itself. As early as 1879, for instance, Francis Galton published the first study of word associations (Galton, 1879). And the year 1900 saw the appearance of Wilhelm Wundt's monumental two-volume work *Die Sprache*. It endeavoured to explain the phylogeny of language in the human mind as an increasingly complex and conscious means of expression in a society, and to describe how language is created time and again in the individual act of speaking. Although Wundt deemed it impossible to study language use experimentally, his contemporaries introduced the experimental study of reading (Huey), of

319

verbal memory and word association (Ebbinghaus, Marbe, Watt), and of sentence production (Bühler, Seltz). They began measuring vocabulary size (Binet), and started collecting and analysing speech errors (Meringer and Mayer). The study of neurologically induced language impairments acquired particular momentum after Paul Broca and Carl Wernicke discovered the main speech and language supporting areas in the brain's left hemisphere. In the absence of live brain tomography, aphasiologists began developing neurolinguistic tests for the purpose of localizing brain dysfunctions.

All of these themes persist in modern psycholinguistics. But developments since the 1950s have provided it with two of its most characteristic features, which concern linguistic *processing* and *representation*. With respect to processing, psycholinguistics has followed mainstream psychology in that it considers the language user as a *complex information processing* system. With respect to representation, psycholinguists stress the gigantic amount of *linguistic knowledge* the language user brings to bear in producing and under-standing language. Although the structure of this knowledge is the subject matter of linguistics, it is no less a psychological entity than is language processing itself (Chomsky, 1968). Psycholinguistics studies how linguistic knowledge is exploited in language use, how representations for the form and meaning of words, sentences, and texts are constructed or manipulated by the language user, and how the child acquires such linguistic representations.

I shall first introduce the canonical setting for language use: conversation. Next I shall consider the mental lexicon, the heart of our linguistic knowledge. I shall then move to the processes of speaking and speech under-standing respectively. Finally I shall turn to other modes of language use, in particular written language and sign language.

CONVERSATION

Our linguistic skills are primarily tuned to the proper conduct of conversa-tion. The innate ability to converse has provided our species with a capacity to share moods, attitudes, and information of almost any kind, to assemble knowledge and skills, to plan coordinated action, to educate its offspring, in short, to create and transmit culture. And all this at a scale that is absolutely unmatched in the animal kingdom. In addition, we converse with ourselves, a kind of autostimulation that makes us more aware of our inclinations, of what we think or intend (Dennett, 1991). Fry (1977) correctly characterized our species as *homo loquens*.

In conversation the interlocutors are involved in negotiating meaning. When we talk, we usually have some kind of communicative intention, and the conversation is felicitous when that intention is recognized by our partner(s) in conversation (Grice, 1968; Sperber & Wilson, 1986). This may take several turns of mutual clarification. Here is an example from Clark and

Wilkes-Gibbs (1986), where subjects had to refer to complex tangram figures:

A: Uh, person putting a shoe on.
B: Putting a shoe on?
A: Uh huh. Facing left. Looks like he's sitting down.
B: Okay.

Here the communicative intention was to establish reference, and that is often a constituting component of a larger communicative goal. Such goals can be to commit the interlocutor or oneself to some course of action, as in requesting and promising, or to inform the interlocutor on some state of affairs, as in asserting, for example. The appropriate linguistic acts for achieving such goals are called *speech acts* (Austin, 1962).

Although what is said is the means of making the communicative intention recognizable, the relation between the two can be highly indirect. Conversations involve intricate mechanisms of politeness control (Brown & Levinson, 1987). What is *conveyed* is often quite different from what is *said*. In most circumstances, for instance, we don't request by commanding, like in "Open the window". Rather we do it indirectly by checking whether the interlocutor is able or willing to open the window, like in "Can you open the window for me?" It would, then, be inappropriate for the interlocutor to answer "Yes" without further action. In that case, the response is only to the question (whether he or she is able to open the window), but not to the request.

How does the listener know that there is a request in addition to the question? There is, of course, an enormous amount of shared situational knowledge that will do the work. Grice (1975) has argued that conversations are governed by principles of rationality; Sperber and Wilson (1986) call it the *principle of relevance*. The interlocutor, for instance, is so obviously able to open the window that the speaker's intention cannot have been to check that ability. But Clark (1979) found that linguistic factors play a role as well. If the question is phrased idiomatically, involving *can* and *please*, subjects interpret it as a request. But the less idiomatic it is (like in "Are you able to . . . "), the more subjects react to the question instead of to the request.

Another important aspect of conversation is *turn-taking*. There are rules for the allocation of turns in conversation that ensure everybody's right to talk, that prevent the simultaneous talk of different parties, and that regulate the proper engaging in and disengaging from conversation (Sacks, Schegloff, & Jefferson, 1974). These rules are mostly followed, and sometimes intentionally violated (as in interrupting the speaker). Turn-taking is subtly controlled by linguistic (especially prosodic) and non-verbal (gaze and body movement) cues (Beattie, 1983).

THE MENTAL LEXICON

Producing or understanding spoken language always involves the use of words. The mental lexicon is our repository of words, their meanings, their syntax, and their sound forms. A language's vocabulary is, in principle, unlimited in size. Take, for instance, the numerals in English. They alone form an infinite set of words. But it is unlikely that a word such as *twenty-three-thousand-two-hundred-and-seventy-nine* is an entry in our mental lexicon. Rather, such a word is constructed by rule when needed. We have the ability to produce new words that are not stored in our mental lexicon.

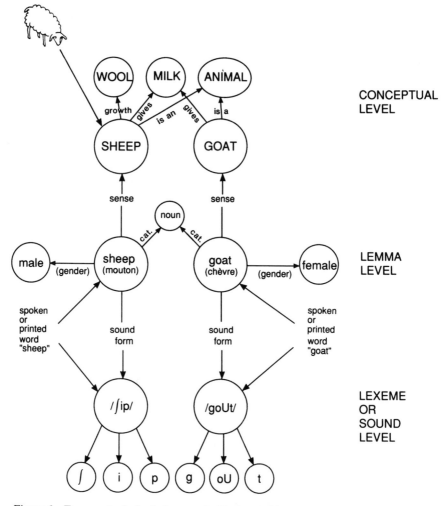

Figure 1 Fragment of a lexical network. Each word is represented at the conceptual, the syntactic and the sound form level
Source: Bock and Levelt, 1993

How many words *are* stored? Miller (1991) estimates that the average high school graduate knows about 60,000 words (under one definition of "word").

One way of representing this enormous body of knowledge is by way of network models. Figure 1 shows a fragment of such a network. Each word is represented by three nodes, one at the conceptual level, one at the syntactic (grammatical) or lemma level, and one at the sound form (phonological) or lexeme level. The lemma is the syntactic representation and the lexeme is the phonological representation. A word's semantic properties are given by its connections to other nodes at the conceptual level (for instance, that a sheep is an animal, gives milk, etc.). A word's syntactic properties are represented by its lemma node's relations to other syntactic nodes (for instance, "sheep" is a noun; French "mouton" has male gender, etc.). The sound form properties, finally, such as a word's phonological segments, are represented in the way a word's lexeme node relates to other sound form nodes ("sheep" for instance contains three ordered phonological segments, $/\int/$, $/i/$, and $/p/$, as shown in Figure 1).

Different authors have proposed different network models (e.g., Collins & Loftus, 1975; Dell, 1986; Roelofs, 1992), and for different purposes. It is unlikely that such networks can adequately represent all complexities of our semantic, syntactic, and phonological knowledge about words. But they can be useful in predicting speed of word access in comprehension and production, as well as in explaining various kinds of errors that we make in speech production and various disorders of accessing words in aphasic speech.

Especially important for theories of language use are the ways that verbs are represented in the mental lexicon. As a semantic entity, a verb assigns semantic roles to its arguments. The verb *walk*, for instance, requires an animate argument that specifies the role of agent, as in *John walked*. The verb *greet* governs two arguments, one for the agent and one for the recipient of the action, as in *Peter greeted the driver*. As a syntactic entity, a verb assigns syntactic functions to the sentence constituents it governs. In the above sentence, *Peter* is the subject and *the driver* the object. A verb's argument-function mapping is not random. Most verbs, for instance, map a recipient argument on to a syntactic object function, but not all. The verb *receive* doesn't. In *Mary received the book*, *Mary* is both recipient and sentence subject. Also, verbs often allow for multiple mappings. In *the driver was greeted by Peter*, the recipient, not the agent appears in subject position.

For each verb, the mental lexicon contains its possible mapping frames. These play an important role in the speaker's syntactic planning and in the listener's syntactic and semantic parsing.

SPEAKING

Speaking is our most complex cognitive-motor skill. It involves the conception of an intention, the selection of information whose expression will make that intention recognizable, the selection of appropriate words, the construction of a syntactic framework, the retrieval of the words' sound forms, and the computation of an articulatory plan for each word and for the utterance as a whole. It also involves the execution of this plan by more than 100 muscles controlling the flow of air through the vocal tract. Finally, it involves a process of self-monitoring by which speech trouble can be prevented or repaired. The following is a bird eye's view over these processes.

Conceptual preparation

The question where communicative intentions come from is a psychodynamic question rather than a psycholinguistic one. Speaking is a form of social action, and it is in the context of action that intentions, goals, and subgoals develop. It is not impossible, though, that the intention *what* to say occasionally arises from spontaneous activity in the speech formulating system itself. It can create rather incoherent "internal speech", which we can self-perceive. This, in turn, may provide us with tatters of notions that we then consider for expression (cf. Dennett, 1991).

Conveying an intention may involve several steps or "speech acts". The speaker will have to decide what to express first, what next, and so on. This is called the speaker's *linearization* problem (Levelt, 1989). It is especially apparent in the expression of multidimensional information, as in describing one's apartment (Linde & Labov, 1975). The conceptual preparation of speech, and in particular linearization, require the speaker's continuing attention. The principles of linearization are such that attentional load is minimized.

Each speech act, be it a request to do X, an assertion that Y, etc., involves the expression of some conceptual structure, technically called a "message" (Garrett, 1975). That message is to be given linguistic shape; it has to become "formulated".

Grammatical encoding

A first step in formulating is to retrieve the appropriate words from the mental lexicon and to embed them in the developing syntactic structure. In normal conversation we produce some two words per second. At this rate we manage to access the appropriate words in our huge mental lexicon. Occasional errors of lexical selection (such as "Don't burn your toes" where *fingers* was intended) show that the lexicon has a semantic organization.

The standard explanation for such errors is that activation spreads through a semantically organized network, as in Figure 1. In such a network, each node has an activation level between 0 and 1. When the lexical concept node SHEEP is active, then activation spreads to semantically related concept nodes, such as GOAT. Both nodes spread activation "down" to their lemma nodes. Which one of the lemmas will then be selected for further processing? Normally it will be the most activated one, in this case the lemma for "sheep". But the occurrence of an occasional error shows that there is a small probability that a less activated lemma gets selected. According to one theory (Roelofs, 1992) the probability that a particular lemma becomes selected within a time interval t is the ratio of its activation to the sum of the activation of all other lemma nodes. For instance, if "sheep" and "goat" are the only two active lemmas during interval t after presentation of the picture, and they have activation levels of 0.7 and 0.1 respectively, the probability that the target word "sheep" will be selected during that interval is 7/8, whereas the erroneous word "goat" will be selected with the probability 1/8. Hence, if there is more than one lemma active in the system, there is always a small probability that a non-intended word becomes selected (and it is likely to be semantically related to the target).

Spreading activation theories of lexical selection are typically tested in picture-naming experiments, where naming latencies are measured. For a review of issues in lexical selection, see Levelt (1992a).

As soon as a lemma is retrieved, its syntactic properties become available. Among them are the lemma's grammatical class (preposition, noun, verb, etc.). Each lemma requires its own specific syntactic environment or "frame". Syntactic planning is like solving a set of simultaneous equations. Each lemma's frame has to fit its neighbour's frames, and since Garrett (1975) there are theories about how this is realized (see Levelt, 1989, for a review). Actually, the equations are not quite "simultaneous"; the lemmas for an utterance are typically not concurrently retrieved. Lemmas for salient concepts, such as animate objects, tend to be retrieved faster than for non-salient concepts (Bock & Warren, 1985), and that affects their position in the developing syntactic structure. For a review of grammatical encoding, see Bock and Levelt (1994).

Phonological encoding

A selected lemma (but only a selected one: see Levelt et al., 1991) spreads its activation to its lexeme node (cf. Figure 1). At this level two kinds of phonological information become available. The first one is the word's segments, which are "spelled out" one after another. The second one is the word's metrical structure. For "sheep" it is the information that it is a one-syllable word. For "father" it is the information that it is a two-syllabic trochaic word. The metrical frames of successive words are often combined, creating so-called phonological word frames. In *Peter gave him it*, the last three words form one phonological word *gavimit*. In a process of *segment-to-frame association* spelled-out segments are inserted one by one into the corresponding phonological word frames. It is during this ordered insertion that phonological syllables are created, one after another (such as *ga-vi-mit*; see

Levelt, 1992b). How this string of phonological syllables determines the precise articulatory gestures to be made by the speech organs is still a matter of much debate (see especially Browman & Goldstein, 1991).

The notion that segments and frames are independently retrieved arose in the analysis of phonological speech errors (Dell, 1986; Shattuck-Hufnagel, 1979). Spoonerisms such as *with this wing I thee red*, or *fool the pill* (instead of *fill the pool*) show that segments can become associated to the right place in the wrong frame.

Phonological encoding also involves the planning of larger units than phonological words. There is, in particular, the planning of intonational phrases. These are units that carry a particular intonational contour. Such contours can be rising, falling or combinations thereof. They often express a speaker's attitude towards what is said: doubt, certainty, or towards the interlocutor: reassuringness, inviting reaction. See Levelt (1989) for a review of phonological encoding.

The output of phonological encoding is an articulatory programme. Phenomenologically, it appears to the speaker as internal speech. This internal speech need not be articulated. It can be kept in an articulatory buffer, ready to be retrieved for articulatory execution (Sternberg, Wright, Knoll, & Monsell, 1980).

Articulation

The articulatory apparatus consists of three major structures. The respiratory system controls the steady outflow of air from the lungs. The breathing cycle during speech is quite different from normal breathing, with very rapid inhalation and very slow exhalation. The laryngeal system has the vocal cords as its central part. It is the main source of acoustic energy. The vocal tract, finally, contains the cavities of pharynx, mouth, and nose. They are the resonators that filter the acoustic energy in frequency bands or *formants*. Vowels are characterized by their formant structure. The vocal tract can be constricted at different places, and these constrictions can be made or released in different manners. In this way a wide range of consonantal and other speech sounds can be made.

The control of this utterly complex motor system has been the subject of much research. Present theories converge on the notion of *model-referenced control* (Arbib, 1981; see also Figure 2). The motor system is given an "articulatory task" (as part of the articulatory programme), such as "close the lips". There are usually many degrees of freedom in executing such a task. For instance, lip closing can be realized by moving the lips, by moving the jaw, or by doing both to various degrees. The internal model computes the least energy-consuming way of reaching the goal, given the actual state of the articulators (there is continuous proprioceptive feedback to the internal model). The output is a set of efferent control signals to the relevant

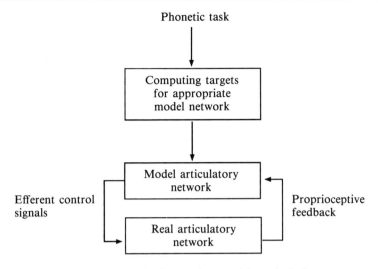

Figure 2 Model-referenced control in articulation
Source: Levelt, 1989

muscles. Saltzman and Kelso (1987) gave a precise mathematical rendering of this theory. See Levelt (1989) for a review of theories of articulation. The output of articulation is overt speech.

Self-monitoring

We can listen to our own overt speech and detect trouble, just as we can listen to the speech of others and detect errors or infelicitous delivery. This involves our normal speech understanding system. We can also detect trouble in our internal speech. When the trouble is disruptive enough for the ongoing conversation, a speaker may decide to interrupt the flow of speech and to make a self-repair.

Not all self-produced trouble (such as errors of selection) is detected by the speaker. Self-monitoring requires attention; we mostly attend to *what* we say, far less to *how* we do it. Detection of trouble is better towards the end of clauses, where less attention for content is required (Levelt, 1989). There are two main classes of trouble that induce repairing. The first one is an all-out error (as in *and above that a horizon-, no a vertical line*); the error can be lexical, syntactic, or phonological. The second one is that something is not really appropriate (as in *to the right is blue − is a blue point*). The speaker then repairs in order to make the utterance more precise, less ambiguous. Upon detecting either kind of trouble, the speaker can self-interrupt. And this ignores linguistic structure; a speaker can stop in the midst of a phrase, a word, or a syllable. But then, the speaker often marks the kind of trouble by some *editing expression*: "no", "sorry", "I mean", for errors; "rather", "that is", for something inappropriate.

Restarting, that is, making the repair proper, is linguistically quite principled. The speaker grafts the repair on to the syntax of the interrupted utterance, which has been kept in abeyance. As a consequence, repairing is like linguistic coordination. One seldom finds a repair such as *is she driving – she walking downtown?* And indeed, the corresponding coordination *is she driving or she walking downtown?* is ill-formed. But *is he – she walking downtown?* is a very common repair type, and it corresponds to a well-formed coordination: *is he or she walking downtown?* (Levelt, 1989).

SPEECH UNDERSTANDING

The canonical objective in speech understanding is to recognize the speaker's communicative intention. How does the listener induce that intention from the speaker's overt speech, a continuous flow of acoustic events?

Several component processes are involved here. First, there is the hearer's acoustic-phonetic analysis of the speech signal, that is, representing it as a *phonetic* not just an *acoustic* event. Second, there is phonological decoding, in particular finding the words that correspond to the phonetic events, and analysing the overall prosodic structure of the utterance. Third, there is grammatical decoding, parsing the utterance as a meaningful syntactic structure. Finally, there is discourse processing, interpreting the utterance in the context of the ongoing discourse, and in particular inferring the speaker's intentions. Let us review these processes in turn.

Acoustic-phonetic analysis

It is very hard, if not impossible, to listen to speech as if it were just a string of chirps, buzzes, hums, and claps. We just cannot help perceiving it as speech. In this so-called "speech mode" (Liberman & Mattingly, 1985) we interpret the acoustic event as resulting from a speaker's articulatory gestures as a phonetic event. There is no unanimity in the literature, though, about what kind of representation the listener derives. According to Liberman and Mattingly, the listener derives the speaker's intended articulatory gestures (even if they were sloppy). Others argue that listeners have special detectors for distinctive events in the speech signal, such as for onsets, for spectral peaks, for the frequencies and motions of formants. The detection of such acoustic events may suffice to derive the presence or absence of phonetic features, such as voicing, nasality, vowel height, stridency, and so on (Stevens & Blumstein, 1981).

Speech segments, clusters, and syllables have characteristic distributions of phonetic features. Hence, if such feature detectors are reliable, they may provide sufficient information for effective phonological decoding. Opinions differ, however, about their reliability. The speech signal is highly variable, dependent as it is on speech rate, sex of the speaker, sloppiness of speech delivery, reverberation or noise in the room, for example. Even if the listener can partial out such effects of the speech context, acoustic-phonetic analysis will often be indeterminate. Still, it may well be sufficient for the purpose. Not every word has to be recognized in order to derive the speaker's intentions. And where a really critical word is missed, the interlocutor will say "what?" or signal difficulty of understanding in other ways.

For an excellent review of acoustic-phonetic processing, see Pisoni and Luce (1987).

Phonological decoding

Whatever the precise character of the phonetic representations, they are the listener's access codes to the mental lexicon. How does a listener recognize words in connected speech? A major problem here is to *segment* the speech, to find out where words begin and end in the continuous flow of speech. There are, basically, two routes here.

The first one is the bottom-up approach, that is, to build on cues in the phonetic representation. Cutler (1990) has argued that English listeners will, by default, segment speech such that there are word boundaries right before stressed syllables. It is a statistical fact of English that 85 per cent of the meaningful words that one encounters while listening begin with a stressed syllable. The segmentation strategy will, therefore, be quite successful. Cutler's theory has meanwhile found substantial experimental support. Also, there are speech sounds that tend to occur at the ends of words, such as [-ng] and [-nd] for English. Speakers may use such phonotactic properties of their language to predict word boundaries.

The second route is top-down. We often recognize a word before it ends. But that means that we can predict the word's end, and hence the upcoming word boundary. That gives us a handle on where to start recognizing the subsequent word.

Given that we know a word's beginning, how do we recognize it? According to the *cohort theory* (Marslen-Wilson, 1989), a small word-initial feature pattern (corresponding to about two segments of the input word) activates all words in the mental lexicon that match it phonologically. Assume the input word is *trespass*, and the cluster [tr] has become available. This will activate all words beginning with [tr], such as *tremble, trespass, trestle, trombone*, etc. This is called the "word-initial cohort". As more phonetic information becomes available, the cohort is successively reduced. When the vowel [ε] is perceived, all items not sharing that vowel, such as *trombone*, are deactivated. This process continues until a single candidate remains. For *trespass* this happens when [p] is reached. The segment [p] is, therefore, called the *uniqueness point* of *trespass*. A word's uniqueness point depends on its word-initial lexical alternatives. For most words the uniqueness point precedes the word's end.

For an optimally efficient system, the word's uniqueness point would also be its *recognition point*. There is good experimental evidence in support of this hypothesis (e.g., Frauenfelder, Segui, & Dijkstra, 1990), though the recognition point may slightly anticipate the uniqueness point in case syntactic or semantic information disambiguates the item from its remaining alternatives (Zwitserlood, 1989). Hence, it will often be possible for a listener to anticipate the upcoming word boundary.

Phonological decoding serves not only the recognition of words, but also their groupings into prosodic constituents, such as phonological and intonational phrases. These constituents carry important information about the syntax of the utterance, and about the communicative intentions of the speaker (cf. Levelt, 1989).

Grammatical decoding

As words are successively recognized and prosodically grouped, the listener will as much as possible interpret these materials "on-line" (Marslen-Wilson & Tyler, 1980). Each recognized word makes available its syntactic and semantic properties. There is, then, concurrent syntactic parsing and semantic interpretation, each following its own principles, but interacting where necessary.

In this connection, one should distinguish between local and global syntactic parsing. Local parsing involves the creation of local phrase structure, combining words into noun phrases, verb phrases, etc. There is increasing evidence that local parsing can run on word category information alone (Frazier, 1989; Tyler & Warren, 1987). We have little trouble parsing "jabberwocky" or semantically anomalous prose such as *the beer slept the slow guitar*. Here we construct phrase structure exclusively by recognizing the words' syntactic categories (Art, Adj, N, V). However, successful local parsing is highly dependent on the intactness of phonological phrases, as Tyler and Warren (1987) could show. For instance, in the above anomalous prose, one should not create a prosodic break between *the* and *slow*, or between *slow* and *guitar*.

Global syntactic parsing, however, interacts with semantic interpretation. In global parsing, semantic roles are assigned to syntactic constituents, and this is to a large extent governed by the verb's argument/function mapping. When the meaning of words or phrases contradicts the semantic roles they should carry, global parsing is hampered (Tyler & Warren, 1987).

One important aspect of global parsing is the resolution of anaphora. In the sentence *the boxer told the skier that the doctor for the team would blame him for the recent injury*, the anaphor *him* can refer back to *the boxer* and to *the skier*, but global syntax prohibits its referring to *the doctor*. Indeed, experimental evidence shows reactivation of both *boxer* and *skier*, but not of *doctor* when the pronoun *him* is perceived. Such reactivation can also be measured for so-called null-anaphors as in *the policeman saw the boy that the crowd at the party accused t of the crime*. Here there is measurable reactivation of *boy* at position *t* (the syntactic "trace" of *the boy*; see Nicol & Swinney, 1989). But also in this respect global parsing is semantically facilitated, for instance if the anaphor's referent is a concrete noun (Cloitre & Bever, 1988).

Grammatical decoding doesn't remove all ambiguity (for instance, the pronoun *him* above is not fully resolved). Here, further discourse processing is needed.

Discourse processing

Partners in conversation construct mental models of the state of affairs they are talking about (Johnson-Laird, 1983; Seuren, 1985). Indefinite expressions (such as in *there is a dog in the room*) make them introduce a new entity (a dog) in the model. Definite expressions (such as *the room* in the same sentence) make them look up an already existing entity. The new information in the utterance is then attached to whichever entity it concerns.

Identifying referents is a major accomplishment of human language processing, still unmatched by any computer program. The problem is that referring expressions can be highly indirect. How can a waitress in a restaurant interpret the referent when her colleague says *the hamburger wants the bill*? Nunberg (1979) argued that there are "referring functions" that map a *demonstratum* (like the hamburger) on to the intended referent (the person who ordered it). But the range of possible referring functions is almost unlimited. Clark, Schreuder, and Buttrick (1983) and Morrow (1986) have argued (and experimentally shown) that such demonstratum-to-referent mapping depends on the mutual knowledge of the interlocutors and on the saliency of entities in their discourse models.

Indirectness is the hallmark of discourse interpretation. As mentioned above, what is said often relates quite indirectly to what the speaker intends to convey. It is not only politeness that governs such indirectness. All figures of speech, whether polite or not, require the listener to build a bridge from the literal to the intended. This holds equally for metaphor (Sperber & Wilson, 1986), irony (Clark & Gerrig, 1984), and hyperbole (Grice, 1975).

Finally, whereas acoustic-phonetic, phonological, and grammatical decoding are largely automatic processes, discourse processing requires the listener's full attention. In that respect, it is on a par with the speaker's conceptual preparation. As interlocutors we are concerned with content. The processing of form largely takes care of itself.

READING

The invention of writing systems, whether logographic, syllabic, or alphabetic, is probably the most revolutionary step in human cultural evolution. It added a powerful means of storing and transmitting information. With the invention of printing, it became a major mechanism for large-scale dissemination of knowledge in a culture.

But equally surprising as this ability to map spoken language on to a visual code is our capacity to efficiently process such a code. When skilled, we silently read five or six printed words per second; this is about twice the rate of conversational speech. This ability has not given us any selective advantage in biological evolution; the invention of writing systems is as recent as about 5,000 years ago. Rather, the ability to read must be due to a happy coincidence of other pre-existing faculties of mind.

One of these is, of course, language. As readers we largely use our parsing potential for spoken language. Visual word recognition feeds into the lemma level of Figure 1. As lemmas are successively activated by the printed words, further syntactic, semantic, and discourse processing operates roughly as for spoken language. There are, admittedly, differences too. There is, for instance, no prosody to help syntactic parsing; instead there is punctuation. Also, there is no external enforcement of rate as there is in speech perception.

Another pre-existing faculty on which reading is parasitic is our enormous ability to scan for small meaningful visual patterns. In a hunter's society these were probably animal silhouettes, footprints, and so on. Words (if not too long or too infrequent) are recognized as wholes; a skilled reader processes a word's letters in parallel. Much ink has been spilled on the question whether the letters individually or the word as a whole activate a phonological code in silent reading, that is, the word's lexeme (see Figure 1). Such phonological recoding indeed exists. But it is only for low-frequent words that this "phonological route" is of any help in lemma access (Jared & Seidenberg, 1991). However, this silent "internal speech" probably does play a role in further syntactic and semantic parsing; it is a way of buffering successive words for further processing.

The ability to scan is optimally used in reading. The basic cycle is this: the reader fixates a word for, on average, one-fifth of a second. The fixation is roughly between the beginning and the middle of the word. During this period lexical access is achieved. In addition, there is some perception of the next word in the periphery of vision. Sometimes this suffices to recognize that next word as well on the same fixation (but the fixation will then last somewhat longer). Usually, however, the information from the periphery of vision is used only to plan a saccadic eye movement (a jump of the eye) to that next word. The size of the saccade depends on the length of the next word; the average saccade is about eight characters in size. The new word is fixated, and the cycle starts all over again.

When a word is quite infrequent, or when the reader has trouble integrating it in the developing syntax or semantics, the fixation duration can be substantially longer. Also, the reader may backtrack and refixate an earlier word when there is serious trouble in comprehension.

For a major review of the reading process and its disorders, see Rayner and Pollatsek (1989).

SIGN LANGUAGE

Contrary to written language, the sign languages of deaf people are not parasitic on spoken language. They are autonomous languages in the visual mode. Their mere existence shows that our faculty of language is not crucially

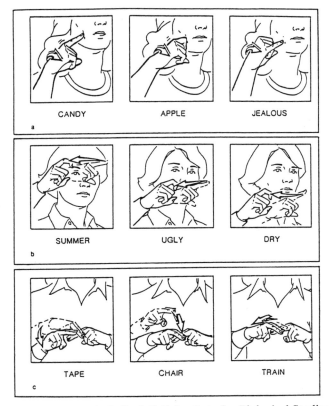

Illustration, copyright Ursula Bellugi, Salk Institute for Biological Studies, La Jolla, CA, 92037

Figure 3 Minimal contrasts between signs in American Sign Language: (a) hand configuration, (b) place of articulation, (c) movement
Source: From Klima and Bellugi, 1979

333

dependent on our ability to speak. Deaf children who grow up in a signing deaf community acquire their language at the same age and in roughly the same stages as hearing children do.

Just as words, signs have form and meaning. The articulators of sign language are the hands, the face, and the body. Where words contrast phonemically (for instance in voicing: *bath* vs *path*), signs contrast in hand configuration, in place of articulation and in hand movement (see Figure 3). Also, facial features may distinguish between signs.

Although the first coining of a sign is often iconic, its meaning is eventually independent of its form, as it is for words in spoken languages. As a consequence, sign languages are mutually unintelligible, just as spoken languages are (contrary to what Wundt suggested in *Die Sprache* – see above).

Sign languages are rich in morphology (for inflection and for derivation of new signs) and have full-fledged recursive syntax. Many syntactic devices are spatial in character. Anaphora, that is, referring back to an earlier introduced entity, is done by pointing to the locus in the signing space (in front of the body) where the original referent was first "established". In American Sign Language the sign for transitive verbs either moves from subject to object locus, or from object to subject locus. Each verb has its own "mapping function" (like in spoken language, see above). For the structure and use of British Sign Language, see Kyle and Woll (1985).

There is increasing evidence that a sign language is subserved by the same areas of the brain that sustain spoken language. Poizner, Klima, and Bellugi, (1987) showed that damage to anterior areas of the left hemisphere in native signers resulted in a style of signing highly comparable to the agrammatism of so-called Broca's patients. Similarly, a form of fluent aphasia resulted when the damage was in a more posterior area of the left hemisphere, comparable to the fluent aphasia of so-called Wernicke's patients. Damage in the right hemisphere left the signing intact, but patients lost the ability to sign coherently *about* spatial relations, such as the layout of their apartment. Their spatial representations were damaged, but not their spatial language.

FURTHER READING

Garman, M. (1990). *Psycholinguistics.* Cambridge: Cambridge University Press.
Levelt, W. J. M. (1989). *Speaking: From intention to articulation.* Cambridge, MA: Massachusetts Institute of Technology Press.
Miller, G. A. (1991). *The science of words.* New York: Scientific American Library.
Rayner, K., & Pollatsek, A. (1989). *The psychology of reading.* Englewood Cliffs, NJ: Prentice-Hall.
Slobin, D. I. (Ed.) (1985). *The crosslinguistic study of language acquisition* (2 vols). Hillsdale, NJ: Lawrence Erlbaum.

REFERENCES

Arbib, M. A. (1981). Perceptual structures and distributed motor control. In V. Brooks (Ed.) *Handbook of physiology: The nervous system. Motor control* (vol. 2, pp. 1449–1480). Bethesda, MD: American Physiological Society.

Austin, J. L. (1962). *How to do things with words*. Oxford: Clarendon.

Beattie, G. (1983). *Talk: An analysis of speech and non-verbal behaviour in conversation*. Milton Keynes: Open University Press.

Bock, J. K., & Levelt, W. J. M. (1994). Language production: Grammatical encoding. In M. A. Gernsbacher (Ed.) *Handbook of psycholinguistics*. New York: Academic Press.

Bock, J. K., & Warren, R. K. (1985). Conceptual accessibility and syntactic structure in sentence formulation. *Cognition, 21*, 47–67.

Browman, C. P., & Goldstein, L. (1991). Representation and reality: Physical systems and phonological structure. *Haskins Laboratory Status Report on Speech Research*, SR-105/106, 83–92.

Brown, P., & Levinson, S. (1987). *Politeness: Some universals in language usage*. Cambridge: Cambridge University Press.

Chomsky, N. (1968). *Language and mind*. New York: Harcourt Brace & World.

Clark, H. H. (1979). Responding to indirect speech acts. *Cognitive Psychology, 4*, 430–477.

Clark, H. H., & Gerrig, R. J. (1984). On the pretence theory of irony. *Journal of Experimental Psychology: General, 113*, 121–126.

Clark, H. H., & Wilkes-Gibbs, D. (1986). Referring as a collaborative process. *Cognition, 22*, 1–39.

Clark, H. H., Schreuder, R., & Buttrick, S. (1983). Common ground and the understanding of demonstratives. *Journal of Verbal Learning and Verbal Behavior, 22*, 245–258.

Cloitre, M., & Bever, T. G. (1988). Linguistic anaphors, levels of representation, and discourse. *Language and Cognitive Processes 3*, 293–322.

Collins, A. M., & Loftus, E. F. (1975). A spreading-activation theory of semantic processing. *Psychological Review, 82*, 407–428.

Cutler, A. (1990). Exploiting prosodic probabilities in speech segmentation. In G. Altmann (Ed.) *Cognitive models of speech processing* (pp. 105–121). Cambridge, MA: Massachusetts Institute of Technology Press.

Dell, G. (1986). A spreading activation theory of retrieval in sentence production. *Psychological Review, 93*, 283–321.

Dennett, D. C. (1991). *Consciousness explained*. Boston, MA: Little, Brown.

Frauenfelder, U., Segui, J., & Dijkstra, T. (1990). Lexical effects in phoneme processing: Facilitatory or inhibitory? *Journal of Experimental Psychology: Human Perception and Performance, 16*, 77–91.

Frazier, L. (1989). Against lexical generation. In W. D. Marslen-Wilson (Ed.) *Lexical representation and process* (pp. 505–528). Cambridge, MA: Massachusetts Institute of Technology Press.

Fry, D. (1977). *Homo loquens*. Cambridge: Cambridge University Press.

Galton, F. (1879). Psychometric experiments. *Brain, 2*, 149–162.

Garrett, M. F. (1975). An analysis of sentence production. In G. Bower (Ed.) *Psychology of learning and motivation* (vol. 9, pp. 133–177). New York: Academic Press.

Grice, H. P. (1968). Utterer's meaning, sentence meaning and word meaning. *Foundations of Language, 4*, 225–242.

Grice, H. P. (1975). Some further notes on logic and conversation. In P. Cole (Ed.) *Syntax and semantics: Pragmatics* (vol. 9, pp. 113–127). New York: Academic Press.

Jared, D., & Seidenberg, M. S. (1991). Does word identification proceed from spelling to sound to meaning? *Journal of Experimental Psychology: General, 120,* 358–394.

Johnson-Laird, P. N. (1983). *Mental models.* Cambridge: Cambridge University Press.

Klima, E. S., & Bellugi, U. (1979). *The signs of language.* Cambridge, MA: Harvard University Press.

Kyle, J. G., & Woll, B. (1985). *Sign language.* Cambridge: Cambridge University Press.

Levelt, W. J. M. (1989). *Speaking: From intention to articulation.* Cambridge, MA: Massachusetts Institute of Technology Press.

Levelt, W. J. M. (Ed.) (1992a). Lexical access in speech production. Special issue of *Cognition, 42,* 1–316.

Levelt, W. J. M. (1992b). Accessing words in speech production: Stages, processes and representations. *Cognition, 42,* 1–22.

Levelt, W. J. M., Schriefers, H., Vorberg, D., Meyer, A. S., Pechmann, T., & Havinga, J. (1991). The time course of lexical access in speech production: A study of picture naming. *Psychological Review, 98,* 122–142.

Liberman, A. M., & Mattingly, I. G. (1985). The motor theory of speech perception revised. *Cognition, 21,* 1–36.

Linde, C., & Labov, W. (1975). Spatial networks as a site for the study of language and thought. *Language, 51,* 924–939.

Marslen-Wilson, W. (1989). Access and integration: Projecting sound onto meaning. In W. D. Marslen-Wilson (Ed.) *Lexical representation and process* (pp. 3–24). Cambridge, MA: Massachusetts Institute of Technology Press.

Marslen-Wilson, W., & Tyler, L. (1980). The temporal structure of spoken language understanding. *Cognition, 8,* 1–71.

Miller, G. A. (1991). *The science of words.* New York: Scientific American Library.

Morrow, D. G. (1986). Places as referents in discourse. *Journal of Memory and Language, 25,* 676–690.

Nicol, J., & Swinney, D. (1989). The role of structure in coreference assignment during sentence comprehension. *Journal of Psycholinguistic Research, 18,* 5–19.

Nunberg, G. (1979). The non-uniqueness of semantic solutions: Polysemy. *Linguistics and Philosophy, 3,* 143–184.

Pisoni, D. B., & Luce, P. A. (1987). Acoustic-phonetic representations in word recognition. *Cognition, 25,* 21–52.

Poizner, H., Klima, E. S., & Bellugi, U. (1987). *What the hands reveal about the brain.* Cambridge, MA: Massachusetts Institute of Technology Press.

Rayner, K., & Pollatsek, A. (1989). *The psychology of reading.* Englewood Cliffs, NJ: Prentice-Hall.

Roelofs, A. (1992). A spreading-activation theory of lemma retrieval in speaking. *Cognition, 42,* 107–142.

Sacks, H., Schegloff, E. A., & Jefferson, G. (1974). A simplest systematics for the organization of turn-taking in conversation. *Language, 50,* 696–735.

Saltzman, E., & Kelso, J. A. S. (1987). Skilled action: A task-dynamic approach. *Psychological Review, 94,* 84–106.

Seuren, P. A. M. (1985). *Discourse semantics.* Oxford: Basil Blackwell.

Shattuck-Hufnagel, S. (1979). Speech errors as evidence for a serial-ordering mechanism in sentence production. In W. E. Cooper & E. C. T. Walker (Eds) *Sentence processing: Psycholinguistic studies presented to Merrill Garrett* (pp. 295–342). Hillsdale, NJ: Lawrence Erlbaum.

Sperber, D., & Wilson, D. (1986). *Relevance: Communication and cognition.* Oxford: Basil Blackwell.

Sternberg, S., Wright, C. E., Knoll, R. L., & Monsell, S. (1980). Motor programs in rapid speech: Additional evidence. In R. A. Cole (Ed.) *Perception and production of fluent speech* (pp. 507–534). Hillsdale, NJ: Lawrence Erlbaum.

Stevens, K. N., & Blumstein, S. E. (1981). The search for invariant acoustic correlates of phonetic features. In P. D. Eimas & J. L. Miller (Eds) *Perspectives on the study of speech* (pp. 1–38). Hillsdale, NJ: Lawrence Erlbaum.

Tyler, L., & Warren, P. (1987). Local and global structure in spoken language comprehension. *Journal of Memory and Language, 26,* 638–657.

Wundt, W. (1900). *Die Sprache* (2 vols). Leipzig: Kröner.

Zwitserlood, P. (1989). The effects of sentential-semantic context in spoken-word processing. *Cognition, 32,* 25–64.

4.4

THINKING AND REASONING

Jonathan St B. T. Evans
University of Plymouth, Plymouth, England

The nature of human thought and the capacity for rational reasoning have been issues of great interest to philosophers and psychologists since the time of Aristotle. Humans have excelled among species in their ability to solve problems and to adapt their environment for their own purposes. We are unique in our possession of a highly sophisticated system of language allowing both representation of complex and abstract concepts and the communication of very precise meaning with one another. We have also developed a new form of evolution — much faster than natural selection — whereby the accumulated knowledge and wisdom of our culture is recorded and passed on through education so that each new generation starts with an advantage on the one before. Despite this impressive record, we also are subject to many systematic errors and biases in our thinking, some of which are discussed in this chapter.

The study of thinking and reasoning in humans can accurately be described as the study of the nature of intelligence. The work described here falls, however, into a quite different tradition from the psychometric study of individual differences in intelligent performance that is usually referred to as the psychology of intelligence. Psychometrics is concerned with the measurement of intelligent performance, whereas the study of thinking and reasoning is focused on understanding the nature of intelligent processes. Strangely enough, these turn out to be two quite different kinds of undertaking.

THE NATURE OF THINKING: AN HISTORICAL PERSPECTIVE

Historically, we can trace three different conceptions of the nature of thinking. The first of these corresponds to what the non-psychologist might respond if asked to define thought. I shall describe this notion as the *contents of consciousness*. Common sense (or *folk* psychology) supposes that we are consciously in control of our actions: we think, therefore we do. When we make a decision or solve a problem it is on the basis of a train of thought of which we are conscious and which we can, if required, describe to another. Such reports of thought are known as *introspections*. The validity of introspection is clearly assumed in our everyday folk psychology, as we all feel able to ask and answer questions about how and why we have taken particular actions. Indeed, a major industry – opinion polling – is based upon introspectionism. Politicians and political commentators alike are absorbed by the results of polls that ask people not only how they intend to vote, but also to identify the issues which will influence their decisions.

Aristotle and other early philosophers were in no doubt that the mind could and should study itself through introspection. This led to a theory of thinking known as *associationism* in which thinking was supposed to consist of a sequence of images linked by one of several principles (see Mandler & Mandler, 1964). Associationism and the equation of thought with consciousness remained more or less unchallenged until the late nineteenth and early twentieth centuries when several separate developments conspired to challenge this idea.

First, there were the systematic experimental studies of introspection carried out at the Würzburg School around the beginning of the twentieth century (see Humphrey, 1951). In these experiments, subjects were asked to perform simple cognitive acts such as giving word associations or judging the comparative weight of two objects and then asked to report on what went through their minds at the time. Much to the initial surprise of the researchers, many of these acts did not appear to be mediated by conscious thoughts. Subjects often reported either no conscious experience at all, or else one of indescribable or "imageless" thought.

A second influential development was that of the Freudian school of psychoanalysis which introduced the notion of unconscious thought and motivation. An introspective report of the reason for an action would certainly be suspect to a Freudian since it might well constitute a *rationalization* of behaviour determined by deep-seated and repressed emotions in the unconscious mind.

The other major influence was the introduction of the school of behaviourism by J. B. Watson (e.g., 1920) whose influence was very strong in

339

psychology up until the 1950s and which lingers on even in the present day. Watson attacked all study of conscious thought as mentalistic and unscientific. Science, he maintained, could concern itself only with the study of phenomena that were subject to objective observation and independent verification – criteria that introspective reports clearly could not meet. Watson and other behaviourists effectively redefined thought as simply complex forms of behaviour which were the result of stimulus–response learning. Study of stimulus–response pairings and reinforcement history were sufficient to explain all phenomena attributed – by the mentalistically inclined – to thinking.

From the viewpoint of a modern cognitive psychologist both introspectionists and behaviourists might be seen as half right. The behaviourists were probably right in their contention that thought cannot be studied effectively via introspection. The mentalists, on the other hand, were correct in asserting that complex behaviour could not be explained without reference to internal mental processes. Their mistake – with the benefit of hindsight – was to assume that such processes were necessarily conscious and reportable. This leads us to the third conception of human thought – that of *information processing*.

Psychologists' own thinking – like that of their subjects – is constrained by the availability of models and analogies. Watson used the analogy of a telephone exchange to explain his notion of learning by stimulus–response connections. Although its origin can be traced to earlier, highly creative thinkers (especially Craik, 1943) the emergence of cognitive psychology in the 1950s and 1960s was largely due to the development of cybernetic systems and then the digital computer. Computers are general-purpose information processing systems. They compute by manipulating symbols which can represent almost anything – numbers and arithmetical operators, permitting arithmetic; letters and words as in word and text processing; collections of facts stored in a database; and so on.

When people perform mental arithmetic, we would describe this as an act of thought. So is a computer also thinking when it performs computations to solve problems? It appears that it is, although some philosophers (e.g., Searle, 1980) maintain that computer intelligence is intrinsically different from that of the human mind. The point of the analogy, however, is that we can see that computers can perform complex acts of information processing – depending upon their programming – but without any need to assume that they are conscious. Once you equate thinking with information processing, then the task of the modern cognitive psychologist is clear: understanding thought is the problem of discovering the software of the human brain. Many psychological theories in fact are formulated as working computer programs which attempt to simulate the behaviour of a human being who is solving a problem or engaged in some other cognitive activity.

In spite of this advance, arguments persist among cognitive and social

340

psychologists as to the value of introspective reports. Some cognitive psychologists disregard them entirely on the basis of much evidence that such reports can be both incomplete and misleading (Nisbett & Wilson, 1977). One interesting line of argument is that verbal reports *are* useful indicators of thought processes but not as used in the tradition of introspective reporting (Ericsson & Simon, 1980). According to this view, verbalizations are the *products* of cognitive processes and can be fruitfully interpreted by the psychologist when subjects are asked to "think aloud" while performing a task or solving a problem. Introspective reports fail because first, they are retrospective rather than concurrent, and second, they invite subjects to describe their thinking or to theorize about the causes of their behaviour.

The psychology of thinking can be broadly defined to cover a wide range of topics. For example, Gilhooly (1982) distinguishes between *directed thinking* – as found in problem solving and reasoning – *undirected thinking* – as in day-dreaming – and *creative thinking*. In this chapter we shall focus on directed thinking: thought aimed at achieving specific goals. This is an area in which reasonable theoretical progress has been made, and for which there are clear practical applications in everyday life.

Studies of directed thinking fall broadly into three main areas which are described as problem solving, reasoning, and decision-making. We shall consider each in turn.

PROBLEM SOLVING

A person has a problem whenever he or she wishes to achieve a goal and is unable to proceed immediately to do so. Problem solving consists of finding a method of getting from where you are to where you want to be, using such resources and knowledge as you have available. This definition obviously covers a vast range of human activity; problem solving is clearly involved in solving crossword puzzles and choosing chess moves, but it is equally involved in finding your way to a new destination, obtaining a ticket for a sold-out sporting contest, or working out how to persuade your boss to give you a pay rise.

One distinction which has helped psychologists think about the vast range of behaviours involved in problem solving is that between well-defined and ill-defined problems. In a well-defined problem, all the information needed and the means of solution are available at the outset. This is typical of things that are set as "problems" in newspapers, and so on, and also typical of much research in the psychological laboratory. An anagram is an example of a well-defined problem. You know the letters that constitute the solution word and also the means of solving the problem – rearrangement of the order of letters – at the outset. Well-defined problem solving thus consists of applying known rules to known information in order to transform the situation and achieve the goal.

341

Some of the most famous studies of well-defined problem solving were conducted by Newell and Simon (1972). An example of one of their problems is cryptarithmetic, in which subjects were given the following problem:

DONALD
+ GERALD

= ROBERT

Subjects are also told that D = 5 and that each letter represents a single digit number between 0 and 9. Given this information and the assumption that the normal rules of arithmetic apply, it is possible – though complicated – to work out what all the letter–number pairings must be. If the reader wishes to attempt this problem, then it is suggested that a good record (on paper) of the sequence of attempts – including errors and correction – be kept.

Newell and Simon (1972) made an important theoretical contribution with the idea of problem solving as a search through a *problem space*. A problem space consists of a number of linked *states* including an initial or starting state and one or more goal states. All problems include *permissible operators* which allows one state to be transformed to another. Thus, solving problem consists in applying operators repeatedly to transform the initial state into a goal state.

As an example consider the game of chess (also studied by Newell & Simon, 1972). The states of the game can be described as the position of the pieces on the board plus some additional information (whose turn is it to move, do players have the right to castle, may a pawn be captured *en passant*, and so on). The initial state is thus the board with the pieces in starting position with White having the right to move. A goal state is any position in which the player has won the game either by checkmating the opponent or making such a mate inevitable. The permissible operators are the laws of chess, which determine the moves that can legally be made in a given situation.

Note that these definitions tell us nothing about the strategy of chess. The problem space consists of all states that can be reached by legal moves – a vast number of possibilities in the case of chess. The strategy of the game obviously consists in choosing between alternative legal moves in such a way as to move towards the goal state of a winning position. In chess, as in many other problems, the problem space is too large for an exhaustive search to be feasible. You cannot consider all moves and all possible replies to more than a very few moves ahead without the number of possible positions becoming enormous. Thus Newell and Simon (1972) emphasize the importance of *heuristic* strategies. An heuristic is a short-cut, rule of thumb method which may lead to a quick solution, but which may also fail. What heuristics do is to drastically reduce the size of the problem space to be searched in the hope that the goal state is not excluded in the process.

Consider the following anagram: GBANRIEK. Since it has eight letters the total problem space includes the 8! = 40,320 possible rearrangements of the letters. A guaranteed, *algorithmic* (i.e., exhaustive search) method of solving this involves constructing all 40,320 letter strings and checking whether each is a word. A typical heuristic method, on the other hand, might involve looking for familiar letter patterns to decompose the problem. For example, we note that the anagram includes the letters I, N, and G and speculate that the word might be of the form ___ING. Thus we have now reduced the problem to solving the five-letter anagram BAREK which has only 5! (120) possible solutions and is thus much easier. We may now spot the solution word BREAKING. Like all heuristics, however, this was not guaranteed to work. Many words contain the letters ING in other configurations, e.g., GELATIN.

Problem space analysis is extremely useful as it provides a common framework in which to describe a very wide range of different problems. Newell and Simon (1972) studied subjects using think-aloud protocols while solving problems such as the cryptarithmetic example given above. They concluded that people have sets of general-purpose problem solving strategies that are used in similar ways to search problem spaces, no matter what particular domain is involved. They implemented their theory in a working computer program called General Problem Solver that was claimed to solve the same problems as the human subjects and in a similar way.

Important though this work has been, the conclusions are somewhat questionable. The first difficulty is that most real-life problems are ill defined. Some aspect of the problem – the information assumed, the means of solution, sometimes even the goal – is incomplete or missing at the outset. Take the case of engineering design which was subjected to detailed psychological study by Ball, Evans and Dennis (in press). An engineer is given a general specification for a device which includes its functionality – what it must do – and a number of constraints, including costs. The engineer must then come up with a technical specification for a device which can be constructed and can be demonstrated to work.

As Ball discovered, such problems are not at all well defined. Nearly all the information required to solve the problem is implicit and must be retrieved either from the existing knowledge and experience of the engineer or by researching technical manuals, and so on. In the process of design, constraints emerge that were not apparent at the outset. The goal initially set may also be modified and rethought as the work progresses. Now such activity can still be usefully described within the problem space framework – a space that is being continually augmented and redefined by the knowledge and experience of the engineer. However, the point is that simply applying the problem space description provides no explanation for some of the most important aspects of the process, particularly the means by which prior knowledge and experience are retrieved and applied.

343

A number of more recent studies of human problem solving have focused on ill-defined problems and the use of prior knowledge. Of particular interest has been the role of analogy in solving problems (see Gick & Holyoak, 1980, 1983; Keane, 1988). Most real-life problem solving – including "expert" problem solving – occurs within contexts where the solver has previous experience. Clearly, people do not solve all such problems as if seen for the first time; they must extrapolate from past experience. The theoretical and practical interest lies in how they actually bring their prior knowledge to bear.

A problem that has featured in many of these studies is the *tumour problem* first introduced by the Gestalt psychologist Duncker (1945). The problem is that of a patient who has a malignant but inoperable tumour that can be destroyed only by radiation. However, the radiation destroys healthy tissue at the same rate as diseased tissue. The solution that subjects must find is to use a lens to converge the rays at the point of the tumour. Hence, the rays accumulate only to sufficient intensity to destroy the tumour and not the healthy tissue they pass through on the way (see Figure 1).

The problem is incompletely defined in that while the goal and constraints are generally indicated, subjects must search their knowledge and imagination for possible means of solution. General knowledge of medical procedures is unhelpful; surgery is out by definition; drug treatments are of no relevance. The problem can, however, be facilitated by provision of a structural analogue such as the General story. The General is trying to attack a fortress which is well defended and which may be reached by a number of different roads. Each road is mined and may be safely crossed only by a small band of men. The General splits his force into small groups which approach

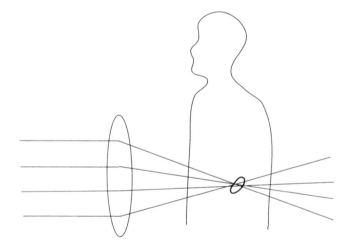

Figure 1 Solution to Duncker's tumour problem

simultaneously from different directions, and converge at the fortress with sufficient force to win the battle.

Gick and Holyoak (1980) showed that presentation of the General story could facilitate convergence solutions to the tumour problem provided that subjects were given a cue as to its relevance. There is a theoretical argument as to whether analogies can work by direct mapping of the elements of the analogy on to the problem, or whether the solution is mediated by an abstract *schema*. Gick and Holyoak suggest that subjects may construct and apply a *convergence schema* which is defined in terms of variables. For example, in the schema the goal is to destroy an obstacle, the means is a sufficient force, the constraint is that direct application is blocked, and so on. The General story could lead to development of a schema which is applied to the tumour problem.

The notion of schema is a useful one, in that it helps us to understand how knowledge may be abstracted, generalized, and applied in new situations. The notion will recur in the discussion of reasoning to which we now turn.

REASONING

Reasoning is the process of drawing conclusions or inferences from given information. An important distinction is that between deductive and inductive inference. Deductive reasoning involves drawing conclusions that are logically valid, that is, they necessarily follow from the premises on which they are based. Thus such inferences do not increase the amount of information contained in the premises; they merely render explicit what was previously latent information. The following are examples of valid deductive inferences:

> The television will work only if it is plugged into the mains;
> The television is not plugged into the mains,
> Therefore, the television will not work.
>
> John is taller than Jim;
> Paul is shorter than Jim,
> Therefore, John is taller than Paul.

The validity of the first example does not depend in any way on our knowledge of television sets, but only on our understanding of the connective "only if". Any argument of the form *p only if q; not-q, therefore not-p* would be logically valid no matter what propositions we substitute for *p* and *q*. Hence, validity depends on the form of the argument, not its actual content. In logic, the statement *p only if q* cannot be true in a world where *p* is the case and *q* is not the case. Hence, once we know that *q* is false we can infer that *p* must be false as well.

The second example requires us to know that the relation taller–shorter is *transitive*. A transitive relation is one where the objects are ordered in a single line so that whenever *A* is higher than *B* on the scale, and *B* is above *C* then *A* is also above *C*. Examples of other transitive relations are better–worse, warmer–colder, and darker–lighter. Many relations, of course, are not transitive. If *A* is next to *B* and *B* is next to *C* it does not follow that *A* is next to *C*.

Deductive inferences are very important in intelligent thinking as they allow knowledge to be stored in generalities and then applied to particular situations. Thus if we want to watch television and discover one that is unplugged, we immediately plug it in. This is a simple example of reasoning in order to solve a problem. The limitation of deductive reasoning, however, is that it adds no new knowledge; thus we cannot learn by deduction. Induction is involved whenever our conclusion has more information than the premises. A typical example is an inductive generalization such as

> The Australian soap operas I have seen were boring, hence all Australian soap operas are boring.

Such an inference is clearly not logically valid, though it could well influence what you watch when you get the TV plugged in.

The British psychologist, Peter Wason, invented two famous problems that have been used extensively to study both inductive and deductive reasoning. The inductive problem was first published by Wason (1960) and is known as the "2 4 6" task. The subjects are told that the experimenter has a rule in mind which applies to "triples" of three whole numbers. An example which conforms to the rule is "2 4 6". The subjects are then asked to discover the rule by generating triples of their own. In each case the experimenter says whether the triple conforms or not. Subjects are told to announce the rule only when they are very sure that they know it.

The actual rule is "any ascending sequence" but the subject is induced by the example to form a more specific hypothesis, such as "ascending with equal intervals". Most subjects have great difficulty in solving the problem initially because all the examples they test appear to conform to the rule. The reason is that subjects test positive examples of their hypothesis which invariably turn out to be positive examples of the experimenter's rule as well. Their hypothesis can be refuted only by testing a negative example of the hypothesis such as "1 2 4" which is revealed as a positive instance of the actual rule. The set relationships involved are shown in Figure 2.

The protocols discussed by Wason (1960) were very interesting, suggesting that some subjects became so convinced of the correctness of their hypotheses that they were led to reformulate the proposed rule in different terms when told it was wrong. A striking example of this is shown in Table 1.

Wason's interpretation of his findings was that subjects have a confirmation bias, meaning that they systematically seek out evidence that confirms rather than refutes their current hypothesis. He suggested that such a confirmation bias is a very general tendency in human thought which may

346

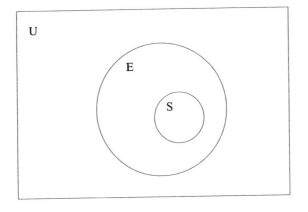

U   Universal set of all triples
E   Experimenter's rule – all
    triples in ascending sequence
S   Subjects' hypothesis, e.g.,
    ascending with equal intervals

Figure 2 Set relationships in Wason's 2 4 6 task

Table 1 Example protocol from Wason (1960)

8 10 12: two added each time; 14 16 18: even numbers in order or magnitude; 20 22 24: same reason; 1 3 5: two added to preceding number.

The rule is that by starting with any number two is added each time to form the next number.

2 6 10: middle number is arithmetic mean of other two; 1 50 99: same reason

The rule is that the middle number is the arithmetic mean of the outer two.

3 10 17: same number, seven, added each time; 0 3 6: three added each time.

The rule is that the difference between two numbers next to each other is the same.

12 8 4: the same number subtracted each time to form the next number.

The rule is adding a number, always the same one, to form the next number.

1 4 9: any three numbers in order of magnitude.

The rule is any three numbers in order of magnitude.

(17 minutes)

account for the maintenance of prejudice and false belief. While a number of authors have accepted this interpretation, it has also been subject to serious challenge (see Evans, 1989; Klayman & Ha, 1987).

The problem is that the subjects in the "2 4 6" experiment have no way of knowing that a positive test cannot lead to refutation of their hypothesis, and in many real-world situations it would do so. For example, in science it is customary to formulate general hypotheses and test if they apply to specific cases. Hence, given the hypothesis "All metals expand when heated" you would test any untried metal to see if the prediction holds – and if it did not you would indeed refute the hypothesis. You would not be likely to try heating non-metal things, and even if you did and they expanded, it would mean only that your rule was insufficiently general.

Arguments such as these have led some authors to suggest that subjects' behaviour on the "2 4 6" is more rational than it at first appears and that if there is a bias, it is towards positive testing rather than to confirmation as such. A particularly interesting experiment reported by Tweney, Doherty, and Mynatt (1980) provides evidence for this. In one study, instead of defining instances in positive and negative terms (right/wrong, belonging/not-belonging) they told subjects that all triples were either MEDs or DAXes and that "2 4 6" was an example of a MED. What happened was that subjects continued to test their hypotheses positively but alternated between testing MED and DAX hypotheses. For example, if the hypothesis was that "triples ascending in equal intervals are MEDs and others are DAXes", then they might test "1 2 5" predicting it to be a DAX. This meant that they effectively tested negative examples of the usual hypothesis and hence solved the problem much more easily. The psychological difference is that the negative test of MED was construed as a positive test of DAX.

A close parallel to these findings occurs with the second and most famous of Wason's problems – the four-card selection task (see Evans, Newstead and Byrne 1993 for detailed review and discussion). This problem requires subjects to test hypotheses via deductive reasoning. In the classic "abstract" version of the task, subjects are told that a set of cards always has a capital letter on one side and a single-figure number on the the other side. They are then shown four such cards lying on a table with the exposed values as shown in Figure 3. The subjects are told that the following rule may be true or false:

If there is an A on one side of the card then there is a 3 on the other side of the card.

The subjects' task is to turn over those cards – and only those cards – that are needed to decide whether the rule is true or false. The task is deceptively simple, since most subjects fail to solve it. The common answers given are A alone, or A and 3. The correct answer is the A and the 7. The reason is that the rule can be shown to be false only if there is an A on one side of a card and number other than a 3 on the other. Only by turning the A and the 7 (not a 3) is it possible to discover such a card. There is also no point

Figure 3 The four cards displayed in a version of Wason's selection task

in turning the 3 since the rule makes no claim that an A must be on the back of a 3.

Wason's original claim was again that card selections reflected a confirmation bias: subjects were trying to prove the rule true rather than false, that is, looking for the combination A and 3, rather than A and not-3. This view was, however, refuted to the satisfaction of Wason as well as other authors by the finding of "matching bias" reported by Evans and Lynch (1973). They pointed out that the preferred selections, A and 3, were not only the verifying choices, but also the positive choices matching the items named in the actual rule. Verification and matching could, however, be separated by introducing negative components into the rule. Consider for example, the rule

If there is an A on one side of the card then there is NOT a 3 on the other side of the card

If subjects have a confirmation bias, then they should now choose the A and the 7 which confirm the two parts of the rule. If, however, they have a matching bias then they should continue to choose A and 3 which are the correct and *falsifying* combination on this rule. Subjects do, in fact, continue to choose predominantly matching values on this and other variants of the rule, thus confirming the predictions of Evans and Lynch. Evans (1989) regards matching as an example of a generalized *positivity bias*, that is, bias to think about positively defined items, which also accounts for subjects' behaviour on the "2 4 6" task.

Dozens of experiments have been published – and continue to be published – in which subjects are asked to solve versions of the Wason selection task. Most of these have been concerned with the so-called thematic materials facilitation effect. This has its origin in two early studies discussed in Wason and Johnson-Laird's (1972) famous textbook on reasoning. In one of these (Johnson-Laird, Legrenzi, & Legrenzi, 1972) subjects were shown envelopes in place of cards, together with the following Postal Rule:

If the letter is sealed then it has a 50 lire stamp on it.

Subjects were then shown four envelopes which were either front side up and showing a 50 or 40 lire stamp, or rear side up showing that they were sealed or unsealed (see Figure 4). The subjects had to decide which envelopes to turn

349

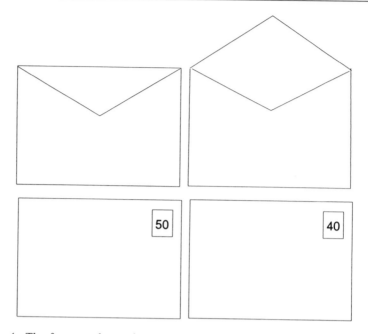

Figure 4 The four envelopes shown to subjects in the Postal Rule version of the selection task

over in order to decide if the rule was true or false. The usual matching response on the abstract task would lead to choice of the sealed envelope and the 50 lire stamp. However, almost all subjects made the logically correct choice of the sealed envelope and the one showing a 40 lire stamp.

The original interpretation offered of this and other similar experiments was that use of thematic materials facilitated logical reasoning on the task. This view has been considerably refined by subsequent research, however. The problem with the Postal Rule is that a very similar rule (involving pence rather than lire) was in force in the UK at the time of the study. Thus it was argued that subjects knew from experience that envelopes with a lower value stamp must not be sealed and that hence no "reasoning" as such was required to solve the problem. This argument was supported by the findings of several later studies which showed that first, the Postal Rule produces no facilitation of performance in American subjects unfamiliar with such a rule, and second, British subjects too young to remember the rule (it was dropped in the 1970s) show no facilitation on the problem whereas older subjects perform much better.

It is not the case, however, that subjects must have direct experience of the context in order for a problem content to facilitate on the selection task. A very effective version, for example, is the Sears Problem in which subjects are asked to play the role of a store manager checking that a company rule has been followed. The rule is

If a purchase exceeds $30, then the receipt must be approved by the departmental manager.

Subjects are shown four receipts, two of which are front side up showing totals of above and below $30 and two of which are front side down and either have or do not have the signature of the departmental manager on them. Few subjects have any difficulty in correctly deciding to turn over the receipt for more than $30, and the one that has *not* been signed by the manager. This is despite the fact that subjects have not worked as managers in department stores.

While arguments exist about the precise reason for facilitation of performance by these kinds of thematic content, the general idea is that where subjects have either direct or analogous experience that can be linked to the problem, then they can solve it. Another line of argument is that it is the introduction of deontic terms such as *may* and *must* which carry with them notions of permission and obligation that causes the facilitation. The idea is that we have generalized reasoning schemas that enable us to understand the logic of any situation in which, for example, a precondition is set for an action. Thus, once we have identified the action (e.g., sealing an envelope, spending over $30) and the precondition (sufficient value stamp, permission of departmental manager) we know what to do: we are applying a generalized permission schema to the problem at hand.

The two problems of Peter Wason discussed in this section have stimulated much interesting psychological work on the nature of human reasoning. The specific findings discussed here invite two general conclusions: first, that reasoning with "abstract" problem material is heavily biased by a tendency to think about positively rather than negatively defined information, and second, that the introduction of thematic problem content, and hence associated prior knowledge, can have a dramatic effect on the reasoning observed, and sometimes produces much better logical performance. The "sometimes" in the latter conclusion is needed. Other research, which there is no space to discuss here, has also indicated that prior knowledge can be a source of bias and error in reasoning. This is especially the case when subjects are asked to evaluate the logic of an argument but have strong prior beliefs about the truth of a conclusion (see Evans, 1989, chap. 4).

DECISION MAKING AND STATISTICAL JUDGEMENT

In a problem solving task, it is normally possible to work out and demonstrate a solution to the problem set. Once you have the solution, you know it and can prove it. In a decision-making task, however, subjects are required to exercise judgement about a choice that will only later prove to work out

351

well or badly. Decision-making means committing yourself to choices between actions by anticipation of what the outcomes will – or may – be. Thus when we make any decision – to accept one job rather than another, to marry someone or not, go to a football match rather than stay at home – we do so in the hope that the future we chose was to be preferred to the one we avoided.

Decision-making is obviously of great importance in the real world, but it is a subject of considerable psychological interest too. Most real-world decision-making is done under conditions of uncertainty: we do not know for sure what will happen as a result of each choice and at best can try to estimate the probabilities of different outcomes. If we are to choose rationally then we need to evaluate the desirability of these outcomes as well. In the parlance of decision theory, we should try to maximize *expected utility* where utility is the subjective value of the outcome and where the term "expectation" means that we weight the various possible outcomes by their likelihood of occurring. Hence, a small chance of a highly desirable outcome might be equally attractive to a much better prospect of a less desirable outcome.

There has been much debate in the psychological literature about whether people choose rationally or not. The notion of rational choice has several components. First, it implies that people will consciously consider the various actions available to them and try to project ahead the possible outcomes and further choices to which they lead in what is termed a *decision tree*. Second, it is assumed that they assign probabilities and utilities to each of these outcomes as accurately as possible in the light of their current beliefs. Finally, rational decision-makers are assumed to apply systematic principles, such as the maximization of expected utility, in order to decide their final choices.

There are many demonstrations of human choice behaviour that appear to depart from this idealized notion. Within the space restriction here I shall discuss just one aspect – the ability of people to judge probabilities or to reason statistically. A famous set of papers by the psychologists Amos Tversky and Daniel Kahneman dating from the early 1970s have apparently demonstrated the frailty of human probability judgement. This research is often cited as evidence of irrationality, although Tversky and Kahneman themselves follow the tradition of work on "bounded rationality" espoused by Newell and Simon (1972). The idea is that people cannot base their probability judgements on probability theory due its computational complexity and instead employ short-cut rules of thumb known as *heuristics*. While often useful, such heuristics can also lead to systematic errors and biases.

Of the heuristics discussed by Kahneman and Tversky, the two most famous are those of *representativeness* and *availability* (see Kahneman, Slovic, & Tversky, 1982 for a collection of relevant papers, including the seminal ones). Probability or frequency of an event is estimated by the availability heuristic when people base their judgement on the ease with which examples can be brought to mind. Such a heuristic would often be effective.

For example, an experienced doctor might base a provisional diagnosis on her recollection of the numbers of previous cases or patients with similar symptoms who turned out to suffer from a particular condition. Assuming that memory was accurate and that experience was representative then this is a good, if rough basis for a judgement.

As Tversky and Kahneman have demonstrated, however, relying on availability of recalled examples can lead to biases. For example, some types of information are easier to retrieve than others, due to the way in which memory is organized. For example, most people will say, if asked, that there are more words in English that start with the letter k than those that have k as the third letter, although the reverse is true. The problem is that it is hard to generate examples of the latter category: they cannot easily be "brought to mind".

Availability is also implicated in biases which preserve false beliefs and theories. An interesting example is the phenomenon of *illusory correlation*. It has been demonstrated in a number of studies that human judges – including experts – hold theories that are not supported by the evidence they encounter. For example, some clinicians maintain that projective personality tests such as the Rorschach ink blot test is useful in diagnosing mental illness despite a lack of any supporting evidence. Research has shown that such judges perceive a correlation between test results and diagnoses in a set of data in which they are in fact randomly related. A plausible explanation of illusory correlation is that the judges selectively remember the cases that confirm their expectations or pet theories. Thus confirming cases are more available in later recall and bias the judgement of the correlation.

The representativeness heuristic is involved in judgements of conditional probability. The likelihood of a sample given a population, or of an event given a hypothesis is dependent upon the perceived similarity of the two. Similarity judgements may, however, cause the subject to overlook the relevance of a critical statistical feature such as the size of the sample, or the base rate occurrence of the event. A simple example is provided by the conjunction fallacy (Tversky & Kahneman, 1983). Subjects are given a description of Bill as follows:

Bill is . . .

They are then asked to rank the likelihood of several statements including the following:

a Bill is an accountant
b Bill plays jazz for a hobby
c Bill is an accountant who plays jazz for a hobby.

What happens is that most subjects rate the order of likelihood of these statements as $a > c > b$. However, there is a statistical impossibility here in that statement c cannot be more likely than statement b. Given two events A and

B the probability of them both occurring – $P(A \cap B)$ – must be less than or equal to the probability of either $P(A)$ or $P(B)$. Whenever *c* is true then *b* is true as well, because Bill plays jazz for a hobby. If all jazz players were accountants then the two statements would be equally likely, otherwise *b* has to be more probable.

The explanation offered for the fallacy is that the description of Bill conforms to our stereotype for accountants but not for jazz players. Thus the statement *c* is more representative of the description than is statement *b* and hence judged more probable.

One of the most famous of Kahneman and Tversky's problems is the Cabs Problem. You are given the following information: in a certain city there are two cab companies: the Blue cab company, which has 85 per cent of the city's cabs, and the Green cab company, which has 15 per cent of the city's cabs. A cab is involved in a hit-and-run accident and a witness later identified the cab as a Green one. Under tests the witness was shown to be able to identify the colour of a cab correctly about 80 per cent of the time under comparable viewing conditions. The subjects are asked if the cab involved in the accident is more likely to have been Green or Blue. Most say Green, although the correct answer is Blue.

The problem is that subjects disregard the base rate or prior probability of the cab colour – 85 : 15 in favour of Blue. In fact, when asked to give a numerical estimate, most subjects say 80 per cent Green – the chance of the witness correctly identifying a cab. If there were no witnesses, it would be obvious that the chance of the cab being Blue was 85 per cent – the base rate. As Figure 5 shows, however, the chance of a Blue cab being identified as Green is 17 per cent which is still higher than the chance (12 per cent) of a Green cab being identified as Green.

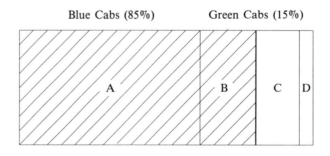

Blue Cabs (85%)   Green Cabs (15%)

A   Probability of Blue identified as Blue   = 80% × 85% = 68%
B   Probability of Blue identified as Green   = 20% × 85% = 17%
C   Probability of Green identified as Green = 80% × 15% = 12%
D   Probability of Green identified as Blue   = 20% × 15% = 3%

Figure 5 Probabilities in the Cabs Problem

Originally, the base rate fallacy was interpreted as the base rate lacking representativeness, although the explanation is probably more fundamental. We find it very difficult to apply abstract statistics to individual cases. Hence, many cigarette smokers are aware of the statistical risks for smokers as a whole, but do not feel that this affects them as individuals. However, we can apply statistics when we see a causal connection. If the cabs problem is slightly reworded, most subjects give the right answer. In this version the number of Green and Blue cabs in the city is the same, but 85 per cent of the cabs *involved in accidents* are Blue. The image of reckless Blue cab drivers conjured up induces subjects to take account of the base rate, although from a statistical point of view the problem is unchanged.

CONCLUSIONS

Psychological research on thinking and reasoning has produced some useful – and sometimes surprising – conclusions. The common-sense view, that intelligent actions are based on conscious and rational acts of thinking, does not fit the evidence at all well. If thought is to be defined as the information processing that underlies problem solving, reasoning, and decision-making, then surprisingly little of this appears to be accessible through introspection.

If human thinking is rational – and the success of the species suggests that it should be – then that rationality is highly constrained by our capacity to process information. In particular, we seem to solve problems and make decisions largely on the basis of heuristic processes which serve us well in some circumstances, but lead us into error and bias in others. We seem to have particular difficulty in understanding probability and uncertainty despite the crucial role that this plays in rational decision-making.

Studies of reasoning also show that we are prone to biases, for example in a strong preference for thinking about positively defined information. Perhaps the most important finding in this area, however, is the discovery that we do not – as was once thought – appear to reason by the use of an abstract mental logic, but instead seem to be highly influenced by the content and context of the problems with which we are faced. The processes of human thought appear to be quite specific to the areas of knowledge which we are involved in applying.

FURTHER READING

Baron, J. (1988). *Thinking and deciding*. Cambridge: Cambridge University Press.
Evans, J. St B. T. (1989). *Bias in human reasoning: Causes and consequences*. Hove: Lawrence Erlbaum.
Johnson-Laird, P. N., & Byrne, R. M. J. (1991). *Deduction*. Hove: Lawrence Erlbaum.

Kahney, H. (1987). *Problem solving: A cognitive approach.* Milton Keynes: Open University Press.

Von Winderfeldt, D., & Edwards, W. (1986). *Decision analysis and human behavioural research.* Cambridge: Cambridge University Press.

REFERENCES

Ball, L. J., Evans, J. St B. T. and Dennis (in press). *Cognitive processes in engineering design: a longitudinal study (Ergonomics).* Unpublished PhD thesis, Polytechnic South West.

Craik, K. J. W. (1943). *The nature of explanation.* Cambridge: Cambridge University Press.

Duncker, K. (1945). On problem solving. *Psychological Monographs, 58,* whole no. 270.

Ericsson, K. A., & Simon, H. A. (1980). Verbal reports as data. *Psychological Review, 87,* 215–251.

Evans, J. St B. T. (1989). *Bias in human reasoning: Causes and consequences.* Hove and London: Lawrence Erlbaum.

Evans, J. St B. T., & Lynch, J. S. (1973). Matching bias in the selection task. *British Journal of Psychology, 64,* 391–397.

Evans, J. St B. T., Newstead, S. E. and Byrne R. M. J. (1993). *Human reasoning: The psychology of deduction.* Hove and London: Lawrence Erlbaum.

Gick, M. L., & Holyoak, K. J. (1980). Analogical problem solving. *Cognitive Psychology, 12,* 306–355.

Gick, M. L., & Holyoak, K. J. (1983). Schema induction and analogical transfer. *Cognitive Psychology, 15,* 1–38.

Gilhooly, K. J. G. (1982). *Thinking: Directed, undirected and creative.* London: Academic Press.

Humphrey, C. (1951). *Thinking: An introduction to its experimental psychology.* London: Methuen.

Johnson-Laird, P. N., Legrenzi, P., & Legrenzi, M. S. (1972). Reasoning and a sense of reality. *British Journal of Psychology, 63,* 395–400.

Kahneman, D., Slovic, P., & Tversky, A. (1982). *Judgment under uncertainty: Heuristics and biases.* Cambridge: Cambridge University Press.

Keane, M. T. (1988). *Analogical problem solving.* Chichester: Horwood.

Klayman, J., & Ha, Y.-W. (1987). Confirmation, disconfirmation and information in hypothesis testing. *Psychological Review, 94,* 211–228.

Mandler, J. M., & Mandler, G. (1964). *Thinking: From association to Gestalt.* New York: Wiley.

Newell A., & Simon, H. A. (1972). *Human problem solving.* Englewood Cliffs, NJ: Prentice-Hall.

Nisbett, R. E., & Wilson, T. D. (1977). Telling more than we can know: Verbal reports on mental processes. *Psychological Review, 84,* 231–295.

Nisbett, R. E., Fong, G. T., Lehman, D., & Cheng, P. W. (1987). Teaching reasoning. *Science, 238,* 625–631.

Searle, J. R. (1980). Minds, brains and programs. *Behavioral and Brain Sciences, 3,* 417–424.

Tversky, A., & Kahneman, D. (1983). Extensional vs intuitive reasoning: The conjunction fallacy in probability judgment. *Psychological Review, 90,* 293–315.

Tweney, R. D., Doherty, M. E., & Mynatt, C. R. (1981). *On scientific thinking.* New York: Columbia University Press.

Wason, P. C. (1960). On the failure to eliminate hypotheses in a conceptual task. *Quarterly Journal of Experimental Psychology*, *12*, 129–140.

Wason, P. C. (1966). Reasoning. In B. M. Foss (Ed.) *New horizons in psychology I* (pp. 135–151). Harmondsworth: Penguin.

Wason, P. C., & Johnson-Laird, P. N. (1972). *Psychology of reasoning: Structure and content*. London: Batsford.

Watson, J. B. (1920). *Behaviorism*. New York: Norton.

4.5

ARTIFICIAL INTELLIGENCE

Alan Garnham
University of Sussex, England

History	Applications
Knowledge representation	Philosophical issues
Vision	Artificial intelligence, cognitive
Thinking, reasoning, problem	psychology, and the future
solving	Further reading
Language	References
Learning	

Artificial intelligence, almost always known as AI, attempts to understand intelligent behaviour, in the broadest sense of that term, by getting computers to reproduce it. "Intelligent behaviour" is taken to include thinking, reasoning, and learning, and their prerequisites (perception, the mental representation of information, and the ability to use language). Indeed, much current work in AI is concerned with modelling aspects of behaviour that would not normally be thought of as requiring any special intelligence. As part of computer science, AI is separate from cognitive psychology, although there is a large overlap in subject area. The two come together (with, most importantly, linguistics and philosophy) in the multidisciplinary approach of cognitive science.

Although AI aims to understand human intelligence, it also aims to produce machines that behave intelligently, no matter what their underlying mechanism. However, although these machines may not model human behaviour, their construction may reflect principles that are useful in studying it.

HISTORY

Since AI depends on computers, it is a relatively new discipline: the name was first used in the mid-1950s, though a few years earlier, pioneers such as Alan Turing in Britain and Claude Shannon in the United States had worked out how to write chess-playing computer programs. The dream of mechanized thought has, of course, a much longer history. The philosophers Blaise Pascal (1623–1662) and Gottfried Leibniz (1646–1716) built small calculating machines, and conceived grander schemes for formalizing thought processes. Charles Babbage (1792–1871) came nearer to building a universal computing machine, but was foiled by the limitations of having to use mechanical parts. Real computers had to wait for electronic components – first vacuum tubes, then semiconductors.

A conference at Dartford College, New Hampshire, in 1956 effectively launched AI research, even though its organizers felt disappointed at the time. In retrospect, the most important line of research discussed at the conference was that of Allen Newell and Herbert Simon (see e.g., Newell, Shaw, & Simon, 1957) on human problem solving. They proposed the idea of a *heuristic* ("rule-of-thumb") procedure for solving problems, and they shunned a line of research based on modelling the properties of networks of brain cells, which only assumed major importance again 25 years later, in the guise of connectionism. Newell and Simon's *information processing* approach was the dominant one in the early days of AI, and it remained influential throughout the 1960s – the so-called *semantic information processing* era. There was, however, a subtle shift of emphasis from a formal analysis of tasks to one based on the meaning of the information being processed. Furthermore, in attempting to tackle broader problems, such as natural language understanding, AI researchers quickly discovered that everyday tasks depend on huge amounts of background knowledge. To keep programs manageable, they were made to work in limited domains, in particular BLOCKSWORLD – a tabletop with prismatic blocks on it. It was hoped that programs that worked in these limited domains would *scale up* to real situations. In practice they did not, and in retrospect it is often obvious why they could not.

The 1970s was a somewhat disappointing period in "traditional" areas of AI research. Indeed, in the UK the Lighthill report (Lighthill, 1972) concluded that AI should not be a priority area for research. The late 1970s saw four important developments. The first was a shift in interest from specific computer programs to general principles. To some extent this development was linked to the second, the emergence of cognitive science, in which AI techniques are used with the primary goal of developing general theories of cognition, rather than with the more applied ("engineering") goal of building intelligent machines. The third development was a shift in the research topics seen as central to AI. In particular, fifteen years of research on the first *expert systems* was beginning to have spectacular payoffs (in the domains of mathematics, medical diagnosis, and determining the structure of complex organic molecules) and suddenly everyone wanted to write an expert system. In the short term, this enthusiasm generated additional funding and research, but it soon became apparent that an expert system in one domain could not necessarily be used as a model for one in another domain. If expert systems showed that real applications had to come to grips with formalizing real knowledge (as opposed to knowledge about toy domains), they also showed that this task was a formidable one. The fourth development was the re-emergence of neural network modelling, of the kind that had been largely set aside by those who espoused the Newell and Simon information processing approach. Theoretical developments together with the availability of larger, faster computers suddenly saw this approach producing important and enticing results.

The 1980s saw the working out of these developments. Although all remain important, all have faced disappointments. It is very hard to make an expert system that replaces an expert, though much easier to write a program that helps one. And it is hard to generalize the lessons learned in one domain of expertise. Cognitive science has not integrated its subdisciplines as closely as was hoped, and neural network modelling has still to show that it can make significant contributions to modelling abilities that call for complex information processing, in particular high-level processes in language understanding and thinking and reasoning.

KNOWLEDGE REPRESENTATION

Intelligent behaviour requires information to be stored, either in a short-term store or a long-term store or, more usually, both. One of the primary tasks of AI is therefore to produce an account of how information is represented in an intelligent system.

We know that the human nervous system has many parts, and that those parts probably operate in different ways. Nevertheless, there are many attractions in proposing that all information is stored in the same format. It may not be the form of information storage that differentiates information processing systems, but the nature of the information and the purpose for which it is used. Partly for this reason, many AI researchers have been attracted to the idea that information should be stored using the logical language known as *first order predicate calculus* (FOPC), and extensions of it that incorporate reasoning about time and modality. An additional attraction of this proposal is that, at least in principle, FOPC is computationally tractable: given a FOPC database, other facts implied by that database can be generated automatically. Other systems of representation are either not known to have or known not to have this property.

Unfortunately, although FOPC appears to have desirable properties, in practice it is extremely cumbersome to use. Partly because of the uniformity of the representation, facts in a large FOPC database can be difficult to find. Similarly, although there is a well-established procedure for drawing inferences from facts in a FOPC database (the resolution method, Robinson, 1965), it very quickly gets bogged down in making all but the simplest inferences. Furthermore, inferences made from a FOPC database cannot be overridden by new information. Everyday inferences can – they are said to be *non-monotonic*. For example, if I know that John is 25 years old and lives in Los Angeles, I infer that he can drive. If I subsequently learn that he suffers from epilepsy, I would probably withdraw my previous conclusion. Since the late 1970s there have been several attempts to construct nonmonotonic logics, similar to FOPC but with additional rules of inference that violate monotonicity. There have also been attempts to formalize nonmonotonic reasoning in other ways. The idea of a truth maintenance system (TMS) (Doyle, 1979) has been important in many of these. A TMS stores information about the justification for beliefs held, and allows *dependency-dependent backtracking*, so that when a belief turns out to be false, the reasons why it was held can be accessed directly and reassessed. None of these attempts to handle non-monotonic reasoning has been entirely successful.

Partly as a result of problems with uniform representation systems, such as FOPC, many AI researchers have proposed non-uniform representations, which allow special procedures for manipulating certain types of information. One of the earliest, and best-known, non-uniform representations is semantic networks (Quillian, 1968). Semantic networks give a special place to the information represented in their links and, in particular, they allow efficient processing of taxonomic information. Quillian's original, and rather simple, networks have been extended and elaborated in various ways, and representation of information in network form has proved a recurrent theme in AI. More complex non-uniform representation schemes that are related to semantic networks include frames and scripts. Scripts represent stereotyped sequences of events, frames have several uses. In one, frames represent particular objects and types of object, and a more recent development is that of object-oriented programming languages. The first widely used object-oriented language was the AI language SMALLTALK. More recently object-oriented versions of the most important AI language, LISP, have appeared, and languages such as C now have object-oriented versions (C++). Indeed, one of the major applications of object-oriented programming is not in AI, but in the development of windows-based interfaces for personal computers and workstations, where windows are treated as objects.

In the framework of semantic networks, the spread of activation through a network is the principal method of extracting information from it. This process has usually been simulated on a serial computer, but it ought to be achieved more efficiently on parallel hardware. Indeed, one of the most important parallel processing computers, the Connection Machine (not to be confused with connectionist neural nets), was inspired by Scott Fahlman's

(1979) suggestion for implementing semantic networks on special hardware. The idea of distributed processing is also found in neural network models of cognitive processing. Neural networks also allow, though they do not demand, distributed representations of the knowledge embodied in them. In particular, those neural networks that *learn* to perform tasks, rather than having information encoded into them by the programmer, are likely to develop distributed representations. Such networks show rule-governed behaviour as an emergent property, and the only way to determine exactly what rules such a network is following is to examine the relation between its inputs and its outputs.

There are many things we cannot be sure of, so a further issue in knowledge representation is the encoding and use of uncertain information. Inferences from uncertain information are modelled mathematically using probability theory and, in particular, Bayes' theorem, which is familiar to psychologists from statistical courses. Complex sets of probabilistic interrelations can be modelled in so-called *Bayesian networks*. Unfortunately Bayesian inference is neither computationally simple nor always the correct model of real world uncertain inference. The early expert system MYCIN (see below) introduced the simplifying idea of *certainty factors* associated with each of its diagnostic rules of inference. In recent years attention has focused on a more sophisticated mathematical approach known as Dempster-Shafer theory and there has also been renewed interest in fuzzy set theory, which enjoyed brief popularity in cognitive psychology in the mid-1970s.

VISION

Traditional AI research on vision was concerned, broadly speaking, with recognition of the objects – the prismatic solids – in the BLOCKSWORLD. For computer vision programs, the objects were matt white, uniformly lit (no shadows), and placed against a black background. In fact, the general problem of object recognition in the BLOCKSWORLD was set aside in favour of two of its component problems: finding lines in an image of a BLOCKSWORLD scene, and *segmenting* the image into sets of regions – each region corresponding to a surface – that belong to the same object. Indeed, this research came to be dominated by attempts to solve the segmentation problem: many programs required line drawings (rather than images) as their inputs.

The most important method of attempting to solve the segmentation problem, originally suggested by Alfonso Guzman (1968), was to use information about the types of vertex in the scene. Guzman's taxonomy was intuitive, but it was systematized independently by Max Clowes (1971) and David Huffman (1971), who stressed the importance of maintaining different descriptions of the image (in terms of lines, line junctions, and regions) and the scene (in terms of edges, vertices, and surfaces), and of making systematic inferences about the scene on the basis of the image. The Clowes-Huffman scheme is limited to scenes with no shadows and in which no more than three lines meet at any point. It has three types of line (corresponding to boundaries, inside edges, and outside edges) and four basic types of line junction (Ts, Ys, Ls, and arrows). From these line types and junction types, 16 *derived* junction types can be constructed, which correspond to possible

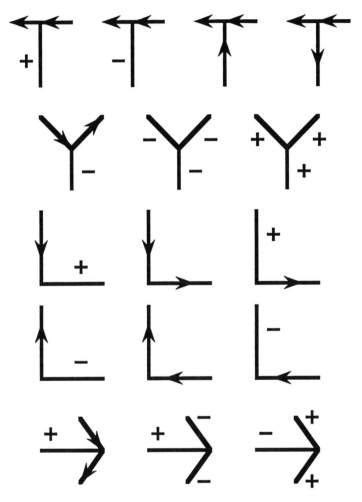

Figure 1 The 16 derived junction types in the Clowes-Huffman scheme – 4 Ts, 3 Ys, 6 Ls, and 3 arrows. An arrow on a line signifies that it represents an occluding edge (boundary between objects), a plus (+) sign signifies a convex (or outside) edge of a single object, and a minus (–) sign a concave (or inside) edge. The direction of the arrow indicates the side of the line on which the occluding object lies (to the right when facing in the direction of the arrow)

configurations in a BLOCKSWORLD scene (see Figure 1). Identification of the basic junction types in the image, plus the application of the constraint that any line should be of the same type along its whole length, allows most images of permissible scenes to be interpreted.

David Waltz (1975) extended the Clowes-Huffman scheme to scenes with shadows and to images in which more than three lines meet at a point. These apparently simple changes increased the number of permissible derived junction types from 16 to about 2,500. Nevertheless, Waltz's program was more successful than those devised by Clowes and Huffman, since he exploited the need for *consistent* labelling of neighbouring junctions. An iterative technique known as *Waltz filtering* or, more generally, as *relaxation* eliminates possible labellings of junctions, using this consistency constraint. In most cases it rapidly converges on a solution to the segmentation problem for the image it is processing.

Steve Draper (1981) and others have identified a number of problems with the junction-labelling technique and with an alternative to it known as the gradient-space method. Draper invented a technique called *sidedness reasoning*. Sidedness reasoning is about whether two points or surfaces are on the same side of a third surface. Draper showed that this technique was able to segment all BLOCKSWORLD images but in doing so he virtually put a stop to work on object recognition in the BLOCKSWORLD. The reason was that his technique wore on its sleeve the fact that it was specific to BLOCKSWORLD: it works only when all surfaces are flat. Thus, the idea of solving the problem of object recognition in a miniature domain and scaling up the solution to the real world would not work.

A quite different approach to the problems of vision is found in the work of David Marr (1982) and his associates. Marr's work integrates ideas from AI, psychology, and neurophysiology in what is usually taken to be the paradigmatically successful piece of research in cognitive science. The work is guided by an underlying philosophy about the study of natural information-processing systems. Marr identified three levels at which such systems should be studied. First, a *task analysis* answers the questions of what the system does and why it does it. This analysis leads to a *computational theory* of the system – an account of the function (in the mathematical sense) it computes. The second level of analysis is that of *representation and algorithm*. The third level is that of implementation. In the case of natural information processing systems, this level of analysis requires the study of the neural mechanisms that support the system. Marr is critical of previous AI work on vision, largely because of its focus on the second level of analysis at the expense of the first, to which Marr attached great importance. He is also critical of neurophysiological work, such as that of Hubel and Wiesel (1962), in which the purpose of certain types of cell is inferred from their properties. According to Marr, the purpose of a system (and of its parts) can be determined only by constructing a computational theory.

In his own work, Marr recognized three main stages of visual processing. In the first of these stages, the array of light falling on the retina is transformed into a representation called the *primal sketch*. The primal sketch is a symbolic representation, but it is a representation of the image, not of the scene. It contains information about lines, boundaries, and regions in the image. The construction of the primal sketch takes place very early in the visual system and proceeds on the basis of local interactions between processing units (cells) that represent adjacent parts of the image. Although these interactions reflect what is known about the early visual system, Marr eschewed theories what were motivated *solely* by neurophysiological evidence. Hence, his demand for independent support – from task analysis and psychological evidence – for the algorithm and representation he proposed.

In the second stage of visual processing, the $2\frac{1}{2}$D sketch is derived from the primal sketch. This sketch is a very short-term memory store into which a set of processes writes information about the surfaces (in the scene) represented in the image, their orientation, and their approximate distance from the viewer: the third dimension is not properly represented, hence $2\frac{1}{2}$D sketch. The most important of these processes are stereopsis, structure from motion, and shape from shading.

Since objects have not yet been recognized, surfaces cannot be identified by reference to information about the objects of which they are part. This aspect of the construction of the $2\frac{1}{2}$D sketch reflects Marr's preference for *bottom-up* (data-driven) theories of visual processing. The only world knowledge that such theories can claim the visual system uses is a set of general principles, such as what very few points in an image correspond to abrupt changes in the surface represented. Specific information about the scene being viewed is not yet available.

In the final stage of visual processing, a *3D model description* is constructed from the $2\frac{1}{2}$D sketch. This representation contains information about the identity and three-dimensional structure of the objects in the scene. Marr's account of this final stage is highly speculative, and less closely linked with the psychological and neurophysiological evidence. Marr's basic idea is that objects can be represented, in a *catalogue* stored in long-term memory, as jointed *generalized cylinders* (cylinders whose cross-section changes along their length). The principal axes of these cylinders make up stick figures of the objects represented. He showed that, subject to certain constraints, generalized cylinder representations could be derived from the $2\frac{1}{2}$D sketch, and then compared with entries in the catalogue, with any necessary rotation and bending at the joints. In practice this matching is difficult, and Marr suggested a process of gradual refinement in the match between the image and the stored representations in the catalogue. This kind of process can be (relatively) time-consuming, and was rejected by Marr in his analyses of the lower levels of visual processing.

Marr's work incorporates, in addition to traditional AI-style programming, much straightforward mathematics. Subsequent work on vision, both theoretical and applied, has become increasingly mathematical and, hence, increasingly inaccessible to psychologists. On the theoretical side, many of the problems of visual analysis have been identified as special cases of what are known as *ill-posed* problems. They are ill posed because, as they stand, they do not have a unique solution. They can be analysed by a technique known as *regularization*, which requires the addition to the problem of the kind of general constraints identified by Marr. On the applied side, specialized hardware in the form of very large-scale integration (VLSI) chips has allowed, for example, stereo algorithms to be used in real-world applications.

THINKING, REASONING, PROBLEM SOLVING

Historically, problem solving was one of the earliest topics of AI research. Furthermore, it has often been argued that it is the central topic, since AI techniques in other domains can be seen as special cases of searching through a "space" of possibilities for a solution to a problem. For example, parsing a sentence can be seen as a search through the (infinite) set of possible syntactic structures defined by the grammar of a language.

Occasionally it is possible to examine all possible solutions to a problem to find the right one. However, for most interesting problems there are too many possibilities to make this approach viable. Usually there are several steps in the solution to a problem, so the number of possible moves multiplies up at each step, producing what is called a *combinatorial explosion* in the number of potential solutions. A *control strategy* for searching through the space of possible solutions is, therefore, required.

Traditionally, there are two ways of representing problems so that a search can be made for their solution. In a *state-space representation*, problems are represented in terms of states of the relevant part of the world, and actions (usually referred to as *operators*) that transform one state into another. In this representation, a single path through the tree of possibilities (= a sequence of operators) represents the solution to the problem. In a *problem-reduction* representation a large problem is broken up into a number of sub-problems, all of which must be solved if the main problem is to be solved. State-space representations are easier to construct. Sensible reductions of problems can be hard to find, but they are very useful when they have been found. In serious AI work on problem solving the two types of representation are combined into AND/OR trees. AND branchings represent problem reductions, where all the sub-goals have to be fulfilled. OR branchings represent alternative possibilities in a state space, only one of which has to be fulfilled.

Various general control strategies for searching problem spaces have been proposed. The most fundamental distinction is between *breadth-first* and *depth-first* search of trees. In breadth-first search all possible one-operator solutions are checked, then all possible two-operator solutions, and so on. In depth-first search one possible solution is followed up until it succeeds or fails, or until a pre-set depth limit is reached, since a branch in an AND/OR tree may never terminate. Simple depth-first and breadth-first search are used only in desperation. Usually some method is introduced for following up the most promising possibilities. Methods for deciding which possibility is the most promising are inevitably heuristic. The most sophisticated method of making the choice is the AO^* algorithm. However, the algorithm itself does not provide the means of measuring which next move is the best. Furthermore, there is no general method for assigning values to moves. A new one must be devised for each domain in which the algorithm is used.

Such methods can, nevertheless, be applied to solving puzzle-book problems and in game-playing computers (e.g., for chess). In chess-playing programs the problem that the computer is trying to solve is not how to win the game, but what move to make next. Successful programs run on very fast super-computers, so that they can examine vast numbers of possible moves. However, they limit the distance ahead (in terms of moves) that they look. Since they typically cannot see ahead to a winning position, they have to evaluate the positions that they can reach in other ways, and then aim to reach the best position that a rational opponent will let them. The play of such programs differs in several ways from that of human chess players. The standard of the best of them, however, is usually reckoned to be in the grandmaster category.

Even if all AI researchers had access to the kind of super-computers that chess programmers use, they would not necessarily want to use the same kind of brute force problem solving methods, particularly if they were interested in modelling human problem solving abilities. Newell, Shaw, and Simon (1957) first introduced the idea of heuristic (rule-of-thumb) problem solving techniques in their Logic Theory Machine, that proved theorems of logic. An alternative way of speeding up problem solving is to use domain-specific techniques, that may be heuristic, but which need not be. An early example of an AI program that used a domain-specific technique was Gelernter's (1963) Geometry Machine, which constructed the equivalent of geometrical diagrams. It is thought that most human mathematicians, except when they are working in completely new areas of mathematics, use domain-specific techniques. More generally, domain-specific techniques are thought to be widely used in all types of problem solving.

LANGUAGE

There is a long history of computational research on all aspects of language processing. Research on speech, both automatic speech recognition and speech synthesis, has been strongly influenced by work on signal processing carried out by electronic engineers. More recently, with the advent of larger and more powerful computers, the field of *speech and language technology* has emerged, which is primarily directed to producing tools for processing large corpora of linguistic data held on computers. Some of the techniques developed may be of interest to AI researchers; others are used to derive statistical information that is of primary interest to, say, lexicographers.

Work on language processing is divided into three parts, concerned respectively with recognizing or selecting words, computing or generating sentence structure, and processing meaning at the level of discourse. Until the 1970s AI research on language processing often produced working systems that understood a substantial portion of a language such as English. Winograd's (1972) SHRDLU, a program that talks about moving blocks around the BLOCKSWORLD, represents the apotheosis of this work. However, it has since become obvious that the component parts of language processing are each so complex that they must be studied separately, if real progress is to be made.

Recent work on word identification has been largely dominated by neural network modelling, in particular the TRACE model of auditory word identification (McClelland & Elman, 1986) and Seidenberg and McClelland's (1989) model of visual word identification. The TRACE model is "hand-coded". It does not use distributed representations, and hence its mode of operation is easy to discern. It has interacting banks of detectors at three levels: for the auditory features of sounds, for phonemes (sounds that correspond roughly to letters), and for words. The Seidenberg and McClelland model, on the other hand, is a model that learns. One of its most interesting features is its eschewal of lexical representations: all its knowledge is encoded in links between orthographic and phonological features.

Investigations of the computation of sentence structure (parsing) have taken two rather different directions. On the one hand, *computational linguists* worry about problems such as the linguistic niceties of describing sentence structure and the computational properties of the procedures that derive the structure for a particular sentence, given a description of how sentences in its language can be structured (a grammar). One of the most important developments in computational models of parsing is the introduction of unification-based approaches (e.g., Kay, 1985). Unification is a technique that is widely used in other branches of AI, in particular theorem proving. Unification-based parsers, like some other parsers, such as chart parsers, have the additional advantage of clearly separating information about how sentences can be structured (the grammar) from information about how sentence structure is computed (the parsing algorithm). In contrast with researchers whose primary interest is in the computational properties of parsing systems, those who attempt to model the way that people derive sentence structure have to take account of well-established empirical findings on, in particular, what happens when people encounter a syntactic ambiguity. It is not yet clear how these two approaches to parsing can be integrated.

Understanding and generating discourse still remain formidable tasks. AI research has often been hampered by a restricted or ad-hoc approach to word meanings. One hope is that linguistically more sophisticated approaches to word meaning, such as Jackendoff's (1990) conceptual semantics, will be taken up by AI researchers. At the level of sentence meaning, AI researchers, at last, agree about the importance of compositional semantics of a broadly Montagovian kind (Dowty, Wall, & Peters, 1981). However, the major problems in describing discourse level processing, which have been known for many years, still resist satisfactory analysis. Some of the most important are figurative and indirect uses of language, coherence, ellipsis, and the role of the other participants' beliefs.

LEARNING

For historical reasons, learning has been a comparatively neglected topic in AI. The information processing approach to understanding intelligent behaviour was seen as a radical alternative to the behaviourism that had dominated psychology, and which placed a strong emphasis on learning. Furthermore, traditional AI aimed to study intelligence at an abstract level, independent of both its genesis (learned or programmed) and its underlying mechanism (carbon or silicon). The study of learning has come back into its own with the increasing importance of connectionist modelling. Nevertheless, a number of important studies of learning have been carried out in the symbolic framework, and the diversity of the learning mechanisms that they investigate contrasts sharply with the behaviourist approach.

Learning by being told often involves little more than adding a fact to a database. However, more abstract pieces of information, such as advice on the best strategy for winning a game, may need to be *operationalized*.

A more complex kind of learning is learning from mistakes. Gerald Sussman's (1975) program HACKER writes its own mini-programs for solving problems of stacking and unstacking blocks in BLOCKSWORLD. However, it can learn only when it can almost solve a problem, and its performance is crucially dependent on its having a "teacher" who presents it with a suitably graded set of problems. Patrick Winston's (1975) program that learns concepts for configurations of blocks (such as arches) in BLOCKSWORLD, similarly learns from almost correct information. When told that something is not quite an arch, it can use that information to deduce what distinguishes arches from non-arches.

As well as recognizing the importance of being almost correct, Winston also emphasized that an important aspect of learning is what is sometimes called *induction* – going beyond the information embodied in the examples presented to the program to form general concepts (in his case) or rules. Positive instances suggest generalizations of the concept or rule, negative instances suggest specializations (or restrictions). Research subsequent to

369

Winston's, particularly that of Ryszard Michalski (e.g., 1983) has systematized the study of induction, and shown that it can be regarded as a special case of search, with the search space being the set of possible generalizations statable in a particular language. Michalski's approach is more powerful than Winston's, but less closely related to human learning. It can also be used for the related task of discrimination learning. Its disadvantage is that it works straightforwardly only if the generalizations are formulated using exactly the same predicates that are used to describe the instances.

Winston's program can learn more complex concepts (such as arch) only because it knows simpler concepts (pillar, lintel). This aspect of the program relates, very crudely, to the question of how much of what we know about language is learned, and how much is innate. In the case of concepts, it has been argued (e.g., by Fodor, 1981) that all concepts must be innate. More generally, it is widely, though not universally, believed that many general principles governing the form of possible languages are innate, and that the availability of these principles to the language learning mechanism explains how it is able to achieve what appears, on mathematical analysis, to be a difficult or impossible task.

Another famous example of learning by generalization is Arthur Samuel's (1963) checkers (draughts) program. This program develops a general method for evaluating board positions by comparing computed evaluations with the way the game actually turns out, and revising, if necessary, the method of evaluation.

A more ambitious, and more controversial, attempt to study a different kind of learning – learning by exploration – is found in Doug Lenat's (1982) AM (Automated Mathematician) and EURISKO programs. AM starts with a collection of set-theoretic concepts and ways of combining them, and creates further mathematical concepts from them (e.g., positive whole number, prime number, the fundamental theorem of arithmetic – that every number can be expressed as a product of prime factors).

None of the programs described so far provides a convincing model of human learning. People can learn things very quickly, though they often make mistakes in doing so. This very quick learning depends on particular ways of using background knowledge. Two lines of research that attempt to model this kind of learning investigate analogy-based learning and explanation-based learning. The importance of analogy in learning and problem-solving has long been recognized in cognitive psychology. None the less the underlying processes are difficult to model computationally, not least because the domain from which an analogy is drawn need not be specified in advance. In explanation-based learning (see e.g., de Jong, 1988) a single event or episode is explained on the basis of a theory about the relevant aspects of the world. That explanation is then generalized so that it will be useful in other situations.

Traditional AI work on learning has embodied a variety of ideas. An alternative tradition, running from the British Empiricist philosophers of the seventeenth and eighteenth centuries to the behaviourists and neo-behaviourists of the twentieth century, has seen all learning as the formation and strengthening of associations between ideas. In a modified form, this notion also underlies recent connectionist accounts of learning. Connec-tionists machines are collections of simple processing units, with levels of

OUTPUT

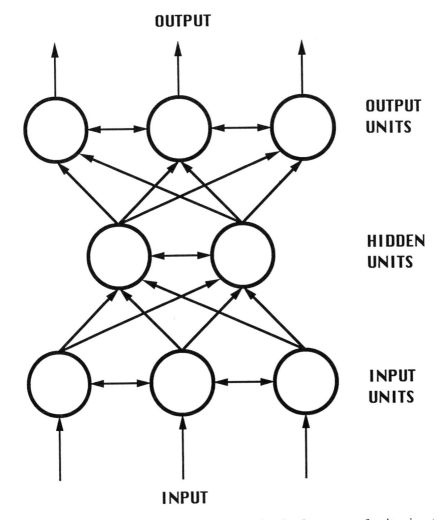

OUTPUT
UNITS

HIDDEN
UNITS

INPUT
UNITS

INPUT

Figure 2   A simple connectionist network showing the three types of unit – input, hidden, and output – and the connections between them

activation that can be passed from one unit to another. A typical machine has three layers of units: input units, hidden units and output units (see Figure 2). Such machines can learn in several ways, but the most popular is known as a *back propagation*. It is a supervised learning method in which a stimulus is encoded at the input units and produces an output at the output units. The supervisor tells the machine what the output should have been, and the difference between the actual and expected outputs is propagated back through the network of units, and used, in a precisely specified way, to adjust the (associative) strengths of the connections between them. Adjustments are small, because the machine must not produce the correct response to the last input at the expense of responding grossly incorrectly to other inputs. Learning is slow, sometimes very slow, but a stable set of associative strengths is usually reached.

Another biological metaphor that has inspired AI work on learning is *evolution. Genetic algorithms* (e.g. Goldberg, 1989) use complex rules to perform tasks. The parts of these rules can be recombined by processes that are analogous to the genetic operations that take place in the germ cells during sexual reproduction. The resulting rules are then allowed to perform their task for some time, and their performance is assessed. Those that do best re-enter the "reproductive" process.

APPLICATIONS

Intelligent machines should be of more than academic interest. However, most of the machines that we interact with in everyday life, for example automatic bank tellers, are not intelligent. More intelligent machines – often referred to as expert systems – do have applications. However, despite the hopes of the early 1980s, it now appears that expert systems will typically be used to assist experts, rather than to replace them. Perhaps the most important area of application for intelligent programs is in medical diagnosis, though there are obviously ethical problems in this domain. One area in which computers play a crucial role is in modern scanning techniques (CAT, PET, NMR, etc.). The basic use of computers in scanning is to generate appropriate images. Intelligent programs might also help to produce diagnoses from images.

One of the earliest, and best known, medical diagnosis systems is MYCIN (Shortliffe, 1976), which diagnoses serious bacterial infections so that life-saving antibiotic drugs can be administered before a culture has been developed. The development of such a system requires the gleaning of information about the diseases in question and their symptoms. Some of this information is elicited from experts, sometimes with difficulty, as the experts cannot necessarily verbalize their knowledge. TEIRESIAS (Davis, 1982) is a program that attempts to automate this knowledge transfer, and also to use the knowledge already in MYCIN to generate user-friendly explanations of its diagnoses. Other diagnostic information comes from statistical records. In an expert system all the information is usually represented in a uniform way, so that new information can readily be added. The rules for making inferences are stored separately, and an attempt is made to keep the inferential processes simple. One of the major aspects of inference in expert systems is combining uncertain bits of information to produce a best guess, for example at a diagnosis. This combination is sometimes achieved using standard statistical (Bayesian) techniques and sometimes using domain specific rules, as in MYCIN (see above).

MYCIN also formed the basis of the first *expert system shell*, E-MYCIN, which is MYCIN stripped of its domain-specific knowledge. Expert system shells were the first of several attempts to make the creation of new expert systems easy. Success has been partial. E-MYCIN, for example, is most successful in other medical diagnosis systems, such as PUFF, which diagnoses pulmonary diseases.

Another well-known expert system is DENDRAL (Lindsay, Buchanan, Feigenbaum, & Lederberg, 1980), which works out the molecular structure of large organic molecules from their mass spectrograms. DENDRAL has been in regular use by research chemists for some time. An additional program, meta-DENDRAL, attempts to formulate new rules using the induction techniques described above.

A second area in which AI has sought to find application is in computer-assisted learning (CAL). With the expansion of higher education in the UK, CAL is likely to become increasingly important, though it is as yet unclear what the contribution of AI techniques will be. The current focus of attention is on multimedia, and in particular hypermedia learning tools, which provide facilities for exploring large databases in various ways, but which rely on much of the intelligence resting in the instructions and with the student.

The intelligent tutoring systems of AI, on the other hand, try to be intelligent themselves. Such systems have three main components: a knowledge base which could, in principle, incorporate multimedia options, a model of the student, and a set of teaching strategies. The knowledge base is used to impart information directly to students, but it is also used to generate explanations of why students' answers to questions are wrong. This process, in turn, makes use of the model of the student to decide what kinds of misconceptions students will have. Such indirect methods of teaching meet with some success, but they prove comparatively difficult to implement in a tutoring system.

PHILOSOPHICAL ISSUES

AI research, more than that in other sciences, has been surrounded by philosophical controversy. Two related issues have provided the major focus of debate. The first is whether machines can think, and the second is what role they should be allowed to play in our lives.

The question of whether machines can think, although one that excites the popular imagination, is not necessarily a clear one. One crucial aspect of it, however, is whether there is a difference between computer programs that model phenomena such as the weather, which simulate processes in the world, but do not reproduce them, and AI programs. In other words: is a computer running such a program really intelligent, or is it just simulating intelligent behaviour? On one view, most programs lack real intelligence because they do not interact with the world. The symbols that they manipulate have meaning only because of the way they are interpreted by their programmers. On this view a robot that based its interactions with the world on its internal computations could be intelligent. An opposing view is that real intelligence can be manifest only in biological systems (Searle, 1980). To support this thesis Searle put forward his famous *Chinese room* argument. If he sat in a room manipulating symbols according to the rules embodied in a computer program, he might, from the outside, be described as reading and answering questions in Chinese. He would not, however, understand Chinese. So, understanding Chinese is not just running a program. However, Searle's view of what else it is, basically being a biological intelligence, appears to have no foundation, and has been dubbed *protoplasm chauvinism* (Torrance, 1986).

If machines, or at least robots, can be intelligent, we might at some time in the future have moral responsibilities towards them, or we might be in danger of being dominated by them. To some extent the moral issues raised by such considerations are just those that arise in the application of any science. The difference is that we might be faced not simply with a substance or technique that might be misused, but with something that is itself an "alien" intelligence. However, it is difficult to pinpoint, as Weizenbaum (1976) has tried to do, the sense in which intelligent computers pose a special threat.

ARTIFICIAL INTELLIGENCE, COGNITIVE PSYCHOLOGY, AND THE FUTURE

Since the mid-1970s there has been an enormous growth in AI research. It is no longer possible, as it once was, for an AI researcher, let alone a psychologist, to keep up with developments in all of its subfields. Furthermore, much of AI has become very technical: much more so than cognitive psychology. Nevertheless, the best science often is technical; if cognitive psychologists are not to risk being usurped, they should keep at least one eye on developments in AI.

FURTHER READING

Boden, M. A. (1987). *Artificial intelligence and natural man*, 2nd edn. London: MIT Press.
Garnham, A. (1988). *Introduction to artificial intelligence*. London: Routledge.
Garnham, A. (1991). *The mind in action*. London: Routledge.
Rich, E., & Knight, K. (1991). *Artificial intelligence*, 2nd edn. New York: McGraw-Hill.

REFERENCES

Clowes, M. B. (1971). On seeing things. *Artificial Intelligence, 21,* 79–116.
Davis, R. (1982). TEIRESIAS: Applications of meta-level knowledge. In R. Davis & D. Lenat (Eds) *Knowledge-based systems in artificial intelligence* (pp. 227–490). New York: McGraw-Hill.
de Jong, G. (1988). An introduction to explanation-based learning. In H. E. Shrobe (Ed.) *Exploring artificial intelligence: Survey talks from the national conferences on artificial intelligence* (pp. 45–81). San Mateo, CA: Morgan Kaufmann.
Dowty, D. R., Wall, R., & Peters, P. S. (1981). *Introduction to Montague semantics.* Dordrecht: Reidel.
Doyle, J. (1979). A truth maintenance system. *Artificial Intelligence, 12,* 231–272.
Draper, S. W. (1981). The use of gradient and dual space in line-drawing interpretation. *Artificial Intelligence, 17,* 461–508.
Fahlman, S. E. (1979). NETL: *A system for representing and using real-word knowledge.* Cambridge, MA: MIT Press.
Fodor, J. A. (1981). The present status of the innateness controversy. In J. A. Fodor, *Representations* (pp. 257–316). Brighton: Harvester.
Gelernter, H. L. (1963). Realization of a geometry-theorem proving machine. In E. A. Feigenbaum & J. Feldman (Eds) *Computers and thought* (pp. 134–152). New York: McGraw-Hill.
Goldberg, D. (1989). *Genetic algorithms in search, optimization, and machine learning.* Reading, MA: Addison-Wesley.
Guzman, A. (1968). Decomposition of a visual scene into three-dimensional bodies. *Proceedings of the American Federation of Information Processing Studies Fall Joint Conference, 33,* 291–304.
Hubel, D. H., & Wiesel, T. N. (1962). Receptive fields, binocular interaction and functional architecture in the cat's visual cortex. *Journal of Physiology, 160,* 106–154.
Huffman, D. A. (1971). Impossible objects as nonsense sentences. In B. A. Meltzer & D. Michie (Eds) *Machine intelligence 6* (pp. 295–323). Edinburgh: Edinburgh University Press.
Jackendoff, R. S. (1990). *Semantic structures.* Cambridge, MA: MIT Press.
Kay, M. (1985). Parsing in functional unification grammar. In D. R. Dowty, L. Karttunen, & A. M. Zwicky (Eds) *Natural language parsing: Psychological, computational, and theoretical perspectives.* (pp. 251–278). Cambridge: Cambridge University Press.
Lenat, D. M. (1982). AM: Discovery in mathematics as heuristic search. In R. Davis & D. M. Lenat (Eds) *Knowledge-based systems in artificial intelligence* (pp. 1–225). New York: McGraw-Hill.
Lighthill, J. (1972). *Artificial intelligence: Report to the Science Research Council.* London: Science Research Council.

Lindsay, R., Buchanan, B. G., Feigenbaum, E. A., & Lederberg, J. (1980). *Applications of artificial intelligence for chemical inference: The DENDRAL project*. New York: McGraw-Hill.

McClelland, J. L., & Elman, J. L. (1986). The TRACE model of speech perception. *Cognitive Psychology*, *18*, 1–86.

Marr, D. (1982). *Vision: A computational investigation into the human representation and processing of visual information*. San Francisco, CA: Freeman.

Michalski, R. S. (1983). A theory and methodology of inductive learning. *Artificial Intelligence*, *20*, 111–161.

Newell, A., Shaw, J. C., & Simon, H. A. (1957). Empirical explorations with the Logic Theory Machine: A case study in heuristics. *Proceedings of the Western Joint Computer Conference*, *15*, 218–230.

Quillian, M. R. (1968). Semantic memory. In M. Minsky (Ed.) *Semantic information processing* (pp. 216–270). Cambridge, MA: Massachusetts Institute of Technology Press.

Robinson, J. A. (1965). A machine-oriented logic based on the resolution principle. *Journal of the Association for Computing Machinery*, *12*, 23–41.

Samuel, A. L. (1963). Some studies in machine learning using the game of checkers. In E. A. Feigenbaum & J. Feldman (Eds) *Computers and thought* (pp. 71–105). New York: McGraw-Hill.

Searle, J. R. (1980). Minds, brains, and programs. *Behavioral and Brain Sciences*, *3*, 417–424.

Seidenberg, M., & McClelland, J. L. (1989). A distributed, developmental model of word recognition and naming. *Psychological Review*, *96*, 523–568.

Shortliffe, E. H. (1976). A model of inexact reasoning in medicine. *Mathematical Biosciences*, *23*, 361–379.

Sussman, G. (1975). *A computer model of skill acquisition*. New York: Elsevier.

Torrance, S. (1986). Breaking out of the Chinese room. In M. Yazdani (Ed.) *Artificial intelligence: Principles and applications* (pp. 294–314). London: Chapman & Hall.

Waltz, D. (1975). Understanding line drawings of scenes with shadows. In P. H. Winston (Ed.) *The psychology of computer vision* (pp. 19–92). New York: McGraw-Hill.

Weizenbaum, J. (1976). *Computer power and human reason*. San Francisco, CA: Freeman.

Winograd, T. (1972). Understanding natural language. *Cognitive Psychology*, *3*, 1–191.

Winston, P. H. (1975). Learning structural descriptions from examples. In P. H. Winston (Ed.) *The psychology of computer vision* (pp. 155–209). New York: McGraw-Hill.

5
LEARNING AND SKILLS

INTRODUCTION

In everyday language, "learning" refers to the acquisition of knowledge, but psychologists use the word in a subtly different sense. For psychologists, the acquisition of knowledge belongs to the field of memory, and the word *learning* is usually reserved for changes in behaviour resulting from experience. The word *skill*, on the other hand, has roughly the same meaning in psychology as in everyday usage, but something needs to be said about the distinction between cognitive, motor, and social skills, all of which are covered in this section. Social skills are simply those that are specifically required for effective social interaction. The distinction between cognitive and motor skills is not entirely clear but, roughly speaking, cognitive skills are defined negatively as skills that do not require bodily or perceptual-motor coordination to any significant degree, and motor skills are those that do.

Nicholas J. Mackintosh opens this section by outlining the fundamental principles of classical and operant conditioning in chapter 5.1. Classical conditioning is sometimes called Pavlovian conditioning, after the Nobel Prize-winning Russian physiologist who first investigated it. Operant conditioning is sometimes called instrumental conditioning, because in this type of learning the occurrence of certain elements of behaviour, called responses, are instrumental in eliciting reward or reinforcement. Among the technical terms that Mackintosh introduces in connection with classical conditioning are *unconditional stimulus* (a stimulus that elicits a response unconditionally) and *conditional stimulus* (one that elicits a response only after a process of learning has taken place): there is a potential source of confusion about these concepts that needs to be cleared up. As a result of a mistranslation of Pavlov's writings into English, these are commonly called *unconditioned* and *conditioned* stimuli, and that is also why the learning process that causes a stimulus to elicit a response has come to be called conditioning (a back-formation from "conditioned").

In chapter 5.2 Donald M. Baer introduces applied behaviour analysis, which involves technological applications of operant conditioning in real-life settings, including hospitals, clinics, schools, and factories. The methods of applied behaviour analysis are sometimes practised in the professions of psychology, notably clinical and counselling psychology (see chapter 13.1, Graham E. Powell), educational (school) psychology (see chapter 13.2, David Fontana), and forensic (criminological) psychology (see chapter 13.4, Clive R. Hollin).

Chapter 5.3, by K. Anders Ericsson and William L. Oliver, focuses on cognitive skills, chapter 5.4, by John Annett, on motor skills, and chapter 5.5, by Michael Argyle, on social skills. These three chapters are obviously closely related to one another; there are also links between these chapters and others in different sections. For developmental aspects, see chapter 8.1 (George Butterworth), which deals briefly with the development of skills, and chapters 8.2 (Sara Meadows) and 8.3 (Peter K. Smith) on cognitive and social development respectively. Ericsson and Oliver's discussion of cognitive skills touches on several of the issues addressed in chapter 4.4 (Jonathan St B. T. Evans) in relation to thinking and problem solving, and their discussion of acquisition of superior memory performance is directly relevant to the contents of chapter 4.1 (Alan Baddeley), which deals with memory in general. John Annett's chapter also touches on memory, and therefore links with chapter 4.1. Michael Argyle's discussion of social skills draws heavily on research into non-verbal communication, which is discussed in greater detail in chapter 9.5 (Peter Bull and Lesley Frederikson).

A.M.C.

5.1

CLASSICAL AND OPERANT CONDITIONING

Nicholas J. Mackintosh

University of Cambridge, England

The laws of association	Associative learning in humans
Pavlovian and instrumental conditioning	Further reading
Hierarchical associations	References

There was a time when standard textbooks of experimental psychology afforded a central place to the study of conditioning and learning in animals. The learning theories of the American psychologists Clark Hull, Edward Tolman, Edwin Guthrie, and B. F. Skinner were regarded, and not only by their authors, as among psychology's most fundamental theoretical contributions to the understanding of human behaviour. Few psychologists would now grant learning theory such an exalted position. Indeed, the study of conditioning is more often derided as artificial or, an even worse fate, ignored as boring and irrelevant. Both the earlier adulation and the later denigration are surely unjustified. The study of conditioning in animals is not the key to all psychology, but it is certainly more interesting and probably more important than its detractors have supposed.

The scientific study of conditioning dates back to the beginning of the twentieth century, to the experiments of Ivan Pavlov (1849–1936) in Russia and Edward Thorndike (1874–1949) in the United States, working in quite different traditions and in total ignorance of one another. Pavlov developed the general procedures for studying classical (or Pavlovian) conditioning, invented a terminology to describe it that is still in use, and advanced an account of what was happening in his experiments, many elements of which

379

are still widely accepted. In the course of his work on the digestive system of the dog, Pavlov had found that salivary secretion was elicited, not only by placing food in the dog's mouth but also by the sight and smell of food, and even by the sight and sound of the technician who usually provided that food. Anyone who has prepared dinner for their pet dog will not be totally amazed by Pavlov's discovery. In a dozen different ways, that include excited panting and jumping and also profuse salivation, dogs show that they recognize the familiar precursors of their daily meal. For Pavlov, at first, these "psychic secretions" merely interfered with the planned study of the digestive system; but he then saw that he had a tool for the objective study of something even more interesting – how animals learn.

Pavlov's experiments on conditioning employed a standard simple procedure (Pavlov, 1927). A hungry dog is restrained on a stand and every few minutes is given some dry meat powder, whose occurrence is signalled by an arbitrary stimulus, such as the illumination of a lamp or the ticking of a metronome. The food itself elicits copious salivation, and after a few trials the ticking of the metronome, which regularly precedes the delivery of the food, will also elicit salivation. In Pavlov's terminology the food is an unconditional stimulus (US), because it invariably (unconditionally) elicits salivation, which is termed an unconditional response (UR). The ticking of the metronome is a conditional stimulus (CS) because its ability to elicit salivation (now a conditional response (CR) when it occurs to the CS alone) is conditional on a particular set of experiences. The occurrence of the CR to the CS is termed a conditional reflex which is reinforced by the presentation of the US (food) – so that the US itself is often termed a reinforcer. In the absence of food the repeated presentation of the CS alone will result in the gradual disappearance or extinction of its CR.

Thorndike's typical experiment involved placing a cat inside a "puzzle box" from which the animal could escape and obtain food only by pressing a panel, operating a catch, or pulling on a loop of string (Thorndike, 1911). Thorndike measured the speed with which the cats gained their release from the box on successive trials, observing that the animals would initially behave aimlessly or even frantically, stumbling on the correct response or responses purely by chance, but would eventually execute these responses efficiently and economically within a few seconds of being placed in the box. Thorndike's procedures were greatly refined by Skinner (1938), who delivered food to the animal inside the box via an automatic delivery device, and could thus record the probability or rate at which animals performed the designated response over long periods of time without having to handle them. Skinner also adopted some of Pavlov's terminology, referring to his procedure as one of operant (or instrumental) conditioning, to the food reward as a reinforcer of conditioning, and to the decline of responding, when the reward was no longer available, as extinction. In Skinner's original experiments, the animals were laboratory rats who were required to depress a small lever protruding from one wall of the box in order to obtain a small pellet of food. Subsequently the "Skinner box" was adapted for pigeons, who were required to peck at a small illuminated disk on one wall of the box in order to obtain some grain.

The traditional theory of conditioning was built round these simple experiments, where learning was evidenced by the animal acquiring a new response. After conditioning the dog now salivates to the ticking of the metronome, the rat presses the lever, the pigeon pecks the illuminated disk. Conditioning then seemed to be a matter of the strengthening of a new conditional reflex, or, in Thorndike's analysis, the formation of a new connection or bond between a stimulus and a response. But as soon as one departs from this one rather limited experimental paradigm, this description immediately seems less appropriate: not all learning seems to be a matter of the acquisition of new responses. The rat in the Skinner box who learns to press a lever if rewarded with a pellet of food for doing so, will learn even more rapidly to refrain from pressing the lever if each lever press results in the delivery of an electric shock as well as a pellet of food (Mackintosh, 1983, p. 124). What *new* response has been acquired, or stimulus–response connection strengthened, as a result of this experience? Similarly, many instances of Pavlovian conditioning are only with difficulty described as the establishment of new reflexes. Thirsty rats will avidly drink a sweet-tasting sucrose solution, but if its ingestion is followed by an injection of lithium chloride, which makes the animal mildly ill, they will condition an aversion to the sucrose solution, refusing to touch it the next day (Revusky & Garcia, 1970). What is the new stimulus–response connection that has been formed? The measure of conditioning is a decline in responding (drinking of sucrose); it seems more plausibly described as a revaluation of the initial attractive solution, so that it is now regarded as aversive.

That the traditional stimulus–response account of conditioning is seriously misleading is confirmed by a slightly more elaborate experiment, illustrated in Table 1 (see Dickinson, 1989; Rescorla, 1991). In the first stage of the experiment, a rat is trained to press a lever in a Skinner box or operant chamber to obtain sucrose pellets. In the second stage, the rat is given cause to revalue the sucrose pellets: after eating some in another environment the rat receives an injection of lithium chloride which conditions an aversion to

Table 1 Design for reinforcer revaluation experiment

Stage 1	*Stage 2*	*Stage 3*
Rat trained to press lever for sucrose pellets	Rat given sucrose pellets to eat followed by lithium injection	Rat given opportunity to press lever (no sucrose pellets available)

sucrose pellets. The test phase simply asks whether the rat will press the lever again when replaced in the operant chamber. Common sense suggests that the rat should not, and common sense is right: the rat does refrain from pressing the lever (significantly more than various control groups). But how is this to be explained by the traditional stimulus–response account? According to this analysis, what the rat learned in the first place was to press the lever whenever it came into view. The function of the sucrose pellet was simply to strengthen a new connection between sight of lever and response of pressing. Once this new stimulus–response connection has been formed, no change in the value of the sucrose will have any further bearing on it: the rat would stop pressing the lever only if given the opportunity to learn something new about the consequences of so doing – that lever pressing was no longer rewarded, for example, or was actually punished. It seemed reasonable to suppose that the rat should refrain from pressing a lever which has previously produced sucrose pellets that are now no longer valued, because we implicitly took it for granted that what the rat had learned, was first, that lever pressing produces sucrose pellets, and second, that sucrose pellets are no longer valuable; we then assume that the rat can put these two pieces of information together. But this is not how learning is represented by stimulus–response theory.

Similar revaluation effects occur in simple Pavlovian conditioning experiments. If a CS is paired with sucrose pellets and comes to elicit an appropriate appetitive CR, this CR will be abolished by subsequently conditioning an aversion to the sucrose pellets (Holland & Straub, 1979). Here we must assume that the original conditioning established an association between some central representations of the CS and the sucrose pellets rather than simply strengthening a new reflex between CS and CR. The implication is that conditioning is not reducible to the strengthening of new reflexes or stimulus–response connections by the automatic action of a process of reinforcement. It is more profitably viewed as the process by which animals detect and learn about the relationship between events in their environment, be those events stimuli, responses, or reinforcers, and adjust their behaviour accordingly.

THE LAWS OF ASSOCIATION

Viewed from this perspective, conditioning experiments arrange contingencies between events, and animals associate those events. In a typical Pavlovian experiment, the experimenter arranges that food will be presented whenever the metronome starts ticking, never at other times. The dog associates the ticking of the metronome with the delivery of food, and the salivary CR that develops is an index of the formation of this association. If the experimenter continued to present food following the metronome alone, but on other trials turned on a flashing light at the same time as the metronome and delivered no food, the dog would presumably learn that the light signalled the absence of the food and the formation of such an 'inhibitory' association would be evident from the dog's tendency not to salivate whenever the light accompanied the metronome – and from the fact that the light would equally inhibit salivation when presented in conjunction with a second independently trained positive CS (Rescorla, 1969).

In a typical operant experiment the experimenter arranges that the delivery of food is dependent on the animal's execution of a particular response – the rat pressing a lever, the pigeon pecking an illuminated disk. By parity of reasoning, we might suppose that this contingency between response and food results in the formation of an association between the two, and that the change in behaviour we observe – an increase in the probability of lever pressing or disk pecking – is an index of this associative change. Of course, if the reinforcer contingent on lever pressing had been an aversive event such as shock, the same association between response and reinforcer would have resulted in a decline in the probability of responding.

The next question to be addressed is what are the conditions under which associations between CSs and reinforcers or responses and reinforcers are formed. Classical associationist theory of British empiricist philosophy, which long antedates the laboratory study of conditioning, usually assumed a very small number of laws of association, of which the most prominent was that of temporal contiguity. Two events will be associated if and only if they occur in strict temporal contiguity. It turns out that, for conditioning at least, this is seriously misleading. Temporal contiguity is certainly important, for the rat that will learn to press a lever when a pellet of food is delivered immediately after each lever press will learn more slowly when a delay of even a few seconds is imposed between lever pressing and food. But even so, learning will occur with intervals of 30–60 seconds (Dickinson, Watt, & Griffiths, 1992); in other conditioning preparations, mostly Pavlovian, successful conditioning can occur with delays of a minute or more between presentation of the CS and the delivery of the reinforcer. The most famous example of this is the food aversion conditioning procedure referred to earlier (Revusky & Garcia, 1970). A rat that consumes a novel-flavoured substance at one time can condition an aversion to that substance, even if the interval between consumption and illness is several hours. This finding has led some investigators to suppose that food aversion conditioning represents a unique adaptive specialization of learning, which may not obey the same laws as other more arbitrary forms of conditioning (Rozin & Kalat, 1971; Seligman, 1970). As Revusky (1971) has noted, however, there are numerous parallels between food aversion conditioning and other more conventional paradigms: for example, although conditioning occurs over longer intervals than those usually effective in other paradigms, it still varies inversely with the length of the interval separating ingestion and sickness; an aversion produced by making a rat sick after ingesting one substance does not generalize completely

:to other flavours (Mackintosh, 1983, p. 203). This can mean only that the aversion is a consequence of associating the specific substance ingested with the subsequent illness.

But it is clear that strict temporal contiguity between response or CS and reinforcer is not absolutely necessary for successful conditioning. More important than this, however, is the demonstration that it is not the *absolute* temporal relationship between, say, a CS and the reinforcer that determines how readily conditioning will occur, but the *relative* temporal proximity of the two. In pigeons, brief illumination of a disk of light before the delivery of food will result in conditioning manifest as pecking the illuminated disk (a phenomenon sometimes termed "autoshaping"). Such conditioning occurs more readily with a reasonably short interval between CS and food. But what is more important is the length of this interval relative to the interval between successive trials; where this inter-trial interval is short, say 24 seconds, conditioning will occur much more rapidly if the interval between onset of CS and food is also short — 4 seconds rather than 8 or 16 seconds. But when the interval between trials is long, the interval between CS and US can also be

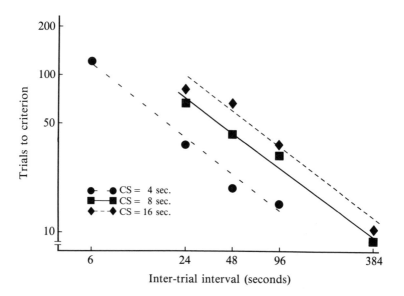

Figure 1 Speed of conditioning (measured by the number of trials required to reach a predetermined level of responding) as a function of the duration of each trial and of the interval between trials. Both axes are plotted on log coordinates. Speed of conditioning was inversely related to trial duration, but within each trial duration (points joined by regression lines) trials to criterion decreased as the intertrial interval increased. But note that, for example, the three groups with trial and inter-trial intervals of 4 and 24 seconds, 8 and 48 seconds, and 16 and 96 seconds all conditioned at the same rate

Source: Gibbon, Baldock, Locurto, Gold, and Terrace, 1977

lengthened without detracting from successful conditioning (Gibbon, Baldock, Locurto, Gold, & Terrace, 1977). Indeed, as Figure 1 shows, Gibbon and colleagues found that across a range of absolute values, a constant ratio between these two intervals resulted in a constant level of conditioning.

Relative temporal proximity is not the only newly established law of conditioning that raises problems for the classical associationist analysis. So does the phenomenon of relative validity. Successful conditioning will occur even if the CS is not always followed by a reinforcer, or if the response is not consistently reinforced. Indeed, Skinner's best-known contribution to the study of operant conditioning was the description and analysis of a variety of schedules of intermittent reinforcement (Ferster & Skinner, 1957), when a rat's lever presses or a pigeon's pecks are reinforced only after a certain passage of time (interval schedules), or after a certain number of responses have been performed (ratio schedules). Such schedules can typically generate rapid and persistent responding. But there is now good evidence that a CS which will elicit reliable CRs even if only intermittently followed by a reinforcer, will cease to do so if the reinforcer also occurs in the absence of the CS. In the limiting case when the probability of the reinforcer is the same in the absence of the CS as it is in its present, one typically finds no evidence of conditioning at all. The classic experiments to demonstrate this were undertaken by Rescorla (1968), studying conditioned suppression in rats, a procedure in which a CS is paired with the delivery of a brief shock while a hungry rat is pressing a lever for occasional food reinforcement. Conditioning to the CS is measured by the extent to which it suppresses the rate at which the rat presses the lever. As Figure 2 shows, the magnitude of conditioned suppression in Rescorla's experiments was not only a direct function of the probability of shock in the presence of the CS, but also an inverse function of the probability of shock in the absence of the CS. When these two probabilities were equal the CS elicited no suppression at all.

The implication of these studies is that conditioning depends on the extent to which a CS signals a *change* in the rate or probability of a reinforcer. One way of understanding this is to turn to a slightly different set of experiments, those on blocking. In experiments on conditioned suppression in rats, Kamin (1969) found that animals exposed to a compound CS, consisting of a light and a noise signalling shock, would normally condition to both elements of the compound. But prior conditioning to one element of the compound alone would attenuate or block conditioning to the other element. The design and results of one of Kamin's experiments are shown in Table 2. It is clear that blocking of conditioning to the light occurred because the light–noise compound signalled the same reinforcer as that signalled by the noise alone; as is shown in the third group in Table 2, when an additional unpredicted shock was programmed after each compound trial, substantial conditioning accrued to the light. Subsequent experiments have confirmed the conclusion

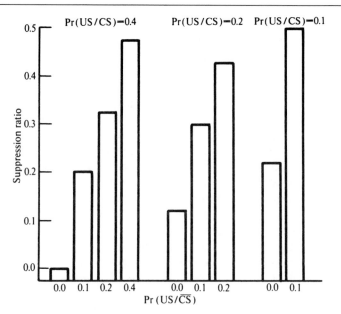

Figure 2 Conditioned suppression in rats as a function of the probability of shock in the presence and absence of the CS. A suppression ratio of 0.50 indicates that the CS did not suppress responding (i.e., no conditioning); one of 0.00 indicates complete suppression (i.e., strong conditioning). The probability of shock is calculated over 2-minute intervals (i.e., the duration of the CS); thus the first four groups received an average of 0.4 shocks per CS and between 0 and 0.4 shocks per 2-minute interval in the absence of the CS

Source: Rescorla, 1968

that blocking is a consequence of the added stimulus predicting no change in reinforcement from that signalled by the pretrained stimulus alone (Dickinson & Mackintosh, 1979; Rescorla & Wagner, 1972).

Rescorla and Wagner (1972) proposed a formal model of conditioning which explains most of these results in a simple and elegant way. They

Table 2 Design and results of Kamin's blocking experiment

Group	Stage 1	Stage 2	Test results
Blocked	Noise → shock	Noise + light → shock	No conditioning to light
Control	—	Noise + light → shock	Conditioning to light
Surprise	Noise → weak shock	Noise + light → strong shock	Conditioning to light

suggest that conditioning depends on the discrepancy between obtained and expected reinforcement. In Kamin's (1969) blocking experiment, the shock is fully predicted by the noise by the end of Stage 1. There was thus no discrepancy between obtained and expected shock when the light was added to the noise, and therefore no conditioning to the light. To explain Rescorla's own experiments on relative validity, and the Gibbon et al. (1977) experiment on the temporal spacing of trials, we need only add the assumption that animals associate the occurrence of a reinforcer not only with a discrete CS, but also with the entire experimental context in which conditioning trials occur. Successful conditioning to the CS thus depends on its signalling an increase in the probability of the reinforcer over that already predicted or expected on the basis of the context alone. One final virtue of Rescorla and Wagner's model is its ability to integrate both excitatory and inhibitory conditioning. As noted above, inhibitory conditioning occurs if CS 1 is paired with a reinforcer but when CS 2 is added to CS 1 no reinforcer occurs: according to Rescorla and Wagner (1972) CS 2 now becomes a conditioned inhibitor because it signals the absence of an otherwise expected reinforcer, that is, a negative discrepancy between obtained and expected reinforcement.

PAVLOVIAN AND INSTRUMENTAL CONDITIONING

Essentially all the laws of association described above for the case of Pavlovian conditioning can also be demonstrated in instrumental or operant conditioning. Operant conditioning occurs only when a response is followed by an otherwise unexpected change in reinforcement: no conditioning will occur when the probability of the reinforcer is the same whether or not the rat presses the lever, and instrumental conditioning will be blocked if the occurrence of the reinforcer is better predicted by any other, discrete signal than by the occurrence of the response (Mackintosh & Dickinson, 1979). Conversely, if the reinforcer is better predicted by the response than by the signal, the response will block conditioning to the signal (Garrud, Goodall, & Mackintosh, 1981). The implication is that the same laws govern the formation of associations between related events regardless of whether those events are stimuli or responses.

But it is equally important to understand the distinction between classical and operant conditioning. The operational distinction, first clearly enunciated by the Polish psychologists Miller and Konorski (1928) and by Skinner (1938), is that in a Pavlovian experiment the experimenter arranges a relationship between a stimulus and a reinforcer regardless of the subject's behaviour; but in an instrumental experiment, the experimenter arranges a relationship between the subject's behaviour and the reinforcer. The argument so far has assumed that animals can associate these related events, and that such associations are formed in accordance with the same laws. The distinction between Pavlovian or classical and operant conditioning concerns the ways in which these associations are translated into changes in behaviour, and arise because reinforcers are events with two distinct properties. They are USs, that is, they unconditionally or reflexly elicit a variety of responses or patterns of behaviour; but they also act as incentives or goals, which animals will work to obtain (or avoid). These two sets of properties lie at the root of the two different ways that conditioning can produce changes in behaviour.

According to Pavlov, the reason why a CS-reinforcer association produces a conditional reflex is because the CS comes to substitute for the reinforcer, thereby acquiring the ability to elicit the same pattern of behaviour – salivation, leg flexion, approach, withdrawal. If dry food in the mouth elicits salivation, a CS associated with that food will also elicit salivation; if the sight of food elicits approach and pecking in a hungry pigeon, a small visual stimulus associated with the delivery of food will equally elicit approach and pecking.

According to Thorndike the principle of instrumental conditioning is the law of effect. A response that produces one class of consequence (roughly, appetitive reinforcers or rewards) will increase in probability; one that produces another class (roughly, aversive reinforcers or punishers) will decrease in probability. Instrumental responses are modified by their consequences, as opposed to Pavlovian CRs, which are simply elicited by a stimulus regardless of their consequences.

There is good reason to accept both Pavlov's and Thorndike's principles of reinforcement. Pavlov is right, because some responses are acquired regardless of their consequences. A dog that salivates to a CS signalling the delivery of food will still salivate even if the experimenter arranges that food never occurs on those trials when the dog salivates in advance of the normal time for its delivery (Herendeen & Shapiro, 1975). The law of effect predicts that dogs should learn *not* to salivate under these circumstances when exposed to this omission contingency, but this is something they seem to find remarkably difficult to do. Similar results have been obtained with other animals and other CRs (Mackintosh, 1983, pp. 30–33). But the Pavlovian principle is quite insufficient to account for all changes in behaviour in all conditioning experiments. For a start, it predicts that only responses elicited by (or at least related to) the reinforcer will be successfully conditioned: it should be impossible for animals to learn to perform wholly arbitrary responses to obtain food or avoid pain. Now it is true that animals often find it difficult to learn an operant response incompatible with their natural reactions to the reinforcer: Breland and Breland (1966) and Boakes, Poli, Lockwood, and Goodall (1978) reported that raccoons and rats were reluctant to drop a ball down a chute in order to obtain food. The problem was that the ball, by virtue of its association with food, elicited food-related CRs: the raccoons rubbed it between their paws, the rats put it in their mouth. While this is testimony to the power of the Pavlovian principle of reinforcement, it does not show it is an all-encompassing account of conditioning: Boakes et al.

(1978), for example, reported that all their rats *did* eventually learn to perform the required operant response.

A rat's lever presses for food or water rewards, or to escape or avoid shock, are not particularly closely related to any of these reinforcers, and since operant contingencies can determine the force, duration, and direction of such responses (Mackintosh, 1983, pp. 41, 138; see also Heyes & Dawson, 1990), it is hard to see how one could deny the operant principle of the law of effect. Moreover, although rats may come to approach and make contact with a manipulandum whose appearance signals the delivery of food, they will rapidly learn to avoid such responses if they cause the omission of food (Locurto, Terrace, & Gibbon, 1976): contrast this outcome with those referred to earlier, where Pavlovian CRs may persist for a long time even though they cause the omission of an appetitive reinforcer.

The distinction between classical and operant conditioning cannot then be merely operational. Some responses appear to be modifiable by their consequences while others seem to be simply elicited by a stimulus associated with a reinforcer regardless of those consequences. The distinction between these two processes is not an absolute one: although many responses may be affected more by one process than by the other, many are affected by both. In the final analysis, the question at issue is not whether a particular response is modifiable only by a stimulus–reinforcer contingency and another response only by a response–reinforcer contingency, it is whether we can separate the effects of the two types of contingencies.

Dickinson (1989) and his colleagues have revealed a further striking difference between Pavlovian and operant conditioning in the way in which a change in the incentive value of the reinforcer is translated into a change in behaviour. If a hungry dog receives conditioning trials with a CS paired with the delivery of meat powder, the salivary CR that emerges will show immediate and appropriate sensitivity to variations in the animal's level of motivation. If satiated for food, the dog will neither swallow the meat powder nor salivate to the CS signalling its delivery. But for an instrumental response to change in this way, the animal must, at some time or other, have had direct experience of the reinforcer under the changed level of motivation. Hungry rats trained to press a lever for sucrose (a reinforcer they have never experienced before) will continue to press the lever when satiated, unless and until they have the opportunity to discover that sucrose is of no value when they are satiated (Balleine, 1992). Similarly, the experiment described earlier on revaluing sucrose pellets by pairing their consumption with an injection of lithium has an immediate effect on Pavlovian CRs, but will produce a decline in instrumental responding only if the rat has a second opportunity to taste the sucrose after its initial pairing with illness (Balleine & Dickinson, 1991). Although these results are both surprising and perhaps puzzling, they certainly strengthen the case for arguing that there is an important distinction between the relatively automatic way in which an association between a CS and reinforcer allows the CS to elicit a change in behaviour, and the more indirect way in which an association between a response and a reinforcer causes a change in the probability of that response.

HIERARCHICAL ASSOCIATIONS

In a typical operant conditioning experiment, rats' lever presses are reinforced at some times but not at others, with the occurrence of reinforcement being marked by a particular discriminative stimulus (see Figure 3a). In due course the rat will learn to respond only in the presence of that stimulus. How is this control exercised? Some theorists have argued that there is a hierarchical or second-order association between the discriminative stimulus and the response–reinforcer relationship: in associative terms, the discriminative stimulus retrieves a representation of the response–reinforcer association (Mackintosh, 1983; Rescorla, 1991). Rescorla has provided evidence for this view with an experiment on blocking. Recall that blocking occurs when an added stimulus signals no change in reinforcement from that already predicted by the first stimulus. In general terms, the blocking experiment provides a powerful technique for inferring how animals encode information about the occurrence of a reinforcer. If blocking is disrupted by a particular change in the conditions under which reinforcement occurs, we can be confident that animals have detected this change. In the first stage of his experiments (as shown in Table 3) Rescorla trained rats in the presence of a single discriminative stimulus (S1) to perform two different responses, R1 and R2, for two different reinforcers Rf1 and Rf2. He then added a second stimulus, either maintaining the same relationship between responses and reinforcers as had been signalled by S1, or reversing that relationship so that now R1 was reinforced by Rf2 and R2 by Rf1. Where the compound signalled exactly the same relationship between response and reinforcer as S1 alone had, the added

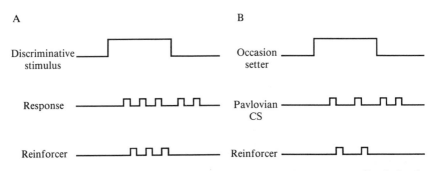
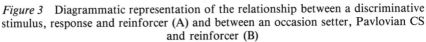

Figure 3 Diagrammatic representation of the relationship between a discriminative stimulus, response and reinforcer (A) and between an occasion setter, Pavlovian CS and reinforcer (B)

390

Table 3 Design and results of Rescorla (1991)

Group	Stage 1	Stage 2	Test results
Blocked	[S1: R1 → Rf1	[S1 + S2: R1 → Rf1	S2 does not control
	[S1: R2 → Rf2	[S1 + S2: R2 → Rf2	responding
Control	[S1: R1 → Rf2	[S1 + S2: R1 → Rf1	S2 does control
	[S1: R2 → Rf1	[S1 + S2: R2 → Rf2	responding

stimulus acquired no control over responding. But where the response–reinforcer relationships were changed, the added stimulus did acquire such control. Note that the only change was in the *relationship* between responses and reinforcers; any direct association between this stimulus and the response or the stimulus and the reinforcer alone was held constant across the two conditions. This study thus provides strong evidence that discriminative stimuli encode the actual relationship between events occurring in their presence.

Analogous effects have been discovered in Pavlovian experiments. A CS paired with a given reinforcer will be associated with that reinforcer, but if (as is shown in Figure 3b) this CS-reinforcer relationship holds only when another stimulus is present, then the second stimulus (the "occasion setter") may acquire hierarchical control over the first-order CS-reinforcer association; the first-order CS will elicit its CR only in the presence of the occasion setter (Holland, 1985; Rescorla, 1985). Of course, other simpler explanations of the establishment of this discrimination are possible, for it might be enough to say that both stimuli are associated with the reinforcer but too weakly for either to elicit a CR on its own. When both are combined, their combined associative strength is greater than some critical threshold and a CR occurs. But it turns out that the occasion setter's ability to control a CR to a target CS can survive substantial changes in its own direct association with the reinforcer. Under some conditions at least, repeated presentation of the occasion setter alone, sufficient to extinguish any such direct associations it may have, does not abolish its ability to control responding to its target CS (Holland, 1991).

There is evidence that the experimental context in which conditioning trials occur can also exert this sort of hierarchical control over associations between a CS or a response and reinforcer (Bouton & Swartzentruber, 1986). Under some circumstances (although by no means all), the effects of a series of conditioning or extinction trials may be largely confined to the context in which they occurred (Hall & Honey, 1990) and if different contingencies between CSs and reinforcers are established in different contexts, animals appear to retrieve the appropriate contingency when placed in the appropriate context.

ASSOCIATIVE LEARNING IN HUMANS

The time is long past when a learning theory based on conditioning experiments with animals was regarded as the key to understanding human behaviour. Many cognitive psychologists have taken it for granted that they could safely ignore both the results of, and the theories derived from, such experiments. Of course, it was acknowledged, CRs such as the eyeblink or GSR can be conditioned and extinguished, and may even show other phenomena found in animal studies (Lovibond, 1988; Martin & Levey, 1991); but what did this have to say of any interest to those studying human learning and memory, let alone thinking, reasoning, or problem solving? In normal adults, the conditioning process can apparently be overridden by instructions: simply telling subjects that the US will not occur again causes instant loss of a CR which would otherwise extinguish only slowly (Davey, 1983). Most subjects in a conditioning experiment are aware of the experimenter's contingencies, and in the absence of such awareness often fail to show evidence of conditioning (Brewer, 1974; but see Baeyens, Eelen, Van den Bergh, & Crombez, 1990, for an important exception to this generalization). Moreover, there are important differences between very young or severely retarded children (on the one hand) and older children and adults (on the other) in their behaviour in a variety of operant conditioning and discrimination learning experiments, differences that seem largely attributable to the development of language (Bentall & Lowe, 1987; Dugdale & Lowe, 1990). All this suggests that people have rather more efficient, language- or rule-based forms of learning at their disposal than the laborious formation of associations between a CS and a US. Even behaviour therapy, one of the apparently more successful attempts to apply principles of conditioning to human affairs, has given way to cognitive behaviour therapy or simply cognitive therapy.

The rise of connectionist theories has perhaps done something to change this perception, for such theories have provided surprisingly powerful explanations of many apparently complex aspects of human cognition (McClelland & Rumelhart, 1986; Morris, 1989; Rumelhart & McClelland, 1986) and have done so by applying little more than some of the basic assumptions of associative learning theory – including an error-correcting learning rule formally identical to that embodied in the Rescorla–Wagner model. The important message here is that it is probably less interesting to look for evidence of simple conditioning in human subjects than to apply the fundamental principles of associative learning (derived from conditioning experiments) to more complex situations. Thus Shanks and Dickinson (1987) have been able to show that the way in which people make judgements about contingencies between events (was one event the cause of another?) can be largely explained by the applications of the Rescorla–Wagner model (see also Wasserman, 1990), while Gluck and Bower (1988) and Shanks (1990) have applied a similar analysis to the way in which people make diagnostic judgements or learn to sort stimuli into different categories, and McLaren, Kaye, and Mackintosh (1989) and Hall (1991) have argued that some simple principles of associative learning can successfully explain many of the well-known, but poorly understood, phenomena of perceptual learning both in people and in other animals. It is not too fanciful to detect opportunities for significant rapprochement between a variety of different areas within experimental psychology.

FURTHER READING

Dickinson, A. (1980). *Contemporary animal learning theory*. Cambridge: Cambridge University Press.
Domjan, M., & Burkhardt, B. (1986). *The principles of learning and behavior* (2nd edn). Pacific Grove, CA: Brooks/Cole.
Flaherty, C. F. (1985). *Animal learning and cognition*. New York: McGraw-Hill.
Mackintosh, N. J. (1974). *The psychology of animal learning*. London: Academic Press.
Mackintosh, N. J. (1983). *Conditioning and associative learning*. Oxford: Oxford University Press.
Pearce, J. M. (1987). *Introduction to animal cognition*. Hillsdale, NJ: Lawrence Erlbaum.

REFERENCES

Baeyens, F., Eelen, P., van den Bergh, O., & Crombez, G. (1990). Flavor–flavor and color–flavor conditioning in humans. *Learning and Motivation*, *21*, 434–455.
Balleine, B. W. (1992). Instrumental performance following a shift in primary motivation depends on incentive learning. *Journal of Experimental Psychology: Animal Behavior Processes*, *18*, 236–250.
Balleine, B. W., & Dickinson, A. (1991). Instrumental performance following reinforcer devaluation depends upon incentive learning. *Quarterly Journal of Experimental Psychology*, *43B*, 279–296.
Bentall, R. P., & Lowe, C. F. (1987). The role of verbal behavior in human learning: III. Instructional effects in children. *Journal of the Experimental Analysis of Behavior*, *47*, 177–190.
Boakes, R. A., Poli, M., Lockwood, M. J., & Goodall, G. (1978). A study of misbehavior: Token reinforcement in the rat. *Journal of the Experimental Analysis of Behavior*, *29*, 115–134.
Bouton, M. E., & Swartzentruber, D. (1986). Analysis of the associative and occasion-setting properties of contexts participating in a Pavlovian discrimination. *Journal of Experimental Psychology: Animal Behavior Processes*, *12*, 333–350.
Breland, K., & Breland, M. (1966). *Animal behavior*. New York: Macmillan.
Brewer, W. F. (1974). There is no convincing evidence for operant or classical conditioning in adult humans. In W. B. Weimer & D. S. Palermo (Eds) *Cognition and the symbolic processes* (pp. 1–42). Hillsdale, NJ: Lawrence Erlbaum.
Davy, G. C. L. (1983). An associative view of human classical conditioning. In G. C. L. Davey (Ed.) *Animal models of human behavior: Conceptual, evolutionary, and neurobiological perspectives* (pp. 95–114). Chichester: Wiley.

Dickinson, A. (1989). Expectancy theory in animal conditioning. In S. B. Klein & R. R. Mowrer (Eds) *Contemporary learning theories* (pp. 279–308). Hillsdale, NJ: Lawrence Erlbaum.

Dickinson, A., & Mackintosh, N. J. (1979). Reinforcer specificity in the enhancement of conditioning by post-trial surprise. *Journal of Experimental Psychology: Animal Behavior Processes*, 5, 162–177.

Dickinson, A., Watt, A., & Griffiths, W. J. H. (1992). Free-operant acquisition with delayed reinforcement. *Quarterly Journal of Experimental Psychology*, 45B, 241–258.

Dugdale, N., & Lowe, C. F. (1990). Naming and stimulus equivalence. In D. E. Blackman & H. Lejeune (Eds) *Behaviour analysis in theory and practice: Contributions and controversies* (pp. 115–138). Hillsdale, NJ: Lawrence Erlbaum.

Ferster, C. B., & Skinner, B. F. (1957). *Schedules of reinforcement.* New York: Appleton-Century-Crofts.

Garrud, P., Goodall, G., & Mackintosh, N. J. (1981). Overshadowing of a stimulus–reinforcer association by an instrumental response. *Quarterly Journal of Experimental Psychology*, 33B, 123–135.

Gibbon, J., Baldock, M. D., Locurto, C., Gold, L., & Terrace, H. S. (1977). Trial and intertrial durations in autoshaping. *Journal of Experimental Psychology: Animal Behavior Processes*, 3, 264–284.

Gluck, M. A., & Bower, G. H. (1988). From conditioning to category learning: An adaptive network model. *Journal of Experimental Psychology: General*, 117, 227–247.

Hall, G. (1991). *Perceptual and associative learning.* Oxford: Oxford University Press.

Hall, G., & Honey, R. C. (1990) Context-specific conditioning in the conditioned-emotional-response procedure. *Journal of Experimental Psychology: Animal Behavior Processes*, 16, 271–278.

Herendeen, D. L., & Shapiro, M. M. (1975). Extinction and food-reinforced inhibition of conditioned salivation in dogs. *Animal Learning and Behavior*, 3, 103–106.

Heyes, C. M., & Dawson, G. R. (1990). A demonstration of observational learning in rats using a bidirectional control. *Quarterly Journal of Experimental Psychology*, 42B, 59–72.

Holland, P. C. (1985). The nature of conditioned inhibition in serial and simultaneous feature negative discriminations. In R. R. Miller & N. E. Spear (Eds) *Information processing in animals: Conditioned inhibition* (pp. 267–297). Hillsdale, NJ: Lawrence Erlbaum.

Holland, P. C. (1991). Transfer of control in ambiguous discriminations. *Journal of Experimental Psychology: Animal Behavior Processes*, 17, 231–248.

Holland, P. C., & Straub, J. J. (1979). Differential effects of two ways of devaluing the unconditioned stimulus after Pavlovian appetitive conditioning. *Journal of Experimental Psychology: Animal Behavior Processes*, 5, 65–78.

Kamin, L. J. (1969). Predictability, surprise, attention and conditioning. In R. Campbell & R. Church (Eds) *Punishment and aversive behaviour* (pp. 279–296). New York: Appleton-Century-Crofts.

Locurto, C., Terrace, H. S., & Gibbon, J. (1976). Autoshaping, random control, and omission training in the rat. *Journal of the Experimental Analysis of Behavior*, 26, 451–462.

Lovibond, P. F. (1988). Predictive validity in human causal judgment and Pavlovian conditioning. *Biosocial Psychology*, 27, 79–93.

McClelland, J. L., & Rumelhart, D. E. (1986). *Parallel distributed processing: Explorations in the microstructure of cognition*, vol. II. Cambridge, MA: Bradford.

Mackintosh, N. J. (1983). *Conditioning and associative learning*. Oxford: Oxford University Press.

Mackintosh, N. J., & Dickinson, A. (1979). Instrumental (Type II) conditioning. In A. Dickinson & R. A. Boakes (Eds) *Mechanisms of learning and motivation* (pp. 143–167). Hillsdale, NJ: Lawrence Erlbaum.

McLaren, I. P. L., Kaye, H., & Mackintosh, N. J. (1989). An associative theory of the representation of stimuli: applications to perceptual learning and latent inhibition. In R. G. M. Morris (Ed.) *Parallel distributed processing: Implications for psychology and neurobiology* (pp. 102–130). Oxford: Oxford University Press.

Martin, I., & Levey, A. B. (1991). Blocking observed in human eyelid conditioning. *Quarterly Journal of Experimental Psychology*, *43B*, 233–256.

Miller, S., & Konorski, J. (1928). "Sur une forme particulière des réflexes conditionnels". *Comptes rendus des séances de la société de biologie*, *99*, 1155–1157.

Morris, R. G. M. (Ed.) (1989). *Parallel distributed processing: Implications for psychology and neurobiology*. Oxford: Oxford University Press.

Pavlov, I. P. (1927). *Conditioned reflexes*. Oxford: Oxford University Press.

Rescorla, R. A. (1968). Probability of shock in the presence and absence of CS in fear conditioning. *Journal of Comparative and Physiological Psychology*, *66*, 1–5.

Rescorla, R. A. (1969). Pavlovian conditioned inhibition. *Psychological Bulletin*, *72*, 77–94.

Rescorla, R. A. (1985). Conditioned inhibition and facilitation. In R. R. Miller & N. E. Spear (Eds) *Information processing in animals: Conditioned inhibition* (pp. 299–326). Hillsdale, NJ: Lawrence Erlbaum.

Rescorla, R. A. (1991). Associative relations in instrumental learning. *Quarterly Journal of Experimental Psychology*, *43B*, 1–24.

Rescorla, R. A., & Wagner, A. R. (1972). A theory of Pavlovian conditioning: Variations in the effectiveness of reinforcement and nonreinforcement. In A. H. Black & W. F. Prokasy (Eds) *Classical conditioning II: Current research and theory* (pp. 64–99). New York: Appleton-Century-Crofts.

Revusky, S. (1971). The role of interference in association over a delay. In W. K. Honig & P. H. R. James (Eds) *Animal memory* (pp. 155–213). New York: Academic Press.

Revusky, S., & Garcia, J. (1970). Learned associations over long delays. In G. H. Bower (Ed.) *The psychology of learning and motivation* (vol. 4, pp. 1–84). New York: Academic Press.

Rozin, P., & Kalat, J. W. (1971). Specific hungers and poisoning as adaptive specializations of learning. *Psychological Review*, *78*, 459–486.

Rumelhart, D. E., & McClelland, J. L. (1986). *Parallel distributed processing: Explorations in the microstructure of cognition*, vol. I. Cambridge, MA; Bradford.

Seligman, M. E. P. (1970). On the generality of the laws of learning. *Psychological Review*, *77*, 406–418.

Shanks, D. R. (1990). Connectionism and the learning of probabilistic concepts. *Quarterly Journal of Experimental Psychology*, *42A*, 209–238.

Shanks, D. R., & Dickinson, A. (1987). Associative accounts of causality judgment. In G. H. Bower (Ed.) *The psychology of learning and motivation* (vol. 21, pp. 229–261). San Diego, CA: Academic Press.

Skinner, B. F. (1938). *The behavior of organisms*. New York: Appleton-Century-Crofts.

Thorndike, E. L. (1911). *Animal intelligence: Experimental studies*. New York: Macmillan.

Wasserman, E. A. (1990). Detecting response–outcome relations: Toward an understanding of the causal texture of the environment. In G. H. Bower (Ed.) *The psychology of learning and motivation: Advances in research and theory* (vol. 26, pp. 27–82). London: Academic Press.

5.2

APPLIED BEHAVIOUR ANALYSIS

Donald M. Baer

University of Kansas, USA

Reinforcement concepts and techniques in applied behaviour analysis	Technological
	Conceptually systematic
	Effective
The definition of applied behaviour analysis	Capable of generalized effects
Applied	**Summary**
Behavioural	**Further reading**
Analytic	**References**

Many practitioners would agree that they practise applied behaviour analysis, but some of them would not agree completely on the definition of their discipline, or that other practitioners who claim to be applied behaviour analysts deserve the title. Of course, that kind of disagreement is true of many disciplines, applied and basic. In the case of applied behaviour analysis, diversity of opinion probably results from a pre-existing diversity in the philosophical approach, behaviourism, from which it is derived, and in the diverse trainings and motivations of its practitioners and researchers.

Zuriff (1985), in *Behaviorism*, reviews the wide variety of logic and definition that operate in modern behaviourism. He shows that even so, a consistent enough core of usage, argument, and procedure can be extracted to define at least one philosophical approach deserving the name; his book is aptly subtitled *A Conceptual Reconstruction*. Much the same deconstructive-reconstructive approach is needed to characterize applied behaviour analysis, because it shows a large overlap with, yet certain small differences from, related disciplines called behaviour modification, behaviour therapy, cognitive-behaviour therapy, cognitive therapy, learning theory, social learning theory, radical behaviourism, methodological behaviourism, neo-behaviourism, and the like.

Inspecting the tables of contents of two definitive texts, *Contemporary Behavior Therapy*, edited by Wilson and Franks (1982), and *Theoretical Issues in Behavior Therapy*, edited by Reiss and Bootzin (1985), will illustrate this breadth. It will also suggest that disciplinary diversity is increasing rather than condensing to an essential core. Those texts will show the reader the larger context of behavioural application, which makes discussion of any one of its variants somewhat arbitrary. However, careful reading of those chapters may also show that although practitioners display great diversity in discussing the meaning of their work, the work itself shows considerably less diversity.

REINFORCEMENT CONCEPTS AND TECHNIQUES IN APPLIED BEHAVIOUR ANALYSIS

In its early years, applied behaviour analysis was mainly an attempt to see whether learning theory, until then essentially a laboratory science based mainly on studies of animal behaviour, could be applied to the problems of real people in their society. The basic principle in learning theory appeared to be reinforcement: whether a behaviour will occur more or less frequently in the future is determined most fundamentally by certain of its consistent, systematic consequences (cf. Skinner, 1938, 1953). Those consequences that affect the future occurrence of the behaviours that precede them are termed *reinforcers*, simply to label the fact that they affect the behaviours that precede them. Some of them are called *positive reinforcers* because they increase the future probability of responses that consistently and systematically produce or increase them, and others of them are called *negative reinforcers* because they increase the future probability of responses that consistently and systematically avoid or reduce them. Increasing a behaviour's future probability by controlling its consequences in either process is termed *reinforcement*. When reinforcement is discontinued, that increased probability of the behaviour's occurrence typically declines to its pre-reinforcement level, and that process is usually termed *extinction*.

Thus, for example, we may discover that many of a person's behaviours exist because they often achieve approval from important other people, and we may then call approval a positive reinforcer for those behaviours of that person; we may discover that many others of the person's behaviours exist because they often avoid or reduce disapproval from important other people, and we may then call disapproval a negative reinforcer for those behaviours of that person; and we may well see that many of those behaviours, once strong, are lost or reduced when they no longer accomplish either process.

If reinforcement is the basic principle of learning theory, then *discrimination* is its most important derivative principle (cf. Skinner, 1938, 1953). The point of discrimination is that in real life, no behaviour leads to the same consistent, systematic consequences at all times and in all places. For example, even breathing does not always produce its natural consequence of the oxygen-nitrogen-pollutants mixture that we call air. Swimming requires that breathing occurs only when the mouth or nostrils are out of the water; singing requires, somewhat less stringently, that we breathe according to the structure of the music rather than at any time we may be a little short of breath. In swimming, the relevant reinforcer is access to the air; in singing, the relevant positive reinforcer is the maximal beauty of the music we produce, and the relevant negative reinforcers are our disapproval (and our audience's disapproval) of any breathing patterns that would mar that beauty.

If there are environmental events – stimuli – that mark the times or places when a behaviour will have consistent, systematic reinforcing consequences, then those stimuli typically will come to evoke those behaviours that will produce or increase positive reinforcers at those times or places, or evoke those behaviours that will avoid or reduce negative reinforcers at those times or places. Thus "out of water" and "end of phrase" are stimuli signalling when breathing will have reinforcing consequences; they are termed *discriminative stimuli* to index the fact that they control our behaviour in that way.

A more fundamental statement is possible: what we mean by learning is behaviour change. What we mean by behaviour change is the selection of some behaviours over others. Learning theory argues that environments select behaviours, and put them under the control of any stimuli that may mark when or where the selection processes operate. The behaviours that environments select are those that produce and increase, or avoid and reduce, the relevant consequences of that environment – its reinforcers. That argument resembles evolutionary theory, which supposes that environments select most the species that survive well enough in them to reproduce best. Over generations, evolution selects species sensitive to certain reinforcers relevant to survival and reproduction, and capable of becoming sensitive to even more; within any organism's life, reinforcers select the behaviours that best produce or avoid them. Both approaches are thereby seen as *selectionist* in philosophy.

Despite the pervasiveness of the reinforcement concept and its techniques in applied behaviour analysis, they are not definitional of it. However, they may well seem so to casual inspection of the field; a very large proportion of conceptualization and practice in the field embodies them. So, while they are not definitional, their frequent operation in the discipline sometimes makes behaviour-analytic diagnosis and intervention rather distinctive, considered alongside more traditional psychological approaches, and that distinctiveness needs description here.

In traditional approaches, problem behaviour is very likely to be seen as expressive; if so, its form or topography becomes a key to its meaning. By contrast, in applied behaviour analysis (as in its parent disciplines, behaviour analysis and operant psychology), behaviour is invariably questioned first for its instrumentality – for what consequences it accomplishes in the behaver's environment. In that case, its form becomes almost irrelevant, because different environments can easily give the same function to an arbitrary range of behaviour topographies.

The aggressive child is a classic example. Suppose that a child in a day-care setting often hits, scratches, pushes, and bites other children, often destroys their constructions and possessions, and often threatens them with these and other forms of violence. Traditional views usually begin with the topography of the child's behaviour, see it as aggressive and destructive, and suppose that it is expressive. The usual assumption is that aggression expresses anger, resentment, or fear. Then a traditional diagnosis asks what has made this child angry, resentful, or afraid (and perhaps singles out what seems a relevant fact, such as a new baby in the family). Subsequent therapy often focuses on reducing those causes (e.g., telling parents to increase their attention to this child, despite the new baby), and perhaps considers teaching the child to respond to them better (e.g., tells the parents to make the child an extravagantly praised helper in caring for the baby). A behaviour-analytic approach asks instead what consequences these behaviours consistently, systematically accomplish, and relies on extensive, intensive, objective, uninterpretative observation to see what they may be.

That kind of observation, to be behavioural, requires the observer to count how often and how long, and where and when, certain physically defined behaviours occur, whether or not they seem to meet the spirit in which the observation is undertaken. Again, the aggressive child is a classic example. An observer of aggression would not be asked to record the child's "aggressions" (and its consequences); that would require interpretation, and we would find ourselves studying the observer's interpretative behaviour, not the child's aggressions. Instead, the observer very likely would be asked to observe all instances of "forceful application of hands/feet/teeth/shoulders to the body/property of another person". That kind of definition is meant to prevent interpretation by the observer. It also allows a small amount of invalid measurement, as, for example, if the child plays a friendly game of leap-frog and necessarily applies hands forcefully to the back of another child. In the applied behaviour-analytic approach, the occasional error of that kind is considered a small price for a better approximation to objectivity of measurement.

A beginning list of the systematic consequences of aggression, so defined, that objective observation often will reveal might take the following form:

1 intense, lengthy, sympathetic adult attention
2 intense, lengthy, angry adult attention

400

3 a temporary lapse in the ongoing demands for work or obedience that adults make on well-behaved children

4 undisputed control of some play space

5 undisputed control of some play materials

6 solitude

7 tears, crying, and retreats by other children.

Any of these systematic consequences may be the positive or negative reinforcer supporting this behaviour, or the reinforcer may be something else that the observer has not yet noticed. And there may be more than one reinforcer operative in this case.

When the list is considered complete, the observer will often ask a helpful question about each item on it: "Do any other easily performed behaviours of the child seem to accomplish this consequence better (more reliably, more quickly, more enduringly, with less effort) than the aggressive behaviours under study?" The answer may already be evident, or it may require further observation. If the answer is Yes, the probability diminishes that this item is the reinforcer responsible for the frequent aggressive behaviour, but not to zero; if the answer is No, the probability rises that this item is the responsible reinforcer, but not to certainty. The question is helpful, but not definitive.

In applied behaviour analysis, the only certain way to decide among these reinforcer possibilities is to perform a set of diagnostic experiments, often called a functional *analysis* (e.g., Carr & Durand, 1985; Iwata, Pace, Kalsher, Caldery, & Cataldo, 1990). These experiments require first that each consequence be controlled systematically, one at a time, to reveal what will happen to the aggressive behaviours when they no longer accomplish this particular consequence. The preceding question can help establish the most cost-effective order in which to test these possibilities. In addition, these experiments require that careful, extensive observation establish if the aggressive behaviour occurs similarly throughout all the child's environments, or only in some places; and whether it occurs similarly at all times, or only at some times.

The combination of answers from these two classes of experiments should guide the intervention that will follow. For example, suppose that the experiments show that it is the consistently consequent lengthy attention from teachers at day-care and parents at home, whether approving or disapproving, that is the reinforcer. Suppose the observations show that aggressive behaviours from this child are seen primarily when teachers or parents are available to answer them with lengthy attention. That pattern means that one appropriate intervention is to discontinue those parental and teacher patterns, so that aggression no longer consistently and systematically produces attention from teachers and parents. Yet aggression cannot simply be ignored, for fear that children will be hurt; thus the parents and teachers may be taught to attend immediately, consistently, and systematically to the aggressor's victim rather than to the aggressor, removing the victim from harm as instantly as possible without a moment's attention to the aggressor (e.g., Pinkston, Reese, LeBlanc, & Baer, 1973). In addition, teachers and parents may be taught to consistently and systematically offer lengthy attention for desirable non-aggressive behaviours by this child, so that the same reinforcer can be gained by child behaviours that are not only more desirable to all, but also easier for the child.

Alternatively, suppose that the experiments show that it is the undisputed control of certain toys and materials that is the reinforcer, and the observations show that aggression is seen only when those particular toys and materials are available for play. Then the intervention could take the form of never making those toys and materials available, or of making sure that aggression always forfeits their control to children other than the aggressor, meanwhile making certain that the child knows better ways to ask to use those toys and materials, and that those ways will prove more efficient than aggression in future access to them.

Alternatively again, suppose that the experiments show that the reinforcer is the sight and sound of other children crying and retreating, and the observations show that aggression against them occurs at any times they are present. Then the intervention may take the form of reducing the reinforcing effectiveness of those particular reinforcers, and increasing the reinforcing effectiveness of their opposites. Two assumptions will be made. One is that these reinforcers have acquired their reinforcing function through unfortunate socialization experiences. The other is that the discrimination process can be used to make and unmake reinforcers: its formulas are that stimuli made discriminative for access to positive reinforcers or escape from negative reinforcers usually become positive reinforcers themselves, that stimuli made discriminative for the loss of positive reinforcers or gaining of negative reinforcers usually become negative reinforcers themselves, and that when stimuli lose their discriminative function, they usually also lose the reinforcing function that discriminative function had lent them (cf. Catania, 1984, pp. 179–185; Kazdin, 1977, p. 3; Reese, 1978, p. 21; Skinner, 1953, chap. 12; Stubbs & Cohen, 1972). Then the intervention might well be to create an environment in which when other children are happy, this child has maximal access to as many as possible of his or her other reinforcers; and when other children cry or run away, this child has as minimal access as possible to as many as possible of his or her other reinforcers.

However, applied behaviour analysis is often practised when prior functional analysis of a problem behaviour is impossible, impractical, or not favoured by the practitioner. (It can be problematic to conduct the necessary experiments and observations in real-life settings, and when they are done in more convenient settings instead, it is easy to doubt their validity for the real-life settings in which the behaviour under investigation is a problem.) In those cases, interventions probably will not attempt to change the current reinforcement contingencies, but instead will try to override their effects with more powerful reinforcement contingencies developed and applied by the practitioner. Many behaviours have been altered effectively by the contingent use of approval and praise, sweets and other favoured edibles, access to specially favoured activities, money, and the like, all without analysis of what reinforcers (if any) were maintaining the problem behaviour.

Indeed, the frequent success of money as a positive reinforcer, when used in adequate amounts, parallels a classic technique in applied behaviour analysis to achieve similar success by mimicking its essential characteristics: the *token reinforcement system* or *token economy* (cf. Kazdin, 1977; Martin & Pear, 1978, pp. 137, 144–145, 335–365). A token economy is constructed by maintaining a shop or store that stocks every practical reinforcer known to be even occasionally effective for the people under study, whether these are tangible things or tickets allowing access to special activities; these are called the *back-ups*, and if possible they are made unavailable from any other source. Back-ups can be bought only with a special currency, the token. Tokens are often small pieces of plastic that token-system clients can get only through the practitioner; sometimes, they are simply marks entered in the client's account book by the practitioner; and sometimes they are merely verbal announcements of having earned points toward something.

The practitioner assigns in advance how many tokens are required to purchase each item in the store, and makes that known to the clients, either by posting prices if the clients have the necessary cognitive skills, or through extensive experience if they do not. If the store is well stocked for the clients at hand, and if the practitioner has successfully taught the clients that these items are available only by purchasing them with tokens, that is, through token exchanges, and has taught the clients all of what back-ups are available, and at what cost, then the token itself becomes an exceptionally powerful reinforcer.

Any client's reinforcers vary in effectiveness from time to time, and from situation to situation; and of course any client may become temporarily satiated with one reinforcer or another. The effectiveness of the token system results from the great variety of potential reinforcers that it stocks, such that there is sure to be at least one effective reinforcer for any client at any time, and very likely to be many. The practicality of the token system is equally great: practitioners can readily carry and dispense tokens as contingent reinforcers, when they could hardly carry or dispense many of the back-ups that the tokens will buy (such as access to a public game, or a container of cold soda, or an hour's TV viewing time, or a hamburger). With tokens, practitioners have the opportunity not only to reinforce the responses they have chosen as clinically desirable for the client, immediately as they occur, but also to teach needful clients the skills of collecting, keeping safe, and eventually exchanging tokens, thereby slowly moving the clients from dependence on only short-term gratifications to much longer-term ones.

403

Even so, the practitioner can easily diminish the value of the tokens by requiring too many of them for the back-ups, by requiring too few of them for the back-ups, by constantly changing prices, by reducing the critical variety of the back-ups, by not maintaining a balance of high-priced and low-priced items, by delaying tokens-for-back-ups exchange times too long for the clients' current abilities to mediate, by not teaching clients the skills necessary to avoid misplacing their accumulating tokens, by allowing some clients to be systematically victimized by others who steal their tokens, or by not keeping up with the clients' changing tastes as the behaviour-change programme proceeds.

Token systems have often been criticized as being artificial, and as teaching inappropriately materialistic values (often by critics whose own behaviour is thoroughly and happily enmeshed in the money system of their culture). In response to these criticisms, many applied behaviour analysts have given up their use, despite their power for otherwise difficult-to-accomplish behaviour changes. Others have learned to use token systems only temporarily, and have them gradually fade out of noticeable existence, at first by systematically making the exchanges later and later. Meanwhile, they begin to replace the physical token awards with symbolic account-book awards and a great deal of approval. Then their approval grows steadily more prominent as the account-book awards grow less prominent and less reliable. Soon, merely very approving verbal agreements about roughly how many tokens have been earned are operating, thus making the eventual exchanges less on the basis of how much credit the client has amassed, and more on the basis of how well the client has behaved since the last exchange. Indeed those two criteria have become essentially identical, and the system has become remarkably like those ordinary, undesigned everyday social systems in which people who behave well are treated well. When applied to developmentally delayed clients, this cosmetic fading of the token system into an unobtrusive natural social arrangement will go more slowly, in part because it will require the early teaching of the necessary cognitive skills before the explicit token system can fade into the implicit one, if it is to remain successful.

Using principles and procedures much like these, or derivative from these, applied behaviour analysts (sometimes using other professional titles) have since the early 1970s made and published several thousand experimental analyses of many problematic behaviours in a wide variety of clients at a wide variety of age levels. The following list notes illustrative examples of the behaviours that have often been targeted:

aggression	biting
alcoholism	blood pressure
anger	bullying
assertiveness	community organization
attendance	compliance
attention span	cooperation

counting
courtesy
door-slamming
drug abuse
elective mutism
energy conservation
enuresis
exercise
grammar
greeting others
hair-pulling
headbanging
heart-rate
hyperactivity
imitation
littering
marital discord
on-task behaviour
over-eating
peer-tutoring
pill-taking
play skills
posture
promptness

property destruction
public speaking
quarrelling
recruiting praise
safety
seizures
self-injury
self-instruction
self-monitoring
self-scratching
sentence construction
sign language
sloppiness
smoking
social skills
staff training
study
tantrums
teasing
thumbsucking
vandalism
volunteering
vomiting
walking skills

The next list notes the settings in which these behaviours have most often been changed:

clinics
delinquency halfway houses
factories
homes
hospitals
mental hospitals
nursing stations
offices
playgrounds
preschool classrooms

public school classrooms
public spaces
retardation halfway houses
retardation institutions
shops and malls
street intersections
streets
university classrooms
waiting rooms

Somewhat more detailed accounts of just how these behaviours were changed in the people living or working in these settings can be gleaned from several texts designed to provide overviews of the field, notably those by Sulzer-Azaroff and Mayer (1991), Martin and Pear (1978), and Reese (1978). Readers will note that the most frequently used techniques are based on the reinforcement and discrimination principles just sketched. Despite its heavy reliance on them, reinforcement concepts and techniques are not definitional of applied behaviour analysis. But, with an appreciation of their prevalence in the discipline, we are in a better position to consider how to define it.

THE DEFINITION OF APPLIED BEHAVIOUR ANALYSIS

The first research journal devoted to the discipline of applied behaviour analysis, the appropriately named *Journal of Applied Behavior Analysis*, was first published in 1968. In its first issue, Baer, Wolf, and Risley (1968) offered a tentative characterization of the field in its first article, "Some current dimensions of applied behavior analysis". That paper, which cited seven essential or ideal dimensions of then-current research and practice, has been widely cited since as either definitive or comprehensively characteristic of the discipline. Nearly twenty years later, an anniversary edition of the journal presented an updated version of that article (Baer, Wolf, & Risley, 1987), which cited the same seven dimensions, as prefaced by its title, "Some still-current dimensions of applied behavior analysis". It noted that twenty years of experience had not changed these seven dimensions, but had greatly broadened the contexts within which each was to be understood.

Those seven prescriptions are that work in the field should be *applied*, *behavioural*, *analytic*, *technological*, *conceptually systematic*, *effective*, and *capable of generalized effects*. Each of these is discussed below.

Applied

The analysis of behaviour is applied, if first, the behaviours under analysis can be categorized as a *problem* by at least the individual troubled by them and the practitioner to whom the troubled individual complains (on the assumption that the practitioner can change them); and second, changing those behaviours does indeed solve or alleviate the complainer's problem (cf. Baer, 1988). The application is perhaps more important if the behaviours are considered a problem by a larger segment of society, but a great deal of application is done for individuals.

It is important to note that especially in the areas of developmental disability and mental illness, and especially when the troubling behaviours reside in children, the people who complain most often to practitioners cite problems not with their own behaviours, but with the behaviours of the delayed or mentally ill individuals, or of the children, with whom they live or for whose habilitation, rehabilitation, or teaching they have been made responsible, or have assumed responsibility.

In this view, it is crucial to note that true application is not achieved simply by changing the targeted behaviours; it must also be true that changing those behaviours solves or alleviates the complainers' problem. In this approach, no behaviours are intrinsically pathological; their problematic status always depends on at least one complainer. A behaviour is problematic only because someone finds it so, or a culture defines it as such, and one or more practitioners agree to attempt its change. Even cultural definitions are contextual: there is hardly a behaviour to which we can object that would not be found desirable or tolerable in some other context. We see killing as murder in a peaceful context but as heroism in a warlike context; we see a person's deliberate self-exposure to death as hurtful or sinful in some contexts, but heroic in others (as when trying to rescue a child from a burning building).

Behavioural

In behavioural application, behaviours are defined to be publicly observable by virtually any observer, rather than only by someone trained in the relevant clinical science. That means that only their physical dimensions will be cited as what the observer is to see or hear and record; it follows that behaviours that have no physical dimensions cannot be observed and so evade analysis and treatment in the discipline. As noted earlier, observers are never told to record something labelled "aggression", but instead something physical requiring much less interpretation on their part, for example "forceful application of hands/feet/teeth/shoulders to the body/property of another person". Similarly, observers usually are not asked to discriminate between "intentional" forceful applications and "accidental" forceful applications, unless we can specify some physical conditions that we believe will reliably separate the two categories. Some practitioners might risk defining "intentional" as only those that occur with an immediately prior (e.g., within 3 seconds) orientation of the aggressor's face to the subsequent target, and the rest as "unintentional"; other practitioners might see this as a reasonable attempt, but too fraught with potential error for ordinary use. This difference between practitioners' development of their measurement systems is one of pragmatic judgement, not principle.

However, if the postulate is that behaviours that have no physical dimensions, or no publicly observable physical dimensions, must be ignored by the discipline, that can lead to apparently principled disputes, and sometimes to invidious comparisons between behaviour-analytic and cognitive approaches. For example, when clients complain of persistent distressing thoughts that they do not know how to stop or prevent, it might appear that behavioural practitioners must on principle confess their helplessness while cognitive practitioners will recognize a problem exactly appropriate to their discipline. In practice, the difference will prove more verbal than real. Both will very likely teach essentially the same "thought-stopping" techniques (cf. Cautela & Wysocki, 1977). The cognitive analysts will report that their intervention was responsive to their clients' thoughts, and that they were successful in stopping those thoughts. The behavioural practitioners will report that their intervention was responsive to their clients' descriptions of their thoughts, and that they were successful in getting their clients to describe an absence of those thoughts. Very likely, both sets of practitioners will have done essentially the same things and have based their conclusions on essentially the same evidence. The cognitive analysts may be a little less troubled about the reality of what they had just accomplished, but not much. Theorists, of course, may continue to see a profound difference of paradigm in how the two sets of practitioners talk about their work.

Analytic

Behaviour analysis is analytic when first: it can convincingly show the origin of, or more likely, what is currently maintaining the problem behaviours under consideration; second, it can convincingly show that the procedures subsequently applied to the problem are responsible for the behaviour changes that occur; third, it makes good theoretical sense that those procedures should have changed those behaviours in that way; and fourth, those changes resolve or alleviate the original complaint about the behaviours to be changed. At their best, practice and research in the field achieve all four; but quite often, usually because of practical limitations, only the second and third are accomplished, and sometimes only the second.

To accomplish even the second – to show convincingly that the procedures applied to a set of behaviours are responsible for the subsequent changes in those behaviours – requires a small experiment. Typically, those experiments are conducted with one subject, the client; hence they use what are called single-subject designs. The single-subject designs, frequently used throughout the history of natural science, are rarely used in social, behavioural, and clinical sciences; thus their use gives applied behaviour analysis (and behaviour analysis) another quite distinctive attribute, and incidentally reveals its strong affinity for the natural rather than the social sciences. One quite common version of single-subject design uses four successive phases: first, the practitioner-researcher observes, measures, and plots the behaviours under study on to a graph, and establishes that measurement is reliable, that the behaviours do indeed have a level that can be considered a problem, and that there is no natural trend in these behaviours that would indicate that they will improve as fast as a practitioner might improve them. Second, an intervention is made: behaviour-change procedures are applied while measurement and graphing continue, to reveal whether these procedures are effective enough to satisfy the practitioner-researcher's judgement of how much change is needed, and how promptly it is needed. Third, if the procedures seem promising, then measurement and graphing continue while the behaviour-change procedures are discontinued, or are replaced by contrasting procedures (e.g., a "placebo"), to show whether the change just observed was coincidental or a systematic result of the behaviour-change procedures applied by the practitioner-researcher. Fourth, if the behaviour-change is reversed, diminished, or halted, then measurement and graphing continue while the behaviour-change procedures applied in the second phase are resumed, and the behaviours are brought to the final state of change desired by the practitioner-researcher, who is now confident that those behaviour changes are not coincidental, but are systematic results of the behaviour-change procedures applied.

An exposition of all of the single-subject designs, and all their procedures, would be prohibitively long here; interested readers might well begin their study with Kazdin's (1982) text, *Single-Case Research Designs.*

Technological

Applied behaviour analysis is presumed to be more of a scientific process than an artful or personal one. Thus, we would not expect it to be practised better by certain experts than others; its effective procedures should have been disseminated perfectly by way of research reports, manuals, training films, and tapes, etc. All its applications are supposed to become matters of recipe, much like the recipes of cookery books. Even modestly trained readers with relatively little experience should always be able to produce the same result simply by following the recipe.

Yet sometimes applied behaviour-analytic practitioner-researchers find that the presumably complete and objective descriptions of their procedures are not sufficient to allow reasonably trained readers to accomplish the same level of results. In that case, a highly appropriate next research target is to discover what ingredients are missing from the recipes that had been offered to the field previously, so as to publish new recipes that are more perfectly technological.

Devotion to technology gives much of the applied behaviour-analytic literature a distinctive character. Readers looking for exact solutions to behaviour-change problems may often find exactly what they need; readers in search of new principles will probably be bored.

Conceptually systematic

The conceptual system of a cookery book lies in physical chemistry, and very few cooks know enough physical chemistry to appreciate the unity and predictability of the recipes in any of their books. When enough properly technological recipes exist to satisfy virtually every eater's needs, cooks need not learn more. However, in a field like applied behaviour analysis, where not nearly enough recipes exist to solve the problems confronting practitioners, the field will advance better if its practitioners can become practitioner-researchers (cf. Pinkston, Levitt, Green, Linsk, & Rzepnicki, 1982, esp. chaps 2, 4, 9, and 10) who can refine existing recipes and invent the new ones necessary for some new problems. That is likely to proceed more efficiently if the practitioner-researchers have a conceptual system that explains how behaviour works, and does so well enough to predict what kinds of behaviour-change interventions are effective, what it may mean when they do not work as expected at first, and, most important of all, what to do next in that case. Many conceptual systems can explain anything that happens, once it is clear what has happened; far fewer seem able to explain a failure in terms that reliably indicate how to produce a subsequent success.

So far, the largely reinforcement-based conceptual system of applied behaviour analysis has met that criterion fairly well. However, it is obvious that if some alternative conceptual system could accomplish the same goals even better, applied behaviour analysts could immediately turn to that new system, and to its distinctive procedures, and still be applied behaviour analysts. Reinforcement theory is not the definitive characteristic of applied behaviour analysis; but one of the field's definitive characteristics is to rely on some conceptual system for these purposes.

Effective

Almost every clinical discipline aspires to effectiveness; the distinctive disciplinary question is how to define it. The internal logic of applied behaviour analysis suggests two sometimes distinctive meanings of effectiveness.

First, because in this approach no behaviour is intrinsically pathological, and problem behaviours are thought to be defined as such only by relevant people and cultural practice, then it follows that any behavioural intervention has been effective not to the extent that it has changed its target behaviours, but to the extent that it has changed the complaints about those target behaviours that provoked the behaviour-change intervention in the first place. Thus, in a school system that grades its students' work as A, B, C, D, and F (failing), changing the study and work behaviours of a student who is constantly awarded Fs into behaviours that will earn Ds will be effective enough, if the originating complaint is merely that the student is failing. If the originating complaint is that the student is shamefully stupid by ordinary social standards, then effectiveness may require that the behaviours be changed enough to achieve Cs. If the originating complaint is that the student will not be able to apply successfully to a medical school, then effectiveness will demand that the behaviours be changed into those that earn As.

Second, even if a behavioural intervention is effective enough to change behaviours sufficiently to reduce or alleviate the originating complaints about them, it may not be considered truly effective unless it also survives, as an intervention, as long as the problem it solves is there to be solved by it. Suppose, for example, that a teacher complains that her students are so unruly that teaching them anything is difficult, and that even when they are reasonably well behaved, they learn little. Suppose that we offer her some of the many behavioural intervention programs that solve such problems (e.g., O'Leary & O'Leary, 1972), and that with our support, she uses these interventions to achieve a classroom of well-behaved, hard-working, high-achieving students. The teacher expresses delight, and reports that her problem has been solved completely. The first meaning of effectiveness has

410

been achieved. And so suppose further that after a year of this thorough success, we withdraw, because it is clear that she knows exactly how to continue these programmes herself, and is well able to do so. But suppose that we check this classroom two years later, and find none of the programmes being practised, and the current children once again rowdy and unaccomplished. The second meaning of effectiveness has not been achieved: some successful programmes were put in place but did not survive, even though the problems for which they are effective solutions are still present and still demanding solution, and those programmes would still solve those problems if applied to them. Then we need a doubly effective programme: one that will reduce all the teacher's complaints, and one that she will continue to use after we are gone. Put differently, we were ineffective because our initial analysis was incomplete: we analysed the children's deportment and academic achievement, but not their teacher's tolerance for the programmes that accomplish that. Thus, for effectiveness, the analysis of her tolerance is the most important next research question.

That research would go better if we could predict reliably when the people who use behaviour-change programmes in our presence will not continue using them in our absence, or when they dislike our programmes but are reluctant to say so in our presence. The interview and questionnaire techniques aimed at accomplishing that kind of prediction have been prescribed and named *social validity* (Wolf, 1978), but they have not yet been studied enough to evaluate their effectiveness for that purpose, and they are very likely still incomplete (Schwartz & Baer, 1991). The evaluation of social validity is one of the major research questions in modern practice.

Capable of generalized effects

A very frequent finding in behavioural intervention is that the target behaviours change readily enough in the setting in which the intervention takes place, but that those changes do not generalize to all the other places where those behaviour changes are desired. Thus a speech therapist will often discover that a child's poor articulation can be improved greatly through imitation and differential reinforcement with the therapist in the clinic, but that the child now articulates better only there and only in the presence of the speech therapist, and not yet with parents, friends, other teachers, and peers in other places. Modern applied behaviour analysis systematically assumes that the desired generalizations of any behaviour change will not occur naturally, and will have to be made to happen: they will require explicit programming. In 1977 Stokes and Baer reviewed what was known about techniques that could foster generalization, and found a surprising number of techniques that succeed at least sometimes (see also Drabman, Hammer, & Rosenbaum, 1979; Marholin & Siegel, 1978): teaching enough of the correct kinds of examples, teaching in a variety of places and with a variety of teachers, obscuring where and when behaviour-change procedures operate or do not, making sure that salient events in the teaching situations also occur wherever else generalization is desired, varying irrelevant aspects of the teaching situation so that they cannot inadvertently acquire inappropriate discriminative control of the new behaviour, establishing mediating rules and other forms of self-control for use in non-teaching settings, and so on.

The current flowering of that line of research is well summarized in the text, *Generalization and Maintenance*, edited by Horner, Dunlap, and Koegel (1988). Perhaps a fair summary of current knowledge and technique is that any behaviour change within the technology of behaviour change can be made to generalize as its teachers desire, if they know this auxiliary technology of generalization, and are willing to do the work that it prescribes, perhaps with some experimentation in finding the optimum technique for the problem in hand.

SUMMARY

Any clinical discipline that meets the criteria defined above, as applied, behavioural, analytic, technological, conceptually systematic, effective, and capable of generalized effects, may fairly be called applied behaviour analysis. At present, that discipline relies greatly on the reinforcement concept and its techniques. That reliance is not part of its definition, however; as more effective concepts and techniques are found − if they are − they will surely be incorporated into applied behaviour analysis, if they can meet the seven criteria; if so, they may well change its character to some extent. Applied behaviour analysis is a discipline about behaviour change whose own behaviour is open to change.

FURTHER READING

Catania, A. C. (1984). *Learning* (2nd edn). Englewood Cliffs, NJ: Prentice-Hall.

Horner, R. H., Dunlap, G., & Koegel, R. L. (Eds) (1988). *Generalization and maintenance: Life-style changes in applied settings*. Baltimore, MD: Paul H. Brookes.

Martin, G., & Pear, J. (1978). *Behavior modification: What it is and how to do it*. Englewood Cliffs, NJ: Prentice-Hall.

Reese, E. P. (with J. Howard & T. P. Reese) (1978). *Human operant behavior: Analysis and application* (2nd edn). Dubuque, IA: W. C. Brown.

Sulzer-Azaroff, B., & Mayer, G. R. (1991). *Behavior analysis for lasting change*. Fort Worth, TX: Holt, Rinehart & Winston.

REFERENCES

Baer, D. M. (1988). If you know why you're changing a behavior, you'll know when you've changed it enough. *Behavioral Assessment, 10*, 219–223.

Baer, D. M., Wolf, M. M., & Risley, T. R. (1968). Some current dimensions of applied behavior analysis. *Journal of Applied Behavior Analysis, 1,* 1–7.

Baer, D. M., Wolf, M. M., & Risley, T. R. (1987). Some still-current dimensions of applied behavior analysis. *Journal of Applied Behavior Analysis, 20,* 313–327.

Carr, E. G., & Durand, V. M. (1985). Reducing behavior problems through functional communication training. *Journal of Applied Behavior Analysis, 18,* 111–126.

Catania, A. C. (1984). *Learning* (2nd edn). Englewood Cliffs, NJ: Prentice-Hall.

Cautela, J. R., & Wysocki, P. A. (1977). The thought stopping procedure: Description, application, and learning theory interpretations. *Psychological Record, 27,* 255–264.

Drabman, R. S., Hammer, D., & Rosenbaum, M. S. (1979). Assessing generalization in behavior modification with children: The generalization map. *Behavioral Assessment, 1,* 203–219.

Horner, R. H., Dunlap, G., & Koegel, R. L. (Eds) (1988). *Generalization and maintenance: Life-style changes in applied settings.* Baltimore, MD: Paul H. Brookes.

Iwata, B. A., Pace, G. M., Kalsher, M. J., Cowdery, G. E., & Cataldo, M. F. (1990). Experimental analysis and extinction of self-injurious escape behavior. *Journal of Applied Behavior Analysis, 23,* 11–27.

Kazdin, A. E. (1977). *The token economy: A review and evaluation.* New York: Plenum.

Kazdin, A. E. (1982). *Single-case research designs: Methods for clinical and applied settings.* Oxford: Oxford University Press.

Marholin, D., & Siegel, L. J. (1978). Beyond the law of effect: Programming for the maintenance of behavior change. In D. Marholin (Ed.) *Child behavior therapy* (pp. 397–415). New York: Gardner.

Martin, G., & Pear, J. (1978). *Behavior modification: What it is and how to do it.* Englewood Cliffs, NJ: Prentice-Hall.

O'Leary, K. D., & O'Leary, S. G. (Eds) (1972). *Classroom management: The successful use of behavior modification.* New York: Pergamon.

Pinkston, E. M., Reese, N. M., LeBlanc, J. M., & Baer, D. M. (1973). Independent control of a preschooler's aggression and peer interaction by contingent teacher attention. *Journal of Applied Behavior Analysis, 6,* 1, 323–334.

Pinkston, E. M., Levitt, J. L., Green, G. R., Linsk, N. L., & Rzepnicki, T. L. (1982). *Effective social work practice: Advanced techniques for behavioral intervention with individuals, families, and institutional staff.* San Francisco, CA: Jossey-Bass.

Reese, E. P. (with J. Howard & T. W. Reese) (1978). *Human operant behavior: Analysis and application* (2nd edn). Dubuque, IA: W. C. Brown.

Reiss, S., & Bootzin, R. R. (Eds) (1985). *Theoretical issues in behavior therapy.* New York: Academic Press.

Schwartz, I. S., & Baer, D. M. (1991). Social validity assessments: Is current practice state of the art? *Journal of Applied Behavior Analysis, 24,* 189–204.

Skinner, B. F. (1938). *The behavior of organisms.* New York: Appleton.

Skinner, B. F. (1953). *Science and human behavior.* New York: Macmillan.

Stokes, T. F., & Baer, D. M. (1977). An implicit technology of generalization. *Journal of Applied Behavior Analysis, 10,* 349–367.

Stubbs, D. A., & Cohen, S. L. (1972). Second-order schedules: Comparison of different procedures for scheduling paired and nonpaired brief stimuli. *Journal of the Experimental Analysis of Behavior, 18,* 403–413.

Sulzer-Azaroff, B., & Mayer, G. R. (1991). *Behavior analysis for lasting change.* Fort Worth, TX: Holt, Rinehart & Winston.

Wilson, G. T., & Franks, C. M. (Eds) (1982). *Contemporary behavior therapy: Conceptual and empirical foundations.* New York: Guilford.

Wolf, M. M. (1978). Social validity: The case for subjective measurement, or how behavior analysis is finding its heart. *Journal of Applied Behavior Analysis, 11,* 203–214.

Zuriff, G. E. (1985). *Behaviorism: A conceptual reconstruction.* New York: Columbia University Press.

5.3

COGNITIVE SKILLS

K. Anders Ericsson
Florida State University, USA

William L. Oliver
Florida State University, USA

Acquisition of simple cognitive skills	Performance of experts on domain-specific tasks
Acquisition of cognitive skills in everyday life	Cognitive processes mediating expert performance
Expertise and expert performance	Acquisition of superior memory performance
Capturing expert performance in the laboratory	**Conclusion**
	Further reading
	References

Skill refers to superior performance that is acquired through extended practice and training. Before its use in psychology, the term was used to distinguish skilled and unskilled labour. A skilled worker had the prerequisite aptitudes to carry out complex jobs, whereas an unskilled worker was limited to perform jobs that could be mastered in relatively short times (Welford, 1968). The aptitudes required of skilled workers often involve knowledge, judgement, and manual deftness developed through years of training. The degree of skill in a domain can obviously vary, and experts and masters can be distinguished from moderately skilled performers. During the years of training to attain skilled performance, there is an incremental improvement on the many different specific tasks needed to perform the skill. Laboratory research in psychology has shied away from studying the acquisition of complex skills. Instead, laboratory research has focused on the ways in which people learn simple tasks for which large improvements can be observed within a few hours of practice.

The skills that people learn vary greatly in the relative emphasis they place on perceptual, cognitive, and motoric processes. For example, the identification of enemy aircraft at a distance would seem to reflect difficulties in perception and would be considered primarily a perceptual skill. Ballet and tight-rope walking would require the production of complex motor sequences and would be considered motor skills. The identification of cognitive skills is more difficult. This difficulty partly arises because extended practice often reduces cognitive involvement so that performance becomes automatic. Mathematicians, for instance, report that they simply "see" the correct solutions for some equations, suggesting that they first perceive and then respond directly to familiar patterns of symbols. As a working definition, *cognitive skills* can be characterized as acquired superior performance on tasks for which perception of stimuli is easy and the required motor responses are simple and part of the subjects' repertoire of responses. This definition clearly includes skill in mathematics, natural science, and other academic subjects. Skill in games, such as chess, bridge, and Go, involve perception of clearly visible configurations of pieces and cards and involve simple movements. Thus, these games meet the defining criteria for cognitive skill. Most laboratory tasks in psychology use readily perceivable stimuli and simple responses, usually button presses or vocalization of single words. Acquired superior performance on these laboratory tasks as a result of practice also qualifies them as cognitive skills.

It is important to note that skills that would *not* be classified as cognitive skills according to our definition none the less include component skills that are cognitive in nature. Skills with cognitive components include skill in sport, surgery, and artistic performance. Improvements of perceptual and motoric aspects of performance predominate in these skills, but there are clearly important cognitive aspects as well (e.g., the decisions a pianist must make on the interpretation of a piece of music). In our conclusion to this chapter we shall briefly comment on the cognitive aspects of these types of skills with cognitive components.

Much of our understanding of cognitive skills comes from the study of real-life expertise. Some insight into cognitive skills can be gained through our observation of the performance of everyday skills. Naturally occurring instances of skilled performance, however, take place in complex social and professional contexts, and it is virtually impossible to gain any general scientific knowledge about cognitive skill through mere observation. Thus, the first step towards studying cognitive skill in some domain is to identify a set of standardized tasks that can be performed in the laboratory. These standardized tasks are designed to be difficult enough to challenge the expert yet easy enough that they can be performed in brief periods of time. The tasks can then be used to elicit expert behaviour in laboratory or classroom settings so that expertise may be assessed or studied. For many academic skills, such as mathematics, there has been a long tradition in the design of test problems that can be used to measure a given individual's level of skill.

For some domains it is more difficult to identify standardized tasks that capture the essence of the real-life skill. Chess skill, for instance, is defined as the ability to defeat opponents in entire games; to measure chess skill it would seem necessary to rely on a chess rating system based on performance of players in tournament games. Fortunately, in the case of chess such a rating system is available. De Groot (1978) found that it was also possible to measure the same chess skill by having players select the best move for a series of unfamiliar chess positions. Similarly, medical skill in radiology has been assessed by testing radiologists' ability to interpret X-rays. The identification of a representative set of standardized tasks is not only important for the measurement of skill, but also necessary for the systematic study of the cognitive processes that underlie skilled performance.

An alternative approach to the study of cognitive skill looks at the acquisition of new skills in the laboratory. Practical concerns usually constrain this research to the study of simple skills that require little background knowledge and that can be acquired within relatively few hours of practice in the laboratory. Few researchers have the resources or time to study a skill that takes many years to acquire.

A comprehensive account of cognitive skill would describe skill acquisition as well as describe the knowledge and strategies used at all levels of skill including the highest international-level performance in a given domain of expertise. Most studies have been focused on some part or aspect of the skill acquisition process. We shall first discuss research on comparatively simple cognitive skills that can be attained within hours so that the entire acquisition process can be monitored in the laboratory. Then we shall review results from studies of everyday skills. Finally, we shall review research on expert performance and try to extend our framework to accommodate those findings on the highest levels of skilled performance.

ACQUISITION OF SIMPLE COGNITIVE SKILLS

Drawing on previous studies of skill acquisition, Fitts and Posner (1967) described three different acquisition stages according to a model originally proposed by Fitts. The "early or cognitive stage" involves understanding the task and its demands as well as learning what information one must attend to. During this stage an individual occasionally makes gross errors reflecting inadequate understanding. With further practice individuals move to "the intermediate and associative stage". This stage is characterized by attempts to identify efficient strategies to allow rapid perception and retrieval of required information and responses. During this stage individuals eliminate errors and increase the speed of performance. The "late or autonomous stage" involves minimizing cognitive control by making the access of correct responses automatic. During this final stage, performance is virtually error free and the speed of performance continues to improve as a result of further practice. Subsequently, Anderson (1982) provided a theoretical model with three different learning mechanisms, each corresponding to a stage of the Fitts model.

The three-stage model of skill acquisition does a remarkably good job in accounting for empirical evidence, even outside the strictly cognitive skills. The acquisition of skill in flying an airplane and telegraphy proceeds in a manner consistent with the model. For these skills, the early cognitive phase is completed within ten hours, after which major errors are rare (Fitts & Posner, 1967). Performance then becomes faster and ultimately "automatic" performance is attained.

Many laboratory tasks used to study skill acquisition are comparatively easy. After the experimenter's instruction and some practice problems, subjects understand the task and the first stage of skill acquisition is completed. An "alphabet arithmetic" task used by Compton and Logan (1991) is a good example of a laboratory task used to study skill acquisition. Subjects are shown problems like those shown in Table 1. The subjects' task is to indicate as quickly as possible whether a given letter falls n letters (given by the addend) beyond another letter in the alphabet. The subjects are to respond as quickly as possible by pressing buttons labelled "True" and "False" depending on whether a correct or incorrect answer appears on a given trial of practice. Compton and Logan found that, when generating an answer to an alphabet arithmetic problem, such as "G + 3 = ", subjects would initially report that they sequentially accessed the following three letters of the alphabet – G, H, I, J – before responding true or false. For trials with reports of sequential access, the observed reaction times increased linearly with the number of letters accessed. With practice subjects became faster and more accurate when counting off the letters (associative stage). With even more practice on the alphabet arithmetic task, subjects reported being able to access the answer directly based on past experience with the specific problems, and the observed reaction time was found to be independent of the number of letters added (autonomous stage). The primary reason for the dramatic speed-up with practice is due to an increase in the frequency of direct retrieval from memory. Consistent with the three-stage model of Fitts, generating answers in the alphabet arithmetic task starts with a fixed sequence of cognitive processes (counting off the letters) and is then transformed through practice into direct retrieval from memory. The first stage is essentially omitted because the subjects understand the task immediately and can begin practising to reduce errors and speed-up their scanning of the alphabet.

Other evidence for the three-stage model comes from research on individual differences. A number of studies have shown that tests of general

Table 1 Example problems and answers for the alphabet task with the appropriate letter sequences generated by the subjects

Problem	Letter sequence	Answer
B + 3 = E	"B–C–D–E"	True
N + 3 = R	"N–O–P–Q"	False
H + 2 = J	"H–I–J"	True

cognitive abilities, such as tests of verbal knowledge and attention efficiency, can predict which subjects will perform well and which will perform poorly when first learning a relatively complex laboratory task (Ackerman, 1987; Woltz, 1988). These same tests do not, however, predict performance level late in the acquisition process. Instead, performance differences among subjects at later stages of learning are better predicted by tests of motor or perceptual skill, depending on which of these component skills are emphasized in the task being learned. This pattern of results is consistent with the view that skill acquisition starts with a cognitive stage stressing verbal, planful processes, when subjects with verbal skills would have an advantage, and then eventually progresses to an autonomous stage stressing automatic

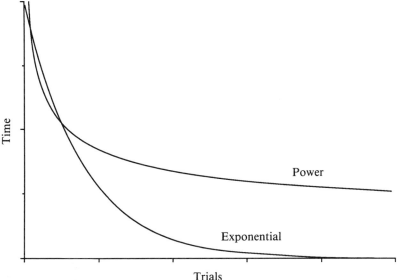

Figure 1 Examples of a power and an exponential function in a graph. Improvement curves that plot the time to perform a task as a function of trials of practice are often well described by power functions

responses, when subjects with efficient perceptual or motor skills would have an advantage.

Improvement during the second and third stages of skill acquisition in laboratory tasks follows very consistent patterns described mathematically by power functions (Newell & Rosenbloom, 1981). The rate of improvement, often measured by how quickly subjects can perform a task, is initially very rapid and then levels off with increasing trials of practice. Researchers have found that practice in relatively pure cognitive tasks, such as generating geometry proofs (Neves & Anderson, 1981), recognition of memorized facts (Pirolli & Anderson, 1985), and the alphabet arithmetic task (Logan, 1988) leads to improvements that follow power functions. In fact, this functional form of improvement is so consistent across task domains that one can now speak of a "power law of practice", and theories of skill acquisition are developed in part to explain why practice curves follow power functions as opposed to other functions, such as exponential functions. A power curve is contrasted with an exponential curve in Figure 1.

ACQUISITION OF COGNITIVE SKILLS IN EVERYDAY LIFE

Many cognitive skills in everyday life have been shown to develop in a way consistent with the three-stage model of skill acquisition. Most children learn to read by sounding out words, and with further practice the reading of words is converted to automatic access of the meaning of words. Children learn to generate sums by sequential counting initially using fingers, then by internalized silent counting, and finally by retrieval of familiar facts of single-digit additions. Similarly, multiplication is initially generated by sequential addition, but with instruction and training this process is replaced by direct retrieval from a memorized multiplication table.

More complex cognitive skills for solving algebra word problems and physics problems show a similar transformation with experience and practice. Beginners (novices) often have to generate their solutions step by step relying on general problem-solving methods like trial-and-error. For example, if a physics problem asks for the velocity of an object, a novice starts to retrieve formulas yielding velocity and then checks whether each formula is consistent with the given information. This method of starting with the question is called backward reasoning. In contrast, more experienced subjects (experts) proceed by forward reasoning and, as part of the comprehension of the physics problem, generate a representation of the problem which allows them to retrieve a solution plan (Simon & Simon, 1978). When experts categorize physics problems, they rely on underlying physical principles (e.g., Newton's second law and conservation of energy), whereas novices categorize problems by surface features, such as "problems involving pulleys". This finding suggests that experts form an immediate representation of problems that systematically cues their relevant knowledge, whereas novices do not have this kind of orderly efficient access to their knowledge (Chi, Glaser, & Rees, 1982).

With increased expertise in a domain, individuals accumulate more as well as better organized knowledge about that domain. With a lot of experience of algebra word problems, students recognize types of problems and can thus retrieve a solution plan from memory instead of generating the equations in step-by-step fashion (Hinsley, Hayes, & Simon, 1977). Experts in a wide range of domains, such as chess (de Groot, 1978) are able to select the appropriate action after a very brief period of exposure to a problem situation. The ability of experts to retrieve rapidly and reliably the appropriate plans and solutions from the vast body of information in long-term memory implies that the expert encodes the presented problem in terms of several patterns which, in combination, serve as memory cues (Chase & Simon, 1973).

Because improving performance of everyday skills requires learning new knowledge and strategies, the course of improvement for these skills does not always follow a trajectory implied by the three-stage model of skill acquisition or by power functions. For instance, Thorndike (1921) observed that clerks often failed to learn to add numbers faster even though they frequently performed the task. Similarly, adults' handwriting does not necessarily become faster or more legible with time. Also, the learning of skills is often very specific and does not transfer to other skills. For instance, Brazilian children who work as street vendors can perform complex calculations to ply their trade, but cannot perform similar calculations in a classroom setting (Carraher, Carraher, & Schliemann, 1985). Skills sometimes do transfer within domains or to very related domains as in the case of text editing or word processing on computers (Singley & Anderson, 1989). A text editor can be learned more quickly after one has used a different text editor because many of the goals are the same across text editors (e.g., moving a block of text), although the commands or keystrokes to achieve the goals differ.

A number of studies have examined the long-term retention of everyday, cognitive skills when the skills are no longer being used. Skills that have not been highly practised appear to be lost fairly rapidly once they are no longer used. Highly practised skills are retained very well, however, so that a student's skill at algebra that is being used in a calculus course is retained for life even though the more tenuously learned skill at calculus is rapidly lost with disuse (Bahrick & Hall, 1991).

EXPERTISE AND EXPERT PERFORMANCE

The highest levels of cognitive skills are generally referred to as expert performance. Typically, an expert is a successful, full-time professional in a domain. Domains of expertise include specialties of medicine, engineering, law as well as academic disciplines. The best individuals in competitive games, such as chess, bridge, Go, and backgammon, are also considered to be experts. The superior achievements and performance of experts are socially recognized by awards, prizes, and promotions to higher-paid jobs. Hence, there is a fair consensus on who the experts are, but the real problem is to characterize how experts differ from less accomplished people in general terms.

Being an expert in a domain, such as medicine or physics, involves superior performance on a vast number of different tasks. An analysis of any one of those tasks reveals a large body of knowledge and skill that are necessary even to be able to complete these tasks. Around 20 years of schooling is often a prerequisite for attaining the necessary knowledge and skills, which would roughly correspond to the early and cognitive phase in Fitts's framework. An additional 10 years of full-time experience is often necessary to attain expert status in the domain (Ericsson & Crutcher, 1990). The highest achievement of an expert in these domains consists of a discovery of a new technique, fact or theory that extends the accumulated knowledge in that domain. These achievements are primarily made by experts in their 30s and early 40s (Lehman, 1953).

Games, such as chess and bridge, differ from academic domains in that the necessary rules can be learned in a matter of hours. There is no prerequisite knowledge learned in schools, and children as young as 5–6 years of age can play these games. Based on the results from tournaments, it is possible to measure the level of performance for a given individual on an objective scale, such as the chess rating system. By examining biographical data on world-class chess players in the nineteenth and twentieth centuries, the time course for learning to play chess at the highest levels of skill can be charted. Simon and Chase (1973) found that all international-level chess players had spent 10 or more years in intensive study of chess before attaining their level of expertise. Outstanding chess players tend to have started playing chess at young ages (on the average between 9 and 10 years of age), and for those players that started later during adolescence, 10 years or more of chess study is still needed to achieve a high level of skill (Ericsson & Crutcher, 1990). The acquisition of chess skill of recent players achieving very high levels can be traced by examining their chess ratings as a function of age. Elo (1978) found that at age 12 these players played at the same level as average adult players. During adolescence there was a steep improvement, levelling off in the early 20s. During this period the international-level players improved more and attained a higher final level. The highest achievement of elite chess players is normally attained between 30 and 40 years of age (Elo, 1965). The parallels between acquisition of expert performance in chess and in more traditional domains of expertise, such as science and medicine, are striking and suggest intriguing commonalities. Research (Charness, 1991) has detailed the vast amount of knowledge about chess – for example, the many thousands of variants of chess openings – that expert chess players know.

422

Capturing expert performance in the laboratory

A central problem in all research on expert performance is that real-life expertise occurs in complex and highly interactive situations. A medical expert diagnosing the disease of a patient engages in an extended interview with the patient, often requiring subsequent medical tests and physical examinations. The chess games played by chess experts last several hours, and each game is different from all of the tens of thousands of other chess games that the chess expert has previously played in his or her life. Hence, a given expert will most likely never play the same chess game twice in his or her life, nor are two different experts ever likely to encounter identical middle-game chess positions. This problem of not being able to observe many experts (as well as novices) in the same situation is a major challenge for research on real-life expertise.

The general solution to this problem is to analyse carefully the real-life expertise to identify brief segments of the experts' behaviour that capture the essence of the naturally occurring task. The researcher then studies these brief segments of behaviour under various experimental conditions to gain insight into the expertise. For example, a chess expert has to select the next move for the current chess position. Due to the wide range of different chess positions that can occur during games with many different opponents, it is reasonable to assume that a stronger chess player would be able to select a better move (on the average) than a weaker chess player. Research (Charness, 1981; de Groot, 1978) has shown that the ability of chess players to select good moves for chess positions is strongly correlated with the standard chess ratings from actual chess tournaments. Thus, research on chess skill has examined the ability of chess experts to generate good moves for selected positions (e.g., under speed conditions) with the confidence that an important component of chess expertise is captured by the task. Similarly, it is possible to present a medical expert with a summary of relevant information about a patient to capture the cognitive processes of diagnosing the patient's disease. This situation would occur naturally when a doctor asks a colleague for help in diagnosing a difficult case. Laboratory studies show that the accuracy of diagnosis increases with the level of medical expertise (Patel & Groen, 1991).

Performance of experts on domain-specific tasks

Research comparing the performance of individuals at different levels of expertise shows that experts select the correct action for representative tasks, whereas less accomplished individuals select inferior or incorrect actions. This important finding implies that the mediating cognitive processes are qualitatively different at different levels of expertise, in contrast to the earlier discussed simpler cognitive skills where the primary differences concerned the speed of generating correct responses. In other words, experts may differ from novices by focusing on different information or by using altogether different strategies to perform a task, and therefore *cannot* be thought of as carrying out the same mental steps as novices in faster and more efficient ways. Another important implication is that improved accuracy of performance cannot be attained by simply doing the same thing again and again. To attain more accurate performance subjects need to change their cognitive processes by learning to allow generation of the correct responses on a subsequent occasion. Consistent with the need for continuous learning in the acquisition of expert performance, the number of years of experience with a domain has often only a relatively weak correlation with actual performance.

In some domains of expertise investigators have been unable to identify superior performance of "experts". Often these domains involve decision-making and forecasting of complex economic, social, and medical events, where the lack of immediate feedback and the probabilistic nature of these events would make learning slow and difficult (Camerer & Johnson, 1991). In many other domains, such as surgery, internal medicine, and academic skill, experts display reliable superior performance on tasks representative of their domain. The performance of these experts can be studied to identify the cognitive processes that underlie their expertise.

Cognitive processes mediating expert performance

There are many types of observations that can be collected on subjects' cognitive processes while they generate their response to a representative task (Ericsson & Oliver, 1988). The most important technique involves instructing subjects to verbalize their thoughts concurrently (think aloud), but subjects can also be asked to recall their thoughts retrospectively once the task is completed.

Comparisons between think-aloud protocols of novices and experts often reveal qualitative differences in the cognitive processes. Studies comparing novice and expert writers show particularly striking differences in their strategies. Novice writers tend to write down ideas on topics as they occur to them, whereas expert writers spend a lot of time planning their text to fit the particular audience and meet the appropriate goals of the genre (Scardemalia & Bereiter, 1991). This planning results in expert writers taking much longer to write texts than novice writers. The texts produced by the experts, however, are qualitatively superior to those of the novices. Medical doctors and students at different levels of expertise differ in their ability to diagnose a disease from a description of a patient. In addition to the experts' more reliable access to and better integration of their knowledge about diseases (Feltovich, Johnson, Moller, & Swanson, 1984), the medical experts were better able to integrate information about the patient and discover inconsistencies. They

424

could also recover more easily from incorrect diagnostic hypotheses they had generated earlier. Patel and Groen (1986) have shown that after a brief review of the patient chart, the medical expert is able not only to recall the relevant information but also to give an integrated account of the underlying pathophysiology of the case. Experts store the relevant information about a case in a well-integrated representation in long-term memory, and their recall of this information is superior to lesser experts when given unexpected tests of memory (Norman, Brooks, & Allen, 1989).

Cognitive processes mediating the selection of chess moves for a given position have been extensively studied and related to expertise in chess. Chess players at all levels of expertise spend several minutes considering alternative moves and mentally exploring the consequences of potential moves by planning. The number of moves chess players plan ahead depends on their level of chess skill (Charness, 1989). The planning and evaluation of consequences of potential chess moves is critical even for international chess masters. Even though a chess master can retrieve several promising moves within seconds of seeing the chess position, systematic planning is necessary to select the best move or occasionally to discover an even better move (de Groot, 1978). Being able to mentally represent the chess position after a sequence of conceived chess moves requires superior memory for chess positions.

Early research in the 1920s showed that chess masters have superior memory for chess positions, but their memory for other types of information was in the normal range. De Groot (1978) found that chess experts could recall the location of most chess pieces after having selected a chess move for a position, and that the amount of recall was related to the level of chess expertise of the subject. In their classic research, Chase and Simon (1973) systematically studied intentional memory for briefly presented chess positions (see the top panel of Figure 2) as well as chess boards with randomly arranged pieces (see the bottom panel of Figure 2). The amount of recall for chess positions increased with chess expertise and the chess master was able to recall the locations of many pieces for chess positions from normal games. However, the recall for random boards was uniformly low (around four pieces) regardless of chess expertise. Chase and Simon argued that chess experts recognize familiar patterns, for example, strings of pawns, in the normal board positions. These patterns are stored in short-term memory, as larger patterns or chunks of information. Both chess experts and novices had difficulty remembering the random boards because few familiar chess patterns could be identified and those patterns that appeared by chance did not form a coherent, larger pattern corresponding to a normal chess board position. Subsequent research has shown that the chess masters' superior memory for chess positions reflects storage in long-term memory (Charness, 1991). In many other types of expert performance, experts show superior memory for information from their domains of expertise (Ericsson & Staszewski, 1989). Expert memory aids in planning, reasoning, and the storage of information

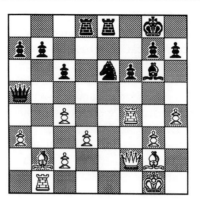

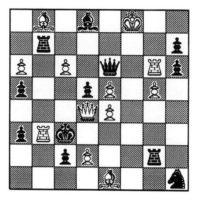

Figure 2 An example of a normal chess board position appears at the top of the figure. A random configuration of the same pieces appears in the board position at the bottom of the figure

in temporary states, such as when experts solve complex physics problems. Insight into how superior memory for a specific domain can be attained is best provided by research on the acquisition of memory skill in the laboratory.

Acquisition of superior memory performance

Improvements in performance on a memory task as function of practice is a cognitive skill and has been studied directly. Chase and Ericsson (1981, 1982) arranged for a college student (SF) to practise on a digit-span task in which subjects must recall a list of digits that is rapidly presented (1 digit/second). The digits must be recalled in their presented order without any errors. During the first practice sessions SF rehearsed the digits to himself and was able to reproduce lists of about seven digits. His initial performance was typical for untrained college students in this task. With practice on the task SF's performance improved steadily (see Figure 3). As shown in the figure, SF is not alone in his ability to recall long digit strings. The subject DD eventually acquired a digit span over 100 digits after over 800 practice sessions (Staszewski, 1988)!

SF's superior memory performance was possible only after qualitative changes in his cognitive processes compared to his initial use of rehearsal to recall the presented digits. Initially, SF reported segmenting the list of presented digits into groups, e.g., 7 digits would be 3 + 4 digits (like a telephone number). During the fifth session SF came up with the idea of encoding digit groups as running times with a dramatic increase in his performance as a result. SF was an experienced runner and knew a lot about running times for different races. For example 352 could be encoded as 3 minutes and 52 seconds and a near world-record time for the mile. Encoding digit groups as running times augmented by numerical patterns allowed SF to think briefly about a given digit group before considering the next digit group. For longer digit strings, SF adopted the strategy of deciding ahead of time how to segment the numbers. For example, 13 digits would be segmented into three 3-digit groups and a single 4-digit group. As SF improved

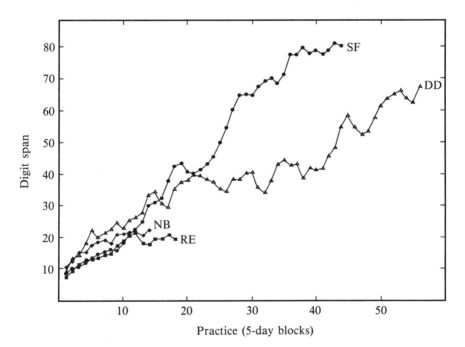

Figure 3   The digit span for four subjects is shown as a function of one-hour practice sessions averaged over blocks of five sessions

427

further, he invented hierarchical structures. For example, a given digit might fall in the second digit group in the last portion (third portion) of the list. At recall he could then regenerate locations in the list as retrieval cues to recall the associated digit groups. The period of arrests in improvement in Figure 3 were associated with problem-solving efforts in extending his retrieval structures to allow reliable retrieval of additional digit groups. SF's acquisition of his memory skill should be seen as successive reorganization of his cognitive processes in line with our general claims about expert performance.

Based on the evidence from SF and the other trained subjects as well as from other individuals with exceptional memory, Chase and Ericsson (1982) proposed a theory of skilled memory. According to skilled-memory theory, superior and exceptional memory reflect acquired ability to store information in LTM in retrievable form. Rapid storage of information in memory requires a body of associated knowledge and patterns. For example, SF relied on running times and other subjects rely on their knowledge of numbers. Information is associated to a retrieval structure at the time of encoding, which allows efficient retrieval at recall. All memory skills are domain-specific and show essentially no transfer to other materials due to the specificity of the encoding processes. For example, when SF's digit-span had increased by over 1,000 per cent, his memory span for consonants remained at only six letters.

Skilled-memory theory has been extended to account for the superior domain-specific memory of experts (Ericsson & Staszewski, 1989). A review of the superior memory of experts shows that it is not an inevitable consequence of expertise, as experts in some domain do not display it (Ericsson & Pennington, 1993). Instead, superior memory in a domain is related to the demands for extended working memory to support planning and reasoning. Superior memory requires the acquisition of encoding processes and retrieval structures uniquely tailored to meet the demands on memory in that domain.

In sum, our characterization of the acquisition of expert performance is not consistent with a linear progression through Fitts's three stages of skills. Instead experts continue to return to the early cognitive phase to improve their understanding of the task and to uncover superior methods and new knowledge to further increase the accuracy of their performance. In many instances, experts develop memory skills to overcome limits on short-term memory so that they can more effectively plan and reason. This continuous restructuring and refinement of the mediating processes by experts implies that doing the same thing over and over (mere repetition) will not lead to expert performance. In support of this claim we noted earlier that the level of performance is often weakly correlated with the amount of experience in that domain. Instead, the attained level of performance in a domain appears to be closely correlated with the amount of time spent deliberately trying to improve one's performance (deliberate practice) (Ericsson, Krampe, &

Tesch-Römer, 1993). For example, chess experts do not rely on simply playing many games to improve; in addition to playing games, they spend up to four hours a day studying published games of international chess masters. Failure to predict a move made by the master in a studied chess game provides an opportunity to analyse the chess position more carefully. Similarly, medical practitioners regularly discuss the diagnosis and treatment of their patients with their colleagues and with their supervising head of the clinic at weekly case conferences. For virtually any domain of expertise there exists deliberate practice activities that maximize opportunities for learning and improvement.

CONCLUSION

Cognitive skill refers to the greatly improved performance on cognitive tasks as a result of practice. The acquisition of simple cognitive skills is well described by Fitts's three-phase model, where the task is first understood (cognitive phase) then responses are learned (associative phase) and finally these responses become directly retrievable (autonomous phase). In these simple tasks, performance becomes accurate relatively soon after practice begins and the speed to perform the task increases as a function of the number of practice trials. Many cognitive skills in everyday life are acquired in a similar manner. In contrast, performance of experts in more complex domains is acquired over many years of training with steadily improved accuracy. The cognitive processes mediating expert performance are continually revised to accommodate new knowledge and better methods to perform the tasks, which include the acquisition of memory skills to support the memory-demanding activities of planning and reasoning. As a result of deliberate efforts to improve their performance, experts acquire strategies and skills that differ qualitatively from the strategies and skills of novices. The changes in strategies and the acquisition of skills to overcome basic information-processing complicate efforts to predict expert level of performance from the individual differences of beginners. The success of such prediction has been found to be surprisingly poor – accounting only for 1–4 per cent of the variance (Ghiselli, 1966).

So far our review has been limited to cognitive skills. Research on typing and expert performance in sports shows the central importance of cognitive factors. Comparisons of typists at different level of expert performance show that the best typists look further ahead of the letters currently being typed. When preview of the text to be typed is eliminated in an experimental condition, the experts' typing speed is reduced to the level of novices (Salthouse, 1991). The experts are able to attain their high typing speed to a great extent by preparing for future key strokes in advance. Similarly, expert tennis players can return hard tennis serves because they learn to perceive their opponents' preparatory movements prior to the actual hitting of the tennis ball (Abernethy, 1991). Through the acquisition of anticipatory processing strategies, experts in motor skills can circumvent the limits imposed by simple serial reaction time. Expert athletes in team sports, such as basketball and field hockey, display superior memory for briefly presented pictures of game situations, but not for random arrangements of players (Allard & Starkes, 1991). The ability to correctly represent a game situation is essential for the quick selection of correct current actions and the preparation for future actions and events. Similarly, research on perceptual skills has shown the importance of cognitive factors. For instance, research has revealed the cognitive strategies used to perform seemingly pure perceptual tasks, such as determining the sex of a chicken (Biederman & Shiffrar, 1987) and identification of different shades of a colour or different pitches of tones (Ericsson & Faivre, 1988). Subjects have been able to use these strategies to develop absolute pitch, an ability that many have viewed as innate. A wide range of exceptional performance has been analysed and successful accounts in terms of acquired skill has been given (Howe, 1990).

Studies of cognitive skill and expert performance have shown that effective methods and strategies allow individuals to attain high levels of performance and circumvent basic processing limits. Further research on cognitive skill is likely to play an important role in advancing our knowledge about human cognition.

FURTHER READING

Chi, M. T. H., Glaser, R., & Farr, M. J. (Eds) (1988). *The nature of expertise*. Hillsdale, NJ: Lawrence Erlbaum.

Colley, A. M., & Beech, J. R. (Eds) (1989). *Acquisition and performance of cognitive skills*. New York: Wiley.

Ericsson, K. A., & Smith, J. (Eds) (1991). *Toward a general theory of expertise*: *Prospects and limits*. Cambridge: Cambridge University Press.

VanLehn, K. (1989). Problem solving and cognitive skill acquisition. In M. I. Posner (Ed.) *Foundations of cognitive science* (pp. 527–580). Cambridge, MA: Massachusetts Institute of Technology Press.

REFERENCES

Abernethy, B. (1991). Visual search strategies and decision-making in sport. *International Journal of Sport Psychology*, *22*, 189–210.

Ackerman, P. L. (1987). Individual differences in skill learning: An integration of psychometric and information processing perspectives. *Psychological Bulletin*, *102*, 3–27.

Allard, F., & Starkes, J. L. (1991). Motor-skill experts in sports, dance and other domains. In K. A. Ericsson & J. Smith (Eds) *Toward a general theory of expertise: Prospects and limits* (pp. 126–152). Cambridge: Cambridge University Press.

Anderson, J. R. (1982). Acquisition of cognitive skill. *Psychological Review*, *89*, 369–406.

Bahrick, H. P., & Hall, L. K. (1991). Lifetime maintenance of high school mathematics content. *Journal of Experimental Psychology: General, 120,* 20–33.

Biederman, I., & Shiffrar, M. (1987). Sexing day-old chicks: A case study and expert systems analysis of a difficult perceptual-learning task. *Journal of Experimental Psychology: Learning, Memory & Cognition, 13,* 640–645.

Camerer, C. F., & Johnson, E. J. (1991). The process-performance paradox in expert judgment: How can the experts know so much and predict so badly? In K. A. Ericsson & J. Smith (Eds) *Toward a general theory of expertise: Prospects and limits* (pp. 195–217). Cambridge: Cambridge University Press.

Carraher, T. N., Carraher, D. W., & Schliemann, A. D. (1985). Mathematics in the streets and in the schools. *British Journal of Developmental Psychology, 3,* 21–29.

Charness, N. (1981). Search in chess: Age and skill differences. *Journal of Experimental Psychology: Human Perception and Performance, 7,* 467–476.

Charness, N. (1989). Expertise in chess and bridge. In D. Klahr & K. Kotovsky (Eds) *Complex information processing: The impact of Herbert A. Simon* (pp. 183–208). Hillsdale, NJ: Lawrence Erlbaum.

Charness, N. (1991). Expertise in chess: The balance between knowledge and search. In K. A. Ericsson & J. Smith (Eds) *Toward a general theory of expertise: Prospects and limits* (pp. 39–63). Cambridge: Cambridge University Press.

Chase, W. G., & Ericsson, K. A. (1981). Skilled memory. In J. R. Anderson (Ed.) *Cognitive skills and their acquisition* (pp. 141–189). Hillsdale, NJ: Lawrence Erlbaum.

Chase, W. G., & Ericsson, K. A. (1982). Skill and working memory. In G. H. Bower (Ed.) *The psychology of learning and motivation* (vol. 16, pp. 1–58). New York: Academic Press.

Chase, W. G., & Simon, H. A. (1973). The mind's eye in chess. In W. G. Chase (Ed.) *Visual information processing* (pp. 215–281). New York: Academic Press.

Chi, M. T. H., Glaser, R., & Rees, E. (1982). Expertise in problem solving. In R. J. Sternberg (Ed.) *Advances in the psychology of human intelligence* (vol. 1, pp. 1–75). Hillsdale, NJ: Lawrence Erlbaum.

Compton, B. J., & Logan, G. D. (1991). The transition from algorithm to retrieval in memory-based theories of automaticity. *Memory & Cognition, 19*(2), 151–158.

de Groot, A. (1978). *Thought and choice and chess.* The Hague: Mouton (original work published 1946).

Elo, A. E. (1965). Age changes in master chess performance. *Journal of Gerontology, 20,* 289–299.

Elo, A. E. (1978). *The rating of chessplayers, past and present.* London: Batsford.

Ericsson, K. A., & Crutcher, R. J. (1990). The nature of exceptional performance. In P. B. Baltes, D. L. Featherman, & R. M. Lerner (Eds) *Life-span development and behavior* (vol. 10, pp. 187–217). Hillsdale, NJ: Lawrence Erlbaum.

Ericsson, K. A., & Faivre, I. A. (1988). What's exceptional about exceptional abilities? In I. K. Obler & D. Fein (Eds) *The exceptional brain: Neuropsychology of talent and special abilities* (pp. 436–473). New York: Guilford.

Ericsson, K. A., & Oliver, W. L. (1988). Methodology for laboratory research on thinking: Task selection, collection of observation and data analysis. In R. J. Sternberg and E. E. Smith (Eds) *The psychology of human thought* (pp. 392–428). Cambridge: Cambridge University Press.

Ericsson, K. A., & Pennington, N. (1993). Experts and expertise. In G. Davis & R. Logie (Eds) *Memory in everyday life.* Amsterdam: North Holland.

Ericsson, K. A., & Smith, J. (1991). Prospects and limits in the empirical study of expertise: An introduction. In K. A. Ericsson & J. Smith (Eds) *Toward a general theory of expertise: Prospects and limits* (pp. 1–38). Cambridge: Cambridge University Press.

Ericsson, K. A., & Staszewski, J. J. (1989). Skilled memory and expertise: Mechanisms of exceptional performance. In D. Klahr & K. Kotovsky (Eds) *Complex information processing: The impact of Herbert A. Simon* (pp. 235–267). Hillsdale, NJ: Lawrence Erlbaum.

Ericsson, K. A., Krampe, R., & Tesch-Römer, C. (1993). The role of deliberate practice in the acquisition of expert performance. *Psychological Review, 100,* 363–406.

Feltovich, P. J., Johnson, P. E., Moller, J. H., & Swanson, D. B. (1984). LCS: The role and development of medical knowledge in diagnostic expertise. In W. J. Clancey & E. H. Shortliffe (Eds) *Readings in medical artificial intelligence* (pp. 275–319). Reading, MA: Addison-Wesley.

Fitts, P. M., & Posner, M. I. (1967). *Human performance.* Belmont, CA: Brooks/Cole.

Ghiselli, E. (1966). *The validity of occupational aptitude tests.* New York: Wiley.

Hinsley, D. A., Hayes, J. R., & Simon, H. A. (1977). From words to equations: Meaning and representation in algebra word problem. In M. A. Just & P. A. Carpenter (Eds) *Cognitive processes in comprehension* (pp. 89–106). Hillsdale, NJ: Lawrence Erlbaum.

Howe, M. J. A. (1990). *The origins of exceptional abilities.* Oxford: Basil Blackwell.

Lehman, H. C. (1953). *Age and achievement.* Princeton, NJ: Princeton University Press.

Logan, G. D. (1988). Toward an instance theory of automatization. *Psychological Review, 95,* 492–527.

Neves, D. M., & Anderson, J. R. (1981). Knowledge compilation: Mechanisms for the automatization of cognitive skills. In J. R. Anderson (Ed.) *Cognitive skills and their acquisition* (pp. 57–84). Hillsdale, NJ: Lawrence Erlbaum.

Newell, A., & Rosenbloom, P. S. (1981). Mechanisms of skill acquisition and the law of practice. In J. R. Anderson (Ed.) *Cognitive skills and their acquisition* (pp. 1–55). Hillsdale, NJ: Lawrence Erlbaum.

Norman, G. R., Brooks, L. R., & Allen, S. W. (1989). Recall by expert medical practitioners and novices as a record of processing attention. *Journal of Experimental Psychology: Learning, Memory and Cognition, 15,* 1166–1174.

Patel, V. L., & Groen, G. L. (1986). Knowledge based solution strategies in medical reasoning. *Cognitive Science, 10,* 91–116.

Patel, V. L., & Groen, G. J. (1991). The general and specific nature of medical expertise: A critical look. In K. A. Ericsson & J. Smith (Eds) *Toward a general theory of expertise: Prospects and limits* (pp. 93–125). Cambridge: Cambridge University Press.

Pirolli, P., & Anderson, J. R. (1985). The role of practice in fact retrieval. *Journal of Psychology: Learning, Memory, and Cognition, 11,* 136–153.

Salthouse, T. A. (1991). Expertise as the circumvention of human processing limitations. In K. A. Ericsson & J. Smith (Eds) *Toward a general theory of expertise: Prospects and limits* (pp. 286–300). Cambridge: Cambridge University Press.

Scardemalia, M., & Bereiter, C. (1991). Literate expertise. In K. A. Ericsson & J. Smith (Eds) *Toward a general theory of expertise: Prospects and limits* (pp. 172–194). Cambridge: Cambridge University Press.

Simon, D. P., & Simon, H. A. (1978). Individual differences in solving physics problems. In R. S. Siegler (Ed.) *Children's thinking: What develops?* (pp. 325–348). Hillsdale, NJ: Lawrence Erlbaum.

Simon, H. A., & Chase, W. G. (1973). Skill in chess. *American Scientist*, *61*, 394–403.

Singley, M. K., & Anderson, J. R. (1989). *The transfer of cognitive skill*. Cambridge, MA: Harvard University Press.

Staszewski, J. J. (1988). The psychological reality of retrieval structures: An investigation of expert knowledge (doctoral dissertation, Cornell University, 1987). *Dissertation Abstracts International*, *48*, 2126B.

Thorndike, E. L. (1921). *The psychology of learning*, vol. II. New York: Teachers College, Columbia University.

Welford, A. T. (1968). *Fundamentals of skill*. London: Methuen.

Woltz, D. J. (1988). An investigation of the role of working memory in procedural skill acquisition. *Journal of Experimental Psychology: General*, *117*, 319–331.

5.4

MOTOR SKILLS

John Annett
University of Warwick, England

The problem of motor control	The acquisition of skills
The neural basis of motor control	Mechanisms of learning
Motor consistency and variability	Cognitive processes
Motor programs	Verbal instruction
Feedback control	Knowledge of results
Complex skills and control hierarchies	**Retention and transfer**
Serial organization and control	Motor memory
	Transfer of training
	Conclusion
	Further reading
	References

Skills occur in great variety, from those involving the whole body in sports like gymnastics, to hand skills used in everyday activities such as using hand tools and playing musical instruments, and intellectual skills such as playing chess or controlling a nuclear power station. Whatever the nature of the activity, behaviour is called *skilled*, or *a skill*, when it is (1) directed towards the attainment of an identifiable goal (for example catching the ball), and (2) so organized that the goal is reliably achieved with economy of time and effort (that is, most catches are held), and (3) has been acquired by training and practice (practice makes perfect). Obviously the topic of skill embraces a very wide range of questions in theoretical and applied psychology. The characteristics and limits of human skilled performance have been of interest to applied psychologists since the beginning of the twentieth century with early studies of morse telegraphy and typing and later of flying skills. More recently, sports psychologists have provided many detailed studies of

434

physical skills. There have been significant advances in the understanding of the neural mechanisms underlying movement, and neurological disorders with motor implications in children (cerebral palsy) and elderly people (stroke and Parkinson's disease) have stimulated interest in assessment and rehabilitation.

To begin to understand any skill it is necessary first to consider three aspects of the problem. First, different skills employ different *effector systems*, that is, functional units of the central nervous system (CNS) connected with various groups of muscles. Second, since skills are by definition goal-directed, there is always an *object*, often some environmental variable, which is manipulated or changed by the operation of the effectors. Third, the particular way in which the effector system acts on the object to achieve the goal state is mediated by a *control system*.

Research on motor skills has given pride of place to the hand as the effector system for manipulative and control skills and, of course, the trunk and limbs are the principal effectors in whole body skills. However, other important effectors include the ocular-motor (eye-movement) system, which is involved in spatially oriented behaviour, and the vocal system, which produces some of the most highly skilled behaviour of which humans are capable. These varied effector systems have different physical properties which must be taken into account in any theoretical analysis of control mechanisms. The skeletal effectors are essentially lever systems in which the angle at the joint is controlled by balanced groups of muscles, the agonists and antagonists. As mechanical systems they have properties of mass and elasticity, which place important limitations on the movements that are physically possible and especially on the speed with which a change of joint angle can take place. But these physical properties can also be exploited in the interest of economy of both physical and computational effort. The eye, by contrast, has low inertia which enables it to make fast saccades to preselected locations, an essential requirement for spatially directed behaviour. The vocal system, which includes the muscles of the diaphragm, larynx, jaw, tongue, and lips, requires very precise integration and timing of movement sequences for the generation of speech. It is, of course, not only the muscles that are controlled but also speech sounds; hence, speech is highly dependent on auditory feedback as shown by its susceptibility to disturbances, especially delay of only a few hundred milliseconds which can induce stuttering.

The second aspect of skill, the properties of objects that are controlled, is also significant in determining the kind of control that is needed. For instance, an ordinary bicycle ridden at reasonable speed is quite stable, and all the rider has to do is control direction and forward speed. Clearly, the physical properties of the object being controlled have profound consequences for the mechanism by which control is exerted.

Control systems may, in general, be of two kinds, characterized as *feedforward* and *feedback*. In a feedforward system, output, that is, muscular activity, is controlled by a program or set of stored instructions that are initiated by a starting signal in much the same way as a domestic washing machine runs through a sequence of actions when a particular program is set up and initiated. In a feedback system a target value for one or more variables is set (often known as the set point) and output is controlled by a signal proportional to the difference between the currently sensed value and the set point. A thermostat-controlled domestic heating system is a familiar example of feedback control.

THE PROBLEM OF MOTOR CONTROL

The central issue for research on skill is how the effector mechanisms are successfully brought to bear on objects in the environment in order to fulfil the goals of the organism. The information processing analysis of human skill, current from the 1950s, although providing a very significant advance on the conditioned reflex models of the 1930s and 1940s, has turned out to be not entirely satisfactory as an account of skill. In the basic model, sensory information is seen flowing through a channel, being filtered by attentional mechanisms, stored in temporary buffers, and processed or transformed by central mechanisms into a motor output. This model followed the classic traditions of Helmholtz, Donders, and Wundt, who used the principle of subtraction to deduce the time course of a sequence of hypothesized internal processes, or black boxes (see Woodworth, 1938, chap. 14).

For example, the time required to make a decision between two courses of action can be determined by subtracting reaction time to a predictable stimulus (simple reaction time) from the time required to respond to one of two possible signals (choice reaction time). This subtraction logic was pursued vigorously and with increasing degrees of sophistication for 100 years in the search for a detailed account of the "black boxes". An important analysis by Hick (1952) showed that reaction time was proportional to stimulus information, analogous to the rate at which physical communication channels can transmit information. Limitations to skilled performance were attributed principally to the capacity of the central channel, and theorizing centred on the results of experiments on serial and choice reaction time, divided attention, and performing two tasks at once. The capacity problem was not satisfactorily resolved within the framework of a static, linear model, and later interpretations of the nature of motor control (Abernethy & Sparrow, 1992) led to the consideration of rather different questions.

The neural basis of motor control

The pathways between sensory input and motor output are neither anatomically nor functionally linear and sequential. Figure 1 (after Brooks, 1986) shows the principal neural pathways involved in voluntary movement. A

436

number of different structures intervene between the senses and the muscles and there is a great deal of interaction between them. Information flows out from the cortex and other parts of the brain to the effectors and also back again to the "higher centres". Figure 1 suggests that intentions or goals, driven originally by the motivational (limbic) system, are formulated in the association cortex, and developed into plans, principally in the frontal lobes. The formulation of a detailed executive program to achieve a goal that requires a postural adjustment must relate bodily equilibrium to the direction and force of the intended action and here structures such as the basal ganglia, thalamus, and lateral cerebellum make essential contributions by preparatory adjustments of muscular tone and by relating muscular forces to externally perceived space. The pyramidal cells of the primary motor cortex make synaptic connections direct to the motor neurons in the spinal cord but there are

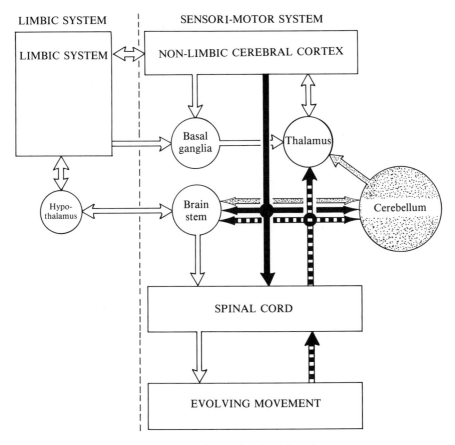

Figure 1 Principal neural pathways involved in voluntary movement
Source: After Brooks, 1986

other direct connections from the brain stem (red nucleus), and furthermore, the motor cortex interacts with the intermediate cerebellum to relate efferent signals to the changing state of sensory information. At the spinal level, both descending systems (cortico- and rubro-spinal tracts) modulate semi-autonomous spinal reflexes that control the relationships between sets of muscles. The rate and extent to which muscles change their length is dependent on a number of factors including their starting position and load and the state of other muscles that are functionally related to them or form a *synergy* or *coordinative structure* (Bernstein, 1967). The messages coming down from the brain have been likened to advice rather than instructions, since the influence of local conditions at the periphery can be strong and the relevant information may not be directly available to the higher centres. However, it is the behavioural evidence as much as the complexity of the physical mechanisms that demands a more sophisticated theory of motor control.

Motor consistency and variability

Highly skilled acts are characterized more by the constancy of their output or results than by the consistency of the muscular contractions used to achieve them. Whenever I aim to hit the *t* on my keyboard my hand comes at it from a slightly different angle, and I can pick up my coffee without first having to adopt precisely the same posture I used last time. A motor control system that depended on a centralized command structure would not be the most effective way of achieving constant goals under varying conditions. A complex joint like the shoulder is controlled by at least ten muscles, each containing a large number of motor units, that is, bundles of fibres controlled by a single nerve ending. If movements were centrally coded in terms of joint angles, then the message specifying a new position of the upper arm would require the specification of ten different values or the control of ten degrees of freedom, to use the phrase of Bernstein (1967). A moderately complex movement involving just the arms, hand, and fingers already involves a formidable number of degrees of freedom that would have to be specified in any centrally computed program. A robotics engineer designing a machine to mimic human action would look for a simpler solution, and debates in the motor skills field relate to proposed solutions. Possible solutions can be divided into those requiring stored information (feedforward models) and those that attribute action to the patterns of external stimulation and the physical properties of the responding system. Fully feedback systems are limited to relatively slow actions due to an unavoidable minimum lag time of about 100 milliseconds associated with sensory feedback.

Motor programs

Simple positioning tasks such as placing a peg in a hole (Fitts, 1954) illustrate two types of control in one movement, a pre-programmed, ballistic or open-loop initial phase followed by a controlled or closed-loop second phase. The pre-programmed phase has been taken as evidence for a general mode of feedforward control by means of a *motor program*. Different authors have slightly different conceptions of the nature of motor programs (see Summers, 1989), but the core idea is of a pattern of motor impulses which may be computed on demand or may be drawn from a memory bank. A motor program for throwing a dart into the bullseye would constitute a pattern of arm acceleration and deceleration with the finger-thumb release being timed for a particular point in the cycle.

Evidence for the existence of motor programs comes from three main sources: first, the degree to which it is possible to modify movement patterns that are subject to unforeseen mechanical forces or new information shortly after initiation; second, the effects of feedback deprivation on the execution of the motor task; and third, the relationship between initiation time and the complexity of a prepared sequence of movements. As an instance of the first type of evidence, Wadman, Denier, van der Gon, Geuze, and Moll (1979) recorded the EMG (electromyogram) signals indicating changes in the electrical potential of the muscles associated with the acceleration/deceleration pattern of a rapid sequence of arm movements. The original pattern of muscle electrical activity was preserved even on trials when the arm was unexpectedly prevented from moving strongly, suggesting pre-programmed control.

As regards feedback deprivation, Lashley (1917) noted that a patient who, due to a spinal injury, had no kinaesthetic sensation (that is, no sensation of movement) in his lower limbs could none the less reproduce movements accurately. He argued this would be possible only if there were a central memory for the motor command. Motor programs are implicated in the control of eye movements. When a pattern of excitation sweeps across the retina, the organism needs to know whether this is a result of movement in the external world or of the organism itself. A copy of the original motor instruction, an efference copy, could be used to detect the difference between self-generated and externally generated visual movement. Experiments on the accuracy of movement in the absence of sensory feedback due to surgical intervention or temporary ischaemia (Laszlo, 1966) provide supportive evidence for motor program theory to the extent that simple reaching movements can still be made in the absence of kinaesthetic feedback. However, fine control is typically lost and there are many more actions in which transformations of external sensory feedback such as delays and geometric transformations seriously disrupt performance.

It has been found that the time to produce the first response in a pre-programmed sequence increases as a linear function of the total length of the sequence. The increased reaction time is taken to reflect the time taken to retrieve the program elements from memory. This would fit with a hierarchical structure for the components of a rapid sequence of finger movements and demonstrates a linear increase in reaction time with the number of nodes in the response hierarchy that would have to be activated to produce the sequence.

Critics of the motor program concept have argued that the amount of information that would have to be retained in memory to specify all the movements of which an adult is capable would exceed the storage capacity of the brain. However, the extent of the problem may have been overestimated. Vredenbregt and Koster (1971) were able to simulate cursive handwriting by using two DC motors to drive a pen across the writing surface. Carefully timed discrete voltage pulses to the motors moving the pen in the horizontal and vertical directions produced recognizable letters due to the natural dynamics (inertia and viscosity) of the mechanical system; in other words, the information needed to specify the response is perhaps not as large as appears at first sight.

Some theories of motor control stress the role of peripheral factors, for example a limb can be considered as a mass-spring system. The angle adopted by a joint depends on the relative tension in the agonist and antagonist muscles which themselves are elastic or spring-like. It has been suggested (e.g., Bizzi, 1980) that the angle of a joint, and hence the position of a limb, can be specified in terms of the relative tension of the opposing muscles. If the initial position of the limb is disturbed by a temporary load, then it will automatically return to its former position when the load is released just as a swing door will return to its closed position after being pushed open. Muscular tension in turn can be determined by the rate of firing of the neurons serving the opposing muscle groups. The particular significance of this solution is that external disturbances caused by sudden changes of load (for instance, by hitting a small object) do not affect the final position and do not require additional processing in the nervous system. The terminal position of limb in space can also be determined by the relative tension of the opposing muscles.

Feedback control

It would be wrong to regard motor programs and feedback as mutually exclusive accounts of motor control. Actions require both some degree of pre-planning and some means of monitoring and adjusting the plan if the intended results are to be achieved under variable conditions. The operation of the feedback principle in the central nervous system (CNS) was noted by Bell as long ago as the 1820s (Bell, 1826), but it is only since the 1940s following the work of Craik and others (Craik, 1947) at Cambridge on the skills of pilots and gun layers that its significance for motor control was appreciated. The essential principle (illustrated in Figure 2) is that the output of a power source, for instance a motor or a muscle, is controlled by a signal

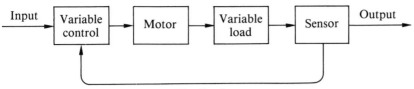

Feedback

Figure 2 A simple servo or feedback loop. The motor provides power, which is applied to a load that varies according to external conditions. The actual output is sensed and fed back to a variable control, which adjusts the power to meet variations in loading and thus maintains a constant output

derived from a discrepancy between the desired value of a variable and its current value. The humble thermostat which switches the boiler on when the temperature falls below the set point serves as a model for motor control in the peg-moving, bicycle riding, and many other tasks. In a purely feedback-controlled system the only information that needs to be stored in the CNS is the set point or goal since it is the environment which holds the information necessary to control movement.

Skills such as catching and hitting fast-moving objects and steering towards or around fixed objects provide some particularly clear examples of direct feedback control of movement. When moving through the environment, the visual field represented on the retina expands outwards from the centre, and similarly as an object approaches the observer textural features on its surface move from central towards peripheral vision. Lee and Young (1986) have shown in a variety of interception tasks that time to contact can be specified by the ratio of retinal size and expansion velocity of a textural feature, and that this variable (tau) is used to control movement directly.

The direct coupling of action to visual feedback is strikingly observed in tasks where mirrors, lenses, or closed-circuit television (CCTV) are used to change the familiar relationship between movement and the visual cues normally used to guide it. In tracing a star pattern seen in a mirror, subjects find it very difficult to change direction at the corners. One feels momentarily paralysed and further progress is possible only by decoupling the visual cue, that is, by not paying attention to it and allowing control to pass to the visual or kinaesthetic imagery system. Perceptual coupling is another way of relieving the motor system of its computational burden, and so we may conclude that both motor program theory and feedback theory have a range of possible answers to Bernstein's degrees of freedom problem.

Complex skills and control hierarchies

Feedback theory has been applied to a wider range of problems than just the control of simple motor acts. A complex skill, be it a straightforward sequence such as assembling a piece of equipment or a set of conditional actions such as might be employed in playing football or running a chemical plant, is characterized by a unique structure. Structured skills can be analysed into behavioural units called "TOTE" ("test-operate-test-exit") units by Miller, Galanter, and Pribram (1960) or "Operations" by Annett, Duncan, Stammers, and Gray (1971). Each unit is specified by a goal state of one or more variables, and the discrepancy between the goal state and the current state drives action. Consider the series of steps required to tie a bow, from grasping the two ends to be tied together to the final tug that tightens the knot (Annett, 1986). Each step can be thought of as a goal to be attained, having one end in each hand is necessary before proceeding to twist them together, and so on. Tying a bow is a simple behavioural sequence, but at the same time it has a vertical or hierarchical structure. A description of bow tying might refer to (1) making a half knot, (2) making two loops with the ends, and (3) making another half knot with the two loops. Stage (1) might be further broken down into sub-operations such as (1.1) grasping the free ends, (1.2) twisting one over the other, (1.3) pulling the half knot tight, and so on. It is even possible to break down (1.1) into detailed finger movements, although it would be less useful to specify these in detail because factors such as the size and flexibility of the material to be tied could vary, making it necessary to change some of the details from one knot to the next.

Serial organization and control

To assert that control of complex skills is hierarchically organized can give the misleading impression that all effective instructions issue from the highest level and are passed down to the effector units unchanged, but not even military hierarchies work in this way. Generals are responsible for strategy, not tactics, and units in a well-organized army have some degree of autonomy. Shaffer (1981) analysed the performance of highly skilled pianists by having them play a piano wired to a computer which timed each keystroke. They played pieces from memory and by sight and in different tempi and moods. A statistical analysis of the variations in the timing of keystrokes revealed that the temporal structure was most constant at the level of the bar, with much of the detailed variation in timing of particular bars being repeated across performances. Expressive temporal features, such as rubato, could be varied between performances while others were left unchanged. Shaffer interpreted these results as indicating that the temporal structure of the music is represented at an abstract level and is not simply determined by the speed with which one keystroke follows the next. In this sense the temporal features represent control at a relatively high level in the hierarchy.

THE ACQUISITION OF SKILLS

Skills are, by definition, learned, and in most cases must be specifically taught. The plasticity of skilled behaviour creates problems for theories of performance and is one of the main reasons for the abandonment of the 1950s-style linear information processing model. The pivotal concept of a capacity-limited information processing channel which could apparently account for choice reaction time data (Hick, 1952) and the trade-off between speed and accuracy in rapid movement tasks (Fitts, 1954) began to collapse when it was shown that extended practice changes the relationship between stimulus information and performance. Experimental results from thousands of trials of choice reaction time could no longer be fitted to Hick's equation

$$RT = k \log_2 (N + 1)$$

where k is a constant and N is the number of equiprobable stimuli requiring a unique response; it was also demonstrated that after weeks of practice two apparently conflicting tasks could be performed simultaneously.

Unfortunately, the investigation of learning was very closely identified with behaviourist concepts of stimulus, response, and reinforcement, and despite some early attempts to account for skill learning in information processing terms (Annett & Kay, 1957), it was not until the end of the 1960s that non-stimulus–response theories of skill acquisition began to emerge (Adams, 1971; Annett, 1969; Schmidt, 1975). These theories all referred to centrally stored data, the traces of previous sensory and motor events, and reinterpreted knowledge of results as information feedback which changes behaviour rather than reinforcement which acts by strengthening stimulus–response connections.

Mechanisms of learning

Practice results in both quantitative and qualitative changes in performance. Early studies with trainee morse telegraphists showed that the number of signals correctly transcribed per minute rises steadily over the first three to four months of practice, remains roughly constant (at a plateau) for the next two months, and then begins to rise again. The later acceleration in learning rate was accompanied by a change in method from transcribing single letters to receiving and writing down whole words. "Grouping", as this process came to be known, is one of the common qualitative changes in performance that results from practice.

A quantitative change occurs with practice in simple repetitive skills, so that the logarithm of time for each repetition is a linear function of the logarithm of the number of practice trials. This relationship is the *log-log-linear law of learning*, and its apparent simplicity suggests that there might be a single underlying learning process. Crossman (1959) suggested that each practice trial draws on a population of perceptual-motor processes and that these are evaluated in terms of the effort required to achieve the goal. On successive trials, each process is negatively weighted in proportion to the effort it entails, such that the probability of effortful processes being selected is progressively reduced. Newell and Rosenbloom (1981) maintained that a power function provides a better fit to skill acquisition data, including results from both motor and mental skills, and they propose that the learning principle is "chunking". Information is said to be chunked when it is dealt with as a single unit, for instance the telegraphist dealing in whole words rather than single letters. In terms of the hierarchical theory described earlier in the chapter, the lowest levels of the control hierarchy are chunked, thus a muscle synergy (a group of muscles operating together) would constitute a single chunk requiring only a single command rather than central specification of the activity in all the individual muscle units. It is hard to distinguish between the selection and the chunking theory on empirical grounds, but if one could look at changes in the detailed components of a skill as a function of practice, the Crossman theory would predict that more effortful components progressively give way to less effortful, whereas the Newell and Rosenbloom theory would predict that relatively stable and consistent groups of components would emerge after practice.

A single process would provide the most parsimonious account of learning, but there is ample evidence to suggest that there are at least two broadly different types of learning process, one type that occurs as a result of repetition *per se* and another in which cognition plays a major role. The log-log-linear law may well indicate not a single slow-acting process but a population of ways of learning that are successively drawn upon until exhausted. Thus, in the early stages, relatively rapid progress can be made by imitating the method of a skilled model or taking the advice of a coach, whereas much later in practice, when major sources of improvement have been exhausted, repetition may refine perceptual and temporal judgements or, according to a classical theory, facilitate the connections between task elements.

Cognitive processes

Observational learning and verbal instruction play an important part in the early stages of learning new skills (Fitts, 1964) but a well-articulated theory of cognitive motor learning is lacking, in part due to the lingering influence of behaviourism on theorizing about learning. Imitation occurs in a variety of animal and bird species, and in humans as young as 12 days (Meltzoff & Moore, 1977). The key to cognitive motor learning lies in elucidating the way in which learned skills are represented in memory.

Coaching hints can exploit the human capacity to form representations of objects and complex movement patterns. For example, a squash coach encourages his pupils to adopt a particular stance when receiving serve by instructing them to "pretend to be a Red Indian on the war-path". The phrase summons up an image of feet apart, knees slightly bent, right arm raised holding the racket/tomahawk head-high, and having a generally alert attitude. To the extent that learners (and you the reader) can both envisage the posture and adopt it is clear evidence of the existence of a high-level representation of a complex, but quite specific, movement pattern. These patterns, or "action prototypes" (Annett, 1979), are active in both the perception and production of actions, so if an action pattern is a perceptible entity it is (barring purely biomechanical limitations) capable of being produced. The theory that perception and action are served by the same rather than different processes has been entertained by a number of authors, for example Prinz (1986) and Weimer (1977). There is strong evidence that in perceiving the actions of other humans certain invariant features are extracted from the complex stimulus array. In a technique developed by Johansson (1973), an actor clad in dark clothes with small lights attached to the principal joints is filmed in high contrast. When the actor is stationary, only a jumble of bright spots is seen, but when the actor moves there is a distinct and immediate impression of human action. It has been shown (Cutting & Proffitt, 1982) that accurate judgements can be made about the actor's sex and the weight of any object being carried.

Studies of learning to ski (Whiting, Vogt, & Vereijken, 1992) illustrate how a learner can use an expert model as a source of information. The task was to learn a particular pattern of movement of the trunk and legs on a ski simulator. This device comprised a spring-loaded platform on which the learner stands and which slides from side to side over runners in response to leg and body movements. The movements were characterized by amplitude, frequency, and fluency the latter being a score derived from an idealized acceleration pattern. All subjects were given knowledge of results on the three scores (frequency, amplitude, and fluency) and all improved with practice, but the subjects who observed the model quickly learned to match the fluency characteristic, although even after five practice sessions, few subjects were able to match the precise frequency and amplitude of the model's movements. This ability to abstract a particular higher-order description or representation of a complex activity is crucial to imitation, but more experimental studies are needed, particularly studies that relate subjects' ability to perceive significant features of action to the ability to perform that action.

Verbal instruction

Motor *skill* is conventionally distinguished from verbal *knowledge* and the former is often inaccessible to the latter. Skilled swimmers cannot answer factual questions about the breast-stroke any faster or more accurately than novices, and subjects can learn to control complex systems, including simulated chemical plant and transportation systems, without being able to express the rules that govern their control decisions.

Neurological evidence points to the likelihood of separate encoding of verbal knowledge and motor capability in the central nervous system. Amnesics who cannot recall facts can learn and remember a motor skill (Cohen & Squire, 1980), and one consequence of damage to the corpus callosum which connects the two hemispheres of the brain is that patients have difficulty in following verbal instructions to carry out simple tasks with the left hand (which is controlled by the right, non-verbal, hemisphere). The problem of how the verbal and non-verbal systems communicate is a matter of conjecture, but it seems likely that the translation is effected through the mechanisms of high-level representations that include both images and abstractions. Experts asked (for the first time at least) to explain how a task is performed frequently resort to imagery, whereas instructors, as was shown in the "Red Indian" example above, often resort to imagery-inducing language in order to convey information about postures and actions.

Knowledge of results

Perhaps the most extensive use of language in skill training is in the provision of knowledge of results, and this topic has received very extensive coverage in the research literature (see summaries by Annett, 1969; Salmoni, Schmidt, & Walter, 1984). Informing the learner of the outcome of each response or trial (knowledge of results, or KR) typically gives the most rapid learning, whereas no-KR, or practice-only conditions, generally show poor learning or none at all. The rate and extent of learning is sensitive to the amount of information given – the more detailed the KR the better the learning – making it clear that the "reinforcement" interpretation is inadequate.

Several theories stress the informative properties of KR. Annett (1969) interpreted KR as a form of feedback used by the learner to adapt responses to the standard specified by the trainer. This very simple theory applied to the acquisition of a linear positioning task proposes a short-term store of the kinaesthetic sensations produced by the preceding movement and the simple strategy of modifying the direction and approximate extent of the next movement according to a simple rule that uses both external KR and internal feedback. The first attempt to produce a movement of the specified extent is guided only by a pre-existing concept of the required direction and amplitude but the second attempt is based on (1) a (fading) memory trace of the first attempt, (2) discrimination between internal feedback from a current response and the trace of the preceding response, and (3) a simple strategy such as, "if the last response was shorter than required make the next one longer, if it was correct reproduce it, if it was too long make it shorter". Evidence from the rate and extent of learning linear positioning tasks with different kinds and amounts of KR provides qualitative support for this basic model.

Adams's (1971) theory, also based on the concept of feedback, proposes a "motor trace" or record of the output specification of a response and a "perceptual trace", a record of the sensory feedback (including KR) associated with that motor trace. Practice strengthens the perceptual trace such that the sensory consequences of motor outputs are anticipated. Outputs can then be preselected on the basis of their expected feedback. Schmidt's "schema theory" (Schmidt, 1975) extended Adams's "closed loop theory" to account for the learning of classes of actions. The choice of motor output is related to expected sensory consequences by information about previous response specifications, previous sensory consequences, and previous outcomes, that is, whether the sensory consequences signal a desired state of affairs. These sources of information are consolidated into a "recognition schema" that encodes the relationships between sensory consequences and outcomes, and a recall schema that relates outcomes to response specifications. The particular merit of the schema theory is that it allows for generalized learning and it makes the specific prediction that learning is most effective when a variety of responses are made, thus practising throwing darts at different targets is as good or better than just practising with the bullseye. This prediction is by and large fulfilled, but none of the three theories makes very strong differential predictions; it can be argued that they provide only a general description of the learning mechanism.

A later theoretical development was the application of connectionist models to simple motor learning. Horak (1992) used a simulated neural network to represent Schmidt's recall schema in learning a unidimensional ballistic skill such as throwing an object at a target at some (variable) distance. The network learns to match its variable force output to different inputs, representing different target distances, by changing the weights of interconnections between its elements (analogous to individual neurons) according to performance outcomes. In a sense, the network discovers the rule relating perceived target distance to appropriate force output in much the same way as suggested by Annett's (1969) account of the role of KR in learning. An especially intriguing feature of this simulation is that it exhibits the *contextual interference effect*. That is, if trials involving roughly the same distance and requiring similar force are given in a block, the network learns quite rapidly but transfers less well to targets set at other distances than when trials at different distances are varied randomly in the practice sequence. In the latter case, learning rate is reduced but transfer between targets at different distances is improved and in this respect the network model mimics the qualitative results of actual learning experiments.

Much of the research on KR has used simple unidimensional positioning tasks, but in more complex skills, such as gymnastics, outcome information may be insufficient to identify critical features of the performance that need to be modified. Kinematic data may be helpful but, as with video recordings, may need expert interpretation to establish the precise link between performance and outcome.

KR is often said to have a motivational role. Even when not very informative, KR seems to boost performance by encouraging persistence in effortful and monotonous tasks (see Annett, 1969, chap. 5). If KR provides information about goal attainment, there is no need to postulate an additional energizing function to account for learning. In the context of current theories of skill as goal-directed action it is unlikely that any activity that is not seen to be making progress towards some goal will be maintained, especially if it consumes resources of energy or information processing capacity, thus in any comparison between KR and no-KR conditions performance under the latter is likely to be less effortful, less concentrated and less persistent. The motivational effect of KR is simply a demonstration of "feedback in action" (Annett, 1969).

RETENTION AND TRANSFER

Motor memory

It is a common observation that a skill once learned is never forgotten. Early studies of typewriting and juggling, using the relearning or *savings* method, showed that after more than a year without practice the level of performance originally reached after 45–50 days of practice was regained with about 10 days of retraining, a saving of 80 per cent of the original learning. Hill (1957), using himself as a subject, measured savings of 70 per cent in typing skill over a retention interval of 50 years! Retention of verbal material is typically less good. A study by Leavitt and Schlosberg (1944) apparently confirmed the superiority of motor memory by comparing savings scores for pursuit rotor tracking and nonsense syllable learning after intervals of 1, 7, 28, and 70 days. They found that retention of the motor task declined from near 90 per cent after a retention interval of 1 day to around 75 per cent after 70 days, whereas savings on the nonsense syllables declined from about 80 per cent after 1 day to 50 per cent after 70 days. This result is not, however, as clearcut as it at first appears since the two tasks were not equated for ease of learning nor for the number of trials or repetitions, and both these factors are known to affect retention.

Short-term retention of skills (short-term motor memory – STMM) has been studied largely through the medium of simple positioning tasks in which subjects attempt to reproduce movements of a specific extent, normally without the aid of vision. Variables such as number of repetitions, duration of the retention interval, and interference have yielded a body of information on kinaesthetic memory and the central, but not very conclusive, debate has been how movement information is encoded, for example as action plans (motor programs) or sensory templates. The evidence (e.g., Laabs, 1973) suggests that what is retained is the location of a target rather than the extent of the movement required to reach it, that is, a spatial rather than strictly motor or kinaesthetic memory.

Using a task analogous to digit span (which entails memorizing short strings of digits), Smyth and Pendleton (1990) found evidence to suggest that memory for bodily movements, such as dance steps, may be distinct from memory for spatial location. Subjects observed, and were asked after a short interval to reproduce, a series of arbitrary body movements. Various interference tasks during the short retention interval reduced the number of items correctly recalled but in different degrees. Verbal interference tasks had little effect, whereas motor tasks such as squeezing a rubber bulb, pointing to a series of targets and watching, or making similar movements, reduced the number of items correctly recalled. The results of the experiments as a whole suggest a dissociation between verbal, spatial and movement coding systems in short-term memory.

Although absolute values of felt force, distance, and direction can be retained with moderate accuracy for short periods, it is unlikely that we rely on simple sensori-motor memory of discrete movements to remember how to perform skilled tasks. The world in which we live and the actions we need to take are far too variable for it to be worthwhile to memorize precise movement information. It is rather through a set of outline plans organized so as to achieve criterion conditions, which may be abstractly defined, that we are able to remember how to solve familiar motor problems (Annett, 1988).

Transfer of training

The element of non-specificity in skill learning makes it possible to transfer the benefits of experience in one situation to others that are related. Having learned to drive a Mini, only a little more training is needed to master a Jaguar or a Rolls Royce; indeed, our whole system of education and training is based on the presumption of transfer, that is, that acquiring some specific skills will enhance the acquisition of others. Transfer of training, like retention, can be measured in terms of the savings in learning Task B that can be attributed to prior experience on Task A. According to Woodworth (1938), E. H. Weber, the father of psychophysics, reported in the 1840s that skills learned with the right hand transferred to the left and vice versa, and that a surgeon trained his students to carry out difficult operations with the left hand so that they would be better able to perform them with the right (see Woodworth & Schlosberg, 1955, pp. 738–743).

The traditional theory of transfer was that practice on any task will develop one or more abilities and that the transfer task will benefit to the extent that it also depends on the same ability. This *formal discipline theory* was at the basis of educational practice, popular at least since the time of

John Locke, which insisted on learning poetry to develop the memory and mathematics to develop logical thinking. An alternative theory of *identical elements* is that transfer occurs only when the original learning task and the transfer task share some common feature or element. Under the influence of behaviourism, the elements soon came to be understood as stimuli and responses and from this narrow interpretation arose the paradox of *negative transfer*.

Negative transfer occurs when previous experience interferes with the learning or performance of a skill, and this can happen when transferring between tasks that are similar in all but a few important respects, such as transferring from a right-hand-drive car to a left-hand-drive, or even changing from driving on the left to driving on the right side of the road. In such cases almost every element is identical. However, a problem can arise when near-identical stimuli must be linked to different responses, for example moving a lever in the opposite direction to that originally learned. For transfer to occur, not only is it important that the two tasks should have common stimuli and responses, but also they should have common stimulus–response connections.

Even with this modification, the identical elements theory is not entirely satisfactory because of the occasional failure of transfer even when the tasks concerned have important common elements (Annett & Sparrow, 1985). Fotheringhame (1984), for example, found no significant transfer between two measurement tasks employing the same principles (the use of micrometers and vernier height gauges) unless the principle linking the two was explicitly taught. The additional, and perhaps essential, factor in transfer is an *awareness* of features or elements common to the old and the new task, and here the trainer or educator can employ training techniques likely to enhance useful transfer (Annett & Sparrow, 1985).

It has been suggested that learning often occurs at two levels, a cognitive and a *meta*cognitive level. Metacognition refers to awareness of one's own cognitive processes, thus it is possible both to learn a skill and to know something about how one is doing it and to have a learning strategy. Less able learners and those who show poor generalization and transfer typically have underdeveloped metacognitive skills (Downs & Perry, 1985), and training programmes in metacognitive skills are being developed for use in schools and the training of less able school-leavers. The role that metacognition might play in the acquisition and transfer of perceptual-motor skills is, however, relatively unexplored territory.

CONCLUSION

Any introductory review of such a broad and active field as motor skill is bound to be incomplete. Little has been said in this survey about the problems that technological advances bring to modern industrial skills or about issues in education and rehabilitation. In the early 1950s researchers in motor skills were among the first to see the relevance of information processing concepts to our understanding of human motor performance. In doing so they provided an important building block for modern cognitive psychology, but it was only later that relations between cognition and skill were explored in depth. The Cartesian dichotomy of body and mind would relegate motor skill to mere mechanism, not involving truly psychological processes, but a conception of skill is emerging that interprets the mechanisms of movement in the context of meaningful action. This recognition of the importance of cognitive processes in the generation and control of action and in the acquisition of skill is leading to exciting new research prospects.

FURTHER READING

Holding, D. H. (1989). *Human skills* (2nd edn). Chichester: Wiley.
Jeannerod, M. (1988). *The neural and behavioural organisation of goal-directed movements.* Oxford: Oxford University Press.
Jeannerod, M. (1990). *Attention and performance: XIII. Motor representation and control.* Hillside, NJ: Lawrence Erlbaum.
Rosenbaum, D. (1991). *Human motor control.* London: Academic Press.
Summers, J. J. (1992). *Approaches to the study of motor control and learning.* Amsterdam: Elsevier.

REFERENCES

Abernethy, B., & Sparrow, W. A. (1992). The rise and fall of dominant paradigms in motor behaviour research. In J. J. Summers (Ed.) *Approaches to the study of motor control and learning* (pp. 3–45). Amsterdam: Elsevier.
Adams, J. A. (1971). A closed loop theory of motor learning. *Journal of Motor Behavior, 3,* 111–150.
Annett, J. (1969). *Feedback and human behaviour.* Harmondsworth: Penguin.
Annett, J. (1979). Memory for skill. In M. M. Gruneberg & P. E. Morris (Eds) *Applied problems in memory* (pp. 215–247). London: Academic Press.
Annett, J. (1986). On knowing how to do things. In H. Heuer & C. Fromm (Eds) *Generation and modulation of action patterns* (pp. 187–200). Berlin: Springer.
Annett, J. (1988). Motor learning and retention. In M. M. Gruneberg, P. E. Morris, & R. N. Sykes (Eds) *Practical aspects of memory: Current research and issues. Clinical and educational implications* (vol. 2, pp. 434–440). Chichester: Wiley.
Annett, J., & Kay, H. (1957). Knowledge of results and skilled performance. *Occupational Psychology, 31,* 69–79.
Annett, J., & Sparrow, J. (1985). Transfer of training: A review of research and practical implications. *Programmed Learning and Educational Technology, 22,* 116–124.
Annett, J., Duncan, K. D., Stammers, R. B., & Gray, M. J. (1971). *Task analysis.* Department of Employment training information paper 6. London: Her Majesty's Stationery Office.
Bell, C. (1826). On the nervous circle which connects the voluntary muscles with the brain. *Philosophic Transactions, 2,* 163–173.

Bernstein, N. (1967). *The coordination and regulation of movements*. Oxford: Pergamon.

Bizzi, E. (1980). Central and peripheral mechanisms in motor control. In G. E. Stelmach & J. Requin (Eds) *Tutorials in motor behavior* (pp. 131–143). Amsterdam: North Holland.

Brooks, V. B. (1986). *The neural basis of motor control*. Oxford: Oxford University Press.

Cohen, N. J., & Squire, L. R. (1980). Preserved learning and retention of pattern analyzing skill in amnesia: Dissociation of knowing how and knowing that. *Science, 210*, 207–210.

Corkin, S. (1968). Acquisition of motor skills after bilateral medial temporal lobe excision. *Neurospychologia, 6*, 255–265.

Craik, K. J. W. (1947). Theory of the human operator in control systems: 1. The operator as an engineering system. *British Journal of Psychology, 38*, 56–61.

Crossman, E. R. F. W. (1959). A theory of the acquisition of speed skill. *Ergonomics, 2*, 153–166.

Cutting, J. E., & Proffitt, D. R. (1982). The minimum principle and the perception of absolute, common and relative motion. *Cognitive Psychology, 14*, 211–286.

Downs, S., & Perry, P. (1985). *Developing skilled learners: Learning to learn in the YTS*. Sheffield: Manpower Services Commission R&D no. 22.

Fitts, P. M. (1954). The information capacity of the human motor system in controlling the amplitude of movement. *Journal of Experimental Psychology, 47*, 381–391.

Fitts, P. M. (1964). Perceptual motor skill learning. In A. W. Melton (Ed.) *Categories of human learning* (pp. 234–285). New York: Academic Press.

Fotheringhame, J. (1984). Transfer of training: A field investigation. *Occupational Psychology, 57*, 239–248.

Hick, W. E. (1952). On the rate of gain of information. *Quarterly Journal of Experimental Psychology, 4*, 11–26.

Hill, L. B. (1957). A second quarter century of delayed recall or relearning at eighty. *Journal of Educational Psychology, 48*, 65–68.

Horak, M. (1992). The utility of connectionism for motor learning: A reinterpretation of contextual interference in movement schemes. *Journal of Motor Behavior, 24*(1), 58–66.

Johansson, G. (1973). Visual perception of biological motion and a model for its analysis. *Perception and Psychophysics, 14*, 201–211.

Laabs, G. J. (1973). Retention characteristics of different reproduction cues in motor short-term memory. *Journal of Experimental Psychology, 100*, 168–177.

Lashley, K. S. (1917). The accuracy of movement in the absence of excitation from the moving organ. *American Journal of Physiology, 43*, 169–194.

Laszlo, J. I. (1966). The performance of simple motor task with kinaesthetic sense loss. *Quarterly Journal of Experimental Psychology, 18*, 1–8.

Leavitt, H. J., & Schlosberg, H. (1944). The retention of verbal and motor skills. *Journal of Experimental Psychology, 34*, 404–417.

Lee, D. N., & Young, D. S. (1986). Gearing action to the environment. In H. Heuer & C. Fromm (Eds) *Generation and modulation of action patterns* (pp. 217–230). Berlin: Springer.

Lee, D. N., Lishman, J. R., & Thomson, J. A. (1982). Regulation of gait in long jumping. *Journal of Experimental Psychology: Human Perception and Performance, 8*, 448–459.

Meltzoff, A. N., & Moore, M. K. (1977). Imitation of facial and manual gestures. *Science, 198*, 75–80.

Miller, G. A., Galanter, E., & Pribram, K. (1960). *Plans and the structure of behavior*. New York: Holt, Reinhart & Winston.

Newell, A., & Rosenbloom, P. S. (1981). Mechanisms of skill acquisition and the law of practice. In J. R. Anderson (Ed.) *Cognitive skills and their acquisition* (pp. 1–55). Hillsdale, NJ: Lawrence Erlbaum.

Paillard, J. (1982). Apraxia and the neurophysiology of motor control. *Philosophical Transactions of the Royal Society of London*, B298, 111–134.

Paillard, J. (Ed.) (1991). *Brain and space*. Oxford: Oxford University Press.

Prinz, W. (1986). Modes of linkage between perception and action. In W. Prinz, & A. F. Sanders (Eds) *Cognition and motor processes* (pp. 185–193). Berlin: Springer.

Salmoni, A. W., Schmidt, R. A., & Walter, C. B. (1984). Knowledge of results and motor learning: A review and critical appraisal. *Psychological Bulletin*, *95*, 355–386.

Schmidt, R. A. (1975). A schema theory of discrete motor skill learning. *Psychological Review*, *82*, 225–260.

Shaffer, L. H. (1981). Performances of Chopin, Bach, and Bartok: Studies in motor programming. *Cognitive Psychology*, *13*, 326–376.

Smyth, M. M., & Pendleton, L. R. (1990). Space and movement in working memory. *Quarterly Journal of Experimental Psychology*, *42A*, 291–304.

Summers, J. J. (1989). Motor programs. In D. H. Holding (Ed.) *Human skills* (2nd edn, pp. 49–59). Chichester: Wiley.

Vredenbregt, J., & Koster, W. G. (1971). Analysis and synthesis of handwriting. *Philips Technical Review*, *32*, 73–78.

Wadman, W. J., Denier, C., van der Gon, J. J., Geuze, R. H., & Moll, C. R. (1979). Control of fast goal-directed arm movements. *Journal of Human Movement Studies*, *5*, 3–17.

Weimer, W. B. (1977). A conceptual framework for cognitive psychology: motor theories of the mind. In R. Shaw & J. Bransford (Eds) *Perceiving, acting and knowing: Towards an ecological psychology* (pp. 267–311). Hillsdale, NJ: Lawrence Erlbaum.

Whiting, H. T. A., Vogt, S., & Vereijken, B. (1992). Human skill and motor control: Some aspects of the motor control–motor learning relation. In J. J. Summers (Ed.) *Approaches to the study of motor control and learning* (pp. 81–111). Amsterdam: Elsevier.

Woodworth, R. S. (1938). *Experimental psychology*. London: Methuen.

Woodworth. R. S., & Schlosberg, H. (1955). *Experimental psychology* (3rd edn). London: Methuen.

5.5

SOCIAL SKILLS

Michael Argyle
University of Oxford, England

Social skills are patterns of social behaviour which make individuals socially competent, that is, able to produce the desired effects on other people. These effects may be related to personal motivations, for example, to be popular, or to task goals, for example, to enhance learning, recovery, or hard work on the part of others. Everyday social skills are mainly about the first, professional skills about the second.

It has been known for some time that social skills can have powerful effects on personal life, including mental health, as well as on successful work performance. As a result there has been a rapid increase in the use of social skills training, for many kinds of patients, for many types of work, and also for loneliness, for heterosexual skills, and for working abroad. We shall discuss later the methods used, and how far they are successful.

"Social skills" is also a model of social behaviour, which uses the analogy between social performance and motor skills, like driving a car (Argyle, 1983). This and other models of social performance will be discussed later. Social skills are usually regarded as the behavioural side of social competence; there are other components, such as knowledge and understanding and the absence of anxiety, which contribute to competence, and lie behind skilled performance.

THE ASSESSMENT OF SOCIAL COMPETENCE

It is necessary to assess individuals' social competence, in order to decide if and how they should be trained, and in order to do research into social skills. The methods which are commonly used are different for the study and training of people at work, and for clinical settings, including loneliness and other everyday problems.

Social skills at work

These may be assessed by research workers, for example studying the effects of different kinds of supervision, or for personnel selection and promotion. *Objective measures of effectiveness*, such as sales, productivity, or other performance measures, have the advantage of face validity – of being direct indices of success on the job. However, it may be difficult to obtain such measures: different individuals may be working in different situations so that the measures are not comparable, and it may be necessary to consider a range of outcomes, some of them difficult to measure, like "goodwill" (for sales). Nevertheless in many work situations it is objective results which often lead to promotion or redundancy.

Ratings by subordinates or colleagues are used in merit rating incentive schemes, and have often been used in leadership research, such as the Fleishman and Harris (1962) Leader Behavior Description Questionnaire.

Such ratings can include a wide range of scales, but it needs to be known which if any are relevant aspects of social skills.

Role-playing is often used in management selection, in assessment centres, with role-playing as leaders or members of work-groups or committees, or dealing with analogue work situations. It has been found to be a good predictor of management success, correlating with management success in the range .25–.35 (Muchinsky, 1986), and also correlates well with behaviour on the job, such as for teachers.

Video role-play can be used when it is difficult to create scaled-down versions of some jobs for role-play purposes; in this there is a video-presentation of a problem, to which the candidate makes spoken replies that are recorded and rated. This has been done in Britain for the police (Bull & Horncastle, 1983).

Interviews are widely used to assess work skills: it is probably a mistake to base judgements on performance in the interview, since it is an unusual situation. It is better to ask for detailed accounts of performance in situations at work or in other similar situations.

SOCIAL SKILLS FOR PATIENTS AND THE GENERAL POPULATION

Interviews can be a rich source of information, to find out the situations or relationships which are found difficult, and what seems to go wrong. *Role-playing* is also often used, with local "stooges" or other trainees, either modelling the situations found difficult, or an open-ended "get to know the other" task. This is video-taped and studied carefully. It is now known that role-played behaviour has only a modest relationship for patients with performance in natural settings (McNamara & Blumer, 1982); nevertheless trainers find it a rich source of data. A more elaborate alternative is the Social Interaction Test, in which patients are confronted by standard social situations (Trower, Bryant, & Argyle, 1978).

A large number of self-report *questionnaires* have been constructed, mostly in the USA, for social competence, usually with between three and seven subscales. These are reviewed by Spitzberg and Cupach (1989). At the present time little is known about their validity and no scales have become generally accepted, or come into clinical use. A short and simple scale, which has had some success as a research measure is the Social Competence Questionnaire (Sarason, Sarason, Hacker, & Basham 1985). Argyle, Furnham, and Graham (1981) used a self-report measure of degrees of difficulty experienced in different social situations – information which is needed by a trainer (Table 1). There is a little more agreement on measures of the main components of social skills, like empathy and assertiveness, and these will be described later.

Table 1 List of difficult situations

1 Complaining to a neighbour who you know well about constant noisy disturbances
2 Taking a person of the opposite sex out for the first time for an evening
3 Going for a job interview
4 Visiting the doctor when unwell
5 Going to close relative's funeral
6 Going round to cheer up a depressed friend who asked you to call
7 Being a host or hostess at a large party (e.g., twenty-first birthday)
8 Give a short formal speech to a group of about fifty people that you don't know
9 Taking an unsatisfactory article back to a shop where you purchased it
10 Going across to introduce yourself to new neighbours
11 Dealing with a difficult and disobedient child
12 Going to a function with many people from a different culture
13 Playing a party game after dinner (charades, musical chairs)
14 Attending a distant relation's wedding ceremony when you know few people
15 Apologizing to a superior for forgetting an important errand

Source: Argyle, Furnham, and Graham, 1981

Finally *ratings by others* can sometimes be made: for example, teachers can rate pupils, pupils can rate each other, and hospital staff can rate patients.

THE NEED FOR TRAINING IN SOCIAL SKILLS

How many people need training – assuming that this can be done success-fully? In one sense everyone's skills could be improved, just as opera singers have teachers and Olympic athletes have coaches. However, there is a smaller group whose lack of social skills is more acute, and who suffer as a result.

In the general population

1 *Children* – who are rejected, usually because they are aggressive or disrup-tive, or who are isolated, or who have no close friends.
2 *Adolescents and young people* – who are lonely, shy, unassertive, or have heterosexual problems. About 40 per cent of students say they are "shy", 55 per cent are often lonely (Argyle, 1984). This is one of the largest groups with social skills problems.
3 *Adults* – who have no friends, or marital difficulties (one-third of couples break up), or can't cope with their children.
4 *Old people* – who are lonely, have difficulty keeping up relations with kin, or are quarrelsome.

Failures in some of these spheres produce great unhappiness and have further consequences: marriages break up, badly handled children become delinquent, and isolated children and young people become mentally disturbed.

Social skills at work

Most jobs involve dealing with people; for teachers, managers, salespeople, and others this is the main task. Socially unskilled managers produce high levels of discontent, and consequent absenteeism and labour turnover among their subordinates. Some salespeople sell four times as much as others, in the same shop. Those who go to work abroad, as salespeople or for organizations like the Peace Corps, have a failure rate of 60 per cent or more in some parts of the Far East and Middle East, that is, they come home before their one- or two-year term is completed (Argyle, 1984). Lack of social skills is one of the main reasons that people lose their jobs. Many jobs require special skills: the only alternative to training is trying to learn these skills on the job by trial and error; evidently this often fails.

Mental patients

All kinds of mental patients have social behaviour problems. Schizophrenics are the worst, and are found very difficult to interact with. Depressives are also found very unrewarding. Many neurotics have social skills deficits. Bryant, Trower, Yardley, Urbieta, and Letemendia (1976) found that 17 per cent of adult neurotics (on a conservative estimate) were socially inadequate in a number of ways, corresponding to the components of social skill (described below) such as low rewardingness or assertiveness, inadequate non-verbal communication, and poor conversational powers.

THE COMPONENTS OF SOCIAL SKILL

What are the basic psychological processes which generate socially skilled behaviour? If we knew the answer, it would be easier to measure and train social skills. There is no agreed answer to this question, though each of the processes described below has been put forward by a number of people, sometimes under different names.

The social skill model

This model uses motor skills, like riding a bicycle or driving a car, as a model for social skills (Figure 1). In each case the performer seeks certain goals (e.g., make others talk a lot), makes skilled moves (e.g., asks closed questions), perceives the effects of this (e.g., short replies), and takes corrective action (e.g., asks more open-ended questions). The model emphasizes the goals of interactors, the specific social behaviour used, and the perception of

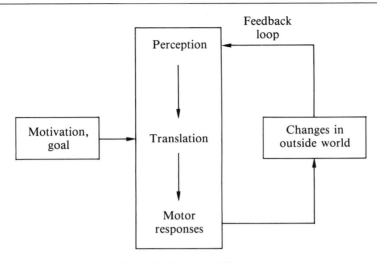

Figure 1 Motor skill model
Source: Argyle, 1983

and reactions to feedback. In the example above the questioner modified the kind of questions asked, just as a driver might adjust the steering wheel of a car. There is continuous flexibility of behaviour in response to the behaviour of the other (Argyle, 1983).

This model has led to emphasis on the elements of social performance, particularly the non-verbal ones, like facial expression and gaze. However, it has become clear that verbal elements are also important, and that global aspects of performance, such as rewardingness and assertiveness, may be more important than any specific elements. We also know that a number of further processes need to be taken into account. Some of these are about particular goals (e.g., assertiveness), others about particular behaviours (e.g., non-verbal communication), or about other parts of the model (e.g., cognition).

Assertiveness

Assertiveness, the ability to influence or control others, has sometimes been equated with social competence. It is contrasted both with aggression and with passive behaviour; a number of scales have been devised which have some validity against behaviour (e.g., Rathus, 1973). It was first introduced by behaviour therapists, in the belief that assertiveness inhibits anxiety, it has been taken up by women to overcome alleged oppression by men (men do score higher on assertiveness scales), and it has been found useful for some professional training, such as for nurses (Galassi, Galassi, & Vedder, 1981).

Lazarus (1973) proposed that assertiveness has four main components: refusing requests, asking for favours and making requests, expressing positive and negative feelings, and initiating, continuing, and ending general conversation. Assertiveness is found to correlate with a range of non-verbal elements (e.g. louder voice, more gaze), and with verbal ones. However, I shall draw instead on the social psychology of social influence. At the heart of any form of social influence there must be a verbal request; to be effective this needs to be persuasive, that is, it motivates and persuades by offering some good reason or incentive for complying with the request. The verbal request should be accompanied by the appropriate non-verbal style, such as tone of voice – a combination of dominant and friendly. Influence is greater if there is already a strong interpersonal relationship of friendship, authority, or both, though this may be strengthened in "ingratiation", where the request is preceded by flattery and agreement. The request should be an appropriate and legitimate one.

Rewardingness, reinforcement

Social psychologists have often regarded this as the key to friendship and interpersonal attraction. Jennings (1950), in a classic study of 400 girls in a reformatory, found that the popular girls were the ones who helped, protected, cheered, and encouraged others. Several theories of interpersonal attraction are based on findings like this. Leadership skills include a dimension of "Consideration", that is, looking after the needs of group members. Marital therapy has often consisted of training spouses in providing greater rewards for one another. Mental patients, especially schizophrenics and depressives, are found to be very unrewarding and "socially bankrupt".

The effect of reinforcement in social situations is to keep others in the situation or relationship, to increase the other's attraction to ego, and to make greater influence possible, when reinforcement is contingent on the desired behaviour. It can take a variety of forms. Verbal reinforcement includes praise, approval, acceptance, agreement, encouragement, and sympathy. Non-verbal rewards are smiles, head-nods, gaze, touch (in some situations), and tone of voice. Rewards can also take the form of help, presents, meals, advice, and information. Engaging in enjoyable shared activities is also rewarding, for example, sport, dancing, music and parties (Hargie, Saunders, & Dickson, 1987).

Non-verbal communication (NVC)

The social moves or signals of the social skills model are partly non-verbal, and perception and feedback is partly of the NVC of others. Assertiveness and rewardingness require special non-verbal styles of voice, face and posture. There is found to be a general factor of non-verbal expressiveness consisting of

1 a lot of facial expression, especially smiling
2 a high level of gaze
3 closer proximity
4 voice louder, higher pitch, more expressive
5 more other-directed gestures, fewer self-directed (e.g., self-touching).

Socially competent and effective people of all kinds are higher on this factor: doctors, teachers, and others do better if they have it. Socially inadequate people are low on it (Argyle, 1988). There is a self-report scale of expressiveness by Friedman, Prince, Riggio, & DiMatteo (1980); people in jobs needing social skills have a higher score. However, it is necessary for such people to be able to control their non-verbal expression: air stewardesses do this partly by simply adopting the appropriate expression, partly by thinking positive thoughts about the passengers (Hochschild, 1983).

It is necessary to decode the NVC of others correctly. There is some evidence that this is important, and some patients are very bad at it, but it is less important than effective encoding. There are several tests of such perceptual sensitivity, such as the PONS test (Rosenthal, Hall, DiMatteo, Rogers, and Archer, 1979), but there is little correlation between these different measures.

Another kind of NVC is used in conjunction with speech, and is described below; non-verbal signals are also used as the main vehicle for self-presentation.

Verbal communication

This lies at the heart of nearly all human social performance and social skill. Most skilled moves or signals are basically verbal, and furthermore have to fit into a conversational sequence. Even one utterance has to be skilfully designed, to be understandable by the recipient. It is a "speech act", a piece of behaviour planned to have some effect on the others. Encoding requires anticipatory decoding. Professional skills, like those of teachers, psychotherapists, or trade union negotiators, need special verbal skills. Socially inadequate individuals are often very poor conversationalists. However, no measure has so far been produced for verbal skills.

Effective management of conversational sequences is important. There are certain common two-step sequences like question–answer. Grice (1975) put forward rules for acceptable utterances: they should be relevant to what went before, provide enough information but not too much, be clear, and true. The social skills model suggests a basic four-step sequence, where the first speaker corrects his first move at step 3.

1 Interviewer: asks question
2 Respondent: gives inadequate answer, or fails to understand

461

3 Interviewer: clarifies and repeats question
4 Respondent: gives more adequate answer.

Another important type of skilled move is the "proactive" or double speech act, for example, where a speaker replies to a question and then asks one in return, instead of bringing the conversation to a halt. Some professional social skills, like teaching, involve repeated cycles, such as repetition of the following: teacher lectures – teacher asks question (a proactive move) – pupil replies (Flanders, 1970).

It is normal for speakers to "accommodate" to each other's speech style, to speak at a more similar speed, loudness, accent, language, and so on. This happens when people like each other or want to be accepted, and it does lead to greater acceptance (Giles & Coupland, 1991).

One of the main ways in which Grice's rules are broken is in the interest of "politeness". The main purpose of politeness is avoiding damaging the other's self-esteem, and it is done by avoiding constraining his or her behaviour, for example by indirect requests ("mitigation"), by praising the other rather than self, and by maximizing agreement. Such politeness is effective, for example in preserving relations between captain and crew of aircraft, though in times of crisis, mitigation should be replaced by "aggravation": "Turn the bloody engine off", not "Excuse me, captain, but how about turning the engine off?" (Linde, 1988).

Conversation is closely coordinated with, and supported by, non-verbal signals. Speakers accompany their words with illustrative gestures, vocal emphasis, and intonation; they look up at grammatical breaks, and at the ends of utterances, to obtain back-channel feedback. Listeners provide continuous feedback by facial expressions, occasional vocalizations, head-nods, and posture. Turn-taking is managed by speakers giving terminal gazes at the ends of utterances, falling pitch, and return of hands to rest, as well as by the verbal structure of utterances (Argyle, 1988).

Empathy, cooperation, and concern for others

Empathy is the capacity to share the perceived emotion of another, and to understand the point of view of others, to "take the role of the other" (Eisenberg & Strayer, 1987). There are a number of measures, of which the best known is that devised by Mehrabian and Epstein (1972). Undue attention to self, including an inability to take much interest in others or their point of view, is found in all kinds of mental patients. In psychotherapy, interviewing, and many other skills, it is important to pay careful attention to the views and feelings of others, and to display this by questions, "reflection", and other techniques.

Cooperation is taking account of the goals of others, as well as one's own, and coordinating behaviour so that both shall be reached. All social activities take more than one to do them, whether play (e.g., see-saw, tennis), social activity (dancing, singing, talking, sex), or work of most kinds. Many kinds of social skill failure can be seen as failure of cooperation. Social life calls for a lot of cooperation:

> You're on a bike hike with five of your friends. One of the girls, who just moved into the neighbourhood, is very slow and is holding the group up. The other girls you are with are all yelling at her and threatening to leave her behind. (Dodge, no date)

One solution might be simply to slow down with her.

Successful leadership skills involve consulting and persuading subordinates. Negotiation consists of finding an "integrative" solution, where each side makes concessions, so that the main goals of each are attained (Argyle, 1991). Concern for others is central to all close relationships; much social skills training (SST) for patients and lonely people is basically about establishing such relationships. In love, marriage, and close friendships, conceptualized as "communal" relationships, social influence and exchange of rewards are less important than concern for the needs of the other (Hays, 1988).

Cognition and problem solving

Cognitive social psychology has become important for the study of judgements and attitudes. How important is it for social skills? A number of aspects of social skill lie outside the field of consciousness, and are evidently the result of lower-level processes. People cannot tell us how they manage to take turns, follow the rules of grammar, respond to small non-verbal signals, fall in love, or manage other relationships (Argyle, 1988; Nisbett & Wilson, 1977), any more than they can explain how they walk or ride a bicycle. In both cases the lower levels are automatic, the higher ones governed by plans and rules.

There are areas of social skill where cognitive factors have been found to be important. First, there are informal rules of behaviour, of which people are aware; if the rules of relationships are broken, the relationship is likely to be disrupted. In the case of friendship, Argyle, Henderson, and Furnham (1985) found that "third party rules" are particularly important – keep confidences, don't criticize others in public, don't be jealous of other relationships, and so on. Second, it is important to understand the true nature of situations and relationships. La Gaipa and Wood (1981) found that disturbed adolescents, who had no friends, had inadequate ideas about friendship: like younger children they thought it was about receiving rewards from others, and they didn't know about loyalty, commitment and concern for the other. Third, it is possible to teach more effective skills of conversation by education in the relevant principles.

463

The level at which conscious control takes over fluctuates: during training, clients are made unusually aware of turn-taking cues or gaze patterns, for example, though attention later passes to higher-level concerns. An important part of the social skill model is called "translation", the process of using feedback information to modify behaviour, for example, what to do if the other doesn't talk enough, becomes hostile, or presents some other problem? Some tests of social skill provide a sample of problems typical of the skill, to see how the client would cope with them. One method of SST is based on problem solving: trainees are taught how to tackle problem situations by thinking up solutions to scripted problems (Shure, 1981). Other methods of SST make use of educational methods, to increase knowledge and understanding of, for example social relationships, or behaviour in another culture.

Self-presentation

This is a special goal of social skill, which is important not only for the self-esteem of interactors, but also to enable others to know how to react. "Grey" or anonymous individuals are difficult to deal with. However, not all claims to identity or status are accepted, and each person's status and role in an encounter has to be negotiated and be acceptable to the others. Failures of skill are often due to failures in the sphere of self, resulting in undue self-consciousness and social anxiety.

The self-image is the whole set of thoughts that individuals have about themselves, including roles (job, social class, etc.), personality traits, and body image. Self-esteem is the extent to which individuals think well of themselves. Self-presentation is behaviour designed to influence the impressions of the self formed by others. Direct verbal claims to fame or status are usually laughed at and disbelieved in western culture, though indirect verbal forms are common ("as I was saying to X", etc.), as well as "face-work", such as excuses, apologies, and justifications to limit damage to face. Non-verbal self-presentation is probably more important: clothes and other aspects of appearance, accent and speech style, and general manner. Such signals can successfully create impressions of social class, group membership, personality, and political views. Self-presentation is often partly inflated, and Goffman (1956) predicted that if exposed this causes embarrassment. This prediction has been confirmed, though there are other sources of embarrassment, especially social accidents (e.g., forgetting someone's name), suddenly becoming the centre of attention, and inappropriate sexual events.

Embarrassment is part of social anxiety, which is partly the result of undue self-attention, and worry about social disapproval, leading to cautious and ineffective social performance (Froming, Corley, & Rinker, 1990). Actual or feared disapproval leads to low self-esteem, as does a gap between aspirations and achievements.

464

Self-disclosure of personal information is normally gradual and reciprocated, and is necessary for close relationships, as a sign of trust. Some individuals spend a lot of time with friends, but still feel lonely, because the conversation is not intimate enough (Jones, Hobbs, & Hockenbury, 1982).

Skills for different situations and relationships

The skills needed vary between different social situations. Some are commonly found difficult and are sources of anxiety: public performance, parties, dealing with depressed people, and conflict situations. Work involves a number of standard situations: committees, presentations, interviews, negotiation, selling, and so on. These all require special moves, sequences and physical settings, and are governed by rules about what should or should not be done (Argyle et al., 1981).

Social relationships similarly need distinctive skills – for friends, spouses, work subordinates, and others. Marriage requires a high level of rewardingness, for example, and the skills and willingness to negotiate and compromise. Again there are distinctive rules for each relationship. Many people do not appear to understand relationships very well, so that there is scope for an educational component to training. They may not realize the importance of networks and third-party rules for friendship, or the number of decisions to be made in marriage, from which conflict can very easily occur (Argyle & Henderson, 1985).

INDIVIDUAL DIFFERENCES IN SOCIAL SKILLS

Gender

Men score higher on measures of assertiveness; the main demands for assertiveness training come from women. However, women score higher on most of the other components of social competence; they score much higher on empathy, and on measures of cooperativeness (Argyle, 1991). Women are found to be more rewarding, they have better verbal skills (more fluent, better grammar, more educated accents), and are more expressive non-verbally (smile a lot more, gaze more, finer gestures). Male non-verbal behaviour reflects their assertiveness – louder voices, more interruptions, take up more space (Argyle, 1988).

Age

All aspects of social skill increase with age, during childhood and adolescence. At student age many young people have difficulty making friends, and with common social situations, though social competence improves rapidly during this period (Bryant & Trower, 1974), and later as the result of having to cope with social tasks at work and in the family.

Social class

Studies of the social skills of children between 8 and 16 show that middle-class children do better on measures of taking the role of the other, reward-ingness, and social understanding, even with IQ held constant (e.g., Gollin, 1958). Middle-class adults do better on some aspects of skill, they are verbally more fluent, and take more account of the point of view of listeners. People in most middle-class jobs require more social skills, since most of them involve dealing with people and with complex social situations (e.g., doctors, lawyers, teachers, managers), compared with manual workers.

Personality

Intelligence is correlated with social intelligence and understanding, and probably with verbal skills. Extraverts are found more friendly and rewarding, and approach social situations in the confident expectation that they are going to get on well with people and enjoy themselves (Thorne, 1987). Argyle and Lu (1990a) found that they particularly enjoy two kinds of social situations – teams and clubs, dances and parties. Neuroticism is associated with social anxiety, lack of self-confidence, self-consciousness, and corresponding lack of social competence.

THE AETIOLOGY OF SOCIAL SKILLS

Social skills correlate with extraversion and intelligence, and negatively with neuroticism and other aspects of mental disorder, all of which are known to be partly inherited, so that there is probably an innate predisposition to become socially skilled, or the reverse.

Popularity and other aspects of social competence in children are caused by early warm relations with their mother, while unpopularity is caused by punitive and controlling styles of discipline and by stresses such as break-up of the family, and poverty (Ladd, 1991).

Parents influence the development of social skills throughout childhood in other ways. They provide models of assertiveness, sociability, cooperative-ness or lack of these, may encourage empathy, cooperation, or the reverse, and may coach and instruct, including such aspects of behaviour as "Look at me when I'm talking to you", "Don't interrupt", "Say hello". They may supervise play between siblings, and teach them to cooperate instead of quarrelling, and may provide peer-group contacts for their children.

Number and ages of siblings have rather complex effects on the develop-ment of social skills. First-born and only children are more independent, and surprisingly the more siblings a child has, the *lower* the child's subsequent extraversion (Eysenck & Cookson, 1970), probably because the child has less practice at sociability with peers outside the family. The skills learned depend on position in the family, so that girls with older brothers may learn indirect and skilful ways of out-witting them (Lamb & Sutton-Smith, 1982). Cooperative fantasy play takes place from an early age inside and outside the family, from 3 to 10, and children learn to follow rules, to see the point of view of others, to cooperate with peers, and in hierarchies, to inhibit aggression. This learning is partly by imitation, partly by trial and error (e.g., Howes, 1988).

Social skills continue to develop at school and at work. Young people learn to work under supervision, in a group, and to supervise others. They learn specialized skills such as committee chairmanship and public speaking. Trial and error is important, as is imitation, and special training courses.

Gender differences in social skill can be traced to childhood socialization. Many studies have shown how boys and girls are handled differently. Parents allow boys greater independence and encourage them to compete; parents are warmer towards girls, punish them less, and supervise them more closely (Huston, 1983). Generally boys model themselves on their fathers, girls on their mothers.

Failure of social competence in young adults can be traced to childhood experience, such as socially inadequate parents, geographical or other isolation, and little experience with the peer group. A study of American students found that socially inadequate male students often had similarly inadequate mothers (Sherman & Farina, 1974).

THE EFFECTS OF SOCIAL SKILLS

Social skills are important, because of the effects they have on relationships, and therefore on health and happiness, and on effectiveness at work. We shall discuss their effects on mental health later. Much of the research on this topic is in the form of correlations, or other statistical relationships, between social performance and such effects. This does not show causation, which requires experimental or longitudinal designs. There are some of these, and there is also research, which we report later, showing the effects of training in these skills.

Everyday life

We have listed the skills which lead to liking and popularity: rewardingness, positive non-verbal signals, following informal friendship rules, taking the role of the other, self-disclosure, and correct understanding of friendship. Rewardingness was first demonstrated by Jennings (1950). Sarason et al. (1985) found that the individuals who had difficulty finding social support were those who were unrewarding, introverted, pessimistic, alienated, intolerant, hostile, and had low self-esteem. Experimental studies have shown that people are liked more if they smile, have a friendly tone of voice, look more, and approach nearer (Argyle, 1988). There are a number of verbal techniques used by extraverts which may be very effective: agreeing, paying compliments, asking questions, finding things in common, use of first names, talking of pleasant events, and humour (Ellis & Beattie, 1986).

Marriage is the most important relationship, in terms of its effects on health and mental health, but about one-third of them fail. The social-skills sources of marital satisfaction include pleasing verbal acts and fewer criticisms, non-verbal acts (kiss, touch, presents, help), a problem solving approach to decisions, and a good sex life. Divorce and unhappy marriages, as judged by complaints, are in part caused by the following factors (Argyle & Henderson, 1985):

1 unfaithfulness
2 too little sex
3 arguing
4 lack of respect for spouse
5 not having interesting conversations
6 violence and drink.

Marital therapy focuses on training in rewardingness, and on negotiation. It would be useful to teach some of the informal rules too, such as faithfulness.

Many studies have shown the importance of social support for health (Schwarzer & Leppin, 1989). To obtain social support, social skills are needed to establish and maintain supportive relationships, especially with family, but also with friends and workmates. Social support leads to good health in several ways; close relationships like marriage produce greater immune system activity; positive emotions as produced by friends do the same; families look after each other, and encourage better health behaviour; and social support helps people cope with stress better, by practical help and emotional support (Sarason, Sarason, & Pierce, 1990).

Argyle and Lu (1990a) found that extraverts are happier than introverts, and in a longitudinal analysis found that this was partly because extraverts are more assertive and cooperative (Figure 2). The numbers are correlations. The top figure shows that extraversion predicts happiness with a correlation of .39, but that this effect is reduced to .28 when the effect of extraversion on assertiveness is taken into account. In another study it was found that extraverts are more cooperative in certain ways, and this too causes happiness at a later date (Lu & Argyle, 1991). A further process may be that extraverts send more positive non-verbal signals, they smile more, look more, and approach nearer, all of which are likely to produce a reciprocal response, and an elevated mood in both.

On the other hand lonely people (who are usually unhappy) suffer from social skills deficits: they are shy, unassertive, have social anxiety and low

A

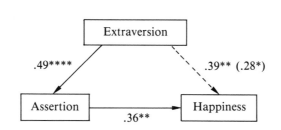

Figure 2a Assertiveness as a mediator of the extraversion–happiness relationship
Source: Argyle and Lu, 1990b

B

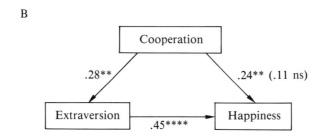

Figure 2b Extraversion as a mediator of the cooperation–happiness relationship
Source: Lu and Argyle, 1991

self-esteem, have negative and distrusting attitudes about relationships, and feel alienated (Jones, Hobbs, & Hockenbury, 1982).

Work effectiveness

Supervisory skills were the first to be studied, and it has often been shown that the productivity of work-groups is higher if supervisors use certain skills. These are a combination of initiating structure (giving instructions, etc.), consideration (looking after group members), and the democratic-persuasive style. There are modest effects on rate of work, greater if the work is not machine-paced, but much greater effects on absenteeism, job satisfaction, and labour turnover (see Figure 3).

These skills probably apply to all situations involving dealing with subordinates, especially groups of subordinates, in leisure groups as well as at work. However, there are also "contingencies", that is different skills are more important in different settings. For example if the task is unrewarding, more consideration is needed, if the best line of action is unclear, or if the group is unlikely to accept the leader's ideas, more participation is needed (Argyle, 1989).

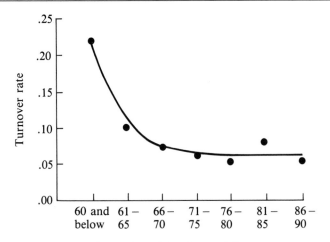

Figure 3a   Effect of consideration on labour turnover
Source: Fleishman and Harris, 1962

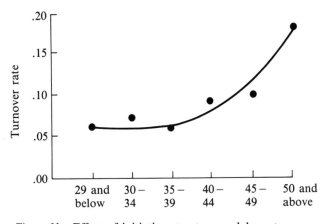

Figure 3b   Effect of initiating structure on labour turnover
Source: Fleishman and Harris, 1962

Many studies have been made of school-teaching skills, and their effect on learning by pupils, and the results have been embodied in training courses. The most effective teaching style is a combination of a number of elements, including the businesslike organization of lessons, the use of examples and illustrations, questions, praise, and making use of pupil's ideas, as well as the usual leadership style (Rosenshine, 1971). Doctor skills are widely taught, but research has so far been directed only towards such sub-goals as accurate history-taking, patient satisfaction, and compliance with doctor's instructions, rather than with the health of patients (Maguire, 1986).

470

Cross-cultural skills are most important for working organizations, because of the very high "failure rate" described earlier. Critical incident surveys have analysed large numbers of instances where members of one culture have got into difficulties in a second culture, the correct skills discovered, and embodied in training texts known as Culture Assimilators (Fiedler, Mitchell, & Triandis, 1971).

SOCIAL SKILLS AND MENTAL HEALTH

Do mental patients have social skills deficits, and if so what kinds? Is lack of social skill a cause of mental disorder?

The social skills of mental patients

Individuals suffering from social anxiety or neuroticism are found to be less socially skilled in several ways. They speak less, and in particular initiate less conversation; they look less, smile less, have more speech disfluencies, and fidget more; they avoid social situations, especially those which they find difficult (e.g., parties, meeting strangers), and are less assertive; they expect that social events will have negative outcomes. These are general findings; there are some socially anxious and neurotic patients who have normal social skills (Trower, 1986).

Depressives have been found to differ from other people in non-verbal style: more depressed faces, less gaze, less proximity, more self-touching gestures, drooping postures, a speech style which is lacking in vitality (low and falling pitch, slow and weak), and drab appearance (Argyle, 1988). However, these deficits are not found in all depressives, and more global effects are more characteristic. Depressives alienate other people quickly, and are avoided; they talk little, mainly about themselves, are unassertive, and above all are unrewarding: this may result in their becoming socially isolated (Williams, 1986).

More than other disorders schizophrenia covers a wide range of patients. However, comparisons of schizophrenics and controls have often found differences in non-verbal communication: schizophrenics show less facial expression but with some grimaces, avert gaze when talking to psychologists about their problems, need a great deal of personal space, direct gestures mainly to themselves, their voices tend to be silent, monotonous, of low volume and flat, they fail to synchronize speech and gesture, or coordinate their behaviour with that of others, and their appearance is characteristically odd and eccentric (Argyle, 1988). Their conversation is incoherent and unresponsive, they form very weak relationships or none, do not like being supervised, and are upset by criticism (Williams, 1986).

471

Delinquents are rated as less socially competent, have lower levels of gaze and smiling, and fidget more than non-delinquent controls. They do less well on tests of how to cope with social situations, especially at dealing with adults in authority, and they suggest aggressive rather than more skilled solutions to problem situations (Henderson & Hollin, 1986). Some violent criminals are overcontrolled and unassertive; some sexual offenders lack heterosexual skills. It seems likely that social skills failure is at least part of the cause of antisocial behaviour in these cases (Howells, 1986).

Psychopaths are different: they are not lacking in social skills, indeed they can be charming and persuasive when it suits them. What they lack is affection for or empathy with other people; they are very impulsive and lack the usual restraints on aggression or sexuality.

Explanations of the link between social skills deficits and mental disorder

First, skills deficits may cause mental disorder. Trower et al. (1978) proposed that, as a result of faulty socialization, some young people become socially unskilled; this leads to rejection and social isolation, which in turn result in depression and anxiety. A similar theory was put forward by Libet and Lewinsohn (1973), who found that depressives are very unrewarding to others; they argue that as a result others avoid them, and they then receive few rewards.

Second, the Sarasons' social support version: Sarason et al. (1985) found that individuals with poor social skills are less likely to be able to establish socially supportive relationships, and are therefore more likely to be upset by stress. Many studies have shown the importance of social support for good mental health, from Brown and Harris (1978) onwards. It is important to be loved, and to be accepted as part of a social network, in order to enjoy companionship, find emotional support, and receive serious help.

The third explanation is that the real cause is anxiety, neuroticism, and so on: certain personalities are predisposed both to mental disorder and to inadequate social behaviour. Henderson, Byrne, and Duncan-Jones (1981) found that neuroticism predicted both lack of social support and mental disorder. They have found that treating socially inadequate patients by desensitization improved both their mental health and their social skills, suggesting that anxiety may have been the real cause. Schizophrenics have inadequate social skills but this may be the result of more fundamental personality disturbance. However, it would still be possible for poor social skills to cause further problems and result in amplification of symptoms.

SOCIAL SKILLS TRAINING: HOW IT IS DONE

The classical method

There are three or four phases:

1 explanation and modelling, live or from video
2 role-playing with other trainees or stooges
3 comments from trainer and playback of videotape
4 repeat performance.

This is typically carried out in groups of six, for one to one-and-a-half hours, once or twice a week. The full package includes all the above features, and the groups may be supplemented by individual sessions. Modelling is an important component of role-playing, that is, showing how the skill should be done. This can be on videotape. There can be more than one example and these should not be too perfectly done. Figure 4 shows arrangements for a social skills training laboratory, with one-way screen, video cameras, and an ear microphone to instruct a trainee during the role-playing.

There may be six, ten, or more sessions. A serious problem is how to achieve generalization to real-life situations. For those not resident in

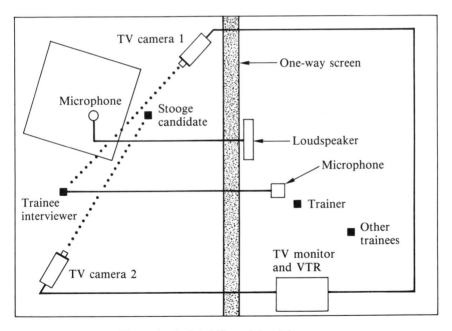

Figure 4   Social skills training laboratory
Source: Argyle, 1983

institutions "homework" is often used: trainees are asked to repeat the exercises (e.g., to make someone else talk more, or less) between sessions in real-life settings, and to report back. For those in hospital or prison, other staff can continue the training between the formal sessions.

Role-playing can deal with a wide range of skills and problems. For example exercises can focus on social relationships, or on situations which are found difficult.

Other laboratory methods

Role-playing is not the best way of training all of the components of social skills which have been described. Sending non-verbal signals, by face and voice, is most effectively trained by simple exercises with mirrors, video and audio-tape recorders. Failures of self-presentation are quite easily dealt with by changes of appearance, and sometimes voice training. Conversational failures may need some instruction on the conduct of conversations, and simple exercises, which may include role-played interviewing. Failure to take the role of the other can be tackled in various ways, including exercises in finding out the opinions of others.

Educational methods

Lecture and discussion methods were abandoned long ago as methods of SST when they were found to be ineffective, and because it is obvious that motor skills cannot be learned in this way. However, various research studies should make us think again. The Culture Assimilator, for inter-cultural training, has been quite successful (see Fiedler et al., 1971); books on assertiveness have been very popular. Our research on rules suggests another area where straightforward instruction is indicated. Much trouble with relationships arises because of misunderstanding the nature of friendship, marriage, and so on. Conversational skills involve some understanding of the principles of conversational structure. In all these cases direct teaching may be the best method. It is particularly important to learn the informal rules of situations and relationships. However, there is more to the performance of skills than knowing the rules, and behavioural practice is necessary too.

Learning on the job

For some jobs it is not possible to create role-play situations which simulate the work situation at all realistically. Police dealing with ethnic situations or managers dealing with trade unions are examples. An alternative to role-playing exercises in the lab is coaching on the job, starting with easy situations, by a trainer who accompanies the trainee and gives immediate coaching and feedback. This has long been done for schoolteachers, and is now done in some areas for police by "tutor constables".

Design of work skills courses

Some preliminary research is needed to discover what the problems are in the situations which, for example, police officers or supervisors find difficult. This could be done by surveys of potential trainees, or of experienced practitioners, or of their clients and subordinates. An example is a critical incident survey of people who have got into difficulty working in another country. Table 2 shows the skills taught on some American supervisory courses.

Table 2 List of skills taught to supervisors on some American courses

1 Orienting a new employee
2 Giving recognition
3 Motivating a poor employee
4 Correcting poor work habits
5 Discussing potential disciplinary action
6 Reducing absenteeism
7 Handling a complaining employee
8 Reducing turnover
9 Overcoming resistance to change

Source: Latham and Saari, 1979

It is then necessary to decide which are the best skills for dealing with these problems, by drawing on relevant research, or seeking the advice of those with a lot of experience of the job, though they can sometimes be wrong. A training course can then be devised to train employees in the approved ways of dealing with the problem situations. This will normally be based on role-playing in groups, but can include training on the job, and some educational input from lectures and discussion.

Design of SST for individual patients

A patient's social behaviour first needs to be carefully assessed by role-playing exercises, interview and questionnaire (described above). The patient can attend a number of role-played training sessions with other patients who have similar needs, such as for basic social skills. Other patients can act as the stooges. The patient can then be given a few individual sessions, to deal with any more idiosyncratic problems, for example, particular social situations that present difficulties. At either stage the training can include laboratory methods other than role-playing, such as non-verbal exercises. At the end of each session the patient can be given written notes about what to think about, and instructions for homework.

SOCIAL SKILLS TRAINING: DOES IT WORK?

For the general population

SST is needed by, and to a small extent provided for, all age-groups. However, adolescents and young adults are the group for whom the need appears to be greatest, and where a high rate of success is reported. There are four main varieties.

Assertiveness courses have been found to be very effective, in before-and-after studies, sometimes using realistic but rather unethical role-play tasks with annoying confederates. Compared with anxiety reduction and cognitive therapy, assertiveness training and other SST have more effect on behaviour, though similar effects on feelings of anxiety and anger.

Heterosexual skills training, mostly with American students, has also been very successful, for example, in terms of number of dates per week, anxiety, and behavioural measures of skill. It is not clear whether improved skills or anxiety reduction are more important; some success has been obtained from simply arranging practice dates, without further training.

Loneliness is mainly caused by social isolation, due to poor social skills, and is common among young people. In extreme cases it is a cause of mental disorder. Training in the skills needed is straightforward and very successful (Furnham, 1986).

Adults of all ages have social skills needs too. One of the greatest is for marital therapy. Positive benefits for 65 per cent of clients are reported for SST focusing on rewardingness, improved communication, and negotiation skills (Argyle & Henderson, 1985).

Work skills

Most jobs require social skills, and most people pick these up by doing them. However, some fail completely and give up, for example many teachers, while others are very ineffective. Follow-up studies have used before-and-after comparisons of SST to find the effect on objective measures or on rated competence or rated social performance.

Managers, supervisors, and leaders of all kinds can be trained successfully, in terms of the effects on productivity, sales, etc., and of the job satisfaction and absenteeism of their subordinates (Burke & Day, 1986). Most firms use some kind of SST for this.

About 80 per cent of British teachers receive some "microteaching", with small classes; all aspects of teaching skills can be improved, including the elimination of errors, both for beginners and the experienced (Brown & Shaw, 1986).

Mental patients

There have been many experimental studies of the effectiveness of SST. The usual design is before-and-after comparisons of patients who are given SST, compared with others on a waiting list or who are given other kinds of treatment. Assessments are made of clinical conditions, social skills (e.g., by role-play measures), and subjective discomfort. Shepherd carried out an analysis of 52 such studies with adult psychiatric patients (Spence & Shepherd, 1983); reviews of follow-up studies of different kinds of patients are given in Hollin and Trower (1986). The conclusions of this research are as follows:

1 SST is better than no treatment, or placebo treatment, for all kinds of patients.
2 It is usually no better than the best alternative treatments, such as desensitization, cognitive therapy, or drugs.
3 However, it does have more effect on social skills.
4 It is the best treatment for neurotics who are socially unskilled or anxious.
5 Outcomes are improved if SST is added to other treatments, e.g., for schizophrenics.
6 It is not clear that improved social skills are always the cause of improvement; other treatments for depression have sometimes led to improved social behaviour as part of general recovery.

CONCLUSIONS

1 Social skills are patterns of social behaviour which make people competent in social situations. They can be assessed by role-playing, interviews, ratings by others, or objective results. There are many questionnaire measures but none has so far been widely accepted.
2 Many people suffer from inadequate social skills, especially adolescents and young adults, most mental patients, and a lot of people at work.
3 Social skills are like motor skills in their hierarchical structure and rapid response to feedback; assertiveness and rewardingness are important components, as are the verbal and non-verbal elements, empathy and cooperation, problem solving and understanding, self-presentation, and the skills for different situations and relationships.
4 There are individual differences in the social skills of men and women, different social classes, and personalities.
5 Social skills are mainly acquired from experience in the family and peer groups, and later at work.

6 Social skills have massive effects on popularity, marriage and other relationships, health and happiness, and effectiveness at work.
7 Most mental patients and many offenders have defective social skills, and
for some of them this is a cause of their trouble.
8 SST is usually done by role-playing, but can be supplemented by other
laboratory methods, educational methods, and training on the job. It is
very effective with non-patients, is as good as alternative methods for
many kinds of patients, or can be a supplement to them, and is effective
for a wide range of work skills.

FURTHER READING

Hollin, C. R., & Trower, P. (Eds) (1986). *Handbook of social skills training* (2 vols).
Oxford: Pergamon.
L'Abate, L., & Milan, M. A. (Eds) (1985). *Handbook of social skills training and
research*. New York: Wiley.
Spence, S., & Shepherd, G. (1983). *Developments in social skills training*. London:
Academic Press.
Trower, P., Bryant, B., & Argyle, M. (1978). *Social skills and mental health*. London:
Methuen.
Wine, J. D., & Smye, M. D. (Eds) (1981). *Social competence*. New York: Guilford.

REFERENCES

Argyle, M. (1983). *The psychology of interpersonal behaviour*, 4th edn.
Harmondsworth: Penguin.
Argyle, M. (1984). Some new developments in social skills training. *Bulletin of the
British Psychological Society*, *37*, 405–410.
Argyle, M. (1988). *Bodily communication*, 2nd edn. London: Methuen.
Argyle, M. (1989). *The social psychology of work*, 2nd edn. Harmondsworth:
Penguin.
Argyle, M. (1991). *Cooperation: The basis of sociability*. London: Routledge.
Argyle, M., Furnham, A., & Graham, J. A. (1981). *Social situations*. Cambridge:
Cambridge University Press.
Argyle, M., & Henderson, M. (1985). *The anatomy of relationships*. London:
Heinemann, and Harmondsworth: Penguin.
Argyle, M., & Lu, L. (1990a). The happiness of extraverts. *Personality and
Individual Differences*, *11*, 1011–1017.
Argyle, M., & Lu, L. (1990b). Happiness and social skills. *Personality and Individual
Differences*, *11*, 1255–1261.
Argyle, M., Henderson, M., & Furnham, A. (1985). The rules of social relationships.
British Journal of Social Psychology, *24*, 125–129.
Brown, G., & Harris, T. (1978). *Social origins of depression*. London: Tavistock.
Brown, G., & Shaw, M. (1986). Social skills training in education. In C. R. Hollin
& P. Trower (Eds) *Handbook of social skills training* (vol. 1, pp. 59–78). Oxford:
Pergamon.
Bryant, B., & Trower, P. (1974). Social difficulty in a student population. *British
Journal of Educational Psychology*, *44*, 13–24.

Bryant, B., Trower, P., Yardley, K., Urbieta, H., & Letemendia, F. (1976). A survey of social inadequacy among psychiatric patients. *Psychological Medicine, 6*, 101–112.

Bull, R., & Horncastle, P. (1983). *An evaluation of the Metropolitan Police recruit training programme.* London: Police Foundation.

Burke, M. J., & Day, R. R. (1986). A cumulative study of the effectiveness of management training. *Journal of Applied Psychology, 71*, 232–245.

Dodge, K. A. (no date). *Cooperation in children.* Unpublished manuscript, University of Indiana.

Eisenberg, N., & Strayer, J. (Eds) (1987). *Empathy and its development.* Cambridge: Cambridge University Press.

Ellis, A., & Beattie, G. (1986). *The psychology of language and communication.* London: Weidenfeld & Nicolson.

Eysenck, H. J., & Cookson, D. (1970). Personality in primary school children: 3. Family background. *British Journal of Educational Psychology, 40*, 117–131.

Fiedler, F. E., Mitchell, R., & Triandis, H. C. (1971). The culture assimilator: An approach to cross-cultural training. *Journal of Applied Psychology, 55*, 95–102.

Flanders, N. A. (1970). *Analyzing teaching behavior.* Reading, MA: Addison-Wesley.

Fleishman, E. A. (1953). The description of supervisory behavior. *Journal of Applied Psychology, 37*, 1–6.

Fleishman, E. A., & Harris, E. F. (1962). Patterns of leadership behavior related to employee grievances and turnover. *Journal of Occupational Psychology, 53*, 65–72.

Friedman, H. S., Prince, L. M., Riggio, R. E., & DiMatteo, M. R. (1980). Understanding and assessing non-verbal expressiveness: The affective communication test. *Journal of Personality and Social Psychology, 39*, 333–351.

Froming, W. J., Corley, E. B., & Rinker, L. (1990). The influence of public self consciousness and the audience's characteristics on withdrawal from embarrassing situations. *Journal of Personality, 58*, 603–622.

Furnham, A. (1986). Social skills training with adolescents and young adults. In C. R. Hollin & P. Trower (Eds) *Handbook of social skills training* (vol. 1, pp. 33–57). Oxford: Pergamon.

Galassi, J. P., Galassi, M. D., & Vedder, M. J. (1981). Perspectives on assertion as a social skills model. In J. D. Wine & M. D. Smye (Eds) *Social competence* (pp. 287–345). New York: Guilford.

Giles, H., & Coupland, N. (1991). *Language: Contexts and consequences.* Milton Keynes: Open University Press.

Goffman, E. (1956). *The presentation of self in everyday life.* Edinburgh: Edinburgh University Press.

Gollin, E. S. (1958). Organizational characteristics of social judgment: A developmental investigation. *Journal of Personality, 26*, 139–154.

Grice, H. P. (1975). Logic and conversation. In P. Cole & J. Morgan (Eds) *Syntax and semiotics: Speech acts.* New York and London: Academic Press. (vol. 3, pp. 41–58).

Hargie, O., Saunders, S., & Dickson, D. (1987). *Social skills in interpersonal communication*, 2nd edn. London: Routledge.

Hays, R. B. (1988). Friendship. In S. W. Duck (Ed.) *Handbook of personal relationships* (pp. 391–408). Chichester: Wiley.

Henderson, M., & Hollin, C. R. (1986). Social skills training and delinquency. In C. R. Hollin & P. Trower (Eds) *Handbook of social skills training* (vol. 1, pp. 79–101). Oxford: Pergamon.

Henderson, S., Byrne, D. G., & Duncan-Jones, P. (1981). *Neurosis and the social environment*. Sydney: Academic Press.

Hochschild, A. R. (1983). *The managed heart*. Berkeley, CA: University of California Press.

Hollin, C. R., & Trower, P. (Eds) (1986). *Handbook of social skills training* (2 vols). Oxford: Pergamon.

Howells, K. (1986), Social skills training and criminal and antisocial behaviour. In C. R. Hollin and P. Trower (Eds) *Handbook of social skills training* (vol. 1, pp. 185–210). Oxford: Pergamon.

Howes, C. (1988). Peer interaction of young children. *Monographs of Society for Research in Child Development*, *53*, no. 1.

Huston, A. C. (1983). Sex-typing. In P. H. Musson & E. M. Hetherington (Eds) *Handbook of child psychology* (vol. 4, pp. 387–467). New York: Wiley.

Ingram, R. E. (1989). Self-focused attention in clinical disorders: Review and a conceptual model. *Psychological Bulletin*, *107*, 156–176.

Jennings, H. H. (1950). *Leadership and isolation*. New York: Longman Green.

Jones, W. H., Hobbs, S. A., & Hockenbury, D. (1982). Loneliness and social skills deficits. *Journal of Personality and Social Psychology*, *42*, 682–689.

Ladd, G. W. (1991). Family–peer relationships. Special issue of *Journal of Social and Personal Relationships*, *3*.

La Gaipa, J. J., & Wood, H. D. (1981). Friendship in disturbed adolescents. In S. Duck & R. Gilmour (Eds) *Personal relationships: Personal relationships in disorder* (vol. 3, pp. 169–189). London: Academic Press.

Lamb, M. E., & Sutton-Smith, B. (1982). *Sibling relationships*. Hillsdale, NJ: Lawrence Erlbaum.

Latham, G. P., & Saari, L. M. (1979). Application of social-learning theory to training supervisors through behavioral modelling. *Journal of Applied Psychology*, *64*, 239–246.

Lazarus, A. A. (1973). On assertive behavior: A brief note. *Behavior Therapy*, *4*, 697–699.

Libet, J., & Lewinsohn, P. M. (1973). The concept of social skill with special reference to the behavior of depressed persons. *Journal of Consulting and Clinical Psychology*, *40*, 304–312.

Linde, C. (1988). The quantification study of communication success: Politeness and accidents in aviation discourse. *Language in Society*, *17*, 375–399.

Lu, L., & Argyle, M. (1991). Happiness and cooperation. *Personality and Individual Differences*, *12*, 1019–1030.

McNamara, J. R., & Blumer, C. A. (1982). Role playing to assess social competence: Ecological validity considerations. *Behavior Modification 6*, 519–549.

Maguire, P. (1986). Social skills training for health professional. In C. R. Hollin & P. Trower (Eds) *Handbook of social skills training* (vol. 2, pp. 143–165. Oxford: Pergamon.

Mehrabian, A., & Epstein, N. (1972), A measure of emotional empathy. *Journal of Personality*, *40*, 525–543.

Muchinsky, P. M. (1986). Personnel selection methods. In C. L. Cooper & I. T. Robertson (Eds) *International review of industrial and organizational psychology* (pp. 37–70). Chichester: Wiley.

Nisbett, R. E., & Wilson, T. D. (1977). Telling more than we know: Verbal reports on mental processes. *Psychological Review*, *84*, 231–259.

Rathus, S. A. (1973). A 30-item schedule for assessing assertive behavior. *Behavior Therapy*, *4*, 398–406.

480

Rosenshine, B. (1971). *Teaching behaviours and student achievement*. Slough: National Foundation for Educational Research.

Rosenthal, R., Hall, J. A., DiMatteo, M. R., Rogers, P. L., & Archer, D. (1979). *Sensitivity to nonverbal communication in the PONS test*. Baltimore, MD: Johns Hopkins University Press.

Sarason, B. R., Sarason, I. G., Hacker, T. A., & Basham, R. B. (1985). Concomitants of social support: Social skills, physical attractiveness, and gender. *Journal of Personality and Social Psychology, 49*, 469–480.

Sarason, B. R., Sarason, I. G., & Pierce, G. R. (Eds) (1990). *Social support: An interactional view*. Chichester: Wiley.

Schwarzer, R., & Leppin, A. (1989). Social support and health: A meta-analysis. *Psychology and Health, 3*, 1–15.

Shepherd, G. (1986). Social skills training and schizophrenia. In C. R. Hollin & P. Trower (Eds) *Handbook of social skills training* (vol. 2, pp. 9–37). Oxford: Pergamon.

Sherman, H., & Farina, A. (1974). Social adequacy of parents and children. *Journal of Abnormal Psychology, 83*, 327–330.

Shure, M. B. (1981). Social competence as a problem-solving skill. In J. D. Wine & M. D. Smye (Eds) *Social competence* (pp. 158–185). New York: Guilford.

Spence, S., & Shepherd, G. (1983). *Developments in social skills training*. London: Academic Press.

Spitzberg, B. H., & Cupach, W. R. (1989). *Handbook of interpersonal competence research*. New York: Springer.

Thorne, A. (1987). A press of personality: A study of conversation between introverts and extraverts. *Journal of Personality and Social Psychology, 53*, 718–726.

Trower, P. (1986) Social skills training and social anxiety. In C. R. Hollin & P. Trower (Eds) *Handbook of social skills training* (vol. 2, pp. 39–65). Oxford: Pergamon.

Trower, P., Bryant, B., & Argyle, M. (1978). *Social skills and mental health*. London: Methuen.

Williams, J. M. G. (1986). Social skills training and depression. In C. R. Hollin & P. Trower (Eds) *Handbook of social skills training* (vol. 2, pp. 91–110). Oxford: Pergamon.

6
EMOTION AND MOTIVATION

INTRODUCTION

The transient mental feelings that we call emotions, which psychologists find notoriously difficult to define, have intrigued inquiring minds at least since the time of the pre-Socratic philosophers of ancient Greece. In contemporary psychology, emotion is nowadays often coupled with motivation, which is an umbrella term for the psychological processes that initiate, energize, and direct behaviour. These two things are linked because emotional arousal of almost any kind characteristically drives people to action; in other words, emotions have powerful motivational effects. Psychologists and mental philosophers of the nineteenth century used to think of emotion as one of the three classes of mental phenomena, the other two being cognition and volition (roughly equivalent to motivation).

In chapter 6.1 Brian Parkinson provides an introductory survey of psychological research into emotion. After grappling with the definition of emotion, he discusses its main components (positive or negative evaluations of situations, bodily changes, expressions of emotion, and motivational effects), and the various factors that are implicated in causing emotional arousal. He then knits the research findings together into a four-factor theory of emotion, and he concludes by discussing the curious relationship between emotion and cognition. Readers who are interested in the expression of emotion, including facial expression, should see also chapter 9.5 (Peter Bull and Lesley Frederikson), which deals with emotional expression in the context of non-verbal communication.

In chapter 6.2, which is devoted to hunger and appetite, John E. Blundell and Andrew J. Hill deal with one of the most primitive motivational states, which usually (though not invariably) results from food deprivation. Much of the research in this area is, unsurprisingly, heavily biological in its approach but, as Blundell and Hill explain, eating is an interaction between an organism and its environment that cannot be properly understood in purely physiological terms. This chapter is concerned chiefly with normal processes of hunger and appetite, but it touches on an eating disorder called bulimia nervosa in which eating patterns become highly disturbed; for more information on bulimia nervosa and eating disorders in general, see chapter 10.4 (Peter J. Cooper).

In chapter 6.3 Russell G. Geen focuses on social motivation, which is a research area concerned with social processes that initiate and energize behaviour. This chapter includes a discussion of research into the motivational effects on an individual's behaviour of the mere presence of other people, a phenomenon that is called social facilitation (rather misleadingly, in view of the fact that the effects are not necessarily facilitative but can impair performance); the attentional and distracting effects of social presence (for more on attention in general, see chapter 4.2, Michael W. Eysenck); the socially activated need of individuals to present favourable impressions of themselves to others; the apparent loss of motivation in groups caused by social loafing and "free riding"; and several other phenomena of social motivation. For a slightly different angle on social facilitation and social loafing, see chapter 9.2 (Peter B. Smith).

John Bancroft discusses sexual motivation and behaviour in chapter 6.4. Before turning to human sexuality, he begins with a comparative discussion of sexuality among primates in general; this has an obvious bearing on behavioural ecology, which is discussed in detail in chapter 2.2 (John Lazarus). He then describes the surprisingly numerous functions of sex, and the mechanisms of human sexuality, including the role of the sex hormones in men and women, cognitive processes, mood and emotional states, and social influences on sexual response; there are obvious links to other chapters in this section.

Finally, chapter 6.5 is on stress and coping. Robert J. Gatchel discusses, among other things, the major theories of stress and the psychological effects of three broad classes of stress-inducing experiences, namely cataclysmic events such as wars and natural disasters, personal misfortunes such as bereavements, and background stressors (everyday hassles). He also outlines the ways in which people appraise stress, and concludes with a discussion of coping processes and the health implications of stress and coping. For a further discussion of that issue, see chapter 11.5 (John Weinman) on health psychology.

A.M.C.

6.1

EMOTION

Brian Parkinson
University of Leicester, England

It has often been remarked that everyone knows perfectly well what emotion is, but no one can define it. In fact, as with most paradoxes, this is not quite true. On the one hand, not everyone agrees about what emotion is. Although most people do seem to have their own intuitive understanding of the term, there is nevertheless some uncertainty about what counts as an emotion, and even how various different emotional conditions such as anger, embarrassment, pride and so on are manifested. People from different cultures and different eras sometimes have very different conceptions of emotions (e.g., Harré, 1986; Lutz, 1988) and their lists of individual states that come under the general heading may differ quite substantially.

On the other hand, there are at least some states, such as happiness and anger, that few people within western culture would disagree are emotional. Similarly, there is a degree of consensus about how to define the phenomenon in question. When we look at the kinds of things most people (including psychologists) want to call emotions, we can see that they share certain common features to a greater or lesser extent, and this certainly allows a provisional definition. But more of this in a moment.

Clearly, there are several ways of approaching the question of what emotion is, and this chapter covers some of these different angles. First, you can define emotion by giving examples of items that belong in the category, and of the conditions that clearly do not. The question of membership in the class of emotions seems more easily answerable for some states than for others. For example, is love an emotion? Is lust? Is shopping? I shall consider the idea that not all examples of emotions are equally good representatives of the category.

A second way of defining emotion is by looking at the different aspects and components of emotional experience, and I shall next follow this approach, concentrating on four important aspects of emotional experience: cognitive evaluations of the situation, bodily responses, facial (and other) expressions, and action impulses. I shall argue that emotions usually possess at least most of these characteristics but that, with the possible exception of the evaluative factor, none of them should be seen as defining or necessary features of emotional experience.

A third way of characterizing emotion is to consider how the various aspects combine with one another, and how they interact to make an emotional episode what it is. I shall look at the internal structure of emotional experience and review some of the alternative causal sequences that have been proposed by psychologists to explain how emotion happens.

Finally, emotion can be defined by relating and contrasting it with other psychological functions. I shall discuss the relationships and contrasts between emotion and cognition in order to clarify how emotion fits in with general psychological functioning.

By the end of the chapter, the reader should be in a better position to know how psychologists might answer the question "What is an emotion?" For now, I shall suggest a provisional definition based upon a common-sense understanding of the concept. What, then, do the states that people think of as emotional have in common with one another?

To make a start on this definition, I want to argue that emotions are characteristically *intentional* states. By this I mean that they take an object of some sort. It is hard to imagine a pure state of pride, anger, or love without the state being directed at something: you are proud of your success, angry with someone who has insulted you, in love with someone in particular, rather than just proud, angry, or in love per se (e.g., Averill, 1980). The apparent exceptions to this rule are states such as happiness, boredom, and depression, which may sometimes seem quite diffuse and unfocused. According to the definition I am suggesting, these conditions would not qualify as bona fide emotions (see below).

So, emotions imply a certain relationship between a person and some object, person (including the self), or event (real, remembered, or imagined).

My second assumption is that this relation is an intrinsically *evaluative* one. A defining feature of emotion seems to be that when emotional we feel good or bad, approving or disapproving, relieved or disappointed about some state of affairs. Third and finally, this evaluative attitude is not a permanent and enduring aspect of our way of relating to the world, but a disruption or break from our background position. Even the derivation of the word "emotion" suggests a *move away* from normal functioning, something that comes over us for a while. Thus, emotions are states that are more or less transient and short lived.

This preliminary definition also allows us to distinguish emotions from related states such as moods (cf. Clark & Isen, 1982). Like emotions, moods have an evaluative component and feel good or bad (i.e., they too are *affective* states); unlike emotions, moods do not usually take a definite object (you can just be grumpy as a result of "getting out of bed the wrong side" without any particular focus to the experience); unlike emotions, moods can persist for relatively long periods of time.

To summarize, although it is not easy to come up with a thoroughgoing definition of emotion that will include all the phenomena that non-psychologists might want to call emotion (and exclude all those that they would not), it is still true that certain characteristics are agreed to be fairly central defining features of emotion. The chances are, if someone is emotional, that person will have a positive or a negative felt reaction to some definite object (whether imagined or real), and this reaction will not last too long. In other words, I shall consider emotions to be evaluative, affective, intentional, and short-term conditions.

THE CATEGORY OF EMOTION

The simplest and most obvious way of explaining what emotion is, is by giving examples. It seems reasonable to assume that once we know what items are included in the category of emotion, we shall have a pretty good idea of what an emotion is. Unfortunately, the problem of defining emotion does not go away this easily because there is less than universal agreement about what conditions count as emotions. Psychologists as well as non-psychologists differ in their opinions of whether certain states are or are not emotional.

Nevertheless, there is some consensus concerning a few clear examples of emotion. Fehr and Russell (1984) asked Canadian college students to rate a series of emotion terms on the basis of how closely they represented the category. *Love* was rated as the best example of an emotion overall, followed by *hate*, *anger*, *sadness*, and *happiness*. These same words also tended to be the ones that most readily sprang to mind when the students were asked to list emotions (see Table 1).

Other words, such as *pride*, *hope*, *lust*, *pain*, and *hunger*, were rated as

Table 1 Two top tens of representative emotions

Common-sense chart	Psychologists' chart
Happiness (152)	Fear (9)
Anger (149)	Anger (7)
Sadness (136)	Disgust (6)
Love (124)	Sadness (5)
Fear (96)	Joy (5)
Hate (89)	Surprise (5)
Joy (82)	Rage (4)
Excitement (53)	Love (3)
Anxiety (50)	Happiness (3)
Depression (42)	Interest (3)

Source: Based on free listings of emotion names by 200 subjects (Fehr & Russell, 1984)

Source: Based on lists of "basic emotions" produced by 14 representative basic emotions theorists (Ortony & Turner, 1991)

Note: Numbers in parentheses reflect number of selections of the emotion names by informants

relatively poorer examples of emotions. Some people thought that these conditions were emotional and some did not. Fehr and Russell concluded that the category of emotion is not one around which any sharp dividing line can be drawn, separating emotions on the inside from other, non-emotional states on the outside. Rather, there are many states that might be labelled as emotions in some circumstances but not others, and by certain people but not everyone. The class of emotional phenomena, in such a view, is bounded by fuzzy rather than distinct edges.

This approach to the structure of categories is known as the *prototype approach* (Rosch, 1978), because the category is considered to be defined by its most central and characteristic example or prototype. Membership of the category then depends upon degree of similarity to this prototype: the closer resemblance a particular item shows to the prototype, the more likely it is to be included in the category, but all-or-none judgements are often difficult. The alternative *classical* view of categories is that it is possible to draw up a list of defining features that allow us to determine exactly what belongs inside a category and what belongs outside. Some concepts have very tight and precise definitions which allow us to make incontestable decisions about what counts as a member of the category and what doesn't. For example, a square *is* a quadrilateral with sides of equal length and vertices of 90 degrees. Given my earlier comments about the difficulty of defining emotion in a precise manner, it will be no surprise that I see problems with a classical approach to the category, the most obvious one being that there are few characteristics that all emotions have in common, but other non-emotional states do not also share (but see Clore & Ortony, 1991, for an alternative point of view).

When psychologists have drawn up their own lists of emotions, they too have often disagreed with one another. Some theorists have suggested that there is a small set of primary emotions, based on the genetic inheritance of the species or the commonalities in human development (see Table 1). For example, Ekman and Friesen (1971) suggested that there are six basic biologically programmed emotions: *happiness*, *sadness*, *fear*, *anger*, *surprise*, and *disgust*, each with its own distinctive facial expression. In the primary emotion view, other non-primary emotions are thought to be blends of the basic ones. However, the fact that psychologists have disagreed about which emotions are basic (and about whether states such as surprise are even emotions, let alone basic emotions) tends to undermine the credibility of the view that certain states are basically, irreducibly, and inescapably emotional. Indeed, some psychologists have denied that there is any good reason to suppose that there are *basic* emotions at all (Ortony & Turner, 1991).

Having considered the various examples of emotion, there still remains the question of how these examples themselves should be defined. Like the concept of emotion in general, particular emotional terms also seem to have prototypical rather than classical definitions. For example, saying that someone is angry implies a variety of claims about that person's experience, expression, and likely behaviour, but not all of these need apply for anger to be a valid description of the state. Next I shall look at the different components of emotion, before considering the ways in which these aspects are interrelated and build the complete experience of an emotional state.

COMPONENTS OF EMOTION

Psychological research into emotion has focused on four variables that are associated with emotional experience. I shall consider each of these factors in turn as characteristics of emotional experience. The four kinds of phenomena are the following: situational evaluations, bodily changes, expressive behaviours, and motivated actions. For example, an angry person will typically evaluate the situation in terms of some kind of insult against himself or herself, will experience physical symptoms such as a quickened heartbeat and flushing of the face, will show a characteristic facial expression with clenched teeth and a knitted brow, and will have the impulse to hit out at the antagonist in some literal or metaphorical way. This represents the prototype of our category of anger. Real-life examples of anger may share a large proportion of these features but usually not all of them. Although it is hard to conceive of someone being angry without evaluating the situation in terms of a personal slight, none of the other aspects of the emotion are necessary to anger.

Situational evaluations and interpretations

Above, I suggested that emotional states typically involve an evaluative relationship between the person and an intentional object. This evaluative aspect appears to be quite central to what we mean by emotion. Unless we are experiencing the situation as positive or negative, in a good or a bad light, it seems to make little sense to claim that we are emotional.

Arnold (1960) emphasized the importance of the evaluative aspect of emotion with her concept of *appraisal*, which refers to the process whereby the personal relevance of the emotional object is apprehended: "To arouse an emotion, the object must be appraised as affecting me in some way, affecting me personally as an individual with my particular experience and my particular aims" (p. 171).

Lazarus (1968) suggested that emotional appraisal has two facets, which he called *primary appraisal* and *secondary appraisal*. In primary appraisal, the individual evaluates the relevance of the current situation to personal well-being, weighing up whether it has good or bad implications for prevailing concerns, and implicitly asking the question: "Am I in trouble or am I OK?" In secondary appraisal, the individual evaluates his or her capacity for dealing with the situation (coping potential), asking, in other words, "What can be done about it?"

Clearly, different emotions are characterized by different evaluations of the situation. For example, positive emotions such as happiness and pride are associated with primary appraisals that the situation is beneficial to personal concerns, whereas negative emotions such as anger, fear, and sadness suggest that the situation is being appraised as detrimental to the individual. Emotions may be further differentiated on the basis of aspects of secondary appraisal: for example, if the situation is appraised as unfavourable, and coping potential is appraised as low and unlikely to improve, then the emotional state experienced is likely to be depression or sadness. On the other hand, if the situation is appraised as unfavourable but coping potential is appraised as high, then the emotion is more likely to be felt as hope (Smith & Lazarus, 1990).

Several studies have investigated the different appraisals that are associated with different emotions. For example, Smith and Ellsworth (1985) asked students to think of occasions in the past when they had experienced fifteen specific emotional states such as pride, anger, and so on. The students then answered various questions about their evaluations of these remembered situations, using a series of rating scales. Smith and Ellsworth found that characteristic patterns of ratings were associated with the different emotions. Other experiments (e.g., Frijda, Kuipers, & ter Schure, 1989) have produced broadly consistent findings.

From this research it can be concluded that a wide variety of emotional experiences can be differentiated using a relatively small set of appraisal dimensions. The most important dimensions relate to the event's pleasantness or unpleasantness; its unfamiliarity or familiarity; its unexpectedness; its beneficial or harmful implications; uncertainty about its implications; your own and other people's responsibility for the event; the controllability or uncontrollability of the event; whether the event is relevant to your well-being or someone else's; and whether the event conforms to or conflicts with your norms. The evidence suggests that these dimensions are differentially *symptomatic* of the different emotions. I shall return to the separate issue of whether they also play a *causal* role in distinguishing emotions in a later section.

Bodily changes

Emotion has a strong intuitive connection with the heart and with the guts (Averill, 1974). Correspondingly, psychologists have been discussing and investigating the bodily accompaniments of emotional states since the 1880s, (e.g., James, 1884).

At the centre of this research is a long-standing controversy about whether distinctive patterns of physiological response accompany the various possible emotional states (Ekman, Levenson, & Friesen, 1983). Cannon (1929) argued that all the excited emotions such as anger and fear are actually accompanied by the same state: a generalized emergency response preparing the body for vigorous activity. This pattern, known as *sympathetic arousal*, is based on a diffuse activation of the sympathetic division of the autonomic nervous system and produces a general increase in metabolic rate and energy mobilization in the body. The following set of responses characteristically occur: increase in heart rate and blood pressure, increased respiratory volume, constriction of the blood vessels in the skin (pallor), dilation of pupils, arrest of gastro-intestinal activity, decreased salivation (dry mouth), and increased action of the sweat glands. The response system is partly mediated by increased adrenaline (epinephrine) secretion, which may also result in trembling, and feelings of cold.

Although there is little convincing scientific evidence that there are definite relationships between distinctive body states and different emotions, people still report different bodily symptoms associated with anger, fear, sadness, and so on (e.g., Nieuwenhuyse, Offenberg, & Frijda, 1987). There are a number of possible reasons for this. First, it may be that intense emotions actually do have distinctive bodily accompaniments, but the weaker reactions that are evoked in the laboratory (for practical and ethical reasons) are less clearly differentiated. In this case, subjects' beliefs about distinctive bodily accompaniments may still be correct. Second, it is possible that cultural stereotypes about what symptoms are supposed to be associated with different emotions distort people's interpretations of their own bodily responses (Rimé, Philippot, & Cisamolo, 1990). Finally, it may be that different emotions focus awareness on different parts of the body because of their symbolic content; although the actual physiological response is diffuse, only the relevant symptoms are picked up by the person having the emotional experience. For example, although embarrassment may be accompanied by a wide variety of physiological responses, the fact that the emotion is concerned with feelings of exaggerated social visibility makes facial flushing the most salient symptom. The best conclusion that can be drawn from the research is that it is important to maintain a distinction between felt bodily symptoms of emotion, and the actual physiological changes that may or may not underlie them.

Emotional expression

One of the most obvious indices of emotional experience, precisely because we are socially attuned to it, is expressive behaviour. By expression, I mean movement and sounds made by someone indicating the presence of emotion to someone else. These movements and sounds may not be deliberate or intentional, but they will still be expressive to the extent that they communicate emotional information. The face is the most important channel of emotional expression, partly because it is capable of a wide variety of subtly patterned movements. In addition, emotion may be expressed through tone of voice, bodily posture, and gestures.

Since Darwin (1872), it has been commonly believed that at least some facial expressions are genetically programmed in humans. Evidence for this idea has come from studies that show that a small set of facial expressions are consistently identified by people coming from a large variety of cultures including some which have had little contact with westerners (Ekman & Friesen, 1971). For example, four facial expressions (anger, disgust, happiness, and sadness) posed by members of a pre-literate culture were recognized at better than chance level by American students. The evidence relating to other emotional expressions is less convincing. Furthermore, real-life emotional states are accompanied by continually changing facial expressions which are rarely as clearcut as those used in the studies mentioned.

Emotional meaning can also be conveyed by body posture, limb movements, and so on. In fact, facial expressions are often part of more general action patterns which include postural changes and integrated movements of the whole body. Finally, emotion may be expressed vocally, in speech intonation and pitch and so on (Scherer, 1986). Research evidence suggests that the emotional meaning of contentless speech is recognized about as well as that of facial expression.

Motivated action

The fourth and final component of emotion is motivated action. Emotions often seem to contain the impulse to act in certain ways appropriate to the particular emotion. For example, when angry, you may feel a strong urge to hit out at someone in some way, when in love to seek out the company of your loved one and get as close as you possibly can to him or her, and when afraid you may feel the strong desire to run away, literally or metaphorically.

A currently popular view is that the evolutionary functions of different emotions serve particular survival-related goal systems and put the organism in a state of readiness for dealing with situations of particular kinds (e.g., Smith & Ellsworth, 1985). According to this perspective, emotions should be seen as inherently *motivational* states, serving particular functions. For example, the evolutionary goal of anger might be to protect oneself from antagonists, so the angry state prepares the organism for aggression and retaliation. Similarly, fear has obvious survival relevance in preparing for rapid escape from a dangerous situation. The direct survival implications of emotions such as happiness, embarrassment, sadness, and so on, however, are a little harder to locate, and it may be that the behaviours associated with these emotions serve social rather than evolutionary functions. For example, we may get embarrassed to distance ourselves from a potential negative evaluation in public: the urge to hide or become invisible may reflect the socially produced need to avoid being a focus of other people's attention at such times (e.g., Modigliani, 1971).

SEQUENCES OF EMOTION: THE INTERNAL STRUCTURE OF EMOTIONAL EXPERIENCE

I have considered some of the factors that are symptomatic of emotion. I shall now look at these same variables again, but this time discussing their possible participation in the causation of emotional experience. My approach will be to consider the roles these factors have been assigned by different theorists in explaining how emotional experience is produced. Finally, I shall attempt to integrate the insights of these alternative models into a more general model of the emotional syndrome as a whole.

Factor 1: appraisal

The first and most central factor in the causation of emotion relates to the evaluation of some situation or event, based on the process of appraisal. Appraisal theorists suggest that emotions are rarely direct reactions to stimulus qualities. Rather, what gives an object emotional impact is its relevance to the individual's personal concerns. Lazarus (1984), for example, argued that before it can cause an emotion, a stimulus, event, or encounter must be interpreted and evaluated to weigh up its personal significance.

An experiment by Lazarus's research team (Speisman, Lazarus, Mordkoff, & Davison, 1964) provides an illustration of how emotional response might depend upon appraisal. The unfortunate subjects in this study were shown a movie depicting a tribal ritual called "subincision" in which adolescent males undergo an apparently painful operation on their genitals. The film was found to be emotionally unpleasant to watch, producing autonomic and self-report reactions of stress. However, these reactions could be reduced by including a soundtrack suggesting an "anthropological perspective" which encouraged subjects to interpret the depicted events in terms of the insights they provided into an alien culture. Correspondingly, a soundtrack emphasizing the trauma of the ritual increased stress reactions. The authors argued that the different soundtracks modified subjects' ongoing appraisal of the emotional content of the movie, allowing them to interpret the material as more or less threatening, and thus intensify or alleviate their emotional reaction.

In contemporary emotion theory, appraisal is the central explanatory concept. Lazarus (1991) has even argued that appraisal is both a necessary and sufficient condition for emotional experience. Other theorists suggest that other variables have a role to play in determining emotional experience (Parkinson & Manstead, 1992). I shall consider some of the other factors that might influence emotional experience, before moving on to a discussion of whether emotion is as exclusively dependent on appraisal as Lazarus has suggested.

Factor 2: arousal

According to William James (1898), who is often credited with devising the first modern psychological theory of emotion, the common-sense idea of how emotion is caused, where a situational encounter directly produces emotional feeling, actually gets things backwards (see Figure 1a and Figure 1b):

> Our natural way of thinking . . . is that the mental perception of some fact excites the mental affection called the emotion, and that this latter state of mind gives rise to the bodily expression. My thesis, on the contrary, is that *the bodily changes follow directly the perception of the exciting fact, and that our feeling of the same changes as they occur IS the emotion*. Common sense says, we lose our fortune, are sorry and weep; we meet a bear, are frightened and run; we are insulted by a rival, are angry and strike. The hypothesis here to be defended says that this order of sequence is incorrect . . . and that the more rational statement is that we feel sorry because we cry, angry because we strike, afraid because we tremble, and not that we cry, strike, or tremble because we are sorry, angry, fearful, as the case may be. (p. 449, emphasis in original)

James (1898) argued that the differences between emotions are a direct result of the different patterns of physiological response associated with them. According to James, seeing something frightening instinctively triggers a whole set of reactions in our bodies. The particular pattern of these reactions is felt by us consciously and experienced as the particular emotion of fear.

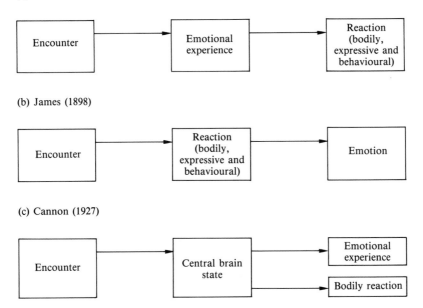

Figure 1 Sequences of emotion: early theories

For example, our feelings of fear might be based on the feeling of raised blood pressure, tightening of our muscles, a certain sensation in our guts.

One of the main problems with James's theory, as pointed out by Cannon (1927), is that the physiological changes that accompany a wide variety of emotions are actually very similar, and certainly not distinct enough to differentiate widely contrasting subjective states such as euphoria and anger. Cannon's alternative theory represented a slight return towards the common-sense view of emotion. Cannon's idea was that emotional encounters directly triggered a central brain process in the thalamus, which had two simultaneous and independent outputs, one to the arousal system which prepared the body to cope with the emergency, and the second to the cortex where the conscious experience of the emotion was registered (see Figure 1c). Thus the symptoms of quickened pulse, sweating, and so on, were simply side-effects of energy mobilization in preparation for responding to emergency, and were irrelevant to the subjective awareness of emotion. In defence of this position, Cannon pointed out that sensory feedback from the body's periphery was simply too slow and too vaguely registered to allow it a causal role in the production of rapid and differentiated emotional experience.

Schachter (1964) revived and revised James's idea that emotions are dependent on feedback from bodily changes, but also accepted Cannon's arguments that emotions mostly share the same bodily response of general-ized sympathetic arousal. Schachter believed that arousal feedback provided the subjective "heat" behind emotional experience, but that the quality of the emotion was derived from a second factor based on situational information.

Specifically, Schachter argued that the kind of emotion that was felt depended on how arousal was interpreted and explained by the person experiencing it. In this view, if you believe that your state of arousal is caused by a wild animal that is chasing you, then you are likely to experience the state as fear. However, if you think that your arousal is triggered by the close presence of somebody attractive, you might well come to feel your reaction as love, or at least as lust, for that person. In other words, emotion consists of an *attribution* of arousal to an emotionally relevant situational cause (see Figure 2).

If Schachter's theory is correct, then it is possible to change the emotions that people experience simply by modifying the way that they interpret their arousal reactions; in a famous experiment, this is exactly what Schachter and Singer (1962) tried to do. In the study, the first thing Schachter and Singer had to do was to get people into a state of arousal that was not linked to any emotional state. They achieved this by injecting the experimental subjects with adrenaline, under the pretext that it was a new vitamin compound called suproxin, whose effects the experimenters were testing (in a control condi-tion, the suproxin injection was actually a saline placebo). Second, the inves-tigators had to convince the subjects that their experienced arousal was produced by either emotional or non-emotional causes. They managed this by accurately informing some subjects that the injection would bring about all the usual side-effects of arousal including heart-rate increase, a rise in body temperature, and so on, but by deceiving other subjects that the injec-tion would have no side-effects (or side-effects unrelated to an arousal reaction). These latter misinformed subjects, therefore, were supposed to

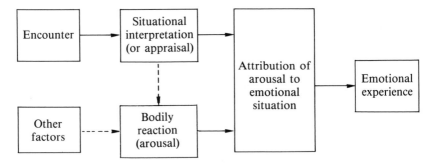

Note: Broken lines represent linkages that are possible rather than necessary

Figure 2 Schachter's two-factor theory

496

experience arousal symptoms without knowing their source, and according to the theory should experience emotion depending upon how they came to explain their felt symptoms.

Schachter and Singer manipulated their subjects' emotional explanations for unexplained arousal by putting them into different situations. This was done while subjects were supposedly waiting for the vitamin compound to be absorbed. Each subject waited with another supposed subject who was actually an accomplice of the experimenter and who acted in one of two different ways, contrived to convey contrasting emotional situations.

In the first condition, the accomplice tried to create a general atmosphere of *euphoria*. For example, he improvised a basket-ball game with screwed up pieces of paper and a waste-bin, made paper planes, aimed a makeshift catapult at a tower he had built from some folders, and finally discovered some conveniently concealed hula hoops and started playing with one of them, leaving the other within easy reach of the subject.

In the second condition, the situational manipulation was intended to occasion the emotion of *anger*. Here, the real subject and the accomplice were asked to fill in a questionnaire while waiting for the suproxin to be absorbed. This questionnaire started out fairly inoffensively, asking about the subject's age, sex, and so on. From then on, the questions became increasingly personal and insulting. For example, one item asked: "With how many men (other than your father) has your mother had extra-marital relationships?" The only response alternatives provided were: "4 and under"; "5 to 9"; and "10 and over"! The accomplice made irritated comments as he answered the questions. Finally, his acted annoyance reached such a pitch that he tore up the questionnaire and threw it on the floor, shouting: "I'm not wasting any more time. I'm getting my books and leaving".

The extent to which subjects got caught up in the general emotional atmosphere of these two contrasting situations was assessed by observers who watched their behaviour from behind one-way glass. Subjects also made self-ratings of their emotional state. According to the experimental predictions, the only subjects who should have got emotional as a function of the accomplice's behaviour were those who had been injected with adrenaline but not warned about the effects it would have on their bodies. Subjects given an accurate warning about symptoms would have a perfectly good non-emotional explanation of their felt reaction and therefore would not take on the mood of the accomplice. Correspondingly, subjects who had been injected with a placebo should have experienced no extra arousal and therefore no increase in emotion. If either arousal or an emotional explanation for arousal were missing, then no emotion should have resulted. On the other hand, subjects who experienced unexplained arousal should have attributed their symptoms to the emotional characteristics of the situation and taken on the emotional state of euphoria or anger depending upon which emotion the accomplice acted out.

In fact, these predicted differences in emotional experience failed to emerge as clearly as Schachter and Singer might have hoped. Although subjects correctly informed about the effects of the injection consistently reported less emotion than those given incorrect side-effects information, subjects who had been injected with an inert placebo did not always differ significantly from misinformed aroused subjects. In other words, the administration of adrenaline did not make a reliable difference to the emotional experience of subjects. An even bigger problem was that subjects in the anger condition did not generally report their mood as negative at all: even when injected with adrenaline, misinformed of side-effects, and subjected to a humiliating questionnaire, they still rated themselves as mildly happy! Subsequent attempts to replicate the study have been similarly inconclusive (see Reisenzein, 1983, for a review).

Although the evidence for Schachter's theory is not completely convincing, his theory was historically influential because it suggested a potentially important role for interpersonal variables in the constitution of emotional experience. Previously, social factors were thought to play a role only in modifying the *expression* of an unchanged underlying biologically determined state (e.g., Ekman's concept of *display rules*), but after Schachter, theorists began to recognize the possibility that social interactions and interpersonal roles could directly shape the experience of emotion (e.g., Averill, 1980).

The second main influence of two-factor theory has been on self-attributional accounts of emotion (e.g., Laird & Bresler, 1992). Schachter suggested that emotion is based on an inferential process through which people come to the conclusion that they are emotional on the basis of the evidence that is available to them. If they believe that a plausibly emotional object has caused them to become aroused, they will conclude that their feelings about that object must be quite strong. This self-perception analysis (Bem, 1972) suggests that other sources of emotionally relevant information might similarly affect emotional judgements. Such information might arise, for example, from awareness of facial expression, or feedback from emotional action.

Factor 3: facial expression

Unlike the signals available from the autonomic nervous system, which as we have seen are too diffuse to provide diagnostic information about emotional quality, facial expressive patterns show at least some consistent relations with specific emotions. Several theorists have suggested that feedback from facial expression is an important source of emotional feelings (e.g., Izard, 1971; Tomkins, 1962).

Darwin (1872) was the first to suggest that facial responses might affect as well as reflect emotional experience. He argued that "the free expression by outward signs of an emotion intensifies it. On the other hand, the repression as far as possible of all outward signs softens our emotions" (p. 22).

Many studies have supported Darwin's insight, showing that facial expressions have a small but reliable influence on the strength of emotional reactions. One of the most convincing demonstrations of a facial feedback effect was provided by Strack, Martin, and Stepper (1988). These investigators apparently succeeded in manipulating facial expression without subjects' awareness. Subjects were told that the study was an investigation of how disabled people manage to perform various tasks using parts of the body that are not normally used for these tasks. In the study, subjects were asked to write while holding the pen in their mouth. One of their assigned tasks was to rate how funny a series of cartoons was. While performing this task, some of the subjects were told to hold the pen between their teeth, a position which puts the face in an expression close to a smile, while others were told they could use only their lips to hold the pen, effectively preventing them from smiling and encouraging more of a frowning face. It was found that subjects who held the pen between their teeth rated their amusement at the cartoons as significantly higher than those who held the pen using their lips. Thus, it seems that our emotional reactions to emotional material can be influenced partially by the expression we have on our face.

How does facial expression affect emotional experience? In Laird's (1974) original facial feedback experiment, one subject explained his reaction as follows: "When my jaw was clenched and my brows down I tried not to be angry but it just fit the position. . . . I found my thoughts wandering to things that made me angry which is sort of silly I guess. I knew I was in an experiment and knew I had no reason to feel that way, but I just lost control" (p. 480). Clearly, this subject was perfectly aware that the position of his face resembled a frown, and this recognition consciously triggered thoughts relating to anger, which in turn made him feel a little more angry. Lard interpreted his results in terms of self-perception theory, arguing that people's emotional feelings are based partly on the evidence from their own facial expressions.

This kind of inferential process seems less likely in Strack, Martin, and Stepper's study where subjects were apparently unaware that they were smiling or frowning. It may be that facial expressions influence emotional experience to the extent that they contribute to, or interfere with, the natural way of reacting in an emotional situation. However, the influence is not usually very great and has been demonstrated only with respect to a limited range of emotions such as amusement and pain.

Factor 4: action readiness

According to Frijda (1986), the awareness of desires and impulses to action is a vital part of the experience of emotion. In this view, active emotions such as anger and fear are characterized by the feeling of action readiness, whereas the experience of more passive emotions such as sorrow and despair includes feelings of loss of interest and disinclination for action. In support of this position, strong correlations have been obtained between self-ascriptions of emotions, and self-reports of modes of action readiness (e.g., Frijda, Kuipers, & ter Schure, 1989). Reports also suggest that the experience of action readiness in emotion is felt as involuntary and impulsive rather than deliberate and controlled. The urge to act in a certain way or to refrain from action seems to be something that comes over people, rather than something they choose to do. Frijda calls this the felt *control precedence* of an emotion and believes that it can be seen as a further defining feature of what is taken to be emotional experience.

Synthesis: four-factor theory

I have considered several possible causal routes to the production of an emotional experience, with different theorists assigning priority to different categories of variable from the four factors of emotion. The reader may feel entitled at this point to ask which of these sequences is the correct one. The simple answer to this is the appraisal sequence: emotion is determined mainly by our evaluations and interpretations of the personal significance of events. However, a more complete answer based on the current state of our knowledge is that most of the suggested sequences may be applicable under certain circumstances. Feedback from any of the four factors of the patterned emotional response may occasionally contribute to the strength or quality of the experience.

To summarize my conclusions from the present section, there are two main kinds of theories of how emotion is caused. The first set of theories focus on how the situation leads to emotion, and are typically based on the concept of cognitive appraisal. The second set concentrate on the role of bodily reactions in emotional experience and rely on notions of feedback. Of course, appraisal and feedback theories are not necessarily mutually exclusive. For example, bodily reactions are often caused by appraisal of the situation (Smith, 1989), and the effects these reactions have on emotion in turn often reflect the way they influence the appraisal process. If you notice your heart is pounding, you may look for a plausible emotional cause for this reaction in the situation, which you will then reappraise in more emotional terms. Laird and Bresler (1992) suggest that feedback or self-perception theory explains how the subjective experience of emotion is constructed out of the various sources of emotional information, but appraisal theory accounts for the bodily changes that produce this feedback information. However, factors other than appraisal may also sometimes influence the various sources of feedback and make their independent contribution to the causation of emotion (see Figure 3).

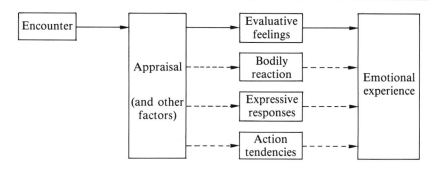

Note: Broken lines represent linkages that are possible rather than necessary

Figure 3   A four-factor theory of emotion

Another way of viewing the emotional process is to see all four kinds of phenomena as manifestations of a common underlying process (Frijda, 1986). From this perspective, the process of emotion can be specified as the impact of a stimulus event, consisting of an appraisal of that event leading to an effect upon action readiness. Feeling is primarily the conscious result of that appraisal. Emotional expression, motivated behaviour, and physiological change are all manifestations of the state of action-readiness, and awareness of these factors also contributes to feeling. In this view, the feeling of anger, for example, is a specific patterned motivational state containing an appraisal of other-blame which directly implies a readiness to hit out at this other person, and is expressed through the body and on the face. In other words, rather than seeing emotional experience as constructed out of various channels of feedback information, we can see emotion as an integrated evaluative process which already includes the various aspects of the response syndrome.

EMOTION AND COGNITION

In this chapter so far, I have tried to understand emotion by looking at it from the inside by asking what kinds of things emotions are, what constituent components they have, and how these components might fit together to make an emotional experience. Finally, I shall consider emotion's external relations with another important psychological function, that of cognition. Thus, I shall try to get a final fix on what emotion is by mapping its relative position in general psychological theory.

In common sense, emotion is often considered as the opposite of rational, considered thought. When emotional, we act impulsively in the heat of the moment rather than coolly calculating the best course of action, the heart rather than the head becomes the crucial metaphoric organ controlling what we do (Lutz, 1988). These intuitive connotations seem to suggest that emotional phenomena might fall outside the range of cognitive theories whose explanatory concepts are phrased in terms of information processing and formal symbol manipulation.

However, as we have seen in this chapter, many psychologists currently believe that the way we feel emotionally about something is crucially dependent upon the way we evaluate and interpret that thing cognitively. Lazarus (1991), for example, argues that emotion is always preceded by cognitive appraisal which determines the quality and the quantity of the response. In other words, emotion is secondary to cognitive activity. Against this view, Zajonc (1980) has suggested that affective reactions can arise in the absence of any prior cognitive processing, and more generally, that cognition and emotion are fundamentally separate systems just as common sense appears to suggest.

One of Zajonc's examples can be used to illustrate his point. He argues that when we meet people, we are sometimes aware of whether or not we like them even before we have remembered who they are. Similarly, Zajonc suggests that our affective judgements of the pleasantness or unpleasantness of all kinds of objects can be immediate and independent of any cognitive interpretation.

There are two obvious problems with this account. First, although most people would accept that emotional reactions sometimes arise without any prior *conscious* evaluative or interpretational work, this does not mean that no information processing of any kind has occurred. In fact, it would be difficult to explain our different emotional reactions to different situations if no recognition processes came first. Zajonc would argue that this recognition may sometimes be affective rather than cognitive. Lazarus (1984), on the other hand, would say that any recognition of the personal significance of an encounter is *appraisal* by definition, even though this appraisal may often be unconscious and automatic. Stating the controversy this way suggests that the only real disagreement between Lazarus and Zajonc may relate to how the processes preceding emotional reaction are defined. In fact, appraisal need not be seen in *purely* cognitive terms anyway (e.g., Parrott & Sabini, 1989), since it clearly includes a strong evaluative element.

The second problem with Zajonc's analysis is that it is not clear whether he is really talking about *emotion* or simply about *affect*. Lazarus (1984) argued as follows: "Cognitive activity is a necessary precondition of emotion because to experience an emotion, people must comprehend – whether in the form of a primitive evaluative perception or a highly differentiated symbolic process – that their well-being is implicated in a transaction, for better or worse" (p. 124). If Lazarus's analysis of what emotion involves is correct, then much of Zajonc's argument does not concern emotional phenomena at all. Like Lazarus, I have argued above that it is hard to imagine a genuine emotional state that does not include at its centre an evaluative relation to some intentional object. However, in my opinion, the issue of causality is not quite as simple as Lazarus sometimes seems to imply. It may be that other non-cognitive factors, such as bodily and facial feedback, also contribute to the causation of both appraisal and emotion (Parkinson & Manstead, 1992).

CONCLUSION

Like the psychology of emotion itself, this chapter began with an apparently simple question: "What is an emotion?" (cf. James, 1884). Much of what I have written here helps to answer this question. An emotion is a relatively short-term, evaluative state focused on a particular intentional object (a person, an event, or a state of affairs). Good examples are anger, fear, love, and hate. Emotional reactions typically include many of the following four components: appraisal of the situation, bodily response, facial expression, and changes in action readiness. None of these factors is completely necessary for emotional experience, but it would be implausible to describe as emotional any state that included none of them. Emotion can be seen as the unfolding pattern of interrelationships of these aspects, as the subjective experience of the episode, or as an underlying process that determines the whole syndrome. In any case, the investigation of emotion requires a range of perspectives (e.g., cognitive, physiological, ethological, and social), all of which have a role to play in our overall understanding of the phenomenon (Averill, 1992). In this chapter, I have tried to give a flavour of the spectrum of possible relevant analyses.

ACKNOWLEDGEMENT

This chapter has been influenced in many not always obvious ways by the work of Nico Frijda, whose contribution is gratefully and respectfully acknowledged.

FURTHER READING

Averill, J. R. (1982). *Anger and aggression: An essay on emotion.* New York: Springer.
Clark, M. (Ed.) (1992) *Review of personality and social psychology: vol. 13. Emotion.* Beverly-Hills, CA: Sage.
Frijda, N. H. (1986). *The emotions.* Cambridge: Cambridge University Press.
Lazarus, R. S. (1991). *Emotion and adaptation.* Oxford: Oxford University Press.
Ortony, A., Clore, G. L., & Collins, A. (1988). *The cognitive structure of emotions.* Cambridge: Cambridge University Press.

REFERENCES

Arnold, M. B. (1960). *Emotion and personality: vol. 1. Psychological aspects*. New York: Columbia University Press.

Averill, J. R. (1974). An analysis of psychophysiological symbolism and its influence on theories of emotion. *Journal for the Theory of Social Behaviour, 4*, 147–190.

Averill, J. R. (1980). A constructivist view of emotions. In R. Plutchik & H. Kellerman (Eds) *Emotions: Theory, research, and experience* (vol. 1, pp. 305–339). New York: Academic Press.

Averill, J. R. (1992). The structural bases of emotional behavior: A metatheoretical analysis. In M. S. Clark (Ed.) *Review of personality and social psychology: Emotion* (vol. 13, pp. 1–24). Newbury Park, CA: Sage.

Bem, D. J. (1972). Self-perception theory. In L. Festinger (Ed.) *Advances in experimental social psychology* (vol. 6, pp. 1–62). New York: Academic Press.

Cannon, W. B. (1927). The James-Lange theory of emotions: A critical examination and an alternative theory. *American Journal of Psychology, 39*, 106–124.

Cannon, W. B. (1929). *Bodily changes in pain, hunger, fear, and rage* (2nd edn). New York: Appleton.

Clark, M. S., & Isen, A. M. (1982). Toward understanding the relationship between feeling states and social behavior. In A. H. Hastorf & A. M. Isen (Eds) *Cognitive social psychology* (pp. 73–108). New York: Elsevier.

Clore, G. L., & Ortony, A. (1991). What more is there to emotion concepts than prototypes? *Journal of Personality and Social Psychology, 60*, 48–50.

Darwin, C. R. (1872). *The expression of emotions in man and animals*. London: John Murray.

Ekman, P., & Friesen, W. V. (1971). Constants across cultures in the face and emotion. *Journal of Personality and Social Psychology, 17*, 124–129.

Ekman, P., Levenson, R. W., & Friesen, W. V. (1983). Autonomic nervous system activity distinguishes among emotions. *Science, 221*, 1208–1210.

Fehr, B., & Russell, J. A. (1984). Concept of emotion viewed from a prototype perspective. *Journal of Experimental Psychology: General, 113*, 464–486.

Frijda, N. H. (1986). *The emotions*. Cambridge: Cambridge University Press.

Frijda, N. H., Kuipers, P., & ter Schure, E. (1989). Relations among emotion, appraisal, and emotional action readiness. *Journal of Personality and Social Psychology, 57*, 212–228.

Harré, R. (Ed.) (1986). *The social construction of emotions*. New York: Basil Blackwell.

Izard, C. E. (1971). *The face of emotion*. New York: Appleton-Century-Crofts.

James, W. (1884). What is an emotion? *Mind, 9*, 188–205.

James, W. (1898). *The principles of psychology* (vol. 2). London: Macmillan.

Laird, J. D. (1974). Self-attribution of emotion: The effects of facial expression on the quality of emotional experience. *Journal of Personality and Social Psychology, 29*, 475–486.

Laird, J. D., & Bresler, C. (1992). The process of emotional experience: A self-perception theory. In M. S. Clark (Ed.) *Review of personality and social psychology: Emotion* (vol. 13, pp. 213–234). Newbury Park, CA: Sage.

Lazarus, R. S. (1968). Emotions and adaptation. In W. J. Arnold (Ed.) *Nebraska symposium on motivation* (vol. 16. pp. 175–265). Lincoln, NE: University of Nebraska Press.

Lazarus, R. S. (1984). On the primacy of cognition. *American Psychologist, 39*, 124–129.

Lazarus, R. S. (1991). *Emotion and adaptation*. Oxford: Oxford University Press.

Lutz, C. (1988). *Unnatural emotions*. Chicago, IL: University of Chicago Press.

Modigliani, A. (1971). Embarrassment, facework, and eye-contact: Testing a theory of embarrassment. *Journal of Personality and Social Psychology, 17*, 15–24.

Nieuwenhuyse, B., Offenberg, L., & Frijda, N. H. (1987). Subjective emotion and reported body experience. *Motivation and Emotion, 11*, 169–182.

Ortony, A., & Turner, T. J. (1991). What's basic about basic emotions? *Psychological Review, 97*, 315–331.

Parkinson, B., & Manstead, A. S. R. (1992). Appraisal as a cause of emotion. In M. S. Clark (Ed.) *Review of personality and social psychology* (vol. 13, pp. 122–149). New York: Sage.

Parrott, W. G., & Sabini, J. (1989). On the "emotional" qualities of certain types of cognition: A reply to arguments for the independence of cognition and affect. *Cognitive Therapy and Research, 13*, 49–65.

Reisenzein, R. (1983). The Schachter theory of emotion: Two decades later. *Psychological Bulletin, 94*, 239–264.

Rimé, B., Philippot, P., & Cisamolo, D. (1990). Social schemata of peripheral changes in emotion. *Journal of Personality and Social Psychology, 59*, 38–49.

Rosch, E. (1978). Principles of categorization. In E. Rosch & B. B. Lloyd (Eds) *Cognition and categorization* (pp. 27–48). Hillsdale, NJ: Lawrence Erlbaum.

Schachter, S. (1964). The interaction of cognitive and physiological determinants of emotional state. In L. Festinger (Ed.) *Advances in experimental social psychology* (vol. 1, pp. 49–80). New York: Academic Press.

Schachter, S., & Singer, J. E. (1962). Cognitive, social, and physiological determinants of emotional state. *Psychological Review, 69*, 379–399.

Scherer, K. R. (1986). Vocal affect expression: A review and a model for future research. *Psychological Bulletin, 99*, 143–165.

Smith, C. A. (1989). Dimensions of appraisal and physiological response in emotion. *Journal of Personality and Social Psychology, 56*, 339–353.

Smith, C. A., & Ellsworth, P. C. (1985). Patterns of cognitive appraisal in emotion. *Journal of Personality and Social Psychology, 48*, 813–838.

Smith, C. A., & Lazarus, R. S. (1990). Emotion and adaptation. In L. A. Pervin (Ed.) *Handbook of personality: Theory and research* (pp. 609–637). New York: Guilford.

Speisman, J. C., Lazarus, R. S., Mordkoff, A., & Davison, L. (1964). Experimental reduction of stress based on ego-defense theory. *Journal of Abnormal and Social Psychology, 68*, 367–380.

Strack, F., Martin, L. L., & Stepper, S. (1988). Inhibiting and facilitating conditions of the human smile: A non-obtrusive test of facial feedback hypothesis. *Journal of Personality and Social Psychology, 54*, 768–777.

Tomkins, S. S. (1962). *Affect, imagery, consciousness: vol. 1 The positive affects*. New York: Springer.

Zajonc, R. B. (1980). Feeling and thinking: Preferences need no inferences. *American Psychologist, 35*, 151–175.

6.2

HUNGER AND APPETITE

John E. Blundell and Andrew J. Hill

University of Leeds, England

Physiological and environmental interactions	Conditioned hunger
Appetite and body weight regulation	Is eating caused by hunger?
Appetite as the output of a biopsychological system	Nutrition, appetite, and the satiety cascade
The identification of hunger	Motivation: order and disorder
Hunger and the satiety cascade	Further reading
	References

Hunger and appetite are phenomena that have always been central to the study of motivation. They both belong to the domain of psychological inquiry that seeks to find the reasons underlying the actions of human beings and animals. The terms "hunger" and "appetite" are widely used both in scientific literature and in non-technical discourse to refer to states and processes that guide food consumption. That is, they describe the drive or the motivational force that constrains us to eat particular foods within a certain pattern of eating. However, we should not think of hunger and appetite as simple entities with a simple causal relationship to eating behaviour. Hunger and appetite are themselves quite different and complex phenomena. By examining their structure and the way in which they operate we shall be drawn into an examination of the mechanisms that control eating and which, in turn, exert an influence over body weight. Accordingly, this exploration of the control of the motivation to eat will lead into a consideration of disorders of motivation (over- and under-eating) and, in addition, disorders of body weight. Indeed, a part of the impetus to study hunger and appetite as

506

motivational forces comes from the need to understand and treat motivation when it is poorly regulated.

In order to generate a clear understanding of hunger and appetite, one major task is to define their relationships with environmental happenings, physiological states, and objectively measured food consumption. Initially, it is necessary to define the terms. Although the reader may discover some disagreement among scientists about the precise meanings of the terms, the following descriptions provide working definitions.

Appetite can refer to the sum total of processes influencing the expression of the willingness to eat. Appetite is the global phenomenon influenced by cultural, economic, physiological, and cognitive factors. Hence it is appropriate to speak about the regulation of appetite and to consider the factors that influence this regulation. It is not necessary to use appetite in any more precise technical sense.

The logical status of the term *hunger* needs clarification, for it is clear that the term is used in more than one sense by psychologists. On the one hand, hunger is a motivational construct with the logical status of a mediating concept or intervening variable (Royce, 1963). That is, the term refers to an explanatory principle which is inferred from other directly observable and measurable events. In this sense the term helps in understanding the motivational processes. On the other hand, hunger may be used to refer to certain conscious sensations or feelings linked to a desire to obtain and eat food. This is the sense in which lay people understand the notion of hunger. It is necessary to emphasize the distinction between the psychological process of hunger with relevance for motivational theory, on the one hand, and the conscious sensation of hunger on the other. It is these hunger sensations that probably exert motivational pressure on behaviour, and it is these that researchers attempt to capture by means of rating scales and other devices.

Throughout this chapter, the term hunger will be used to represent a subjective experience or feeling that is associated with the desire to eat and obtain food. From a functional point of view, hunger achieves a purpose as that nagging, irritating feeling whose presence constantly serves to stimulate thoughts about food and eating. Hunger can also be present as a latent disposition which becomes activated in the presence of food stimuli. Hunger is therefore useful and reminds us that the body needs food. In this way hunger can be seen to possess a clear biological function.

How important is hunger in the expression of appetite? To what extent is appetite influenced by physiological and environmental factors? What role do cognition and attitudes play in changing the intensity or direction of appetite? How does nutrition influence the strength of the disposition to eat which is the essence of appetite? The answers to these questions will provide a framework for understanding appetite as a motivational phenomenon.

PHYSIOLOGICAL AND ENVIRONMENTAL INTERACTIONS

Appetite represents the constellation of forces that control eating, and eating is an activity that links alterations in the physiological domain (under the skin) with events taking place in a domain beyond the skin (the environment). Indeed, eating behaviour represents a particularly intimate form of interaction between organisms and their environments, for it involves consumption of part of the environment, which in turn forms part of the organism and influences the interaction. Moreover, eating is an episodic activity and the processes of appetite control must account for this.

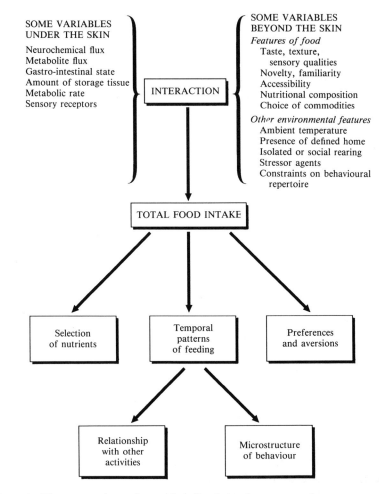

SOME VARIABLES
UNDER THE SKIN

Neurochemical flux
Metabolite flux
Gastro-intestinal state
Amount of storage tissue
Metabolic rate
Sensory receptors

INTERACTION

SOME VARIABLES
BEYOND THE SKIN
Features of food
   Taste, texture,
     sensory qualities
   Novelty, familiarity
   Accessibility
   Nutritional composition
   Choice of commodities

Other environmental features
   Ambient temperature
   Presence of defined home
   Isolated or social rearing
   Stressor agents
   Constraints on behavioural
     repertoire

TOTAL FOOD INTAKE

Selection
of nutrients

Temporal
patterns
of feeding

Preferences
and aversions

Relationship
with other
activities

Microstructure
of behaviour

Figure 1 The expression of appetite (food intake, temporal patterns, nutrient selection, etc.) reflecting an interaction between internal and external factors

The particular patterns of eating observed at any time represent an interaction between two constellations of factors (Blundell, 1979). Figure 1 draws attention to the fact that eating depends not only on the neurochemical and metabolic state of organisms but also on environmental features such as the taste, texture, novelty, accessibility, and choice of food, and on other external features such as the presence of other organisms. This notion of appetite as the consequence of an interaction provides a framework for thinking about appetite in animals as well as in humans. Indeed, Figure 1 emphasizes the way in which food consumption can be broken down into specific components (nutrient selection, micro-structure of behaviour, etc.) so as to diagnose the effects of various factors on the expression of appetite. The pattern of eating provides a sensitive way of assessing the impact of physiological or environmental features (Blundell, 1984). Of course, for humans, the subjective experiences or cognitions surrounding eating can similarly be regarded as being constructed out of physiological signals and the characteristics of the external environment (Blundell, 1981). Reynolds (1976) has referred to these cognitions as culturally defined knowledge entering the mind to give contours to the world, thus making sense out of physiological functioning.

As a first stage in understanding appetite, the interactional concept is important, for it lets us know that the phenomenon is not controlled by a single dominant cause. The analysis of appetite will therefore require an appreciation on the interrelationships among a number of factors from quite separate domains. This approach is equally important for the study of appetite in animals and in humans. However, for the investigation of human appetite a further conceptual scheme is appropriate.

APPETITE AND BODY WEIGHT REGULATION

It has been noted above that appetite can be considered a phenomenon that links biological happenings (under the skin) with environmental happenings (beyond the skin). This interaction has implications for the regulation of body weight. This is inevitable because energy balance is dependent upon the relationship between energy intake (food consumption) and energy expenditure (physical activity, energy used to maintain bodily processes, and energy involved in the processing and storage of consumed food). A positive energy balance (intake greater than expenditure) means that body weight will be gained, whereas a negative energy balance leads to weight loss. Any factors that influence appetite will naturally adjust energy intake, and this will alter energy balance. It is normally considered that body weight is a variable subject to homeostatic control. That is, body weight is biologically regulated. However, because appetite is also influenced by environmental factors, an examination of the principles of weight regulation should tell us something about the strength of biological and environmental influences on appetite. What basic principles can be uncovered?

Figure 2 illustrates how appetite is shaped by the principles of biological regulation and environmental adaptation. All living organisms require food (a nutrition supply) for growth and maintenance of tissues. This supply is achieved through eating. The expression of this behaviour is controlled according to the state of the biological system. A complex system of signals operates to ensure the appropriate direction and quality of this (eating) behaviour. The extension of Claude Bernard's principle of homeostasis to include behaviour is often referred to as the behavioural regulation of internal states (Richter, 1943). However, the expression of behaviour is also subject to environmental demands, and behaviour is therefore adapted in the face of particular circumstances.

In the case of human appetite, attention must be given to the conscious and deliberate (external) control over behaviour. Human beings can decide to alter their own behaviour in order to meet particular objectives, for example, a display of moral conviction (political hunger strike) or a demonstration of aesthetic achievement (dieting). In both of these examples, eating is curtailed with an ensuing interruption of the nutritional supply. Regulatory mechanisms will tend to oppose this undersupply and generate a drive to eat. In the technically advanced cultures of Europe and North America, the nutritional supply may be adjusted in another way. The existence of an abundant supply of palatable, energy-dense food promotes overconsumption. This in turn, in an interaction with genetic susceptibility, leads to an increase in fat deposition (Bouchard, 1985). However, an oversupply of calories leading to the deposition of body fat does not generate a biological drive to undereat. Hence, the operation of the regulatory system is not symmetrical:

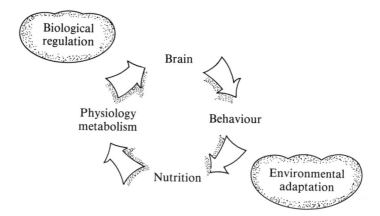

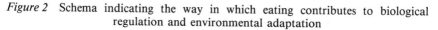

Figure 2 Schema indicating the way in which eating contributes to biological regulation and environmental adaptation

510

there is a strong defence against undernutrition and only weak response to the effects of overnutrition.

These principles appear to tell us that appetite is actively stimulated whenever there is any reduction in food intake and a threat to bodily integrity. However, the appetite control system can passively accept an excess of food (or at least of some types of foods) which in turn can lead to a positive energy balance. The existence of these principles may help to explain the increasing prevalence of obesity in many affluent cultures in the final decade of the twentieth century.

Because the control of appetite is so fundamental to the existence of all living organisms, we can expect that the principles governing this control will have obvious functional value. Do the principles make sense? For human beings it can be supposed that during most of the tens of thousands of years of human evolution the biggest problem facing humankind was the scarcity of food (Boyd Eaton & Konner, 1985). Hence, powerful mechanisms will have developed to signal this deficit and to generate an appropriate motivational response. However, the existence of an abundance of food, highly palatable and readily available, is a very recent development in evolutionary terms. Accordingly, it is unlikely that evolutionary pressure has ever led to the development of mechanisms to prevent overconsumption. Indeed, the presence in the body of depots of adipose tissue (fat) ensures that any excessive intake of calories can be readily accommodated. Consequently, we should not necessarily expect to find a simple symmetrical relationship between appetite control and body weight regulation. This asymmetry may help us to understand the way in which appetite is deregulated in the eating and weight disorders.

APPETITE AS THE OUTPUT OF A BIOPSYCHOLOGICAL SYSTEM

One useful strategy for understanding the variety of factors that influence the expression of appetite is to consider the operation of a biopsychological system. This system incorporates the interactions between physiology and the environment set out in Figure 1, and includes the principles of regulation described in Figure 2. A simple outline of the biopsychological system for appetite control is sketched out in Figure 3. This conceptualization draws attention to the interrelationships between particular spheres of interest including the external environment (cultural and physical), the behavioural act of eating (quantitative and qualitative aspects), processes of ingestion and assimilation of foods, the storage and utilization of energy, brain mechanisms implicated in the control system, and mediating subjective states such as attributions and cognitions (Blundell & Hill, 1986).

The essence of the biopsychological system is that it functions in an integrated fashion. That is, an adjustment to any particular component (say, energy intake) will lead to consequences elsewhere (for example, in energy

511

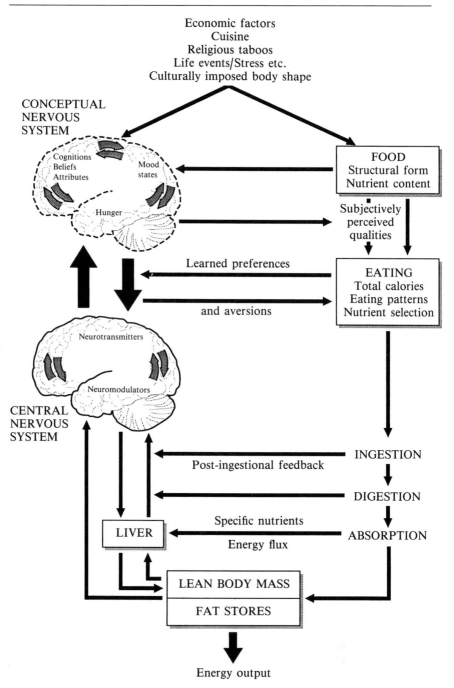

Figure 3 Conceptualization of certain major components involved in the biopsychological system underlying the expression of appetite

output). This is why dieting behaviour (self-enforced restriction of food intake) is likely to be self-defeating, because the suppression of energy consumed results in a fall in the rate at which the body utilizes energy. Energy balance tends to be preserved. The fact that eating behaviour is one component built into a biopsychological system containing many self-regulating mechanisms indicates how difficult it is to adjust eating through volitional action or by behaviour modification procedures. Although some adjustment can be made, the forces within the system exert a pressure to keep behaviour in harmony with biological actions. The force can be called motivation. One aspect of this motivation which is expressed through subjective feelings is hunger.

THE IDENTIFICATION OF HUNGER

How do we describe the experience of hunger as it occurs in everyday life? The first serious attempt to investigate this issue was made by giving people a questionnaire to complete which asked about physical sensations in a number of bodily areas, moods, urges to eat and preoccupation with thoughts of food (Monello & Mayer, 1967). The questionnaire was completed before and after eating. It was found that the observation, "I feel hungry", is typically based on the perception of bodily feelings which at times may be very strong. Gastric sensations, a hollow feeling or stomach rumbling, are frequent indicators of hunger, although people also report sensations in the mouth, throat, and head. These accompany more diffuse feelings of restlessness and excitability as well as an urge to eat. In one celebrated project known as the Minnesota experiment, a group of volunteers were placed on a semi-starvation diet for six months (Keys, Brozek, Henschel, Mickelsen, & Taylor, 1950). Their experience of hunger was extreme. Nearly two-thirds reported feeling hungry all the time and a similar proportion experienced physical discomfort due to hunger. Subjects experienced a marked increase in what was referred to as "hunger pain". For some, this pain, vaguely localized in the abdomen, was of mild discomfort. For others, it was intensely painful.

Eating changes both the pattern of physical sensations and the accompanying emotional feelings, with unpleasant and aversive sensations being replaced by more pleasant ones. So for example, an aching stomach becomes relaxed and the feeling of excitement and irritability replaced by one of contentment.

Despite a great deal of individual variability in the perception of these sensations, hunger can be associated with clear symptoms. And it is partly through reference to these that people can make judgements about the intensity of their hunger experience. The measurement of hunger, desire to eat, or urge to eat, is most commonly conducted using fixed-point or visual analogue scales. Respectively, these require the subject to choose a number from a scale or point on a line that corresponds to their current state of hunger. Careful presentation of these scales to people who understand what is being asked of them yields meaningful information. Most importantly, quantifying the subjective experience of hunger makes it a state that is amenable to scientific investigation. Consequently, hunger can be described qualitatively in terms of the sensations with which it is associated and can also be measured quantitatively. This means that the significance of hunger can be understood through its structure and by its intensity.

If hunger is the feeling that reminds us to seek food, then the consumption of food is the action that diminishes hunger and keeps it suppressed for a certain period of time, perhaps until the next meal or snack. The capacity of food to reduce the experience of hunger is called satiating power or satiating efficiency (Kissileff, 1984). This power is achieved by certain properties of the food itself engaging with various physiological and biochemical mechanisms within the body that are concerned with the processing of food once it has been ingested. The satiating power of food therefore results from a variety of biological processes and is an important factor in the control of hunger. Some foods have a greater capacity to maintain suppression over hunger than other foods.

How is hunger related to the overall control of human appetite and food consumption? The feeling of hunger is an important component in determining what we eat, how much we eat, and when we eat. However, hunger must also be seen within the context of social and physiological variables. Eating patterns are maintained by enduring habits, attitudes, and opinions about the value and suitability of foods and an overall liking for them. These factors, derived from the cultural ethos, largely determine the range of foods that will be consumed and sometimes the timing of consumption. The intensity of hunger experienced may also be determined, in part, by the culturally approved appropriateness of this feeling. However, normal hunger is more importantly associated with the events surrounding meals (so-called periprandial circumstances) and the periods between meals. Therefore, hunger can be considered to arise from an interaction between the physiological requirement of the body for food (or particular nutrients) and the capacity of food to satisfy these requirements. It follows that hunger will be successively stimulated and suppressed, giving rise to a diurnal rhythm. This rhythm, and the relationship between hunger and eating, may be altered by certain other social factors (e.g., distressing psychological events) or interrupted by some disease states.

HUNGER AND THE SATIETY CASCADE

When food consumption reduces hunger and inhibits further eating, two processes are involved. For technical precision and conceptual clarity it is useful to describe the distinction between "satiation" and "satiety". Both terms may be assigned workable operational definitions (i.e., definitions that depend on measurable events). Satiation can be regarded as the process that develops during the course of eating and that eventually brings a period of eating to an end. Accordingly, satiation can be defined in terms of the measured size of the eating episode (volume or weight of food, or energy value). Hunger declines as satiation develops and usually reaches its lowest point at the end of a meal. Satiety is defined as the state of inhibition of further eating which follows at the end of an eating episode and which arises from the consequences of food ingestion. The intensity of satiety can be measured by the duration of time elapsing until eating is recommenced, or by the amount consumed at the next meal. The strength of satiety is also measured by the duration of the suppression of hunger. As satiety weakens so hunger is restored.

In the view of some researchers, satiation and satiety can be referred to as within-meal satiety and between-meal satiety respectively (Van Itallie & Vanderweele, 1981). What mechanisms are responsible for these processes? It is clear that the mechanisms involved in reducing hunger and in continuing this suppression range from those that occur when food is initially sensed, to the effects of metabolites on bodily tissues following the digestion and absorption of food (across the wall of the intestine and into the blood stream). By definition, satiety is not an instantaneous event but occurs over a considerable time period. It is therefore useful to distinguish different phases of satiety that can be associated with different mechanisms. This concept is illustrated in Figure 4. Four mediating processes are identified: sensory,

MEDIATING PROCESSES

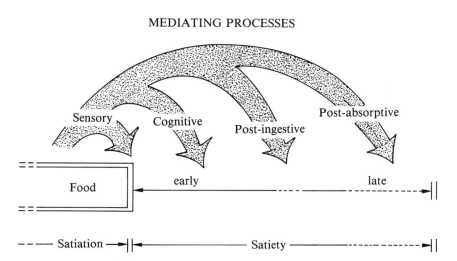

Figure 4 The satiety cascade. This diagram represents the mediating processes, arising from food consumption, which influence the feeling of hunger and the expression of appetite. One important aspect of this conceptualization is the distinction between satiation and satiety

cognitive, post-ingestive, and post-absorptive. These maintain inhibition over hunger (and eating) during the early and late phases of satiety. Sensory effects are generated through the smell, taste, temperature, and texture of food, and it is likely that these factors inhibit eating in the very short term (e.g., Rolls, Rowe, & Rolls, 1982). Cognitive effects represent the beliefs held about the properties of foods and these factors may help inhibit hunger in the short term. The category identified as post-ingestive processes includes a number of possible actions including gastric distension and rate of gastric emptying, the release of hormones such as cholecystokinin, and the stimulation of certain receptors along the gastro-intestinal tract (Mei, 1985). The post-absorptive phase of satiety includes those mechanisms arising from the action of metabolites after absorption across the intestine and into the blood stream. This category includes the action of chemicals such as glucose and amino acids, which may act directly on the brain after crossing the blood–brain barrier or which may influence the brain indirectly via neural inputs following stimulation of peripheral chemoreceptors. The most important suppression and subsequent control of hunger is brought about by post-ingestive and post-absorptive mediating processes.

CONDITIONED HUNGER

It should be kept in mind that the biopsychological system for appetite control has the capacity to learn. That is, it has the capacity to form associations between the sensory and post-absorptive characteristics of foods (e.g., Booth, 1977). This means that it will be useful to distinguish between the unconditioned effects of foods, that is, those in which the natural biological consequences of food processing are reflected upon satiety, and the conditioned effects that come into play due to the links between sensory aspects of food (particularly those that are tasted) and later metabolic effects generated by the same food. The sensory characteristics (or cues) therefore come to predict the impact that the food will later exert. Consequently, these cues can suppress hunger according to their relationship with subsequent physiological events.

This mechanism has much in common with the cue-consequence learning used to account for taste aversions (Garcia, Hankins, & Rusiniak, 1974). However, the potency of this mechanism depends on the stability and reliability of the relationship between tastes (sensory cues) and physiological effects (metabolic consequences) of food. When there is distortion or random variation between sensory characteristics and nutritional properties, then the conditioned control of hunger is weakened or lost. Learned hunger is therefore not an important factor when the food supply contains many foods with identical tastes but differing metabolic properties.

IS EATING CAUSED BY HUNGER?

An answer to this question can begin by considering whether hunger is a necessary or a sufficient condition for eating to occur. Because people may deliberately prevent themselves from eating in spite of hunger (fasting for moral or political conviction), hunger is not a sufficient condition. Occasions can also be imagined where a person would eat if food were particularly tempting, but where no hunger was being experienced. Therefore, it appears that hunger is neither a sufficient nor a necessary condition for eating. That is, the relationship between hunger and eating is not based on biological inevitability. However, under many circumstances there is a close relationship between the pattern of food intake and the rhythmic oscillation of hunger. Indeed, the results of many experimental studies confirm the strong relationship between the intensity of experienced hunger sensations and the amount of food consumed (e.g., De Castro & Elmore, 1988). For example, when hunger and eating have been monitored continually it has been reported that hunger ratings at the start of each hour were correlated with reported intake in the hour following each hunger rating (Mattes, 1989). The strong correlations found in almost all studies indicate that in many circumstances the measured intensity of hunger reliably predicts the amount of food that will be consumed. This fact has led to the proposal that there is a causal connection between hunger and the size of a following meal.

These observations are sufficiently strong and reliable to allow us to act as if hunger were a cause of eating. In actuality, it is probably the case that common physiological mechanisms induce changes both in hunger and in the eating response. Therefore, we can consider an appetite control system in which hunger, eating, and physiological mechanisms (of the satiety cascade) are coupled together. However, the coupling is not perfect, and there will be circumstances where, for example, a physiological treatment will change eating but not hunger. In other words, uncoupling can occur. This may take place under certain conditions of fasting or in disordered eating, and instances such as this can provide useful information about the role of hunger in the overall control of appetite.

NUTRITION, APPETITE, AND THE SATIETY CASCADE

The concept of the satiety cascade (Figure 4) implies that foods of varying nutritional composition will have different effects on the mediating processes and will therefore exert differing effects on satiation and satiety. There is considerable interest, for example, in whether the macronutrients (protein, fat, and carbohydrate) differ in their satiating efficiency or capacity to reduce hunger.

A procedure widely used to assess the action of food on satiety is the preload strategy. Precisely prepared foods (identical in taste and appearance but varying in energy and/or nutrient composition) can be consumed in the preload. Effects of consumption are then measured over varying periods by ratings of hunger and other sensations, food check-lists, accurately monitored test meals and, if necessary, food diaries. The procedure sounds simple, but the conduct of such experiments needs to be governed by a strong methodology to prevent incidental features from interfering with the monitoring process. For example, it is important to prevent the occurrence of any appetite-modulating stimuli during the interval between preload and test meal. Such interruption would obviously contaminate the measurement of the satiating efficiency of the preload.

Using the preload strategy and related procedures, it is possible to assess the satiating power of a wide variety of foods varying in nutrient composition (Blundell, Rogers, & Hill, 1988). One issue of clinical and theoretical interest is the comparative effect of carbohydrate and fat on appetite. It is clear that following consumption of carbohydrates, the digested carbohydrate influences a number of mechanisms involved in satiety. These include peripheral detectors and central nervous system monitoring of glucose. These mechanisms collectively form the basis of the energostatic control of feeding (Booth, 1972), or what has been called the caloric control of satiety (Blundell & Rogers, 1991). Although sweet carbohydrates induce some positive feedback for eating through stimulating sweet taste receptors in the mouth, this should be countered by the potent inhibitory action of the post-ingestive and post-absorptive mechanisms. Appropriate experiments should demonstrate whether or not this is the case.

One clear finding from these studies is that carbohydrates are efficient appetite suppressants. That is, they contribute markedly to the satiating efficiency of food and exert a potent effect on satiety (e.g., Rogers, Carlyle, Hill, & Blundell, 1988). A variety of carbohydrates, including glucose, fructose, sucrose, and maltodextrins, have rather similar effects when given in a preload. They suppress later energy intake by an amount roughly equivalent to their caloric value, although the time course of the suppressive action may vary a little according to the rate at which the carbohydrate loads are metabolized.

In contrast, only a few studies have systematically investigated the extent to which dietary fat contributes to the satiating power of food. However, there is a widespread belief that high-fat diets are responsible for an elevated energy intake that in turn leads to weight gain through fat deposition. For example, researchers have shown that subjects undereat when forced to eat low-fat foods for three weeks, and overeat (relative to a balanced diet) when obliged to consume from an assortment of high-fat foods (e.g., Lissner, Levitsky, Strupp, Kackwarf, & Roe, 1987). These findings suggest that fat stimulates caloric intake. It is known that the fat content of food alters texture and palatability and may increase food acceptability. This factor, coupled with the high-energy density of fat, probably facilitates dietary excess within a meal or snack (by passive overconsumption). In addition, when subjects (lean or obese) consume large amounts of fat from a range of high-fat foods, this excessively large intake exerts only a weak braking action on subsequent eating (Blundell, Cotton, Lawton, & Burley, 1992). In other words, fat has a disproportionately weak action on satiety. Taken together, these findings show why diets high in fat can promote weight gain and lead to obesity. In addition, this relationship between nutrition and the expression of appetite confirms that the biopsychological system has only a weak defence against overconsumption (Figure 2).

MOTIVATION: ORDER AND DISORDER

Consideration of the relationship between nutrition and appetite illustrates clearly the interactive processes underlying the expression of the motivation to eat. The forces that impel and guide people to eat do not arise entirely internally, but are the result of mechanisms "under the skin" acting in concert with events in the environment. One of the most prominent of these environmental events is the type of food that people have available. In turn, this food has sensory and nutritional components. The sensory aspects of food (taste, smell, texture, mouth-feel) contribute to the perceived palatability (liking) of food, and this represents a hedonic quality. Together, the hedonic and nutritional components of food influence the pattern of the motivation to eat.

Of course, the emerging pattern of motivation arises from the processing of food by physiological and metabolic actions and by the events represented in the satiety cascade (Figure 4). The pattern of motivation takes the form of discrete episodes of behaviour (meals, snacks, etc.) along with oscillations in the strength of subjectively perceived hunger. As noted earlier, hunger is usually closely related to eating events. Consequently, there is a synchrony between the profile of hunger and the pattern of eating behaviour. In turn, this pattern of events is synchronized with peripheral physiological actions concerned with the handling of food in the body. A third level of events involves neural mechanisms in the brain that reflect physiological and behavioural happenings. It follows that the orderly expression of motivation involves a synchrony between the behavioural (and subjective) pattern, peripheral physiological events, and brain mechanisms (see Blundell, 1991, for a detailed account).

This well-synchronized control of motivation (expression of appetite) is an important factor in the maintenance of general health. One aspect of this synchrony involves the modulation of hunger in accordance with biological needs and environmental demands. In societies where food is plentiful, the relatively mild experience of hunger plays a biologically useful role in the orderly regulation of eating patterns. When food is scarce, however, the power of hunger can drive people to desperate deeds.

In addition, there are some clinical conditions that appear to reflect some disorder in the control of motivation. This occurs, for example, in extreme forms of dieting, periods of bingeing and fasting, and in the condition of bulimia nervosa (which often involves self-induced vomiting after food ingestion). These behavioural patterns create a de-synchrony among the behavioural, physiological, and neural levels. In addition, there is a disorderly relationship between the profile of hunger and the pattern of eating (Blundell & Hill, 1990). This labile or unregulated hunger reflects a pathology of appetite.

The view of appetite as the output of a biopsychological system indicates how the motivation to eat plays a natural role in maintaining the well-being and biological functioning of human beings (and animals). The system also indicates the role of hunger and its relationship to the expression of appetite. Given the complexity of the system, we should expect to find that appetite is influenced by many factors. This is certainly the case, but the potential complexity of these issues should not prevent us from comprehending the principles that regulate the form of this motivation.

FURTHER READING

Friedman, M. I., Tordoff, M. G., & Kare, M. R. (1991). *Appetite and nutrition*. New York: Marcel Dekker.

Hill, A. J., & Blundell, J. E. (1993). A practical guide to the measurement of eating behaviour and food intake. *International Journal of Obesity*.

LeMagnen, J. (1988). *Hunger*. Cambridge: Cambridge University Press.

Loge, A. W. (1991). *The psychology of eating and drinking* (2nd edn). New York: Freeman.

Shepherd, R. (1989). *Handbook of the psychophysiology of human eating*. Chichester: Wiley.

REFERENCES

Blundell, J. E. (1979). Hunger, appetite and satiety: Constructs in search of identities. In M. Turner (Ed.) *Nutrition and lifestyles* (pp. 21–42). London: Applied Science.

Blundell, J. E. (1981). Deep and surface structures: A qualitative approach to feeding. In L. A. Cioffi, W. P. T. James, & T. Van Itallie (Eds) *The body weight regulatory system: Normal and disturbed mechanisms* (pp. 73–82). New York: Raven.

Blundell, J. E. (1984). Serotonin and appetite. *Neuropharmacology, 23*, 1537–1551.

Blundell, J. E. (1991). Pharmacological approaches to appetite suppression. *Trends in Pharmacological Sciences, 12*, 147–157.

Blundell, J. E., & Hill, A. J. (1986). Biopsychological interactions underlying the study and treatment of obesity. In M. J. Christie & P. G. Mellet (Eds) *The psychosomatic approach: Contemporary practice of whole person care* (pp. 115–138). Chichester: Wiley.

Blundell, J. E., & Hill, A. J. (1990). Serotonin, eating disorders and the satiety cascade. In G. B. Cassano & H. S. Akiskal (Eds) *Serotonin-system-related syndromes (SRS): Psychopathological and therapeutic links* (pp. 125–129). London: Royal Society of Medicine.

Blundell, J. E., & Rogers, P. J. (1991). Hunger, hedonics and the control of satiation and satiety. In M. I. Friedman, M. G. Tordoff, & M. R. Kare (Eds) *Appetite and nutrition* (pp. 127–148). New York: Marcel Dekker.

Blundell, J. E., Rogers, P. J., & Hill, A. J. (1988). Uncoupling sweetness and calories: Methodological aspects of laboratory studies on appetite control. *Appetite, 11* (suppl. 1), 54–61.

Blundell, J. E., Cotton, J. R., Lawton, C. L., & Burley, V. J. (1992). Dietary fat and appetite control: Weak effects on satiation (within meals) and satiety (between meals). In D. J. Mela (Ed.) *Dietary fats: Determinants of preference, selection and consumption* (pp. 79–103). London: Elsevier.

Booth, D. A. (1972). Postabsorptively induced suppression of appetite and the energostatic control of feeding. *Physiology and Behavior, 9*, 199–202.

Booth, D. A. (1977). Satiety and appetite are conditioned reactions. *Psychosomatic Medicine, 39*, 76–81.

Bouchard, C. (1985). Inheritance of fat distribution and adipose tissue metabolism. In J. Vague, P. Bjorntorp, B. Guy-Grand, M. Rebuffe-Scrive, & P. Vague (Eds) *Metabolic complications of human obesities* (pp. 87–96). Amsterdam: Excerpta Medica.

Boyd Eaton, F., & Konner, M. (1985). Paleolithic nutrition: A consideration of its nature and current implications. *New England Journal of Medicine, 312*, 283–289.

De Castro, J. M., & Elmore, D. K. (1988). Subjective hunger relationships with meal patterns in the spontaneous feeding behavior of humans: Evidence for a causal connection. *Physiology and Behavior, 43*, 159–165.

Garcia, J., Hankins, W. G., & Rusiniak, K. W. (1974). Behavioral regulation of the milieu interne in man and rat. *Science, 185*, 24–31.

Keys, A., Brozek, J., Henschel, A., Mickelsen, O., & Taylor, H. L. (1950). *The biology of human starvation* (vol. 2). Minneapolis, MN: University of Minnesota Press.

Kissileff, H. R. (1984). Satiating efficiency and a strategy for conducting food loading experiments. *Neuroscience and Biobehavioral Reviews, 8*, 129–135.

Lissner, L., Levitsky, D. A., Strupp, B. J., Kackwarf, H., & Roe, D. A. (1987). Dietary fat and the regulation of energy intake in human subjects. *American Journal of Clinical Nutrition, 46*, 886–892.

Mattes, R. (1989). Hunger ratings are not a valid proxy measure of reported food intake in humans. *Appetite, 15*, 103–113.

Mei, N. (1985). Intestinal chemosensitivity. *Physiology Reviews, 65*, 211–237.

Monello, L. F., & Mayer, J. (1967). Hunger and satiety sensations in men, women, boys and girls. *American Journal of Clinical Nutrition, 20*, 253–261.

Reynolds, V. (1976). *The biology of human action*. San Francisco, CA: Freeman.

Richter, C. P. (1943). Total self-regulatory functions in animals and human beings. *Harvey Lecture Series, 38*, 63–103.

Rogers, P. J., Carlyle, J., Hill, A. J., & Blundell, J. E. (1988). Uncoupling sweetness and calories: Comparison of the effect of glucose and three intense sweeteners on hunger and food intake. *Physiology and Behavior, 43*, 547–552.

Rolls, B. J., Rowe, E. A., & Rolls, E. (1982). How sensory properties of foods affect human feeding behavior. *Physiology and Behavior, 29*, 409–417.

Royce, J. R. (1963). Factors as theoretical constructs. *American Psychologist, 18*, 522–528.

Van Itallie, T. B., & Vanderweele, D. A. (1981). The phenomenon of satiety. In P. Bjorntorp, M. Cairella, & A. N. Howard (Eds) *Recent advances in obesity research* (vol. 3, pp. 278–289). London: Libbey.

6.3

SOCIAL MOTIVATION

Russell G. Geen
University of Missouri, USA

Motivation refers, in a general sense, to processes involved in the initiation, direction, and energization of individual behaviour. The term *social motivation* refers to the activation of these processes by situations in which other people are in close contact with the individual. It is usually assumed that the social situation does not provide specific cues for the behaviour of the individual. Such topics as direct social influence, persuasion, conformity, and social reinforcement are not, therefore, considered to be part of social motivation.

HISTORICAL BACKGROUND

The study of social motivation was begun by Triplett (1898), who observed that sport bicyclists pedalled with greater speed when they rode in the company of other cyclists than they did when riding alone. Among possible causes for this effect, Triplett suggested that "another can . . . be the means of releasing or freeing nervous energy for [the individual] that he cannot of himself release" (p. 516). In the first experimental study of this "dynamogenic" phenomenon, Triplett showed that subjects performed a reel-cranking task more rapidly when accompanied by another person performing the same task than they had done in isolation. This study introduced to psychology the phenomenon of *social facilitation* of performance, in which the presence of others produces an increase in individual motivation. Triplett studied situations in which the other persons present performed a task in concert with the individual; these became known as *coaction* settings. In 1904 Meumann reported the first study in which social facilitation was achieved by a passive *audience* that merely observed the individual perform (Cottrell, 1972).

Several years later, Ringelmann reported a series of studies (which had actually been conducted prior to Triplett's research) in which the presence of others appeared to lead to a loss in motivation (Kravitz & Martin, 1986). Ringelmann showed that when people are added to a group engaged in a physical task like rope-pulling, the amount of force exerted per person decreases as the size of the group increases. Although Ringelmann thought that this effect was due chiefly to loss of coordination as the group grew in size, he conceded that loss of motivation could also be involved.

The earliest studies in social motivation, therefore, showed that under some conditions the presence of others leads to motivational gains whereas under other conditions it produces motivational decrements. Interest in motivational losses in social settings – the so-called "Ringelmann effect" – declined sharply in the decades immediately following the original reports, but investigations of social facilitation, involving both the coaction and audience paradigms, were conducted sporadically during that period. The findings from these studies were mixed, however, and tended to show that the presence of audiences or coactors facilitated performance or had the opposite effect – what I shall designate as *social inhibition* of performance – about equally often. Research was seriously hampered by a lack of theoretical formulations that could explain these contradictory effects with a single set of premises.

SOCIAL FACILITATION

The modern era of research on social facilitation began with a major theoretical paper by Zajonc (1965). Attempting to explain the mixed evidence from previous studies, Zajonc proposed that (1) the presence of others elicits a drive-like state of arousal, (2) drive multiplies with habit strength for all responses in a situation, increasing the probability of a dominant response relative to a subordinate one, and (3) the dominant response is more likely to be the correct one on easy tasks than on difficult ones. From this, Zajonc concluded that the presence of others leads to social facilitation of performance on easy or overlearned tasks, but to social inhibition of performance on difficult ones. This finding had been reported earlier by Allport (1924) but not explained in theoretical terms.

The decade following the appearance of Zajonc's paper yielded numerous experimental investigations of social facilitation, most of them animated by Zajonc's arguments. Some sought to test his viewpoint and others to challenge it with alternative explanations. In 1977 Geen and Gange reviewed this literature and concluded that at that time the most parsimonious explanation for both social facilitation and social inhibition was the drive-theoretical viewpoint. In the years since that review the situation has changed; such a confident conclusion of the primacy of drive theory is no longer warranted.

To understand the changes that have come about in conceptualizations of social facilitation, it is necessary to note that theoretical explanations have generally involved two sequential steps. The first is the impact of the presence of others on the individual, which places the individual in a state that mediates subsequent behaviour. The second is a process activated by that state that produces facilitation or inhibition of behaviour. Figure 1 illustrates these two processes as they were described by drive theorists: the presence of others elicits drive, which energizes responses. The outcome of this energization process is either an increment or a decrement in performance, depending

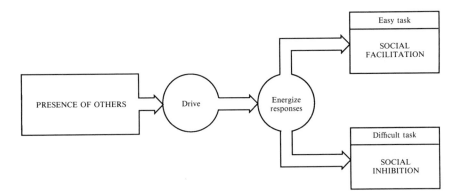

Figure 1 Schematic representation of drive theory of social facilitation. Rectangles containing terms in upper-case letters represent independent and dependent variables, respectively. Units labelled in upper-and-lower case letters represent hypothetical intervening variables. Of these, circles represent the two stages in the process described in the text

on task difficulty. Alternatives to the drive theoretical approach have involved departures from that theory at each of the two steps.

AROUSING EFFECTS OF SOCIAL PRESENCE

Evaluation apprehension

An early criticism of Zajonc's position concerned the nature of the social presence required for increased drive. Whereas Zajonc (1965) had concluded that the mere presence of others is sufficient to have this effect on the individual, certain investigators argued that the others must be regarded by the individual as potential judges and critics. The immediate precursor of increased drive is therefore thought to be anxiety or *evaluation apprehension*. For example, Cottrell and his associates (Cottrell, Wack, Sekerak, & Rittle, 1968) found that social facilitation of performance in the presence of others did not occur when the others were inattentive and unaware of what the individual was doing. Other studies have shown that audiences having a high social status exert a greater impact than audiences of lower status (e.g., Henchy & Glass, 1968), suggesting that the former may elicit stronger evaluation apprehension than the latter. In a study supporting this conclusion, Seta, Crisson, Seta, and Wang (1989) showed that the status of other persons present plays a role in generating arousal. Whereas the addition of high-status persons to an observing group leads to increased arousal in the observed individual, the addition of lower-status persons may actually reduce arousal by diminishing the overall level of anxiety over being evaluated.

Distraction/conflict

An alternative to both the mere presence and evaluation apprehension hypotheses is the idea that the presence of others distracts the individual from the task and thereby engenders response conflict. This conflict, in turn, causes increased arousal or drive. In a number of studies, Baron and his associates (e.g., Baron, Moore, & Sanders, 1978) have shown both that predicted social facilitation effects occur in audience settings and that the subjects in such settings are distracted by the observers. In many of these studies, it has been difficult to disentangle the effects of distraction from those of social facilitation, but in one experiment the two effects were successfully separated operationally. The results of this study (Groff, Baron, & Moore, 1983) clearly support the distraction/conflict hypothesis.

Uncertainty and social monitoring

In speculating on possible reasons that the "mere presence" of others generates increased arousal, Zajonc (1980) elaborated upon his earlier position by suggesting that socially generated drive may be the product of *uncertainty*. The presence of others implies the possibility of action on their part, and that the individual must always be alert to possible changes in the environment caused by the behaviour of others. Often such actions cannot be anticipated and therefore may elicit uncertainty.

Guerin and Innes (1982) have extended Zajonc's analysis to the process of *social monitoring*. Because others have the potential to create uncertainty by their presence, the individual must observe them periodically in an attempt to predict their actions. It is assumed that others who are present elicit less arousal when they can be observed and monitored than when they cannot. It is further predicted that the greatest amount of uncertainty is caused by others when they are nearby, attending to the individual, and outside the latter's range of monitoring. Guerin (1986) performed a meta-analysis of all studies in which the "mere presence" of others led to increased arousal (i.e., in which possible effects of evaluation apprehension were controlled). He concluded that in every such study the effects of the presence of others were attributable to either uncertainty or the absence of ability to monitor. In some the behaviour of the others was unpredictable whereas in others the others' behaviour was predictable but could not be monitored.

All of the proposed antecedents of socially induced arousal – evaluation apprehension, distraction-induced conflict, and uncertainty – have some empirical support. As has already been noted, separating the effects of evaluation apprehension from those of distraction has often been difficult. In the same way, a clear line between evaluation apprehension and uncertainty is difficult to draw: the person who is not being monitored may, without the individual's being able to discern, be evaluating the individual's performance.

ATTENTIONAL EFFECTS OF SOCIAL PRESENCE

Cognitive overload

Later formulations of social facilitation departed from the once-dominant view that drive constitutes the major intervening variable in the process. In an extension of his distraction/conflict model, Baron (1986) argued that the distraction from a task caused by being observed by others results in stimulus overload. This is a departure from the previously held idea that distraction engenders drive, because the consequences of cognitive overload are different from those of increased drive. Whereas drive energizes all responses in a situation (manifesting the second of the two steps in the social facilitation process outlined above), cognitive overload produces selectivity and narrowing of attention (Figure 2).

More specifically, Baron proposed that attentional conflict produced by distraction places demands on the person that may exceed the person's

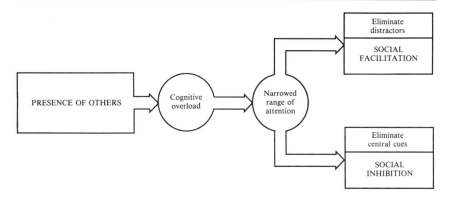

Figure 2 Schematic representation of cognitive overload theory of social facilitation. See legend to Figure 1 for explanation

capacity for attention. It is assumed that every person has a finite attentional capacity, and that as demands arise, the smaller is the spare capacity left over for such activities as problem solving. One result of overload is increased effort to pay attention, which can produce a momentary increase in arousal. The significance of this arousal does not lie in its energizing task-related responses, however, as drive theory would hold. Instead, it is a concomitant of effortful attention. The main functional response to cognitive overload is a narrowing of attention to a relatively narrow range of central cues, thereby reducing the load on the attentional system. Reduction in the range of cue utilization under such conditions has been described by several investigators (e.g., Easterbrook, 1959; Geen, 1980).

This reduction in the range of stimuli to which the person attends has effects on the performance of simple and complex tasks similar to those previously attributed to increased drive. Simple tasks require attention to a relatively small number of central cues, whereas complex tasks demand attention to a wide range of cues. Stimulus overload produces a narrowing in the range of cue utilization for both simple and complex tasks. When the task is simple, this narrowing terminates attention to irrelevant distractors, but when the task is complex, the same process leads to the elimination of important task-related information.

Only a few studies have examined the role of being observed on attentional processes. Bruning, Capage, Kozuh, Young, and Young (1968) found that being observed by the experimenter was associated with better performance by subjects who had been given additional irrelevant (and hence potentially distracting) information about their task, relative to the performance of subjects who were not observed. In addition, being observed was harmful to subjects given additional relevant information. Both findings suggest that being observed led subjects to be less influenced by the additional information than were non-observed subjects. This is what would be expected if being observed produced a narrowing of attention to central task cues. Geen (1976) replicated the results of Bruning et al. (1968) and found in addition that individual differences in test anxiety moderated the narrowing of cue utilization. This finding suggests that the cognitive overload produced by observation may be exacerbated when evaluation apprehension is also present.

Automatic and controlled processing

An approach to social facilitation and inhibition that is similar to the foregoing has been proposed by Manstead and Semin (1980), who emphasize the difference between automatic and controlled processing of information. Automatic processing develops with increasing familiarity with the task and a concomitant decreasing need for sustained attention. Once performance has become routine, attention is no longer required. Controlled processing is used when performance has not become routine and requires continuous attention to task demands. It follows from this that automatic processing is not limited by attentional capacity, whereas controlled processing is. Manstead and Semin (1980) propose that performance on novel or complex tasks, which require considerable controlled processing, is impaired by the presence of others, who make competing demands on attention. Performance on easy, familiar, or overlearned tasks, which are processed automatically, is not affected by such demands. Instead, the presence of others may prompt a focus of attention on otherwise ignored behavioural sequences and thereby bring about improved performance.

SELF-PRESENTATIONAL CONCERNS AND SOCIAL FACILITATION

The presence of others has effects on the individual that go beyond both arousal and cognitive overload by engaging and activating a need to present a desired or idealized self-image to others. Self-presentation motives have been shown to play a role in several studies. The findings of these studies are sometimes cited as evidence against the drive theoretical explanation of social facilitation, and it is true that they often report effects that cannot be accounted for by that approach. For example, Bond (1982) designed an experiment in which drive theory and self-presentation theory made directly opposite predictions and found that the latter accounted for the social facilitation effect. Other studies (reported below), while being less directly crucial in comparing the two theories, have adduced evidence that under some conditions the self-presentation theory can explain results that are inexplicable in terms of drive theory. Three approaches to social facilitation that employ the concepts of self-presentation have been proposed.

Self-awareness

Carver and Scheier (1981) have proposed that the effect of the presence of others increases the individual's sense of self-awareness, making him or her more cognizant of not only personal behaviour but also an ideal standard of performance for the task at hand. In keeping with their general theory of behaviour, in which action is generated to reduce or eliminate discrepancies between one's actual level of performance and a standard, Carver and Scheier propose further that the decision to undertake such action depends on the perceived probability of successful matching-to-standard. When the task is easy, and the probability of successfully matching the ideal is high, the person proceeds to complete the task; in this case, the presence of others, by bringing the real-ideal discrepancy into focus, therefore facilitates performance. However, when the task is difficult, the person is more likely to perceive the probability of success as too low and to give up. The presence of others, therefore, causes effort, and subsequent task performance, to cease or to become minimal (Figure 3).

Impression management

Another self-presentational approach to social facilitation is based on the premise that people strive to present the best possible appearance to others so that they may make a favourable impression. Observers or co-actors may not only motivate individuals to work hard at tasks but also exacerbate the person's sense of embarrassment when performance leads to failure. Such

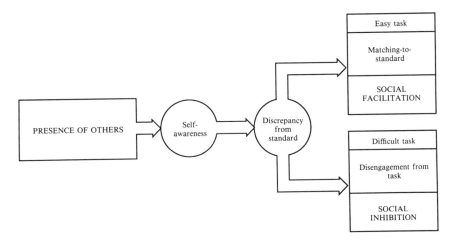

Figure 3 Schematic representation of self-awareness theory of social facilitation. See legend to Figure 1 for explanation

failure is less likely when the task is easy than when it is hard, so that the increased motivation may be sufficient to produce performance of high quality. Difficult tasks often result in failure, however, at least at the outset. Embarrassment evoked by such failure may cause stress and cognitive interference that disrupts subsequent performance. The previously cited study by Bond (1982) was conducted in the context of this approach.

Thus evaluation apprehension, which was earlier shown to be an antecedent of arousal, also plays an important role in presentation of the self. Baumeister (1982) makes this point in asserting that the desire to make a good impression is a fundamental motive and that fear of negative evaluation arises whenever the person has some concern over being able to present the self adequately.

Consistent with this line of reasoning, several studies have shown that when the person is subjected to an experience of failure just before performing a task (which should increase feelings of evaluation anxiety), subsequent performance before observers is poorer than it is when no prior failure is experienced (e.g., Seta & Hassan, 1980). Geen (1979) obtained similar findings among observed subjects who had first been exposed to failure, and in addition found that when a success experience preceded the task, performance among observed subjects was *superior* to that of subjects who performed the task without preliminary treatment. Because the task used by Geen was a difficult one, this finding goes against what would have been predicted from drive theory, but it is consistent with the self-presentational approach. In a subsequent study, Geen (1981) showed that subjects who are observed following success are more persistent at a second task than those who work alone, suggesting that self-presentation needs lead to greater motivation to succeed.

Response withholding

Evaluation apprehension arising from the presence of others can also influence performance by motivating the individual to refrain from behaving in ways that may be socially undesirable. This may have several effects. An early experiment in social facilitation by Matlin and Zajonc (1968) revealed that subjects gave more common associates in a word association task while being observed than when performing alone. Although this finding was interpreted as evidence for drive theory inasmuch as drive could have energized dominant verbal habits at the expense of subordinate ones, subsequent research suggests another interpretation. In replicating the Matlin and Zajonc study, Blank, Staff, and Shaver (1976) found that the major difference between observed subjects and those working alone was that the latter emitted a greater number of unusual and idiosyncratic associates than the former. The results were interpreted as indicating that observed subjects suppressed unusual responses in favour of more common ones in order to avoid looking strange to the observer.

Response suppression has also been demonstrated in a series of studies by Berger and his associates (Berger et al., 1981), who found that the presence of an audience motivates subjects to suppress overt practice (e.g., moving one's lips while reading, counting out loud) while performing a task. Because these devices assist learning, their suppression should inhibit performance on difficult tasks. Elimination of such overt practice on easy tasks may have the beneficial effect of compelling the person to use more symbolic processing, which should improve performance on such tasks. The upshot of all this is that if for any reason the person feels constrained to inhibit overt motoric practice, learning unfamiliar material will be hindered but learning familiar material will not. Berger further suggests that persons who are observed while learning will feel such constraints because of a cultural norm that discourages such overt activity. Thus the presence of an audience should facilitate performance on familiar tasks but inhibit performance on unfamiliar ones. In several experiments, Berger and his associates have found support for this hypothesis.

A third line of research that has linked the presence of an audience to response inhibition is constituted by several studies by Geen (1985; 1987) on the relationship of evaluation apprehension to passive avoidance. Briefly stated, the major hypothesis of this research is that when people are anxious in an evaluative situation and are also unable to leave the situation physically, they withhold or restrain responding in an effort to avoid making errors. If the presence of observers elicits evaluation apprehension, one reaction to audience settings may be cautiousness in responding, reflected in a low response rate. Furthermore, because complex and difficult tasks evoke more anxiety than simple ones, the greatest amount of response withholding should come on difficult tasks. This would lead to relatively poor performance, whereas on simple tasks the relatively moderate response withholding would have no such effect. Instead, a slightly slower response rate could facilitate greater attention to simple tasks because the person is not distracted by his or her own action, and this could lead to a slight facilitation of performance (Figure 4).

Geen (1985) found some support for this hypothesis in a study in which subjects who were high in test anxiety (as measured by a standard test anxiety scale) attempted to solve fewer anagrams while being watched by an evaluating experimenter than while either being observed in a non-evaluative way or while working alone. Subjects in the high anxiety-evaluated condition also reported higher levels of state anxiety than highly test anxious subjects in the other two conditions. In addition, the correlation between state anxiety and number of anagrams attempted was negative in every condition of the experiment and the highest negative correlation was found in the high anxiety-evaluated group. The results showed, therefore, that being observed by an

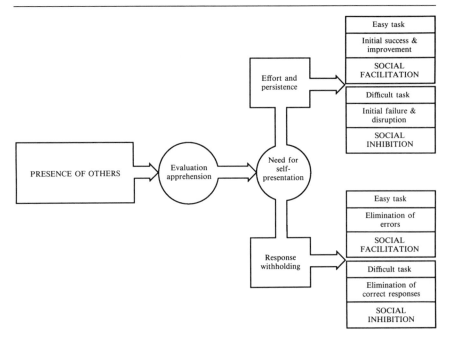

Figure 4 Schematic representation of impression management theory of social facilitation. See legend to Figure 1 for explanation

evaluator creates state anxiety, and that state anxiety produces a depressed rate of task-relevant responding.

In a second study of response withholding, Geen, Thomas, and Gammill (1988) tested the joint effect of observation and co-action on performance, following a hypothesis suggested by Geen (1980) that co-action effects should be greater when the experimenter is present and observing during the task. Subjects who performed with three co-actors while the experimenter was observing attempted fewer anagrams and reported higher levels of state anxiety than did subjects who performed under co-action conditions with the experimenter absent. When the experimenter was absent, no overall co-action effect was found, suggesting that the co-action effect was mediated by experimenter presence. Geen (1980) had argued that the presence of co-actors influences social facilitation by creating competition among the co-actors which, in turn, leads each subject to fear being outperformed by the others. If the experimenter, who is usually regarded as the purveyor of rewards and punishments, is present and evaluating each subject's performance, the evaluation apprehension in the situation is even higher. It is this heightened apprehension that leads to response inhibition and state anxiety in the co-action-experimenter present condition.

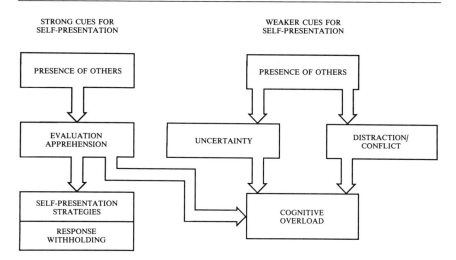

STRONG CUES FOR
SELF-PRESENTATION

WEAKER CUES FOR
SELF-PRESENTATION

PRESENCE OF OTHERS

PRESENCE OF OTHERS

EVALUATION
APPREHENSION

UNCERTAINTY

DISTRACTION/
CONFLICT

SELF-PRESENTATION
STRATEGIES

RESPONSE
WITHHOLDING

COGNITIVE
OVERLOAD

Figure 5   Overview of theories of social facilitation and inhibition
Source: Adapted from Geen, 1989

Conclusion

Geen (1989) has proposed a model of the processes involved in social facilitation that summarizes most of what has been covered in this discussion (see
Figure 5). It is based on a few assumptions. First, all social situations contain
some cues informing the person that he or she should strive to make a good
self-presentation. Some situations contain strong cues, such as prior success
(e.g., Geen, 1979) or tasks having the potential for embarrassment (e.g.,
Berger et al. 1981); other situations contain weaker cues. Second, when
strong self-presentation cues are present, the person experiences a high level
of evaluation apprehension, accompanied by behaviour calculated to protect
the person from making a bad impression (i.e., strategic self-presentation
and response withholding). Third, when self-presentation cues are weaker,
the dominant response of the individual to the social presence will be uncertainty or distraction. These will contribute to cognitive overload. Evaluation
apprehension may also lead to cognitive overload in addition to any self-
presentational effects that it has. The effects of self-presentational concerns,
response withholding, and cognitive overload on social facilitation or
inhibition of performance have already been discussed (see Figure 4).

SOCIAL LOAFING

The phenomenon of apparent motivation loss in groups studied by
Ringelmann (see above) was resurrected in the late 1970s by Latané and his

associates, who gave the phenomenon the name of *social loafing*. Early tests of social loafing involved simple physical acts such as shouting and hand clapping individually or in groups, with the general result that the intensity of output per person declined as additional members were added (e.g., Latané, Williams, & Harkins, 1979). Later studies showed considerable generality in the effect, with loafing occurring in several non-physical activities. The data on social loafing are consistent with one of the major premises of social impact theory (Latané & Nida, 1980): when a person is a member of a group subjected to social forces, the impact of those forces on each person in the group is diminished in inverse proportion to, among other things, the number of people in the group.

Several explanations for social loafing have been proposed: free riding, equalization of perceived output, evaluation apprehension, and matching to standard.

"Free riding" and the "sucker" effect

One reason for a loss of individual motivation is what Kerr (1983) has called the *free rider* effect. This occurs when each member of a group perceives that there is a high probability that some other member of the group will solve the problem at hand and that the benefits from this person's performance will go to all members. Given this view of things, each person concludes that his or her output is dispensable and exerts little effort as a result. As the size of the group increases, the probability likewise increases that someone else in the group will solve the problem. The importance of individual effort therefore become less and less as the size of the group increases.

Related to this effect is that of equalizing what may be perceived to be an inequitable output. If subjects in groups expect their partners to become free riders, they may respond by loafing for the purpose of bringing equality of effort to what they perceived to be an inequitable situation. By doing this the subjects avoid looking like "suckers" who work hard for a group goal while those about them do not. In support of this idea, Jackson and Harkins (1985) found that subjects shouted more while alone than they did when in pairs (i.e., they loafed) only when they had no information concerning their partners' intended level of effort. When informed that the partner intended to expend either a high or a low effort, subjects matched their outputs to those of the partner.

Evaluation apprehension

Social loafing has also been explained as a normal response to tasks that are tiring, uninteresting, and otherwise not likely to engage the person's involvement. This argument rests on the assumption that the tasks commonly used in research on social loafing are boring and meaningless. People therefore try to avoid doing them, and will unless social constraints are implemented. Kerr and Bruun (1981) call this the "hide-in-the-crowd" explanation, indicating that group members provide a cover of anonymity for the unmotivated individual. This cover is usually facilitated in experiments on loafing by the usual practice of pooling the outputs of the group members. Making each person's output identifiable eliminates social loafing (Williams, Harkins, & Latané, 1981).

This finding introduces the possibility that subjects become apprehensive about being evaluated by the experimenter (as has already been demonstrated in research on social facilitation), and that this is why they do not loaf under non-anonymous conditions. Such is especially the case when subjects believe that their performance is being compared to that of their co-actors, so that they are effectively in competition with the others. This will be more likely to occur, moreover, when all of the persons in the group are performing the same task than when they are working on different tasks. Harkins and Jackson (1985) found support for this hypothesis by showing that social loafing was least likely to occur in a group when the outputs of the individuals were identifiable and when all subjects worked at the same task. Thus, the condition in which the highest level of evaluation apprehension was created was also the one in which the least loafing occurred.

If experiments on group performance involve tasks that engage the interest or concern of the individual, a necessary condition for social loafing is absent and the effect is not obtained (Brickner, Harkins, & Ostrom, 1986). Social loafing is, therefore, attributable not so much to a loss of motivation in the group setting as to an absence of motivation due to the nature of the task that becomes manifest in behaviour under group conditions. Evaluation apprehension in this setting causes the individual to suppress the preferred response – inactivity – in favour of more socially desirable behaviour. Viewed in this way, absence of social loafing appears to represent a special case of response withholding under conditions of evaluation anxiety quite similar to that shown in studies reviewed above.

Matching to standard

The third explanation of social loafing involves the concept of matching-to-standard. This explanation assumes that apprehension over the possibility of being evaluated by the experimenter causes the person to match a standard for performance set by the experimenter (and that this matching is avoided under conditions that allow social loafing). Several studies have shown in addition that even when cues signalling evaluation by the experimenter are not present, social loafing may be eliminated by the invocation of other salient standards to which the person's output can be compared. These standards need not be social. Harkins and Szymanski (1988), for example, found that merely reminding the persons in a group of a personal performance standard for the behaviour in question was sufficient to eliminate social loafing, and Harkins and Szymanski (1989) obtained the same result by reminding individuals of a group standard.

Conclusion

Social loafing, once thought to be the product of a loss in motivation under group conditions, now appears to be a form of avoidance behaviour prompted by uninteresting and non-involving tasks. It is reduced or eliminated by establishing conditions that either remove the anonymity of the persons involved or remind the persons of certain standards of behaviour pertinent to the activity. The idea that the introduction of social, personal, or group standards increases motivation is consistent with certain theoretical formulations pertaining to the self. For example, Breckler and Greenwald (1986) have proposed that individuals select their behaviours in order to secure a favourable self-image, to make a good impression on other people, and to live up to the standards of important reference groups. People foreswear social loafing in spite of low motivation for the task because of salient personal, social, and collective standards for behaviour. These three standards may, in turn, all be the products of a larger superordinate motive: the motive to be included in the social collective. To understand this, we must consider the motivational bases for evaluation apprehension, social anxiety, and self-presentation.

THE NEED FOR SOCIAL INCLUSION

Theory and research on both social facilitation and social loafing suggest that evaluation apprehension is an important motive for human behaviour in social settings. Each phenomenon may therefore be thought of as a manifestation of a more general influence of *social anxiety*, which has been defined as a state brought about by a person's being motivated to make a certain impression on others but doubting that this impression can be made (Schlenker & Leary, 1982). To avoid this state the person adopts various strategies of self-presentation and impression management in the hopes of creating a favourable impression and, as a consequence, of maintaining self-esteem. That is, the person adopts a course of action that enables him or her to overcome doubts about securing a desirable social outcome.

The impression management strategy in social facilitation, seen in such behaviour as trying harder to succeed in the presence of an audience following success than following failure (Geen, 1979; 1981), typifies such behaviour. The person appraises the social situation as one that threatens to be embarrassing should the person fail and, as a consequence, the person increases effort to avoid failure. Inhibiting socially undesirable responses in social settings may also be seen as behaviour calculated to avoid the possibility of making a bad impression and hence avoiding social anxiety. Suppressing a desire to loaf in a group during a boring task because of fear of exposure or of not meeting an internalized standard may also be interpreted as behaviour aimed at avoiding anxiety.

Why should the fear of making a bad impression be such a powerful motive for individual behaviour? One answer is that people may wish to make a good impression in order to avoid social rejection or exclusion. Humans have a strong need to be accepted by, and included within, society.

Fear of death

One reason that people need to be included within the collective may be that human culture, which society represents, provides a buffer against facing one's own vulnerability and mortality (Greenberg, Psyzczynski, & Solomon, 1986). Society provides a "cultural drama" that gives meaning to life and without which the person would experience existential dread. The person is therefore motivated to fulfil an approved role in that drama. Meeting cultural standards brings approval, social acceptance, and self-esteem; failing to meet those standards and social expectations invites rejection. Avoiding failure and suppressing socially undesirable action is only part of the motivational complex elicited by fear of death and non-being. The same motive also elicits positive pro-social behaviours aimed at enhancing and strengthening the authority of social customs and demands (e.g., Rosenblatt, Greenberg, Solomon, Psyzczynski, & Lyon, 1989).

Exclusion anxiety

A theory related to that of Greenberg and his associates has been proposed by Baumeister and Tice (1990), who place less emphasis on existential concerns and more on the potentially adaptive side of social anxiety. Social anxiety may serve as a warning signal that social disapproval will occur unless an ongoing course of action is modified. Any behaviour that might make the person seem unattractive or useless to the group could invite social exclusion and thereby elicit the warning signal. Anxiety therefore interrupts behaviour, focuses attention on what is being done wrong, and motivates the person to seek an alternative course of action.

Among these alternatives, as already noted, are acts that help the person avoid failure or other negative outcomes by controlling behaviour, becoming more motivated to do some things and to refrain from doing others. The phenomena of social facilitation and social loafing fall within this broad domain of behaviour. However, it is also possible that the person will resort to other courses of action and sample from a wide range of cognitive strategies demonstrated in research on the maintenance of self-esteem, such as self-handicapping, a self-serving attributional bias, excuse-making, or symbolic self-completion (Geen, 1991). Each strategy can be thought of as a process whereby the person attempts to escape blame or criticism from others for failure or other socially undesirable outcomes.

SUMMARY

A common thread that connects the problem of social facilitation with that of social loafing is the construct of evaluation apprehension. Situations that evoke this affective state can elicit a number of intervening processes that lead in turn to the improvement or inhibition of performance. Such situations can also eliminate tendencies toward social loafing that may be evoked in group settings by boring or uninvolving tasks. Evaluation apprehension, in turn, is a facet of social anxiety, a state called forth whenever the person wishes to make a good impression on others but fears that others' evaluations will be negative. Finally, social anxiety may be a product of a larger and more general motivational state based on a need for inclusion in the social collective and its corresponding fear of social exclusion. Social motivation may, therefore, be a manifestation of basic social processes that have adaptive and even existential consequences.

FURTHER READING

Baron, R. S. (1986). Distraction-conflict theory: Progress and problems. In L. Berkowitz (Ed.) *Advances in experimental social psychology* (vol. 19, pp. 1–40). New York: Academic Press.

Carver, C. S., & Scheier, M. F. (1981). The self-attention-induced feedback loop and social facilitation. *Journal of Experimental Social Psychology*, *17*, 545–568.

Geen, R. G. (1989). Alternative conceptions of social facilitation. In P. Paulus (Ed.) *The psychology of group influence* (2nd edn, pp. 15–51). Hillsdale, NJ: Lawrence Erlbaum.

Harkins, S. G. (1987). Social loafing and social facilitation. *Journal of Experimental Social Psychology*, *23*, 1–18.

REFERENCES

Allport, F. H. (1924). *Social psychology*. Boston, MA: Houghton Mifflin.

Baron, R. S. (1986). Distraction-conflict theory: Progress and problems. In L. Berkowitz (Ed.) *Advances in experimental social psychology* (vol. 19, pp. 1–40). New York: Academic Press.

Baron, R. S., Moore, D., & Sanders, G. S. (1978). Distraction as a source of drive in social facilitation research. *Journal of Personality and Social Psychology*, *36*, 816–824.

Baumeister, R. F. (1982). A self-presentational view of social phenomena. *Psychological Bulletin*, *91*, 3–26.

Baumeister, R. F., & Tice, D. M. (1990). Anxiety and social exclusion. *Journal of Social and Clinical Psychology*, *9*, 165–195.

Berger, S. M., Hampton, K. L., Carli, L. L., Grandmaison, P. S., Sadow, J. S., & Donath, C. (1981). Audience-induced inhibition of overt practice during learning. *Journal of Personality and Social Psychology, 40,* 479–491.

Blank, T. D., Staff, I., & Shaver, P. (1976). Social facilitation of word associations: Further questions. *Journal of Personality and Social Psychology, 34,* 725–733.

Bond, C. F. (1982). Social facilitation: A self-presentational view. *Journal of Personality and Social Psychology, 42,* 1042–1050.

Breckler, S. J., & Greenwald, A. G. (1986). Motivational facets of the self. In R. M. Sorrentino & E. T. Higgins (Eds) *Handbook of motivation and cognition* (vol. 1, pp. 145–164). New York: Guilford.

Brickner, M. A., Harkins, S. G., & Ostrom, T. M. (1986). Effects of personal involvement: Thought-provoking implications for social loafing. *Journal of Personality and Social Psychology, 51,* 763–769.

Bruning, J. L., Capage, J. E., Kozuh, J. F., Young, P. F., & Young, W. E. (1968). Socially induced drive and the range of cue utilization. *Journal of Personality and Social Psychology, 9,* 242–244.

Carver, C. S., & Scheier, M. F. (1981). The self-attention-induced feedback loop and social facilitation. *Journal of Experimental Social Psychology, 17,* 545–568.

Cottrell, N. B. (1972). Social facilitation. In C. G. McClintock (Ed.) *Experimental social psychology* (pp. 185–236). New York: Holt.

Cottrell, N. B., Wack, D. L., Sekerak, G. J., & Rittle, R. H. (1968). Social facilitation of dominant responses by the presence of an audience and the mere presence of others. *Journal of Personality and Social Psychology, 9,* 245–250.

Easterbrook, J. A. (1959). The effect of emotion on cue utilization and organization of behavior. *Psychological Review, 66,* 187–201.

Geen, R. G. (1976). Test anxiety, observation, and the range of cue utilization. *British Journal of Social and Clinical Psychology, 15,* 253–259.

Geen, R. G. (1979). Effects of being observed on learning following success and failure experiences. *Motivation and Emotion, 3,* 355–371.

Geen, R. G. (1980). Test anxiety and cue utilization. In I. G. Sarason (Ed.) *Test anxiety: Theory, research and applications* (pp. 43–61). Hillsdale, NJ: Lawrence Erlbaum.

Geen, R. G. (1981). Effects of being observed on persistence at an insoluble task. *British Journal of Social Psychology, 20,* 211–216.

Geen, R. G. (1985). Evaluation apprehension and response withholding in solution of anagrams. *Personality and Individual Differences, 6,* 293–298.

Geen, R. G. (1987). Test anxiety and behavioral avoidance. *Journal of Research in Personality, 21,* 481–488.

Geen, R. G. (1989). Alternative conceptions of social facilitation. In P. Paulus (Ed.) *The psychology of group influence* (2nd edn, pp. 15–51). Hillsdale, NJ: Lawrence Erlbaum.

Geen, R. G. (1991). Social motivation. *Annual Review of Psychology, 42,* 377–399.

Geen, R. G., & Gange, J. J. (1977). Drive theory of social facilitation: Twelve years of theory and research. *Psychological Bulletin, 84,* 1267–1288.

Geen, R. G., Thomas, S. L., & Gammill, P. (1988). Effects of evaluation and coaction in state anxiety and anagram performance. *Personality and Individual Differences, 6,* 293–298.

Greenberg, J., Psyzczynski, T., & Solomon, S. (1986). The causes and consequences of a need for self-esteem: A terror management theory. In R. F. Baumeister (Ed.) *Public self and private self* (pp. 189–212). New York: Springer-Verlag.

Groff, B. D., Baron, R. S., & Moore, D. S. (1983). Distraction, attentional conflict, and drivelike behavior. *Journal of Experimental Social Psychology, 19,* 359–380.

Guerin, B. (1986). Mere presence effects in humans: A review. *Journal of Experimental Social Psychology, 22,* 38–77.

Guerin, B., & Innes, J. M. (1982). Social facilitation and social monitoring: A new look at Zajonc's mere presence hypothesis. *British Journal of Social Psychology, 21,* 7–18.

Harkins, S. G., & Jackson, J. M. (1985). The role of evaluation in eliminating social loafing. *Personality and Social Psychology Bulletin, 11,* 456–465.

Harkins, S. G., & Szymanski, K. (1988). Social loafing and self-evaluation with an objective standard. *Journal of Experimental Social Psychology, 24,* 354–365.

Harkins, S. G., & Szymanski, K. (1989). Social loafing and group evaluation. *Journal of Personality and Social Psychology, 56,* 934–941.

Henchy, T., & Glass, D. C. (1968). Evaluation apprehension and the social facilitation of dominant and subordinate responses. *Journal of Personality and Social Psychology, 10,* 446–454.

Jackson, J. M., & Harkins, S. G. (1985). Equity in effort: An explanation of the social loafing effect. *Journal of Personality and Social Psychology, 49,* 1199–1206.

Kerr, N. L. (1983). Motivation losses in small groups: A social dilemma analysis. *Journal of Personality and Social Psychology, 45,* 819–828.

Kerr, N. L., & Bruun, S. E. (1981). Ringelmann revisited: Alternative explanations for the social loafing effect. *Personality and Social Psychology Bulletin, 7,* 224–231.

Kravitz, D., & Martin, B. (1986). Ringelmann rediscovered: The original article. *Journal of Personality and Social Psychology, 50,* 936–941.

Latané, B., & Nida, S. (1980). Social impact theory and group influence: A social engineering perspective. In P. Paulus (Ed.) *The psychology of group influence* (1st edn, pp. 3–34). Hillsdale, NJ: Lawrence Erlbaum.

Latané, B., Williams, K., & Harkins, S. G. (1979). Many hands make light the work: The causes and consequences of social loafing. *Journal of Personality and Social Psychology, 37,* 822–832.

Manstead, A. S. R., & Semin, G. (1980). Social facilitation effects: Mere enhancement of dominant responses? *British Journal of Social and Clinical Psychology, 19,* 119–136.

Matlin, M. W., & Zajonc, R. B. (1968). Social facilitation of word associations. *Journal of Personality and Social Psychology, 10,* 435–460.

Rosenblatt, A., Greenberg, J., Solomon, S., Psyzczynski, T., & Lyon, D. (1989). Evidence for terror management theory: I. The effects of mortality salience on reactions to those who violate or uphold cultural values. *Journal of Personality and Social Psychology, 57,* 681–690.

Schlenker, B. R., & Leary, M. R. (1982). Social anxiety and self-presentation: A conceptualization and model. *Psychological Bulletin, 92,* 641–669.

Seta, J. J., & Hassan, R. K. (1980). Awareness of prior success or failure: A critical factor in task performance. *Journal of Personality and Social Psychology, 39,* 70–76.

Seta, J. J., Crisson, J. E., Seta, C. E., & Wang, M. A. (1989). Task performance and perceptions of anxiety: Averaging and summation in an evaluative setting. *Journal of Personality and Social Psychology, 56,* 387–396.

Triplett, N. (1898). The dynamogenic factors in pacemaking and competition. *American Journal of Psychology, 9,* 507–533.

Williams, K., Harkins, S. G., & Latané, B. (1981). Identifiability as a deterrent to social loafing: Two cheering experiments. *Journal of Personality and Social Psychology, 40,* 303–311.

Zajonc, R. B. (1965). Social facilitation. *Science, 149,* 269–274.

Zajonc, R. B. (1980). Compresence. In P. Paulus (Ed.) *Psychology of group influence* (1st edn, pp. 35–60). Hillsdale, NJ: Lawrence Erlbaum.

6.4

SEXUAL MOTIVATION AND BEHAVIOUR

John Bancroft

MRC Reproductive Biology Unit, Edinburgh, Scotland

Reproduction by sexual means is a universal characteristic of multicellular living organisms. In bringing the male and female germ cells together, nature has evolved an extraordinarily rich variety of biological strategies. In plants, intermediate devices are often employed – insects, water, wind, and so on. In the animal kingdom some specific pattern of behavioural interaction of male and female is nearly always involved.

In most animal species, this process is dangerous; vigilance is reduced and vulnerability to predators increased. As a consequence, reproductive behaviour is restricted to whatever is needed for optimum reproductive consequences, timed to occur during the fertile phase of the female's reproductive cycle. Sexual behaviour has therefore evolved to be under control of the same hormones that determine other aspects of the reproductive process, in particular the gonadal steroid hormones testosterone, oestradiol, and progesterone.

In mammals, the pattern of hormonal control of the female's sexual behaviour varies across species. Males are more consistent, with testosterone being necessary for both adequate sexual behaviour and male fertility in virtually all species. However, sexual behaviour is by no means under absolute control of such hormones. Genetic influences are important; some individuals are more responsive than others to these hormonal effects on behaviour. Learning is also crucial; in most mammalian species that have been studied, disruption of normal relationships between the young animal and the mother and/or the peer group results in impairment of later sexual behaviour, particularly in the male, which, in primates, may be quite intractable (Larsson, 1978).

PRIMATE SEXUALITY: THE COMPARATIVE APPROACH

Darwin (1871) described two types of sexual selection: *intrasexual*, best exemplified by competition between males for access to the female, and *intersexual*, when characteristics of one gender increase the likelihood of being accepted or chosen as a mate by the other. These two types of selection often interact, as when the female is most attracted to the male who dominates the male–male competition.

Whatever the process of mate selection, the investment in parenting differs for the male and the female. There is no biological constraint on the number of offspring fathered by a male; there are clear constraints on the female, whether she has only one partner or many. Such contrasts contribute to the evolution of male–female differences in behavioural aptitudes.

We find that in any particular species of mammal, the pattern of mating and adaptation to the environment interact to have powerful influences on social structure. In those species where male–male competition is preeminent, the associated social structure will depend on the needs for environmental adaptation. The orang-utan, for example, lives in an environment which, in terms of food supply, can sustain only the occasional animal. Male–male competition determines which male occupies a particular territory, usually a quite extensive area. A small number of females may also inhabit the same territory but keep away from the male, usually for long periods of lactational infertility, making themselves available to the male only when they are in heat. The gorilla, by contrast, lives among relatively abundant food supply and the successful male keeps a harem of females to himself, driving male offspring away when they approach maturity and maintaining his position until he succumbs to a younger more powerful male.

The chimpanzee has evolved to live in social groups in which the males cooperate to protect the group from external threats. The mating pattern is very different again (Tutin, 1980); when a female in the group is in heat (or oestrus), all or most of the males will mate with her. This pattern serves to reduce male–male competition and foster group cohesiveness. Its non-reproductive function is also aided by the relatively long period of oestrus, which encourages sexual activity for more than one-third of the female's reproductive cycle and is much longer than that required for reproductive purposes.

In the case of the gorilla (and orang-utan), the *polygynous* pattern of mating is associated with marked sexual dimorphism, the larger male being most successful in gaining access and winning the attraction of the female (the male is approximately twice the size of the female). The male chimpanzee is only slightly larger than the female, perhaps reflecting his defensive role in the group. The chimp's pattern of mating, relatively unusual among primates, is *promiscuous*, and characterized by a greater capacity for sperm production. The male gorilla ensures his reproductive success by his bodily size and strength; the chimpanzee by the number of ejaculations and sperm that he can produce during frequent mating. This is reflected in a high testis–body weight ratio, much higher in the chimpanzee than in the gorilla (Short, 1981).

Primates who show monogamous mating patterns, and who live in family groups (e.g., the gibbon or marmoset) show no sexual dimorphism and relatively low testis–body weight ratios. In such monogamous family groups sexual interaction between the maturing offspring and the parents is not tolerated. The integrity of the family group is maintained by socially induced delay of puberty and the driving away of the offspring once puberty is reached.

This variety of socio-sexual structure is also reflected in the level of sexual activity of the male and/or female that characterizes a species. The male orang-utan is relatively highly sexed and will mate with any female he comes across, whether she is receptive or not. That is why the female keeps out of his way until she is in heat. The male gorilla, by comparison, is relatively uninterested in sex and requires the particular stimulation of the oestrous female to activate his behaviour. This depends not only on the female's attractiveness to him when in heat, but also on her behaviour in soliciting his interest. Thus one can see that a female gorilla, or a female orang-utan, whose behaviour is not influenced appropriately by the hormonal changes that accompany her fertile period, is unlikely to reproduce herself.

This comparison of three of the Great Apes, who in evolutionary and genetic terms are probably among the closest relatives of the human primate, illustrates the three components of female sexuality, first defined by Beach

(1976), that have dominated much of the biological investigation of animal sexual behaviour: first, *attractiveness*, shown by the female chimp in heat who emits hormonally determined signals, both olfactory and visual (the extraordinary and very obvious enlargement of her external genitalia), which sexually excite the males in the group; second, *proceptivity*, the active behaviour of the female that elicits a sexual response from the male, as shown by the female gorilla in oestrus or, in a somewhat different way, by the female orang-utan, who when in oestrus makes herself available to the male; and third, *receptivity*, the acceptance by the female of the male's advance and attempted mounting.

This analysis has facilitated our understanding of the role of hormones in the sexual behaviour of female primates as well as other mammals. In most species oestrogens play a crucial role in attractiveness (though learning, by the male, of the sexual significance of olfactory or visual cues may also be of importance), and perhaps particularly in the sub-primate mammals, in receptivity. Testosterone, possibly in combination with oestrogens, plays an important role in female proceptivity (Dixson, 1983). Interestingly, investigation of male sexuality has been somewhat more simplistic – little attention has been given to the notion of attractiveness or receptivity of the male. In a somewhat chauvinistic way, the male is seen as simply "proceptive".

This "three species" comparison also shows us that sexuality can evolve to serve non-reproductive purposes to a degree that is not simply determined by the level of evolutionary complexity. The role of sexual behaviour in the social organization of the chimpanzee is striking. By comparison, sex has little non-reproductive purpose for the gorilla. But in other primate species we see the function of sexual intimacy in affectional bonding between animals, which has relevance to parental relationships as well as to other aspects of the social process.

The type of analysis so far presented is relatively uncontroversial when confined to non-humans. There are, of course, many differences to be found among non-human species in the biological mechanisms that influence sexual behaviour. But there are also many commonalities. It would make little sense to assume that the biological mechanisms involved in human sexuality are unique to humans, any more than are mechanisms involved in eating behaviour, or aggression, or cardiovascular physiology. It would also be unwise to assume that social determinants of non-human primate behaviour are irrelevant to the human. On the other hand, there are crucial features of the human situation that are uniquely human. The challenge is to place those features and mechanisms into perspective.

Nevertheless, the use of this cross-species comparative approach to further our understanding of the human situation tends to elicit a polarity of attitudes which, while of general relevance, is particularly marked when our sexuality and issues of gender are concerned. This is the contrast between those who seek to explain human behaviour in either predominantly biological or predominantly sociological terms. For many thinking people such polemic is futile, the importance of both biological and sociological determinants are obvious; the intellectual challenge is to understand how they interact. But the polemic continues almost unabated. An analysis of its origins is beyond the scope of this chapter, although the political implications are among the most relevant. Emphasis on the "biological imperative" reinforces acceptance of the status quo, which is of particular relevance to the position of women in our society. Hence, notions of biological determination of gender differences are particularly contentious and many feminist thinkers are intolerant of such explanations. Emphasis on social determination reinforces the aspirations of those who seek social change, whether or not such change is facilitated by such a view.

In a multi-authored volume (Geer & O'Donohue, 1987), a variety of theoretical approaches to understanding human sexuality was presented. These included sociological approaches such as scripting theory, feminist psychology, cognitive psychology, psychoanalysis, learning theory, anthropology and the evolutionary approach. While the interest and relevance of most of these approaches is apparent, what is intriguing is the extent to which some of the proponents regard their explanatory systems as sufficient. In contemplating the fundamental complexity of sexuality, especially of the human, one is reminded of the blind men and the elephant. We can obtain a variety of views of this complexity, each of which has its own validity and heuristic value, but which is inevitably incomplete. The goal should be to establish, not the real or correct explanation of human sexual behaviour, but rather a way of looking at it that serves a useful purpose. The most appropriate view will therefore vary according to that purpose. Educationalists may find an explanatory model emphasizing sociological and/or learning mechanisms more helpful than one emphasizing the biological. The feminist, concerned with improving the status of women in society, will need to emphasize the extent to which societal expectations of male sexual behaviour involve dominance over or exploitation of women. The clinician or professional, seeking to help those with problems in their sexual lives, requires a psychosomatic approach to understanding how psychological processes, and their social influences, interact with physiological mechanisms. It is from this background that this chapter has been written, attempting the difficult task of integrating sociological, psychological, and biological mechanisms (Bancroft, 1989).

HUMAN SEXUALITY

In the process of building our integrated view of human sexuality we can usefully consider two broad dimensions, the functions that sexual behaviour serves, and the mechanisms involved in implementing those functions.

The functions of sex

Although for most mammalian species the non-reproductive functions of sex are limited, we have already seen how in some primates they are more extensive, and for most humans they have a pervasive influence. Apart from reproduction we therefore have to consider the following:

Pleasure

Perhaps the primary, or most basic, reinforcer of sexual behaviour is the pleasure that can be experienced, a combination of sensual pleasure and the uniquely sexual pleasure associated with orgasm.

Pair-bonding and fostering intimacy

The vulnerability of being actively sexual is relevant to this function. In most species, as mentioned earlier, the dangers are physical, but for humans they are predominantly psychological. It can be argued that exposing oneself in this way in a sexual relationship, and finding oneself safe in the process, provides a particularly powerful form of bonding between two people. This is the essence of sexual intimacy. Experiencing and giving pleasure no doubt contribute to this process, but they may be less crucial to bonding than the experience of emotional security that is engendered. It is for this reason that the bonding effect of sexuality within a relationship is so readily threatened by sexual involvement outside the relationship.

Asserting masculinity or femininity

The issue of gender identity – how we feel about ourselves as male or female, and how we express that identity as behaviour – is a uniquely human issue deriving from our use of language and the consequent need to label and categorize various aspects of ourselves, others, and our environment (Money & Ehrhardt, 1972). During childhood, sexuality is relatively unimportant to our gender identity; pre-pubertal boys and girls establish their sense of gender in terms of their non-sexual interests, activities, and peer group relationships. Following puberty, when their bodies begin secondary sexual development, and their hormonal and social milieu change, sexuality becomes important. How attractive or effective one is in sexual terms becomes an important reinforcer of one's sense of gender, among other things. Much of early adolescent sexuality can be understood in this way. However, throughout our lives, particularly at times when our gender identity is threatened in other ways (e.g., a woman having to undergo a hysterectomy, a man being made redundant, the effects of ageing), we may use our sexuality for this purpose.

547

Bolstering self-esteem

Feeling sexually attractive to others, or succeeding in one's sexual endeavours, may generally improve our self-esteem (and conversely, in the face of sexual failure, lower it).

Achieving power or dominance

The "power" of sexuality tends to be regarded as an aspect of masculinity, with the male, for both social and physical reasons, typically being in a position of dominance. Sex can be used to control relationships, however, by both men and women, and is often an important aspect of the dynamics of a relationship. Power may be exerted by controlling access to sexual interaction, or determining the form that a sexual encounter takes. While in the clinical context it is most usual to encounter this aspect within an established relationship, it is also an important and interesting aspect of early "courtship" behaviour. Whereas women have legitimate reasons for fearing the abuse of power by men in sexual interaction, the extent to which women control normal sexual exchanges, determining when an interaction can progress to the next stage, is perhaps underestimated and under-researched. Perper (1985) studied this aspect of male–female interaction in the social context of "singles bars".

Expressing hostility

An important aspect of the "dominance" issue of male–female sexual interaction is the use of sexuality to express hostility. This is of most relevance to the problem of rape and sexual assault. Whereas many instances of sexual assault or coercive sex can be seen as an extension of dominance or power, usually by the male over the female, there are also instances when the sexual assault can be understood as an expression of anger, either against the individual woman, or against the woman as a representative of other women, or against the man whose property the assaulted woman is seen to be. This latter pattern is common in interracial rape (e.g., the black man raping the white woman) or rape during wartime (Brownmiller, 1975). There is much controversy about the extent to which rape should be understood as either an act of aggression or a sexual act. It is likely that, to understand many cases of rape and sexual assault, we shall need to understand how aggression and sexual arousal can interact (see below).

Reducing anxiety or tension

The reduction in arousal that typically follows orgasm may be used as a device to reduce anxiety or tension. While this is an occasional function for most people, it is most likely to become established as an habitual pattern when solitary masturbation is the main sexual outlet. In such circumstances, masturbation may increase in frequency when anxiety or tension is high.

Risk taking

For some individuals, taking risks is a form of excitement that they seek. Sexual interaction provides a variety of risks, ranging from the relatively benign, such as being found out, to the serious, such as pregnancy or sexually transmitted disease.

Material gain

Offering oneself as a sexual partner for payment or other material benefits is a well-established aspect of human sexuality, as well as being evident among primates. Prostitution, the institutionalized form of such sexuality, has been established in most human societies. The social function of prostitution, that is, the extent to which it serves the needs of a society, has been an issue of considerable debate at various times. Thus when there was a moral outrage against the level of prostitution and its consequences towards the end of the nineteenth century, the social benefits were often stressed implicitly if not explicitly, by those who wished to maintain the status quo (Davenport-Hines, 1990).

The mechanisms of human sexuality

Given the variety of functions that have been considered, what is it that endows an experience with a specifically sexual quality? Is it, as some sociological theorists would have us believe, mainly a question of whether the experience is labelled as sexual in the social context? Or are there intrinsically sexual characteristics, and if so what are they?

We can draw a useful parallel with eating behaviour. A hungry person experiences a subjective state we call appetite which motivates him or her to obtain food, focusing attention on that goal. The subjective state is accompanied by and partly consists of various physiological changes, many of which are in preparation for food intake. Both biochemical processes, such as hypoglycaemia, and psychological processes, such as thinking about food, are involved. We learn to feel hungry at certain times and in certain situations. Our appetite is increased by the sight or smell of food, and we learn to like certain foods more than others. As with sex, a variety of functions other than nutrition, some social, are met by the varieties of eating behaviour.

In the sexual context, what we experience as sexual appetite, or sexual desire, and what may subsequently become a state of sexual arousal, is also

549

a complex interaction between cognitive processes, neurophysiological and biochemical mechanisms, and mood. How we behave in such circumstances will reflect the "scripts" that our social group has provided us. We can therefore view this complex interactive situation through these various "windows" and consider (1) neurophysiological arousability, (2) cognitive processes, (3) mood and emotional states, and (4) social influences or "scripts" for sexual action.

Neurophysiological arousability

The increase in central arousal or alertness that typically occurs when responding to a sexual stimulus focuses attention on the stimulus, and is accompanied by a range of physiological responses particularly involving the genitalia – penile erection in the male and genital tumescence and lubrication in the female. Orgasm, the culmination of this arousal process, is a uniquely sexual phenomenon, about which little is known (Bancroft, 1989). There are important sex differences; the frequency of orgasm (and ejaculation) in the male is limited by a "refractory period" of unarousability, which is relatively short in the adolescent but progressively lengthens as the man gets older. The frequency of orgasm in women is not restricted in the same way, perhaps because the reproductive consequences of frequent orgasms in the female would be unimportant, whereas in the male, infertility would result.

The localization of these various "sexual" functions within the central nervous system (CNS), at least in lower animals, is becoming established. The hypothalamus and other parts of the limbic system are important. The universality of such mechanisms across species is well illustrated by the function of the medial preoptic area of the hypothalamus. Lesions of this area result in deficits in sexual response in virtually all mammalian species that have been studied. The deficits are complex; they do not impair motivation for sexual interaction (a lesioned primate, for example, may continue to masturbate), but result in disruption of the complex motor and communicative responses that normally enable the animal to copulate with a mate (Hart & Leedy, 1985).

Central mechanisms are involved in *information processing*, that is, the recognition of a potentially sexual situation or partner, *genital responses*, and the complex pattern of motor behaviour and interaction with a sexual partner that results in *copulation and orgasm*. It is reasonable to assume, from the evidence that we have so far, that many of these neurophysiological mechanisms are involved in the sexual responses of the human, though how those responses are expressed and experienced will obviously be shaped by the uniquely human aspects of the information processing (Everitt & Bancroft, 1991).

Animal studies have shown that the neurotransmitters involved in the control of sexual behaviour are also involved in many aspects of brain function and are widely distributed in the CNS. By contrast, reproductive hormones such as testosterone and oestradiol have receptors that are more restricted in their distribution, located in areas involved in sexual responses and other brain mechanisms essential for reproduction. It is the interaction of the neurotransmitters with the hormones in specific brain areas that is crucial for many aspects of sexual response and behaviour.

The role of hormones: the male

The principal androgenic hormone in the male, testosterone, has a clear and fundamental role in the sexuality and fertility of men, as well as that of the male in most mammalian species (Bancroft, 1988). Increasing levels of testosterone in early adolescence are accompanied not only by development of secondary sexual characteristics, such as growth of the penis, sexual hair, and the onset of spermatogenesis, but also by increased sexual arousability, as shown by spontaneous erections during sleep and at other times. In one study, the sexual interest of the early adolescent boy, and his likelihood of masturbating and engaging in sexual interactions, were correlated more strongly with his level of free (i.e., biologically active) testosterone than with his stage of pubertal development (Udry, Billy, Morris, Groff, & Raj, 1985). A deficiency of testosterone in adult men is typically associated with a lack of sexual interest or desire, which can be improved by hormone replacement. The effects of testosterone on erectile function are more complex. Spontaneous erections, such as those that occur during sleep, are testosterone-dependent, and are impaired in states of hormone deficiency. By contrast, erections in response to visual erotic stimuli are relatively unaffected by testosterone lack, suggesting that there are aspects of sexual responsiveness in men that are testosterone-dependent, and others that are not. The erectile response to erotic imagery or fantasy may come into the hormone-dependent category, though the evidence is less clear. Testosterone is also necessary for normal spermatogenesis, and the hypogonadal man will be infertile. While seminal emission is testosterone-dependent, it is not yet clear whether this is the case for orgasm per se.

Testosterone, therefore, is necessary for normal sexual interest in men, but it is not sufficient. The considerable variation in the level of sexual interest among men cannot be explained in terms of variation in testosterone level, though genetic differences in the behavioural responsiveness to hormones may contribute. Other factors, not as yet understood, must contribute to an individual's constitutional level of sexual responsiveness.

The role of hormones: the female

Do women show a menstrual-cycle-related pattern of sexual interest or responsiveness comparable to the oestrus of most primates? In particular, are they more sexually interested or responsive, or attractive to their partners, around the time that they ovulate? The evidence remains inconclusive. The various studies that have relied on women's retrospective recall have found that a mid-cycle peak in sexuality is the least common pattern, women being more likely to report their peaks postmenstrually, premenstrually, or even during menstruation, or to be unaware of any particular cyclical pattern. The few studies in which hormonal changes have been measured in parallel with behaviour have produced conflicting results. Thus in some studies, peaks of sexuality have been postmenstrual (during the mid-follicular phase) rather than periovulatory (Bancroft, 1989). Others have shown evidence of a mid-cycle peak, the most convincing coming from a study of newly married African women, who showed peaks of coital activity around ovulation (Hedricks, Piccinino, Urdry, & Chimbia, 1987). One possible explanation for this variability is that the behavioural effect of the reproductive hormones will depend on the social and reproductive circumstances. In other words, if a woman is seeking pregnancy, as a young African woman is likely to be at the start of her marriage, then the behavioural effects of the periovulatory hormones may be interpreted differently, leading to desire for sexual intercourse. If fertility is not the goal, the effects may have a different significance. This implies an interaction between hormonal and cognitive processes, influenced by societal expectations. This would also be consistent with hormones having a different impact on the sexuality of women at different stages of their life cycle.

The interaction between mood and sexuality is also important. In one study one-third of the variance in sexual interest through the menstrual cycle was attributable to variations in well-being (Sanders, Warner, Backström, & Bancroft, 1983). Thus in women who experience noticeable changes in well-being through the cycle, peaks of sexual interest will be more likely at times when well-being is highest (e.g., postmenstrually).

Oestradiol, which is crucial to oestrus in many species, shows a very uncertain relationship to the sexuality of women, apart from its unequivocal role in the normal lubrication response of the vaginal wall to sexual stimulation. This latter effect is important for many post-menopausal women whose oestradiol levels have fallen. Testosterone is normally present in the circulation of women in approximately one-tenth of the quantity found in men, with about 50 per cent coming from the ovaries and 50 per cent from the adrenals. Its ovarian source varies cyclically, resulting in maximum levels around mid-cycle. This androgen appears to be relevant to sexual interest in women, as in men, though the evidence is much less consistent. The most convincing evidence comes from hormone replacement for women following the removal of their ovaries (Sherwin, 1991). However, such positive effects on sexuality involve supraphysiological levels of hormone. It is more difficult to demonstrate a relationship between sexuality and testosterone levels that vary within the woman's physiologically normal range.

In so far as testosterone is important for female sexuality, we are left with an intriguing riddle. It is often assumed that during the early organizing stages of our development, mainly prenatally, the relevant target organs of the male are sensitized to testosterone so that later, when androgens rise at puberty, the testosterone activates secondary sexual development, and sexual responsiveness, along male lines. By implication the female is less responsive to testosterone. But if women are responsive to testosterone, then even with the supraphysiological amounts referred to above, they are responding to levels which, in the male, would be in the hypogonadal range. This suggests that males are *less* sensitive to the behavioural effects of androgens than females, perhaps permitting them to be exposed to the much higher levels of androgens that are necessary for male muscular development and growth. If this is the case, then the initial exposure of the male foetus to consistently high levels of androgens must *de*sensitize the target cells in the brain. Females by comparison will be exposed to both lower and more variable levels of androgens during early development, resulting in more variable levels of target organ sensitivity. This offers one theoretical explanation for the apparently greater variability among women in the importance of testosterone for their sexuality.

Other explanations are worth considering. Given the pattern of sexual behaviour in human relationships, where frequency of sexual intercourse is greater than that required for optimum fertility, and the uncertain evidence of an oestrus in relation to the woman's ovarian cycle, it would be less important in terms of reproduction whether or not a woman responded behaviourally to her reproductive hormones. By contrast, for the man, for whom both fertility and sexual interest are clearly dependent on testosterone, any lack of responsiveness to testosterone would reduce his likelihood of reproducing himself. It is therefore possible that women have evolved to be genetically more variable than men in their behavioural responsiveness to reproductive hormones.

In general, we see more evidence that social influences are important to the sexuality of women than of men. Whether this is because the hormonal effects in women are generally weaker, or whether there are other explanations, is not yet clear.

Cognitive processes

Information processing is no less important for the sexuality of the rat than for that of the human. The situation has to be appraised, the availability of a suitable mate determined and the interaction with the mate negotiated. For the human, however, this information processing involves the appraisal of "meaning", and the repercussions of such meaning add a higher level of complexity.

Thus the sexuality of a situation, as perceived, will be susceptible to the full weight of human learning and the "social scripts" for sexual action, which we shall consider further below. At a more fundamental level of cognitive function, we need to consider the extent to which the individual is focusing attention not only on the sexual stimulus, but also on the physiological responses to it. Thus, if there is no distraction, there will be an escalation in which, confronted with a potentially sexual stimulus, the recognition of the response as sexual will lead to further response and associated arousal (Dekker & Everaerd, 1988). This process, it should be said, will not be independent of the neurophysiological substrate considered above. In a hypogonadal man, for example, whose arousability is impaired by testosterone deficiency, this process will be limited.

The importance of the cognitive component involves both the scope for altered meaning that it permits (a stimulus that is potentially sexual may be interpreted as non-sexual or even threatening) and the scope for distraction by other types of information processing that interfere with this escalating feedback process. There is now a substantial body of experimental evidence indicating how distracting stimuli impair the erotic response to a sexual stimulus (Cranston-Cuebas & Barlow, 1990). Interestingly, men can be more readily distracted from the erotic effects of auditory stimuli than of visual stimuli; women are distracted equally from both types of erotic stimuli (Przybyla & Byrne, 1984). This raises the interesting possibility that visual stimuli have a particular importance in the male, which is relatively independent of information processing, involving perhaps more direct links between the visual cortex and the hypothalamus.

Interestingly, when men who experience problems with their sexual response (e.g., erectile dysfunction of a psychogenic kind) are compared with "normal" men, distracting cues are less disruptive or may even enhance their response to erotic stimuli, presumably because in their usual situation, their concern about sexual failure is a more powerful form of distraction whose negative effects, including inhibiting or otherwise negative emotional responses, may be reduced by distracting stimuli that have no sexual connotations.

Erotic imagery or fantasy, while of undoubted relevance, does not fit easily into this scheme of things. Variability in the importance of imagery is partly a function of its general use. Whereas "thinking about imaginary situations", or "cognitive rehearsal", is universal, we vary considerably in the extent to which we produce images, either visual or auditory, or even tactile. If such images are more powerful in eliciting a sexual arousal response than simple cognitive rehearsal, their use could account for much of the individual variability in sexual arousability and sexual interest. Furthermore, an erotic image needs to be seen *both as a stimulus and a response*; it can occur as a manifestation of sexual arousal. The hypogonadal man, as a consequence, produces less in the way of erotic imagery.

Mood and emotional states

It has been widely assumed that anxiety or fear is incompatible with sexual response, and the principal theoretical explanations for sexual dysfunction, both psychoanalytic and behavioural, have emphasized the central role played by anxiety. Similarly, it is often assumed that it is difficult to be angry and sexually aroused at the same time. Such negative effects of anxiety or anger on sexual response were attributed to non-specific activation of the sympathetic nervous system in the periphery, leading to inhibition of erection, and so on. There is now little reason to support this view: if sympathetic activation does have an adverse effect, it is by direct and specific inhibition of sexual response, and not as part of generalized sympathetic activation.

Experimental manipulation of emotional states has shown these earlier assumptions to be oversimplifications. In many subjects, particularly those without obvious sexual problems, the induction of any form of arousal, even those with qualities of anxiety or anger, can increase the likelihood of a sexual response to a sexual stimulus (Cranston-Cuebas & Barlow, 1990). On the other hand, situations inducing anxiety or anger may act as distractors, or, if anxiety (or threat) is perceived as related to the sexual stimulus, this may lead to inhibition of sexual response. What is therefore apparent is that neither anxiety nor anger per se are incompatible with sexual response. Their significance in a sexual situation, depend on their origins and their perceived meaning to the subject (Bancroft, 1989).

There has been much less investigation of the relationship between depressed mood and sexual response, perhaps because depression is more difficult to invoke experimentally. The link between mood and sexuality has already been discussed in relation to the menstrual cycle. It is not surprising to find that, in most circumstances, feelings of depression and sexual arousal do not go together. This reflects the negative valence that the mood imparts both to the situation and to the subject's feeling of self-worth. It also reflects the state of inertia rather than arousal that typically characterizes depression. It is, however, possible that biochemical changes associated with depression can have adverse effects on sexual arousability. This is suggested by the impairment of spontaneous sleep erections in states of depression, and their recovery when the depression remits (Thase et al., 1987), together with a common link between the onset of loss of sexual interest and a depressive illness (Schreiner-Engel & Schiavi, 1986).

Social influences and "scripts"

The meaning we attribute to a physiological state will influence reaction to it, and, because of the effects of feedback, how that state evolves. There is an important sex difference in this respect: boys have a physiological signal of sexual response, penile erection, which is not only obvious but also readily labelled as sexual. Once that labelling has occurred, the boy has a ready method of assigning sexual significance to experiences or situations. Not only are girls provided with much less in the way of labels for their genitalia, when they respond physiologically, but also the changes are also less obvious and the attribution of sexual meaning to them less likely. The fact that most girls are older than boys when they recognize their genital responses as sexual may partially explain why social factors appear to have greater influence on the emerging sexuality of adolescent girls than of boys (Udry, Talbert, & Morris, 1986).

The sources of socially derived meanings or "scripts" for sexual behaviour are obviously highly complex (Gagnon & Simon, 1973) and can be considered only in outline in this chapter. At the individual level, the most immediate sources are the family and peer group. These, in turn, will reflect not only cultural patterns, but also religious and socio-economic factors within cultures. Anthropological evidence clearly indicates how such scripts vary across cultures, with some cultures being predominantly "sex positive" and others "sex negative" (Ford & Beach, 1952). The explanations for these cultural contrasts are of considerable interest. Attempts to understand the social evolution of such varied cultural patterns have emphasized the levels of sexual stratification (i.e., the extent to which one gender, usually the male, exerts the power in the social system) and sexual segregation (i.e., the extent to which males and females spend most of their time apart). These in turn reflect the type of social adaptation to the environment, and in particular whether social structure has evolved to the point when property and its inheritance becomes an important issue (Hotvedt, 1990). Thus in hunter-gatherer societies, now virtually extinct, small social groups moved through the environment to where food was available. For them, not only was property of little consequence, but also the patterns of male–female relationships were relatively egalitarian, and attitudes to sexuality relatively positive. This pattern was possibly facilitated by long periods of adolescent infertility, allowing the exploration of sexual relationships before the limitations of child-rearing intervened. As social systems became more settled and more complex, first with pastoral societies, gathering herds of livestock, and later agricultural societies, with the possession of land by a minority and the development of structured social hierarchies, the relevance of sexual stratification and segregation increased, with those of affluence having a particular need to protect the transfer of property by controlling paternity. We can do little but speculate about these very early origins. In more recent historical times, we see strong evidence of striking regional contrasts. Thus, the sexual norms of early Mediterranean societies were dominated by the importance of virginity. Sexual taboos were aimed at avoiding cuckoldry and ensuring that the husband, usually much older than his wife, was the father of any offspring. In contrast, the northern European tradition, possibly derived from "hunter-gatherer" types of fishing communities, emphasized fertility before marriage, with the "bundling" pattern of courtship, in which the couple paired off and progressed towards sexual intercourse, with marriage following pregnancy (Bancroft, 1989). The socio-political significance of these two contrasting systems is profound, with the northern European pattern more consistent with egalitarian male–female relationships and a single standard of sexual morality. The picture was further complicated by the impact of the Industrial Revolution, its dispersive effect on the extended family, the new opportunities for sexual exploitation of working-class women and the reinforcement of a "double standard" of sexual morality (Schmidt, 1977; Shorter, 1975). Nevertheless, these contrasting patterns are still evident today, in both Europe and the New World.

In more recent times, we have evidence of substantial changes in the pattern of premarital sexual behaviour from the mid-1960s. This was mainly manifested as a narrowing of the differences in sexual experience of adolescent boys and girls, reflecting a weakening of the "double standard" and increase in the ability of girls to enjoy their emerging sexuality (Clement, Schmidt, & Kruse, 1984). Such changes can be explained only in terms of changing social attitudes and "scripts", although the availability of modern methods of fertility control may have aided the process. The contrast between the exceptionally high levels of teenage pregnancy in United States and low levels in European countries such as Sweden and The Netherlands, and the associated contrast in attitudes to sex education and provision of contraceptive advice, is further evidence of the impact of social factors on the pattern of sexual behaviour (Jones et al., 1986).

CONCLUSIONS

We can now consider how these various factors interact to shape the sexuality of our "man" and "woman".

The man's level of sexual interest or desire will be a function of his neurophysiological state of arousal, his awareness of his arousal responses and the meanings he attributes to them, his rehearsal of the sexual "scripts" he has acquired by thoughts and internal images, and his mood. The origins of these components will include genetic and hormonal influences, the effects of learning, and the nature of his relationship with his social group.

His likelihood of expressing such interest as sexual behaviour will depend on his opportunities for action and his ability to enact the scripts appropriately. The likelihood of his repeating the behaviour will depend on its success in meeting his emotional needs at the time, whether it generates positive or negative emotional reactions, and whether it conforms to the norms of the social group that most influences him.

The sexuality of the woman can be understood in basically similar terms. There are potentially important differences in sexual physiology, particularly in relation to the "refractory period". Also, as there may be less emphasis on genital response in her early sexual development, and more emphasis on scripts in which relationships dominate, her constitutional capacity for sexual arousal will be relatively less important than her psychological susceptibility to interpersonal and social pressures. This may explain why, in general, the role of hormones in the sexuality of our woman is less clear than it is with our man.

FURTHER READING

Bancroft, J. (1989). *Human sexuality and its problems* (2nd edn). Edinburgh: Churchill Livingstone.

Ford, C. S., & Beach, F. A. (1952). *Patterns of sexual behaviour*. London: Eyre & Spottiswoode.

Gagnon, J., & Simon, W. (1973). *Sexual conduct: The social sources of human sexuality*. Chicago, IL: Aldine.

Kinsey, A. C., Pomeroy, W. B., Martin, C. F., & Gebhard, P. H. (1953). *Sexual behavior in the human female*. Philadelphia, PA: Saunders.

Masters, W. H., & Johnson, V. E. (1966). *Human sexual response*. Boston, MA: Little, Brown.

REFERENCES

Bancroft, J. (1988). Reproductive hormones and male sexual function. In J. M. A. Sitsen (Ed.) *Handbook of sexology: The pharmacology and endocrinology of sexual function* (vol. 6, pp. 297–315). Amsterdam: Elsevier.

Bancroft, J. (1989). *Human sexuality and its problems* (2nd edn). Edinburgh: Churchill Livingstone.

Beach, F. A. (1976). Sexual attractivity, proceptivity, and receptivity in female mammals. *Hormones and Behavior, 7,* 105–138.

Brownmiller, S. (1975). *Against our will! Men, women and rape*. New York: Simon & Schuster.

Clement, U., Schmidt, G., & Kruse, M. (1984). Changes in sex differences in sexual behaviour: A replication of a study of West German students (1966–1981). *Archives of Sexual Behavior, 13,* 99–120.

Cranston-Cuebas, M. A., & Barlow, D. H. (1990). Cognitive and affective contributions to sexual functioning. *Annual Review of Sex Research, 1,* 119–162.

Darwin, C. (1871). *The descent of man and selection in relation to sex*. London: John Murray.

Davenport-Hines, R. (1990). *Sex, death and punishment*. London: Collins.

Dekker, J., & Everaerd, W. (1988). Attentional effects on sexual arousal. *Psychophysiology, 25,* 45–54.

Dixson, A. F. (1983). The hormonal control of sexual behaviour in primates. *Oxford Reviews of Reproductive Biology, 5,* 131–219.

Everitt, B. J., & Bancroft, J. (1991). Of rats and men: The comparative approach to male sexuality. *Annual Review of Sex Research, 2,* 77–117.

Ford, C. S., & Beach, F. A. (1952). *Patterns of sexual behaviour*. London: Eyre & Spottiswoode.

Gagnon, J., & Simon, W. (1973). *Sexual conduct: The social sources of human sexuality*. Chicago, IL: Aldine.

Geer, J. H., & O'Donohue, W. T. (Eds) (1987). *Theories of human sexuality*. New York: Plenum.

Hart, B. L., & Leedy, M. G. (1985). Neurological bases of male sexual behavior: A comparative analysis. In N. Adler, R. W. Goy, & D. W. Pfaff (Eds) *Handbook of behavioral neurobiology* (vol. 7, pp. 373–422). New York: Plenum.

Hedricks, C., Piccinino, L. J., Udry, J. R., & Chimbia, T. H. (1987). Peak coital rate coincides with onset of luteinizing hormone surge. *Fertility and Sterility*, *48*, 234–238.

Hotvedt, M. E. (1990). Emerging and submerging adolescent sexuality: Culture and sexual orientation. In J. Bancroft & J. M. Reinisch (Eds) *Adolescence and puberty* (pp. 157–172). New York: Oxford University Press.

Jones, E. F., Forrest, J. D., Goldman, N., Henshaw, S. K., Lincoln, R., Rossoff, J. I., Westoff, C. F., & Wul, D. (1986). *Teenage pregnancy in industrialized countries*. New Haven, CT: Yale University Press.

Larsson, K. (1978). Experiential factors in the development of sexual behaviour. In J. Hutchison (Ed.) *Biological determinants of sexual behaviour* (pp. 55–86). Chichester: Wiley.

Money, J., & Ehrhardt, A. A. (1972). *Man and woman, boy and girl: Differentiation and dimorphism of gender identity from conception to maturity*. Baltimore, MD: Johns Hopkins University Press.

Perper, T. (1985). *Sex signals: The biology of love*. New York: Institute for Scientific Information Press.

Przybyla, D. P., & Byrne, D. (1984). The mediating role of cognitive processes in self-reported sexual arousal. *Journal of Research in Personality*, *18*, 54–63.

Sanders, D., Warner, P., Backström, T., & Bancroft, J. (1983). Mood, sexuality, hormones and the menstrual cycle: I. Changes in mood and physical state: Description of subjects and method. *Psychosomatic Medicine*, *45*, 487–501.

Schmidt, G. (1977). Introduction, sociohistorical perspectives. In J. Money & H. Musaph (Eds) *Handbook of sexology* (pp. 269–282). Amsterdam: Excerpta Medica.

Schreiner-Engel, P., & Schiavi, R. C. (1986). Lifetime psychopathology in individuals with low sexual desire. *Psychosomatic Medicine*, *43*, 199–214.

Sherwin, B. B. (1991). The psychoendocrinology of aging and female sexuality. *Annual Review of Sex Research*, *2*, 181–198.

Short, R. V. (1981). Sexual selection in man and the Great Apes. In C. E. Graham (Ed.) *Reproductive biology of the Great Apes* (pp. 319–341). London: Academic Press.

Shorter, E. (1975). *The making of the modern family*. New York: Basic Books.

Thase, M. E., Reynolds, C. F., Glanz, L. M., Jennings, J. R., Sewitch, D. E., Kupfer, D. J., & Frank, E. (1987). Nocturnal penile tumescence in depressed men. *American Journal of Psychiatry*, *144*, 89–92.

Tutin, C. E. G. (1980). Reproductive behaviour of wild chimpanzees in the Gombe National Park, Tanzania. In R. V. Short & B. J. Weir (Eds) *The Great Apes of Africa. Journal of Reproduction and Fertility*. suppl. 28, 43–57.

Udry, J. R., Billy, J. O. G., Morris, N. M., Groff, T. R., & Raj, M. H. (1985). Serum androgenic hormones motivate sexual behavior in adolescent boys. *Fertility and Sterility*, *43*, 90–94.

Udry, J. R., Talbert, L. M., & Morris, N. M. (1986). Biosocial foundations for adolescent female sexuality. *Demography*, *23*, 217–229.

6.5

STRESS AND COPING

Robert J. Gatchel
University of Texas Southwestern Medical Center, USA

Early conceptualizations of stress	Cataclysmic events
	Personal stressors
Walter Cannon	Background stressors
Hans Selye	**Appraisal of stress**
John Mason	**Coping behaviour**
Marianne Frankenhaeuser	**Stress, coping, and health**
Psychological stress	**Further reading**
Types of stressors	**References**

The term *stress* has become part of the lay vernacular, and is widely used as a ready explanation for a number of problems from health complaints to work "burnout" and job dissatisfaction. Moreover, from a scientific point of view, there has been a great deal of research conducted that has demonstrated a relationship between stress and these mental and physical health problems. In these contexts, the term stress is often viewed as a well-delineated construct which has been carefully defined and is quite specific in its effects. However, in this chapter, it will be highlighted how the construct of stress is far from specific, and why there is quite a bit of debate concerning its precise definition.

A major problem associated with defining and measuring stress is that, rather than being an actual entity or "thing", stress is a construct which is inferred in order to account for some form of behaviour. Stress is usually viewed as a mediator, that is, an unobservable inferred construct which is hypothesized to account for a certain observable behaviour such as health or illness differences between individuals. Of course, if one uses a construct to explain some form of behaviour, it is essential that one develops a precise operational definition and employs objective and quantifiable behavioural referents as measures of the construct. As will be seen, this attempt at a precise operational definition is no easy task. Stress is a broad process that involves complex biochemical, physiological, behavioural, and psychological dimensions, many of which are directly or indirectly related to health. At the outset, a rather broad definition of stress will be used: stress is the process by which environmental events threaten or challenge an organism's well-being and by which that organism responds to this threat (Gatchel, Baum, & Krantz, 1989). The environmental events that cause stress are called *stressors*. When such stressors occur, a complex physiological and psychological response mechanism is evoked. When these stressors are intense or become chronic, there are often negative health consequences or outcomes that are produced by them.

EARLY CONCEPTUALIZATIONS OF STRESS

The ancient Greek physician, Hippocrates (c.460–c.370 BC), who initially proposed that bodily fluids or humours were responsible for certain personality or temperament types, as well as for physical and mental illness, also highlighted the potential negative impact of stress. In his writings, Hippocrates separated suffering caused by disease (*pathos*) from the toil involved in resisting and fighting it (*ponos*). Thus, he suggested a stress-like feature of illness – the energy and wear caused by attempts to combat disease. Since that time, there have been similar notions appearing in the literature (Selye, 1956).

Walter Cannon

It was not until the beginning of the twentieth century, however, that the concept of stress became more scientifically formalized through the work of the physiologist Walter Cannon. Cannon was among the first to actually use the term *stress*, and he clearly indicated that both physiological and psychological components were important. In his physiological studies, he used the term "great emotional stress" to describe a powerful psychophysiological response process that appeared to influence emotion in animals (Cannon, 1928, 1929). His studies clearly demonstrated that emotional stressors such as pain, fear, and rage could cause significant changes in physiological functioning. Cannon pointed out the important "emergency function" of the catecholamines, epinephrine (adrenalin) and norepinephrine (noradrenalin). He suggested that epinephrine played an important role in adaptation by arousing the organism and thereby enabling it to respond more rapidly to danger. Thus, when extremely frightened or enraged, the organism may experience an arousal that may be uncomfortable, but which readies it to act against the stimulus that frightens or angers it.

Initially, these stress-related increases in catecholamines produced by sympathetic nervous system activation, or the "fight or flight" model derivable from Cannon's work, may facilitate adaptive behaviour. This arousal was seen as quite adaptive in helping to increase the ability to resist or enhance the ability to flee the threatening situation. Indeed, some studies have demonstrated superior performance on certain tasks when subjects are injected with epinephrine (Frankenhaeuser, Jarpe, & Mattell, 1961), and also among individuals who produce greater levels of catecholamines in the face of challenge (see Frankenhaeuser, 1971). However, it should also be pointed out that such arousal has been found to be associated with impaired performance on complex tasks (see Evans, 1978).

In Cannon's later writings (Cannon, 1935), stress is clearly seen in terms of both physiological as well as emotional or psychological responses to dangers in the environment. Although stress is seen as an important aid in survival since it mobilizes the organism to take some important action, Cannon also saw it as possibly causing a significant disruption of emotional and physiological stability or homeostasis. He described *critical stress levels* as stress or dangers that affect an organism to such a degree as to disrupt homeostasis or equilibrium which can cause disruption of physiological functioning. Aside from the wear and tear on our bodies generated by repeated or prolonged stress, a variety of negative outcomes is likely to occur when stress does not abate or when there is repeated exposure to stress. Among these consequences are decrements in the ability to cope with subsequent stressors, after-effects, and, in certain cases, physiological dysfunction, tissue damage, or even death (Gatchel et al., 1989).

It should also be noted that Cannon documented the importance of neuroendocrine system responses in the stress response. The "stress hormones" epinephrine and norepinephrine are now often used in research investigations of the stress process: this is an important system operative in the physiological stress response. Stimulation of the sympathetic nervous system causes the adrenal medulla to secrete large amounts of catecholamines, which are neurotransmitter hormones that increase cardiovascular activity, produce vasoconstriction, inhibit gastro-intestinal activity, and increase a number of other bodily functions. In a second major system involved in the stress response process, the pituitary gland secretes the hormone *adrenocorticotropic hormone* (ACTH) that stimulates the adrenal cortex to produce corticosteroids, particularly cortisol. Cortisol affects carbohydrate metabolism and is an anti-inflammatory agent (see Figure 1).

Hans Selye

The early physiological research on emotional stress by Cannon basically laid dormant for many years until Hans Selye's investigations of stress appeared in the literature (Selye, 1956). This research by Selye popularized the notion

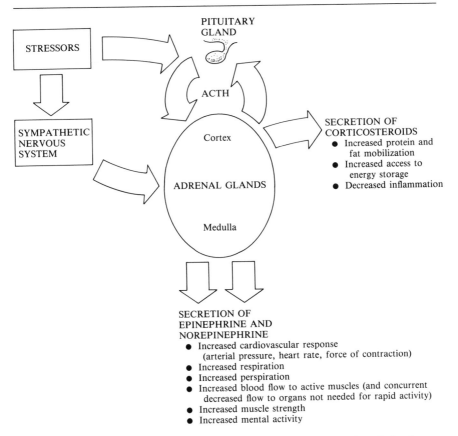

Figure 1 Illustration of the stress-related activities of the adrenal glands

of stress and brought it to the attention of scientists in many different disciplines. As is now well known, Selye's work on stress began quite accidentally in his investigation of sex hormones. Selye found that injections into rats of extracts of ovary tissue produced an unexplainable triad of responses: (1) an enlargement of the adrenal glands which secrete catecholamines and corticosteroids, (2) shrinkage of the thymus gland, and (3) bleeding ulcers. Stimulated by these puzzling findings, Selye subsequently found that extracts of other organs caused the same triad of responses, and that substances not derived from bodily tissue could also cause these responses. He eventually found this same "non-specific" triad of responses to be characteristic of such disparate stimuli as injection of insulin, application of cold or heat, exposure to X-rays, exercise, and so on. His studies clearly showed that each time an alien or aversive stressor agent was applied, changes in the adrenal and thymus glands and the development of ulcers in the acid sensitive stomach lining were observed. This triad of responses was called *non-specific* because it appeared to be caused by *any* noxious or aversive event. Selye (1956) illustrated this notion of a non-specific stress response by comparing it to a burglary:

> Suppose that all possible accesses to a bank building are connected with a police station by an elaborate burglar-alarm system. When a burglar enters the bank, no matter what his personal characteristics are – whether he is small or tall, lean or stout – and no matter which door or window he opens to enter, he will set off the same alarm. The primary change is therefore non-specifically induced from anywhere by anyone. The pattern of resulting secondary change, on the other hand, is highly specific. It is always in a certain police station that the burglar alarm will ring and policemen will then rush to the bank along a specified route according to a predetermined plan to prevent robbery. (p. 58)

Thus, a consistent triad of responses is non-specifically induced. In using this concept of non-specific response, Selye then went on to define the stress syndrome as all of the non-specifically induced changes that were produced by a noxious agent. Stress itself was considered a specific state that was the "common denominator of all adaptive reactions in the body". Exposure to a stressor, such as injection of a pathogen, created a response pattern involving, among other things, the original triad of physiological responses.

Selye also introduced the concept of the *General Adaptation Syndrome* (GAS). According to Selye, the GAS consists of three distinct stages of responding (Figure 2). In the first stage, termed the *alarm reaction*, the organism becomes aware of the stressor, or the presence of noxious stimulation. The organism prepares to resist the stressor by mobilizing and activating physiological functioning (e.g., increasing adrenal activity, as well as cardiovascular and respiratory functions, as a means of increasing the body's readiness to respond). The second stage, called the *stage of resistance*, refers to that period when the physiological reserves are ready and circulating levels of corticosteroids have increased. Various coping mechanisms are employed in order to achieve suitable adaptation. During this stage, there is a relatively

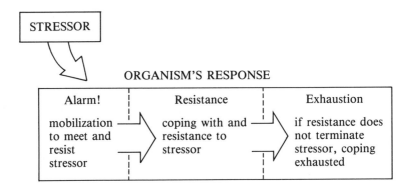

Figure 2 The three stages of Selye's General Adaptation Syndrome

constant resistance to this stressor, but this may be accompanied by a decrease in resistance to other stimuli. When these reactions are repeated many times, or when they are prolonged because of recurring problems, the organism may be placed at risk for irreversible physiological damage. Selye believes that this is the result of the third stage of the GAS, which he refers to as the *exhaustion stage*. During this stage, adaptive reserves are depleted by long-term or repeated conflict with stressors, and resistance is then no longer possible. The result of this exhaustion is likely to be the onset of *diseases of adaptation*. Such illnesses as kidney disease, arthritis, and cardiovascular disease can occur. For example, cardiovascular damage and arthritis may be linked to prolonged elevated levels of catecholamines (Ross & Glomset, 1976). Likewise, high concentrations of inflammatory corticosteroids may be precursors to the onset of arthritis. Also, there is evidence that suggests that prolonged stress can affect immunity (Gatchel et al., 1989). Thus, like Cannon, Selye emphasizes that negative physiological consequences result from prolonged exposure to stressors.

John Mason

Research on the importance of the GAS and how it might be associated with significant health problems caught the attention of the scientific and medical community because of its obvious theoretical and clinical implications. Attention and further development of stress theory increased following the popularization of Selye's work. Moreover, like what happens often in science, criticism of Selye's work also began to appear. One such criticism was the fact that his notion of non-specificity appeared to rule out the possible importance of psychological mechanisms in determining response to a stressor (Mason, 1975). For example, if the same triad of responses were produced regardless of the type of stressor, how might you account for potential individual differences in appraisal and subsequent reaction to the same stressor? Researchers such as John Mason suggested that the process of *psychological appraisal* was very important in determining the type of response produced by a stressor. For example, Mason suggested that stress is neither non-specific nor unitary and that psychological awareness or appraisal of noxious events is an important component necessary for stress to occur. He reported that different patterns of epinephrine, norepinephrine, and corticosteroid secretion were associated with stressors varying in degree of uncertainty or anger and fear elicitation. These are all stressors, but they have different emotional consequences. According to Mason, psychological distress precedes adrenal-pituitary response and may be necessary for physiological reaction to occur.

Mason states that there may be circumstances in which the non-specific stress response of Selye occurs without any psychological input, but the best evidence suggests that awareness of a noxious condition and attempts to deal

565

with it are very crucial in this process. Mason indicates that this awareness need not be conscious in the common use of the term because of the body's ability to attack foreign substances without conscious awareness of the individual. Mason's own work has also demonstrated that physical stressors, such as application of heat, do not elicit adrenal activity when psychological factors involved in the perception and sensation of the stressor are eliminated (see Mason, 1975). Another study reported by Mason compared two groups of dying patients, one composed of people who remained in a coma until they died and the other made up of patients who remained conscious until they passed away. After death, autopsy indicated that the conscious group showed symptoms of stress, such as enlarged adrenal glands, while those who were not conscious showed no such symptoms (Symington, Currie, Curran, & Davidson, 1955).

In fairness to Selye, it should be noted that the notion of psychological appraisal in the stress process can be integrated in the Selye model if one assumes that the non-specific nature of stress is limited to the organism's initial response to a stressor during the alarm stage. If the alarm stage response alone is seen as non-specific, then psychological appraisal or interpretation may still affect subsequent responses during the resistance and exhaustion stages. Thus, one can modify Selye's original model to incorporate some of the more recent research documenting the importance of psychological appraisal and coping mechanisms on the stress response.

Marianne Frankenhaeuser

The work of Marianne Frankenhaeuser and her fellow Swedish colleagues has clearly revealed the strong psychological component involved in the stress response. For example, she has demonstrated that epinephrine and norepinephrine levels can significantly affect the emotional and cognitive functioning in subjects, and that they are secreted in response to purely psychological events (Frankenhaeuser, 1972). In one such study, increases in levels of epinephrine and norepinephrine were associated with decreasing amounts of control over electric shock (Frankenhaeuser & Rissler, 1970). In another study, both understimulation (not having enough to do) and overstimulation (having too much to do) were associated with rises in epinephrine and norepinephrine levels (Frankenhaeuser, Nordheden, Myrsten, & Post, 1971).

In another interesting study, Patkai (1971) demonstrated that increased output of the "stress hormones" epinephrine and norepinephrine were associated not only with noxious or aversive events but also with pleasant but uncontrollable events. In this study, subjects participated in four sessions. During one session, they played a game of chance (a modified bingo game that was generally regarded as being pleasant). In another session, they viewed gruesome surgery films; and in a third session, unpleasant and tedious tasks were performed. Subjects also spent one session in "neutral inactivity" in order to provide a baseline or control for their other experiences. It was found that epinephrine secretion was highest in the pleasant but uncontrollable setting (playing a game), next highest in the less pleasant conditions (tedious task session, film session), and lowest in the inactivity session. Thus, both pleasant and unpleasant events evoke biochemical symptoms of stress (see Figure 3).

This above work is important because it demonstrates the pervasive role that psychological factors can play in eliciting a primary physiological symptom of stress (epinephrine and norepinephrine secretion). This physiological

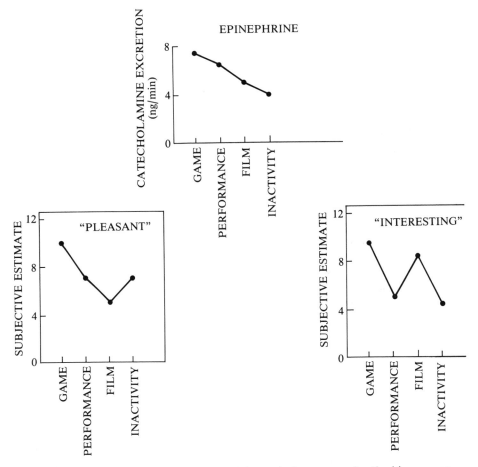

Figure 3 Mean epinephrine levels and ratings of pleasantness for the bingo game (pleasant condition), task and film (less pleasant conditions), and inactivity sessions. Note that higher levels of epinephrine were associated with pleasant and unpleasant events

Source: Patkai, 1971

response, in turn, is associated with psychological responses such as emotionality and cognitive ability. It also suggests a kind of non-specific specificity not unlike Selye's. The same bodily response – secretion of epinephrine and norepinephrine – seems to occur in the face of a wide range of psychological events. Included in a list of stressors that elicit this response are urban commuting, job dissatisfaction, loss of control, conflict, taking examinations, noise, anticipation of an aversive event, and boredom (see Collins & Frankenhaeuser, 1978; Lundberg & Frankenhaeuser, 1976). However, psychological processes can affect the degree or magnitude of this response.

PSYCHOLOGICAL STRESS

This early research on stress clearly documented the importance of biological bases of the stress process. The more recent research has started to focus on the psychological dimension of the stress concept. This has attracted a great deal of interest in the psychological community because, if psychological factors are demonstrated to actually alter bodily function in ways that might facilitate illness, an important link between psychology and health will have been revealed. Indeed, the relationship between the mind and the body has long been a controversial topic among philosophers, physiologists, and psychologists. The Greek physician Hippocrates proposed one of the earliest temperamental theories of personality and suggested that various bodily fluids or humours were associated with specific personality attributes or temperaments. This view of the interrelationship between mind and body, however, lost favour in the seventeenth century with the advent of physical medicine during the Renaissance and the belief that it was unscientific to view that the mind influenced the body. The understanding of the mind and soul was relegated to the areas of religion and philosophy, while the understanding of the body was considered to be in the separate realm of physical medicine. This perpetuated the dualistic viewpoint that mind and body functioned separately and independently. This dualistic viewpoint was further formalized and consolidated by the French philosopher René Descartes, with his Cartesian dualism of mind and body becoming the pre-eminent philosophical basis of medicine. The discovery in the nineteenth century that micro-organisms caused certain diseases produced further acceptance of the dualistic viewpoint. During this new scientific era of medicine, mechanical laws or physiological principles became the only permissible explanations of disease.

Strict dualism mellowed somewhat during the mid-nineteenth century, primarily because of the work of the prominent French physician Claude Bernard, who began to emphasize the contributions of psychological factors to physical ailments. Subsequently, Sigmund Freud was very influential in stressing the interaction of psychological and physical factors in various disorders. Though emphasis was still placed on the body, micro-organisms, and biological determinants of illness, gradually we were becoming more aware of other sources of influence.

The research on stress has renewed the interest in the significant influence of psychological factors in health and illness. The contemporary researcher who has been most responsible for the delineation of the importance of psychological factors in the stress process is Richard Lazarus (1966). By pointing out that stressors can be psychological, Lazarus made the study of stress much more complex and challenging. This is because another level of influence is added to this research area. That is to say, like other aspects of behaviour, psychological stress cannot be measured directly. Instead, it must be inferred from responses or defined in terms of the situations in which it arises.

In dealing with a construct such as stress, it is best to define it operationally as a complex of responses consisting of three broad components of behaviour: (1) subjective or self-report (i.e., asking people how they feel); (2) overt motor behaviours measured by observing performance on certain tasks; and (3) physiological arousal involving primarily the sympathetic branch of the autonomic nervous system, and measuring responses such as epinephrine and norepinephrine levels. What makes the study and measurement of the stress response so difficult is that one cannot always assume that these three broad behaviour component measures will be highly correlated to one another. An individual may verbally report that he or she does not feel "stressed" but yet display increased catecholamine levels and be observed performing poorly on a task requiring concentration. Obviously, it is important to assess all three components of behaviour in specific situations whenever possible, with the expectation that there may be complex interactions among components that may differ from one type of situation to the next.

Indeed, it is useful to group or label stressors in terms of where they occur, what they entail, or their characteristics. As a result, we can discuss occupational stress, urban stress, and the like. The problem is that the impact of the death of a parent, losing a job, or being exposed to crowding is greater than the sum of its effects. What does it mean to experience such stress? This is the real challenge for stress researchers.

TYPES OF STRESSORS

Many external events or situations carry a range of potential problems. Some or all of these problems may be perceived as stressful under certain conditions. In an attempt to categorize types of stressors along a number of dimensions, including how long the stressor persists, the magnitude of response required by the stressor, and the number of people affected, Lazarus and Cohen (1977) have delineated three general categories as stressors: cataclysmic events, personal stressors, and background stressors or daily hassles.

Cataclysmic events

These are stressors that have sudden and powerful impact and are more or less universal in eliciting a stress response. Such events usually require a great deal of effort for effective coping. War, natural disaster, and nuclear accidents are unpredictable and powerful threats that generally affect all of those touched by them. The powerful onset of such cataclysmic events may initially produce a freezing or dazed response by victims. Coping is difficult and may bring no immediate relief. For example, when a severe storm hits an area or when an earthquake occurs in a region, it can be extremely frightening and dangerous to residents, causing severe disruption of people's lives, and causing damage or loss whose impact will not fade for years. However, because the actual event is brief, the severe and threatening aspects of such a stressor dissipate rapidly. Some cataclysmic events, though, cause little physical damage but do not fade quickly. For example, at Love Canal in upstate New York, the discovery of toxic waste and dangers to urban residents was a slow process with little physical destruction. The same was the case for the nuclear accident at Three Mile Island. In these situations, where rebuilding is not what is needed (nothing was actually destroyed), and the damage already done is less important than damage that may yet occur in future years, recovery may be much more difficult. Thus, even within this broad category of cataclysmic events, there may be significant differences in terms of the immediate impact and the long-term consequences on recovery from such a stressor.

Personal stressors

Similar to cataclysmic events, personal stressors are strong and may be unexpected. These types of stressors include events that are powerful enough to challenge adaptive abilities in the same way as the cataclysmic events, but they affect fewer people at any one point in time. This distinction is important to make, since it has been demonstrated that social support has a moderating effect on stress (see Gatchel et al., 1989). In other words, having people around to provide support, help, comparison for emotional and behavioural responses, and other assistance can reduce the negative impact of the stressor. With cataclysmic events, people are able to share distress with others undergoing the same difficulties. However, the second class of stressors (personal stressors) affect fewer people at a time, resulting in fewer people with whom to share the experience. Such events include response to illness, death, or losing one's job.

The death of a parent, for example, is generally an intensely painful loss, and is not always anticipated. The event itself is acute (the death and the immediate period of grief are relatively short) even though, like a disaster, it may leave scars or problems that continue for years. Most typically, the occurrence of the stressor and its immediate aftermath are the most stressful aspects of the experience. Typically, things gradually improve and people may begin to cope with the loss of a loved one by believing that things will continue to improve steadily. However, again, there may be wide individual differences that occur that need to taken into account.

Background stressors

These are persistent, repetitive, and almost routine stressors that are part of one's everyday life. Lazarus and Cohen (1977) have labelled this third group of stressors as daily hassles – stable, repetitive, low-intensity problems encountered daily as part of one's routine. These daily hassles are different from other stressors in many ways. First of all, they are much less powerful than the other two categories of stressors noted above. Cumulatively, over time they may pose threats equally serious, but individually the stressors do not generally pose severe threats. Second, they are chronic. Their impact persists over long periods of time, and the effects of the exposure are gradual. Thus, living in a very noisy neighbourhood may not pose severe threats all at once. That is to say, one exposure to noise is easily coped with and not particularly threatening. However, noise is not usually a one-time event. Rather, it is often repeated and may persist indefinitely. In this context, the notion that things are getting better may not be common: the point at which the worst is over may never occur as things slowly become worse and worse. People can cope with individual episodes of noise even if it is uncontrollable (Glass & Singer, 1972), but the cumulative effects of chronic exposure to noise over time appear to be more severe (Cohen, 1980).

Other chronic stressors include job dissatisfaction, neighbourhood problems, and commuting. In an evaluation of another type of chronic stressor, Thorell, Knox, Svensson, & Waller (1985) reported greater systolic blood pressure elevations among those in high-demand–low-control occupations (such as waiters, drivers, and cooks) than among those in more controllable or less demanding settings. Moreover, Karasek and colleagues have suggested that work stress, which they again operationalized as low control over the work process *and* high work demand, is associated with greater risk for coronary heart disease (Karasek, Theorell, Schwartz, Pieper, & Afredson, 1982). Frankenhaeuser and colleagues have also shown that work stress is associated with coronary risk factors involving catecholamine production, cigarette smoking and sedentary behaviour (e.g., Frankenhaeuser & Johansson, 1982).

Finally, the benefits of social support in order to cope may not be as important with these types of stressors. Even if large numbers of individuals are affected, the duration and magnitude of individual exposure may be too brief to raise the need for affiliation or support. A crowded commute to work is an episodic bout with stress. However, the stress is not severe and can usually be coped with (although it may become increasingly difficult to do so over time). Such an aversive experience probably will not be of sufficient intensity to cause people to band together to provide each other with support and comfort.

In summary, background stressors or daily hassles are chronic, affect large numbers of people *on an individual basis*, and alone do not require a great deal of coping. Yet, the cumulation of stress over a long period of time may result in deceptively severe consequences. Regular and prolonged exposure to low-level stress may require more adaptive responses in the long run than exposure to other stressors. Background stressors generally push an individual's abilities toward their limit. By requiring that people allocate attention and effort to them, they may gradually reduce an individual's ability to cope with subsequent stressors.

APPRAISAL OF STRESS

In his work, Lazarus (1975) emphasizes the role of perception and cognitive appraisal in the stress response process. He argues that unless we perceive the situation as threatening, we will not experience stress. Thus, it could be argued that animals in Selye's experiments may have had to perceive danger before an alarm reaction and the subsequent phases of the GAS could occur. Indeed, in support of this hypothesis, the earlier reviewed study by Symington and colleagues (1955) found that patients who were dying from disease showed no stress response, as measured by adrenal activity, as long as they were unconscious. Lazarus argues that blocking a person's ability to appraise his or her situation as stressful can prevent the onset of the stress response period.

Lazarus has demonstrated the significance of psychological stress over the course of more than twenty years of research. In an initial series of studies conducted during the 1960s, he demonstrated that, by altering the interpretations or appraisals people made while exposed to a stressor, different stress reactions would occur. For example, in one such study, Lazarus, Opton, Nomikos, and Rankin (1965) required that subjects view a gruesome and stressful film depicting woodshop accidents such as a worker cutting off a finger and a worker being killed by a wooden plank driven through his body. Subjects were provided with different narratives when viewing the film. One group of subjects was told that the events had been staged and that no one was really being hurt. Another group was told that events were real but the film would help improve safety in such settings. A third group of subjects was given no explanation. Results demonstrated that both sets of instructions were effective in reducing arousal during the film, relative to the group given no explanation, presumably because such instructions allowed the appraisal of the film in a less threatening manner.

These results were similar to those reported in an earlier study by Lazarus and colleagues (Speisman, Lazarus, Mordkoff, & Davidson, 1964). In this study, subjects were shown a film depicting primitive initiation rites that included rather unpleasant circumcision surgery performed on young adolescents. Subjects viewed the film accompanied by one of three different sound tracts. One group of subjects heard a narration accompanying the film which emphasized the pain, mutilation, and possible disease consequences associated with the circumcision rites (trauma condition); a second group heard a narration in which the pain and consequences were denied and that the participants in the rites were willing and happy because this provided transition from adolescence to adulthood (denial condition); the third group heard a detached description of the rites from an anthropological perspective (intellectualization condition); a fourth group was shown the film with no narration accompanying it. The results of this investigation showed that the psychological stress responses were significantly reduced for subjects in the denial, intellectualization, and no-narration conditions, relative to subjects in the trauma group. Thus, once again, instructions tailored to denial and intellectualization allowed subjects to appraise the situation as less threatening, while instructions given to trauma subjects emphasized those aspects of the film that were more likely to be seen as stressful. Thus, these studies, as well as a number of other studies conducted by Lazarus and his colleagues, provide strong evidence that stress is not well understood in situational terms alone. The films that different groups of subjects saw were the same, and the setting in which they viewed them was similar. However, by altering the interpretations people made while viewing the films (through the narrative or soundtrack manipulation), Lazarus and his colleagues were able to observe different stress reactions.

It should also be pointed out that in some of the studies conducted by Lazarus and colleagues, another source of important variance in stress reactions was also revealed — personality dispositions or tendencies to appraise events in particular ways. For example, in the study of responses to the film depicting circumcision rites, Speisman et al. (1964) found that subjects predisposed to the use of psychological denial as a means of coping with aversive events demonstrated more stress in response to the detached intellectualization soundtrack than to the denial soundtrack. The opposite was true of those subjects who tended to routinely cope by intellectualizing a threat. Differences in appraisal were still found to be responsible for variations in the magnitude of the stress response, but a different source of these differences was demonstrated — situational and personality-based variation in the ways in which a stressor was normally appraised by subjects.

Of course, one must keep in mind the important differences between the type of chronic stressors that were used by investigators such as Selye in demonstrating the biological stress response, and the more acute psychological stressors used by investigators such as Lazarus. There may well be different underlying psychophysiological mechanisms involved in these two types of stress processes. Nevertheless, the significance of the work by Lazarus cannot be overlooked in clearly demonstrating the role that appraisal processes can have on certain stress processes. Thus, we evaluate stressors we encounter, and only those appraised to be threatening evoke the stress response. For example, if one fails an examination, a number of factors will enter into an individual's appraisal of this event. Individuals may consider how much the failure will affect their final grades, whether they feel the failure was their fault or the fault of a bad test, how the failure will affect their self-image, or the extent to which they care about grades or tests. If the failure will not count toward their grade, if they do not care how they do on an exam, or if it does not threaten their self-esteem, the individual will not experience stress. If, on the other hand, the failure is perceived as threatening, stress is more likely to occur.

The role of appraisal mechanisms in the stress process has been widely demonstrated and generally accepted. This has led to important additional research focusing on long-term coping and the kinds of appraisals that can be made to modify the magnitude of stress responses displayed. Such coping processes will be discussed next.

COPING BEHAVIOUR

The above research clearly demonstrates that the impact of any potentially stressful event is significantly influenced by how a person appraises or copes with it. When exposed to a potentially stressful situation, we appraise the setting and make judgements about how threatening it is to us. Lazarus and Launier (1978) have delineated a number of possible appraisals of situations: the evaluation of an event as *irrelevant* (the event in question will not affect the individual); *benign* (the event is positive); and *harmful or threatening interpretations* which may lead to stress. These stressful appraisals may, in turn, be harm or loss assessments involving analyses of damage that already occurred; or threat appraisals concerned with future damages; or challenge appraisals focused on the possibility of overcoming the stressor.

After a situation is judged to be threatening and stressful, secondary appraisals are then made. Now, no longer concerned with assessment of danger, we turn our attention and resources to the dangers or benefits of different modes of coping with the perceived threats. Thus, the perception of danger motivates us to search for coping responses that will reduce this threat.

Gatchel et al. (1989) provide the following example of appraisal of a threat:

> Consider an example of this sequence in a familiar and relatively low-threat event. You feel as if your peers at college exclude you from their activities. When impromptu parties come up, you are the last to find out. People go to the movies without inviting you to go along or go to dinner without waiting for you. You feel

isolated from your fellow students. If you are the kind of person that derives self-esteem or gratification from being part of the "gang," you are more likely to appraise this as threatening and aversive than if you prefer the role of "loner". Let us say you are of the former persuasion. You are upset by this situation and wish to respond. During a second appraisal of the situation, you may consider several approaches. You can do nothing or even withdraw further – the benefits of which are that you do not have to expend energy or risk the rejection that might result from a blatant attempt to join the group. The costs of this coping option are continued isolation and loss of self-esteem. On the other hand, you may make a strong effort to join the group, risking embarrassment and rejection for the possible benefit of being accepted into the group. A third alternative might be to slowly increase your participation in the group. The risks and benefits are similar to those of the second alternative except that the risk of embarrassment is reduced and the period of time before you can feel that you "belong" is greater. You may try to find out why you are being treated as you are so that you understand it better. Finally, you may reinterpret the situation, deciding that you do not want to join the group. By reinterpreting rejection by the group in a positive light, you may reduce loss of self-esteem, but you are still not a member of the group. (pp. 47–48)

Thus, the individual's response to the situation will depend on two kinds of appraisal. First, the individual must interpret the situation and consider its potential threats, harm, or challenge. Is it appraised as threatening or stressful? Second, the individual must consider the response choices. Obviously, evaluation of your choices is based on your interpretation of the situation and nature of the threat you see. By weighing the costs and benefits of these choices, you select an appropriate coping strategy. Thus, the relationship between a stressful event and coping represents a dynamic interplay or process. Coping behaviour can be seen as a series of transactions between an individual who has a certain set of resources, values, and commitments with a particular environment with its own demands and constraints.

Coping behaviour is an important part of the stress response. Moreover, there are literally hundreds of different coping strategies a person might utilize in dealing with a stressful event. For the sake of convenience, these coping strategies have been grouped into five general categories by Cohen and Lazarus (1979):

1 *Direct action responses*, where the individual tries to directly manipulate or alter his or her relationship to the stressful situation. For example, an individual may change the setting, flee, or otherwise remove the physical presence of the stressor.

2 *Information seeking*, in which an individual may seek information about the situation so that he or she can understand it and predict related events. Gathering information about the stressful event may be helpful in use for problem solving or emotional regulation. For example, the individual exposed to chronic commuting stress might seek more information about the commuting situation either to reduce his or her anxiety or to make decisions about alternative possibilities.

3 *Inhibition of action*, which involves doing nothing in a situation. This may be the best course of action in some situations, especially if it is seen as a short-term impact or event.
4 *Intrapsychic or palliative coping*, in which the individual accommodates the stressful situation by reappraising the situation or by altering his or her "internal environment". Taking drugs, drinking alcohol, learning to relax, creating or using psychological defence mechanisms, and engaging in meditation are examples of this type of coping.
5 *Turning to others* for help and emotional support involves mobilizing one's social support network to help with the situation. Thus, an individual who is attempting to cope with a particular problem might try to mobilize support from within the family.

An individual will use a wide variety of different coping strategies in managing a single stressor. The same individual may, for example, engage in intrapsychic coping, turning to others for support, and information seeking at different points in time in coping with the event. Which specific coping behaviour will be used at a particular point in time depends in large part on the nature of the stressor itself and the potential problems that may be present in a particular setting within which the stressful event has arisen.

STRESS, COPING, AND HEALTH

As we have seen in this chapter, stress is a major behavioural/psychological link to illness. Chronic stressors can cause neural and endocrine change that alters the normal functioning of the organism (e.g., change in cardiovascular activity or immune system functioning). This physiological response to stress is also accompanied by behavioural responses. Individuals will respond to stress with a variety of coping mechanisms. Stress and the subsequent behavioural response to it can affect health and facilitate, if not cause, some illnesses. Stress has direct physiological effects on the body, and the cumulative wear and tear on the system caused by recurring stress can eventually cause damage to the system. There is abundant evidence that stress can cause a number of physiological and biochemical changes. There is also a growing literature indicating that some of these changes can be linked directly to illness.

There have thus been attempts to develop stress management techniques in order to help individuals deal with stress and avoid negative psychophysiological consequences. Indeed, health psychologists have paid great attention to developing techniques of stress management that can be taught to large groups of people. This is because stress-related disorders appear to account for as much as $17 billion per year in lost productivity, with some estimates placing the annual cost of stress-related illnesses at $60 billion (Adams, 1978). This has caused increased motivation on the part of businesses and organizations to help their workers identify and cope more effectively with a variety of stressful events that they may experience on the job.

It is beyond the scope of this chapter to review the major components and types of stress management programmes. There is a rapidly growing literature on this topic. It should be noted, though, that these stress management programmes have been developed and utilized extensively with populations that already suffer from a stress-related illness or that are at high risk for a stress-related illness. Thus, individuals with psychophysiological disorders such as essential hypertension, headache, and gastro-intestinal problems have been treated with such techniques (Gatchel et al., 1989). Moreover, stress management techniques have also been developed as a means of modifying type A behaviour which is associated with increased risk of coronary heart disease (e.g., Roskies et al. 1986). Such programmes have been documented to be helpful, and results demonstrating a decrease in physiological symptomatology again point to the close link between stress, behaviour, and illness/health.

In conclusion, stress has been a topic of concern for centuries, and was formalized in the early twentieth century by Cannon. Subsequent scientific study of stress by investigators such as Selye, Mason, Frankenhaeuser, and Lazarus further demonstrated the important physiological and psychological concomitants of the stress process. This research has revealed that behavioural factors and stress are involved in the development of many illnesses, and highlights the important role that psychological factors play in health and illness.

FURTHER READING

Antonovsky, A. (1987). *Unraveling the mystery of health: How people manage stress and stay well*. San Franciso, CA: Jossey-Bass.

Friedman, H. S. (Ed.) (1991). *Hostility, coping and health*. Washington, DC: American Psychological Association.

Gatchel, R. J., Baum, A., & Krantz, D. S. (1989). *An introduction to health psychology*. New York: Random House.

Lazarus, R., & Folkman, S. (1984). *Stress, appraisal and coping*. New York: Springer.

REFERENCES

Adams, J. D. (1978). Improving stress management: Action-research based on intervention. In W. W. Burke (Ed.) *The cutting edge*. La Jolla, CA: University Associates.

Cannon, W. B. (1928). Neural organization for emotional expression. In M. L. Reymert (Ed.) *Feelings and emotions: The Wittenberg symposium*. Worcester, MA: Clark University Press.

Cannon, W. B. (1929). *Bodily changes in pain, hunger, fear and rage*. Boston, MA: Branford.

Cannon, W. B. (1935). Stresses and strains of homeostasis. *American Journal of Medical Science, 189*, 1–14.

Cohen, F., & Lazarus, R. (1979). Coping with the stresses of illness. In G. C. Stone, F. Cohen, & N. E. Ader (Eds) *Health psychology: A handbook*. San Francisco, CA: Jossey-Bass.

Cohen, S. (1980). Aftereffects of stress on human performance and social behavior: A review of research and theory. *Psychological Bulletin, 88*, 82–108.

Collins, A., & Frankenhaeuser, M. (1978). Stress responses in male and female engineering students. *Journal of Human Stress, 4*, 43–48.

Evans, G. W. (1978). Human spatial behavior: The arousal model. In A. Baum & Y. M. Epstein (Eds) *Human response to crowding*. Hillsdale, NJ: Lawrence Erlbaum.

Frankenhaeuser, M. (1971). Behavior and circulating catecholamines. *Brain Research, 31*, 241–262.

Frankenhaeuser, M. (1972). *Biochemical events, stress and adjustments*. Reports from the Psychological Laboratories, University of Stockholm, no. 368.

Frankenhaeuser, M., & Johansson, G. (1982). *Stress at work: Psychobiological and psychosocial aspects*. Paper presented at the 20th International Congress of Applied Psychology, Edinburgh, July.

Frankenhaeuser, M., & Rissler, A. (1970). Effects of punishment on catecholamine release and efficiency of performance. *Psychopharmacologia, 17*, 378–390.

Frankenhaeuser, M., Jarpe, G., & Mattell, G. (1961). Effects of intravenous infusions of adrenaline and noradrenaline on certain psychological and physiological functions. *Acta Physiological Scandinavia, 51*, 175–186.

Frankenhaeuser, M., Nordheden, B., Myrsten, A. L., & Post, B. (1971). Psychophysiological reactions to understimulation and overstimulation. *Acta Psychologia, 35*, 298–308.

Gatchel, R. J., Baum, A., & Krantz, D. S. (1989). *An introduction to health psychology*. New York: Random House.

Glass, D. C., & Singer, J. E. (1972). *Urban stress*. New York: Academic Press.

Karasek, R. A., Theorell, T. G., Schwartz, J., Pieper, C., & Afredsson, L. (1982). Job, psychological factors and coronary heart disease: Swedish prospective findings and U.S. prevalence findings using a new occupational inference method. *Advances in Cardiology, 29*, 62–67.

Lazarus, R. S. (1966). Story telling and the measurement of motivation: The direct versus substitutive controversy. *Journal of Consulting Psychology, 30*, 483–561.

Lazarus, R. S. (1975). A cognitively oriented psychologist looks at biofeedback. *American Psychologist, 30*, 553–561.

Lazarus, R. S., & Cohen, J. B. (1977). Environmental stress. In I. Attman & J. F. Wohlwill (Eds) *Human behavior and the environment: Current theory and research* (vol. 2). New York: Plenum.

Lazarus, R. S., & Launier, R. (1978). Stress-related transactions between person and environment. In L. A. Pervin & M. Lewis (Eds) *Internal and external determinants of behavior*. New York: Plenum.

Lazarus, R. S., Opton, E. M., Jr, Nomikos, M. S., & Rankin, N. O. (1965). The principle of short-circuiting of threat: Further evidence. *Journal of Personality, 33*, 622–635.

Lundberg, U., & Frankenhaeuser, M. (1976). *Adjustment to noise stress*. Reports from the Department of Psychology, University of Stockholm, no. 484.

Mason, J. W. (1975). A historical view of the stress field. *Journal of Human Stress, 1*, 22–36.

Patkai, P. (1971). Catecholamine excretion in pleasant and unpleasant situations. *Acta Psychologica, 35*, 352–363.

Roskies, E., Seraganian, P., Oseasohn, R., Martin, N., Smilga, C., & Hanley, J. A. (1986). The Montreal Type A intervention project: Major findings. *Health Psychology, 5*, 45–60.

Ross, R., & Glomset, J. A. (1976). The pathogenesis of artherosclerosis. *New England Journal of Medicine, 295*, 369–377.

Selye, H. (1956). *The stress of life.* New York: McGraw-Hill.

Speisman, J., Lazarus, R. S., Mordkoff, A., & Davidson, L. (1964). Experimental reduction of stress based on ego defense theory. *Journal of Abnormal and Social Psychology, 20*, 156–164.

Symington, T., Currie, A. R., Curran, R. S., & Davidson, J. (1955). The reaction of the adrenal cortex in conditions of stress. In *Ciba Foundations Colloquia on Endocrinology* (vol. 8). Boston, MA: Little, Brown.

Theorell, T., Knox, S., Svensson, J., & Waller, D. (1985). Blood pressure variations during a working day at age 28: Effects of different types of work and blood pressure level at age 18. *Journal of Human Stress, 11*, 36–41.

579

7
INDIVIDUAL DIFFERENCES
AND PERSONALITY

INTRODUCTION

One of the most important ways in which psychology differs from physics and the natural sciences in general arises from the existence of individual differences. Two litres of hydrogen that are treated identically respond identically, but any two human beings, even identical twins, are likely to respond quite differently to identical stimuli of many types. The reason for this is that people differ from one another, not only in appearance (that is, physically), but also in behaviour (that is, psychologically). Psychological differences between people have been investigated since ancient times (see chapter 1.1, Andrew M. Colman, and chapter 1.2, Raymond E. Fancher) and some progress has been made in understanding them.

Differences in intelligence have received more sustained attention from researchers than any other class of individual differences. Scientific research in this area dates back to the work of Francis Galton (1822–1911), grandson of the poet and physician Erasmus Darwin and half-cousin of the biologist Charles Darwin, in the latter half of the nineteenth century. In chapter 7.1 Robert J. Sternberg provides an outline of what is known about intelligence and cognitive styles – people's characteristic ways of thinking. After discussing lay views of intelligence and comparing them with expert opinions, Sternberg examines the major theories of intelligence – psychometric, information-processing, biological, developmental, culture-sensitive, and systems theories – and he concludes by outlining general theories and specific examples of cognitive styles. This chapter touches on the work of Jean Piaget and Lev Vygotsky and other aspects of cognitive development that are discussed in more detail in chapter 8.2 (Sara Meadows) and on the cognitive style of authoritarianism, which is covered in chapter 9.4 (James Vivian and Rupert Brown) in connection with prejudice and intergroup conflict.

Chapter 7.2, by Sarah E. Hampson, on the construction of personality, covers all major approaches to the study of personality under the theoretical umbrella of constructivism, which views personality as a social construction involving actors, observers, and self-observers. Hampson points out (and Paul Kline makes the same point in chapter 7.5) that there is an emerging consensus of opinion in the light of accumulating research evidence that the structure of personality consists of five major factors, which are sometimes called the Big Five: extraversion, agreeableness, conscientiousness, emotional stability, and intellect.

In chapter 7.3 H. J. Eysenck defends his own influential theory of personality, based on only three major factors, and discusses it in the light of other trait theories. He also comments briefly on a number of specific personality traits and addresses the question of the influence of hereditary factors (for a more detailed discussion of this issue, see chapter 2.1, C. P. Kyriacou) and biological determinants of personality.

Chapter 7.4, by Richard Stevens, is devoted to Freudian theories of personality. Stevens outlines and comments on the three major aspects of Freud's view of personality, namely the unconscious, psychosexual development, and psychodynamics. He then goes on to discuss briefly some further aspects of psychoanalysis, most of which are dealt with in chapter 13.5 (Peter Fonagy) from the slightly different point of view of psychoanalysis as a profession. Stevens ends by discussing the scientific evidence for Freud's theories and their implications for the study of personality.

In chapter 7.5, finally, Paul Kline provides a survey of personality tests. He describes personality questionnaires or inventories, projective tests, and objective personality tests, and discusses the advantages and disadvantages of each. He does not dwell on intelligence tests, which are dealt with in chapter 7.1 (Robert J. Sternberg).

A.M.C.

7.1

INTELLIGENCE AND COGNITIVE STYLES

Robert J. Sternberg
Yale University, Connecticut, USA

Loosely speaking, intelligence is the ability to make sense of and function adaptively in the environments in which one finds oneself, and a cognitive style is a preferred way of using that ability. In this chapter we shall consider each of these concepts in much more detail, trying to understand what they are and what some of the ways to frame them are.

INTELLIGENCE

In order to understand intelligence, we must first consider just what it is. This question turns out to be much more complex than it might at first seem. There are several different approaches to the problem, including expert opinions, implicit theories, and explicit psychological theories.

Expert opinions

One way to find out what intelligence is involves asking experts. Back in 1921, the editors of the *Journal of Educational Psychology* did just that. Fourteen experts defined intelligence in fourteen different ways. Two themes ran through their definitions, however: the capacity to learn from experience, and to adapt to one's environment. Much later, Sternberg and Detterman (1986) did a similar study of contemporary experts: although there were differences in emphasis, the themes of learning from experience and adapting to the environment proved to be important again.

Adaptation can occur in a variety of situations: a student learning material to pass a course in school, a patient learning how to live with a chronic disease, a husband or wife learning how to live successfully with a spouse. For the most part, adapting involves making a change in oneself in order to cope more effectively, but sometimes effective adaptation involves either changing the environment or finding a new environment altogether.

Implicit theories

In implicit theorizing about intelligence, one asks non-psychologists what they believe intelligence to be, in order to discover an "ordinary-language" definition. This approach was suggested by Neisser (1979), and was implemented by Sternberg, Conway, Ketron, and Bernstein (1981), who found three major aspects of people's conceptions of intelligence: the ability to solve practical problems (e.g., balancing a chequebook), verbal ability (writing and speaking well), and social competence (getting along with other people).

It is important to realize that there are serious limitations in this ordinary-language view of intelligence. One is with respect to age. Siegler and Richards (1982) asked adult subjects to characterize intelligence as it applies to people of different ages. They found that adults tended to view intelligence as increasingly less perceptual-motor and as increasingly more cognitive with increasing age. Thus, coordination of hand and eye was seen as more important to the intelligence of an infant whereas reasoning ability was more important to the intelligence of an adult. When children are asked to characterize intelligence, their answers differ from those of adults. Yussen and Kane (1985) asked children at roughly 6–7, 8–9, and 11–12 years of age what their conceptions of intelligence were. They found that older children's conceptions of intelligence included more aspects than younger children's and that older children were less likely than younger children to think that certain kinds of overt behaviour signal intelligence.

Another limitation of the Sternberg et al. (1981) results is with respect to culture. Different cultures perceive intelligence in different ways, and a view held in one culture may be diametrically opposed to that held in another culture. For example, Wober (1974) investigated conceptions of intelligence among members of different tribes in Uganda as well as within different subgroups of the tribes. Wober found differences both within and between tribes. The Baganda, for example, tended to associate intelligence with mental order, whereas the Batoro associated it with some degree of mental turmoil. Super (1983) found that among the Kokwet of western Kenya, different concepts of intelligence applied for adults and children. Intelligence in children carried connotations of responsibility, verbal quickness, the ability to comprehend complex material quickly, and management of interpersonal relations. The word as applied to adults suggested inventiveness, cleverness, and sometimes, wisdom and unselfishness. In sum, then, whether or not intelligence actually is the same across and even within cultures, it is certainly not perceived as the same.

Most theorists of abilities have argued that whatever the differences may be across cultures, there are at least some aspects of intelligence that are the same. Let us consider next what some of the major explicit theories of intelligence are.

Explicit theories

Explicit theories of intelligence are those proposed by psychologists (or others) and tested by comparing the theories' predictions to data collected from human subjects. Explicit theories can be of various kinds. We shall consider here psychometric, information-processing, biological, developmental, contextual or cultural, and systems theories.

Psychometric theories

Psychometric theories are so-called because they are based on the measurement (-metric) of psychological (psycho-) properties. Usually, such theories are tested by the measurement of individual differences in people's psychological functioning. The individual-differences approach has people perform a large number of tasks that seem to predict intelligent performance (such as in school or on the job), including recognizing meanings of words, seeing verbal or figural analogies, classifying which of several words does not belong, solving simple arithmetic problems, completing series of numbers, or visualizing spatial relationships between abstract forms. The psychologist uses data from these and similar tasks to analyse patterns of individual differences in task performance. These patterns have usually been statistically analysed through the use of a method called factor analysis. The idea is to identify the basic underlying factors of human intelligence.

The earliest factorial theory of the nature of human intelligence was formulated by Spearman, who also invented factor analysis. His theory is called the two-factor theory. Spearman (1927) suggested that intelligence comprises two kinds of factors – a general factor and specific factors. General ability, or *g*, is required for performance of mental tests of all kinds. Each specific ability, as measured by each specific factor, is required for performance of just one kind of mental test. Thus, there are as many specific factors as there are tests, but only a single general factor. Spearman suggested that the ability underlying the general factor could best be understood as a kind of mental energy.

Thomson (1939) suggested an alternative interpretation. He disputed Spearman's claim that the general factor represented a single underlying source of individual differences. Instead, he proposed that the appearance of a general factor was due to the workings of a multitude of mental bonds, including reflexes, learned associations between stimuli, and the like. Performance of any particular task activates large numbers of these bonds. Some bonds will be required for the performance of virtually any task requiring mental effort, and these bonds will in combination give rise to the appearance of a general factor.

Thurstone (1938), like Thomson, accepted Spearman's hypothesis of a general factor, but he disputed its value. He argued that it is a second-order factor or phenomenon, one of little importance. What are really important, according to Thurstone, are factors which he called primary mental abilities. Thurstone suggested that they include verbal comprehension (measured by tests such as knowledge of vocabulary), word fluency (measured by tests requiring rapid word production, e.g., a listing of as many words as possible with *c* as their third letter), number skill (measured by tests of arithmetical reasoning and computation), spatial visualization (measured by tests requiring mental manipulation of geometric forms), perceptual speed (measured by tests requiring rapid visual scanning, e.g., skimming a page looking only for instances of the letter *a*), memory (measured by tests of recall and recognition of previously presented information), and reasoning (measured by tests such as completing a number series).

Guilford (1967) parted company from the majority of factorial theorists by refusing to acknowledge the existence of any general factor at all. Instead, he proposed that intelligence comprises 120 elementary abilities, each of which involves the action of a mental operation upon some sort of content (e.g., figural, symbolic, verbal) to produce an intellectual product. An example of an ability in Guilford's structure of intellect model is cognition of verbal relations. This ability involves recognition (mental operation) of a conceptual connection (product) between two words (verbal content), for example, that a *peach* is a kind of *fruit*.

Probably the most widely accepted factorial description of intelligence is a hierarchical one. A good example of this class of description was proposed by Vernon (1971). He suggested that intelligence can be described as comprising abilities at varying levels of generality: at the highest level of generality (the top of the hierarchy) is general ability as identified by Spearman;

at the next level are major group factors, such as verbal-educational ability (needed for successful performance in courses such as English or history) and practical-mechanical ability (needed for successful performance in courses such as craftsmanship and car mechanics); at the next level are minor group factors, which are obtained by subdividing the major group factors; and at the bottom of the hierarchy are the specific factors as proposed by Spearman. This description of intelligence may be viewed as filling the gaps between the two extreme kinds of factors proposed by Spearman: between the general and specific factors are group factors of intermediate levels of generality.

Psychometric approaches to intelligence have been realized in practice through the use of intelligence (IQ) tests. These tests yield a so-called intelligence quotient, or IQ, which represents the standing of a person on the test relative to other individuals of the same age. The average IQ within the population is 100, and slightly more than two-thirds of scores fall between 85 and 115. Scores on such tests are used in part to identify people as mentally retarded (a label sometimes assigned to people with IQs below 70) or gifted (a label sometimes assigned to people with IQs above a certain point, such as 130). IQ, however, should be used only as one of several indications of retardation, of giftedness, or even of intelligence in general. Typically, these tests ask individuals to perform such tasks as recognizing meanings of vocabulary words, solving verbal analogies, completing number series, and the like. Some samples of such problems are shown in Figure 1.

Information-processing theories

Information-processing theories seek to understand intelligence in terms of the processing of information that people do when they solve challenging mental problems. What mental processes do people use to complete such tasks? These theories differ in terms of the complexity of the mental processes that they posit as key to intelligence.

Some psychologists have chosen to study basic mental processes. For example, Hunt and his colleagues (e.g., Hunt, Lunneborg, & Lewis, 1975) had subjects perform an extremely simple task. The individual is shown a

1 *Meliorate* means to
  (a) sharpen   *(b) improve   (c) waste   (d) coarsen

2 LAWYER is to CLIENT as DOCTOR is to
  (a) nurse   (b) medicine   *(c) patient   (d) practice

3 Which number should come next in this series: 2, 6, 12, 20, ?
  (a) 28   *(b) 30   (c) 32   (d) 36

Figure 1 Sample IQ test items

pair of letters, such as "A A", "A a", or "A B", and is asked to respond as quickly as possible to one of two questions: "Are the two letters the same physically?" or "Are the two letters the same only in name?" In the first pair the letters are the same physically, and in the second pair the letters are the same only in name. In the third pair, of course, they are different in both physical appearance and name.

The psychologists hypothesized that a critical ability underlying intelligence is that of rapidly retrieving lexical information, such as letter names, from memory. Hence, they were interested in the time needed to react to the question about letter names. They subtracted the reaction time to the question about physical match from the reaction time to the question about name match in order to set aside the time required for sheer speed of reading letters and pushing buttons on a computer, and more importantly, to isolate the time for additional reflection about the more complex name question. The critical finding was that the time differences seemed to predict psychometric test scores, especially those on tests of verbal ability, such as verbal analogies and reading comprehension. The Hunt group concluded that verbally facile people are those who have the underlying ability to absorb and then retrieve from memory large amounts of verbal information in short amounts of time.

A few years later, Sternberg (1977) suggested another approach to studying the cognitive processes underlying human intelligence. He argued that Hunt and his colleagues had found only a weak relation between basic cognitive tasks and psychometric test scores, because the tasks they were using were too simple. Although low-level cognitive processes may be involved in intelligence, according to Sternberg, they are peripheral rather than central. He proposed that psychologists should study the tasks found on the intelligence tests and then determine the mental processes and strategies that people use to perform these tasks.

Sternberg used problems from typical mental tests. An example is a verbal analogy, such as LAWYER : CLIENT :: DOCTOR :?. He determined that the solution to such an analogy requires a set of component cognitive processes, such as the encoding of the analogy terms (i.e., retrieving from memory the attributes of the terms LAWYER, CLIENT, and so on), inferring the relation between the first two terms of the analogy (i.e., figuring out that a lawyer provides professional services to a client), applying this relation to the second half of the analogy, and so on. Using techniques of mathematical modelling applied to reaction-time data, Sternberg proceeded to isolate the components of information processing. He determined whether or not each experimental subject did, indeed, use these processes, how they were combined, how long each took, and how susceptible each process was to error. Sternberg (1983) later showed that the same cognitive processes are involved in a wide variety of intellectual tasks, and he suggested that these and other related processes underlie scores on intelligence tests.

Other cognitive psychologists have pursued different paths in the study of human intelligence. For example, some cognitive psychologists, such as Newell and Simon (1972), have emphasized the study of very complex problem solving, and especially computer-simulation techniques whereby a computer is programmed to perform in ways that mimic human beings. Schank (1980) has also taken an artificial-intelligence approach, concentrating especially upon how computers can understand language. All of these theorists, however, subscribe to the potentially controversial underlying idea that human intelligence is, at heart, a symbol-processing system, and that therefore, computers can provide a good model for what is unique about human intelligence.

Biological theories

Various biological theories of intelligence have been proposed. One of the most well-known is that of Hebb (1949), who suggested that the word intelligence has been used in three different ways and that these different meanings are often confused with each other.

Intelligence A is innate potential. It is biologically determined and represents the capacity for development. Hebb describes it as "the possession of a good brain and a good neural metabolism" (p. 294). Intelligence B is the functioning of a brain in which development has occurred. It represents an average level of performance by a person who has matured. Although some inference is necessary in determining either intelligence, Hebb suggests that inferences about intelligence A are far less certain than inferences about intelligence B. Hebb argues that most disagreements about intelligence are over intelligence A, or innate potential, rather than over intelligence B, which is the estimated mature level of functioning. Hebb has also distinguished an intelligence C, which is the score one obtains on an intelligence test. It is the basis for inferring either of the other intelligences.

Hebb's main interest was intelligence A, and his theory, the neuropsychological theory of the organization of behaviour, can be seen in large part as an attempt to understand what intelligence A is. The core of Hebb's theory is the concept of cell assembly. Hebb proposed that repeated stimulation of specific receptors slowly leads to the formation of an assembly of cells in the brain. More intelligent people have more elaborate sequences of cell assemblies.

Another biologically based theory with great impact on intelligence research is that of Luria (1980). Luria believed that the brain is a highly differentiated system whose parts are responsible for different aspects of a unified whole. In other words, separate cortical regions act together to produce thought and action of various kinds. Luria suggested that the brain comprises three main units. The first, a unit of arousal, includes the brain stem and midbrain structures. Included within this first unit are the medulla, reticular activating system, pons, thalamus, and hypothalamus. The second unit of the brain is a sensori-input unit, which includes the temporal, parietal, and occipital lobes. The third unit includes the frontal cortex, which is involved in organization and planning. It comprises cortical structures anterior to the central sulcus of the brain.

A different kind of theory of intelligence has concentrated upon hemispheric specialization in the brain (see Springer & Deutsch, 1985). This work traces back to a study by an obscure country doctor in France, Marc Dax, who in 1836 presented a little-noticed paper to a medical society meeting in Montpellier. Dax had treated a number of patients suffering from loss of speech as a result of brain damage. This condition, now known as aphasia, had been reported even in ancient Greece. But Dax noticed a connection between loss of speech and the side of the brain in which damage had occurred. Dax noticed that in every case, there had been damage to the left hemisphere of the brain. He was not able to find even one case in which damage had occurred to the right hemisphere only. At the time, the paper aroused no interest.

Many people have now followed up on the lead of Dax, most notably Sperry (1961), who has argued that each hemisphere of the brain behaves in many respects like a separate brain. His work led to the conclusion that visual and spatial functions are primarily localized in the right hemisphere, whereas linguistic functions are primarily localized in the left hemisphere, with exceptions (Farah, 1988). A student of Sperry, Levy (1974), has taken things one step further and argued that the left hemisphere tends to process information analytically, whereas the right hemisphere tends to process it holistically. Continuing with this line of reasoning, Bogen (1975) has suggested that the difference in processing of stimuli in the two hemispheres can be characterized in terms of what he refers to as propositional versus appositional information processing. "Propositional" applies to speaking, writing, and other verbal activities which are dominated by the left hemisphere, whereas "appositional" emphasizes the figural, spatial, non-verbal processing of the right hemisphere. The right hemisphere, in his view, understands patterns and relationships that are not susceptible to propositional analysis and that may not even be logical.

Gazzaniga (1985), also a student of Sperry, argues that the brain is organized modularly into relatively independent functioning units that work in parallel. Moreover, many of these modules operate at a level that is not even conscious, but which parallels our conscious thought and contributes to conscious processing. In particular, the left hemisphere tries to assign interpretations to the processing of these modules. Thus, the left hemisphere may perceive the individual operating in a way that does not make any particular sense or that is not particularly understandable. Its job is to assign some meaning to that behaviour. Gazzaniga gives the example of attending a Christmas party where one's beliefs in marital fidelity are seriously challenged as one is sexually attracted to a new acquaintance. The attraction may be the work of one of the modules of the brain. But as the left hemisphere perceives what is happening, it starts to question the value of fidelity, and beliefs thereby change on the basis of behaviour, rather than the other way around.

A final biological approach uses evoked potentials to measure electrical activity in the brain. Evoked potentials are electrical responses of the brain during neuronal transmission. This approach seeks to relate such activity to various measures of intelligence or cognition more generally. For example, McCarthy and Donchin (1981) found that one evoked potential (P300) seems to reflect the allocation of cognitive resources to a given task. P300 – so-named because it is a positively charged response occurring roughly 300 milliseconds after the stimulus is perceived – seems to increase in strength with the amount of surprise a subject experiences as a result of the presentation of a stimulus.

Schafer (1982) has suggested that the tendency to show a large P300 response to surprising stimuli may be due to individual differences. He believes that a functionally efficient brain will use fewer neurons to process a stimulus that is familiar and more to process a stimulus that is novel. In other words, according to Schafer, more intelligent individuals should show greater P300 responses to unfamiliar stimuli, as well as smaller P300 responses to expected stimuli, than would less intelligent ones. Schafer reported a correlation of .82 between an individual-differences measure of evoked potential and IQ. The higher the IQ, the greater the difference in evoked-potential amplitude between expected and unexpected stimuli. This result suggests that more intelligent individuals are more flexible in responding to novel stimuli than are less intelligent ones.

Hendrickson and Hendrickson (1980) have conducted a programme of research attempting to link electrophysiological responses to observed intelligence. Their measurements are obtained while the subject is at rest. Their basic theory suggests that errors can occur in the passage of information through the cerebral cortex. These errors, which probably occur at synapses, are alleged to be responsible for variability in evoked potentials. Thus, it would follow that individuals with normal neural circuitry that conveys information accurately will form correct and accessible memories more quickly than individuals whose circuitry is "noisy" and hence makes errors in transmission. The Hendricksons have collected data showing a strong correlation between complexity of an evoked potential measure and IQ. The meaning of this correlation, however, is unclear, and it does not necessarily support the Hendricksons' theory.

Developmental theories

How does intelligence develop with age? Indeed, is it the same thing at different ages? The implicit theories we considered earlier suggested that

591

perhaps it is not, and developmental theories in many cases are consistent with this point of view.

By far the most influential developmental theory has been that of Piaget. Piaget (1952, 1972) recognized the importance of adaptation to intelligence. In adaptation, the individual learns from the environment and learns to address the changes in the environment. Adaptation consists of two complementary processes: assimilation and accommodation. Assimilation is the process of absorbing new information and fitting it into an already existing schema about what the world is like. A schema, for Piaget, is a mental image or action pattern. It is essentially a way of organizing sensory information. For example, we have schemata for going to the bank, eating a meal, or applying for a job.

The complement of assimilation is accommodation, which involves forming a new schema when no existing cognitive structure seems adequate to understand new information. The complementary processes of assimilation and accommodation constitute what Piaget refers to as equilibration. Equilibration is the balancing of the two and it is through this balance that people either add to old schemata or form new ones.

According to Piaget, the intelligence of children proceeds through four discrete stages, or periods of development. Each of these periods builds upon the preceding one, so that development is essentially accumulative.

The first period is the sensori-motor one, from birth to approximately 2 years of age. During this time, the newborn baby exhibits only innate, pre-programmed reflexes, such as grasping and sucking. Intelligence begins to exhibit itself as the innate reflexes are refined and elaborated. Understanding of the world is only through direct perception. Instrumentality – the discovery of how actions can lead to outcomes – develops through trial and error. Eventually, however, simple plans can be constructed. By the end of the sensori-motor period, the infant has started to acquire object permanence, or the realization that objects can exist apart from him or herself.

The second period is the pre-operational one, which takes place roughly from ages 2 to 7. The child is now beginning to use symbols and images, but they are directly dependent upon the child's own immediate perception. The child is still essentially egocentric, seeing the world only from his or her own point of view, both literally and figuratively. A pre-operational child seated at a table with a glass of milk on her left, for example, has difficulty understanding that a person opposite her will see the glass as on her right.

The third period is one of concrete operations, and occupies approximately ages 7 to 11. In this period, the child is able to perform concrete mental operations. Thus, the child can now think through sequences of actions or events that previously had to be enacted physically. The hallmark of concrete operational thought is reversibility. It is now possible for the child to reverse the direction of thought. The child comes to understand subtraction, for example, as a reverse of addition and division as the reverse of multiplication. A major acquisition of this period is conservation, which involves a child's recognizing that objects or quantities can remain the same despite changes in their physical appearance. Suppose, for example, that a child is shown two glasses, one of which is short and fat and the other of which is tall and thin. If the pre-operational child watches water poured from the short, fat glass to the tall, thin one, she or he will say that the tall, thin glass has more water than the short, fat one had. The concrete-operational child, able to conserve quantity, will recognize the amounts of liquid as equal.

Formal operations begin to evolve at around age 11, and usually will be fairly fully developed by the age of 16, although arguably, some adults never completely develop formal operations. In the period of formal operations, the child comes to be able to think abstractly and hypothetically, not just concretely. The individual can view a problem from multiple points of view and can think much more systematically than in the past. For example, if asked to list all possible permutations of the numbers 1, 2, 3, and 4, the child will approach the task systematically rather than randomly.

Piaget's theory has been criticized on a number of grounds (e.g., Brown & Desforges, 1979; Siegel & Brainerd, 1978). In particular, it appears that children can often do things at ages younger than those believed by Piaget to be the minimum ages for the performance of certain functions. Development also appears to be more domain-specific than Piaget thought, proceeding more rapidly in some areas than in others. Most importantly, perhaps, intelligence appears not to be as limited in scope and as logical as Piaget made it out to be. But no other single investigator has had more influence on our thinking about the development of intelligence than has Piaget, and many of his ideas are still important in the field of intellectual development.

Although Piaget believed that intellectual development stops its stage-like growth during the period of formal operations, other investigators have suggested that there may be one or more stages beyond formal operations. For example, Arlin (1975) has suggested that such a fifth stage might be one of problem-finding, in which one's intelligence is directed toward finding interesting problems to solve rather than merely solving them. The idea is that an important part of intelligence is not just in solving problems, but in finding the right ones to solve.

Other investigators, such as Pascual-Leone (1987), have suggested that beyond formal operations is a period of dialectical thinking – the realization that in many endeavours there is no absolute truth that is out there for us to know. Rather, our knowledge proceeds in the fashion of a Hegelian dialectic, with successive theses, antitheses, and syntheses. The fundamental notion in both this view and that of Arlin is that the end of development for thinking is not the development of the supreme logician, but rather of someone who both thinks logically and at the same time recognizes the limitations of formal logic.

It would be impossible to move on from the developmental point of view without mentioning the seminal contributions of Vygotsky. Two of Vygotsky's (1978) concepts are particularly key for an understanding of how intelligence develops.

The first is the concept of internalization, which is the internal reconstruction of an external event. The basic notion is that we observe those in the social environment around us acting in certain ways and we internalize their actions so that they become a part of us. For example, we might learn how to speak or ride a bicycle by watching how others do it. Much of what we learn, then, is by modelling rather than by being taught explicitly.

The second key concept is that of the zone of proximal development. The basic idea is that what we typically measure through tests of intelligence is not one's underlying capacity, but rather one's developed ability. However, what we want to measure ultimately is the underlying capacity, or better, the difference between that capacity and developed ability, which is what Vygotsky meant by the zone of proximal development. Vygotsky hoped that we could measure this zone through a procedure of dynamic assessment. Instead of an examiner's asking a child questions and refusing to help the child answer them, the examiner asks questions and then provides graded feedback to help the child solve each problem. The examiner's interest is in the child's ability to profit from guided instruction. A child with a larger zone of proximal development is one who has greater ability to profit from such instruction. In other words, even if a given child has not reached the level he or she is capable of reaching, that child is more likely to reach it if he or she is able to capitalize on guidance. In Vygotsky's view, then, we may be measuring only a small part of a child's potential through conventional static testing. What we need to do is look not only at what the child is now doing, but also at what the child potentially could do.

The culture-sensitive approach

The "culture-sensitive approach" could be given many names, but the core idea is that, consistent with implicit-theories research, intelligence may vary from one culture, or even subculture, to the next. Using standard tests of intelligence, we miss the subtleties that distinguish intelligence from society to society.

The most extreme form of this point of view is called radical cultural relativism. Proposed by Berry (1974), it entails the rejection of assumed psychological universals across cultural systems and requires the generation from within each cultural system of any concept that is applied to it. Thus, this position requires that indigenous notions of cognitive competence be the sole basis for the generation of cross-culturally valid descriptions and assessments of cognitive capacity.

The very same behaviour that is intelligent in one culture may be stupid in another. For example, in a study of sorting behaviour, Cole, Gay, Glick, and Sharp (1971) asked adult Kpelle tribespeople to sort 20 familiar objects into groups. Their subjects separated the objects into functional groups (e.g., a knife with an orange because a knife cuts an orange). The researchers had expected to see taxonomic groupings (e.g., tools, then foods) from these adults, because western adults typically sort taxonomically. The Kpelle proved to be perfectly capable of taxonomic sorting, however: when the subjects were asked specifically to sort the objects the way a stupid person would do it, they immediately arranged them into neat piles of tools, foods, clothing, and utensils. Their notion of the intelligent way to do things was simply different from the researchers'.

Different cultures may also foster the development of different abilities. Serpell (1979), for example, hypothesized that of English and Zambian children, the English children would have more experience with the two-dimensional representations of a pen-and-paper task, and the Zambian children would have more practice moulding wire into two-dimensional objects. Indeed, Serpell found that English children did better at a drawing task, and Zambian children did better on a wire-shaping task. In a similar vein, cross-cultural studies of memory (Wagner, 1978) have found that whether people do well depends very heavily on the familiarity of the content. People tend to do better with more familiar content, so that the relative scores of two cultural groups will depend in large part upon what kinds of materials are used in testing.

To summarize, we need to take into account culture in considering both the nature and the assessment of intelligence. Simply translating a test from one language to another scarcely constitutes doing so. Rather, we need to be sensitive to cultural differences that may artificially inflate the scores of one group over another due to the kinds of materials or tasks used to measure intelligence.

Systems approaches

Finally, we shall consider two examples of systems theories, which attempt to incorporate diverse elements from the various approaches that we have considered so far. Two such theories are Gardner's (1983) theory of multiple intelligences and Sternberg's (1985) triarchic theory.

According to the theory of multiple intelligences (Gardner, 1983), there really isn't one thing that constitutes intelligence at all. Rather, multiple aspects exist. Gardner has isolated seven distinct intelligences.

The first, linguistic intelligence, is involved in reading and writing, listening and talking. The second, logical-mathematical intelligence, is involved in numerical computations, deriving proofs, solving logical puzzles, and most scientific thinking. The third, spatial intelligence, is used in marine navigation, as well as in piloting a plane or driving a car. The fourth, musical intelligence, is seen in singing, playing an instrument, conducting an orchestra, composing, and, to some extent, in appreciating music. The fifth, bodily-kinaesthetic intelligence, involves the ability to use one's body or various portions of it in the solution of problems, in the construction of products, or in athletics. The sixth, interpersonal intelligence, is involved in understanding and acting upon one's understanding of others. And the seventh, intrapersonal intelligence, is the ability to understand oneself – to know how one feels about things, to understand one's range of emotions, to have insights about why one acts the way one does, and to behave in ways that are appropriate to one's needs, goals, and abilities. According to Gardner, these intelligences are relatively independent, and are located separately in the brain.

Sternberg's (1985) triarchic theory is rather different. It posits that to understand intelligence, we must know how it relates to (1) one's internal world, (2) one's external world, and (3) one's experience, which mediates between the internal and the external worlds. Three subtheories deal with each of these aspects of intelligence separately.

The componential subtheory handles the relation of intelligence to the internal world. It specifies the components that people use to process information. For example, metacomponents are used to plan, monitor, and evaluate an activity. Performance components are involved in the actual doing, and knowledge-acquisition components learn how to do things in the first place. The three kinds of components interact and provide feedback to one another. For example, if one travels to a foreign country, metacomponents plan and supervise the trip, while performance components coordinate day-to-day actual needs. Knowledge-acquisition components are used to learn about the country, both in preparation for and during the trip.

The experiential subtheory postulates that the above components are applied to levels of experience ranging from the novel to the familiar. Intelligence is most heavily involved in the accomplishment of tasks that are relatively novel. Thus, good measures of intelligence are unfamiliar, but not too much; if so, the individual simply has no experience to bring to bear (e.g., giving calculus problems to first-grade children).

The contextual subtheory states that the components are applied to experience in order to serve one of three practical purposes in real-world contexts: adaptation to existing environments, shaping of existing environments into transformed ones, or selection of new environments altogether. The intelligent person is able to do all three of these, and knows when to do which.

The nub of the triarchic theory is that intelligent people are those who know their strengths and weaknesses, and who capitalize upon their strengths at the same time that they compensate for or remediate their weaknesses.

Clearly, theories of intelligence vary markedly in their approach, testability, complexity, and even their definition of the construct. Each theory, however, contributes to the ongoing debate of what intelligence is and how it can be measured.

COGNITIVE STYLES

Cognitive styles are links between cognition and personality. In essence, they are ways of exploiting one's intellectual abilities. There are two major streams of literature on cognitive styles, one dealing with general theories and one dealing with specific styles.

General theories

Consider first some of the general theories of cognitive styles. Myers (1980) proposed a series of psychological types, based upon the theorizing of Jung. According to her, there are 16 types, resulting from all possible combinations of Jung's two ways of perceiving (sensing versus intuition), of judging (thinking versus feeling), of dealing with self and others (introversion versus extraversion), and of dealing with the outer world (judgement versus perception). A sensing person has a predilection for seeking the fullest possible experience of what is immediate and real. An intuitive person, in contrast, seeks the broadest view of what is possible and insightful. A thinking person likes to make decisions based on rational and logical planning, whereas a feeling person likes to make decisions based on harmony among subjective values. An extraverted person leans toward the outer world of objects, people, and actions, whereas an introverted person prefers the inner world of concepts and ideas. A judging person tends to be concerned with making decisions, seeking closure, planning or organizing activities. A perceiving person, in contrast, tends to be attuned to incoming information, open to new events and changes, and eager to miss nothing.

Gregorc (1985) proposed an alternative view, suggesting four main types or styles, based on all possible combinations of just two dimensions – concrete versus abstract and sequential versus random. A concrete person tends to engage with the physical and observable world, whereas an abstract person tends to engage with the conceptual, non-concrete world. A random person tends to order events in a web-like or non-linear manner. In contrast, a sequential person tends to order events in a step-by-step or branch-like manner.

Taking a more educationally oriented slant, Renzulli and Smith (1978) suggested that individuals have various learning styles, with each style corresponding to a method of teaching: projects, drill and recitation, peer teaching, discussion, teaching games, independent study, programmed instruction, lecture, and simulation. Holland (1973) took a more job-related orientation and proposed six styles that are used as a basis for understanding job interests. These styles are measured on the Strong-Campbell Interest Inventory, a measure used to determine how people's patterns of interests can be matched to jobs. Holland's typology includes six types of personality: realistic, investigative, artistic, social, enterprising, and conventional.

A rather different conceptual approach was taken by Sternberg (1988) in his theory of mental self-government. Sternberg has suggested that the various forms of government can be viewed as external mirrors of what is internal to the mind – that they suggest various alternatives for ways in which people can organize themselves. According to Sternberg, mental self-government has many aspects, a few of which are mentioned here: function, level, and form.

Three functions of government are the legislative, executive, and judicial. In Sternberg's theory, a person with a legislative style has a predilection for creating, formulating, and planning. A person with an executive style likes tasks and situations that provide structure, procedures, or rules with which he or she can work. A judicial person likes to judge and evaluate existing things and ideas.

Two levels of government are the local and the global. In the theory, a person with a local style has a predilection for tasks and projects that require engagement with specific, concrete details. A global person prefers projects that involve all-encompassing and abstract ideas.

Four forms of government are the monarchic, anarchic, hierarchic, and oligarchic. A monarchic person prefers tasks, projects, and situations that allow focusing fully on one aspect at a time and staying with that until it is complete. An anarchic person prefers tasks that lend themselves to great flexibility of approaches. A hierarchic person likes projects that allow creation of a priority ladder. And an oligarchic person likes tasks that allow working with competing approaches, with multiple aspects or goals that are equally important.

Specific cognitive styles

The other approach to cognitive styles has been the proposal of specific styles of functioning. Consider some examples.

Adorno, Frenkel-Brunswick, Levinson, and Sanford (1950) suggested a style that they referred to as authoritarianism, which displays rigidity and intolerance of ambiguity. People with the authoritarian style tend to see things in black and white and to be intolerant of emotional ambivalence. They tend to hold rigid stereotypes and to be attracted to fascist thought.

A related style, proposed by Rokeach (1954), is that of dogmatism. A dogmatic person organizes information rigidly and is relatively closed to new ways of organizing information; he also believes in absolute authority, and tends to be intolerant of individual differences.

Quite different from these two styles is one proposed by Witkin et al. (1954) called cognitive differentiation. In their view, two basic styles for perceiving the world are field-dependent or field-independent. A field-dependent person relies on the structure of the visual field, and is unable to separate him or herself from it. Such people when tilted at an angle (such as in an aircraft), tend to perceive themselves as right-side-up. Witkin et al. suggested that field-dependent people tend to be more passive and lower in self-esteem than are field-independent people, who can separate themselves from the surrounding perceptual field. A field-independent person could easily distinguish right-side-up with respect to the earth from right-side-up with respect to the plane. Field-independent people tend to do better on most cognitive tests, especially spatial ones, than do field-dependent people.

Finally, we consider reflectivity, a style studied extensively by Kagan (1966) and others. The reflective individual thinks before acting and is thoughtful, in general, about what he or she does. In contrast, an impulsive individual tends to act without thinking, and to have poor control of impulses. Reflective children tend to do considerably better in school than do impulsive ones, and to have more success in a variety of endeavours.

In sum, then, cognitive styles can be understood either in terms of a single integrated theory or mini-theories of specific cognitive styles. In either case, the goal is to understand how people use their intelligence in combination with their personality characteristics, so that we may gain a full understanding of one of humankind's most valuable resources.

FURTHER READING

Ceci, S. (1990). *On intelligence . . . more or less*. Englewood Cliffs, NJ: Prentice-Hall.
Gardner, H. (1983). *Frames of mind: The theory of multiple intelligences*. New York: Basic Books.
Sternberg, R. J. (Ed.) (1982). *Handbook of human intelligence*. New York: Cambridge University Press.
Sternberg, R. J. (1985). *Beyond IQ: A triarchic theory of human intelligence*. New York: Cambridge University Press.
Sternberg, R. J. (1990). *Metaphors of mind: Conceptions of the nature of intelligence*. New York: Cambridge University Press.

REFERENCES

Adorno, T. W., Frenkel-Brunswick, E., Levinson, D. J., & Sanford, R. N. (1950). *The authoritarian personality*. New York: Harper & Row.
Arlin, P. K. (1975). Cognitive development in adulthood: A fifth stage? *Developmental Psychology*, *11*, 602–606.
Berry, J. W. (1974). Radical cultural relativism and the concept of intelligence. In J. W. Berry & P. R. Dasen (Eds) *Culture and cognition: Readings in cross-cultural psychology* (pp. 225–229). London: Methuen.

Bogen, J. E. (1975). Some educational aspects of hemispheric specialization. *UCLA Educator*, *17*, 24–32.

Brown, G., & Desforges, C. (1979). *Piaget's theory: A psychological critique*. Boston, MA: Routledge & Kegan Paul.

Cole, M., Gay, J., Glick, J., & Sharp, D. W. (1971). *The cultural context of learning and thinking*. New York: Basic Books.

Farah, M. J. (1988). Is visual imagery really visual? Overlooked evidence from neuropsychology. *Psychological Review*, *95*, 307–317.

Gardner, H. (1983). *Frames of mind: The theory of multiple intelligences*. New York: Basic Books.

Gazzaniga, M. S. (1985). *The social brain: Discovering the networks of the mind*. New York: Basic Books.

Gregorc, A. (1985). *Inside styles: Beyond the basics*. Maynard, MA: Gabriel Systems.

Guilford, J. P. (1967). *The nature of human intelligence*. New York: McGraw-Hill.

Hebb, D. O. (1949). *The organization of behavior*. New York: Wiley.

Hendrickson, A. E., & Hendrickson, D. E. (1980). The biological basis for individual differences in intelligence. *Personality and Individual Differences*, *1*, 3–33.

Holland, J. L. (1973). *Making vocational choices: A theory of careers*. Englewood Cliffs, NJ: Prentice-Hall.

Hunt, E. B., Lunneborg, C., & Lewis, J. (1975). What does it mean to be high verbal? *Cognitive Psychology*, *7*, 194–227.

Kagan, J. (1966). Reflection-impulsivity: The generality and dynamics of conceptual tempo. *Journal of Abnormal Psychology*, *17*, 17–24.

Levy, J. (1974). Psychobiological implications of bilateral asymmetry. In S. Dimond & J. Beaumont (Eds) *Hemisphere function in the human brain* (pp. 121–183). New York: Wiley.

Luria, A. R. (1980). *Higher cortical functions in man* (2nd edn). New York: Basic Books.

McCarthy, G., & Donchin, E. (1981). A metric for thought: A comparison of P300 latency and reaction time. *Science*, *211*, 77–79.

Myers, I. B. (1980). *Gifts differing*. Palo Alto, CA: Brooks/Cole.

Neisser, U. (1979). The concept of intelligence. In R. J. Sternberg & D. K. Detterman (Eds) *Human intelligence: Perspectives on its theory and measurement* (pp. 179–189). Norwood, NJ: Ablex.

Newell, A., & Simon, H. A. (1972). *Human problem solving*. Englewood Cliffs, NJ: Prentice-Hall.

Pascual-Leone, J. (1987). Organismic processes for neo-Piagetian theories: A dialectical causal account of cognitive development. *International Journal of Psychology*, *22*, 531–570.

Piaget, J. (1952). *The origins of intelligence in children*. New York: International Universities Press.

Piaget, J. (1972). *The psychology of intelligence*. Totowa, NJ: Littlefield, Adams.

Renzulli, J., & Smith, L. (1978). *Learning styles inventory*. Mansfield Center, CT: Creative Learning Press.

Rokeach, M. (1954). The nature and meaning of dogmatism. *Psychological Review*, *61*, 194–204.

Schafer, W. W. P. (1982). Neural adaptability: A biological determinant of behavioral intelligence. *International Journal of Neuroscience*, *17*, 183–191.

Schank, R. C. (1980). How much intelligence is there in artificial intelligence? *Intelligence*, *4*, 1–14.

Serpell, R. (1979). How specific are perceptual skills? A cross-cultural study of pattern reproduction. *British Journal of Psychology*, *70*, 365–380.

Siegel, L. S., & Brainerd, C. J. (Eds) (1978). *Alternatives to Piaget: Critical essays on the theory*. New York: Academic Press.

Siegler, R. S., & Richards, D. D. (1982). The development of intelligence. In R. J. Sternberg (Ed.) *Handbook of human intelligence* (pp. 897–971). New York: Cambridge University Press.

Spearman, C. (1927). *The abilities of man*. New York: Macmillan.

Sperry, R. W. (1961). Cerebral organization and behavior. *Science, 133*, 1749–1757.

Springer, S. P., & Deutsch, G. (1985). *Left brain, right brain* (2nd edn). New York: Freeman.

Sternberg, R. J. (1977). *Intelligence, information processing, and analogical reasoning; The componential analysis of human abilities*. Hillsdale, NJ: Lawrence Erlbaum.

Sternberg, R. J. (1983). Components of human intelligence. *Cognition, 15*, 1–48.

Sternberg, R. J. (1985). *Beyond IQ: A triarchic theory of human intelligence*. New York: Cambridge University Press.

Sternberg, R. J. (1988). Mental self-government: A theory of intellectual styles and their development. *Human Development, 31*, 197–224.

Sternberg, R. J., & Detterman D. K. (Eds) (1986). *What is intelligence? Contemporary viewpoints on its nature and definition*. Norwood, NJ: Ablex.

Sternberg, R. J., Conway, B. E., Ketron, J. L., & Bernstein, M. (1981). People's conceptions of intelligence. *Journal of Personality and Social Psychology, 41*, 37–55.

Super, C. M. (1983). Cultural variation in the meaning and uses of children's "intelligence". In J. B. Deregowski, S. Dziurawiec, & R. C. Annis (Eds) *Explorations in cross-cultural psychology* (pp. 199–212). Lisse: Swets & Zeitlinger.

Thomson, G. H. (1939). *The factorial analysis of human ability*. London: University of London Press.

Thurstone, L. L. (1938). *Primary mental abilities*. Chicago, IL: University of Chicago Press.

Vernon, P. E. (1971). *The structure of human abilities*. London: Methuen.

Vygotsky, L. (1978). *Mind in society*. Cambridge, MA: Harvard University Press.

Wagner, D. A. (1978). Memories of Morocco: The influence of age, schooling and environment on memory. *Cognitive Psychology, 10*, 1–28.

Witkin, H. A., Lewis, H. B., Hertzman, M., Machover, K., Meissner, P. B., & Wapner, S. (1954). *Personality through perception*. New York: Harper.

Wober, M. (1974). Towards an understanding of the Kiganda concept of intelligence. In J. W. Berry & P. R. Dasen (Eds) *Culture and cognition: Readings in cross-cultural psychology* (pp. 261–280). London: Methuen.

Yussen, S. R., & Kane, P. (1985). Children's concept of intelligence. In S. R. Yussen (Ed.) *The growth of reflection in children* (pp. 207–241). New York: Academic Press.

7.2

THE CONSTRUCTION OF PERSONALITY

Sarah E. Hampson
Oregon Research Institute, USA

Learning about personality psychology can be a bewildering instead of an enlightening experience. The typical introductory personality textbook is an anthology of theories in which many different ways of viewing human nature are advanced. Indeed, the gamut of theory in personality is probably wider than for any other aspect of psychology. Personality theories can be grouped according to their underlying similarities (e.g., into trait theories, psychodynamic theories, or phenomenological theories) but within these broad categories there is still much room for variation.

However, one feature common to the majority of personality theories is the emphasis on the individual. The underlying assumption is that the appropriate unit of analysis for personality psychology is the person. Every individual "has" a personality that can be described, perhaps measured, and maybe even changed, by working with the person to whom this personality "belongs". This chapter proposes a different view in which several perspectives on the person are taken into account. According to the constructivist approach, personality is constructed in the course of social interaction from a person's self-presentation, the perception of this presentation by an audience, and self-awareness. These three components of constructed personality will be referred to as the actor, the observer, and the self-observer.

The goal of this chapter is to introduce the reader to the richness and variety of personality psychology by viewing personality as a social construction. The constructivist approach is a metatheory (a theory about theories) of personality. Psychology has tended to study the contributions of the actor, observer, and self-observer as separate fields of inquiry. The actor has been studied in personality psychology, the observer in social psychology, and the self in social and clinical psychology. In this chapter, these three topics will be integrated under one theoretical umbrella. Thus, the constructivist approach provides a framework for the multitude of personality theories, as well as for aspects of social psychology that have been studied independently and yet are closely related to personality psychology.

After providing an overview of the construction of personality, the origins of this approach are explored before describing the three components in more detail. The process of personality construction is discussed in the final part of the chapter, when the structure and dynamics of personality are examined from a constructivist perspective.

THE CONSTRUCTION OF PERSONALITY

The prevailing assumption in personality psychology has been that personalities, however conceived by any particular theorist, originate within individuals. Such an assumption reflects the emphasis on the individual that is typical of western conceptualizations of human beings (Triandis, 1989). The contrasting assumption is that personalities are created collectively by interpersonal processes. The constructivist approach combines both an individuated and a collective view of human nature.

The aspects of personality that are associated with the individual make up the contribution of the *actor* to personality construction. The actor represents a combination of hereditary and environmental influences, including a cumulative history of past experiences. Typically, the study of personality has been concerned exclusively with the study of the actor. However, in the constructivist approach, the actor is viewed as just one of the components in the construction process. The three components of constructed personality are shown in Figure 1.

According to the constructivist view of personality, the actor's behaviour, and the context in which it occurs, is interpreted by an audience of one or more observers. The observer can be another person (or persons) who is (or are) actually present, or the actor can imagine being observed by another.

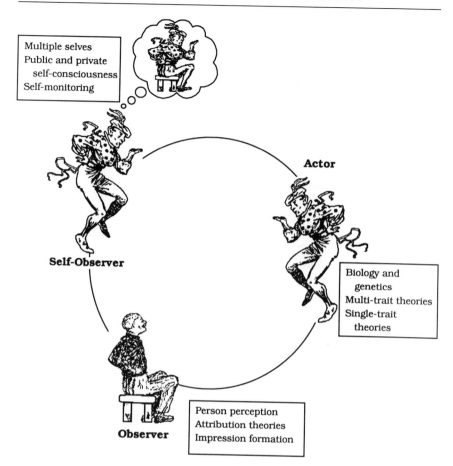

Figure 1   The components of constructed personality: the actor, the observer, and the self-observer

Whether observers are real or imagined, they construe the actor's personality on the basis of information available such as behaviour, appearance, and possessions. In Figure 1, the theatrical metaphor has been exaggerated to emphasize the different roles of actor and observer. The actor is seen in costume, and she or he is performing for the observer who is seated watching.

The observer's perspective has typically been studied independently from personality psychology as a part of social psychology known as "person perception". Here, the term "observer" will be reserved for the non-psychologists' theories and perspective about personality (as opposed to those of the professional psychologist or scientist). The figure depicts an actual observer watching the actor's performance. However, the observer need not be physically present. When we imagine another person's reactions to our self-presentation we are, in a sense, playing to an imaginary audience that may affect our performance just as strongly as any physically present observer.

The third component of constructed personality is the self-observer. This element refers to the human capacity to be self-aware. Self-awareness means that we can attempt to see ourselves as others see us (even though we can never know how successful we are in this endeavour). This capacity permits us to imagine, and even attempt to control, the personality that observers see. The self-observer is depicted in Figure 1 by showing the actor thinking about observing her or his performance. All three components are placed on the same circle, which implies their interconnectedness and interdependency.

The figure also shows some of the topics of psychological study that are traditionally associated with each of the components of actor, observer, and self-observer. They are shown here to demonstrate how the constructivist approach provides a framework for organizing topics in personality and social psychology. Moreover, these topics will be discussed later in the chapter as we consider each component.

THE ORIGINS OF THE CONSTRUCTIVIST APPROACH TO PERSONALITY

The theatrical metaphor implied by the use of the terms "actor" and "observer" reflects the influence of the *dramaturgical* view of personality and identity, which may be traced to the sociology of Goffman (1959), the social psychology of impression management (e.g., Schlenker, 1980), and symbolic interactionism (e.g., Mead, 1934).

Goffman introduced the metaphor of the theatre for interpersonal events, with the stage and actors representing social situations and the people in them. In interpersonal behaviour, the actor performs roles for an audience. A successful performance involves presenting the desired image of oneself and having this image acknowledged by others. For example, most of us have learned that it is unwise to lay claim to an expertise that one does not possess because, if the falsity of the claim is discovered, one's desired image will be rejected by others. Impression-management theorists have developed these ideas further by examining actors' manipulations of their effects on others. Self-presentation is not necessarily done consciously, nor is it inevitably cynical or deceitful. We use self-presentation in our attempts to have others see us as we see (or wish to see) ourselves.

Impression-management theorists are particularly interested in people's behaviour when their self-presentations are threatened. Given that most people wish to be seen in positive terms, being perceived as responsible for a negative event requires an explanation. These explanations are designed to create favourable impressions of one's personality. They are different from the causal explanations studied by attribution theorists. Indeed, the dramaturgical approach provides a different emphasis for person perception, one in which perceivers determine *who a person is trying to be* rather than *why* a person behaved in a certain way (Babcock, 1989).

A prerequisite for self-presentation is awareness of oneself, or consciousness. Accordingly, the self is an essential component in the construction of personality. The symbolic interactionists (e.g., Cooley, 1902; Mead, 1934) were concerned with how self-awareness develops, and the role of language in this process. The "symbolic" part of the name for this school of thought refers to the view that objects in our world are really symbols: they all have social meaning. The "interactionist" part refers to the special role of symbols in human communication. In order for us to communicate, we must be able to adopt the other's perspective. In the process of taking the other's perspective we also learn to see ourselves as another symbolic object in the world; we become self-aware. The construction of personality is rooted in a symbolic interactionist view of what it means to be a person: self-awareness enables communication, communication enables self-presentation, and personality is constructed from the interpretation of self-presentations.

The final important origin of the view that personality is a construction is to be found in the more generic theory of the social construction of reality developed by the sociologists Berger and Luckmann (1967). Like sociology, and in contrast to the physical sciences, much of psychology is concerned with the study of abstract concepts that have no direct counterparts in the physical world (Gergen, 1985). For example, stages in the life cycle such as "old age" have acquired a social reality because our culture enriches them with specific meanings. Thus, at an arbitrary retirement age, a person joins the ranks of "the elderly" and is subjected to a pervasive separatism that reflects our negative constructions of ageing (Estes, 1979). A person's identity or personality may also be viewed as having a social reality constructed by cultural beliefs and practices (Gergen & Davis, 1985).

In sum, the construction of personality, as a metatheory for personality psychology, draws on the dramaturgical approach and the social constructionist theory of social reality. The constructivist approach to personality was developed to achieve two related purposes: (1) to integrate the study of personality and the study of person perception, and (2) to provide a broad theoretical framework within which the various perspectives on personality can be placed (Hampson, 1988). The framework will now be presented in more detail.

THE ACTOR IN PERSONALITY CONSTRUCTION

The emphasis on the actor in past personality psychology is the result of the view that personality in some sense "resides" within the individual. This view has been pursued through biological, psychodynamic, and trait theories. This position is most easily appreciated in a biological approach to personality, such as Eysenck's (see Eysenck, 1967, 1991). The idea that personality has a biological substrate is as old as the ancient Greek theory of the four humours. According to Eysenck, personality may be reduced to three biologically based dimensions of individual variation: extraversion, neuroticism, and psychoticism.

In his biological theory of extraversion, Eysenck (1967) claimed that differences in degrees of extraverted behaviour are the result of functional differences in a particular structure in the brain. Specifically, he related extraversion to the ascending reticular activating system, which is a part of the brain known to be associated with cortical arousal. He theorized that introverts are characteristically more aroused than extraverts, and that the same stimulus will produce a greater increase in arousal for introverts than for extraverts. This difference in biology translates into the introvert's behavioural tendency to avoid stimulation (e.g., to prefer a quiet dinner to a noisy party), and the extravert's stimulus-seeking behaviour (e.g., to prefer adventurous activities to staying home with a good book). Evidence for this particular biological basis of extraversion is, however, inconclusive. Nevertheless, there have been significant advances since the mid-1980s in our understanding of the genetics of personality. As a result of large-scale twin, adoption, and family studies, it is now widely concluded that about 50 per cent of the variance in self-report personality measures may be accounted for by heredity (Loehlin, Willerman, & Horn, 1988).

The investigation of the biological basis of personality and its genetic determinants is just one approach to the study of the actor. There are many other approaches that do not investigate biological or genetic determinants. Hypothetical personality structures – such as Freud's id, ego, and superego, or Cattell's 16 personality factors (Cattell, Eber, & Tatsuoka, 1970) – are postulated to be located within the individual, even though they are not identified with any particular biological substrate. The range of conceptualizations of the structure of personality is partly the result of a diversity of opinion as to what the basic unit of analysis for personality should be.

Candidates for the basic unit of actor-focused personality theories include types, motives, cognitive strategies, personal projects, life tasks, and life paths. The most tried and tested, however, is the *trait*. Traits have been used in personality theories in two ways: as *descriptions* of the actor's behaviour, in which they summarize a person's pattern of behaviour, and as *explanations* of the actor's behaviour, in which they are viewed as causal or generative mechanisms (Wiggins & Trapnell, 1993). An example of the first use of traits is Buss and Craik's (1983) act frequency approach. In this approach, traits are defined as the sets of partially overlapping behaviours or acts that they describe. Personality is assessed by having individuals rate the frequency with which they engage in these acts, or by having other people rate them on the same list of acts. Past behaviour patterns measured in this way are used to predict future behaviours.

However, many personality theories based on traits have adopted the view that traits cause and explain behaviour (Alston, 1975). These theories assume that traits cause predictable behaviours that are relatively stable across situations and across the lifespan. Trait theories may be classified into two varieties: in single-trait theories, only one aspect of personality is under investigation, whereas multi-trait theories aim to be comprehensive. For a single-trait theory to be useful it must identify a trait that determines a large number of important behaviours, and a reliable and valid measure of the trait must be developed. The most successful single-trait theories are also embedded in a broader psychological theory.

Rotter's concept of locus of control is an example of a highly successful single-trait approach (Rotter, 1966). It distinguishes between people with relatively internal locus of control, who believe that they have control over the good and bad things that happen to them, and people with relatively external locus of control, who believe that what happens to them is a consequence of chance, fate, or powerful others. Locus of control is a way of viewing the world that Rotter referred to as a *generalized expectancy*, and it forms one part of Rotter's social learning theory (Rotter, 1954). Rotter developed a general measure of locus of control (Rotter, 1966), which has since been followed by numerous more specific measures for expectancies about locus of control in particular behavioural domains. For example, the importance of sense of control is stressed by health psychologists who wish to increase preventive behaviours and adherence to treatment regimens (Peterson & Stunkard, 1989).

Multi-trait theories attempt to include all aspects of personality. They assume that individual differences can be described in terms of particular profiles on the same set of personality traits. Multi-trait theories all use similar data and analytic methods but have generated somewhat different models of personality structure. The data include self-report questionnaires about behaviours, feelings, thoughts, and opinions; trait ratings; and objective tests, so called because the person taking the test is unaware of what is being assessed. The preferred analytic method is factor analysis, which identifies groups of interrelated responses that can all be described by the same underlying traits.

There is a growing consensus among multi-trait theorists that the structure of personality may be divided into five broad domains (Digman, 1990; Goldberg, 1992). These are shown in Table 1. They are Factor I, Extraversion (or Surgency); Factor II, Agreeableness; Factor III, Conscientiousness; Factor IV, Neuroticism (or Emotional Stability); and Factor V, Openness to Experience (or Intellect) (see Goldberg, 1993). Theorists differ about the details of this model. For example, McCrae (1990) argued that the domain (V) had previously been improperly identified as Intellect and really should be called "Openness to experience". Eysenck (1991) persists in his claim that the Big Five can be reduced to a Giant Three: Psychoticism (a combination of

Table 1   The Big Five personality factors and illustrative traits

I EXTRAVERSION (or SURGENCY)	II AGREEABLENESS
extraverted – introverted	agreeable – disagreeable
talkative – silent	kind – unkind
bold – timid	generous – stingy
energetic – unenergetic	warm – cold
dominant – submissive	unselfish – selfish
III CONSCIENTIOUSNESS	IV NEUROTICISM (or EMOTIONAL
organized – disorganized	STABILITY)
hardworking – lazy	stable – unstable
reliable – unreliable	relaxed – tense
thorough – careless	calm – angry
practical – impractical	unemotional – emotional
V OPENNESS TO EXPERIENCE (or	at ease – nervous
CULTURE, or INTELLECT)	
intelligent – unintelligent	
sophisticated – unsophisticated	
creative – uncreative	
curious – uninquisitive	
analytical – unanalytical	

Agreeableness and Conscientious), Extraversion, and Neuroticism (the opposite of Emotional Stability). Nevertheless, the differences among multi-trait theorists seem relatively trivial now in comparison to earlier disputes when Cattell claimed that at least sixteen traits were necessary to describe personality (e.g., Cattell, 1973).

It has been assumed that trait theories describe the personality of the actor. However, a closer look at the methodology underlying trait theories reveals that there is some confusion over just what exactly is being studied. This confusion is best illustrated by personality ratings. When raters judge ratees on a series of personality traits, is this a study of the personality of the ratees (the actors), or is it a study of the impressions of personality held by the raters (the observers)? The next section takes up this question in a discussion of the observer's contribution to the construction of personality.

THE OBSERVER IN PERSONALITY CONSTRUCTION

The constructivist approach emphasizes the interpersonal nature of personality. Both the dramaturgical model and symbolic interactionism helped shape the view of personality as a construction, and both these influences stress the importance of the observer. Observers form impressions of actors' personalities on the basis of information supplied (wittingly or unwittingly) by actors. This information includes actors' behaviours, appearance, material possessions, and the situations in which they place themselves. Indeed, virtually any information that is available to the observer about the actor may be used to construct an impression of that person. However, typically the actor's behaviour is the most important source of information for personality construction. The actor brings certain biological and learned characteristics that interact with situational factors to result in behaviours. In the process of impression formation, these behaviours are comprehended by the observer in terms of personality constructs or categories. Accordingly, personality construction entails both an actor and an observer: the process requires an actor's behaviours, and the interpretation of those behaviours in personality terms by an observer.

The observer of personality has traditionally been studied by social psychologists investigating person perception. Person perception has now become a central topic in social cognition, which is the study of the way observers process information about actors (Fiske & Taylor, 1991). In order to interact successfully, it is necessary for the participants to understand what each other is doing and why. The level of understanding and explanation necessary depends on the nature of the interaction. Brief encounters where there is a well-defined script, such as interacting with the checkout person at the supermarket, can proceed smoothly without making elaborate personality inferences. Where the situation is more ambiguous, and holds the possibility of future interaction, such as a first date, then it is likely that the participants will work harder at forming impressions of one another.

When observers try to understand and explain actors, they do so with the aid of personality language. Indeed, personality language is the medium of personality construction. It consists of the nouns, adjectives, and verbs that describe individual differences. These terms are used to categorize behaviours and the people performing them. The way observers use personality categories differs depending on whether they are categorizing behaviours or people. The categorization of behaviour involves matching the attributes of the behaviour to those of the personality category (e.g., when Jane is late for the meeting, she is *unpunctual*). In order to decide whether Jane is an *unpunctual* person, the observer needs different information, such as whether she shows a consistent pattern of being late. The rules used by observers for making inferences about the actor's personality traits are the subject of attribution theory. Here, I shall focus on observers' choices of personality traits for constructing the actor's personality.

Observers' choices of personality traits are influenced by characteristics of the observer and characteristics of the situation. Observers typically use only a subset of the many personality categories that are available. Moreover, they tend to apply the same subset of categories across different actors. Likely candidates for these widely used categories are the ones that we apply to ourselves. That is, we evaluate others in terms of the personality traits that we believe are important aspects of own personalities.

Despite these individuating preferences, there is also considerable agreement among observers about the meaning of personality-descriptive terms and the relations among them. For example, personality traits are perceived to vary on a dimension of category breadth. There are many ways in which a person can manifest broad traits (e.g., *kind*, *reliable*), whereas narrow traits (e.g., *helpful*, *punctual*) are expressed by a more restricted range of behaviours. Moreover, groups of traits that describe the same aspect of personality are organized hierarchically. Being *helpful* is perceived as a subset of being *kind*, and being *punctual* is perceived as a subset of being *reliable* (Hampson, John, & Goldberg, 1986). John, Hampson, and Goldberg (1991) examined people's preferences for traits at various hierarchical levels when describing themselves and others. They found a reliable preference for broad traits over more narrow ones (e.g., *kind* is preferred to *helpful*).

Although observers tend to use their particular subset of personality terms to describe others, and these terms are likely to be broad ones, observers are also affected by immediate contextual factors. Observers are susceptible to "priming effects", particularly when the actor's behaviour is open to a number of interpretations. That is, they are likely to see the actor in terms of categories that they have recently used, or that are relevant to their current goals. In addition, when observers expect to interact again with an actor, or believe they will be asked to predict the actor's subsequent behaviour, they tend to make more extreme personality inferences (Monson, Keel, Stephens, & Genung, 1982). Contextual factors can even moderate observers' pervasive preferences for broad traits. When describing characteristics that are inconsistent with their overall impression of the actor (such as describing something negative about a person they like), observers tend to minimize the inconsistency by using a narrow trait category to describe this discrepancy (John et al., 1991).

In addition to studying the personality categories that observers use to construct personality, social psychologists have also studied how personality categories are combined to form coherent impressions. This work dates back to Asch's (1946) seminal studies of impression formation in which he discovered that some traits in a personality description, called "central" traits, were far more influential than others. For example, the inclusion of *cold* in an otherwise positive set of traits resulted in an overall negative impression. More recently, Asch has studied how people reconcile such inconsistencies by examining their explanations for them (Asch & Zukier, 1984). The process of forming a coherent impression from sometimes conflicting information requires active constructions by the observer in the form of explanations and elaborations. For example, Casselden and Hampson (1990) found that subjects found it more difficult to construct impressions of imaginary people described by two inconsistent traits than by two consistent ones. However, when subjects could think of an example of a person characterized by the two

611

inconsistent traits, such as "Mozart" for a "creative and immature person", an impression fell easily into place.

According to the view of personality as a social construction, the way observers form impressions of actors' personalities is an integral part of personality psychology. The dramaturgical approach regards personality as a performance in which personality is constructed in the process of actors performing for observers. The key to the construction process is self-awareness. Actors must be able to imagine the impression that the observer is constructing of them in order to modify their performance. Therefore, the ability to observe oneself is a critical component of personality construction (see Figure 1).

THE SELF IN PERSONALITY CONSTRUCTION

The human capacity for self-awareness permits us to attempt to see ourselves as others see us. When personality psychologists study personality via self-reports such as questionnaires, they are assessing people's perceptions of themselves. Social psychologists also study people's self-perceptions in their investigations of the concept of self. A major issue in the study of the self has been whether people have a unified self-concept, or whether they have many different selves. Personality psychologists have assumed that self-report data assess a unitary self. For example, the typical instructions at the beginning of personality questionnaires do not specify which self the respondent should describe. However, social psychologists recognize the possibility of multiple selves.

William James (1892) said that we have as many selves as people with whom we interact, and the idea of multiple selves is consistent with symbolic interactionism and the dramaturgical approach. Most people would agree that they modify their behaviour to some extent depending on with whom they are interacting. Different observers bring out different aspects of our personalities. For example, a woman may be dominant and stern with her colleagues at work, but gentle and caring with her family at home. Observers who interact with this person only at work would form very different impressions of her from those who interact with her only at home. Goffman equated personality with the various roles a person plays in life, such as co-worker and mother. However, the Jamesian idea of multiple selves goes further than this by suggesting that different personalities are constructed in the context of every relationship that one has.

In social cognition, the idea of multiple selves has been studied extensively by Markus and her colleagues. In addition to role-specific, relationship-specific, and ideal selves, Markus and Nurius (1986) have proposed that our "possible" selves are also important parts of the multiple self-concept. Visions of our future possible selves may determine how we make important life decisions such as career choices. The notion of multiple selves raises the question of whether there is any one self that is more authentic than the others. People sometimes say that they feel more "real" in some relationships, whereas they feel they are putting on an act in others. It may be the case that we feel the most "real" when we are with someone we believe is seeing us as we wish to be seen. There is a feeling of falseness when one tries to live up to someone else's ideal of what one should be like.

The self-concept develops as the result of self-awareness, which permits us to imagine seeing ourselves as others see us. We could not have a sense of self, and hence an impression of our personality, without self-awareness. Although self-awareness is essential for the construction of personality, people vary in the extent to which they are concerned with personality construction. We can think of people we know who seem to be highly sensitive to feedback and concerned with how they are evaluated by others, as well as those who appear to be oblivious to such matters. Personality psychologists have formalized these individual differences in self-awareness, and there are now two theories devoted to this subject: public versus private self-consciousness (Fenigstein, Scheier, & Buss, 1975), and self-monitoring (Snyder, 1979).

People who are high on public self-consciousness tend to rely on external sources of information about themselves, whereas people who are high on private self-consciousness use their inner thoughts and feelings and self-observations of behaviour. The dimension of public self-consciousness seems particularly relevant to personality construction, and differences in self-presentational behaviours have been found between people high versus low on this dimension. For example, individuals high on public self-consciousness are more likely to change their behaviour in response to their perception of the situation than are individuals low on public self-consciousness.

The self-monitoring dimension is probably very similar to public self-consciousness. High self-monitors are described as being sensitive to other people's self-presentations and are able to modify their own accordingly. The self-monitoring scale even includes the item "I would probably make a good actor". However, findings on differences between high and low self-monitors have been rather inconsistent. This may be due to deficiencies in the measure of self-monitoring, and revisions of the scale may yield more consistent findings.

Although people differ in the degree to which they are aware of their effects on others, self-awareness is critical for personality construction. Without self-awareness, the actor's personality is only a projection of the observer. Proud pet owners may tell you about Joey the parrot's great personality, or Harry the horse's cute character. However, such anthropomorphism is misleading because it projects the human concept of personality on to creatures with an entirely different (and unknowable) form of self-awareness to our own. The contrast between human and non-human animals is extreme, but the same argument applies in a more moderate form to cross-cultural comparisons. People from different cultures have different concepts of self that may result from subtle differences in forms of self-awareness (White & Kirkpatrick, 1985).

I have outlined the three components of constructed personality, and showed how much of personality psychology (the study of the actor), social cognition (the study of the observer), and the study of the self (which has been conducted within a number of traditions in psychology ranging from ethology to psychoanalysis) may all be subsumed by this metatheoretical framework. I shall now examine some issues of personality structure and dynamics from a constructivist perspective.

Personality-descriptive language (nouns, verbs, and adjectives) provides the medium of personality construction both for informal (lay, implicit) theorizing about personality in everyday person talk, and for more formal (scientific, explicit) theories. The structure of personality is described in everyday language. Moreover, to the extent that personality is a social construction, language shapes the way we think about ourselves and others.

THE STRUCTURE OF CONSTRUCTED PERSONALITY

Contemporary philosophers of the social sciences advocate that the everyday language of personality description is the place to begin an inquiry into the construction of personality. As Greenwood (1989, p. 144) has stated, "our folk psychology is conceptually fundamental". Similarly, Harré (1983, p. 34) grounded his argument on what it means to be a person in the assumption that "it is in terms of commonsense psychologies that everyday folk construct themselves as persons". By "folk" or "commonsense" psychology these authors mean the concepts in everyday use to categorize human actions and practices. These concepts (e.g., "aggression") are the subject matter for personality psychology. Their scientific study will enhance folk psychology, and may reveal errors in our lay theories, but will always have to relate back to folk concepts. For example, there is no point developing a neuropsychology of aggression if the behaviours one can explain in neuropsychological terms are not perceived as aggressive.

The Big Five structure of personality (see Table 1) is firmly embedded in the folk psychology of personality because it originated in the natural language of personality description (Goldberg, 1981, 1993). As we saw in the section on the actor, multi-trait theories of personality have reached a broad consensus on a taxonomy of personality traits, and this taxonomy looks similar in many respects to the structure of personality that emerges from the study of informal personality theories, or the observer component of personality. When raters rate complete strangers on a series of personality traits, or when they rate the semantic similarity of trait terms, the pattern of their ratings reflects the same underlying Big Five taxonomy (Peabody & Goldberg, 1989).

Personality ratings provide highly ambiguous data, and are a good illustration of the constructed nature of personality. Ratings are the product of the characteristics of the individuals being rated, *and* beliefs about personality held by the people doing the ratings. It is never possible to completely unconfound these two determinants of trait ratings. In order to use personality ratings as a way of studying the beliefs held by those making the ratings (the observers), the ratees should provide no individuating clues as to their personalities. However, even when rating complete strangers, raters will draw inferences from appearance (e.g., inferring intelligence from wearing spectacles). Conversely, when studying the actor's personality through trait ratings, it is impossible to remove the influence of the rater's implicit personality theory. Although it may be possible to minimize idiosyncratic biases by using clearly defined scales and reliability checks, the point of using a human rater is to benefit from her or his ability to categorize diverse behaviours as instances of particular traits.

A consideration of the ambiguous nature of personality ratings leads naturally to the issue of the accuracy of personality judgements. If an actor's self-report is inconsistent with the observer's ratings, which of the two represents a "true" assessment of the actor's personality? Accuracy is a much-debated issue in personality and social psychology (e.g., Kruglanski, 1989), but a view of accuracy that is consistent with the construction of personality is now emerging. For example, we recognize intuitively that some people are better judges of personality (are more "accurate") than others. Funder and Harris (1986) proposed that people's self-reports of their personalities (the actor) and their awareness of self-presentations (the self), as well as raters' assessments of personality (the observer) should all be taken into account in an assessment of people's "social acuity" or ability to make personality judgements. This is a social constructivist approach to accuracy.

Personality structure has been discussed here in terms of the taxonomy of personality concepts that has emerged in studies of actors and of observers. This taxonomy is rooted in the natural language of personality description and therefore takes the social construction of personality as its starting-point. I shall now examine the dynamics of personality from a constructivist perspective.

THE DYNAMICS OF PERSONALITY CONSTRUCTION

For the sake of simplicity, it has been easier to present the contributions of the actor and observer to the process of personality construction as if one person may be designated the actor and another the observer. However, to develop the dramaturgical metaphor further, the actor and the observer are really interpersonal *roles* that may be exchanged during the course of an interaction or over the course of a relationship. Moreover, both the actor and the observer can also be self-observers. Consider a simple interpersonal encounter, one in which only two people are involved. Let us say that John is a job candidate and he is meeting with his potential supervisor, Jane. While John is describing his qualifications, Jane is forming an impression of John. She may draw personality inferences from his appearance and other aspects of his non-verbal behaviour as well as from his self-description. At this stage in the encounter, John is primarily in the role of actor and Jane is primarily in the role of observer. However, let us imagine that at some point in the interview, Jane invites John to ask questions, and he asks Jane about her preferred management style. Now John has adopted the observer role while Jane becomes the actor. Thus the same individual switches from being in the role of actor and observer depending on the nature of circumstances.

A further layer of complexity is added when we consider the self-observer. The capacity for self-awareness is an essential component of personality. As a result of self-awareness, actors monitor their behaviours in an effort to manage the impressions that they make on their observers. Similarly, observers monitor their observations of actors, directing attention to particular aspects of behaviour and evaluating actors in terms of particular personality categories. Moreover, as a result of situational demands as well as individual characteristics, participants in an interaction will vary in the extent to which they allocate attention to self-observation.

Interpersonal encounters often involve more than two participants, which adds further complexity to the construction process. Imagine that John is being interviewed by a panel of six. In this case, six observers are engaging in personality construction, and John has the difficult task of attempting to manage his impression with respect to all of them. In addition to observers who are physically present, there are also the ones in our heads (see Figure 1). For example, John may be thinking about the way his wife would react to him telling the panel that he was looking forward to the opportunity for travel that the job entailed.

The dynamic nature of personality construction is difficult to study. Typically, the process is broken down into components that are then studied separately. The constructivist approach predicts that actors adapt their behaviour in response to observers' behaviours. For example, Sally, typically a bouncy extravert, may tone down her behaviour in the presence of Ruth, a restrained introvert. Furthermore, according to the constructivist approach, Sally will come to see herself as more of an introvert when she is with Ruth because a person's self-concept is derived at least in part from that person's understanding of how they are viewed by others. The effects of observers on actors have been studied by social psychologists interested in what are called "expectancy effects" on the interpersonal process.

Research into expectancy effects has demonstrated that observers expecting to interact with a certain kind of person will ask questions that have a tendency to confirm their initial expectations (rather than ask questions with the potential to refute them). In Snyder & Swann's (1978) study, subjects were asked to select questions from a list that would determine whether a target person was extraverted. Subjects chose questions that called for an answer containing instances of extraversion (e.g., "What would you do if you wanted to liven things up at a party?"). The same tendency to choose questions with a confirmatory bias was observed in subjects instructed to determine whether a target person was introverted. They chose questions like "What things do you dislike about loud parties?" Moreover, judges listening to the target person's answers rated them as responding in a confirmatory way. Fazio, Effrein, and Falender (1981) took this experiment one step further. First, like Snyder and Swann, they induced confirmatory extraverted or introverted behaviour in their subjects by asking them to respond to either extraverted or introverted questions. Immediately after this, they examined subject's self-perceived and judged levels of extraversion and introversion. Subjects who had responded to the extravert questions described themselves as more extraverted and were rated as more extraverted than subjects who had responded to the introvert questions. Both of these studies were highly artificial. Indeed, targets never actually engaged in a face-to-face interaction with the persons questioning them.

The steps assumed by the expectancy confirmation process are quite complex, and typically no one study can encompass them all (Darley & Fazio, 1980). (1) The perceiver forms an expectancy about the target (e.g., Jane is told that John is extraverted). (2) As a result of this expectancy, the perceiver behaves in a certain way toward the target (e.g., Jane asks John a question calling for an extraverted response). (3) The target responds (e.g., John gives instances of extraverted behaviour). (4) The perceiver interprets the target's response (e.g., Jane interprets John's response as evidence of his extraversion), and (5) the target interprets her or his response (e.g., John sees himself as more extraverted as a result of his response).

Studies such as those of Snyder and Swann (1978), and Fazio et al. (1981) have examined some of these steps under artificial conditions. Their findings suggest that observers can shape actors' personalities. However, the question remains whether these expectancy effects generalize to situations where actors are permitted to play a more active role. In real-life interactions, the actor and the observer switch roles, and both are active in personality construction. In laboratory studies of expectancy effects, such as those described above, there is no actual interaction between the two participants. In more naturalistic studies, expectancy effects have been found to be moderated or even outweighed by the influence of the active participation of the actor (Pennington, 1987).

Accordingly, the actor should not be viewed as a puppet whose strings are pulled by observers. Rather, the constructivist approach is a liberating and empowering approach to personality. It does not regard personality as

617

shaped by others or set in stone at some early age. To some extent, the actor can decide to be a particular kind of person, behave accordingly, and have her or his self-definition confirmed by others. I have known a person for many years who is very sociable and outgoing. She is the kind of person that everyone immediately likes and who brings cheerfulness and light to every encounter. Wendy will tell you that she has not always been like this. She remembers that when she was a little girl she was extremely shy around other children, and felt miserable in social situations. She also remembers the day when she decided that kids who got on with other kids had a much better time and were much happier than she. So she decided to be like those other kids. As she remembers it, she soon became the sociable and outgoing person she is today.

The importance of the actor's agenda in the construction of personality has been studied by psychologists interested in impression management. They view the actor's identity as emerging in the process of negotiation between the actor and the observer (Swann, 1987). In impression-management theory, the contribution of the actor to the construction of her or his personality is referred to as the actor's self-presentation. It is recognized that there are individual differences in the extent to which actors are aware of their self-presentations and the degree to which they are motivated to control how they are perceived (Leary & Kowalski, 1990). Thus impression-management theory includes all three components of constructed personality (actor, observer, and self-observer).

However, impression-management theorists may have overestimated the extent to which personality is open to negotiation (Buss & Briggs, 1984). People differ in the extent to which they can vary their self-presentations. As a result of heredity and environment, there are boundaries or limits to our versatility as actors. Nevertheless, within these limits, there is still scope for the actor to be an active participant in the construction of her or his personality.

SUMMARY AND CONCLUSIONS

In this chapter, I have presented the view of personality as a social construction. According to this view, personalities are created in the process of social interaction as a result of the combination of three components: the actor, the observer, and the self-observer. This approach to personality is an overarching metatheory within which to locate other more specific theories in personality and social psychology. It also generates a new way of looking at personality structure and dynamics. The constructivist approach does not reject past personality research, or deny that a science of personality is possible, as have other constructivist approaches in social psychology. Instead, it increases the scope of personality psychology by providing an expanded view in which a variety of theories and methodologies are drawn together.

FURTHER READING

Briggs, S. R., Hogan, R., & Jones, W. H. (Eds) (1993). *Handbook of personality psychology*. Orlando, FL: Academic Press.
Hampson, S. E. (1988). *The construction of personality: An introduction* (2nd edn). London: Routledge.
Pervin, L. A. (Ed.) (1990). *Handbook of personality theory and research*. New York: Guilford.

REFERENCES

Alston, W. P. (1975). Traits, consistency, and conceptual alternatives for personality theory. *Journal for the Theory of Social Behaviour, 5*, 17–47.
Asch, S. E. (1946). Forming impressions of personality. *Journal of Abnormal and Social Psychology, 41*, 258–290.
Asch, S. E., & Zukier, H. (1984). Thinking about persons. *Journal of Personality and Social Psychology, 46*, 1230–1240.
Babcock, M. K. (1989). The dramaturgical perspective: Implications for the study of person perception. *European Journal of Social Psychology, 19*, 297–309.
Berger, P. L., & Luckmann, T. (1967). *The social construction of reality*. New York: Anchor.
Buss, A. H., & Briggs, S. R. (1984). Drama and the self in social interaction. *Journal of Personality and Social Psychology, 47*, 1310–1324.
Buss, D. M., & Craik, K. H. (1983). The act frequency approach to personality. *Psychological Review, 90*, 105–126.
Casselden, P. A., & Hampson, S. E. (1990). Forming impressions from incongruent traits. *Journal of Personality and Social Psychology, 59*, 353–362.
Cattell, R. B. (1973). *Personality and mood by questionnaire*. San Francisco, CA: Jossey-Bass.
Cattell, R. B., Eber, H. W., & Tatsuoka, M. M. (1970). *Handbook for the Sixteen Personality Factor Questionnaire* (3rd edn). Champaign, IL: Institute for Personality and Ability Testing.
Cooley, C. H. (1902). *Human nature and the social order*. New York: Scribners.
Darley, J. M., & Fazio, R. H. (1980). Expectancy confirmation processes arising in the social interaction sequence. *American Psychologist, 35*, 867–881.
Digman, J. M. (1990). Personality structure: Emergence of the five-factor model. In M. R. Rosenzweig & L. W. Porter (Eds) *Annual review of psychology* (vol. 41, pp. 417–440). Palo Alto, CA: Annual Reviews.
Estes, C. L. (1979). *The aging enterprise*. San Francisco, CA: Jossey-Bass.
Eysenck, H. J. (1967). *The biological basis of personality*. Springfield, IL: C. C. Thomas.
Eysenck, H. J. (1991). Dimensions of personality: 16, 5, or 3? – Criteria for a taxonomic paradigm. *Personality and Individual Differences, 12*, 773–790.
Fazio, R. H., Effrein, E. A., & Falender, V. J. (1981). Self-perceptions following social interaction. *Journal of Personality and Social Psychology, 41*, 232–242.
Fenigstein, A., Scheier, M. F., & Buss, A. H. (1975). Public and private self-consciousness: Assessment and theory. *Journal of Consulting and Clinical Psychology, 50*, 522–527.
Fiske, S. T., & Taylor, S. E. (1991). *Social cognition* (2nd edn). New York: McGraw-Hill.

Funder, D. C., & Harris, M. J. (1986). On the several facets of personality assessment: The case of social acuity. *Journal of Personality*, *54*, 528–550.

Gergen, K. J. (1985). The social constructionist movement in modern psychology. *American Psychologist*, *40*, 266–275.

Gergen, K. J., & Davis, K. E. (Eds) (1985). *The social construction of the person*. New York: Springer-Verlag.

Goffman, E. (1959). *The presentation of self in everyday life*. New York: Doubleday.

Goldberg, L. R. (1981). Language and individual differences: the search for universals in personality lexicons. In L. Wheeler (Ed.) *Review of personality and social psychology* (vol. 2, pp. 141–165). Beverly Hills, CA: Sage.

Goldberg, L. R. (1992). The development of markers for the Big-Five factor structure. *Psychological Assessment*, *4*, 26–42.

Goldberg, L. R. (1993). The structure of phenotypic personality traits. *American Psychologist*, *48*, 26–34.

Greenwood, J. D. (1989). *Explanation and experiment in social psychological science: Realism and the social constitution of action*. New York: Springer-Verlag.

Hampson, S. E. (1988). *The construction of personality: An introduction* (2nd edn). London: Routledge.

Hampson, S. E., John, O. P., & Goldberg, L. R. (1986). Category breadth and hierarchical structure in personality: Studies of asymmetries in judgments of trait implications. *Journal of Personality and Social Psychology*, *51*, 37–54.

Harré, R. (1983). *Personal being*. Oxford: Basil Blackwell.

James, W. (1892). *Psychology: The briefer course*. New York: Henry Holt.

John, O. P., Hampson, S. E., & Goldberg, L. R. (1991). The basic level in personality-trait hierarchies: Studies of trait use and assessability in different contexts. *Journal of Personality and Social Psychology*, *60*, 348–361.

Kruglanski, A. W. (1989). The psychology of being "right": The problem of accuracy in social perception and cognition. *Psychological Bulletin*, *106*, 395–409.

Leary, M. R., & Kowalski, R. K. (1990). Impression management: A literature review and two-component model. *Psychological Bulletin*, *107*, 34–47.

Loehlin, J. C., Willerman, L., & Horn, J. M. (1988) Human behavior genetics. *Annual Review of Psychology*, *39*, 101–133.

McCrae, R. R. (1990). Traits and trait names: How well is Openness represented in natural languages? *European Journal of Personality Psychology*, *4*, 119–129.

Markus, H., & Nurius, P. (1986). Possible selves. *American Psychologist*, *41*, 954–969.

Mead, G. H. (1934). *Mind, self, and society*. Chicago, IL: University of Chicago Press.

Monson, T. C., Keel, R., Stephens, D., & Genung, V. (1982). *Journal of Personality and Social Psychology*, *42*, 1014–1024.

Peabody, D., & Goldberg, L. R. (1989). Some determinants of factor structures from personality trait descriptors. *Journal of Personality and Social Psychology*, *57*, 552–567.

Pennington, D. C. (1987). Confirmatory hypothesis testing in face-to-face interaction: an empirical refutation. *British Journal of Social Psychology*, *26*, 225–235.

Peterson, C., & Stunkard, A. J. (1989). Personal control and health promotion. *Social Science and Medicine*, *28*, 819–828.

Rotter, J. R. (1954). *Social learning and clinical psychology*. Englewood Cliffs, NJ: Prentice-Hall.

Rotter, J. R. (1966). Generalized expectancies for internal versus external control of reinforcement. *Psychological Monographs*, *80*, whole number 609.

Schlenker, B. R. (1980). *Impression management*. Monterey, CA: Brooks/Cole.

Snyder, M. (1979). Self-monitoring processes. In L. Berkowitz (Ed.) *Advances in experimental social psychology* (vol. 18, pp. 247–305). New York: Academic Press.

Snyder, M., & Swann, W. B., Jr (1978). Hypotheses testing processes in social interaction. *Journal of Personality and Social Psychology, 36*, 1202–1212.

Swann, W. B., Jr (1987). Identity negotiation: Where two roads meet. *Journal of Personality and Social Psychology, 53*, 1038–1051.

Triandis, H. C. (1989). The self and social behavior in differing cultural contexts. *Psychological Review, 96*, 506–520.

White, G. M., & Kirkpatrick, J. (Eds) (1985) *Person, self, and experience: Exploring Pacific ethnopsychologies*. Berkeley, CA: University of California Press.

Wiggins, J. S., & Trapnell, P. D. (1993). Personality structure: The return of the Big Five. In S. R. Briggs, R. Hogan, & W. H. Jones (Eds) *Handbook of personality psychology*. Orlando, FL: Academic Press.

7.3

TRAIT THEORIES OF PERSONALITY

H. J. Eysenck

University of London Institute of Psychiatry, England

When we try to describe someone's personality, we nearly always use trait names, usually adjectives; we may say that the person in question is sociable, persistent, reliable, sporting, or affected. Or we may use nouns – the person has a good sense of humour; makes a powerful impact; has chutzpah. Traits like these are the "small change" of psychologists also, but a good deal of research and theorizing has to go into their exploration before they are of any use scientifically. Traits are *relatively enduring descriptive characteristics of a person*: if they were not enduring, they would not be very useful, and follow-up studies lasting for up to 40 years have shown reasonable persistence of the various traits measured.

Traits are usually conceived of as *predispositions* to *behaviour* having *cross-situational consistency*, that is, leading to similar behaviour in a variety of situations. The concept of "trait" is often contrasted with the concept of "state", that is, the *momentary* evocation of a particular type of behaviour. Thus a person who has the *trait* of anxiety is nevertheless not always in a *state* of anxiety, and even a person who is very low on the trait of anxiety may on occasion manifest some degree of anxiety — say when going to an important interview ill-prepared and likely to fail! Traits may be regarded as the summation of states; a person who frequently shows anxiety (is often in a *state* of anxiety) is considered to evince the *trait* of anxiety.

The concept of type is also relevant. In the older literature this concept used to be employed to characterise people as belonging to a *group*, as in the "four temperaments" of the ancient Greeks; a person was either choleric, sanguine, melancholic, or phlegmatic. Such a classification was absolute: you belonged to one type or another, and no mixture was allowed. This is clearly not in line with experience, and nowadays the term is either not used at all, or reserved for combinations of traits found to correlate together; thus extraversion is a type concept based on the observed correlations of several traits — sociability, liveliness, activity, dominance, surgency, etc. But we are dealing with a continuum, from an extreme of extraversion to an extreme of introversion, with few people at the extremes and the majority in the middle.

Personality is a term used to combine the many trait measures of a given person; another term often used is "temperament".

The two terms "personality" and "temperament" are often used synonymously by psychologists, and are in a sense not dissimilar to popular usage as defined in modern dictionaries. Personality in the *Concise Oxford Dictionary* is defined as "distinctive personal character", and temperament as "individual character of one's physical constitution permanently affecting the manner of acting, feeling, and thinking". Given the biosocial nature of our species (Eysenck, 1980) the suggested distinction (behavioural or biological) is often difficult to make (no behaviour without physiological, neurological, or hormonal antecedents), but some psychologists (e.g., Strelau, 1983) do insist on treating the terms as referring to different contexts.

In essence, the study of personality deals with non-cognitive individual differences, while the study of cognitive differences is more concerned with the study of intelligence and differential abilities, even though of course cognitive factors also emerge in the study of personality (Kreitler & Kreitler, 1990), but not in the form of differential ability. In the study of personality, we are mainly concerned with aspects of behaviour (sociable, persistent, Machiavellian, suggestible, anxious); these behaviours are of course accompanied by cognitions of one kind or another which guide the expression of these divergent behaviours.

The study of personality may be divided into *descriptive* or taxonomic, on the one hand, and *causal*, on the other. A taxonomy of behaviours, however provisional, must of course precede any type of causal analysis; traits as popularly conceived clearly cannot as they stand serve as the basis for any

623

kind of scientific study. We must try and establish a firm basis for conceptualization and measurement; as Lord Kelvin said: "One's knowledge of science begins when he can measure what he is speaking about, and express it in numbers". How can we transmute popular concepts into measurable quantities? There are many different ways of doing this, some better than others. All must be preceded by a proper conceptualization of the traits to be measured; we must know what we are looking for if we are to have any hope of finding it.

USES AND ABUSES OF PERSONALITY QUESTIONNAIRES

The most widely used measures of personality are ratings and self-ratings (questionnaires). These have encountered many objections. Do subjects tell the truth, indeed do they know the truth about themselves? Do raters know the subject well enough to give a valid assessment? Cannot a person's behaviour change from day to day, so that no meaningful assessment can be made? These and many other questions have of course engaged psychologists for many years, and the answers to most of them are known. We are concerned with two major questions. The first relates to *validity*: does our measurement really measure what it is supposed to measure? The second relates to *reliability*: carrying out our measurement several times, do we get similar answers? There are many ways of answering these questions, most of them involving statistical treatment of the data collected.

Suppose we have a 50-item questionnaire on sociability. We can correlate the sum of the 25 odd-numbered questions with the sum of the even-numbered questions; if the correlation is high (as it would be in any properly constructed questionnaire) then clearly the answers cohere together in a reliable fashion. Repeat the measurement after six months, and correlate the scores for the two occasions; if the correlation is high, then clearly our measure is consistent over time.

A reliable measure is not necessarily valid. We might correlate our score on the questionnaire with the outcome of a rating experiment, or with observations of behaviour, or with a miniature situation experiment; if the outcome is positive, then several quite distinct methods agree on the outcome, which suggests validity. In fact the experiment has been done many times, usually with positive results: social behaviour, self-rated, correlates quite well with ratings given by friends, with the observations of behaviour, with miniature situations, and so on. Agreement is less, although still positive, when less obvious types of behaviour are rated, for example anxiety.

In addition to testing reliability and validity, psychologists have invented techniques to trap subjects resorting to inaccurate or fraudulent reporting. Lie scales have been developed which ask questions that should be answered in a socially undesirable way by an honest subject, for example, "Do you never tell lies?" Subjects who answer "Agree" are obviously trying to put themselves in the best light. (One would of course not rely on just one question and answer for such a conclusion, but score a whole set of questions.) Some subjects show a "yea-saying" tendency, that is, they answer "Yes" much more frequently than "No". Hence, most questionnaires employ items half of which are written in such a form that the trait positive score demands an affirmative, half a negative answer, thus avoiding any influence of the "yea-saying" tendency.

There are many such tricks to make sure that dishonest or false answers are caught; there is no absolute certainty, but as we shall see, such questionnaires have been found to predict with considerable accuracy everyday behaviour in real life. Some critics have suggested that traits and their measurement may be pretty useless because human behaviour is situation-based (Mischel, 1968); in other words, it is the situation that determines what we do. We do not smoke on parade, we do not socialize in church during the sermon, we do not indulge in drunken driving under the eyes of the police. Such a criticism is mistaken because personality study is concerned with the differential behaviour of people in identical situations; of two people invited to a party, one accepts with joy, another refuses; the situation is identical, but one person is sociable, the other not (Eysenck & Eysenck, 1985).

It is impossible to list all the objections that can be (and have been) made to the use of the methods of measuring personality outlined above, or the answers made by exponents of the methods used to obviate relevant criticisms. A well-designed measure of personality must demonstrate reliability and validity before it is accepted by psychologists as a proper instrument that can be used in clinical, social, industrial, or research work; the standards recommended by professional bodies are high, and adherence compulsory.

As an example of validation, consider Figure 1, which shows the scores on an anxiety questionnaire filled in by 1,000 neurotic and 1,000 normal subjects. High scores are characteristic of neurotics, only 28.6 per cent of whom score below 9 points on the questionnaire; of the normals, only 10.6 per cent score above that point. Nor are all of these misclassified; it is usually

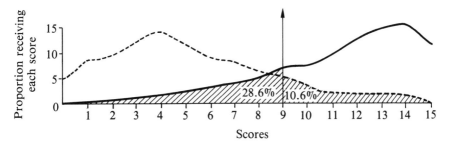

Figure 1   Proportion of neurotics (solid curve) and normals scoring at various levels of an anxiety scale

625

considered that in a normal population, some 10 per cent are in fact neurotic, but decline to go for treatment. There is no one-to-one agreement, but the data show a clear differentiation between the groups.

Internal consistency is often tested by means of a statistical technique called factor analysis; we correlate the items of a questionnaire, or the ratings received, and test whether they hang together as factors in the manner anticipated. Thus a questionnaire of "social shyness" would be expected to show positive correlations between items, and to disclose a single factor of "social shyness". This technique has often been criticized as meaningless; we deduce a factor of "social shyness" from the observed intercorrelations, and then use this factor to explain the observations on which it is based! But such a criticism is unwarranted. We do not use our factor to *explain* (in a causal sense) our observations; as we shall see, causal explanations are of quite a different kind. What we have done is "simply" to objectify our hypothesis; because

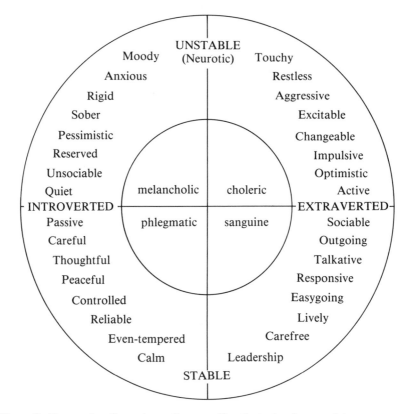

Figure 2 Two major dimensions of personality, the traits characterizing extremes on each dimension, and the relation of the dimensions to the four Greek temperaments
Source: Eysenck, 1970, by courtesy of London University Press

we believe that all our items measure a single trait of "impulsivity" does not *prove* that they do, and indeed more often than not the statistical analysis of data reveals that our original hypothesis was erroneous. Eysenck (1956) factor analysed a well-established questionnaire of social shyness, to test the hypothesis that there were two quite unrelated types of social shyness. One was associated with anxiety, leading to a *fear* of other people, the other was associated with introversion, leading to a dislike of being with other people. The analysis disclosed two unrelated factors, corresponding to these two types of social shyness. Correlational analysis enables us to test our descriptive theories and improve them; it is not intended to serve the role of disclosing *causal* agencies.

HUMAN TYPOLOGY

The search for a reliable and valid measurement of personality traits is only a first step. The traits we find are not independent of each other; they *correlate* in certain patterns that suggest more complex entities that might be called types. The search for such types, higher-order factors, or dimensions of personality is usually conducted by means of factor analysis, a statistical technique designed to discover *patterns* in a table of intercorrelations we have already encountered in the last section. Two such patterns are Extraversion–Introversion (E) and Neuroticism–Stability (N), two dimen-

Table 1 Six typical extraversion and six typical neuroticism questions

	Questions	Key
1	Do you sometimes feel happy, sometimes depressed, without any apparent reason?	N
2	Do you have frequent ups and downs in mood, either with or without apparent cause?	N
3	Are you inclined to be moody?	N
4	Does your mind often wander while you are trying to concentrate?	N
5	Are you frequently "lost in thought" even when supposed to be taking part in conversation?	N
6	Are you sometimes bubbling over with energy and sometimes very sluggish?	N
7	Do you prefer action to planning for action?	E
8	Are you happiest when you get involved in some project that calls for rapid action?	E
9	Do you usually take the initiative in making new friends?	E
10	Are you inclined to be quick and sure in your actions?	E
11	Would you rate yourself as a lively individual?	E
12	Would you be very unhappy if you were prevented from making numerous social contacts?	E

Source: Eysenck, 1970

sions already anticipated in a rather primitive fashion by the ancient Greeks, in the form of their four "temperaments". Figure 2 shows the traits that define E and N, and their relation to the four temperaments.

To illustrate, in a very brief form, how such higher-order constructs originate, consider Table 1, which contains six E and six N questions, according to theory. These were administered to a large group of subjects, and answers intercorrelated and factor analysed. Figure 3 shows the outcome − two clear clusters of items, defining the two factors. Normally, we would of course intercorrelate whole scales, not single questions, but the logic is the same.

Exhaustive research in many parts of the world, and by many investigators, has shown that there are three major dimensions of personality which appear in practically any large-scale analysis, and in many different countries and civilizations (Eysenck & Eysenck, 1985). In addition to E and N, we have psychoticism-superego control (P), and Figure 4 shows the traits whose

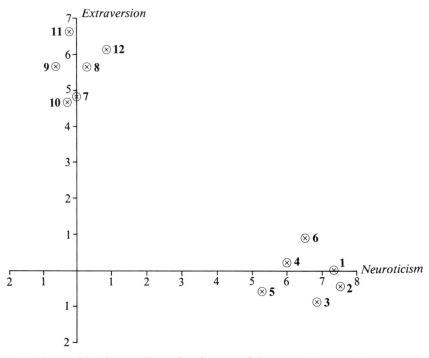

− Relative position in two-dimensional space of six neuroticism and six extraversion questionnaire items

Figure 3 Position of six E and six N items on two factors derived from intercorrelations of items shown in Table 1

628

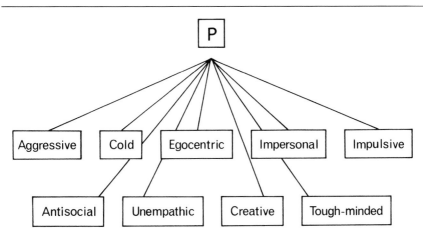

Figure 4 Traits the intercorrelations between which give rise to second-order factor
"psychoticism" (P)
Source: Eysenck and Eysenck, 1985

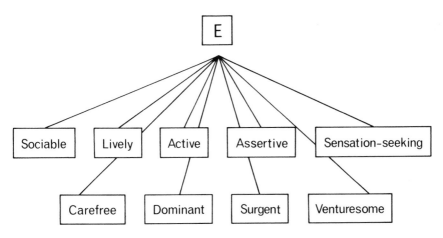

Figure 5 Traits the intercorrelations between which give rise to second-order factor
"extraversion" (E)
Source: Eysenck and Eysenck, 1985

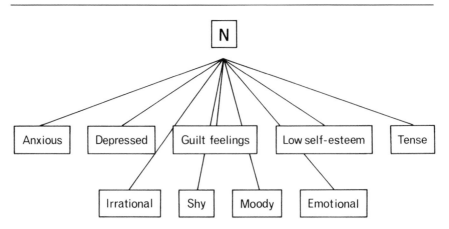

Figure 6   Traits, the intercorrelations between which give rise to second-order factor
"neuroticism" (N)
Source: Eysenck and Eysenck, 1985

intercorrelations establish these dimensions of personality as independent entities forming the centre of human personality.

It is important to distinguish between neuroticism and neurosis, psychoticism and psychosis. The personality dimension measures a *predisposition*, the clinical entity an actual psychological disorder. The psychological variable constitutes the diathesis; under strong stress this diathesis can become a psychiatric illness (Claridge, 1985). Figure 7 shows how the psychoticism dimension is conceived. It constitutes a continuum (abscissa) ranging from schizophrenia on the extreme right to highly altruistic, socialized conduct (superego) on the extreme left (Eysenck & Eysenck, 1976). The normal curve shows the distribution of this variable, that is, roughly normal. The conception is based on the observed fact that all types of functional psychosis are related; that this psychotic kernel extends to "spectrum disorders", schizoid states, psychopathic-type personality disorders, and so on, and that this continuum extends to perfectly "normal" conditions. P_A indicates the probability that a person anywhere on the continuum would become schizophrenic, given environmental stress.

There are other typologies aiming to deal with the major dimensions of personality. The oldest and most widely known is Cattell's Sixteen Personality Factor system (16 PF) (Cattell, Eber, & Tatsuoka, 1970). This system was based on the factor analysis of traits selected from an overview of all trait-similar constructs, and so on. Fifteen traits emerged, in addition to intelligence which Cattell also scheduled. However, these fifteen traits are primaries which are themselves intercorrelated; when the resulting table is factor analysed we obtain three "superfactors" that closely resemble P, E, and N (Eysenck, 1991a). In its time (1960–1970) this system was revolu-

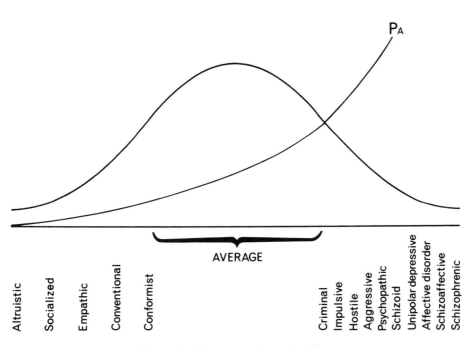

Figure 7 The nature of psychoticism

utionary, and widely used. It is subject, however, to a number of criticisms. First, it has been impossible for many investigators in many countries to obtain factor-analytic results in any way similar to Cattell's; usually only seven or eight primary factors appear that do not resemble Cattell's. Second, the Cattell factors are very unreliable, with estimates quite unacceptably low. Third, items on one scale sometimes correlate better with another scale than the one they are supposed to measure.

A more modern system, which is getting quite popular, is that of the so-called "Big Five" (John, 1990; Goldberg, 1993). This system originated from a survey of adjectives related to personality, and favours five factors: Factor I, Extraversion (or Surgency); Factor II, Agreeableness; Factor III, Conscientiousness; Factor IV, Neuroticism (or Emotional Stability); and Factor V, Openness to Experience (or Culture, or Intellect). It has been found that Conscientiousness and Agreeableness correlate negatively with Psychoticism, so highly that it would seem that these two factors use primaries which help to define Psychoticism as a higher-order factor. Openness to Experience is the latest name for a factor that has had several quite different names, and is difficult to pin down. The system is so new that (apart from E and N) there has been too little work on its theoretical basis, experimental study, or physiological correlates to evaluate it properly.

PERSONALITY TRAITS

Not all questionnaires aim to measure the main dimensions of personality; a scale may aim at a particular theoretical concept. Below is given a list of the most popular of these traits, together with a brief statement about their nature, and the theory on which they are based. Information concerning authors and publishers of the scales, and detailed critical reviews, will be found in the Buros (1970) book, *Personality: Tests and Reviews*, and the later *Handbook of Personality* (Pervin, 1990).

Field dependence-independence

This is conceived as a perceptual test measuring the degree to which an individual depends on input from the environment in judging, say, the position of an upright at an angle with the vertical; the upright is seen in a tilted frame. While intended as a measure of personality, this correlated much more with visuo-spatial ability, a measure of intelligence.

Locus of control

This trait is based on the hypothesis that people may attribute their successes and failures to themselves (internal) or external circumstances, or other people (external locus of control). Externality correlates with anxiety and neuroticism.

Repression-sensitization

Some people seem to exaggerate their emotional reactions (sensitizers), while other people repress or deny them (repressers). These reactions are supposed to be linked with psychopathological types, and have some connection with somatic diseases – repressers are more likely to develop cancer, sensitizers coronary heart disease (Eysenck, 1991b).

Type A-Type B

This typology was developed in the search for personality variables linked with coronary heart disease (CHD). Type A is believed to be CHD-prone; persons of this type are supposed to be hyperactive, suffer time stress, and be liable to anger, hostility and aggression (AHA). Some of these traits, particularly the AHA ones, have in fact been shown to predict CHD (Eysenck, 1991b).

Achievement motivation

The nature of this concept is apparent from the title; it is usually measured by some form of projective technique, but there are also questionnaires that attempt to do so. The concept has been measured in social and national groups, in an attempt (partly successful) to account for group differences in achievement (Lynn, 1991).

Authoritarianism

This is a concept relating mainly to social attitudes, namely those of the follower and the leader. The personality attributes were deduced from psychoanalytic theory, and have not found much support. The original questionnaire used to establish the concept has been severely criticized for its poor psychometric properties, particularly because it confuses "yea-saying" with authoritarianism, all the questions being worded in such a way that saying "yes" counts positively for authoritarianism.

The Myers-Briggs type indicator

This questionnaire attempts to embody Jung's theory of introversion–extraversion; it measures I–E as well as function scales (thinking versus feeling; judging versus perceiving; sensing versus intuition) (Thorne and Gough, 1991).

Sensation-seeking

This concept was developed by Zuckerman (1979) to encapsulate notions of seeking variety and danger, and avoid boredom. The scale has both reliability and validity, and has been widely used internationally.

There are many hundreds of such tests, all of which are listed in the most recent Buros *Mental Measurement Year Book*, but these eight are the most prominent at present.

PERSONALITY: HEREDITY AND ENVIRONMENT

It is important to turn now to causal factors in the determination of personality differences, and of primary importance is the demonstration that genetic factors are equally as important as environmental ones, possibly more so (Eaves, Eysenck, & Martin, 1989). The evidence here is based on twin studies and adoption studies, often using very large groups of 12,000 and 15,000 pairs of twins, and complex modern methods of analysis which set up models of genetic and environmental action and interaction, and then test the adequacy of the models against the data obtained from the samples tested.

The fact that genetic factors are the most important single determinants of individual differences in personality is perhaps not surprising; while for long unpopular among psychologists it has never been seriously denied. What is probably more important is the finding that of the two major environmental influences (*common* environment or between-family influence, and *specific* environment or within-family influence), it is the latter that appears from the analyses as important, not the former. In other words, the influence of the family is almost exclusively genetic; environmental influences come from events that happen to children and adolescents regardless of their family provenance, for example having a specially good or bad teacher, having or not having an accident or illness, marrying a good or bad partner. This finding, replicated many times, goes counter to most psychological or psychiatric teaching, and illustrates the weak foundation on which most previous theories were constructed. Future theories will have to start *de novo*, and take into account these decisive findings.

Certain consequences follow from these considerations. Psychiatrists are often faced with the question: "To what extent do (extreme) environmental experiences influence personality development?" Early sexual abuse, domestic violence, broken homes, deprivation, being brought up in a home with parents showing neurotic or even psychotic symptoms *may* have some bearing on the development of personality, but there are two major problems in proving such theories. In the first place, the influence may be genetic rather than environmental. Children who are frequently beaten by their parents often grow up aggressive and even sadistic, but it may be a case of sadistic children inheriting bad genes from sadistic parents (Eaves et al., 1989). Many prostitutes complain of early sexual abuse, but the correlation may not be environmental; sexually abnormal behaviour may be inherited (Eysenck, 1976). The evidence is inherently ambiguous, and investigations that neglect the possibility of genetic influences cannot be regarded as convincing.

In the second place, identical environmental conditions may have different and even contrary effects on children differing in genetically determined personality. "The flame that melts the wax tempers the steel". A poor environment may cause some children to give up and submit, others to fight against it and achieve. Again, no account that looks *only* at environmental effects can be regarded as sufficient. We always deal with the *interaction* between nature and nurture, and our experiments have to be geared to that fact. Studies of criminality and antisocial behaviour illustrate the methodology appropriate to such investigations (Eysenck & Gudjonsson, 1989). For a detailed discussion of the whole problem, Hoffman (1991) should be consulted; he tried to build a bridge between genetic and developmental psychologists, and indicate ways of resolving differences in methodologies and findings.

It follows from the fact that genetic factors are important in producing individual differences in personality that there must be observable physiological, neurological and/or hormonal differences that can serve to mediate the genetic and behavioural sides; DNA cannot directly determine behaviour! This fact has led to the construction of theories which in turn have produced experimental studies to support or disconfirm theoretical predictions. These form an important part of the scientific study of personality because they enable us to test the validity of our measurements against experimentally testable predictions.

Consider the following chain: (1) Tests are constructed to measure various traits. (2) The traits intercorrelate to suggest a higher-order factor, for example E. (3) E is shown to be highly heritable. (4) A biological theory is suggested to account for extraverted behaviour in terms of certain testable physiological/neurological/hormonal factors. (5) Experimental studies verify the theoretical predictions (Eysenck, 1967). Such a progression would seem to give confirmation of the validity of our original measures, and their reliability, as well as the essential correctness of the theory; had the measures been unreliable and/or invalid, the whole chain of arguments and demonstrations would have collapsed ignominiously.

BIOLOGICAL DETERMINANTS OF PERSONALITY

There is now a huge literature on this topic (Zuckerman, 1991), and I shall give only a very brief example of the logic in question. It has been suggested that extraverted behaviour is due to habitual low cortical arousal; extraverts need strong external stimulation to achieve a satisfactory level of arousal (Eysenck, 1967). Introverts on the other hand have a habitual high level of cortical arousal, and hence avoid such strong stimulation. Figure 8 illustrates the theory; incoming ascending afferent pathways not only take information to the cortex but also send collaterals to the ascending reticular activating system which in turn sends arousal messages to the cortex to enable it to deal properly with the incoming signals. Extraverts have a *sluggish* reticular formation, introverts an *overactive* one, with ambiverts in the middle. There are many additional features to this system, but in essence this is what it says.

Strelau and Eysenck (1987) have edited a book that summarizes the empirical evidence to date, which is largely physiological (EEG, contingent

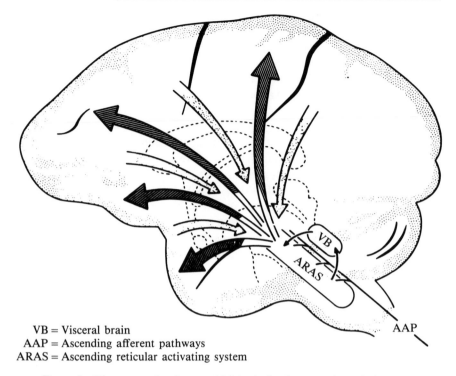

VB = Visceral brain
AAP = Ascending afferent pathways
ARAS = Ascending reticular activating system

Figure 8 Diagrammatic picture of biological substrate of cortical arousal
Source: Eysenck, 1965

negative variation, evoked potentials, positron emission tomography, electrodermal responses, etc.); the verdict is a cautiously optimistic one. Consider one study to illustrate modes of proof. Wilson (1990) measured skin conductance in his subjects once every hour, and also got them to write down what they were doing at the time. (The measures were taken by day, when skin conductance, as a measure of arousal, was higher in introverts than in extraverts.) The two scales come together late at night because extraverts resort to arousal-producing activities (parties, etc.) to increase their arousal, while introverts shun such activities, and resort to arousal-reducing activities like reading and watching TV.

This study is also important because it demonstrates the weakness of the Mischel situationist theory. People are not usually free during the working day to choose what they would like to do; choice is constrained, and hence arousal is determined by personality. But in the evening personality dictates the choice of *situation*; it is personality traits that select appropriate situations, not situations that determine conduct. Many other experiments than this one have given support to the theory (Eysenck & Eysenck, 1985), and

N and P also have been shown to have strong connections with hormonal, physiological and neurological indices (Zuckerman, 1991). There is no universally agreed theory as yet concerning the biological causation of the major dimensions of personality, but suggestions for such theories certainly exist, and have received some degree of support from empirical studies.

One interesting set of studies has tried to relate *drug* action and personality. The arousal theory links introversion and arousal, hence stimulant drugs should increase introverted behaviour, depressant drugs (like alcohol!) extraverted behaviour. In a similar vein, anxiolytic drugs should increase emotional stability, adrenergic drugs decrease it. Hallucinogens should increase psychoticism, anti-psychotic drugs decrease it. Figure 9 shows the suggested set of relations. On the whole, empirical studies have borne out the causal relationships there suggested (Eysenck, 1983).

It is possible to make testable deductions from the causal theories here discussed very briefly, and these deductions may be tested in the laboratory or in real-life situations. Thus the low arousal level of extraverts leads them to seek constant change, as existing stimuli lose their arousal value. In the

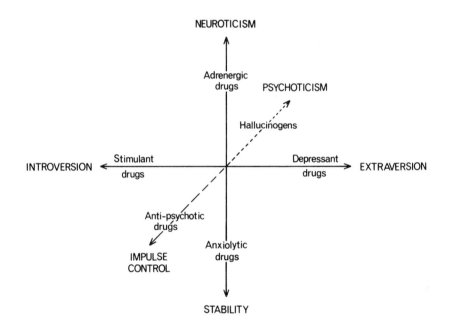

PSYCHOTROPIC DRUGS AND PERSONALITY

Figure 9 Drug action and personality
Source: Eysenck, 1983

637

laboratory we may test their vigilance, which is low, or their desire for change, by offering them a chance to alter the stimuli offered. In real life we predict (and find) that extraverts change jobs more frequently, change sex partners more frequently, and are more likely to divorce, have less product-loyalty in their shopping behaviour, move house more frequently, and so on. Many such verifications have been found in the experimental literature (Eysenck, 1965; Eysenck & Eysenck, 1985).

The point is an important one. Students of traits and higher-order factors have often been accused of subjectivity, and of accepting the verbal statements of their subjects uncritically. Such criticism can be rebutted only by formulating and testing personality theories that go beyond simple trait measurements and provide them with a causal background that leads to testable deductions. In so far as these deductions can be verified experiment-ally or observationally, in so far does trait measurement cease to be subject-ive. Traits are the stepping stones to more complex theories of personality, and form an integral part of these theories. In addition, they are important in dealing with social matters of much concern, such as criminality (Eysenck & Gudjonsson, 1989), education (Eysenck, 1978), sexual behaviour (Eysenck, 1976), and many more (Wilson, 1981).

SUMMARY AND CONCLUSIONS

The study of personality and temperament has come a long way since the 1940s, as a look at a modern handbook of personality (Pervin, 1990) will demonstrate. Its richness is suggested by the huge area covered, and by the amount of social behaviour it explains (Wilson, 1981). Large areas of psychology depend on personality theory and an accurate measurement of personality variables, and the scientific study of these fields has separated them most markedly from the former reliance on Freudian speculation and untestable interpretations. Studies of the genetic basis of personality, and the biological intermediaries that translate DNA into behaviour, promise us ever-more precise information on the fundamental question of why we do what we do. Trait theories have had many critics, but in spite of much undeserved hostility they have led to theories that can integrate much of human behav-iour into meaningful wholes, and that provide testable propositions. More cannot be asked of any scientific concept.

FURTHER READING

Eysenck, H. J., & Eysenck, M. W. (1985). *Personality and individual differences: A natural science approach*. New York: Plenum.
Hall, C. S., & Lindzey, G. (1985). *Introduction to theories of personality*. New York: Wiley.

638

Pervin, L. A. (Ed.) (1990). *Handbook of personality: Theory and research*. New York: Guilford.

Strelau, J., & Eysenck, H. J. (Eds) (1987). *Personality dimensions and arousal*. New York: Plenum.

Zuckerman, M. (1991). *Psychobiology of personality*. Cambridge: Cambridge University Press.

REFERENCES

Brengelmann, J. C. (1960). Expressive movements and abnormal behaviour. In H. J. Eysenck (Ed.) *Handbook of abnormal psychology* (pp. 62–107). London: Pitman.

Buros, O. K. (1970). *Personality: Tests and reviews*. Highland Park, NJ: Gryphon.

Cattell, R. B., Eber, H. W., & Tatsuoka, M. M. (1970). *Handbook for the Sixteen Personality Factor Questionnaire* (3rd edn). Champaign, IL: Institute for Personality and Ability Testing.

Claridge, G. (1985). *Origins of mental illness*. Oxford: Basil Blackwell.

Davey, D. M., & Harris, M. (1982). *Judging people*. London: McGraw-Hill.

Eaves, L., Eysenck, H. J., & Martin, N. (1989). *Genes, culture and personality: An empirical approach*. London: Academic Press.

Eysenck, H. J. (1956). The questionnaire measurement of neuroticism and extraversion. *Rivista di Psicologia*, *50*, 113–140.

Eysenck, H. J. (1965). Extraversion and the acquisition of eyeblink and GSR conditioned responses. *Psychological Bulletin*, *63*, 258–270.

Eysenck, H. J. (1967). *The biological basis of personality*. Springfield, IL: C. C. Thomas.

Eysenck, H. J. (1970). *The structure of human personality*. London: Methuen.

Eysenck, H. J. (1976). *Sex and personality*. London: Open Books.

Eysenck, H. J. (1978). Personality and learning. In S. Murray-Smith (Ed.) *Melbourne studies in education* (pp. 134–181). Melbourne: University of Melbourne Press.

Eysenck, H. J. (1980). The biosocial model of man and the unification of psychology. In A. J. Chapman & P. M. Jones (Eds) *Models of man* (pp. 49–62). Leicester: British Psychological Society.

Eysenck, H. J. (1983). Psychopharmacology and personality. In W. Janke (Ed.) *Response variability to psychotropic drugs* (pp. 127–154). Oxford: Pergamon.

Eysenck, H. J. (1991a). Dimensions of personality: 16, 5 or 3? – Criteria for a taxonomic paradigm. *Personality and Individual Differences*, *12*, 773–790.

Eysenck, H. J. (1991b). *Smoking, personality and stress: Psychosocial factors in the prevention of cancer and coronary heart disease*. New York: Springer-Verlag.

Eysenck, H. J., & Eysenck, M. W. (1985). *Personality and individual differences: A natural science approach*. New York: Plenum.

Eysenck, H. J., & Eysenck, S. B. G (1976). *Psychoticism as a dimension of personality*. London: Hodder & Stoughton.

Eysenck, H. J., & Gudjonsson, G. (1989). *Causes and cures of criminality*. New York: Plenum.

Eysenck, M. W., & Eysenck, H. J. (1980). Mischel and the concept of personality. *British Journal of Psychology*, *71*, 191–204.

Gattaz, W. F. (1981). HLA-B27 as a possible genetic marker of psychoticism. *Personality and Individual Differences*, *2*, 457–460.

Gattaz, W. F., Seitz, M., & Beckman, N. (1985). A possible association between HLA-B27 and vulnerability to schizophrenia. *Personality and Individual Differences*, *6*, 283–285.

Goldberg, L. R. (1993). The structure of phenotypic personality traits. *American Psychologist, 48*, 26–34.

Hall, C. S., & Lindzey, G. (1985). *Introduction to theories of personality*. New York: Wiley.

Hoffman, L. W. (1991). The influence of the family environment on personality: Accounting for sibling differences. *Psychological Bulletin, 110*, 187–203.

John, O. P. (1990). The "big five" factor taxonomy: Dimensions of personality in the natural language and in questionnaires. In L. A. Pervin (Ed.) *Handbook of personality* (pp. 66–100). London: Guilford.

Kline, P. (1981). *Fact and fantasy in Freudian theory*. London: Methuen.

Kreitler, S., & Kreitler, H. (1990). *The cognitive foundations of personality traits*. London: Plenum.

Lynn, R. (1991). *The secret of the miracle economy*. London: Social Affairs Unit.

Mischel, W. (1968). *Personality and assessment*. London: Wiley.

Pervin, L. A. (Ed.) (1990). *Handbook of personality: Theory and research*. New York: Guilford.

Strelau, J. (1983). *Temperament-personality-activity*. London: Academic Press.

Strelau, J., & Eysenck, H. J. (Eds) (1987). *Personality dimensions and arousal*. New York: Plenum.

Thorne, A., & Gough, H. (1991). *Portraits of type*. Palo Alto, CA: Consulting Psychologists Press.

Wilson, G. D. (1981). Personality and social behaviour. In H. J. Eysenck (Ed.) *A model for personality* (pp. 210–245). New York: Springer-Verlag.

Wilson, G. D. (1990). Personality, time-of-day and arousal. *Personality and Individual Differences, 11*, 153–168.

Zubin, J., Eron, L. D., & Schumer, F. (1965). *An experimental approach to projective techniques*. London: Wiley.

Zuckerman, M. (1979). Sensation-seeking: Beyond the optimal level of arousal. Hillsdale, NJ: Lawrence Erlbaum.

Zuckerman, M. (1991). *Psychobiology of personality*. Cambridge: Cambridge University Press.

7.4

FREUDIAN THEORIES OF PERSONALITY

Richard Stevens

The Open University, Milton Keynes, England

Sigmund Freud
The unconscious
  Free association
  Dreams
  "Faulty achievements"
  Listening with the third ear
Psychosexual development
Psychodynamics
Further aspects of
  psychoanalysis

Neurosis
Therapeutic method
Other developments
The evidence for Freud's ideas
The nature of Freudian theory
  and its implications for the
  study of personality
Further reading
References

Freudian theories of personality, indeed psychoanalytic theories in general, are quite different from other approaches to personality found in academic psychology. The difference is essentially one of methodology. This is an issue that will be taken up in greater depth later, but it refers to the fact that Freud, like other psychoanalysts, was more concerned with generating ideas to make sense of the behaviour and feelings he encountered in his patients and in his own life than with testing to ensure the validity of his ideas. The result has been an extraordinary paradox. Freudian theories have been enormously influential not only on the way in which people in our culture think about personality and behaviour but also on the ideas and work of psychologists themselves. Yet, because of the methodological difference noted above, his ideas are not taught in many psychology departments in the USA and the UK or, when they are, are often treated as of essentially historical interest rather than as making a fundamental contribution to our knowledge and understanding of human behaviour and experience. You will be in a better position to assess the appropriateness of that position after reading this chapter.

Psychoanalysis represents a cluster of varied theories and therapeutic procedures which are still evolving. All, however, stem from the work of Freud and, in spite of the fact that it is about one hundred years since his first ideas were formulated, they still provide the core of the psychoanalytic approach. First in this chapter we shall look in detail at Freud's own ideas about personality and the ways in which these developed. Then, after briefly examining some other aspects of psychoanalysis, we shall discuss the important issue of the nature of psychoanalytic theories and try to assess their contribution to our understanding of personality and their significance to psychology in general.

SIGMUND FREUD

To understand Freud's ideas it is helpful to consider them in the context of the life and personality of their creator. Outwardly, the pattern of Freud's life seems undramatic. He was born in 1856 into a middle-class but not particularly wealthy family which, although Jewish, was not especially observant of religious practices. At the *Gymnasium* Freud was top of his class, adept not only in Latin and Greek but also in several modern languages and well versed in both literature and philosophy. At the University of Vienna, Freud specialized in science, eventually settling down to six years of research in physiology. Freud loved research and only the need to enter medicine in order to earn his living pushed him to take his medical degree and to become a junior physician.

At the age of 29, he was appointed occasional lecturer at the university. In the same year, with the aid of a scholarship, he spent a formative five months with the French psychiatrist Charcot in Paris. Charcot impressed Freud and stimulated his interest in the psychological as opposed to the physiological basis of neurosis.

Freud married when he was 30 (after being engaged for four and a half years, of which three were spent apart from his fiancée), and started his own private practice as what we would now call a psychiatrist. His initial concern was to develop new methods for the treatment of what were then called "nervous diseases". After trying and later discarding hypnosis, he took up the "talking" or "cathartic" method which had been developed by an older colleague, Breuer. This involved relaxing and encouraging the patient to talk about anything that came into his or her head and to re-experience in the process the emotions aroused by the episode recollected. He also began to make use of free association (see below) which was to become a core feature of his technique.

In the closing years of the nineteenth century came a period of intense self-analysis. By analysing his own dreams and checking background details with his mother (his father had died at about this time) Freud tried to confront the repressed residues of his own childhood experiences. In this way he generated the groundwork for much of this theory to come. In the year 1900 he published the first major work of psychoanalysis, *The Interpretation of Dreams*. In this, Freud set out his theory of the unconscious and repression and attempted to show how mental phenomena such as dreams as well as neurosis are a product of conflict between different mental systems. *Three Essays on the Theory of Sexuality* came out in 1905. In this, his next seminal work in psychoanalysis, he formalized his ideas on the development of the sexual drive from infancy to maturity and argued that there is a relationship between its development in early childhood and sexual perversion, neurosis and personality in the adult.

A band of devoted followers, later to become the Vienna Psychoanalytical Society, gradually began to gather round Freud. By now he had been appointed to a professorship and, with the growing international recognition of psychoanalysis, he was invited in 1909 to Clark University in the USA to receive an honorary doctorate and to deliver a series of guest lectures. Psychoanalysis began to grow into a flourishing movement. Congresses were held, a journal established and in 1910 the International Psychoanalytic Society was formed.

In the immediately ensuing years Freud generated a steady stream of publications on psychoanalytic technique and theory including studies based on literature and biography. But it was a time also marked by growing dissension in the close-knit psychoanalytic circle which culminated in the secession of Adler from the group in 1911 followed, to Freud's especial sorrow, by Jung in 1914. Psychoanalysis as an international movement was disrupted further by the advent of the First World War. In 1920, quite probably stimulated by the violence of the war, Freud published the most controversial and least accepted of all his works, *Beyond the Pleasure Principle*, in which he postulated *thanatos*, the drive within us all which strives for death and which, when directed outwards, may take the form of aggression against others.

Freud's work in the 1920s largely centred on the development of ego psychology, in particular on the different ways on which the ego is able to defend itself against the anxiety aroused both by the external world and repressed instinctual drives. His daughter Anna, the only one of Freud's children to follow in his footsteps, was subsequently to elaborate his ideas. There is then a decided shift in several of Freud's later writings, as for example *Civilization and its Discontents* (1930), to an analysis of the relationship between the individual and society and the societal origins of guilt.

While he was now enjoying world fame, Freud was also beginning to suffer from cancer of the jaw, which eventually led to 33 operations and was to torment him to the end of his life. Even though his books had been burned in Germany, it was not until the Nazis invaded Austria in 1938 that Freud moved with his family to England. There he died in September 1939.

This synopsis of Freud's life hints at how his theories evolved over his lifetime. The account of his ideas in this chapter reflects the chronological order of this development as outlined above. There are three sets of ideas which form the core of Freudian theory: *the unconscious, psychosexual development*, and *psychodynamics*. These will each be dealt with in turn.

THE UNCONSCIOUS

One of Freud's first realizations was that much of the motivation for our behaviour is unconscious and not necessarily accessible to us. Early in his career he had seen a dramatic illustration of this in Charcot's demonstrations when, by the use of hypnotic suggestion, Charcot could induce or remove at will paralyses and anaesthesias in patients suffering from "hysteria" (a condition where physical symptoms occur which appear to have no organic basis). Further evidence came from Freud's work with Breuer which resulted in their joint publication *Studies in Hysteria* – the first articulation of psychoanalytic ideas. One of Breuer's patients, Bertha Pappenheim (referred to in the *Studies* as Anna O), had suffered, in spite of the hot weather, from a difficulty in drinking. Under hypnosis, she recounted how she had come across her governess encouraging her pet dog to drink from a glass (a story of which previously she had seemed consciously unaware). She vehemently expressed her disgust as she did so and apparently she was able subsequently to drink without difficulty. Freud and Breuer were convinced that the origins of Anna's phobia lay in the associations the act of drinking had with feelings of disgust (and perhaps also dislike of her governess) which she not only had been unable to express at the time but had blocked or repressed from her own awareness.

In a later paper (*The Ego and the Id*, 1923) Freud made the distinction between the *pre-conscious* ideas and memories that an individual can bring to consciousness almost at will, and *unconscious* thought which, because of its disturbing nature, is not easily made conscious even though it may still indirectly influence behaviour. Freud's earlier work was directed at developing methods to find out about unconscious feelings.

Free association

Freud found that many of his patients could not be hypnotized, and he gradually came to abandon hypnosis in favour of "free association" or *freier Einfall* (literally "free coming to mind"). The essence of this technique, which is frequently used in psychoanalytic therapy both on its own and as an adjunct to other methods, is that patients are encouraged to express freely everything that comes into their minds and to avoid any attempt to structure their thought or to check or filter what they say aloud. This was to become the fundamental rule of psychoanalysis, the only rule that patients are obliged and expected to follow at all times in therapeutic sessions. In positive contrast to hypnosis, free association provides material that is quite easily shared with and acceptable to patients, as they experience themselves as producing it and come to recognize recurrent themes.

Dreams

For Freud, though, the "royal road", as he called it, to the unconscious was dream analysis and he regarded *The Interpretation of Dreams*, published relatively early in his career in 1900, as his most significant book. In it he illustrated his theory with extensive examples of dreams from his patients and colleagues as well as his own. Freud considered that dreams essentially represent wish-fulfilments. Sometimes, as in the case of children's dreams of sweets and toys, the wish is portrayed directly in the content of the dream. The motivations underlying the dreams of adults are more likely to be unconscious, often originating in repressed experiences of childhood. Although the unconscious censoring mechanisms of the mind are relaxed during sleep, they are still operative to some extent. Unconscious wish fulfilment is therefore represented in disguised and distorted form. The underlying motivation will be fused with experiences and thoughts from the previous day or even events occurring during the course of the night such as the covers slipping off, a light switched on, or indigestion.

The task of the analyst is to interpret the *latent* content of the dream (that is, its underlying meaning) from the *manifest* content as reported by the dreamer. One of Freud's major contributions was to show the kinds of distortion that latent meaning undergoes. The main distorting processes Freud distinguished as *condensation, displacement, dramatization, symbolization*, and *secondary elaboration*. By *secondary elaboration*, Freud meant the distortions that occur due to the conscious restructuring that takes place when the dreamer recalls or reports his or her dream. Freud considered that although dreams are often remembered as being brief, they may in fact represent *condensations* of several underlying themes. A single figure in a dream, for example, may represent two or more people. A remembered phrase may encapsulate several different meanings (a situation referred to as "over-determination").

Displacement is where the intention underlying the dream is disguised by transferring an act or emotion on to some person or object other than the one that, in actuality, arouses the unconscious feeling. Thus, one patient dreamed of strangling a little white dog. Free association suggested that the dog represented her sister-in-law, who not only was of a notably pale complexion but also had previously been accused by the dreamer of being "a dog who bites". To express her hostility directly in the form of a dream in which she killed her sister-in-law would be too disturbing. So the underlying wish was displaced on to a disguised representation of the sister-in-law – the dog.

In dreams, according to Freud, unconscious feelings often express themselves, as in the example above, in *dramatized* or pictorial form. The associative links between image and feeling are often personal to the dreamer and can be uncovered only with the help of other information about the patient and free association. Some images, however, are commonly found in our culture to represent significant objects, events, or emotions. These are what Freud means by *symbols*. So he considered, for example, that objects that resemble the penis in shape (e.g., elongated things like snakes, sticks, neckties, trains, or trees) or in function (e.g., intrusive things like guns or daggers or erective things like planes or umbrellas) may symbolically represent it. Likewise, "small boxes, chests, cupboards, and ovens correspond to the female organ; also cavities, ships and all kinds of vessels" (Freud, 1900a, p 242). The actions of climbing ladders, stairs, inclines, or flying may be used to symbolize sexual intercourse; having a haircut, a tooth pulled, or being beheaded, may symbolize castration.

"Faulty achievements"

Soon after *The Interpretation of Dreams* came *The Psychopathology of Everyday Life* (1901), a readable book which elaborates on ways in which our unconscious influences us in everyday life. One way is through accidental actions; another is through slips of the tongue (the famous "Freudian slip"). Though Freud's translators coined the term *parapraxes* to refer to such phenomena, Freud's original term *Fehlleistung* is perhaps better more directly translated (as Bettelheim, 1985, has suggested) as "faulty achievement". *Fehlleistungen* offer another source of information to the psychoanalyst. A patient's continuous late arrival for the analytic session, for example, might indicate hostility or resentment towards the analyst. An impressive sequence of "accidental" mishaps might indicate aggression against the self.

Listening with the third ear

The analyst's primary skill and art is in interpretation, looking out for unconscious meanings and motivations, feeling for underlying themes. Reik (1954) has called this process "listening with the third ear". Initial interpretations, be they based on dreams, free associations, or behaviour, are inevitably tentative, no more than working hypotheses to be matched against further evidence. Gradually, consistencies may begin to appear. If only seen as through a glass darkly, a pattern emerges. Psychoanalytic interpretation is rather like doing a jigsaw in which one can never be sure that all the pieces are there!

PSYCHOSEXUAL DEVELOPMENT

In 1905 Freud published his *Three Essays on Sexuality*, perhaps the most important of his books after *The Interpretation of Dreams*. In the course of his work with Breuer, Freud had formed a conclusion that some kind of sexual disturbance invariably underlay hysterical neurosis. In these essays he explored the complex nature and significance of sexuality and its relationship with personality development. In particular, he claimed that sexual development takes place in the first five years of life and that what happens then is of crucial significance for the later adult – not just in terms of sexual life but personality as well.

Freud conceived of development as a complex interaction between a biologically programmed timetable of development and the environment and social context of the child. To describe the biological component he used the concept of *Trieb*, usually translated as instinct or drive, which he conceptualized as a tension system arising from bodily functioning. All psychic energy arises from the operation of the drives. Initially, Freud classified drives into two basic types. There are those drives that promote preservation of the self: hunger and thirst come into this category. But it is sexuality or *libido* whose goal is the continuation of the species that Freud considers of greatest significance psychologically. He uses the term "sexual" in its broadest sense to refer to any kind of body stimulation that produces pleasure.

According to Freud, during the first five years of life, the source and nature of the stimulation that is most pleasurable to the child changes as a result of biological development. For the very young infant, the mouth is the source, and pleasure is derived initially from sucking and later, as teeth develop, from biting (the oral stage). (You may have noticed how, once children begin to be able to handle objects, everything is held to the mouth.) At some time, usually in the second year, excretion is likely to become the focus of attention, pleasurable stimulation being derived from the retention and elimination of faeces (the anal stage). Still later, in about the fourth year, the focus of interest shifts to the genitals. This is reflected in curiosity about sex differences and pleasure in masturbation and physical stimulation from rough play (the phallic stage). From about the age of 5 until adolescence, there is a "latency period", during which attention shifts to the world of school, to learning skills and developing peer relationships. At adolescence, according to Freud, sexuality becomes directed outwards and, instead of the child's own body being the primary source of gratification, becomes focused (if only in fantasy) on another partner. The "pre-genital" modes of childhood sexuality will be incorporated into this. Thus, oral stimulation, for example in the form of kissing, is usually involved in sexual relations.

Each developmental stage involves not only a particular body *zone* but also a *mode* of activity. So the oral phase involves sucking and biting. They also each involve a characteristic *psychological quality*, reflecting the nature of the predominant relationship at that time (which is why it is described as a theory of *psycho*sexual development). The oral stage, for example, comes at a time when the child is entirely dependent on others for the satisfaction of its comfort, contact and sustenance needs. Psychoanalysts (e.g., Erikson, 1950) have argued that if these needs are met, the result is a general optimism, a sense of the world as a positive place; if they are not, this lays the basis for a generally pessimistic emotional orientation. The anal phase is the prototype for relationships with authority. For the first time, perhaps, demands may be made on the child for some kind of control of body functions. In other words, the child has to control impulses and desires in response to the demands of others. Freud associates the phallic phase in boys with *Oedipal* conflict (named after the Greek story of Oedipus who unknowingly killed his father and married his own mother). Because the erogenous zone of stimulation at this stage is the penis, the close affection a boy is likely to feel for his mother becomes "sexualized". With his growing awareness of the relationships of others, the boy comes to see his father as a rival for his mother's affections. This can result in increased hostility towards his father and perhaps also fear of him. According to Freud, the usual way this conflict is resolved is through increased identification with the father, taking on his role and characteristics, and "introjecting" or assimilating his perceived values and attributes. In this way the basis for conscience or superego is established.

Bear in mind when thinking about Freud's ideas here that young children's thought (as the work of Piaget, among others, has demonstrated) is not based on principles of logic and causality like that of most adults, but is much more a world of fantasy and imagination. Freud believed, for example, that because of the boy's focus on his penis at the time of Oedipal conflict, the fear of his father is likely to be experienced as anxiety over losing it (castration anxiety). If this idea may seem odd, it is worth considering the powerful appeal of fairy stories which involve themes that are strange, to say the least, unless they are regarded as fantasies relating to psychosexual stages (see Bettelheim, 1976). For example, characters are often eaten, heads are cut off, and a beanstalk soars magically into the sky until it is cut down to destroy a threatening giant.

How is this relevant to understanding adult personality and behaviour? A key concept here is the general notion of *transference*. This is the idea that the emotional feelings that characterized an early relationship stay with us and, at least on an unconscious level, are "transferred" into relationships in adult life. If the response to parental pressure at the anal phase, for example, was overly submissive or rebellious, this may carry over into later relationships with authority. Or, to take another example, one way a young boy may resolve Oedipal conflict may be by over-idealizing and repressing the sexual feelings his mother arouses in him. This may result in an adult man who has difficulty in integrating sexuality and affection: who uses one woman as a sexual partner but who puts another on a pedestal as a potential wife.

Another key notion in psychoanalytic theory is *fixation*. Fixation can occur if a child is either overstimulated or deprived at one or other of the developmental stages. This may result in an overemphasis in later life on the characteristics or satisfactions associated with the corresponding phase. For example, fixation at the oral stage is likely to result in an adult who is overly concerned with oral gratification. This may take the form of sucking or chewing sweets, smoking, drinking or even excessive talking. Or fixation may express itself in over-use of the modes of action associated with this stage — passivity, dependency, concern with incorporating the values, the "goodness", of others. In a later paper, Freud (1908) explored in some detail the various characteristics that can result from fixation at the anal stage. If the pleasure a child takes in playing with his or her faeces is severely constrained by parents, for example, the child may develop defences against such forbidden pleasures which may express themselves later as obsessive orderliness and cleanliness. If parents reinforce a child's production on the potty, this may lay the foundation for later pleasure in creating. And miserliness may result from a child developing an unwillingness to "let go".

It is interesting, in view of the fact that the majority of his patients were women, that Freud has relatively little to say about the development of girls. Perhaps this is a reflection of his dependence on his own self-analysis as a source of ideas. He believed that for the little girl the crucial issue equivalent to the Oedipal conflict in boys is the realization that she has no penis. This is experienced as a sense of loss which leads her to devalue women and turns her towards her father. Later she will come to identify with her mother because she is in the same position, but her underlying emotional desire to possess a penis will remain. Freud considered that fantasies of being pregnant or even a desire to possess or rival men may represent unconsciously and symbolically attempts to acquire the "missing" part. Many psychoanalysts (e.g., Ernest Jones) and others, however, have criticized Freud's concept of penis envy as too "phallocentric" and alternative accounts of girls' development have been put forward by later writers (see e.g., Chodorow, 1978).

There has also been criticism of Freud's account of male sexual development. Instead of the Oedipus complex being universal as Freud supposed, some critics have suggested that it is peculiar to a particular kind of family structure where the father remains dominant and aloof — as in the patriarchal Jewish family in which Freud himself was reared. The idea of the Oedipus complex certainly had a personal foundation. In his self-analysis and interpreting his own dreams, Freud had been surprised at the hostility and guilt he had discovered in relation to his father and the almost erotic nature of his feelings for his mother.

The theme for Freud's psychosexual theory, then, is that the child is the "parent of the person". Not only later sexual proclivities and neurosis but also personality have their origins in fixation at infantile phases of psychosexual development.

PSYCHODYNAMICS

In *The Ego and the Id* (1923) Freud drew together ideas initiated in earlier works and presented a more formalized conceptualization of the psyche or mind as an energy system taking the form of the confluence of interacting forces which may, and often do, conflict. These forces, Freud suggested, were broadly of three types. First, there is the drive for the satisfaction of biological needs. Gratification through actions or fantasy results in *pleasure*, frustration in tension. Because it is rooted in the body, Freud described this aspect as the "It" (*das Es*). As the child grows older, perceptual and logical capacities develop, bringing increasing understanding of the world around. A child can both do things and learn from experience. The goal of *pleasure* becomes tempered by the demands of *reality*. This reality-testing, perceptual aspect of the self Freud designated the "I" (*das Ich*), denoting that it includes consciousness and is concerned with integrating the different aspects of self. As noted in the discussion of the Oedipus conflict, children, as they grow older, may introject or assimilate values and attitudes through identification with the adults who care for them. This is the basis for the development of the third aspect, the "Above-I" (*das Über-Ich*) as Freud called it to indicate its moral, regulatory power. It is worth noting in passing that such assimilation of values is one way in which the ideological beliefs of the prevailing culture may begin to be taken in by the growing child.

(In the standard translation of Freud's works, the "It", the "I" and the "Above-I" are translated as *id, ego* and *superego*, respectively. However, it is perhaps preferable to use literal English translations of Freud's original words as these convey better that they refer to aspects of the self rather than actual parts of the mind. As Bettelheim (1985) notes, the translators' use of Latin terms rather than everyday words gives them a spurious scientific or medical character, and the ultimate effect has been to reify or "make a thing of" the concepts and thus do a disservice to our understanding of Freud's ideas.)

These aspects may come into conflict with one another. For example, sexual desire, say the desire to masturbate (the drive for pleasure of the It or *id*), may be countered either by a fear that this may lead to punishment (the concern of the I or *ego* for the consequences of reality) or by guilt that it is wrong (the introjected inhibitions of the Above-I or *superego*). Psychodynamics refers to the conflicting forces of these different aspects of the psyche and explores the ways in which conflict may be played out.

In his later formulations, Freud considered that one consequence of intra-psychic conflict is the experience of *Angst*. (While this is translated as "anxiety", it conveys perhaps a more pervasive sense of fear and anguish.) The anxiety may be alleviated by reducing conflict by means of defensive devices. Anna Freud noted that scattered throughout her father's writings are

650

suggestions for nine varieties. In her book *The Ego and Mechanisms of Defence* (1936), she (along with other analysts) has extended the list.

The most pervasive and significant of all defence mechanisms is *repression*. Impulses that in some way are disturbing are shut out of consciousness. In the masturbation example above, sexual desire might be repressed. Freud was using this idea to explain his patients' symptoms as early as his studies with Breuer on hysteria (1895).

With *displacement* (discussed above), the impulse is redirected towards a more acceptable or less threatening target. For example, jealousy of siblings may create resentment in a child towards a parent that conflicts with existing feelings of affection. Such a conflict might be alleviated by displacing the aggression on to a parent substitute such as a teacher or a relative. One kind of displacement which psychoanalysts consider to be of fundamental significance, both for the adjustment of an individual and the development of civilization, is *sublimation*. Freud had made reference to this as early as 1905 in the *Three Essays on Sexuality*. Sublimation is the displacement of libido to non-sexual ends in a way that not only avoids conflict but also actively promotes the individual's adjustment to the social context. So, according to Freud, sexual feelings may be converted into warm friendliness and concern for others or into creative effort.

Projection is where unacceptable feelings (say aggression or sexuality) are projected on to other persons so that *they* are seen as aggressive or sexually motivated (even though they may not be so). This process may underlie some forms of prejudice as well as the dynamics of some relationships. In *reaction formation*, a repressed impulse is held in check by exaggerating the opposite tendency. Thus an extremely gentle and unassertive personality may merely represent a way of coping with strong aggressive feelings which arouse unconscious fear of retaliation or conflict with moral ideals.

These are some of the kinds of transformations which analysts consider desires can undergo when they arouse conflict. There is no finite number of defensive processes but others mentioned by Freud include denial, isolation, regression, rationalization, and identification.

It should not be assumed that defence mechanisms are inherently pathological. In some form, they pervade the fabric of our everyday lives. We may forget to pay that annoying bill, be over-polite to a person we dislike, or displace irritation from the individual who arouses it to a less threatening or more innocuous target such as the cat! But what particularly interests the psychoanalyst are those defences that are rooted in the character and past of an individual. Although chronological classification of defence mechanisms cannot be carried very far, it does seem likely that different defence mechanisms tend to assume prominence and to be appropriate at different stages of development. For example, the use of *projection* is quite natural for very young children. Desires to do forbidden acts may be projected on to pets or dolls and they may be criticized and chastised accordingly. Where fixation has occurred at an early stage of development or where a particular mechanism has been habitually resorted to, this may become the characteristic way in which the adult learns to reduce anxiety. In part, personality emerges from the typical defences we come to employ.

FURTHER ASPECTS OF PSYCHOANALYSIS

This chapter is focused on Freudian theories of personality. There is space for only brief comments on other aspects such as Freud's ideas about neurosis and therapeutic procedure, and other theoretical developments in psychoanalysis.

Neurosis

Freud in effect draws no strict dividing line between normals and neurotics. It is a difference of degree rather than kind. All the ingredients for understanding Freud's views of neurosis have already been presented in considering his idea of a dynamic unconscious, his theory of psychosexual development and the operation of defence processes.

Two kinds of neurosis occupied his attention in particular. One was *hysteria* (this includes conversion hysteria, now rarely seen, which expresses itself in non-organic physical symptoms, and anxiety hysteria which typically takes a form of a phobic reaction as illustrated by Anna O's refusal to drink – see above). The other was *obsessional neurosis*, a condition characterized by obsessional thoughts and compulsive behaviours often of a stereotyped, ritualized kind which, if not followed through precisely, result in a great deal of anxiety. A classic example of obsessional neurosis is Freud's study of Lorenz, often called the "rat-man" because of his obsessive fantasy about his father and girlfriend in which a pot of rats was fastened to their buttocks to gnaw into the anus (Freud, 1909).

With practically all his patients, Freud found that the analytic trail led eventually to a repressed conflict centred on some kind of sexual experience or "seduction" as a child. The hysterics he considered had been passive partners, whereas the obsessional neurotics had taken a more active, interested role. By the time of the *Three Essays on Sexuality*, he had revised this seduction theory, attributing the accounts of his patients to childhood fantasy rather than actual adult abuse of them as children. It has been suggested (e.g., Masson, 1984) that Freud deliberately suppressed his seduction theory because of the opposition it might arouse. Current evidence about the prevalence of sexual abuse in children may make his earlier view now seem more plausible.

Therapeutic method

Like his theory, Freud's therapeutic technique developed over his lifetime. Initially, therapy was aimed at catharsis – releasing repressed feelings. Later, emphasis was placed on interpretation of unconscious motivations. The *resistances* of the patient to interpretations offered, and hesitations or blocks when recounting memories or experiences, were treated as being indicative of sensitive areas and typical defensive strategies. The most important procedure for Freud became the analysis of *transference*. Emotional feelings (towards parents in particular) are thought to be transferred on to the therapist and analysis of the patient's attitude towards him or her may provide important insights. The fact that transference typically goes through a positive phase of emotional attachment to the analyst and then into a negative and critical phase reflects, Freud believed, a working through the ambivalence experienced in the child's relationship with his or her parents. To facilitate transference it is important for analysts to remain neutral and somewhat unresponsive and to undergo analysis themselves in order to alert them to the kinds of projection (or counter-transference) they themselves may be prone to.

Other developments

Both Adler and Jung, who were among the first to break away from Freud, disagreed with what they considered to be Freud's overemphasis on sexuality. Adler saw the drive for power, striving for superiority in compensation for infantile feelings of inferiority, as the primary motivating force. Jung substituted a more general life energy and developed a theory of personality types based on people's different styles of relating to the world (for example, introducing the ideas of introversion and extraversion) He also postulated a "collective unconscious" inherent in us all and the source of "archetypes" which, according to Jung, are symbols originating in the central universal experiences of humankind.

In the 1930s, several analysts (such as Fromm, Horney, and Erikson) left Nazi-dominated Germany for the USA. These "neo-Freudians", as they have been called, place much more emphasis than Freud on the significance for individuals of the society in which they live.

In Britain, stimulated by, among others, Freud's daughter Anna who had previously worked as a schoolteacher, one emphasis has been to extend psychoanalysis to include work with children. Melanie Klein, who had been analysing children long before Freud arrived in Britain, has also been a significant figure here. Klein differs from Freud in that she assumes that the most critical developmental phases come in the first year of life. During that time, she believed, even Oedipal conflict can be experienced and the vestiges of ego and superego functioning are already apparent. The infant's primitive differentiation of self and world leads to projection of feelings on to the key objects in his or her world. These take on both negative and positive qualities (e.g., the "good" and "bad" breast) depending on their often dual role in frustrating and gratifying at different times. Klein's focus is not so much on sexuality as on the child's handling of aggression and rage induced by frustration. The task of analysis is to help reduce the anxiety the child inevitably feels and so to reduce aggressiveness. Klein was prepared to take on children below the age of 6 and she used their play as both a diagnostic and therapeutic medium. Her ideas have brought her a considerable British following and helped lead to the development of the influential "object relations" group.

A more recent development in the USA has been the work of Kohut. This has focused on problems in the way the self is experienced (for example, over-sensitivity to rejection or insatiable need for admiration) and how these relate to difficulties in the transition that confronts us all from the experience as infants of being the centre of the world to growing awareness as we grow older of separateness. Yet another approach has been the (often wilfully obscure) attempt in France by Lacan to re-interpret Freudian theory in the light of structural linguistics and semiotics (the study of signs).

THE EVIDENCE FOR FREUD'S IDEAS

Although Freud often states or implies that his propositions have been derived from his observations of patients, he has left us no direct record of the original data by which we might evaluate his claims. He did, of course, publish case histories, but these are reconstructions of what happened after the event, and Freud made a point of not taking notes during sessions lest this interfere with the relationship between himself and the patient. What is perhaps surprising also is that Freud reported on so few patients. Only twelve are discussed in depth, and in some of these the details are far from complete. Even though much of his work concerns development in childhood, Freud published only one study of a child and in this the analysis was carried out not by Freud himself but the boy's father with Freud's guidance.

Rather than seeing Freud's theories as being derived from observations of patients, it is perhaps more accurate to regard them as a distillation or integration of understanding from a variety of sources: his own self-analysis and observations of everyday life as well as work with patients, and his broad background in philosophy, the arts, and science. Most of the core ideas of psychoanalysis had been postulated, at least in embryonic form, before Freud. The significance of unconscious thought had been anticipated by philosophers like Nietzsche and Schopenhauer and clinically demonstrated by Charcot. Theories of childhood sexuality had been put forward by Moll and Ellis. Freud's genius was to extend, elaborate, and link such elements into a coherent theory; and then to modify and evolve his theory to accommodate observations from both clinical work and life experience.

There are those, however, who have suggested that Freud imposed his interpretations on his patients rather than deriving them from or developing them by observations, and that he even distorted or fabricated evidence to fit with his theories (e.g., Esterson, 1993). Such doubts as these reinforce the need for more explicit demonstration of the validity of psychoanalytic ideas. Unfortunately, psychoanalysts have followed Freud's lead: they have regarded their theories as being adequately "proved upon the couch" and have been inclined to question the appropriateness of more formal kinds of tests. Many attempts have been made, however, by psychologists, to bring experiment, structured observation and cross-cultural comparison to bear on psychoanalytical propositions. (For a summary of the findings see Stevens, 1983; for more detailed reviews see Kline, 1981, and Fisher & Greenberg, 1977.)

The pattern of results is often supportive of Freud's ideas. As just a few examples, findings from dream studies are consistent with the notion that dreams are a reflection of mental life (though they do not necessarily represent wish fulfilments). Cross-cultural studies, as well as comparisons of dreams and projective test responses from boys and girls, suggest that males are more likely to to be preoccupied by Oedipal themes. There is evidence for an anal personality syndrome and some (although less clear-cut) for an oral personality type. The effects of repression on perceptual processes and the displacement of aggression in response to frustration have also been reasonably well demonstrated experimentally.

What support the findings provide, however, take the form of being suggestive or "consistent with" rather than definitive. Several Freudian hypotheses have proved impossible to test adequately. The key problem here lies in the nature of the propositions themselves. They are not grounded in observables but are expressed in terms of other hypothetical concepts proposed by psychoanalytic theory. Repression, for example, can really be defined only by reference to *id*, *ego*, and *superego* and the concept of the unconscious. Even where specific hypotheses are more explicit than this, because they are likely to concern the *meaning* of an action or experience, they are not easy to test in a way that excludes other possible interpretations of the results.

A second kind of problem is that psychoanalytic propositions are almost always couched in probabilistic terms – they predict what is *likely* to happen rather than what definitely will. So strict toilet training will *tend* to lead to later anal characteristics, but there is no guarantee that these will result. A related aspect is that psychoanalytical attributes very often have more than one manifestation. Anal character can show itself as stinginess or creativity. The presence of an unconscious desire may express itself directly or, because of the operation of the defence mechanisms, only in partial form or even in actions of a totally unrelated kind. Conversely, very different, even opposite determinants may give rise to similar behaviour. Fixation, for example, can arise from both deprivation and overindulgence. This variability between determinant and effect makes it extremely difficult, if not impossible, to decisively refute many psychoanalytic propositions. Strictly speaking, they are *unfalsifiable*.

THE NATURE OF FREUDIAN THEORY AND ITS IMPLICATIONS FOR THE STUDY OF PERSONALITY

It is clear that psychoanalysis is not a scientifically grounded theory of personality whose propositions have been demonstrated beyond all reasonable doubt. What value then does it have?

One value is that it does provide a way of interrelating the different forces – from biology, social context, and individual development – which help to make us what we are: it is an *integrative theory*. A second quality is what we might call its *hermeneutic strength*, that is, its provision of methods and concepts to interpret and unpack underlying meanings. It could be argued, however, that the special value of psychoanalytic theory lies in its *epistemological implications*; for, when we examine carefully what it represents and the difficulties involved in testing it, this alerts us to the *nature* of human behaviour and personality as a subject-matter, and the *kind of understanding* that is possible and appropriate in this area. It leads, in particular, to the realization that personality and behaviour are premised on and constituted by *meanings* (both conscious and unconscious). These are not measurable in any precise way and are constructed, in that we actively make sense of the world in terms of our past experiences and the concepts we have acquired and developed. Meanings are also open to reconstruction. Psychotherapy could be regarded as largely a matter of renegotiation of meanings, particularly those concerned with the ways in which the self and others are regarded and thought about. Although Freud wanted to create a nomothetic theory (that is, a series of universal, causal laws to explain how and why we act and experience as we do), in effect he finished up with a set of "hermeneutic tools" – concepts and techniques that help us to interpret underlying meanings. The problem is that it is not easy to find ways of evaluating such interpretations that are comparable to the precision of the empirical testing of causal hypotheses. The best measures of the value of such interpretations would seem to be first, their consistency with other information about the patient and his or her situation, and second, their therapeutic value in helping patients move to a more satisfying experience of their life. Both criteria are difficult to evaluate.

When viewed in this way, we begin to see why personal experience has an important influence on psychoanalytic theorizing, for this provides the groundwork of meanings on which a theorist's ideas are based. We see too how psychoanalysis can influence so powerfully our thinking about ourselves, for the hermeneutic tools that the theories provide can become part of our vocabulary of motive by means of which we explain and account for the actions of ourselves and others.

Hermeneutic theories are not open to the satisfying precision of a theory expressed in observable, testable form. They offer a different form of understanding but one which, arguably, is more appropriate to study of human experience and actions because of the fact that these are so largely constituted by meanings. While psychoanalysis may be usefully regarded as a set of hermeneutic tools, we must resist any claim it may make to be a definitive account of personality. Other theories (as one example, social constructionism) also offer the potential for providing us with other kinds of hermeneutic insights into why we make sense of the world and experience ourselves in the ways that we do.

FURTHER READING

Freud, S. (1900). *The interpretation of dreams* (standard edn, J. Strachey, trans., vols IV and V). London: Hogarth.

Freud, S. (1905). *Three essays on sexuality* (standard edn, J. Strachey, trans., vol. VII). London: Hogarth.

Freud, S. (1938). *An outline of psychoanalysis* (standard edn, J. Strachey, trans., vol. XXIII). London: Hogarth.

Jones, E. (1964). *The life and work of Sigmund Freud* (abridged edn). Harmondsworth: Penguin.

Stevens, R. (1983). *Freud and psychoanalysis: An exposition and appraisal.* Milton Keynes: Open University Press.

REFERENCES

Bettelheim, B. (1976). *The uses of enchantment: The meaning and importance of fairytales*, London: Thames & Hudson.

Bettelheim, B. (1985). *Freud and man's soul.* Harmondsworth: Penguin.

Breuer, J., & Freud, S. (1895). *Studies in hysteria* (standard edn, J. Strachey, trans., vol. II). London: Hogarth.

Chodorow, N. (1978). *The reproduction of mothering: Psychoanalysis and the sociology of gender.* Berkeley, CA: University of California Press.

Erickson, E. H. (1950). *Childhood and society.* New York: Norton.

Esterson, A. (1993). *Seductive mirage: An exploration of the work of Sigmund Freud.* Chicago, IL: Open Court.

Fisher, S., & Greenberg, R. P. (1977). *The scientific credibility of Freud's theory and therapy.* Brighton: Harvester.

Freud, A. (1936). *The ego and mechanisms of defence* (C. Baines, trans.). London: Hogarth.

Freud, S. (1900a). *The interpretation of dreams* (standard edn J. Strachey, trans., vols IV and V). London: Hogarth.

Freud, S. (1900b). *The interpretation of dreams* (A. A. Brill, trans., 1950). New York: Random House.

657

Freud, S. (1901). *The psychopathology of everyday life* (standard edn, J. Strachey, trans., vol. VI). London: Hogarth.

Freud, S. (1905). *Three essays on sexuality* (standard edn, J. Strachey, trans., vol. VII). London: Hogarth.

Freud, S. (1908). *Character and anal eroticism* (standard edn, J. Strachey, trans., vol. IX). London: Hogarth.

Freud, S. (1909). *Notes upon a case of obsessional neurosis* (standard edn, J. Strachey, trans., vol. X). London: Hogarth.

Freud, S. (1920). *Beyond the pleasure principle* (standard edn, J. Strachey, trans., vol. XVIII). London: Hogarth.

Freud, S. (1923). *The ego and the id* (standard edn, J. Strachey, trans., vol. XIX). London: Hogarth.

Freud, S. (1930). *Civilization and its discontents* (standard edn, J. Strachey, trans., vol. XXI). London: Hogarth.

Jones, E. (1964). *The life and work of Sigmund Freud* (abridged edn). Harmondsworth: Penguin.

Kline, P. (1981). *Fact and fantasy in Freudian theory* (2nd edn). London: Methuen.

Masson, J. M. (1984). *The assault on truth: Freud's suppression of the seduction theory*. London: Faber & Faber.

Reik, T. (1954). *Listening with the third ear: The inner experience of a psychoanalyst*. New York: Farrar, Straus.

Stevens, R. (1983). *Freud and psychoanalysis: An exposition and appraisal*. Milton Keynes: Open University Press.

7.5

PERSONALITY TESTS

Paul Kline
University of Exeter, Devon, England

There are three kinds of personality tests:

1 personality questionnaires and inventories
2 projective tests
3 objective tests

NOMOTHETIC AND IDIOGRAPHIC TESTS

All three kinds of personality tests can themselves be classified under two headings: nomothetic and idiographic. Nomothetic tests are concerned with variables common to individuals. Anxiety would be a typical personality variable of this type. Idiographic tests, on the other hand, attempt to assess those aspects of personality that are peculiar to each individual – the things unique to a person. Although this classification cuts across the three types of personality tests, in practice personality inventories tend to be nomothetic and projective techniques idiographic, while objective tests are of both types.

PERSONALITY QUESTIONNAIRES AND INVENTORIES

The terms questionnaires and inventories are interchangeable. For example, Eysenck produced one test, the Eysenck Personality Inventory, which was later modified into the Eysenck Personality Questionnaire (see below). Test constructors describe their tests arbitrarily by either term, and I shall do so throughout this chapter.

Personality inventories consist of sets of items, varying in number from 10 to more than 500. These items are statements or questions, relevant to the personality variables that the tests measure, to which subjects have to respond appropriately. A few examples of typical personality inventory items will clarify the description.

1 Do you enjoy mountain-climbing?   Yes   No
2 I always lock my door at night.   Yes ? No
3 Sometimes I feel afraid for no apparent reason. True False

As can be seen from the examples above, the statements and questions of personality inventories refer to behaviour and feelings. Subject have to indicate whether these apply to them. The commonest forms of items are as follows:

1 Yes No items
2 Yes ? No items
3 True False items
4 Forced choice items, e.g., If I had a free afternoon I would prefer to (a) Look round a sweet factory (b) Play tennis (c) Read a good novel
5 Like-dislike items, where words and phrases constitute the item and subjects have to indicate whether they like or dislike them
6 Items with a rating scale, e.g., Abortion should be illegal: strongly disagree, disagree, uncertain, agree, strongly agree.

There are other varieties of items used in personality inventories, but these six types include those to be found in most of the best ones.

PRINCIPLES OF PERSONALITY INVENTORY CONSTRUCTION

It will be useful to discuss briefly how personality tests are constructed because this will throw considerable light on the nature of these tests.

Choice of variable

In our discussion of item types, no mention was made of the content of items. Indeed the choice of variable is a complex matter. However, over the years it has been shown that the vast number of personality traits which might be measured (there could be as many traits as there are descriptive terms for behaviour) in fact overlap. This can be demonstrated by correlations between them and by the statistical method of factor analysis which groups together similar variables. In fact there are about fifty relatively independent traits and five broad traits which account for a surprisingly large amount of the variation in personality (Digman, 1990). This work was pioneered by Cattell (1957) and has been fully described in Kline (1992).

The Big Five

The five broad factors or traits are often called the Big Five and they are set out below (see also Goldberg, 1993).

I *Extraversion (or Surgency)* The extravert is noisy, outward looking, sociable, and cheerful. The introvert, at the other end of the dimension, is quiet, aloof, and somewhat cold and reserved.

II *Agreeableness* High scorers tend to obey rules and adopt the mores of the society in which they live. Low scorers are the opposite of this. This may be related to tough-mindedness. It has been shown, for example, that Fascists and Communists are both high on tough-mindedness, whereas liberals are much lower, being tender minded. Most effective politicians (regardless of party) are high on this variable.

III *Conscientiousness* This refers to such traits as organization, thoroughness, and reliability, attention to duty, and self-discipline.

IV *Neuroticism (or Emotional Stability)* There is a wide variation in how anxious people generally feel when there is no specific cause to be anxious. Highly anxious people are constantly worried, while at the other end stolid individuals would barely notice if the world collapsed around their ears. This trait anxiety must be distinguished from state anxiety, which fluctuates according to our experiences. Dental appointments, driving tests, and examinations of every kind are obvious sources of state anxiety.

V *Openness to Experience (or Culture, or Intellect)* This factor refers to people's general receptivity to new ideas and new approaches.

Statistical procedures of test construction

These will now be described, using a measure of anxiety as an example. There are two possible methods. First, in factor analysis, items are written which appear relevant to anxiety and are administered to a large trial sample. The correlations between these items are then subjected to factor analysis, which groups together all items measuring the same variable. The items which "load" the factor best (correlate most highly with it) are then selected for the test. Such a method demonstrates that the items measure one factor but it is then necessary to show what this factor is.

Second, item analysis is a similar method of test construction but is statistically less complex. Here the items are administered to a trial sample, as above, but then the correlation between each item and the total score is computed. Items are selected for the final test which correlate most highly with the total score and which are discriminating, that is, the possible responses to the item are more or less evenly split. It should be obvious that an item to which 99 per cent, for example, put the same response is virtually useless since it discriminates so few of the subjects.

In most conditions these methods give highly similar results. The principle behind them is identical: both aim to produce tests that measure only one variable. Tests constructed by either of these methods certainly must measure some variable, although precisely what this is must be demonstrated in validity studies. For example, it could be acquiescence or social desirability that rendered the test homogeneous.

Criterion-keyed method of test construction

Factor and item analysis are sound methods of test construction which can yield valid and reliable tests and are widely used in the construction of personality tests. However, there is a further method which deserves mention because one of the most famous personality tests (the Minnesota Multiphasic Personality Inventory – MMPI) was thus constructed. This is the criterion-keyed method of test construction. In this method items are administered to subjects and selected if they can discriminate one criterion group (in this case the anxious group) from other groups and a non-anxious control group.

There are various problems with criterion-keyed test construction which make its use dubious except, perhaps, for a test designed for screening purposes. Thus there are difficulties in setting up the criterion groups, in almost all areas of psychology. For example, how would one set up a criterion group for a test of extraversion? Furthermore, even if groups can be established, they may differ on a variety of variables so that any resulting test will not be unidimensional. All that can be said of a criterion-keyed test is that it does discriminate the groups.

This is a serious criticism because it means that these tests have no psychological meaning, even if they work efficiently. However, in army selection, where it is necessary to screen out highly psychotic and neurotic individuals who are unlikely to make good military personnel (to put it mildly), this is not important. The reasons for their neurosis or psychosis are irrelevant in this situation and for this a criterion-keyed test is satisfactory.

ADVANTAGES OF PERSONALITY INVENTORIES

Reliability

It is relatively simple to construct reliable personality inventories, thus one can expect a good personality inventory to be reliable. Reliability, as applied to psychological tests, has two meanings: internal consistency and test-retest reliability. First, a test should be internally consistent, that is, each part of it should be measuring the same variable. It is manifestly a bad measure if this is not so. Internal consistency is measured by Cronbach's alpha, a correlation-like index, on a scale from 0 to 1 which shows a higher consistency as it approaches 1. Any good tests should have a reliability greater than .70.

Second, tests if given to the same individuals on different occasions should yield the same scores, provided that the subjects have not changed in respect of the test variables. Test-retest reliability, an index of test stability, is measured by a correlation between the two sets of scores and this again should be beyond .70. That personality test items are objectively scored contributes considerably to their reliability. If tests are to be reliable it is essential that the individual judgement of scorers is eliminated.

Validity

A test is said to be valid if it measures what it claims to measure. This may seem a banal and circular definition. However, the vast majority of personality tests of all kinds are not valid. To demonstrate that a personality test is valid is not an easy matter and it will be necessary to describe how this may be done. There are several different types of validity; each needs to be treated separately.

Face validity

A test is face valid if it looks valid, that is, it seems to the subject to measure, in this instance, some aspect of personality. This is a minor aspect of true validity since, in fact, face validity is not a good guide as to what a test does measure. Indeed the only reason for requiring a test to be face valid is to increase the cooperation of subjects. If a test appears to be patently absurd, subjects do not complete it properly.

Concurrent validity

To demonstrate concurrent validity a test will be correlated with another test of the same variable. The higher the correlation the more valid the test. It is obvious that concurrent validity is fine where there is another valid test. However, in the field of personality this is rarely the case. Furthermore, if there is a benchmark, criterion test, one might ask what the point of the new test is. It would have to be briefer, or easier and cheaper to administer, to make it worthwhile.

Predictive validity

A test has predictive validity if it is able to predict some particular criterion. It might be performance at school or university, scores on another test or membership of a category, for example being neurotic or psychotic. If such predictive validity can be demonstrated, which is not easy, it is impressive support for a test.

Construct validity

Because there are problems with each of these types of validity, the construct validity of personality tests is often demonstrated. In this approach to validation, hypotheses are set up concerning how the test would behave if the test were valid. For example, in the case of a test of anxiety, the following hypotheses might be formulated; if the majority were not refuted, the test could be said to possess construct validity.

1 High scorers would be more likely to seek outpatient psychiatric treatment than low scorers.
2 There would be high correlations with other tests of anxiety.
3 Low scorers would be found in stressful jobs.
4 Frequent attenders at general practitioners' clinics would tend to be high scorers.

These are just examples of hypotheses which could be developed from the nature of anxiety as a variable, and if supported the test could be regarded as valid.

Since clear numerical scores are obtained from personality questionnaires their reliability and validity can be demonstrated and thus good tests can be selected.

Ease of use

Personality inventories, compared with some of the other types of personality tests that are discussed later in this chapter, are easy to use. This is particularly important in applied psychology. Thus they are quick to administer. Even the longest, the MMPI (see below) takes only about an hour. Many can be completed easily in half an hour. They can be administered to large groups at one time: this should be compared with a test that has to be given individually. They can be administered and scored by people who have no considerable training in psychology. The interpretation requires more knowledge, but even this may be acquired on brief week-long courses for the majority of personality questionnaires.

Standardization

Perhaps, most important of all, personality inventories can be standardized. This means setting up norms (scores of various sample groups). Without norms, test scores are almost impossible to interpret. Thus a score of 50 on a test means one thing if this score is obtained only by the top 1 per cent of the population and quite another if 90 per cent of the population reach this score. It is not difficult, although it is time-consuming and expensive, to develop good norms for personality questionnaires. However, to do this for a projective or objective test it is extremely difficult.

Computer presentation

Finally, personality inventories can be computerized. It is a simple procedure to administer an inventory by computer. The items appear on the screen and subjects have a choice of buttons to press to register their responses. Although one computer per person is required, in a large and wealthy organization this presents no problem and group testing by computer is no more difficult than normal testing. However, such group testing needs a large number of computers or work stations since to test many applicants one at a time is not a practicable selection procedure.

There are real advantages to computer presentation of tests. All responses to each item are stored in the computer, which simplifies later statistical analysis in order to investigate the efficiency of the test. Scoring the test is automatic and errorless. Virtually immediately on completion a printout of the scores can be obtained. In some applied settings, such as clinical assessment, vocational guidance or career counselling and development, this is a great advantage, because the results can be discussed there and then with the subjects. Norms can be stored in the computer so that a simple interpretation can be quickly printed out for subjects to keep. All results can be stored so that a database of results with tests can be built up. In-house norms, for example, can be developed and with other data (e.g. on job success) the predictive validity of the test can be easily investigated. However, all these advantages of computer presentation are costly in terms of computers, and thus are suited only to large organizations where large numbers of subjects are tested.

These are the main advantages of personality inventories and it has made them by far the most popular type of personality test in most applied settings, especially for occupational psychology. Nevertheless, there are certain problems with personality questionnaires which must be discussed.

DISADVANTAGES OF PERSONALITY INVENTORIES

The items

Items must be short or they are unanswerable. Yet such brevity often leads to their being simplistic. As Alice Heim (1975) has argued, some test items are offensive to subjects on this account. In brief, it is difficult to believe on reading through personality questionnaires that their sets of simple items can have captured the full richness of human personality.

Deliberate distortion

In selection, especially, distortion is a major problem in personality questionnaires. Few candidates for a job as a salesperson would admit to being shy, to finding it difficult to talk to people, or to getting on badly with people.

Response sets

In addition to deliberate faking there are various *sets* which affect people's responses to personality questionnaires. Two are common. First, acquiescence is the tendency to agree with an item regardless of content. The best tests minimize this by having half the items keyed negatively, so that if a subject answers "Yes" to a large number of items, a high score will not be registered. Second, social desirability is the tendency to respond to an item according to how socially desirable it is. For example, it is socially undesirable to admit prejudice against ethnic or religious groups. Items relating to these will be distorted by this response set. Careful item writing, however, can eliminate most of this bias.

From this discussion of the advantages and disadvantages of personality questionnaires, it is clear that although there are problems over their simplistic nature and factors which distort the responses to them, they have some powerful arguments in their favour, the best tests being reliable, valid, and well standardized.

USES OF PERSONALITY INVENTORIES

As was discussed earlier in this chapter, it is relatively easy to construct reliable personality inventories. If a test is not reliable, it should not be used to make decisions about individuals: the less reliable it is, the greater the error band around any obtained score. This is known as the standard error of measurement. Thus because they can be reliable, personality inventories are the chosen personality tests in applied psychology.

Although applied psychology is an enormous topic (see Jewell and Siegall, 1990, for a good summary) there are three branches in which personality testing finds an obvious place – school (educational), industrial (occupational), and clinical psychology. Their use in these fields will be briefly discussed.

School (educational) psychology

In school psychology, personality inventories have been used in the study of the determinants of educational success. For example, Cattell and Butcher (1968) showed that at the high school (secondary school) level, personality variables played an important role, additional to factors of ability, in academic achievement. Extraverts tend to do better at the primary level, presumably on account of the organization of primary schools, while at secondary and university level introverts have the advantage. It is also the case that anxiety is positively correlated with educational achievement (it drives one on) although too much anxiety has a disabling effect.

Given these significant correlations, in a rational society personality inventories should be incorporated into selection procedures. If they were, however, in our egalitarian age, there would be no little outrage. Nevertheless, they are used in occupational selection and appraisal.

Industrial (occupational) psychology

Personality inventories are widely used in occupational psychology, especially in job selection. The rationale is simple, namely that for each post there is an ideal specification in terms of ability and personality and the aim of testing is to find the best possible match to this specification. It is assumed that where the fit is good, the job is better done, and the individual is happier in the post. This, of course, reduces wastage: when occupants leave unsuitable jobs for which the training has been expensive, it is a serious matter for the employers.

It is clear that good personality tests are likely to be useful in occupational selection since personality variables are important factors in most occupations. Highly sociable people would not enjoy being librarians or archivists and a shy person would be a poor publican or hotel-keeper; similarly airline pilots must be conscientious and decisive under stress. In occupational selection there are two tasks: to discover the psychological characteristics essential to each job and to measure these with reliable and valid tests.

A similar rationale can be applied to vocational guidance, although in this application of psychological tests the results are usually discussed with the subjects and form only one aspect of the process of counselling and guidance, the test scores constituting a useful description of the subject.

Clinical psychology

Here the emphasis is on diagnosis between clinical groups. For example, if it can be shown that a specific clinical group differs from others on particular personality variables or from normals, then this may provide useful insight into the nature and psychology of mental illness. Using Cattell's 16PF test it has been shown that neurotics, of all kinds, tend to be more guilt prone and be more indecisive (less ego strength) than normal controls.

EXAMPLES OF PERSONALITY INVENTORIES

Eysenck Personality Questionnaire (EPQ)

The Eysenck Personality Questionnaire (EPQ: Eysenck and Eysenck, 1975) measures N (neuroticism), E (extraversion), P (psychotism or tough-mindedness), and L (social desirability). This test is one of the best validated personality questionnaires and three of these variables, (N, E, and P) are among the Big Five factors accounting for much of the variance in personality questionnaires.

Sixteen Personality Factor Questionnaire (16PF)

The EPQ measures three broad factors plus a social desirability factor. The 16PF (Cattell, Eber, & Taksuoka, 1970) was developed (as was the EPQ) through factor analysis, but measures sixteen narrower, though correlated factors. This should make the test more useful, but it has turned out that these sixteen primary factors are difficult to replicate, although it is possible to measure the broader dimensions of the EPQ with this test. Despite these problems there is a huge body of research into the correlates of these factors: it is widely used in applied psychology. Indeed this test is of historic interest: Cattell was one of the pioneers in the use of factor analysis in personality measurement and has been responsible for many of the advances in methods and techniques in the field (see Cattell, 1973, 1978).

Minnesota Multiphasic Personality Inventory (MMPI)

The Minnesota Multiphasic Personality Inventory (MMPI: Hathaway & McKinley, 1951) has been superseded by a new (and highly similar) version (MMPI-2: Graham, 1990). However, I shall briefly discuss the original test because this is the personality inventory with the greatest number of references (more than 12,000). With more than 550 items, it is also the largest, at least of the well-used tests. Unlike the EPQ and 16PF, this is a criterion-keyed test, items originally being selected for the nine clinical scales if they could discriminate the groups, one from another and from normal controls. In fact, the authors of this test regarded the items as a pool from which other scales could be developed; over the years more than 200 such scales have been developed.

The problem with criterion-keyed tests is that even if they discriminate between groups, the psychological meaning of the scales is dubious and has to be discovered often by factor analysis. In the case of the MMPI, factor analyses have not supported the validity of the scales, despite their frequent use, since in general the whole test measures little more than the willingness of subjects to admit to symptoms, a factor which is probably the same as the N factor of the EPQ, but measured with some imprecision.

Personality Research Form (PRF)

Jackson has been responsible for a series of tests, of which the Personality Research Form (PRF: Jackson, 1974) is the most frequently used. In the USA at least, these tests are beginning to replace older tests such as the 16PF and MMPI. The PRF uses item analysis as the basis of its construction and has been meticulously constructed so that its parallel forms are, item by item and scale by scale, virtually identical. All scales are highly reliable and in many respects it is a model of test construction with item analytic methods.

However, its validity has never been attested. This is a serious defect because Jackson chose to measure the needs postulated as important in Murray's (1938) theory of personology. Since it has never been demonstrated that these, or any other set of needs, are highly salient to human personality, this choice of variables seems unfortunate. In brief the PRF is an excellent exercise in test construction but one which needs considerable support for its validity before it could be recommended as a substantive personality test.

CONCLUSION

Further details of these and many other personality inventories can be found in Kline (1992). Personality inventories are simple to administer and score, can be made highly reliable and given good norms. However, despite the modern agreement over how to carry out factor analyses, there are still a large number of factored tests with their own sets of factors which their authors all believe to be best. Nevertheless the consensus among informed researchers is that there are at the most five factors, three of which are measured by the EPQ. These factors, especially those of Eysenck, which are substantially genetically determined, should form the basis of any theory of personality.

In applied psychology the main use of personality questionnaires is in occupational selection, where they can provide useful additional information over and above tests of ability. In brief, personality inventories are useful both for personality measurement and theory.

PROJECTIVE TESTS

The second category of personality tests consists of projective tests or techniques. Most projective techniques consist of vague or ambiguous stimuli which subjects are required to describe. Their descriptions are held, in projective test theory, to reflect the deeper, hidden aspects of personality, the conflicts and anxieties which are peculiar to the individual being tested – their idiodynamics. This is in complete contrast to personality inventories, which measure variables common to all individuals. It is assumed, in projective testing, that subjects identify with the main character in the stimulus. For this reason, there are often different cards for men and women (female figures for the latter) while for children, animals are sometimes used because it is considered that these aid identification. Two comments need to be made about this general description.

First, not all projective techniques consist of ambiguous stimuli. One technique is sentence completion, on the rationale that how an incomplete sentence is completed reflects the personality of the subject. For example, subjects might have to complete the sentence "My mother is . . . ". Another well-known test (the House-Tree-Person Test – discussed below), requires subjects, as the name suggests, to draw these three objects. These are then interpreted according to the manual for the test (Buck, 1970).

Second, the stimuli are ambiguous because if they were not, the responses would simply reflect what was there. A lifelike picture of an apple, for example, would produce the somewhat uninteresting response of "apple" other than from the psychotic. For these no test would be necessary.

PRINCIPLES OF PROJECTIVE TEST CONSTRUCTION

Deliberately ambiguous materials of almost any description, usually visual or pictorial but occasionally verbal, are assembled and presented in a manner that encourages respondents to use them as stimuli for imaginative expression. The responses of subjects studied during the construction of the test are examined to see whether they are diagnostic of particular personality characteristics.

ADVANTAGES OF PROJECTIVE TESTS

First, the experience of administering projective tests is highly interesting. As different subjects produce different responses to the stimuli, there is a strong feeling that something fundamental is emerging from the test, that the academic, scientific evaluation of projective measures as invalid is quite simply mistaken. I have certainly experienced this illusion, if that is what it is. They are rich sources of data.

Second, projective tests are usually used by clinicians, who have to deal with subtle aspects of human personality which are not easy to categorize and describe. They feel that the crudities of personality questionnaires are quite unable to measure these almost ineffable characteristics. Certainly such a

671

view makes some sense. Is it really possible that all the richness and uniqueness of human personality can be captured by five variables, as is suggested in the Big Five: extraversion, agreeableness, conscientiousness, neuroticism, and openness to experience? As the philosopher A. J. Ayer once said: nothing can be that simple, let alone everything.

Third, in the hands of certain expert testers some brilliant results appear to have been achieved with projective tests. One example springs to mind. Carstairs (1957) carried out a study of the Rajputs in central India; he interviewed them and administered the Rorschach (see below). From his data he conjured a convincing and apparently insightful account of these highly interesting people whose fundamental belief in reincarnation fuels their whole lives.

Finally, not only are the data yielded by projective tests rich, as has been argued above, but also they are unique. If the Rorschach (a series of inkblots) is administered, for example, it is virtually certain that the subject has never done such a task before (other than having been previously administered the test). Rorschach responses are, therefore, unique data, for which there is no other substitute. For these reasons alone, the argument goes, they should be studied.

DISADVANTAGES OF PROJECTIVE TESTS

Reliability and validity

There are a number of problems with projective tests. In general they tend to be of low reliability; this arises from the subjectivity of scoring, which affects their validity. Furthermore, studies of the validity of projective techniques show usually rather low validity. As Eysenck (1959) pointed out, the more rigorous the experiment, the lower the validity appears to be. Vernon (1963) argued that in selection, the Rorschach test (one of the most famous projective techniques – discussed below) usually added in error. In fact, Eysenck has claimed that projective tests are nothing more than vehicles for the riotous imaginations of clinicians. Even Semeonoff (1971), who is quite favourable to projective methods, is forced to accept that there are definite shortcomings in respect of reliability and validity.

Rationale

There is no real theory of projective testing. As was mentioned above, the rationale of projective tests is that subjects project their inner conflicts and anxieties on to the stimuli which thus tap the deeper recesses of the mind. There are several points to note here. First, this use of projection is quite different from the psychoanalytic usage: in that theory projection is a mechanism of defence in which traits which are unacceptable to an individual are projected on to others. Racist attitudes might be seen as a form of projection. Clearly the projection of projective tests is a different process. Second, there is no theory in psychology to suggest that people might project their own feelings on to ambiguous stimuli. If it is a theory, then it is special to projective tests. In other words, there is no real or convincing rationale on which to base the interpretation of the responses to the test.

Notice the use of the terms "inner" and "deeper". These arise from a psychodynamic or psychoanalytic notion of personality involving unconscious aspects of personality. Generally, indeed, interpretations and scoring of projective tests make use of psychoanalysis in the broad sense of utilizing concepts such as conscious and unconscious, stressing the importance of parental figures and invoking defence mechanisms, to interpret particular responses.

Practical problems

There are several practical problems in projective testing. Most projective tests require considerable training in their administration, scoring, and interpretation, have to be administered individually, and take a long time to complete and score. This means that before they could be used in applied psychology (e.g., occupational and clinical practice) there would have to be strong evidence concerning their reliability and validity. However, as has been seen, projective tests are, generally, of low reliability and validity.

Contextual effects

Vernon (1963) has shown that there are contextual effects on scores: race of tester; race of subject; what the subjects believe the tests to be about; the attitudes of the tester (strict or playful and relaxed); the gender of the tester. If this is the case, then it is difficult to argue that projective tests are tapping the fundamental deep layers of personality.

Given all these problems, it is reasonable to ask why any psychologists should be bothered with projective tests, which are still popular in the USA.

EXAMPLES OF PROJECTIVE TESTS

Rorschach

The Rorschach test (Rorschach, 1921) consists of ten symmetrical inkblots which subjects have to describe. From these descriptions, which are minutely recorded, inferences about every aspect of a subject's personality and, indeed, ability are drawn. For example, if the subject produces long and elegant descriptions, high fluency and verbal ability are scored. A lot of bizarre or aggressive responses are held to be clinically significant, while a response that it is an inkblot is considered to be highly defensive. As has been indicated, the scoring schemes, of which there are three major ones, are detailed and complex and require considerable training to master.

Holtzman Inkblot Test (HIT)

In the Holtzman Inkblot Test (HIT: Holtzman, 1981), 45 inkblots are presented to subjects who have to choose one response to each card. Scoring of the 22 variables is highly reliable and for purposes of retesting there is even a parallel form. These 22 variables have been factored and external correlates of the factors are reported in Holtzman (1981). This is, therefore, a projective test which has the psychometric efficiency of an inventory, although more work is required on discovering what these factors measure.

Thematic Apperception Test (TAT)

The Thematic Apperception Test (TAT: Murray, 1938) is a famous projective test which Murray used (inter alia) in the extensive and brilliant studies of personality reported in his *Explorations in Personality* (Murray, 1938). Murray called his approach to the study of personality "personology", because he believed that personality inventories, which measured elements of the personality, were flawed for that reason. Rather, the whole person, hence the name, should be studied and for this purpose projective tests were superior to inventories.

The stimuli consist of cards portraying people in ambiguous situations. The expressions and feelings of the human figures are also ambivalent. Murray originally interpreted the responses to the cards in terms of needs (the drives of the individual) and presses, the corresponding relevant pressures in the environment. Indeed, he argued that any stimuli would reveal these aspects of personality although his cards had shown themselves well suited to the task. Later workers have used other broadly psychoanalytic principles to interpret the responses. Murstein (1963) described a number of objective scoring schemes.

House-Tree-Person Test (HTP)

In the House-Tree-Person Test (Buck, 1970), the subject is required to draw a house, a tree, and a person; the subject then answers questions about them. On this basis interpretations concerning personality are made. For example, the age of the tree is thought to represent the emotional age of the subject; drawing curtains over the windows is held to represent a defensive person who resists others getting to know them, as does the failure to draw a garden path. These typical interpretations indicate both the highly subjective nature of the scoring system, for which no empirical evidence is provided in the manual, and the fact that the rationale is a somewhat simple-minded metaphor between drawings and thinking.

CONCLUSION

The dilemma of projective testing is that, in the argument concerning the utility and validity of projective tests, both sides are right, although their claims are antithetical. It is true that there is little evidence for the validity of projective tests and that apparently irrelevant contextual variables influence responses. Furthermore, there is no strong theoretical reason why they should work. However, it is also true that personality inventories are simplistic, that projective tests yield rich and unique data, and that certain individuals appear able to use them with great skill and insight.

Careful analysis of this dilemma suggests a solution. If it is accepted that some individuals can find psychological insights in the responses to objective tests, it means that the tests are not useless. Examination of the problems (listed above) shows that the subjectivity of scoring the tests presents a severe difficulty, which training does not overcome. Thus projective tests, it could be argued, might become viable if objective scoring schemes were devised for them.

In fact a number of objective scoring methods have been tried and these appear to make some improvement, although it has to be said there is no agreement, yet, as to how this should be done. One projective tester, Holtzman (1981), has produced an objective version of the Rorschach test (described above).

There can be no doubt that projective tests are full of problems. In their standard form they cannot be regarded as satisfactory personality tests. They are unreliable and their interpretation is far too subjective. The argument that a few gifted individuals can use them well is unsatisfactory for a scientific test. Any scientific measuring instrument should yield accurate results when used by reasonably intelligent trained people. This is not the case with projective tests.

However, because they yield rich and unique data it would seem worthwhile to attempt to overcome the problems and devise objective scoring schemes. Of course, such schemes would have to be shown to be reliable and valid, as is the case with any test. Preliminary studies suggest that this is possible (see Kline, 1992, for a summary of findings in this area) and this should be the aim of further research.

OBJECTIVE TESTS

I shall conclude this chapter with a brief discussion of objective personality tests. This is a category of tests which has been mainly studied by Cattell and his colleagues (Cattell and Warburton, 1967). These tests are defined as tests which can be scored objectively and whose meaning is impenetrable to subjects. In the compendium of these objective test devices (Cattell and Warburton, 1967), which includes around 800 tests from which more than 2,000 variables can be scored, it is clear that the majority of these tests are impenetrable not only to subjects but to most psychologists as well. It should be noted that projective tests, when objectively scored (as was suggested previously) are by this definition objective tests; as such they are included in the compendium.

PRINCIPLES OF OBJECTIVE TEST CONSTRUCTION

Cattell (1957) has discussed the principles behind objective test construction in considerable detail. In summary there are two essentials. The first is that there should be variance on the test. Any task on which individual differences can be noted and which is not a test of ability may be regarded as an objective personality test provided, of course, it can be objectively scored and subjects cannot guess its purpose. The second principle, because the first allows an infinity of tests, is that there should be some rationale in experimental or clinical psychology for the measure. Needless to say all tests must be validated; this is critical in the case of objective tests because, by definition, they lack face validity.

ADVANTAGES OF OBJECTIVE TESTS

Because their purpose cannot be guessed they are difficult to fake. This is particularly important where tests are to be used in the applied setting, and especially in selection. Furthermore, the response sets of acquiescence and social desirability should, in many cases, be avoided. Finally, to study personality cross-culturally, objective tests, especially physiological measures, may prove valuable.

DISADVANTAGES OF OBJECTIVE TESTS

The validity of all these tests is not well proven. Cattell and Warburton (1967) admit this point and argue that further research is required urgently. However, because the tests are difficult to administer (they have to be carefully timed and are often suited only to individual administration) and do not appear valid few researchers have seriously investigated their validity. Kline and Cooper (1984) carried out just such an examination of the validity of the ten best objective tests which have been published as a battery – the Object-ive Analytic (OA) Battery (Cattell and Schuerger, 1976). However, they could find little support for the validity of its scales and were forced to conclude that, in the UK at least, the OA Battery should not be used.

EXAMPLES OF OBJECTIVE TESTS

Fidgetometer

The fidgetometer is a special chair with electrical contacts at various points which are closed by movements. The score is the amount of movement recorded over a fixed period of time. The rationale of the test is that the anxious individual would fidget more. Clearly this is difficult to fake, even if subjects know that their movements are being recorded. How would one know whether it was better to keep still or to move a lot?

Slow line drawing

Subjects are required to draw a line as slowly as possible across a page. Two scores can be extracted from this test: the length of the line, and whether the subject cheated by lifting the pencil. The rationale here was that the cheating score would load negatively on measures of conscientiousness, while the length of line would be related to inhibition and control. Again faking this test or guessing what it measures is no easy matter.

Willingness to play practical jokes

This is a questionnaire in which subjects have to express their willingness to play practical jokes. The rationale for this test was that timid subjects should be more willing – the jokes being an outlet for aggression.

Basic metabolic rate

This is a physiological test, where subjects' smallest oxygen consumption for six minutes is converted to calories per hour per square metre of body area. It was hypothesized that this factor would load on extraversion – extraverts being vigorous and active.

Tests measuring anxiety and assertiveness

To give a better idea of the scope of objective tests, I shall list a few tests which have stronger evidence for validity than the four tests described above. The titles reveal the nature of these tests.

677

1 Greater number of admissions of minor wrongdoings and frailties.
2 Greater acquiescence in answering questionnaires.
3 Higher score on a checklist of annoyances.
4 Little confidence that good performance could be reached on a wide variety of skills.

All these tests measure anxiety, thus showing how difficult they are to fake. The next set of tests measure assertiveness.

1 Preference for socially acceptable book-titles compared to questionable titles.
2 Faster tapping speed.
3 Faster normal reading speed.
4 Faster in reading poetry and copying stick figures.
5 Greater preference for sophisticated or highbrow activities.

CONCLUSION

There are several points deserving of note which are illustrated by this small sample of objective personality tests. It is clear that faking is difficult because it is hard to guess what the tests measure. Questionnaires are used but the scores are not the obvious ones. Thus, for example, the number of acquiescent responses is counted regardless of item content. However, the validity of objective tests is not well established.

From this discussion and description of objective personality tests it can be concluded that at present they should not be used for substantive psychological testing. However, potentially they are the most promising type of test and it would be valuable to undertake a systematic scrutiny of their validity.

SUMMARY

From this chapter a few simple conclusions may be drawn. Of the three kinds of personality tests, only personality inventories are sufficiently developed to be used in applied psychology with any confidence. The best of these tests are reliable and valid. However, questionnaires are inevitably crude. The much richer and more subtle projective tests, however, are insufficiently reliable and of dubious validity so that their use must be confined to research, until objective scoring schemes, which have been devised for them, have been shown to be viable and valid. Finally, objective tests appear to overcome many of the defects of the older techniques. However, they have almost no evidence for validity and the discovery of which objective tests, if any, are valid should be the next task of personality research.

FURTHER READING

Cattell, R. B., & Kline, P. (1977). *The scientific analysis of personality and motivation*. London: Academic Press.

Kline, P. (1992). *Handbook of psychological testing*. London: Routledge.

Kline, P. (1993). *Personality: The psychometric view*. London: Routledge.

Nunnally, J. O. (1978). *Psychometric theory*. New York: McGraw-Hill.

REFERENCES

Buck, J. N. (1970). *The House-Tree-Person technique: Revised manual*, Los Angeles, CA: Western Psychological Services.

Carstairs, G. M. (1957). *The twice-born: A study of a community of high caste Hindus*. London: Hogarth.

Cattell, R. B. (1957). *Personality and motivation structure and measurement*. Yonkers, NY: World Book.

Cattell, R. B. (1973). *Personality and mood by questionnaire*. San Francisco, CA: Jossey-Bass.

Cattell, R. B. (1978), *The scientific use of factor analysis*. New York: Plenum.

Cattell, R. B., & Butcher, H. J. (1968). *The prediction of achievement and creativity*. Indianapolis, IN: Bobbs-Merrill.

Cattell, R. B., & Schuerger, J. (1976), *The O-A (Objective-Analytic) Test Battery*. Champaign, IL: Institute for Personality and Ability Testing.

Cattell, R. B., & Warburton, F. W. (1967). *Objective personality and motivation tests*. Urbana, IL: University of Illinois Press.

Cattell, R. B., Eber, H. W., & Tatsuoka, M. M. (1970). *Handbook for the Sixteen Personality Factor Questionnaire*. Champaign, IL: Institute for Personality and Ability Testing.

Digman, J. N. (1990). Personality structure: emergence of the five factor model. *Annual Review of Psychology*, *41*, 417–440.

Eysenck, H. J. (1959). The Rorschach. In O. K. Buros (Ed.) *The Vth mental measurement yearbook* (p. 581). Highland Park, NJ: Gryphon.

Eysenck, H. J., & Eysenck, S. G. B. (1975). *The Eysenck Personality Questionnaire*. Sevenoaks: Hodder & Stoughton.

Goldberg, L. R. (1993). The structure of phenotypic personality traits. *American Psychologist*, *48*, 26–34.

Graham, J. R. (1990). *MMPI-2 assessing personality and pathology*. New York: Oxford University Press.

Hathaway, S. R., & McKinley, J. C. (1951). *The Minnesota Multiphasic Personality Inventory manual (revised)*. New York: Psychological Corporation.

Heim, A. W. (1975). *Psychological testing*. London: Oxford University Press.

Holtzman, W. H. (1981). Holtzman inkblot technique. In A. I. Rabin (Ed.) *Assessment with projective techniques* (pp. 47–83). New York: Springer.

Jackson, D. N. (1974). *Personality research form*. New York: Research Psychologists Press.

Jewell, L. N., & Siegall, M. (1990). *Contemporary industrial/organisational psychology* (2nd edn). New York: West Publishing.

Kline, P. (1992). *Handbook of psychological testing*. London: Routledge.

Kline, P., & Cooper, C. (1984). A construct validation of the Objective Analytic Test Battery (OATB). *Personality and Individual Differences*, *5*, 328–337.

Murray, H. A. (1938). *Explorations in personality*. New York: Oxford University Press.

Murstein, B. I. (1963). *Theory and research in projective techniques*. New York: Wiley.

Rorschach, H. (1921). *Psychodiagnostics*. Berne: Hans Huber.

Semeonoff, B. (1971). *Projective tests*. Chichester: Wiley.

Vernon, P. E. (1963). *Personality assessment*. London: Methuen.